ARCHITECTURAL
DRAWING

ARCHITECTURAL DRAWING

A Visual Compendium of Types and Methods

Rendow Yee

JOHN WILEY & SONS, INC.

New York • Chichester • Weinheim • Brisbane • Singapore • Toronto

This text is printed on acid-free paper.

Copyright © 1997 by Rendow Yee.

Published by John Wiley & Sons, Inc.

All rights reserved. Published simultaneously in Canada.

Library of Congress Cataloging in Publication Data:
Yee, Rendow.
    Architectural drawing: a visual compendium of types and methods/
by Rendow Yee.
        p.   cm.
    Includes bibliographical references and index.
    ISBN 0–471–16573–5 (pbk. : alk. paper)
    1. Architectural drawing--Technique.   I. Title.
NA2708.Y439   1997
720" .28"4--dc20   96-34307

Printed in the United States of America

10 9 8 7 6 5

Dedicated to Each Student Studying This Book

Past and Present,

Always a Source for Insightful and Innovative Ideas.

To My Parents

Always a Source for Inspiration.

Contents

Preface

In the visual world of design education and the design professions, message (design) and language (graphics) are so interrelated that they cannot be separated. The design process always includes graphic skills to clarify and communicate the issues in question. This book's goal is to communicate a broad range of design-drawing methods; it is not intended to be a handbook on acquiring design skills.

People learn to communicate through language at an early age. They learn to speak, read, and write. The primary type of communication in any kind of design work, whether fashion or building, is drawing. To communicate our design ideas to others, we must learn how to draw. We must draw with enough facility to make our ideas clear. Furthermore, we need to be able to communicate graphic ideas to ourselves because as we work on any design our ideas are constantly changing and evolving.

The language of graphics requires the use of all aspects of the brain —analytical, intuitive, synthetic, and even emotional. The intent of this primer is to provide students and practitioners with graphic tools essential to visual communication methods in the design process. It will reinforce methods of perceiving existing reality in order to create an awareness of the visual world. It will also develop and build confidence in one's analytical and intuitive graphic skills and abilities.

It is quite common to find students with a wide range of backgrounds in drawing upon entering a beginning course in architectural drawing/graphics; some students may have had numerous courses in middle school and high school mechanical drawing and art; other students have never used or been exposed to drafting or sketching equipment. Also, there are students who show a strong potential on aptitude tests related to spatial visualization; but, for one reason or another, they never had an opportunity to develop this potential. This book can be used for those who have little knowledge of geometry or basic mathematics. However, it is also designed for intermediate and advanced students in architectural drawing. Students and practitioners with a prior knowledge of pictorial drawing or perspective will find this book to be a convenient reference guide for presentation work.

The first three chapters are basic to the study of architectural design-drawing methods and provide the necessary fundamental framework to pursue the major areas of two- and three-dimensional pictorial drawings. The next five chapters, —**Orthographic and Paraline Drawing, Representational Sketching, Linear Perspective Drawing, Perspective View Development,** and **Light, Shade, and Shadow**—form the major body of this primer due to their importance for graphic communications. Representational freehand "soft-edge" sketching precedes hardline perspective drawing in the sense that perspective should develop from approximate, freehand, and proportional to constructed, precise, and measured. If design-drawing can be seen as a continuum, the computer (discussed in 3D Modeling) has come onto the scene in the precise measured phase and is moving toward the conceptual phase. Therefore, teaching design-drawing using freehand methods develops skills that are complementary to and not redundant with the computer.

The chapters on paralines, perspectives, and shadows illustrate the most common manual methods in current practice with detailed but simple explanations on the theory behind their use. The use of these procedures will help both the student and the professional in communicating and presenting design ideas. The remainder of the book is devoted to a brief introduction to the topic areas of **Delineating and Rendering Entourage, Diagramming, Conceptual Sketching, 3D Modeling,** and **Presentation Formats.** The final chapter is titled **Exotics** and includes unusual presentation drawings, such as composite drawings. The variety of drawings illustrates a large number of diverse styles; and the medium used, the original size, and the scale used (if applicable) are given for each drawing where this information was available. In this sense, the book acts as a springboard to stimulate readers to explore each topic in more detail by investigating the extensive bibliography. Many of the images illustrated are residential building types, but a large variety of other building types are shown as well. In view of today's global culture, many drawing exhibits from outside the United States are also included.

This comprehensive guide attempts to elaborate equally on each of the currently used architectural design-drawing methods. However, the last quarter of the 20th century has seen an upsurge in the use of paraline drawings. This is due to their ease of construction and their impressive ability to allow the viewer to see and to comprehend the total composition of a design. For this reason, a large number of professional paraline examples are included. Architecture and other design professions have been expanding their expressive vocabulary to include the emerging methods of three-dimensional computer imaging, animation, film, and video. This visual compendium of diverse graphic images done in a variety of both traditional and avant-garde media is rich in its content. Many illustrations are supported by personal commentary by their originators to help shed light on why each type of drawing was chosen to express the design.

Both students and design professionals are continually striving to come up with new ways to represent and express their designs. The graphic image examples that I have chosen are by no means exhaustive. These examples are meant to extend basic techniques that the students learn to a more advanced level as well as to provoke their imagination. They are not meant to dogmatically lead students into a narrow path of particular styles or "isms"; instead, their goal is to encourage students to start their own journey of discovery and exploration.

As a reference for precise graphic constructions the book is laid out in a simple, easy-to-follow step-by-step format. Although mechanically constructed pictorials are emphasized, freehand visualization techniques are encouraged. Most architectural schools have courses covering architectural design-drawing in a time frame from one to three semesters. In many cases the material is covered as an adjunct to the design-drawing studio. This book can be used under any kind of flexible time schedule as a student text, a studio reference, or an office reference for practitioners. For ease of reference, design-drawing types have been categorized in such a way that both students and design professionals will find them handy for reviewing design-drawing methods or for obtaining ideas (the encylopedic nature of the book encourages browsing and wandering) for their own creative presentation compositions.

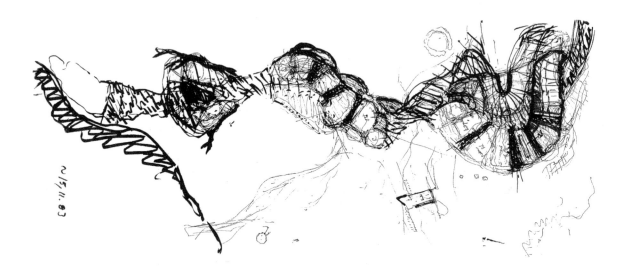

Plan sketch diagrams: Mica Moriane, Official residence of the President of Finland
Mäntyniemi, Helsinki, Finland
Medium: Color felt pens
Courtesy of Raili and Reima Pietilä, Architects

Acknowledgments

This book on architectural drawing developed from an expression of need over many semesters by the architecture faculty and the students enrolled in the basic architectural drawing course at the City College of San Francisco.

I would like to express my gratitude to my fellow staff members in architecture, Lawrence J. Franceschina, Ernest E. Lee, Enrique Limosner, and the late Gordon Phillips, without whose help and advice the reality of this textbook would not have been possible. Gordon gave me the necessary encouragement during the early stages of this book. In particular, I would like to recognize Ernest E. Lee, who along with Julian D. Munoz reviewed the book in its preliminary format. The latest edition is a result of continual revisions due to frequent consultations with colleagues:

Robin Chiang	Norman C. Hall	Harry Leong	Curtis Poon
Alexander Diefenbach	Robert L. Hamilton	Pershing Lin	Nestor Regino
Jim Dierkes	Patrick Houlihan	Jerry W. Lum	Will S. Revilock
Olallo L. Fernandez	Spencer Jue	Ryszard Pochron	Russell Wong

A word of special thanks to Bernard Kuan for endless hours of typing the preliminary manuscript, and to Tony Ho and Winnie Chun for endless hours of pasteup work. I have always appreciated ideas and feedback from my students. A note of special appreciation goes to the following group of students who assisted me in small but significant ways:

Henry Beltran	Randy Furuta	Wilson Lee	Ann-Marie Ratkovits
Ed Broas	Randa Fushimi	Clarissa Leong	Suheil Shatara
Woo Sok Cha	Dennis Hodges	Hedy Mak	Lily Shen
Jason Chan	James Ke	Amos Malkin	Carl Stensel
Keng Chung	Andrew Kong	Amy Man	Gorran Tsui
Ken Cozine	Kenneth Lau	Corvin Matei	Nguyen N. Trong
Fred Dea	Albert Lee	Henry Ng	Kam Wong

I am deeply appreciative to *Architectural Record* and *Progressive Architecture* magazines for giving me permission to reprint many of the drawings that were published in these magazines. Other magazines that I used as rich sources for graphic images were *GA Houses, GA Document International, Architecture California,* and *World Architecture.* Numerous illustrations are from student work contributed by various schools of architecture. Those contributing included Washington University in St. Louis, the University of Texas at Arlington, Savannah College of Art and Design, Southern University, Columbia University, the University of Virginia, Cal Poly San Luis Obispo, The Catholic University of America, the University of Maryland, Texas A & M University, Andrews University, and the City College of San Francisco.

I am grateful to two former professors of mine for stimulating my interest in the field of architectural drawing techniques: the late Professor Emeritus Alexander S. Levens of the University of California at Berkeley and the late Professor Emeritus Roland W. Bockhorst of Washington University. Also, I would like to make a note of Dr. Wayne D. Barton of the City College of Sacramento for sharing his teaching experiences with me in basic drawing courses, and I would like to acknowledge Professor Zenryu Shirakawa of Boston University for improving my writing skills during my high school and college years. A final note of thanks to all those who contributed illustrations to this book. The process of contacting everyone was both an arduous and an enjoyable task.

I am deeply indebted to the group of exceptional architectural teaching professionals who have reviewed my book. Their suggestions have been constructive and positive in helping me to sharpen my focus on elements that may need improvement. I want to give my heartfelt thanks to Dick Davison for his most significant page by page extensive review. Other major review contributors also included Owen Cappleman and Thomas L. Turman. William Benedict shared his excellent syllabus with me and excerpts from it have particularly strengthened the linear perspective drawing and the delineating and rendering entourage chapters.

William R. Benedict, Assistant Professor, Cal Poly San Luis Obispo
Donald J. Bergsma, Professor, St. Petersberg Junior College (Florida)
Derek Bradford, Professor, Rhode Island School of Design
Owen Cappleman, Assistant Dean and Associate Professor, University of Texas at Austin
Ann Cederna, Assistant Professor, The Catholic University of America (Washington, D.C.)
Rich Correa, Professor, Yuba College (California)
Dick Davison, Associate Professor, Texas A & M University
Phillip R. Dixon, Professor, College of San Mateo (California)
Jonathan B. Friedman, Dean and Professor, New York Institute of Technology
Robert Funk, Professor, Bakersfield College (California)
Todd Hamilton, Assistant Dean and Associate Professor, University of Texas at Arlington
Hiro Hata, Associate Professor, State University of New York at Buffalo
Paul Laseau, Professor, Ball State University (Indiana)
Harold Linton, Assistant Dean, Lawrence Technological University (Michigan)
George Martin, Professor, The Catholic University of America
Valerian Miranda, Associate Professor, Texas A & M University
David Pollak, Adjunct Professor of Design, Roger Williams University (Bristol, Rhode Island)
Arpad Daniel Ronaszegi, Assistant Professor, Andrews University (Michigan)
James Shay, AIA Architect
Michael Stallings, Chair and Professor, El Camino College (California)
Paul Stevenson Oles, FAIA, The American Society of Architectural Perspectivists–President Emeritus
Martha Sutherland, Assistant Professor, University of Arkansas
Stephen Temple, Lecturer and Architect, The University of North Carolina, Greensboro
Thomas L. Turman, Professor, Laney College (Oakland, California)
Mohammed S. Uddin, Associate Professor, Southern University (Louisiana)
Dr. Osamu A. Wakita, Chair and Professor, Los Angeles Harbor College
Lee Wright, Associate Professor, University of Texas at Arlington
Lindy Zichichi, Professor, Glendale Community College (California)

The following illustrations were "Reprinted with permission of Progressive Architecture, Penton Publishing."

Anti-Villa, Batey & Mack, Architects
Armacost Duplex, Rebecca L. Binder, FAIA
Casa Canovelles, MBM Arquitectos
Central Chiller Plant, Holt Hinshaw Pfau Jones Architecture
Church of Light, Tadao Ando, Architect
Clybourne Lofts, Pappageorge Haymes Ltd., Architects
Franklin/La Brea Family Housing, Adèle Naudé Santos and Associates, Architects
J.B. Speed Art Museum addition, GBQC Architects
Kress Residence, Robert W. Peters FAIA, Architect
Louisiana Department of Health and Hospitals, R-2 ARCH Designers/Researchers
Museum of Modern Art, Hans Hollein, Architect
Private Studio, William Adams, Architect
Springwood Drive Residence, David Lee Van Hoy and George Patrick Elian, Architects
The Stainless Steel Apartment, Krueck & Sexton, Architects
Waterfront Development Plan, Koetter, Kim & Associates, Inc., Architects and Urban Designers

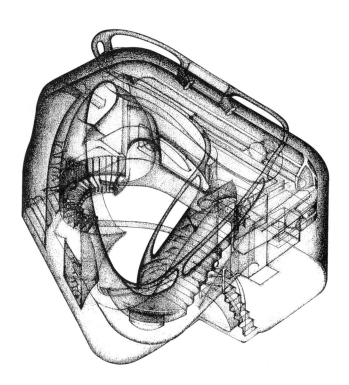

Drawing: Truss-Wall House, Machida, Tokyo, Japan
Transparent Isometric
Courtesy of Eisaku Ushida & Katheryn Findley
of the Ushida-Findley Partnership

Tool
Fundamentals

A surgeon cannot properly function without operating instruments; a contractor cannot properly function without building tools; likewise an architect or designer cannot properly function without drafting or drawing tools. These tools should be treated with meticulous care with the goal of making them last a lifetime. Always purchase the best quality that you can afford. These tools are a necessity for clarity of graphical expression.

The intent of this chapter is to show the variety of instruments that are available, and how to properly use them.

A **metal drafting stand** is characterized by an adjustable table top which can be fitted with a parallel straightedge (see p. 14).

A **four-post table** is usually made of wood or a combination of steel and wood. It has a tool drawer and a large shallow reference drawer. Concealed raising rods can prop the drawing surface to any comfortable drawing angle.

An economical **homemade table** can be made from a flush hollow core door placed on top of adjustable wooden horses.

Types of Drawing Table or Drawing Board Covers

1. **Plastic-coated Paper**
   A green paper underlay with ⅛" horizontal and vertical coordinates.

2. **Borco***
   A vinyl cover which is stain resistant, non-eye straining, and self-healing in the event of scratches or punctures.

3. **Illustration Board**
   A cover that should be hot press, heavy, white, and dense.

4. **Print Paper Sheets**
   Three or four sheets of print paper make a good cover that is not too hard.

5. **Rubber Pad**
   A pad with very little resistance or give.

Avoid drawing on hard surfaces such as glass or wood or hard plastic.

*Borco is a registered trademark of Safco Products Co., Minneapolis, Minnesota.

A highly recommended **drawing board** is one that is hollow with plywood faces or laminated white pine. The technology for types of drawing board and table covers is continually changing. Always check drafting supply catalogues for new surfaces being used. Likewise, there are many new designs for drafting tables that can be found in supply catalogues. Also use the catalogues as a guide for other important accessories such as lamps, chairs, plan files, and spiroll (attaches to drawing table or board to allow drawing to be rolled in to prevent working in cramped positions).

TABLE TYPES AND BOARD COVERS

GRAPHITE DRAFTING PENCILS

Architectural drawings (drafted or sketched) are best produced by using leads in the grade range from 4H to 6B. Shown below are three equally good types of pencils that are commonly used. Experience each pencil type to determine which is most suitable for you. Cylindrical pencil leads are classified by a notation which ranges them from the smallest diameter (hardest—9H) to the largest diameter (softest—6B).

PENCIL GRADE CHART

HARD						MEDIUM								SOFT		
9H	8H	7H	6H	5H	4H	3H	2H	H	F	HB	B	2B	3B	4B	5B	6B

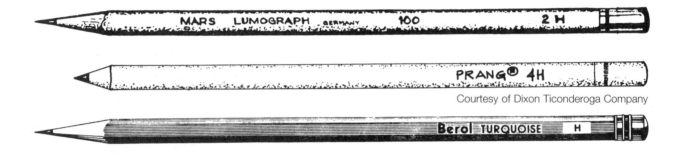

Courtesy of Dixon Ticonderoga Company

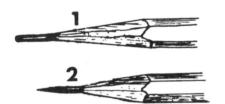

There are many good brands of wood graphite drawing pencils; three are shown above. "H" is the code for hard and "B" is the code for black. The softer leads (B to 6B) are used primarily for freehand sketching. A wood lead pencil must be sharpened by first (**1**) cutting away the wood with small deliberate movements using a scalpel or a razor blade, and then (**2**) making a conical point on a sand paper pad. Clean the graphite from the lead with paper or cloth.

A mechanical leadholder or clutch pencil is shown above. It uses a standard size 2-mm lead which can be drawn out or pulled back by the push-button on the end. Some variations include pocket clips and double end holders. Leads in most tone qualities can be interchanged to suit drawing conditions. Use a pencil pointer to sharpen the leads to a taper similar to a common wood pencil.

A fine-line leadholder with push button lead advance (propelling) is shown above. Using a 0.3-mm to a 0.9-mm lead that is protected by a sliding sleeve (0.5 mm is a popular size), this type of pencil does not need to be sharpened. This pencil type is used for drafting rather than sketching.

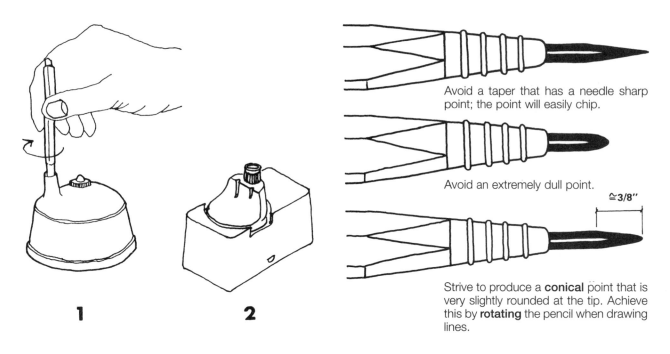

Avoid a taper that has a needle sharp point; the point will easily chip.

Avoid an extremely dull point.

≅3/8″

Strive to produce a **conical** point that is very slightly rounded at the tip. Achieve this by **rotating** the pencil when drawing lines.

1   **2**

To sharpen your lead to a conical point, use either (**1**) a sandpaper desk-top pointer or (**2**) a cutting-wheel lead pointer. The sandpaper pointer works well with graphite lead but not with polyester lead. The sandpaper pointer sharpens by rotating your pencil-holding hand in a clockwise motion. The cutting-wheel pointer has one slot to give a sharp point and one to give a slightly dull point (for lettering). Electric pencil sharpeners cost more but are much faster.

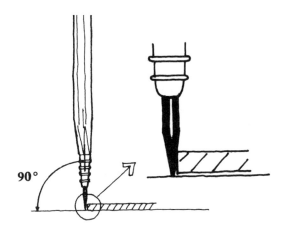

90°

Always draw with a small space between the conical lead point and the straightedge (T-square, parallel bar, or triangle). This is best achieved by either keeping the pencil in a 90° vertical position, or tilting the pencil toward you at a slight angle from the vertical. Never tilt it away from the straightedge. Horizontal, vertical, or oblique (slanted or angled) lines are best achieved by leaning the pencil at approximately 60° from the drawing surface. The pressure should be adequate to give a dark and crisp line.

A typical sandpaper block is shown above. It is a piece of wood with sandpaper sheets stapled to one end. Rotate the pencil and move it in a side-to-side motion to obtain a tapered conical point. Apply minimum pressure to avoid snapping the lead. Also use this block to produce a tapered compass lead point (see p. 10).

SHARPENING AND USING DRAFTING PENCILS

ink cartridge   **pen body**   **nib**

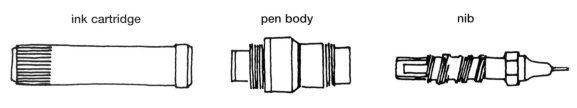

Technical pens are designed with a tubular point within which is a fine wire that controls the ink flow. The tubes are long enough to clear the thickness of drafting instruments. They give excellent control and consistency of line.

TECHNICAL PENS

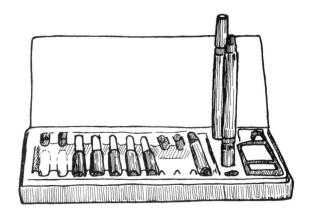

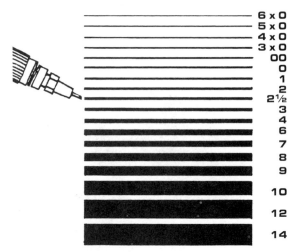

	6 x 0
	5 x 0
	4 x 0
	3 x 0
	00
	0
	1
	2
	2½
	3
	4
	6
	7
	8
	9
	10
	12
	14

The most common problems encountered are clogging, drying up, touchdown blobs, leaking, and line feathering. Pens with good seals can prevent drying. New pen technology has made most pen brands virtually clog-free when not in use. There are also many brands of clog-free waterproof drawing inks. Waterproof inks will not fade if exposed to light whereas most nonwaterproof inks will. Vertical storage should be maintained with the point up and the cap on.

Technical pen sets come in a variety of sizes depending on the number of pen points desired. The primary advantage of technical drawing pens is that they produce clear even lines of constant width. 000 through 4 are the most commonly used pen points for freehand drawing, delineation, and drafting. The line widths shown can slightly vary depending on the type of surface or ink used as well as the speed at which they are drawn.

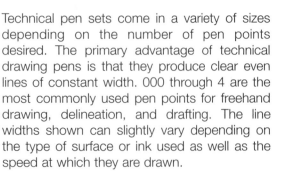

eradicating fluid   **waterproof ink**

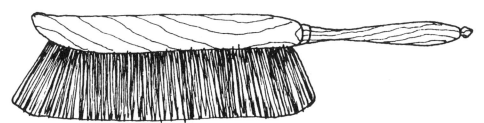

A drafting duster with horse hair or natural bristle is used to keep the drawing surface clean and free of graphite.

Pounce powder is used to prepare a surface for ink or pencil. The pad absorbs dirt and powdered graphite. Skum-x dry cleaning powder keeps the surface clean while one is drafting.

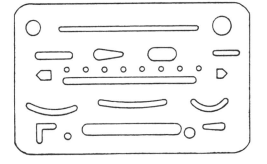

An eraser shield is a thin metal shield that protects lines in close proximity. Hold the eraser shield and erase desired line or lines in small areas.

An electric cord style eraser can also be used with an eraser shield. It is very effective for ink drawings.

Soft erasers that are very pliable and smudge free give the best results. Some excellent brands include Staedtler Mars and Koh-I-Noor as well as Pink Pearl, Magic Rub, and Kneaded Eraser, all from Faber Castell. More dense than a soft eraser is the very effective plastic eraser. The Kneaded Eraser can be molded to any shape.

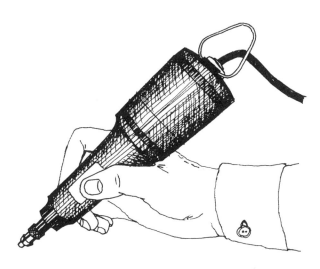

All of the small equipment mentioned in this chapter can be stored and transported efficiently in an art box or a fishing tackle box. Drawings (especially large sheets) should be transported using protective tubes which can be commercially purchased.

CLEANING AND ERASING AIDS

Small triangles (4") are ideal for vertical strokes in aiding hand lettering.

Plastic triangles can be clear or fluorescent with fingerlifts. The most commonly used triangles are 8" to 10" in their longest vertical height. Triangles can come with edges cut back for inking.

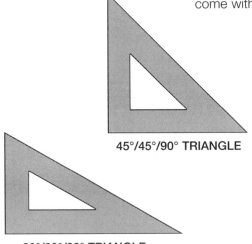

45°/45°/90° TRIANGLE

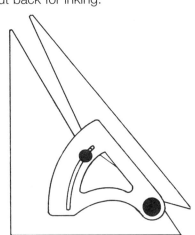

30°/60°/90° TRIANGLE

Triangles are used to draw vertical lines or lines at a specific angle (30°, 45°, and 60°) when used with a T-square or parallel bar. The adjustable triangle is extremely useful for drawing a variety of inclined lines at any desirable angle. A minimum 12" size is best.

T-squares come in lengths of 18", 24", 30", 36", 42", and 48". Good blades have a rigid head and are made of stainless steel or of wood with acrylic edges for visibility. 42" is an all-purpose length.

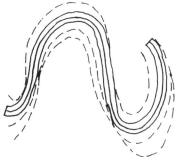

A flexible curve rule can draw almost any curve by shaping and bending. The curve rule is made of plastic with a flexible core.

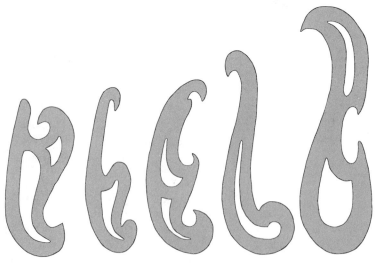

French curves are irregular curves that have no constant radii. Those made of hand-finished acrylic are best.

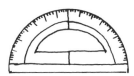

Protractors can be circular or semicircular. They are used to measure angles.

T-SQUARES, TRIANGLES, AND FRENCH CURVES

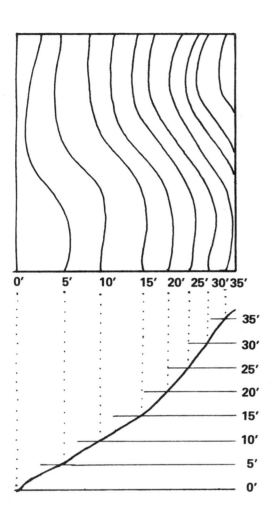

0'   5'   10'   15'   20' 25' 30'35'

35'
30'
25'
20'
15'
10'
5'
0'

Contour lines are lines of constant elevation. Every point passes through the same elevation on the surface of the ground.

Contour intervals can be 1', 2', 5', or 10', depending on the conditions of the terrain and the size of the area being studied.

In the drawing on the left, note how the slope steepens when the contours become more closely spaced. It is less steep at the bottom since the spacing here is greater than at the top. Remember that contour lines should never cross one another.

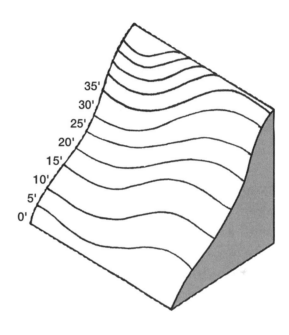

35'
30'
25'
20'
15'
10'
5'
0'

Contour lines can be drawn accurately by using a french curve. The french curve is used for noncircular curves. When fitting the curve through a series of points, be sure that the direction in which its curvature increases is the direction in which the curvature of the line increases. Tangents at each conjunction should coincide to avoid breaks and to allow for a smooth continuity. At sharp turns, a combination of circle arcs and french curves may be used.

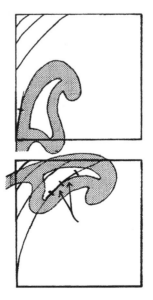
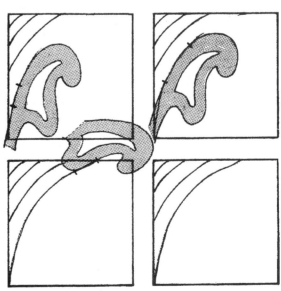

SITE TOPOGRAPHY/USE OF THE FRENCH CURVE

COMPASSES, DIVIDERS, AND THEIR USAGE

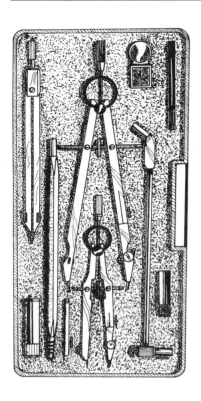

The divider and the bow compass are the major instruments in a drafting set. A **divider** divides lines and transfers lengths. A proportional divider is graduated for lines and circles. A **compass** is used primarily for drawing large circles.

A typical large drafting set includes the following:

(1) Dividers
(2) Large pen-pencil compass
(3) Small pen-pencil compass
(4) Mechanical leadholder pencil
(5) Pencil pointer
(6) Ruling pen handle
(7) 6" extension beam
(8) Lead holder
(9) Lined protective case

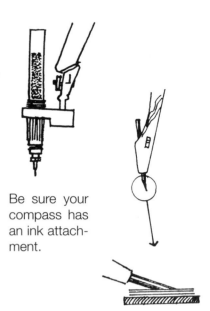

Be sure your compass has an ink attachment.

Keep a low angle when tapering the compass lead.

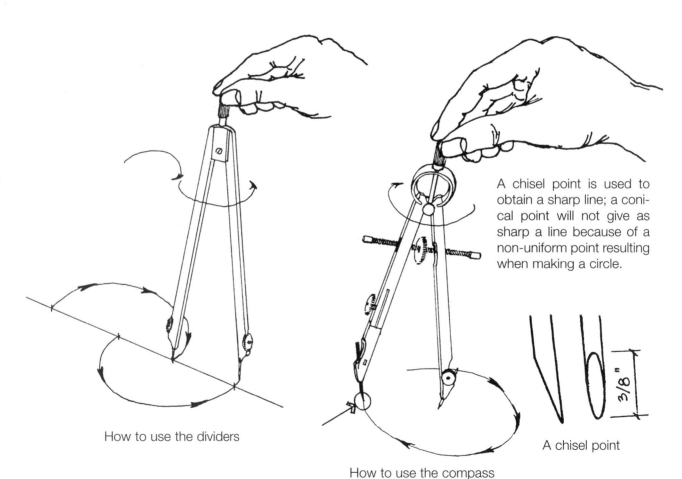

How to use the dividers

How to use the compass

A chisel point is used to obtain a sharp line; a conical point will not give as sharp a line because of a non-uniform point resulting when making a circle.

A chisel point

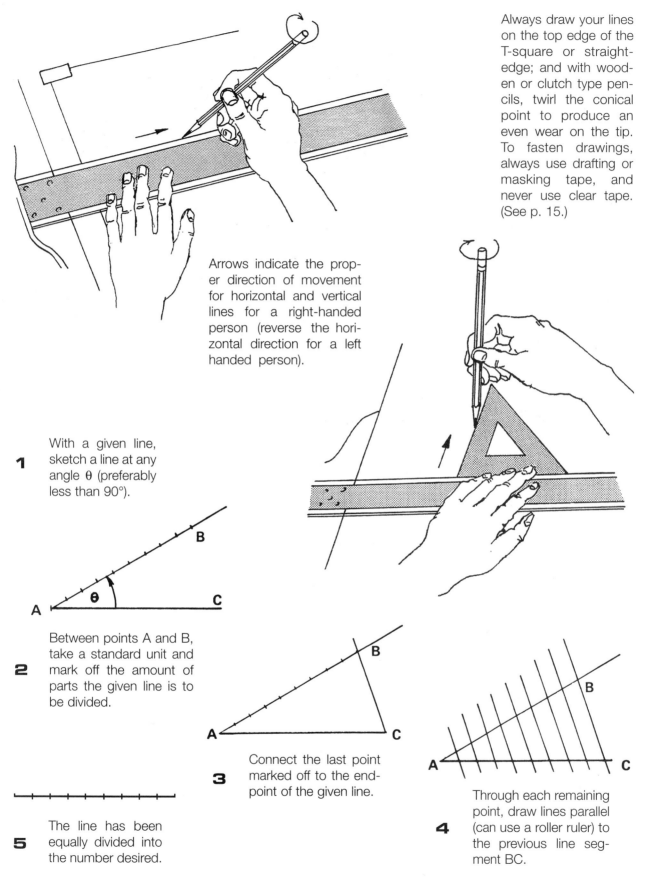

Always draw your lines on the top edge of the T-square or straight-edge; and with wooden or clutch type pencils, twirl the conical point to produce an even wear on the tip. To fasten drawings, always use drafting or masking tape, and never use clear tape. (See p. 15.)

Arrows indicate the proper direction of movement for horizontal and vertical lines for a right-handed person (reverse the horizontal direction for a left handed person).

1 With a given line, sketch a line at any angle θ (preferably less than 90°).

2 Between points A and B, take a standard unit and mark off the amount of parts the given line is to be divided.

3 Connect the last point marked off to the endpoint of the given line.

4 Through each remaining point, draw lines parallel (can use a roller ruler) to the previous line segment BC.

5 The line has been equally divided into the number desired.

USE OF BASIC DRAFTING TOOLS

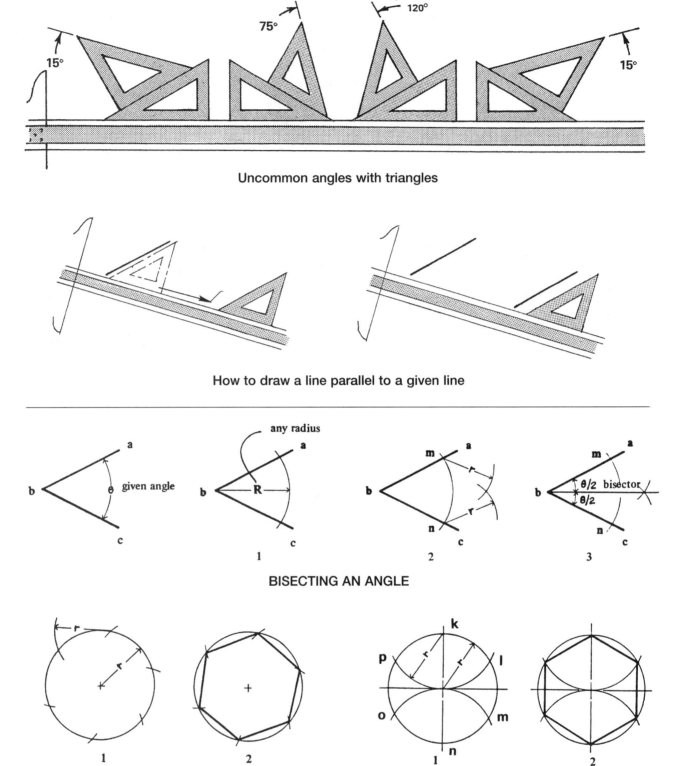

Uncommon angles with triangles

How to draw a line parallel to a given line

BISECTING AN ANGLE

CONSTRUCTING A HEXAGON

Familiarity with drafting tools can be achieved by doing simple geometric operations and constructing various geometric shapes.

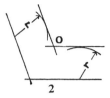
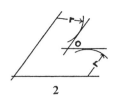
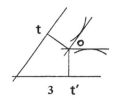
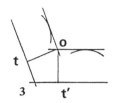
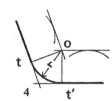
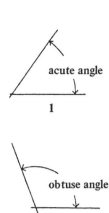

acute angle
1

obtuse angle
1

2

2

3 t t'

3 t t'

4 t t'

4 t t'

CONSTRUCTING TANGENT ARCS

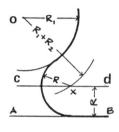
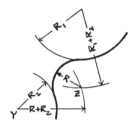
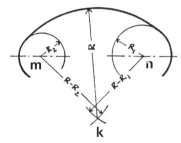
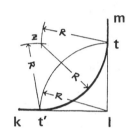

An arc tangent to a straight line and a circle. An equidistance is required.

An arc tangent to two circles. The arc center must be equidistant from both circles.

An arc tangent at a right-angle corner. An equidistance R is required.

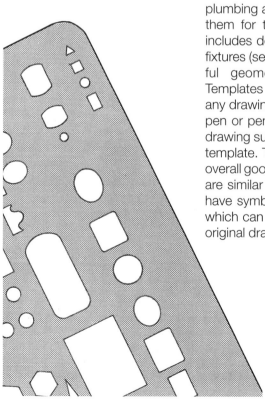

Architectural templates have many standard plumbing and furniture symbols cut through them for tracing. This floor plan template includes door swings, sinks, and bathroom fixtures (see bathroom plan). It also has useful geometric forms such as circles. Templates come in a variety of scales to suit any drawing requirement. Always keep your pen or pencil perpendicular (vertical) to the drawing surface when using an architectural template. This insures a uniform line and an overall good result. **Underlays** and **overlays** are similar to templates. These time-savers have symbols printed or drawn on a sheet which can be traced or transferred onto an original drawing.

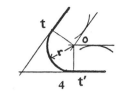

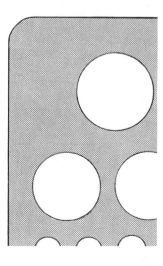

If the desired diameter of a small circle is known, a plastic circle template may be used in place of a compass. Other popular templates are classified as general purpose and elliptical.

ARCHITECTURAL TEMPLATES AND OTHER TEMPLATES

The **parallel roller rule** with its effortless movement has made the T-square relatively obsolete. A slight push with either hand can glide the parallel rule into any desired position on the drawing board. Since it rolls on ball bearings, smudges on drawings commonly found with the use of a T-square are eliminated. It also has the advantage over a T-square of having both ends fixed; thus, a drawn horizontal line cannot deviate from its correct position. Special types of rules can have a built-in cutting edge.

THE PARALLEL RULE

When installing the parallel rule (also termed bar or straightedge), be sure that

(1) Corner plates A and B are firmly attached with ½"-long screws.

(2) The cable wire is parallel to the edge of the drawing board on both sides.

(3) The cable wire passes between the clamping washer and the plate.

(4) The spring is centered between A and B.

(5) The cable wire is moved in the directions indicated below.

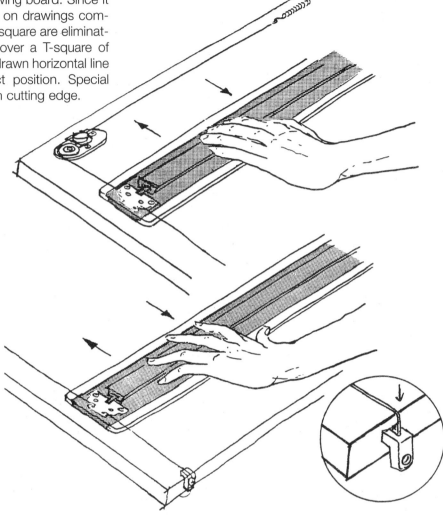

The cable wire is inserted through the hole on top of the stop and aligned with the slot on the rear of the stop. Trim any excessive cable, but leave enough for future adjustments.

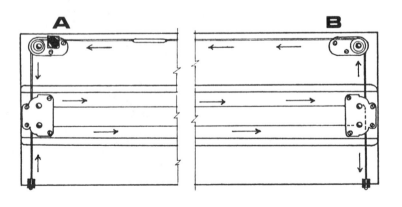

Long, continuous, parallel horizontal lines are a frequent occurrence on architectural drawings. The rule can also be adjusted to many inclined positions slightly away from the horizontal. Rules come in lengths of 36", 42", 48", 54", and 60". Highly recommended is the 42" rule, which permits one to work on a 30" × 40" sheet.

Provide yourself with a comfortable work space with adequate tack surface to pin up your work for reference. Architectural drawing is normally done in a sitting position, but it can also be done in a standing position. Avoid slouching; don't arch your back and collapse your abdominal regions. Sit erect and keep a good posture. Designing and drawing require long hours of sitting in one position. Poor posture will lead to a tired feeling, reduced drawing capacity, and a deteriorated physical state.

A tilted work table reduces the need to lean over the work surface. Most drafting/drawing tables can be adjusted to tilt at various angles. An adjustable stool is ideal for varying the seat height and the back rest. If possible place one foot on a pile bar or footrest in order to raise one knee above the hips. Elevating one leg at a time helps to keep the pelvic region tilted forward. It also preserves the natural curvature of the lower lumbar region, preventing undue physical stress and fatigue.

Purchase the best quality table light source that you can afford in order to prevent eyestrain. An incandescent/fluorescent combination light is excellent. The light should have an adjustable counterpoise to give it flexibility to be positioned over your work.

Line up the drawing sheet horizontally and vertically using the T-square or parallel straightedge and triangle. It is best to apply the drafting tape as shown (broadside) to prevent slippage and movement of the drawing sheet. Drafting dots can also be used to secure drawings to a board or table. Try to make the T-square length match the board or table length. The head of the T-square should always be firmly placed up against the edge of the drawing board or drawing table. If the head is not firm, then there will be vertical movement at the end of the T-square. Also note that, with a T-square, it is common practice to use a metal angle to keep a true edge. A clean thin rag or towel can be used as a forearm rest and sheet protector for long drawing stints.

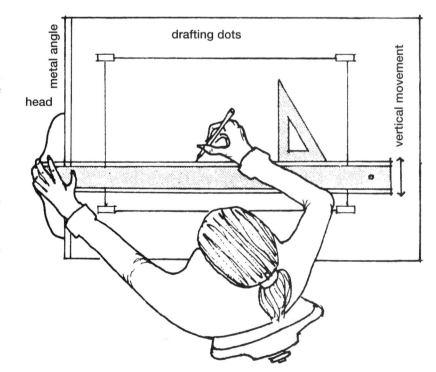

WORKSTATION SET UP: GETTING STARTED

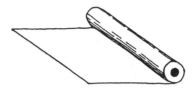

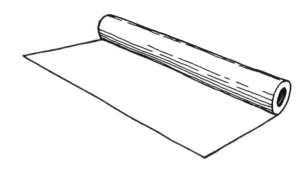

Light yellow or white tracing paper (termed flimsy or talking paper) is excellent for sketching with pencils or markers but not for erasing. It is used for rough sketches, overlays, and preliminary drawings.

Tracing pad sizes are 8½" × 11", 11" × 17", and 17" × 22"

With a fade-out grid

Vellums are quality 100% rag tracing papers with excellent erasing qualities. They are available in either rolls or pads. Clearprint 1000H is widely accepted. Tracing papers are classified by weight, color, and rag content. Heavy and white are normally used for finished drawings. **Plastic film** from polyester (Mylar) gives the highest quality reproductions. It is wonderful for ink.

Both graphite and ink are used extensively with various types of architectural design-drawing methods. These media are frequently used on both translucent and transparent tracing papers. Rag is the cotton fiber in the paper. The higher the percentage of rag content, the better the quality. The peaks and valleys (fiber arrangement) on a tracing paper's surface are its "tooth" quality. Slick paper with less tooth is better for ink work, whereas paper with more tooth is better for pencil work. Sizes can vary from an 8.5" × 11" pad to a 24" × 36" roll. Gridded paper is used to make the drawing of horizontals and verticals much easier. Other good qualities are (1) no harshness on the eyes and (2) no "ghosts" (grooves) showing after pencil lines are redrawn in the same location. Original drawings must "read" well in order to reproduce well for the use of others. Refer to the bibliography for sources that discuss the variety of reproduction processes (reprography).

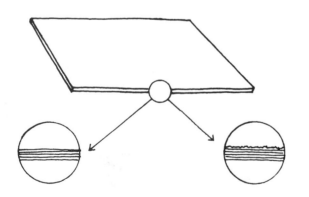

Hot press (less tooth)   Cold press (more tooth)

White **illustration board**, which comes in a variety of thicknesses, is heavier than tracing paper. This sturdiness makes it suitable for both finished drawing presentations and fine presentation models. Cold press boards have a more textured surface than the smoother hot press boards.

Preliminary study models are usually made of gray **chipboard**. Chipboard also comes in a variety of thicknesses. **Foamcore board** is a strong lightweight board that is excellent for modelmaking.

TRACING PAPERS AND BOARDS

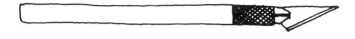

An X-Acto knife uses blades of several different shapes. The one illustrated is most commonly used. It is excellent for small detailed cuts (small apertures).

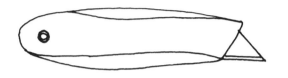

A utility knife is used primarily for long cuts on heavy materials such as thick illustration board, mat board, or cardboard. It is excellent for scoring. Stanley is a highly recommended brand (Stanley Tools, Division of the Stanley Works, New Britain, CT).

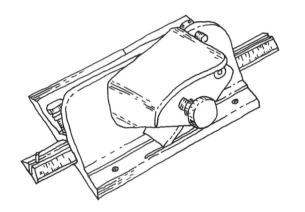

Good-quality cutters can cut a clean crisp 45° bevel. Highly recommended is a series 4000 Logan Mat cutter, which has a built-in marking system. With a pivoting blade holder, it can be used against any suitable straightedge.

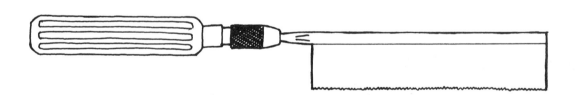

A razor saw with a thin blade and fine teeth is used for extrafine cuts on small pieces of wood such as balsa wood.

Adhesives or **glues** are used to fasten material together for modelmaking. A water-soluble glue is commonly used for cardboard. Rubber cement is excellent for collage work. Spray adhesives are most efficient for mounting drawings or photographs on cardboard as well as for laminating porous smooth sheets together.

A basic cutting rule of modelmaking is **never** to make only one pass when cutting materials (especially thick cardboard). Make a series of light cuts. This will give better control and accuracy. Cutting on a soft surface such as illustration board or a self-healing plastic cutting surface will extend the life of your cutting blade.

MODELMAKING AIDS

The following are architect's scales:

12"=1'0"	1"=1'0"	¼"=1'0"
6"=1'0"	¾"=1'0"	³⁄₁₆"=1'0"
3"=1'0"	½"=1'0"	⅛"=1'0"
1½"=1'0"	⅜"=1'0"	³⁄₃₂"=1'0"

For architectural work, all of the above scales are used. Least used are the scales of 12"=1'0" and 6"=1'0". The scale is usually notated within the title block of an architectural drawing. It can also appear underneath the view of a particular detail. The choice of the proper scale size is dependent on the building size, the amount of detail to be drawn, and the size of paper used. Sometimes common practice dictates the size; for example, floor plans for residential buildings are normally drawn at ¼"=1'0". Construction details can use scales ranging from ½"=1'0" to 3"=1'0".

The actual size of the architect's scale. This scale is ⅛"=1'0"

The **architect's** scale is used primarily for drawing buildings, architectural details, structural details, and mechanical systems in buildings. The purpose is to represent large objects at a reduced scale to fit on drafting paper size sheets. The best quality scale is unbreakable plastic with color-coded, engraved, calibrated graduations. Scales come in three beveled types and one triangular type (see below). Choose the one most suitable for your needs.

The **civil engineer's** or **engineer's** scale is used primarily for site plans, location plans, and land measurements in map drawing.

The following are civil engineer's scales:
10, 20, 30, 40, 50, 60, or 80 divisions to the inch representing feet, 10 ft, 100 ft, rods, or miles.

Be careful not to confuse "scale" and "size."
¼"=1'0" is referred to as "quarter scale" in the architect's language, whereas ¼" to 1" is referred to as "quarter size."

SCALES

OPPOSITE BEVEL
Easy to pick up and handle.

DOUBLE BEVEL
A good pocket scale.

FLAT BEVEL
Easy to keep flat to a board.

TRIANGULAR
The triangular scale has the advantage of having many scales on the same stick. Always observe the scale from directly above.

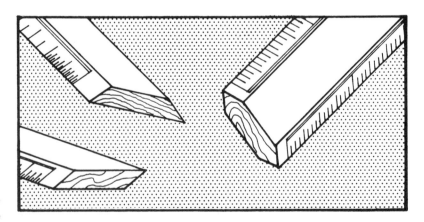

Remember to keep the scale clean, don't mark on it, and never use it as a straightedge!

Determining How Much Each Subdivision Represents

The best procedure is to ask yourself the following question: Each subdivision represents what part of one foot?

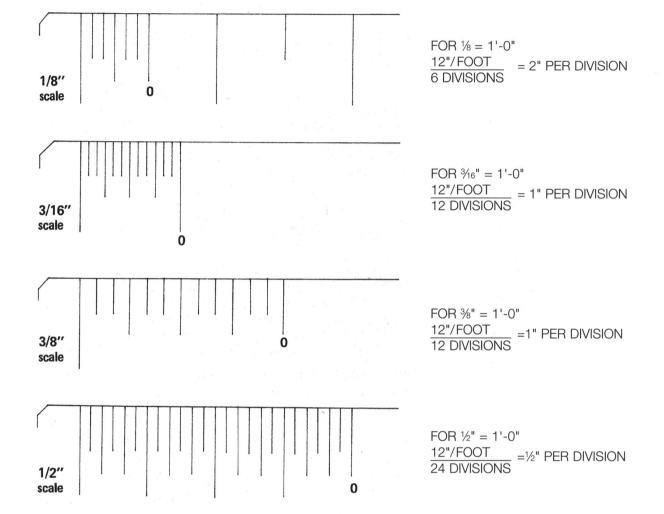

1/8″ scale

FOR ⅛ = 1'-0"

$$\frac{12"/FOOT}{6\ DIVISIONS} = 2"\ PER\ DIVISION$$

3/16″ scale

FOR 3⁄16" = 1'-0"

$$\frac{12"/FOOT}{12\ DIVISIONS} = 1"\ PER\ DIVISION$$

3/8″ scale

FOR ⅜" = 1'-0"

$$\frac{12"/FOOT}{12\ DIVISIONS} = 1"\ PER\ DIVISION$$

1/2″ scale

FOR ½" = 1'-0"

$$\frac{12"/FOOT}{24\ DIVISIONS} = ½"\ PER\ DIVISION$$

1/4″ scale

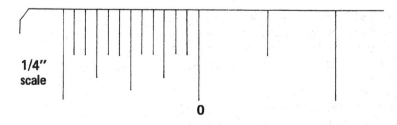

FOR ¼" = 1'-0"

$$\frac{12"/FOOT}{12\ DIVISIONS} = 1"\ PER\ DIVISION$$

THE ARCHITECT'S SCALE

Note that in all of the reduced scales, the major divisions represent feet and their subdivisions represent inches and fractions thereof. Therefore, ½ means ½ inch = 1 ft, not ½ inch = 1 inch.

To facilitate the counting of subdivisions, the above scales have been enlarged from their actual size.

THE ENGINEER'S SCALE

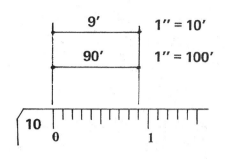

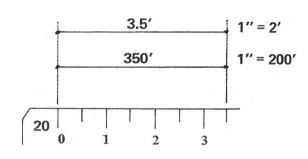

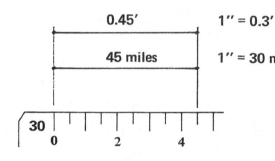

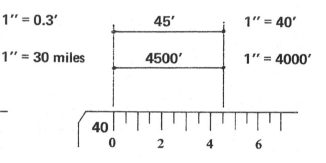

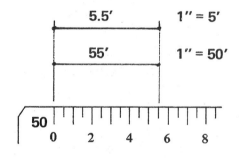

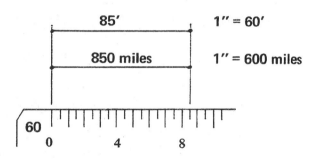

Shown above are the six standard scale units found on the **engineer's scale.** There are many possibilities for each scale unit since different lengths can be indicated for the scale unit. For example, in the case of a 10 scale, 1" can equal any one of the following: 0.1', 1', 10', 100', or 1000' (miles). Two possibilities are shown above for each of the six standard scale units. Divisions to the inch represent feet, rods, or miles.

Think of the scale number such as 10 as the number of divisions per inch. Thus, 40 would indicate 40 increments or parts per inch. A 1" = 40' scale would have 40 increments, each increment being one foot. These incremental divisions are then continued along the full length of the scale. The engineer's scale is used primarily for site plans and location plans.

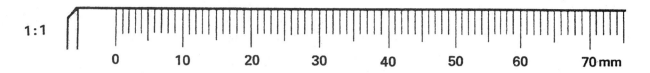

1:1

0   10   20   30   40   50   60   70 mm

This metric scale has a 1:1 ratio and should be used for **full-size** drawings.

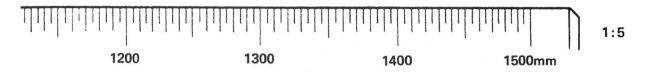

1:5

1200   1300   1400   1500mm

This metric scale has a 1:5 ratio and should be used for drawings **one-fifth full size**.

As with the architect's scale, the metric scales above have been enlarged for easier reading of the subdivisions. These scales are appropriate for architectural details (3"=1'0", etc.). The English system, which is still in use in the United States, is based on the inch and the foot. The **metric system** uses the **meter** (m) as its standard dimension; it has been accepted as the standard outside the United States and Great Britain. A meter is 3.281 feet in length. It is easy to manipulate because one only needs to add equal steps of 1000 parts to change to another multiple of the metric scale. For example, 1000 millimeters (mm) equals 1.0 meter (m). The metric scale is 150 millimeters long (about 6 inches). Architects use various metric scales for various types of drawings. For example, 1:500 is a common scale reduction ratio for site plans, whereas 1:100 is used for floor plans and elevations. Ratio reductions of 1:1 and 1:5 are seen frequently with architectural details. These examples show architectural drawings each requiring a different metric scale.

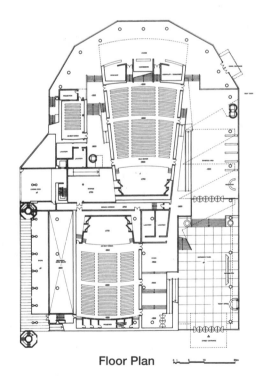

Floor Plan

Palazzo del Cinema, Venice, Italy
38 x 53 cm (15"x20.9")
Medium: Ink on Mylar
Courtesy of Maki and Associates

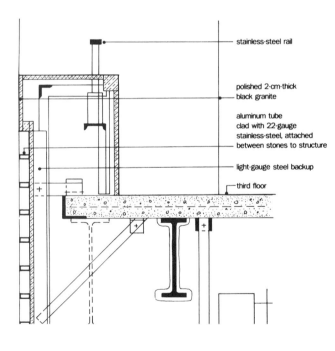

Partial section detail
One O'Hare Center
Rosemont, Illinois

Courtesy of Kohn Pedersen
Fox Associates, Architects

THE METRIC SCALE

2

Lettering Typography, and Line Types

In drafting as well as in the design-drawing process, knowledge of line types, control of line quality, typography, and lettering are important. Well executed hand lettering and proper line quality are needed for clear working drawings and design-drawings.

The intent of this chapter is to develop your ability first to recognize and ultimately to execute proficient lettering, typography, and line quality.

Lettering, Typography, and Line Types

Topic

Lettering

References

Ching, Francis D. K. 1996. Architectural Graphics, third edition. New York: Van Nostrand Reinhold. 148–150.

Lin, Mike. 1993. Designing and Drawing with Confidence. New York: Van Nostrand Reinhold. 75–76.

Sutherland, Martha. 1989. Lettering for Architects and Designers. New York: Van Nostrand Reinhold.

Topic

Typography

References

Berryman, Gregg. 1990. Notes on Graphic Design and Visual Communication. Los Altos: William Kaufmann, Inc.

Burden, Ernest. 1992.
Grid Systems & Formats Sourcebook.
Van Nostrand Reinhold.

Carter, Rob, Ben Day and Philip Meggs. 1985.
Typographic Design: Form and Communication. New York:
Van Nostrand Reinhold.

Lin, Mike. 1993. Designing and Drawing with Confidence.
New York: Van Nostrand Reinhold. 77–78.

Cross References

For pp. 25, 28–31   See pp. 527–532
For pp. 25–27   See pp. 534, 536, 542–543, 547–553
For pp. 36–37   See p. 373

Precise architectural hand lettering for working drawings and presentations will be needed for the immediate future despite the growing use of computer type styles in professional practice. Remember when doing hand lettering to work from the top to the bottom of the sheet; this prevents smudging. If it is not possible to move downward, then cover previously lettered lower parts of the sheet with some clean paper to prevent hand–graphite contact. The example below shows the lettering of a partial wall detail from a set of working drawings. Working drawings are the drawings used by a contractor to erect a structure.

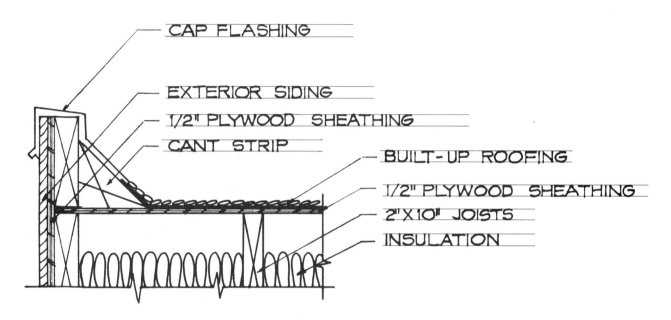

**Evanston Public Library
Design Competition**

Evanston Public Library Design Competition
Courtesy of Michael Blakemore/Sandy & Babcock, Inc.
Architecture & Planning

P E N I N S U L A   R E G E N T
BACKEN ARRIGONI & ROSS, INC.

The Peninsula Regent, San Mateo, California
Courtesy of Backen Arrigoni & Ross, Inc.
Architecture, Planning & Interior Design

An appropriate visual hierarchy of typography should be used for presentations. When we lay out a presentation, the drawings must be referred to using titles, heads, and text material in different styles, sizes, and weights. These bits of information are normally arranged in order of visual importance from heads to titles to text in that order. There must be a hierarchy of heads and titles for any kind of presentation. Presentation drawings can use mechanical lettering methods such as stencils in the form of templates, pressure transfer lettering sheets, traceable sheets in a variety of scales, and traceable typefaces available in computers. Stencilled lettering can achieve a handsome uniformity for a series of drawings; they are commonly used for titles. Stencils are cut in clear plastic templets so that guidelines can be viewed. Opaque color can be applied with brush, flair pens, or ink pens. The highest quality computer type is attained by using PostScript or TrueType printers and fonts. The advantage of these fonts is that they can retain their sharp clear form at any scale size.

When architectural lettering exceeds a height of ½", use larger block typefaces. **Pressure transfer** lettering catalogs give a variety of excellent typefaces. This kind of typographic lettering comes in sheets that can easily be traced over to add a professional quality to drawings. They are divided into two major groups: **serifs** and **sans** (without) **serifs.** Serifs were originally the terminations of parts of a letter that were chiseled by the Romans.

PRESENTATION TYPOGRAPHY

Serif and sans serifs are further divided into **light, medium,** and **heavy** weight types as shown in the three samples below. Always use serifs consistently for any set of drawings.

dining   SECTION

60 pt. l.c.   60 pt. CAPS   Helvetica Light

bath   ELEVATION

54 pt. l.c.   66 pt. CAPS   Folio Medium Extended

A RESIDENCE

36 pt. CAPS   Microgramma Bold Extended

Some nicely proportioned lettering typefaces are Imperial Roman (serif), Bauhaus Demi (sans serif), and Katrina Heavy (serif.) Note these examples below.

kitchen   DETAIL

48 pt. l.c.   72 pt. CAPS   Imperial Roman

Preliminary PLAN

48 pt. l.c.   60 pt. CAPS   Bauhaus Demi

storage   NORTH

60 pt. l.c.   48 pt. CAPS   Katrina Heavy

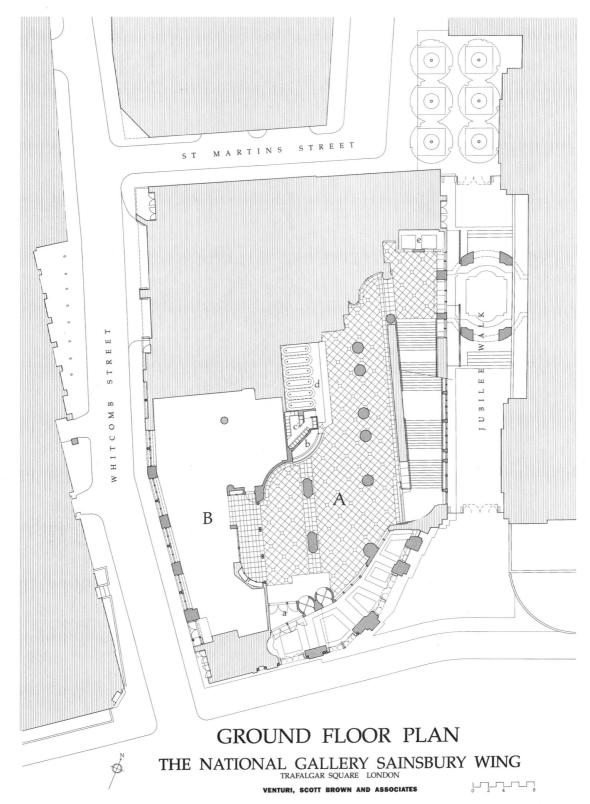

PRESENTATION TYPOGRAPHY

GROUND FLOOR PLAN

THE NATIONAL GALLERY SAINSBURY WING

TRAFALGAR SQUARE LONDON

VENTURI, SCOTT BROWN AND ASSOCIATES

Drawing: Ground Floor Plan, The National Gallery, Sainsbury Wing. Trafalgar Square, London, England
Medium: Ink on vellum (CAD) 30.25" × 43.5" (76.8 × 110.5 cm)
Courtesy of Venturi, Scott Brown and Associates, Inc., Architects

Note the clear hierarchy of titles on this presentation drawing.

Architectural lettering is derived from uppercase Gothic letters; the relative proportions of each letter is easily seen using a gridded background. In actual practice a grid system is not used; try to "eyeball" the correct proportions for each letter. The suggested stroke order need not be followed; individuals differ in hand–eye coordination and may differ in the number of strokes needed to complete a letter. It is important to be consistent in forming the same proportioned letter each time. For a left-handed person, the direction of the vertical strokes and curvilinear strokes remains the same, but the direction of horizontal strokes reverses.

HAND LETTERING

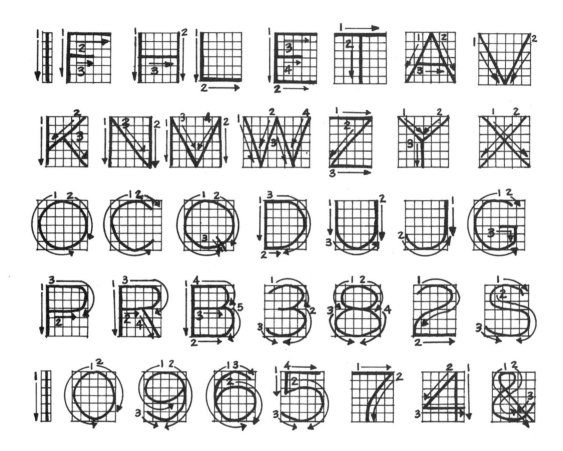

Notice that letters and numerals can be grouped in similar family types: the horizontal and vertical family (I through T); the horizontal, vertical, and angular family (A through X); and the curvilinear family (O through S). The numeral family has all the strokes. With time and practice, your overall goal should be to make controlled **quick, even strokes.** This is especially relevant to the rounded letters and numerals. Be sure the strokes are dark and crisp for good reproducibility. Good architectural hand lettering is the art of mastering basic motions: horizontal, vertical, angular, and curvilinear.

Lettering exercise: Become accustomed to the relative proportions shown for each letter by tracing or copying the letters and numerals on vellum. Repeat this exercise at two more heights: ¼" and ⅛".

The block lettering above is illustrated to help you develop your basic strokes. However, this type of lettering has the shortcoming of using too much space due to being very wide. In architectural work, a narrower proportioned alphabet as shown on the subsequent pages is more suitable.

Lettering Examples

"I LIKE COMPLEXITY AND CONTRADICTION IN ARCHITECTURE. I LIKE ELEMENTS WHICH ARE HYBRID RATHER THAN "PURE," COMPROMISING RATHER THAN "CLEAN," DISTORTED RATHER THAN "STRAIGHTFORWARD," AMBIGUOUS RATHER THAN "ARTICULATED," PERVERSE AS WELL AS IMPERSONAL, BORING AS WELL AS "INTERESTING," CONVENTIONAL RATHER THAN "DESIGNED," ACCOMMODATING RATHER THAN EXCLUDING, REDUNDANT RATHER THAN SIMPLE, VESTIGIAL AS WELL AS INNOVATING, INCONSISTENT AND EQUIVOCAL RATHER THAN DIRECT AND CLEAR. . . . "

I LIKE COMPLEXITY AND CONTRADICTION IN ARCHITECTURE. I LIKE ELEMENTS WHICH ARE HYBRID RATHER THAN "PURE," COMPROMISING RATHER THAN "CLEAN," DISTORTED RATHER THAN "STRAIGHTFORWARD," AMBIGUOUS RATHER THAN "ARTICULATED," PERVERSE AS WELL AS IMPERSONAL, BORING AS WELL AS "INTERESTING," CONVENTIONAL RATHER THAN "DESIGNED," ACCOMMODATING RATHER THAN EXCLUDING, REDUNDANT RATHER THAN SIMPLE, VESTIGIAL AS WELL AS INNOVATING, INCONSISTENT AND EQUIVOCAL RATHER THAN DIRECT AND CLEAR. I AM FOR MESSY VITALITY OVER OBVIOUS UNITY. I INCLUDE THE NON SEQUITUR AND PROCLAIM THE DUALITY.

(VENTURI 1966, 16)

COMPUTER-GENERATED LETTERING

Architectural statement: Reprinted with permission from Robert Venturi's "Complexity and Contradiction in Architecture" 1977 2nd edition, New York: The Museum of Modern Art

1. Computer-generated lettering: Tekton
   Used with express permission. Adobe® and Image Club
   Graphics ™ are trademarks of Adobe Systems Incorporated.
2. Additional software from Handy by Epiphany Design Studio

HAND LETTERING

BASIC GUIDES TO ARCHITECTURAL LETTERING

(1) ALWAYS USE LIGHTLY DRAWN GUIDELINES WHICH ARE THE UPPER AND LOWER LIMITS OF THE AREA BEING LETTERED.

(2) LETTERING SHOULD BE SIMPLE BLOCK VERTICAL CAPITALS.

(3) MINIMUM HEIGHT FOR ANY LETTERING IS 1/8".

MAJOR TITLES SHOULD BE 1/4" HIGH.
3/16" HEIGHT CAN BE USED FOR MINOR TITLES.

(4) MANY INDIVIDUALS ARE INVOLVED WITH THE PRODUCTION OF WORKING DRAWINGS. THERE IS A TREND TOWARDS THE ISSUING OF REDUCED DRAWINGS. THUS, A CLEAR UNIFORM TYPE OF LETTERING IS NEEDED. USE AN HB, H, OR F PENCIL LEAD WEIGHT WITH A ROUNDED CONICAL POINT FOR YOUR LETTERING.

(5) THE AREA BETWEEN VARIOUS ADJACENT | 1/8"
LETTER COMBINATIONS IN ANY WORD IS | 1/16" OR 1/8"
| 1/8"
BASED ON GOOD JUDGMENT. GOOD | 1/16" OR 1/8"
| 1/8"
SPACING DECISIONS BETWEEN LETTERS | 1/16" OR 1/8"
IS AN ART.   AREA IS ~ EQUAL | 1/8"
| 3/16"
DETAIL SCALE PLAN BRICK | 1/4"
| 3/16"
EQUAL SPACING IS BASED ON GOOD | 1/8"
| 1/16" OR 1/8"
VISUAL JUDGMENT. | 1/8"

(6) EXAMPLE: ALPHABETS & NUMERALS
ABCDEFGHIJKLMNOPQRSTUVWXYZ

1 2 3 4 5 6 7 8 9 0

THE USE OF A SMALL TRIANGLE TO KEEP
VERTICAL STROKES OF LETTERS VERTICAL
IS ACCEPTABLE AND IS COMMONLY DONE IN
PROFESSIONAL PRACTICE AS A QUICK
TECHNIQUE, HOWEVER, IT IS BEST TO
EXECUTE FREEHAND VERTICALS IF YOU HAVE
THE ABILITY TO KEEP LINES VERTICAL.

SLIGHT STYLIZATION OF LETTERS IS OFTEN
DONE IN PROFESSIONAL PRACTICE; ANY
DEVELOPMENT OF STYLE SHOULD ALWAYS
EXHIBIT CONSISTENCY IN SPACING, PROPORTION,
AND OVERALL APPEARANCE. FOR EXAMPLE,
THE LETTERS ON THE PREVIOUS PAGE CAN
BE STRETCHED HORIZONTALLY AND HORIZONTAL
STROKES CAN BE DONE AT A SLIGHT ANGLE
TO THE HORIZONTAL. "I" AND "J" ARE EXCEPTIONS
IN ATTEMPTING TO MAKE LETTERS AS
WIDE AS THEY ARE HIGH. SOMETIMES IT
TAKES YEARS TO MASTER THE ART OF GOOD
ARCHITECTURAL LETTERING; BE PATIENT
WITH YOUR PROGRESS.

HAND LETTERING

EXAMPLE: ALPHABET AND NUMERALS,

A   B   C   D   E   F   G   H   I
J   K   L   M   N   O   P   Q   R
S   T   U   V   W   X   Y   Z
1   2   3   4   5   6   7   8   9   0

Hand lettering (pp. 25, 30, 31, 33): Student project by Kam Wong
Medium: Pencil on vellum
Courtesy of the Department of Architecture
City College of San Francisco

A graph paper underlay is an alternative to guidelines (on translucent paper).

LINE TYPES AND LINE WEIGHTS

PENCIL LINES (for architectural drafting)	GRADE OF PENCIL TO USE
PROFILE LINE	H, F, or HB
VISIBLE/ELEVATION LINES	H, F, or HB
CONSTRUCTION/LAYOUT/GRID LINES	2H or 4H
SECTION LINE	H, F, or HB
SECTION LINING	H, F, or HB
HIDDEN/DASH LINES	H or 2H
CENTER LINE	2H or 4H
DIMENSION LINE / EXTENSION LINE	2H or 4H

Slashes and dots are alternatives to arrowheads for terminating dimension lines.

Drawing: National Gallery, Sainsbury Wing
London, England
2" × 26.5" (5.1 × 67.3 cm) Scale: 1:25
Medium: Ink on vellum
Courtesy of Venturi, Scott Brown and
Associates, Inc., Architects

Architectural drawing in the broad sense includes both architectural drafting and architectural sketching. Pencils are the simplest drawing medium in both areas. Pencil leads are made of compressed graphite and clay. The most common grades for architectural drafting work are 4H, 2H, F, H, and HB. To save time, it is common practice to use one lead and vary the pressure to give the desired line weight. An initially drawn line must be bold and uniform, not weak and tentative. Architectural sketching work (see p. 128) is commonly done with grades of 2B, 4B, and 6B, which are softer and allow for more expression.

Some drafting pointers:

Avoid corners that do not touch

A very small overlap is permissible

Keep an even line quality.
See pages 43 and 48

Just touching is the generally accepted correct procedure

Pointing or slightly emphasizing the end helps to strengthen its presence.

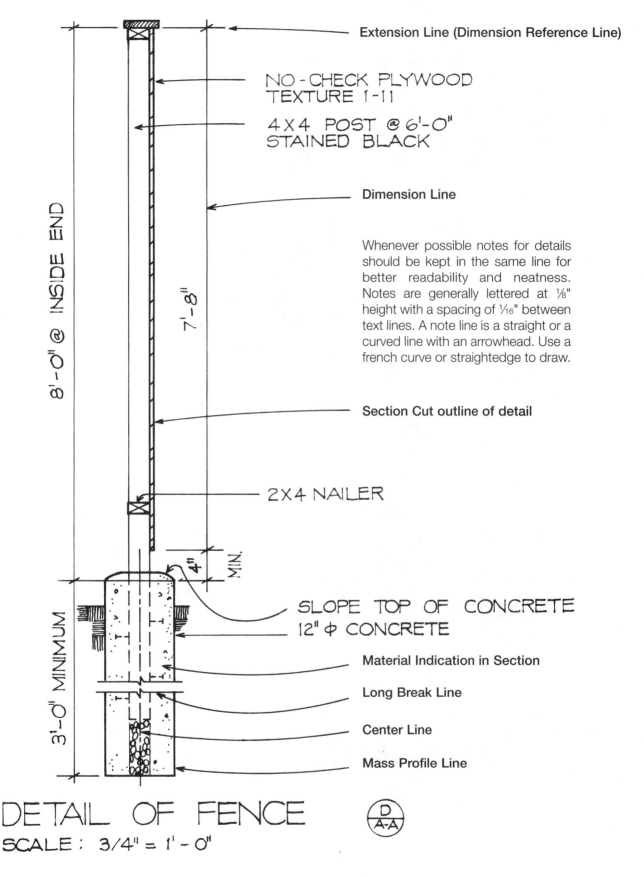

Extension Line (Dimension Reference Line)

NO - CHECK PLYWOOD
TEXTURE 1-11

4 X 4 POST @ 6'-0"
STAINED BLACK

Dimension Line

Whenever possible notes for details should be kept in the same line for better readability and neatness. Notes are generally lettered at ⅛" height with a spacing of ¹⁄₁₆" between text lines. A note line is a straight or a curved line with an arrowhead. Use a french curve or straightedge to draw.

Section Cut outline of detail

2 X 4 NAILER

8'-0" @ INSIDE END

7'-8"

4" MIN.

3'-0" MINIMUM

SLOPE TOP OF CONCRETE
12" ⌀ CONCRETE

Material Indication in Section

Long Break Line

Center Line

Mass Profile Line

DETAIL OF FENCE
SCALE : 3/4" = 1'-0"

LINE TYPES AND THEIR USAGE

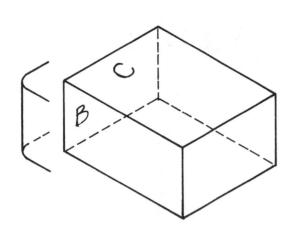

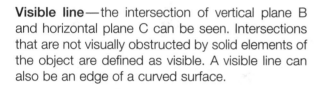

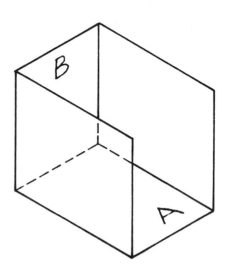

Visible line—the intersection of vertical plane B and horizontal plane C can be seen. Intersections that are not visually obstructed by solid elements of the object are defined as visible. A visible line can also be an edge of a curved surface.

Hidden line—vertical plane B and horizontal plane A intersect, resulting in an intersection line that cannot be seen from the observer's position. This is represented by a dashed line.

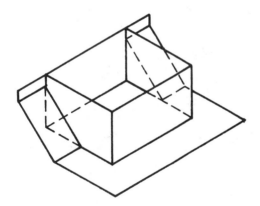

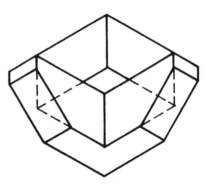

These pictorials (defined as pitch pockets) are part of construction documents for a contractor to use in the erection of a building. Note the use of hidden dashed lines to enhance the visualization of the details. When visible lines, hidden lines, and center lines coincide on a drawing, it is important to know which line takes precedence. A visible line takes precedence over a center line or a hidden line. A hidden line takes precedence over a center line.

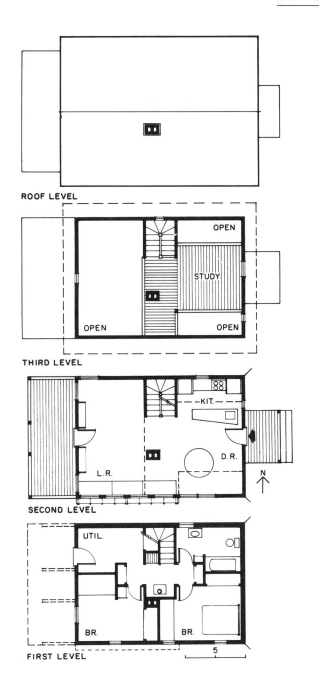

ROOF LEVEL

THIRD LEVEL

SECOND LEVEL

FIRST LEVEL

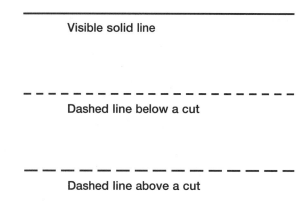

Visible solid line

Dashed line below a cut

Dashed line above a cut

Visible solid lines and dashed hidden lines are two of the most important lines in finished architectural drawings. These lines are drawn with H, F, or HB lead weights. HB drawn lines erase easily, but they tend to smear the most. Note that the dashed line below a cut is proportionally smaller than the one used above a cut. Strive to produce a consistent spacing and length for each dash.

Drawing: Hog Hill House
12" × 30" (30.5 × 76.2 cm) Scale 1/8"=1'0"
Medium: Ink on Mylar
Courtesy of B FIVE STUDIO

Visible lines in architectural drawings can be used for the outline of plan or section cuts (see example above) and any other intersection of planes (wall intersections in plan or elevation, etc.).

Dashed lines in architectural drawings express lines above a plan cut that the observer cannot see, such as roof overhangs (see example above), roof perforations, and skylights, as well as lines below a plan cut that are obscured by the floor, such as partitions.

LINE TYPES AND THEIR USAGE

LINE WEIGHT AND LINE QUALITY

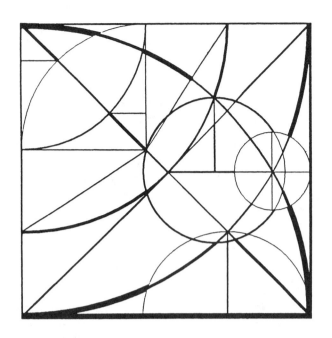

Drawing: Student project by Stephanie Slack
Medium: CAD
Courtesy of California Polytechnic State University, San Luis Obispo
College of Architecture & Environmental Design

Example Line Weights

Line quality refers to the crispness and the darkness (weight intensity) of a line. The darkness of a line is governed by the pencil used and the pressure applied. Inked lines generally have uniform value but can vary in width. It is extremely important to be consistent in drawing the same type of lines.

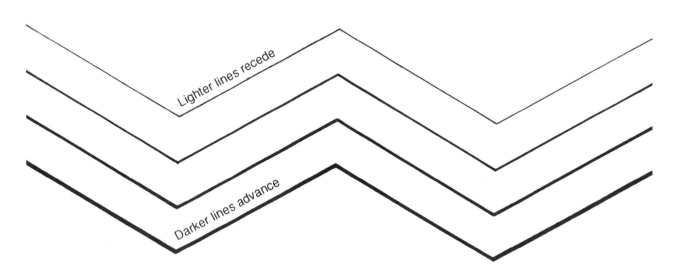

Lighter lines recede

Darker lines advance

As you develop your design-drawing skills, you will realize the importance of line weight and line quality in any composition. As line weights vary, they impact on any composition. Design parameters like variety, spatial depth, and visual hierarchy can be affected.

Drawings: Student project by Ben Ragle
Medium: CAD
Courtesy of California Polytechnic State University, San Luis Obispo
College of Architecture & Environmental Design

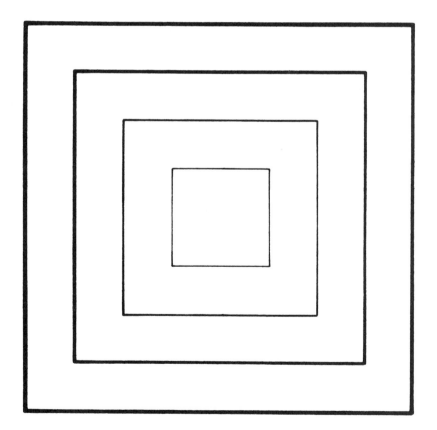

Emphasis is using line weight to create the illusion of space. The more variation of hierarchical line weight from thick to thin, the more implication of depth in the drawing.

EMPHASIS

3

Conventional Orthogonal Terminology

Scaled plans, elevations, and sections are drawings that depict a building or an urban landscape at a smaller size than true size. These drawings follow the principles of "orthographic projection" (see orthographic–paraline section) and help to depict an object in different but related two-dimensional views. Some other architectural drawing conventions (paraline, perspective) require detailed investigation, which accounts for their description in subsequent separate chapters.

The intent of this chapter is to introduce the potential and capabilities of these drawings and symbols and the kinds of information they can communicate.

Conventional Orthogonal Terminology

Topic

Conventional Orthogonal Terminology

References

Drawing: A Creative Process (Ching 1990)
       2-Dimensional Views: 146–153

Graphics for Architecture (Forseth 1980)
       Multiviews: 21–76

Projection Drawing (Wang 1984)
       The Types of Projections: 16–28

Cross References

For p. 41   See p. 431
For pp. 42–43   See pp. 70, 76
For p. 53   See pp. 432, 434–435, 454–457
For p. 56   See p. 546, 578
For p. 59   See pp. 264–265

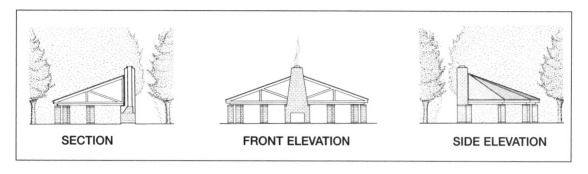

SECTION   FRONT ELEVATION   SIDE ELEVATION

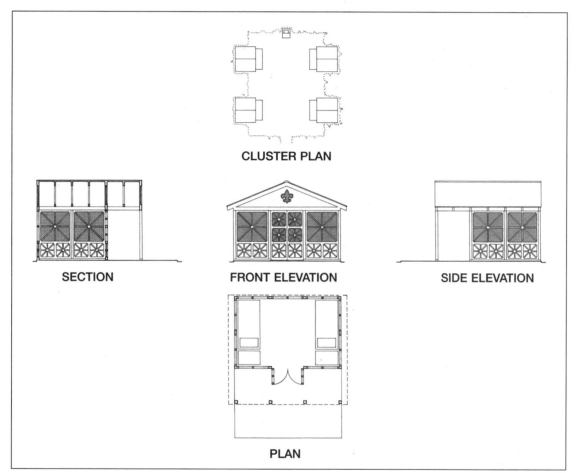

CLUSTER PLAN

SECTION   FRONT ELEVATION   SIDE ELEVATION

PLAN

INTRODUCTION

Drawings: Hoover Camping Cluster in the Hoover Outdoor Education Center
        Yorkville, Illinois
Medium: Ink on Mylar
Courtesy of Tigerman McCurry Architects

Historically, buildings have been described using an **orthogonal** (right-angled) two-dimensional drawing system. The nomenclature used for the various orthogonal views are shown here. Popular architectural terminology such as "floor plan" is common knowledge for the layperson.

Small building types like residences are usually orthogonally drawn at a scale of ⅛"=1'0" or ¼"=1'0". A smaller scale (1⁄16"=1'0") can be used for larger building types such as hospitals and schools. A knowledge of orthogonal conventions and graphic symbols is necessary for architectural drawings and presentations. This chapter isolates and explores these topics in detail.

PRINCIPAL PLANES OF PROJECTION

The horizontal **plan** plane is always parallel to the level ground.

The profile **elevation** plane is always at right angles (perpendicular—90°) to the other two planes.

Ortho literally means "right angle." **Orthographic projection** refers to the transfer of images created by perpendicular projector rays striking a transparent glass plane. The rays are always parallel to each other.

The frontal **elevation** plane is always vertical and 90° to the level ground.

The principal planes along with three additional adjoining planes (back or rear, left profile, and bottom) form a closed **glass box**.

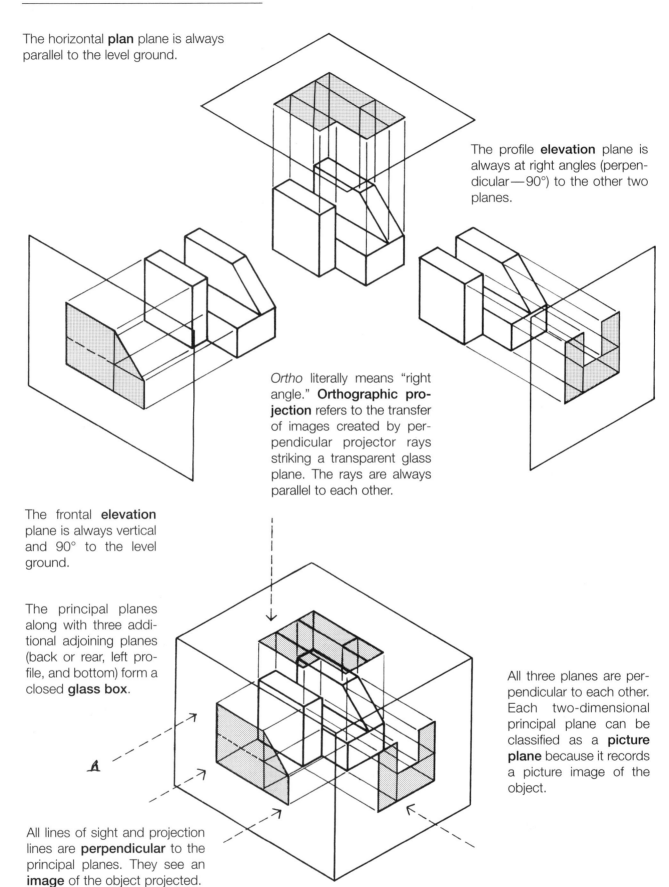

All three planes are perpendicular to each other. Each two-dimensional principal plane can be classified as a **picture plane** because it records a picture image of the object.

All lines of sight and projection lines are **perpendicular** to the principal planes. They see an **image** of the object projected.

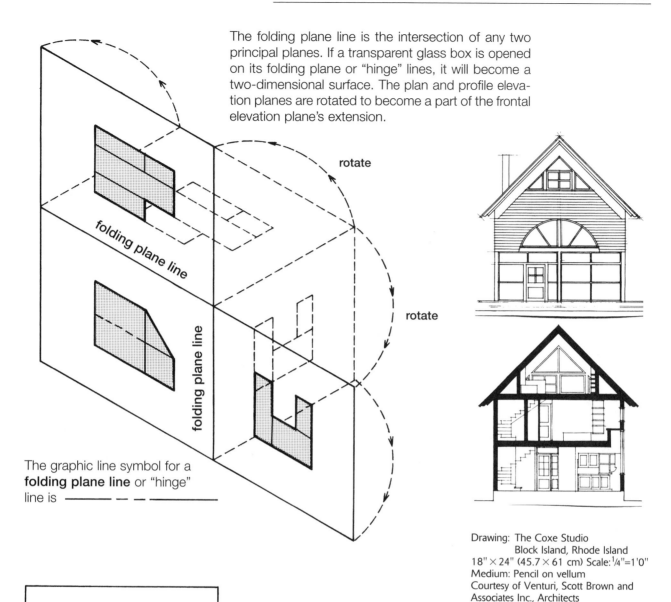

The folding plane line is the intersection of any two principal planes. If a transparent glass box is opened on its folding plane or "hinge" lines, it will become a two-dimensional surface. The plan and profile elevation planes are rotated to become a part of the frontal elevation plane's extension.

rotate

rotate

folding plane line

folding plane line

The graphic line symbol for a **folding plane line** or "hinge" line is ———— — — ————

Drawing: The Coxe Studio
            Block Island, Rhode Island
18" × 24" (45.7 × 61 cm) Scale: $\frac{1}{4}$"=1'0"
Medium: Pencil on vellum
Courtesy of Venturi, Scott Brown and
Associates Inc., Architects

ORTHOGRAPHIC VIEWS

a K

K

a   K a

The above example shows two true-size profile views (elevation and section). **Orthographic** drawings are true-size and true-shape views that are linked and related on a two-dimensional surface.

Remember that when two planes are perpendicular to a third plane, any point in space (such as **a**) will be seen twice an **equal** distance (K) behind the third plane. K can be any distance.

ELEVATION/PLAN/SECTION

An **elevation** primarily shows vertical dimension relationships and the scale of the fenestration.

In an elevation, the image is projected onto a vertical picture plane. Only the ground plane which is outside of the building will be shown as a solid cut. The ground line under the elevation of the building is commonly made thinner and thus lighter than the ground line not touching the building. By tracing over sections and using the plan, elevations can be created.

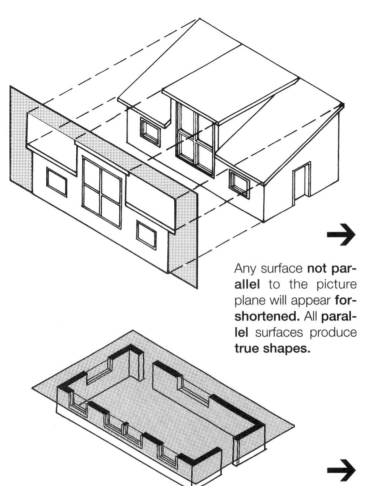

Any surface **not parallel** to the picture plane will appear **foreshortened.** All **parallel** surfaces produce **true shapes.**

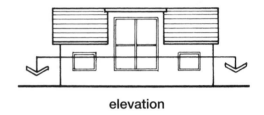

elevation

In a **plan,** a horizontal plane cuts through the building so as to remove that part of the building above the cutting plane.

To help facilitate the understanding of viewer direction and location on sectional cuts, a line with labeled direction arrows (in this case B-B) should always be shown in the plan view.

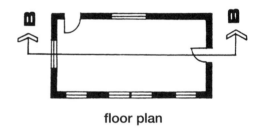

floor plan

In a **section,** a vertical plane cuts through the building so as to remove that part of the building in front of the cutting plane.

Design sections normally do not show the foundation piers to reference the datum line but rather show a toned or solid cut ground mass or an edge line between sky and ground.

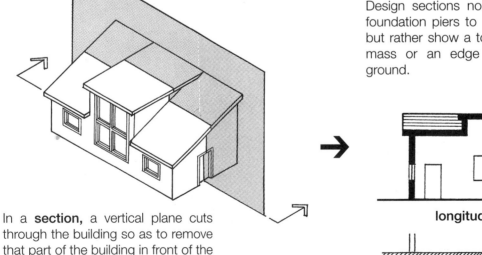

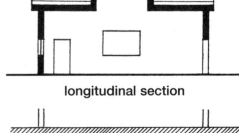

longitudinal section

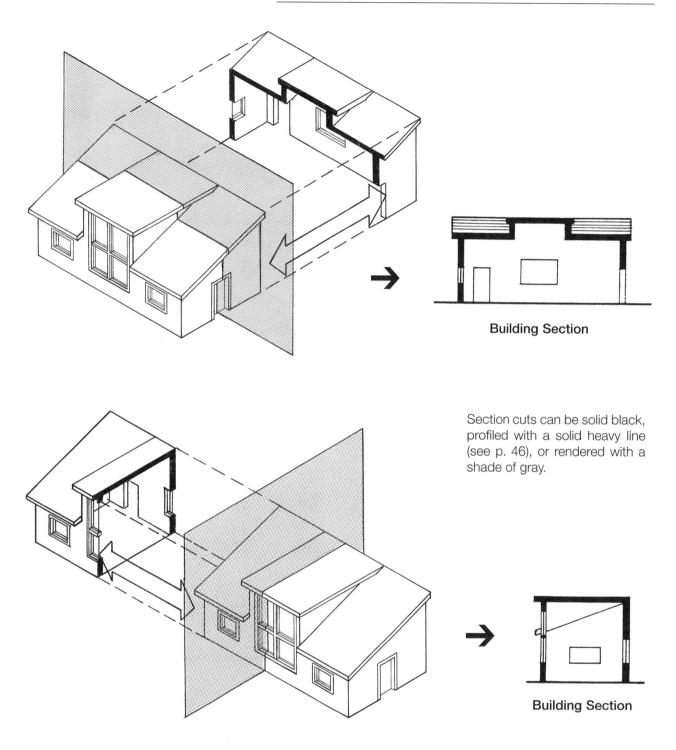

Building Section

Section cuts can be solid black, profiled with a solid heavy line (see p. 46), or rendered with a shade of gray.

Building Section

BUILDING SECTION

A **building section** is analogous to the horizontal cut section (plan) except that the cutting plane is **vertical.** Removing that part of the building in front of the plane reveals a cut pictorial section which allows us to take a glimpse of the interior space. Sectional cuts in architectural drawings are primarily done either prallel to the front or the side elevation. These sections are then properly annotated as explained on the previous page. The location of the cut and the direction of view is left to the decision of the architect/designer. Try to be most descriptive in showing spatial relationships.

The contour that defines where the sky (or space above) meets the building mass and the ground line determines the configuration of any **site section.** The primary function of a site section is to relate any building design to its **contextual environment.**

SECTION TYPES

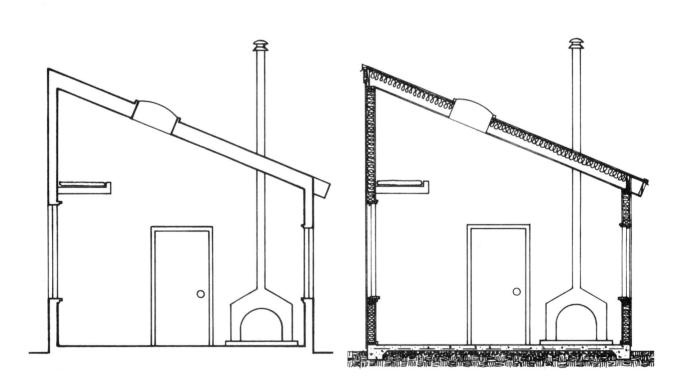

A **design section** shows no structural or construction details in the section area that is cut. The section is profiled with a heavy line to help define the interior spaces and overall form of the building. A **construction section** shows the details required to fabricate the building.

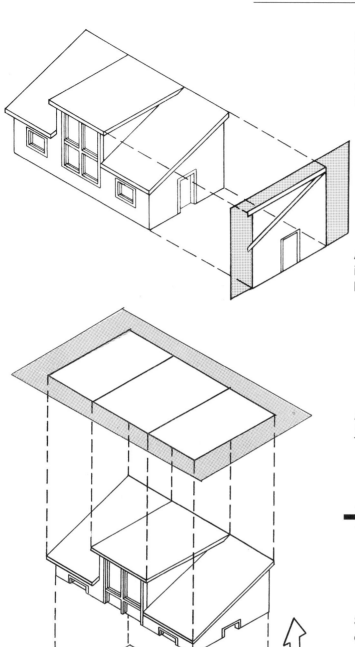

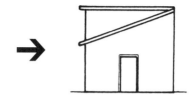

Elevation views are identified by the compass directions (e.g., North Elevation, Southwest Elevation). An elevation shows the relationship of a building's mass to the ground plane as well as its scale and exterior material texture.

A **reflected ceiling plan** is the image reflected into an imaginary mirror placed on the floor plan below.

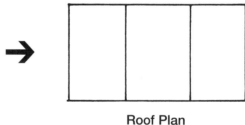

A **roof plan** shows the roof configuration projected on a horizontal plane.

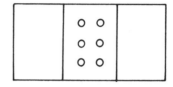

Roof Plan

Section arrows shown in plan indicate the observer's direction of sight.

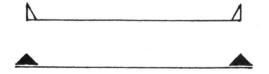

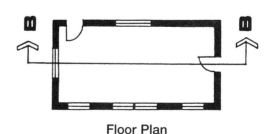

Floor Plan

A **plan** is represented best if the horizontal cut is taken through all openings (such as doors and windows) as well as important vertical elements (such as columns).

ELEVATION VIEWS AND PLAN TYPES

DRAWING THE PLAN: STEP-BY-STEP

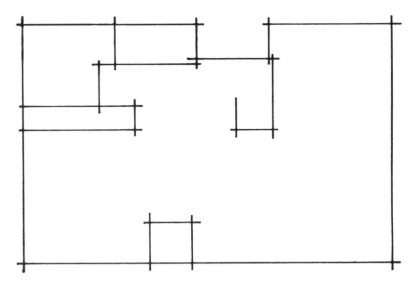

Pages 48 and 49 give a step-by-step process for drawing the plan. In general, the best procedure is to draw the building shell first, then all of the elements contained within the shell. Be sure to locate the center lines of all windows and doors.

(1) Lightly draw the building outline with a single line. Use a single line and lightly draw the center line for interior walls.

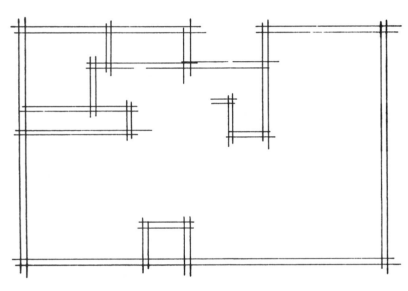

(2) Add wall thickness for both exterior and interior walls.

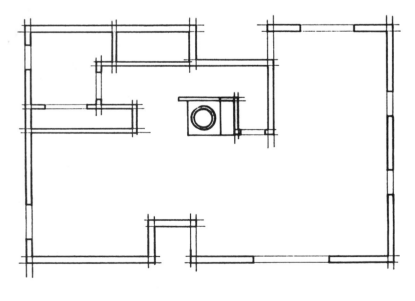

(3) Locate and draw wall openings such as windows, doors, fireplaces, and stairs.

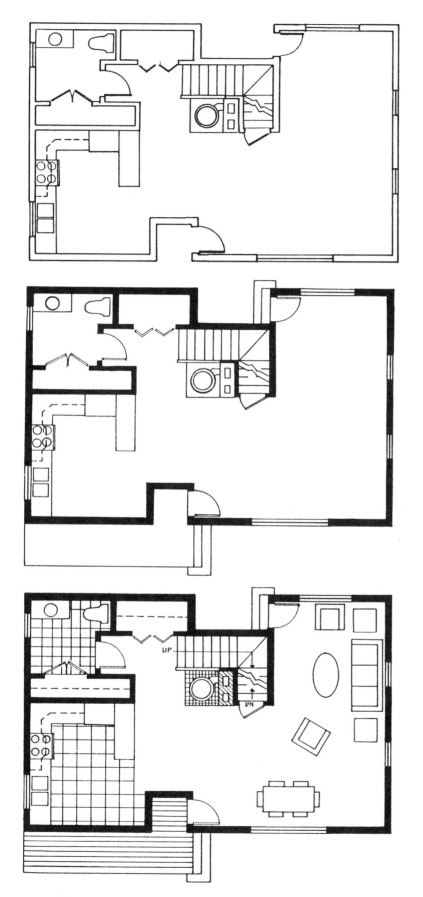

(4) Locate and draw bathroom and kitchen fixtures as well as plan details for doors and windows.

(5) Draw any plan view wall indications with its proper tone value (see p. 50). In this case the wall is toned solid black. If it were left white, the wall outline could be made heavier to make it read better.

(6) Draw the proper material symbol (tone and texture) for the floors in each room.

This step-by-step procedure applies to both freehand or mechanically drawn plans.

The main purpose of furniture and built-in elements (stoves, sinks, etc.) in the plan view is to show function and scale. For an accurate interpretation, the plan view, as with all orthogonal views, must have a constant scale.

DRAWING THE PLAN: STEP-BY-STEP

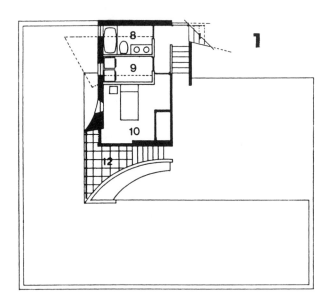

Drawing: The Hague Villa Project
          The Hague, The Netherlands
8" × 10 (20.3 × 25.4 cm) Scale ¼"=1'0"
Medium: Pen and ink
Courtesy of Hariri & Hariri, Architects

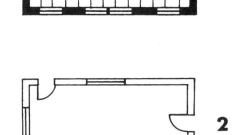

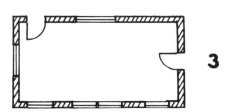

1

2

3

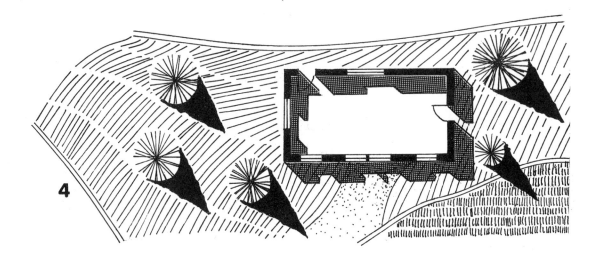

4

Floor plan wall indications can be given different tonal values. In **1**, more contrast is desired; thus, the walls are toned solid black. In **2**, no contrast is needed; thus, the walls are left white with a profile line. In **3**, a sketched line or hatched tone is used for intermediate contrast (can also indicate building material). In **4**, a solid black wall is used to contrast with surrounding ground textures (see section on delineating and rendering entourage) or outdoor patio/deck areas. Condition **2** is least distractive and is most often preferred in the presentation of design drawings. Shadows are sometimes cast within the plan view (p. 342) to give added contrast (condition **4**).

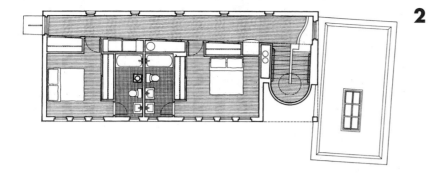

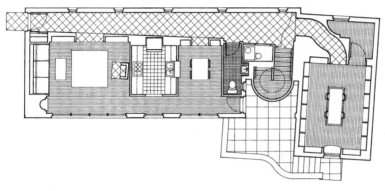

2 Floor plans express and communicate the intent of a design as well as the feasibility of a layout. The patterns, values, and colors of floor furnishings (see pp. 383, 402, and 404) are equally as important as indications for the walls. Condition **2** can be effective if both the floorscape and surrounding groundscape receive a moderately dark value. Darken the outline of the plan cut to provide more "punch." Condition **3** shows a plan wall material indication for concrete block.

Drawing: Son of Chang, Augusta, Georgia
24" × 24" (61x61 cm) Scale 1/4"=1'0"
Medium: Ink
Courtesy of Anthony Ames, Architect

3

4

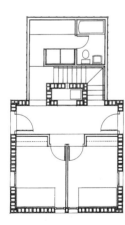

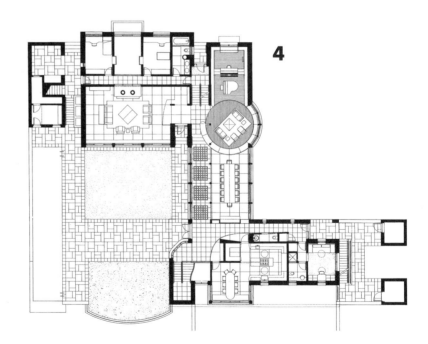

Drawing: Reid House
      Johns Island, South Carolina
20" × 30" (50.8 × 76.2 cm) Scale: ¼"=1'0"
Medium: Ink on Mylar
Courtesy of Clark & Menefee, Architects

Drawing: Private residence, Zumikon, Switzerland
48" × 36" (121.9 × 91.4 cm) Scale: 1:50
Medium: Ink on Mylar
Courtesy of Gwathmey Siegel & Associates, Architects

PLAN WALL INDICATIONS

NORTH ARROWS/GRAPHIC SCALES

SCALE

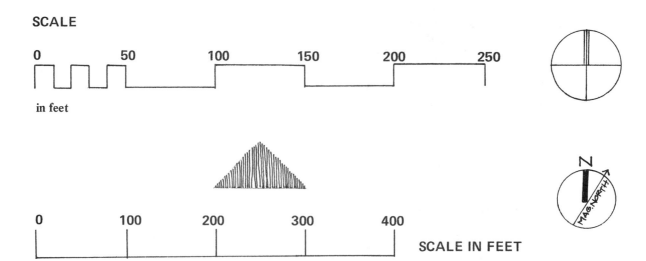

in feet

SCALE IN FEET

North arrows and graphic scales should be **clean, simple,** and **legible.** They should be placed adjacent to each other in a presentation drawing. These symbols facilitate the understanding of the **orientation** and the **scale** of the building. North arrows should never be a distraction on a drawing.

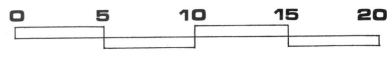

SCALE IN FEET

SCALE ¼" = 1"- 0"

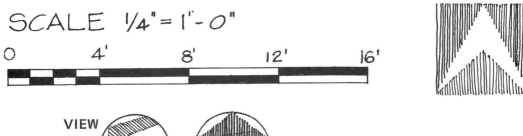

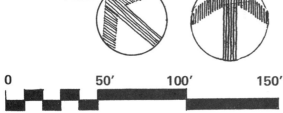

The choice of a graphic scale size is dependent on the **size** and the **complexity** of the drawing. Note that 1" can be represented by whatever multiple you want to make it (i.e., 1" can be equal to 4' or 5'). For convenience, use 1"=1' unit of length regardless of the length represented.

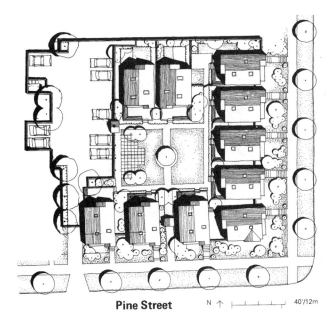

Pine Street

N ↑ |‒‒‒‒‒| 40'/12m

Drawing: Pine Street Cottages, Seattle, Washington
Kucher/Rutherford, Inc. Developer and Contractor
Courtesy of Marcia Gamble Hadley, Designer

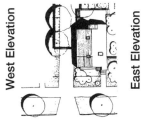

North Elevation

West Elevation

East Elevation

**South Elevation or
Pine St. Elevation**

If the front of a building faces north then the proper notation is North Elevation, and likewise for any direction the various sides of the building may face (i.e., Southwest Elevation). An important site feature such as a major street or a body of water can be used in place of the direction.

Site plans show the orientation and the location of a building (below) or many buildings (above). They can be precise pictorial drawings as shown on this page or schematic drawings (see pp. 432, 434, 435, 456). They are commonly drawn at 1/16"=1'0" or at engineering scales such as 1"=20', 1"=40', and 1"=50'. The boundaries of the site which should enclose all site elements as well as the building complex must be clearly defined as shown below. Shadows help to reveal the building's height and its overall configuration (see pp. 369 and 382).

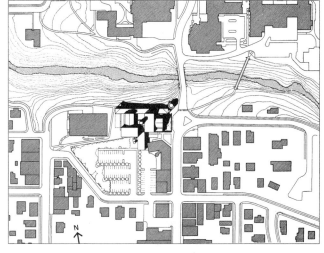

Drawing: Cornell University Center for the
Performing Arts, Ithaca, New York
Scale: 1"=50'0"
Courtesy of James Stirling Michael Wilford
and Associates, Architects

A **location plan** is a variation of the site plan which takes a larger regional context. Important site features like transportation arteries, surrounding buildings, and the physical topography are commonly drawn. These environmental elements usually play an important role in influencing the design of the proposed building.

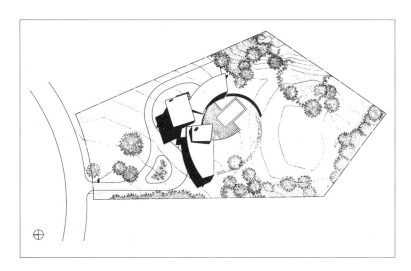

Drawing: Kreindel residence, Cresskill, New Jersey
Courtesy of Frank Lupo and Daniel Rowen, Architects

THE SITE PLAN

DESIGN SECTION: CUTS AND LIGHT STUDIES

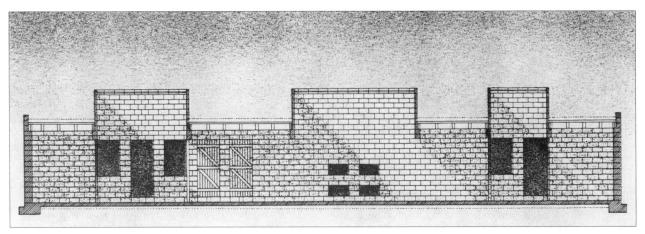

Drawing: Anti-Villa, Napa Valley, California
Medium: Airbrush
Courtesy of Batey & Mack, Architects

Section through hallway

A **building design section** must reveal design objectives as much as possible. To this end, slices are taken through important solids and voids. Light studies are frequently done to reinforce how directional sunlight comes through window or skylight openings. Human figures are also added to give a proper scale to the drawing.

Sections are normally cut through **1** door and window openings, **2** circulation change of level elements (i.e., stairs and ramps), and **3** ceiling or roof openings such as skylights. Foundation elements may or may not be shown, depending on their significance in the overall design, and columns should never show section cuts through them.

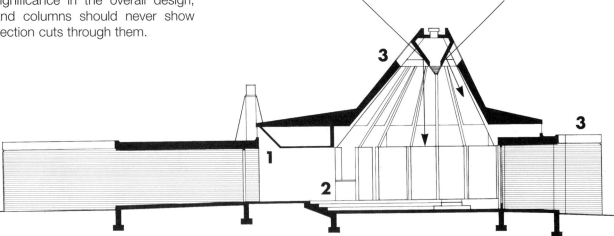

Drawing: Freeman residence, Grand Rapids, Michigan
30" × 20" (76.2 × 50.8 cm) Scale: 1/8"=1'0"
Medium: Ink on vellum
Courtesy of Gunnar Birkerts and Associates, Inc., Architects

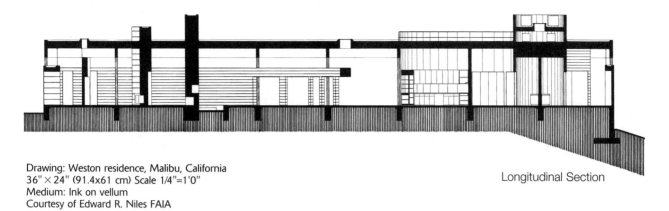

Drawing: Weston residence, Malibu, California
36" × 24" (91.4x61 cm) Scale 1/4"=1'0"
Medium: Ink on vellum
Courtesy of Edward R. Niles FAIA

Longitudinal Section

Lines within the longitudinal section showing the interior elevation above have slightly different line weight intensities. Note the close spacing of vertical lines to indicate a cut ground section. Also note the unequal spacing of fine lines in the interior elevation to imply a curved surface (see p. 319).

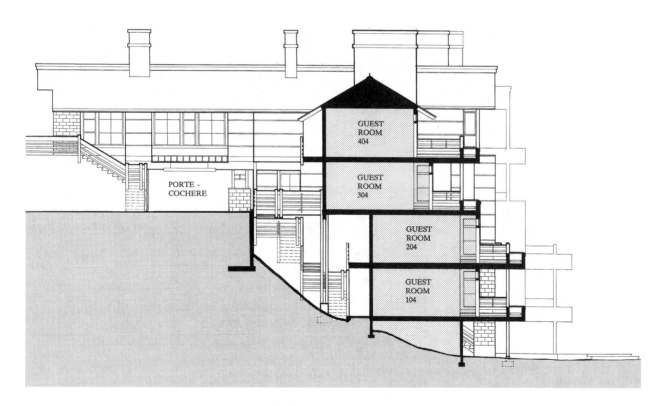

PORTE - COCHERE

GUEST ROOM 404

GUEST ROOM 304

GUEST ROOM 204

GUEST ROOM 104

Drawing: The INN at Langley, Whidbey Island, Washington
Courtesy of GGLO Architecture and Interior Design

It is common to see a hierarchy of elevation lines in a design section. The elevation line weights diminish in intensity as the distance from the observer increases. This contrast in line weights is an excellent depth cue.

DESIGN SECTION: ELEVATION LINES BEYOND

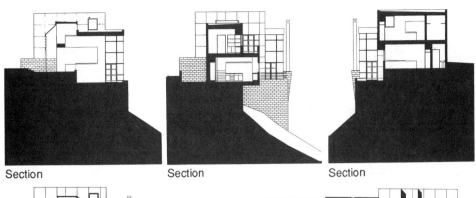

Section   Section   Section

Drawings: Naiditch residence
                Altadena, California
Scale: ⅜"=1'0"
Medium: Pen and ink on Mylar
Courtesy of Dean Nota Architect

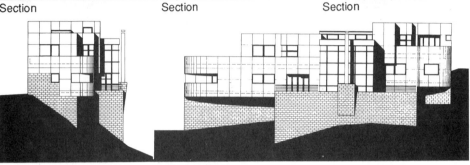

South Elevation   East Elevation

In this compact presentation of sections and elevations, the sectional cut is toned solid black, which allows the viewer to see a clear relationship between the building design and the groundline. This area is a convenient location (within or adjacent to) for labeling and identifying the drawings.

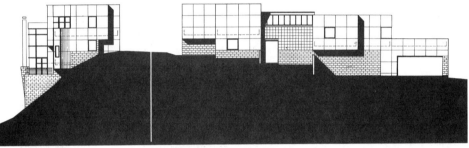

North Elevation   West Elevation

SECTION/ELEVATION LABELING

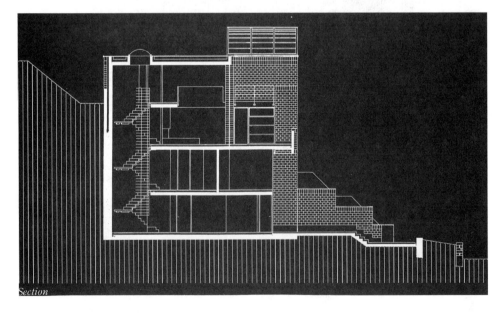

Section

Drawing: Single-family house, Daro, Bellinzona, Switzerland
Courtesy of Mario Botta, Architect, Lugano, Switzerland

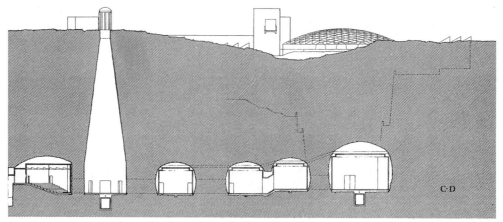

Section C-D showing auditorium, light-shaft and galleries

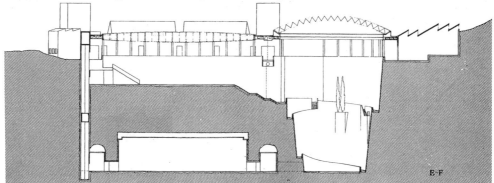

Section E-F showing "Sunk" and galleries

Drawings: The Guggenheim Museum, Salzburg. Salzburg, Austria
Courtesy of Hans Hollein, Architekt

The identification of these sections are placed within the area of the section cut.

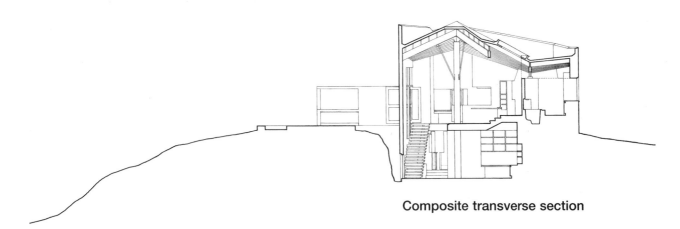

Composite transverse section

Drawing: Barnes House. Nanaimo, British Columbia, Canada
18" × 36" (45.7 × 91.4 cm) Scale: 1/4"=1'0"
Medium: Ink on vellum
Courtesy of Patkau Architects

SECTION LABELING

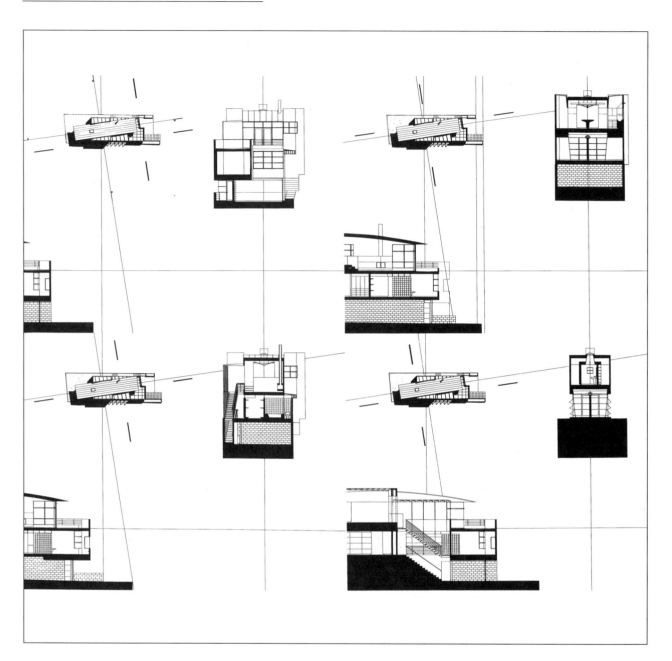

COMPOSITE SECTIONS

Drawings (two facing pages): Elliot residence, Hermosa Beach,
California
Scale: 3/8"=1'0"
Medium: Pen and ink on Mylar
Courtesy of Dean Nota Architect

The use of **composite sections** allows the viewer to examine a multitude of sections for a building. The sections are taken at selected intervals. With the advent of computer-generated drawings, sectional cuts can be immediately examined at an infinite number of locations. This is analogous to a CAT scan in medical technology.

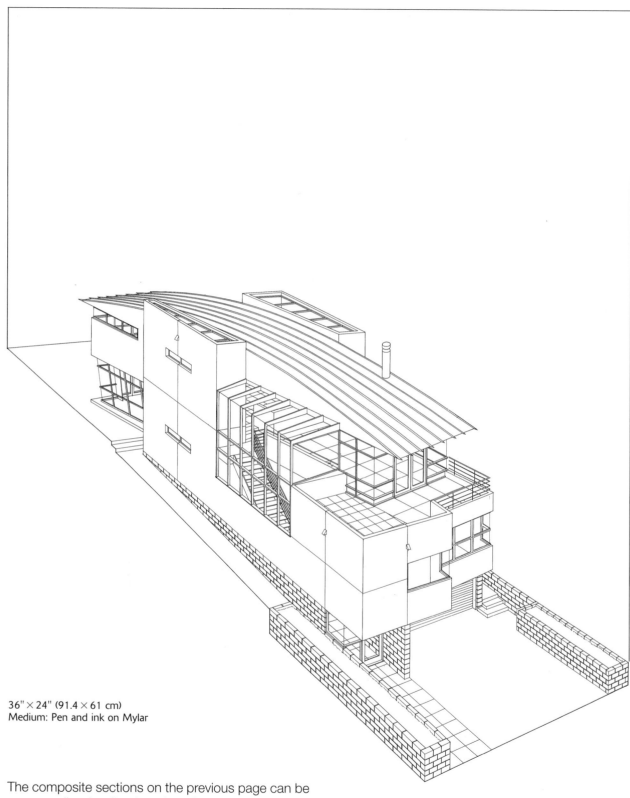

36" × 24" (91.4 × 61 cm)
Medium: Pen and ink on Mylar

PICTORIAL FOR COMPOSITE SECTIONS

The composite sections on the previous page can be more easily visualized and understood by relating them to the above pictorial.

STAIRWAYS

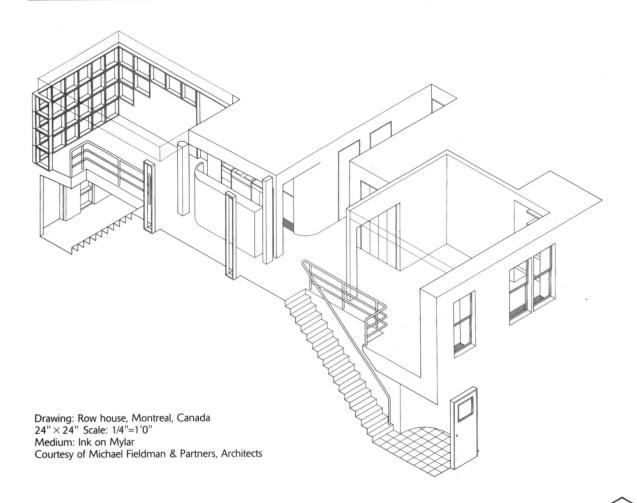

Drawing: Row house, Montreal, Canada
24" × 24" Scale: 1/4"=1'0"
Medium: Ink on Mylar
Courtesy of Michael Fieldman & Partners, Architects

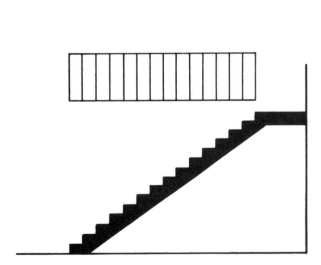

Straight run

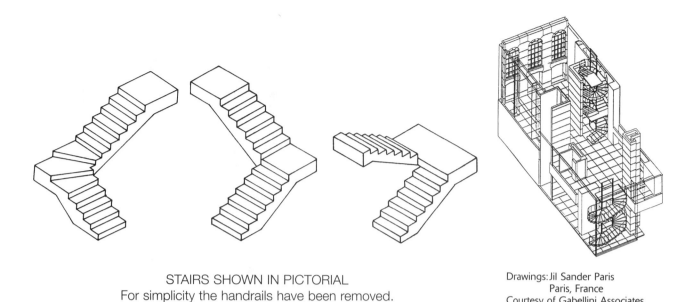

STAIRS SHOWN IN PICTORIAL
For simplicity the handrails have been removed.

Drawings: Jil Sander Paris
Paris, France
Courtesy of Gabellini Associates

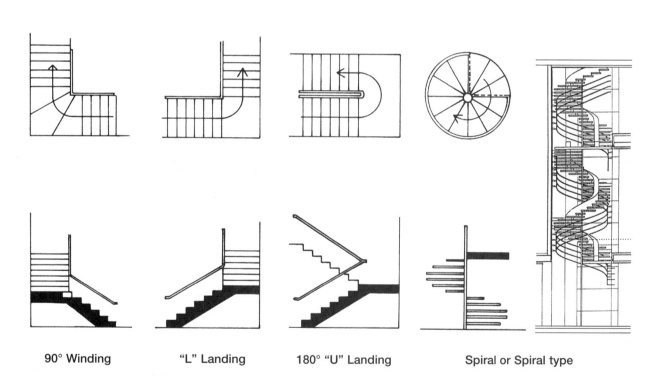

90° Winding   "L" Landing   180° "U" Landing   Spiral or Spiral type

STAIRWAYS

Stairways are the sequence of steps that connect two or more floors in a building. The four examples above are typical (straight stairs are also common) stairway situations seen in plan and in section. In a floor plan, the up or down direction arrow is from the level of the floor plan.

WINDOWS

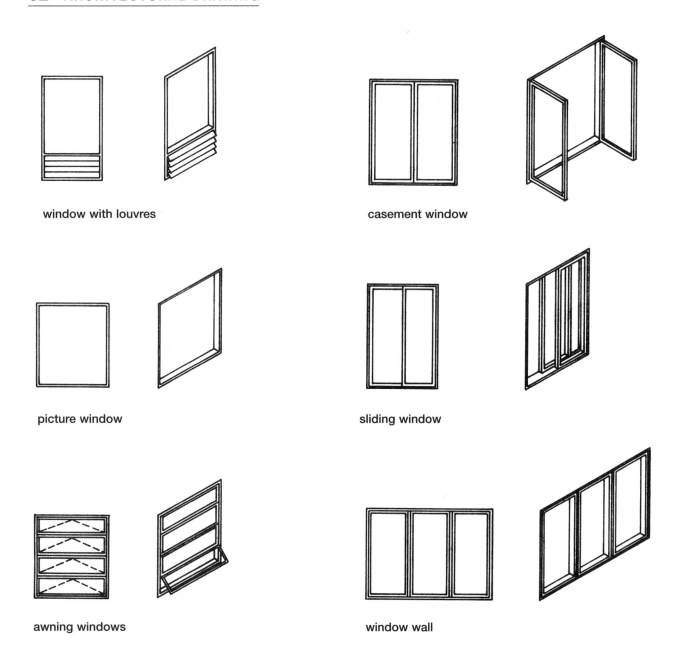

window with louvres

casement window

picture window

sliding window

awning windows

window wall

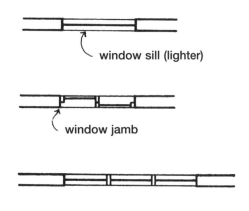

window sill (lighter)

window jamb

Six typical types of windows and five typical types of doors are shown in elevation and in pictorial on p. 62 and p. 63. A plan window is the result of a horizontal cut through the window glass, its frame (jamb), and the wall on both sides.

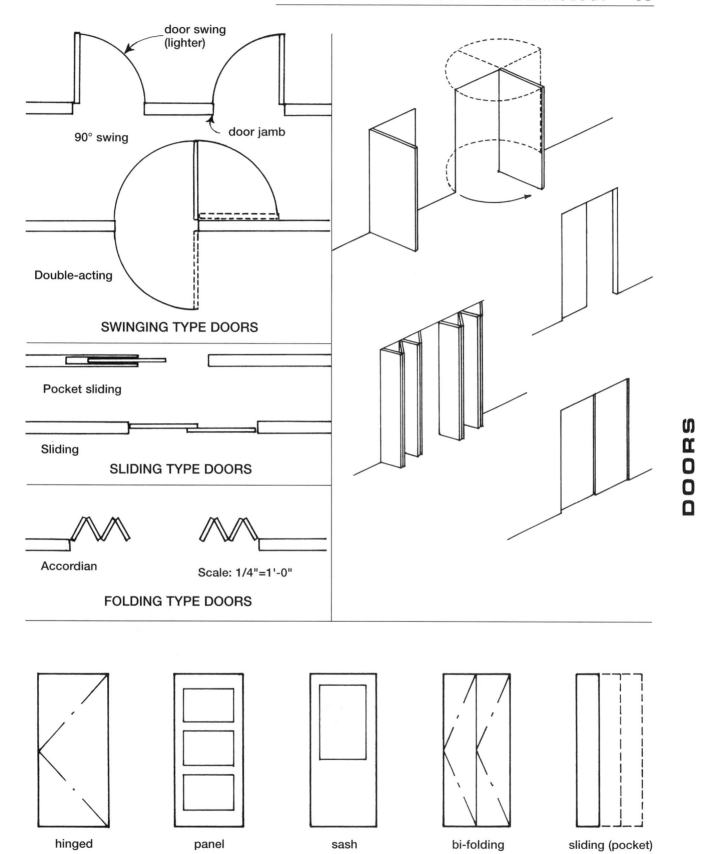

door swing (lighter)

90° swing

door jamb

Double-acting

SWINGING TYPE DOORS

Pocket sliding

Sliding

SLIDING TYPE DOORS

Accordian

Scale: 1/4"=1'-0"

FOLDING TYPE DOORS

DOORS

| hinged | panel | sash | bi-folding | sliding (pocket) |

TYPICAL TYPES OF DOORS

4

Orthographic and Paraline Drawing

It is important that the student of environmental design develop the ability to visualize and graphically express forms and spaces in three dimensions. The design-drawing process begins with two-dimensional expressions in the form of orthographic projections. These multiview drawings are the plan, elevation, and section vocabulary that an architect/designer uses. They are followed by three-dimensional single-view drawings, paralines, and perspectives. Single-view drawings express volumetric forms by combining the parameters of length, width, and depth.

The intent of this chapter is to develop your ability to visualize and communicate form and space by relating orthographic drawings to three-dimensional paraline drawings such as isometrics, axonometrics, and obliques.

Orthographic and Paraline Drawing

Topic

Orthographics

References

Drawing: A Creative Process (Ching 1990) 146–153.

Architectural Graphics (Ching 1985) 17–45.

Drawing and Perceiving (Cooper 1992) 125–132.

Graphics for Architecture (Forseth 1980) 21–75.

The Language of Visual Art (Myers 1989) 112–114.

Basic Visual Concepts and Principles
(Wallschlaeger and Busic-Snyder 1992) 60–61.

Topic

Paralines (axonometrics and obliques)

References

Drawing: A Creative Process (Ching 1990) 154–159.

Architectural Graphics (Ching 1985) 46–53.

Drawing and Perceiving (Cooper 1992) 139–145.

Graphics for Architecture (Forseth 1980) 77–97.

The Language of Visual Art (Myers 1989) 110–111.

Basic Visual Concepts and Principles
(Wallschlaeger and Busic-Snyder 1992) 62–65.

Cross References

For p. 83	See p. 573
For p. 84	See p. 61, 131, 465
For p. 89	See pp. 114–115
For p. 90	See p. 389
For p. 91	See p. 321
For pp. 102–103	See p. 579
For p. 108	See p. 117
For p. 109	See pp. 114, 118
For pp. 114–117	See pp. 582–585
For pp. 120–121	See pp. 588–589

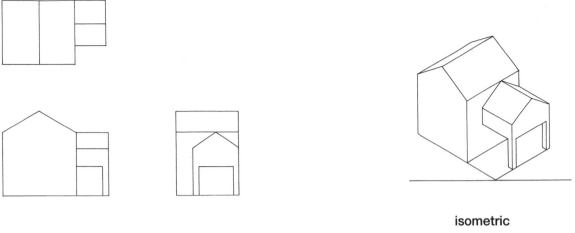

orthographic drawings

isometric

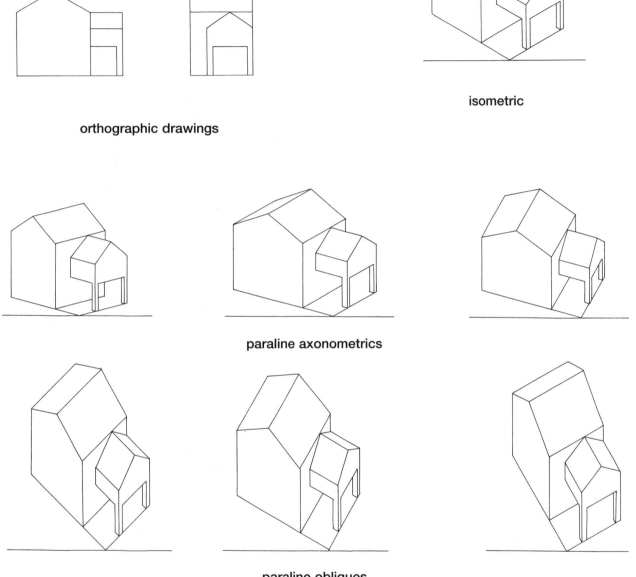

paraline axonometrics

paraline obliques

INTRODUCTION

Plans, elevations, and sections are **orthographic (multiview)** drawings (two dimensional). In **paraline (single view)** drawings, sets of lines are infinitely parallel to each other, giving a three-dimensional character to the pictorial. The proper preparation for the study of **orthographic–paraline drawings** consists of a proven proficiency in handling drafting tools, lettering, and line quality. This, coupled with a brief introduction to drawing conventions, provides the essential background for a survey of these types of pictorial drawings. The family of **axonometrics** (includes **isometric**) drawings and the family of **oblique** drawings can be classified under the general term of **paraline drawings.** Paraline axonometrics are also termed **dimetrics.**

Any building form is composed of the basic elements of points, lines, and planes. Intuitively we sometimes grasp why a shape appears the way it does. However, it is only through an understanding of how these geometric elements interact in orthographic projection that we can fully grasp what we see. The study of this interaction is called **descriptive geometry.**

In elevation, the building form displays true-length vertical lines (**1**) which can appear as either a point or a true-length line in the adjacent views. Likewise, true-length horizontal lines (**2**) also appear as either a true-length line or a point in adjacent views. True-length inclined lines (**3**) appear foreshortened in the adjacent views.

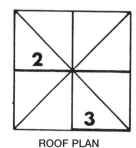

ROOF PLAN

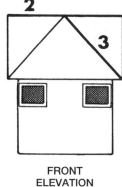

FRONT
ELEVATION

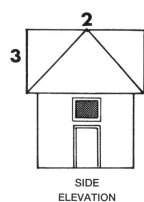

SIDE
ELEVATION

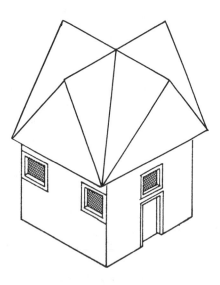

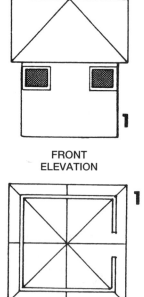

FRONT
ELEVATION

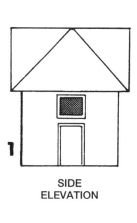

SIDE
ELEVATION

WORM'S-EYE
PLAN

PRINCIPAL LINES

In the drawing (below right), note that the edge view contains a true-length line (outer soffit line) which appears as a point. Edge views of a plane show the plane as true shape in the adjacent view. The concepts of a point view from a true-length line, edge view (true-length as a point), and true shape (true size) become readily apparent as one visualizes the roof structure of this house. Correlate the orthographic views with the pictorial (true shape is toned area).

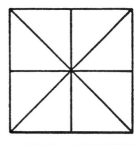

ROOF PLAN EDGE VIEW

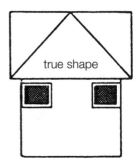

true shape

FRONT ELEVATION

SIDE ELEVATION

see edge view

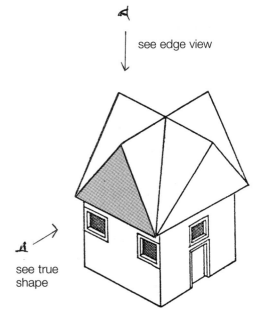

see true shape

edge view (true-length as a point)

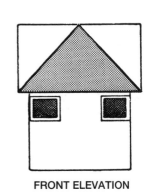

FRONT ELEVATION

SIDE ELEVATION

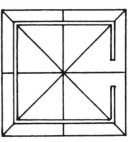

WORM'S EYE PLAN

POINT VIEW/EDGE VIEW/TRUE SHAPE

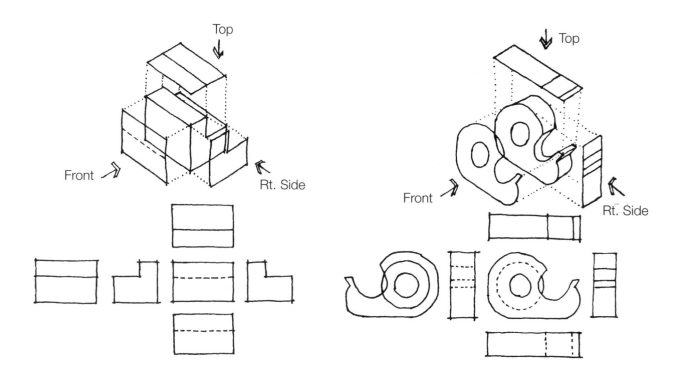

As we have seen in the chapter on drawing conventions, architects and designers represent a three-dimensional building by utilizing "right-angle" or orthographic views. The many orthographic images allow us to comprehend the totality of a design. These images are reproduced through a process of **visualization** and the consequent sketching of the visualized shape. This freehand graphic process begins with the sketch of a three-dimensional pictorial image, the pulling of the two-dimensional orthographic images away from the various surfaces of the object (or building) in question, and the transfer of these images to a two-dimensional orthographic drawing.

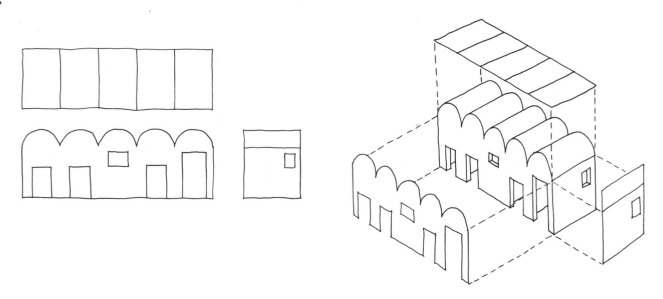

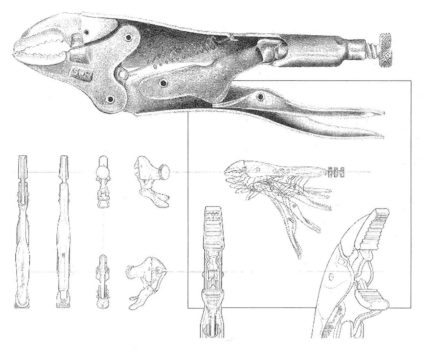

Drawing: Student project by Chris Ernst   Vise Grip
Courtesy of the School of Architecture
The University of Texas at Austin

Being confident and competent in this visualization sketching process requires a lot of practice. The mental visualization process can begin with objects that you can hold in your hand and rotate. An orthographic image by itself cannot be descriptive enough to give us clues as to the spatial composition of the three-dimensional form; but when many orthographic views are related to each other, they become a powerful tool in deciphering the object in question.

Before you can develop the skill of visualizing objects that exist only in the imagination, you must hone your skills in visualizing real objects from several different directions.

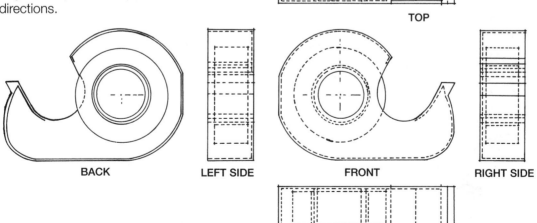

Drawing: Student project by Jacquelyn Mujica   Tape dispenser
Courtesy of the City College of San Francisco, Department of Architecture

SIX VIEWS/VISUALIZATION SKETCHES

VISUALIZATION SKETCHES

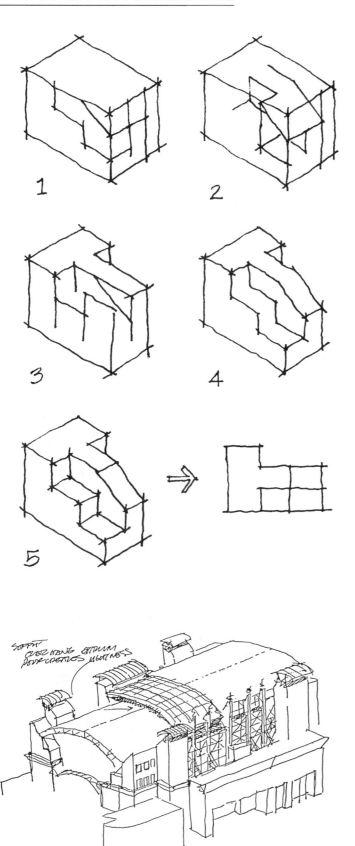

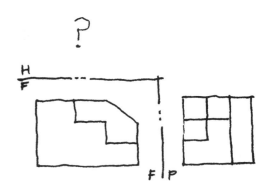

Design professionals often use paraline sketches as well as other types of sketches to help them visualize their designs. Refer to the chapter on conceptual sketching in order to understand how it is used as a communications tool. The best way to develop your visualization skills is to practice seeing the relationship between orthographic and paraline drawings.

This example shows a missing horizontal (top) view. To resolve the missing view, sketch the front and profile planes as shown in sketch #1. Project related points toward the interior of the rectilinear box. Start with the basic or rough forms as shown in sketch #2. Proceed with more detailed parts of the object as shown in sketches #3, #4, and #5.

The ability to develop rough freehand sketches in the orthographic-paraline conversion process will enhance visualization. When an impasse is reached in the resolution of the problem, it is much better to be "loose" than "stiff"; this helps to avoid communicative inhibitions in the design-drawing process that may develop later on.

Sketch: Charing Cross Station
        London, England
Medium: Black ink line with colored pencil
Courtesy of the Terry Farrell & Partners, Architects

Honing your skills in the visualization of simple block forms will enhance your ability to understand the building forms shown in the latter part of this chapter.

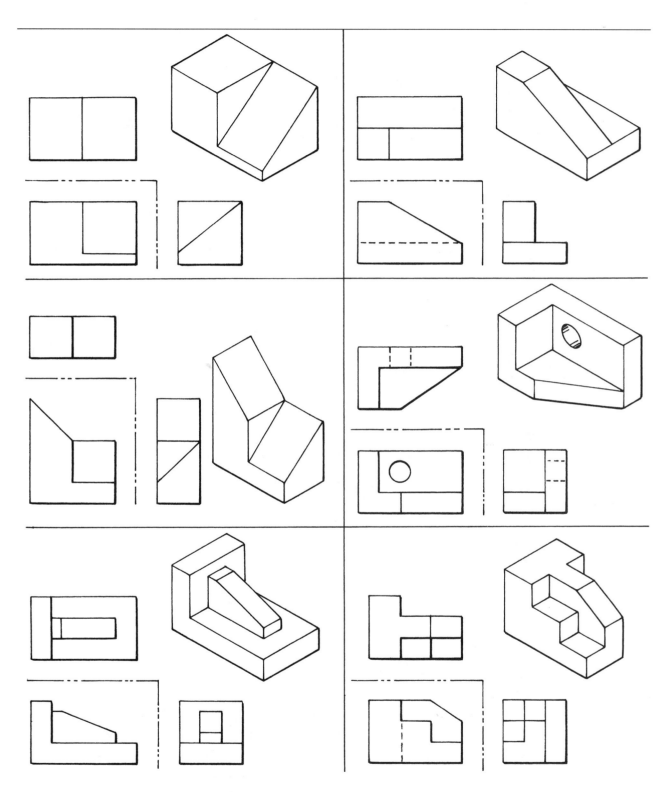

BLOCK VISUALIZATION

BLOCK VISUALIZATION

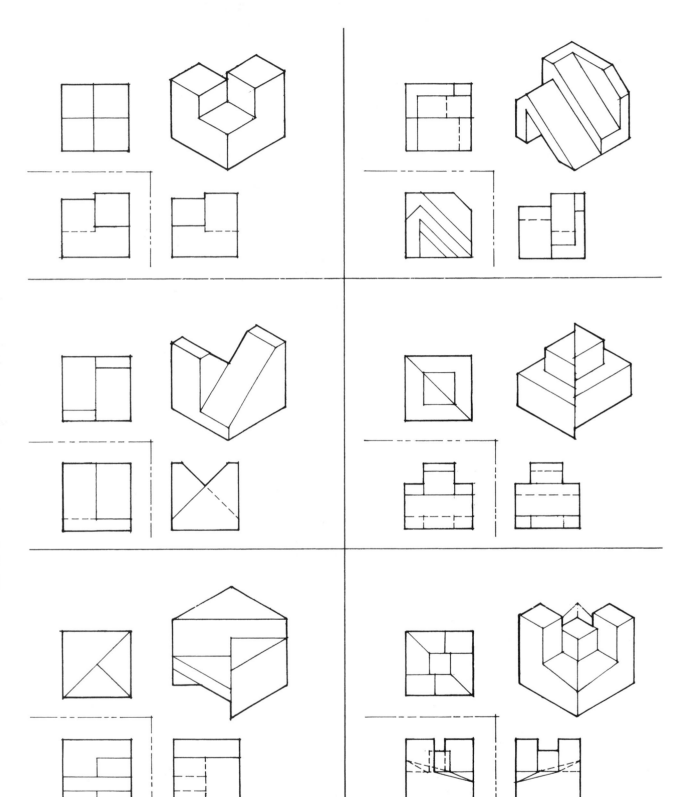

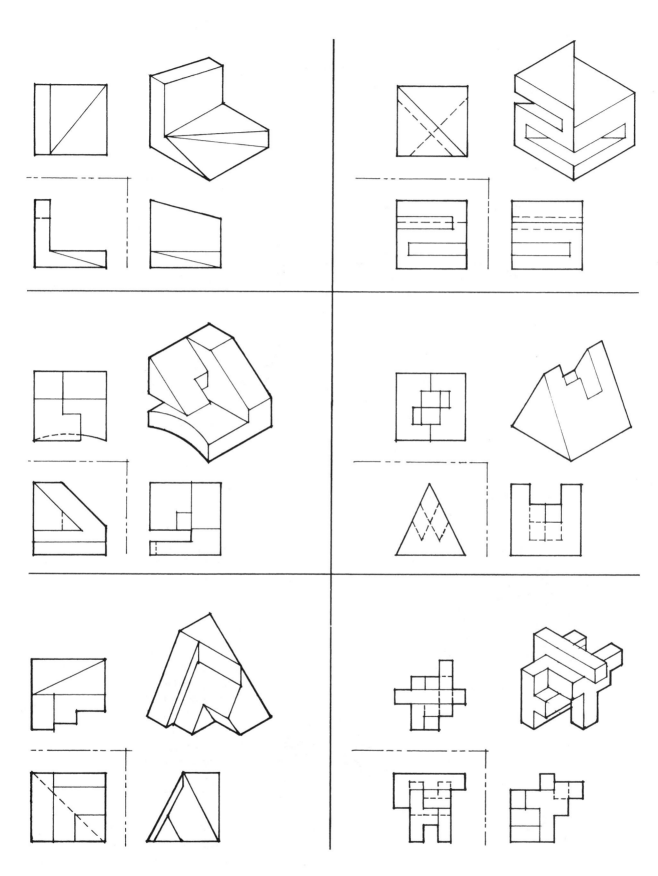

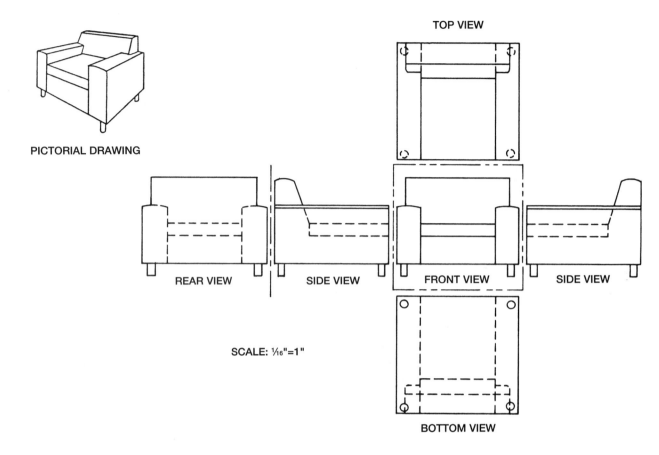

PICTORIAL DRAWING

TOP VIEW

REAR VIEW   SIDE VIEW   FRONT VIEW   SIDE VIEW

SCALE: ¹⁄₁₆"=1"

BOTTOM VIEW

ORTHOGRAPHIC DRAWINGS

SIX VIEW DRAWINGS

Pictorial and Orthographic drawings:
Student project by Ellen Lew
Medium: Pencil on vellum
Courtesy of the City College of San Francisco
Department of Architecture

After drawing hand-held-size objects, examine larger objects like furniture and small buildings and draw them with six or fewer views as needed. The drawing to the left shows six views of a chair projected on the surfaces (picture planes) of an opened glass box. In orthographic projection we use a folding plane line to help understand how the six views are positioned in relation to each other. Henceforth, this line will not be shown between views because in actual architectural practice the line is not drawn.

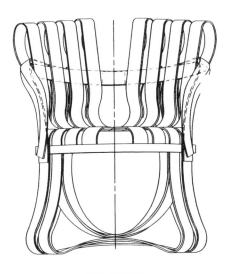

FRONT VIEW

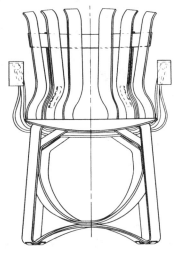

FRONT VIEW

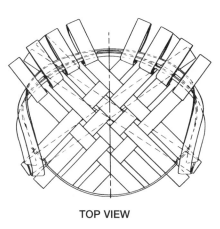

TOP VIEW

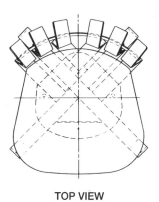

TOP VIEW

BOTTOM VIEW

Drawing: The Frank Gehry Bentwood Collection
Medium: Ink on paper
Courtesy of Knoll

With just a front view and a top view, you can visualize the shape of most chairs and other pieces of furniture. With small objects like chairs, two or three views (top, front, and side) are adequate. With buildings, it is normal to use four or more views (see p. 81).

ORTHOGRAPHIC VIEWS

PROJECTION SYSTEMS COMPARED

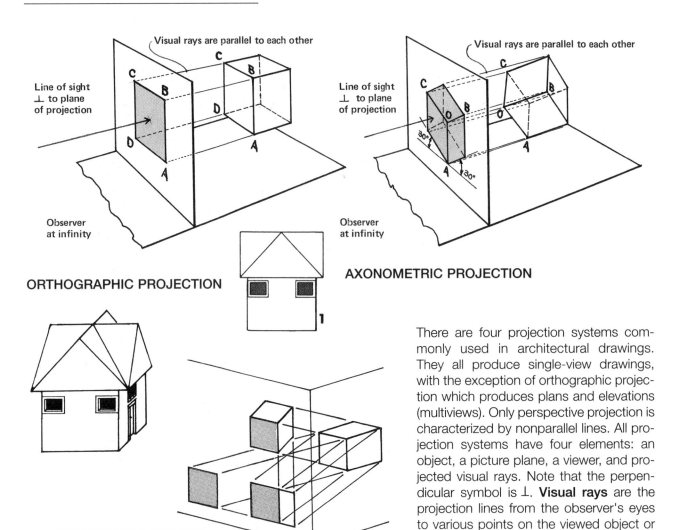

Visual rays are parallel to each other

Line of sight ⊥ to plane of projection

Observer at infinity

ORTHOGRAPHIC PROJECTION

Visual rays are parallel to each other

Line of sight ⊥ to plane of projection

30°   30°

Observer at infinity

AXONOMETRIC PROJECTION

OBLIQUE PROJECTION

There are four projection systems commonly used in architectural drawings. They all produce single-view drawings, with the exception of orthographic projection which produces plans and elevations (multiviews). Only perspective projection is characterized by nonparallel lines. All projection systems have four elements: an object, a picture plane, a viewer, and projected visual rays. Note that the perpendicular symbol is ⊥. **Visual rays** are the projection lines from the observer's eyes to various points on the viewed object or scene.

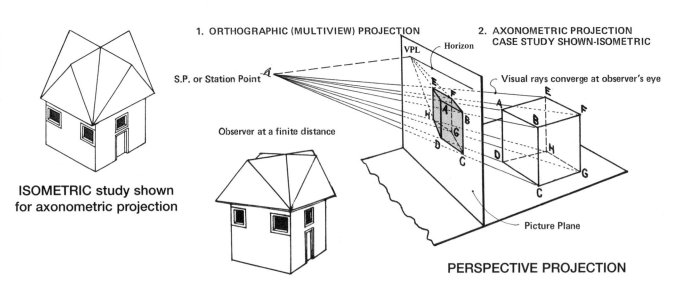

ISOMETRIC study shown for axonometric projection

1. ORTHOGRAPHIC (MULTIVIEW) PROJECTION

2. AXONOMETRIC PROJECTION CASE STUDY SHOWN-ISOMETRIC

VPL   Horizon

S.P. or Station Point

Observer at a finite distance

Visual rays converge at observer's eye

Picture Plane

PERSPECTIVE PROJECTION

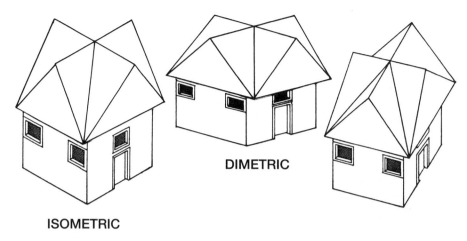

DIMETRIC

ISOMETRIC

Isometric—All three primary axes are set at the same scale: 1:1:1.*

Dimetric—Any two of the three primary axes are set at the same scale. Examples shown are 1:1:¾.

Trimetric—All three primary axes are set at different scales. Seldom used in professional practice

*Scale ratios for the length, height, and depth of the building.

Paraline axonometrics (from Greek) or **axiometrics** (from English) exhibit projectors that are **perpendicular** to the picture plane and **parallel** to each other. They exhibit a vertical front edge with nonconverging side planes.

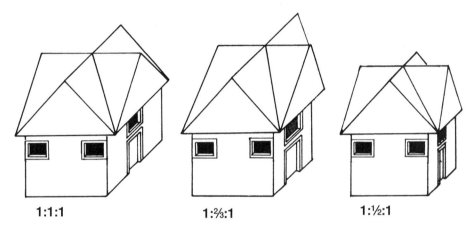

1:1:1   **1:⅔:1**   **1:½:1**

Paraline obliques (here in the form of elevational obliques) exhibit projectors that are **oblique** to the picture plane and **parallel.** They exhibit a flat, true-size frontal shape with nonconverging side planes.

These **elevation obliques** are identified with length, depth, and height ratios, in that order. In an elevation oblique, one elevation is parallel to the picture plane and seen in true size and true shape. Often the receding planes seem too elongated in their true-length. In practice they are usually shortened by as much as one-third to one-half to give visual comfort.

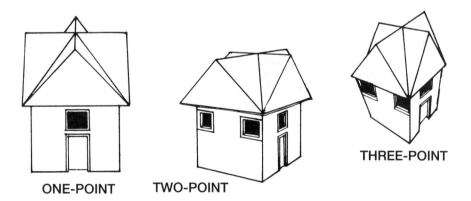

THREE-POINT

ONE-POINT   **TWO-POINT**

Perspectives, which will be covered in detail in the following chapter, are single-view drawings that approach a person's optical perception. For two-point and three-point perspectives, the various surfaces are at a variety of angles to the picture plane, whereas one surface is parallel to the picture plane for a one-point perspective.

Perspectives exhibit projections that are at a variety of angles to the picture plane and they display the characteristics of **point convergence.** They show converging side planes.

PROJECTION SYSTEMS COMPARED

MULTIVIEW AND SINGLE-VIEW DRAWINGS

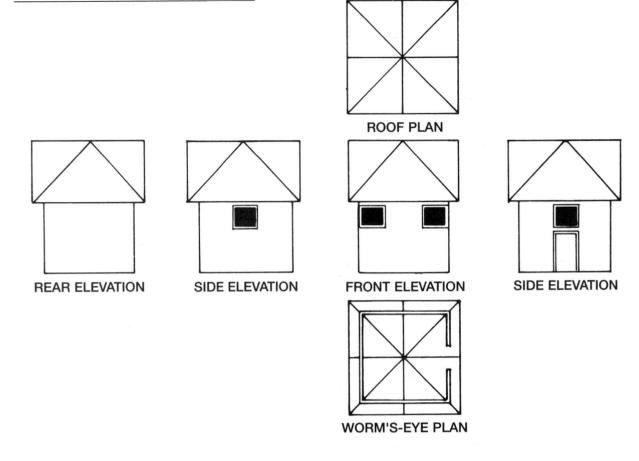

ROOF PLAN

REAR ELEVATION   SIDE ELEVATION   FRONT ELEVATION   SIDE ELEVATION

WORM'S-EYE PLAN

The drawing above shows six orthographic views of a building. This is a **multiview** drawing. Each view would be placed on a separate drawing sheet due to the large scale of building projects.

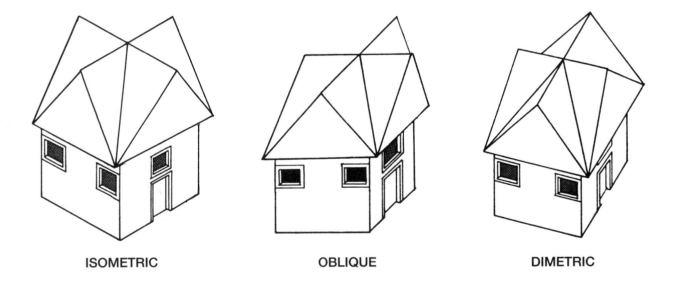

ISOMETRIC   OBLIQUE   DIMETRIC

Isometric, oblique, and dimetric are three types of **single-view** drawings. These are called **paraline** drawings since they all have sets of infinitely parallel lines. A fourth type of single-view drawing is called perspective (see opposite page).

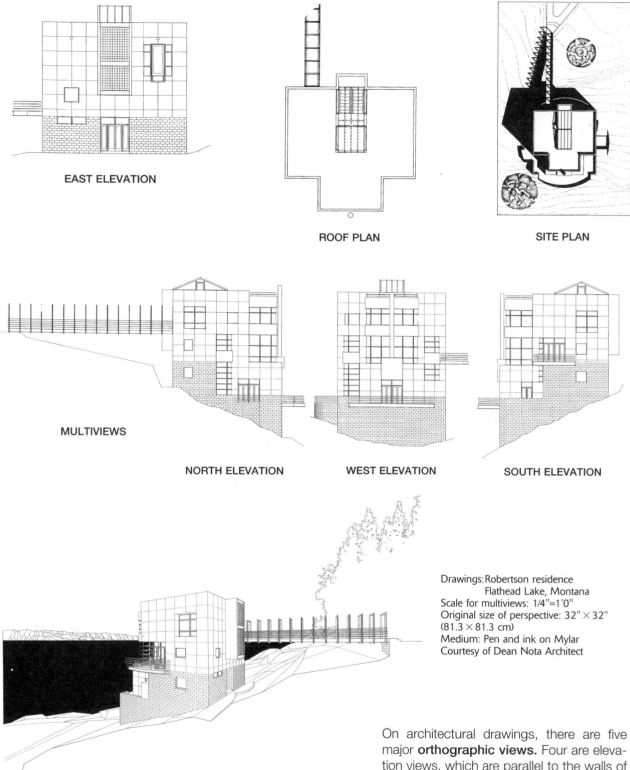

EAST ELEVATION

ROOF PLAN

SITE PLAN

MULTIVIEWS

NORTH ELEVATION

WEST ELEVATION

SOUTH ELEVATION

SINGLE VIEW DRAWING

Drawings: Robertson residence
Flathead Lake, Montana
Scale for multiviews: 1/4"=1'0"
Original size of perspective: 32" × 32"
(81.3 × 81.3 cm)
Medium: Pen and ink on Mylar
Courtesy of Dean Nota Architect

On architectural drawings, there are five major **orthographic views.** Four are elevation views, which are parallel to the walls of the building, and one is a site plan/floor plan view, which is parallel to the ground. Any views that are not parallel to the primary walls of the building are classified as **auxiliary views.**

MULTIVIEW AND SINGLE-VIEW DRAWINGS

CONSTRUCTING ISOMETRIC DRAWINGS

Isometric, when literally translated, means "has equality of measurement." Lengths parallel to any of the orthographic axes will be the **same** as in the isometric. An isometric projection is not composed of true angles, whereas a plan oblique (see p. 87) projection does have a true angle. A bird's-eye view gives the illusion of parallel lines when in reality the lines are converging.

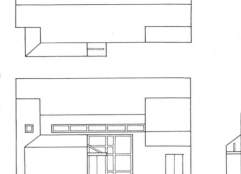

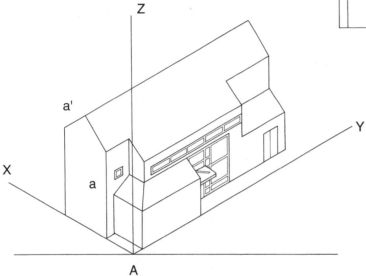

The **isometric** drawing is one of the most important types of **axonometric drawings.** Principles for its construction are as follows:

- The axes *(AX* and *AY)* on the ground plane always are drawn 30° from the horizontal.
- Measure all orthographic distances along the three axes: *AX, AY,* and *AZ* and only along these axes.
- Any line that is not along the isometric axes (inclined lines) should be located by locating the end points of the line (see *a'-a* above). These lengths will not be the same in the isometric view and the orthographic views.
- Parallel lines in an orthographic drawing remain parallel in the corresponding isometric drawing.
- Vertical lines in an orthographic drawing remain vertical in an isometric drawing.
- Hidden lines are normally not drawn in an isometric, but they can be used to help visualization.
- Corner points may be labeled in each orthographic view and the isometric view to help visualize the isometric drawing.
- One disadvantage of the isometric is that it cannot use the orthographic view in the actual orthographic (plan/elevation) layout.

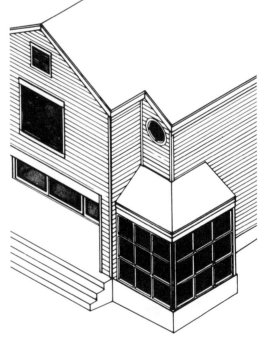

Drawing: Partial isometric
Sprague Lakehouse
Lake Cypress Springs, Texas
24" × 36" (61 × 91.4 cm), Scale: ¼"=1'0"
Medium: Ink on vellum
Courtesy of Todd Hamilton, Architect

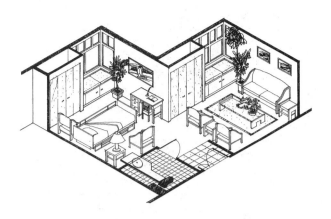

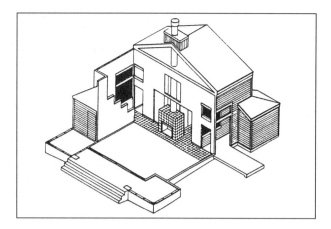

Drawing: Glacier Hills Retirement Health Center, Ann Arbor, Michigan
Medium: Ink on Mylar
Org. size: Approx. 20" × 30" (50.8 × 76.2 cm)
Courtesy of Ellerbe–Becket, Inc.,
designed by Dale Tremain, AIA

Drawing: Sprague Lakehouse
    Lake Cypress Springs, Texas
24" × 36" (61 × 91.4 cm   Scale 1/4"=1'0"
Medium: Ink on vellum
Courtesy of Todd Hamilton, Architect

An **isometric drawing** shows a more mechanistic type of perception. Perspective drawing, which will be studied in a later chapter, is much closer to natural human perception. Nevertheless, isometrics are used because seeing three nonconverging faces of an object is still quite convincing in understanding its form. The observer is limited to viewing only bird's-eye views (above 30') in an isometric. Due to its low angle of view, an isometric drawing does not permit the viewer to see interior spaces unless the roof and side walls are removed. The examples above have all three of these elements absent and also show a partial isometric plan. The examples below show two other ways to reveal the interior configuration. The lower right drawing uses a cutaway partition as well as an isometric section. The lower left drawing requires a transparent isometric (see p. xi).

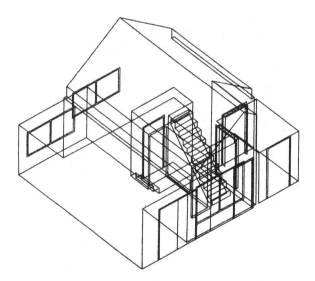

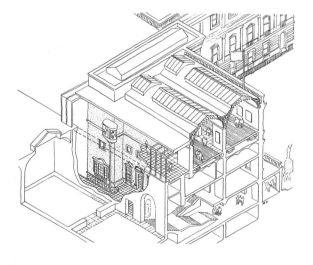

Drawing: Student project by Haden Smith
    Graduate Student Housing
10" × 8" (25.4 × 20.3 cm),   Scale: ¼"=1'0"
Medium: CAD
Courtesy of Washington University
School of Architecture, St. Louis, MO

Drawing: Sackler Galleries, Royal Academy, London, England
Medium: Pencil on trace 418 × 291 mm (16.5" × 11.7")
Courtesy of Sir Norman Foster and Partners
Drawn by Sir Norman Foster

ISOMETRIC DRAWINGS—INTERIOR APPLICATIONS

CONSTRUCTING ISOMETRIC CIRCLES

In paraline drawings all circles appear as ellipses except when they appear in planes parallel to the picture plane (true circles). The four-center ellipse procedure below is the most precise method for approximating true ellipses. See procedures to construct other elliptical forms on pages 278–279.

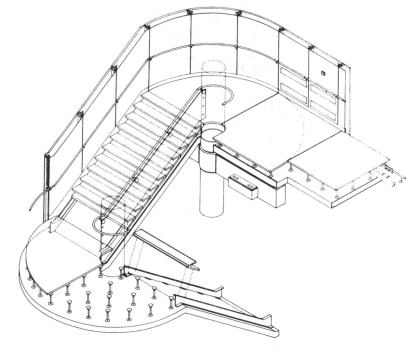

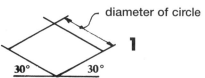

diameter of circle

1

30° 30°

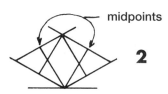

midpoints

2

Drawing: Staircase isometric, Lloyd's of London
London, England
33" × 45.5" (83.8 × 115.6 cm)
Medium: Rottering pen on tracing
Courtesy of the Richard Rogers Partnership, Architects

3

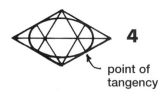

4

point of tangency

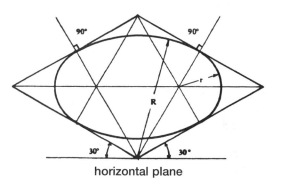

90° 90°

r

R

30° 30°

horizontal plane

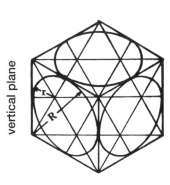

vertical plane

r

R

Procedure for the Four-Center Ellipse

(1) Draw an isometric square using the desired circle's diameter.
(2) Find adjacent side midpoints. Large radius *R* has two centers at the closest corners of the parallelogram. The intersections of the perpendiculars to both opposite sides determines the terminal points of the arc.
(3) Construct the arcs.
(4) Small radius *r* has two centers at the intersections of the perpendiculars within the parallelogram. These small arcs meet the large arcs to complete the ellipse.

The entire construction can be made with a T-square and 30° × 60° triangle. The same procedure applies for both circles in vertical planes or horizontal planes.

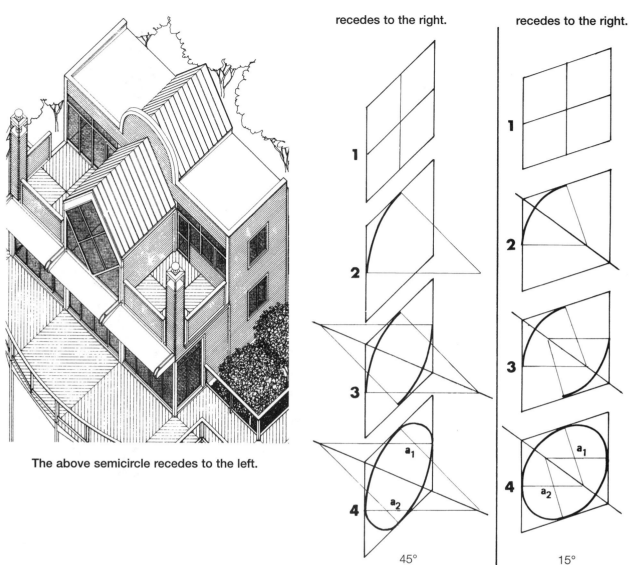

The above semicircle recedes to the left.

recedes to the right.

recedes to the right.

45°

15°

Drawing: Compact House, Bayview, Lake Pend
          O'Reille, Idaho
18" × 24" (45.7 × 61 cm)   Scale: ¼=1'0"
Medium: Ink on vellum
Courtesy of David A. Harris, DHT² Architects & Planners
Reprinted from NEW COMPACT HOUSE DESIGNS, edited by Don
Metz, with permission of Storey Communications/Garden Way
Publishing, Pownal, VT.

CONSTRUCTING PARALINE CIRCLES

The four-center ellipse method shown on the previous page applies for non-30°–30° axonometric circles in left and right receding vertical planes only. Note that in the horizontal plane, circles are seen in true shape.

(1) Draw a paraline square.
(2) Find adjacent side midpoints and construct intersecting perpendiculars. The intersection becomes an arc-center.
(3) Repeat the process for a symmetrical mirror image arc on the opposite side.
(4) Using points a_1 and a_2, complete smaller arcs to accomplish the total axonometric circle.

COMPARING AXONOMETRICS AND OBLIQUES

AXONOMETRICS

PLAN OBLIQUES

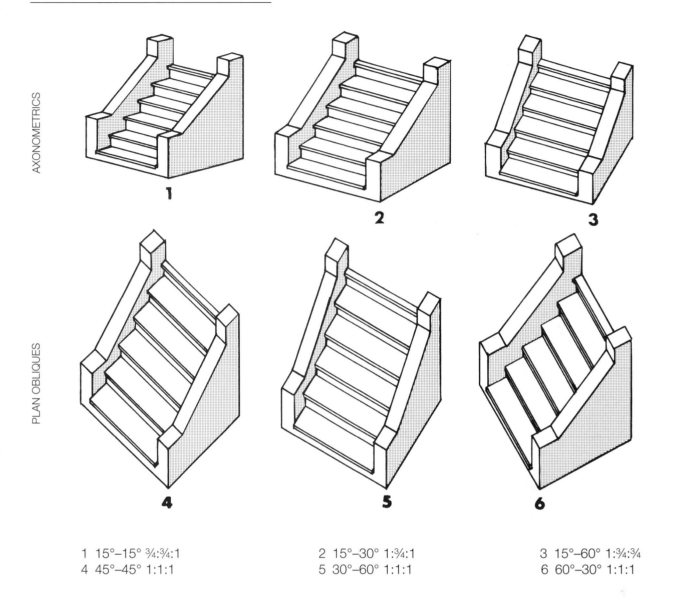

1

2

3

4

5

6

1 15°–15° ¾:¾:1
4 45°–45° 1:1:1

2 15°–30° 1:¾:1
5 30°–60° 1:1:1

3 15°–60° 1:¾:¾
6 60°–30° 1:1:1

Paraline **axonometrics** (axis measure) and paraline **plan obliques** allow for a great variety of choices in deciding which viewpoints are best relative to the type of object being depicted. The six alternatives shown are some of the more common angle and axes scale combinations that are used. In the oblique views of the staircase, all horizontal surfaces such as the tread (horizontal part of the step) areas are shown in their **true shape** and **true size** (actual plan dimensions). A small percentage of the actual riser (vertical part of the step) area is visible in the oblique situations. By contrast note that in all of the axonometric views, the percentage of actual tread area is less and more riser area becomes visible. One must first decide what is most important to show or emphasize before selecting the desired angle and axes scale combinations. This decision process will become more apparent as you study the various examples shown toward the end of this chapter. Note that through many years of professional usage it has become popular to classify "plan obliques" as "axonometrics." Loosely defined the terms are **interchangeable** even though technically they are two separate terms with distinct definitions.

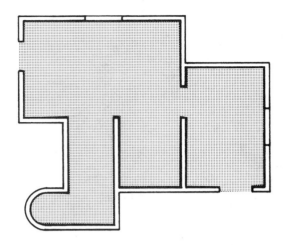

The **plan** view is essential for drawing both **isometric** and **plan oblique** drawings for interior spaces. In professional practice, the plan is always available at common scales such as ¼"=1'0". This same scale would be used for plan obliques. The plan becomes a three-dimensional drawing when the vertical dimension is added. When done manually, the easy and quick transfer of the plan view dictates its preferable use for interiors. However, the time difference is insignificant if the isometric or plan oblique drawings are computer-generated.

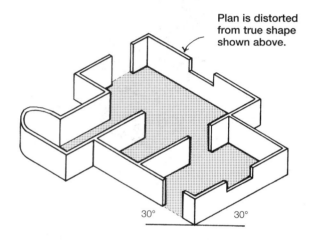

Plan is distorted from true shape shown above.

30°   30°

In a 30°–30° isometric, the interior partitions conceal a large part of the rooms, making it difficult to see the interior furniture, plants, people, etc. **Isometrics** are more commonly used for building **exteriors,** whereas **interiors** are best displayed with **plan obliques** as shown below. An exception for the use of interior isometric drawings is the use of transparent partitions (see p. 83). Note also that the walls are more visible in the isometric than in the 45°–45° drawing below.

Axes angles such as 45°–45° (see example), 60°–30°, and 75°–15° allow the observer to obtain a **higher** vantage point than the 30°–30° isometric. The partitions conceal less of the rooms in the 45° axes and the plan becomes a **true shape.** These drawings can be termed **true-shape plan obliques** and they are simply a variation of the general oblique. As a drawing type, plan obliques give the best simultaneous representation of plan and elevation. They give an excellent analytical view of the spatial organization of the plan. All paralines are excellent tools for verifying three-dimensional relationships.

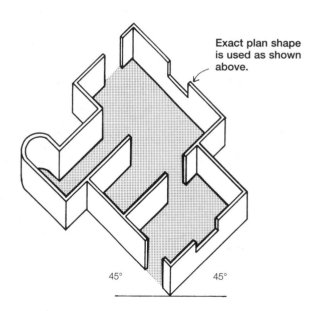

Exact plan shape is used as shown above.

45°   45°

ISOMETRIC AND PLAN OBLIQUE DRAWINGS

PLAN OBLIQUE CONSTRUCTION

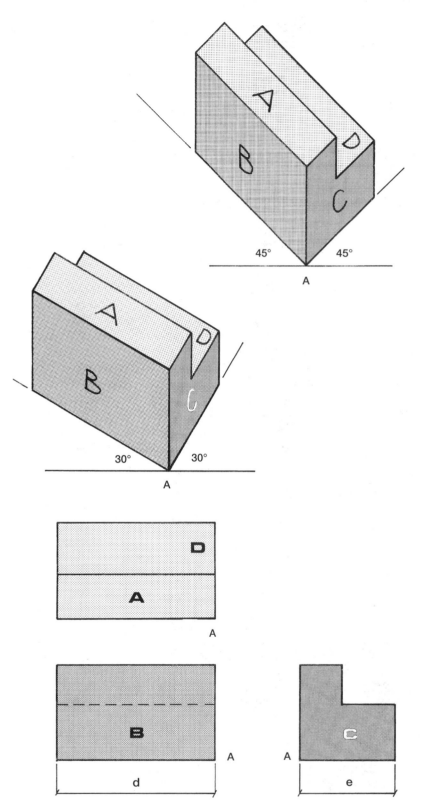

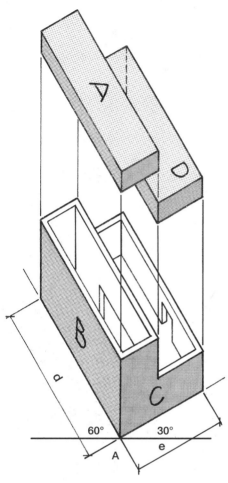

The principles for constructing **plan obliques** are the same as for isometrics. Orthographic lengths such as *d* and *e* are measured along the selected plan oblique axes angles. All vertical lines in the orthographic drawings (elevations) remain vertical and parallel to the *Z*-axis in the plan oblique. The selection of a set of appropriate plan oblique or axonometric angles depends on how the object will be emphasized. At appropriate angles these drawings become a powerful tool for showing the scale, mass, and bulk of a design.

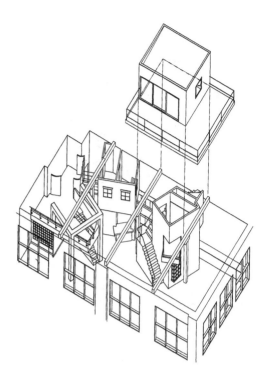

Drawing: Clybourne Lofts
                    Chicago, Illinois
30" × 40", Scale: ¼"=1'0"
Medium: Ink on Mylar
Courtesy of Pappageorge Haymes Ltd., Chicago,
Architects

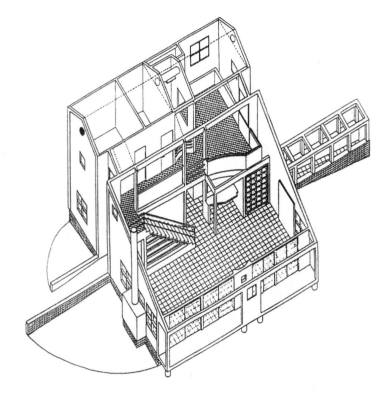

Drawing: Peele residence, North Andover, Massachusetts
±24" × 36" (61 × 91.4 cm), Scale: ⅛"=1'0"
Medium: Ink with Pantone film colors
Adam Gross, Project Associate
Courtesy of Perry, Dean, Rogers, and Partners: Architects
Reprinted from THE COMPACT HOUSE BOOK, edited by Don Metz with
permission of Storey Communications/Garden Way Publishing, Pownal, VT.

PLAN OBLIQUE INTERIORS

Roof removal from a building form helps to reveal the interior spaces drawn at plan oblique axes angles. Plan obliques (either looking down or looking up as on pp. 120–121) provide an unnatural but informative way of looking at architecture. As a procedural rule, always construct the wall or roof outline first (as in the Clybourne Lofts) before adding material wall or floor texture (as in the Peele residence). Spatial definition can be enhanced by the generous use of tonal values. These values produce contrast between the horizontal and vertical planes.

PLAN OBLIQUE HORIZONTAL CIRCLES

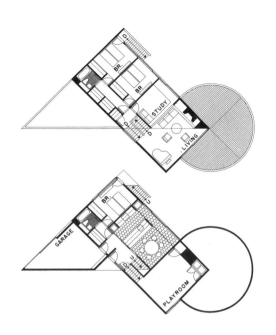

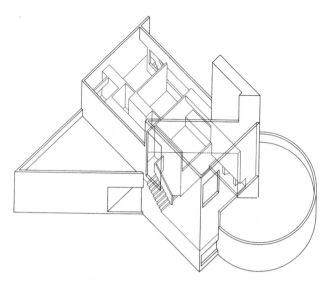

Drawings: House, Oldfield, New York
13.5" × 15.5" (34.3 × 39.4 cm), Scale: ¹⁄₄"=1'0"
Medium: Ink
Courtesy of Hobart D. Betts, Architect

The popularity of plan obliques (interchangeably termed axonometrics) is due to their ease of construction. All geometric shapes are transferred true size (note triangle, rectangle, and circle above).

Drawing: Schuh Box (unbuilt), Hills above San Francisco Bay
11" × 17" (27.9 × 43.2 cm)   Scale: ¹⁄₈"=1'0"
Medium: Ink on trace
Courtesy of David Baker Associates Architects

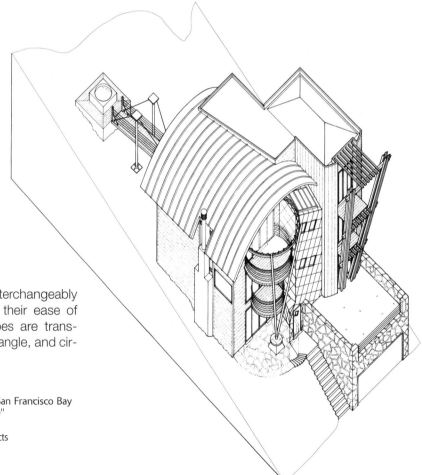

Drawings: Meyer residence, Malibu, California
Both 24" × 36" (61 × 91.4 cm), Scale: ¼"=1'0"
Medium: Ink on Mylar
Courtesy of Gwathmey Siegel & Associates, Architects

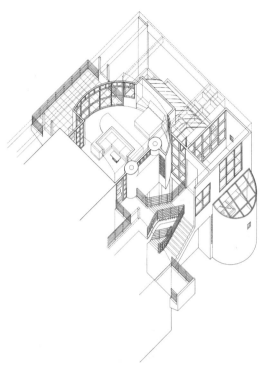

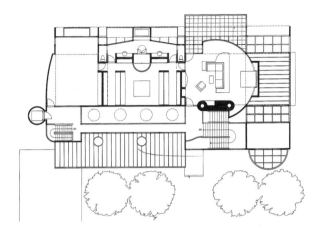

In the plan view and the plan oblique view, sometimes geometric solids are shortened by cutting off a part (truncated). The truncated semicylinder in the above design has a circle that will appear true shape in neither the plan view (foreshortened) nor the plan oblique view. The circle must always be in the horizontal plane to be true shape in the plan view.

Regardless of the axes angles combination, **circles** and other curvilinear forms in horizontal planes retain their **true size** and **shape** in the plan oblique since the plan view is a true-shape view.

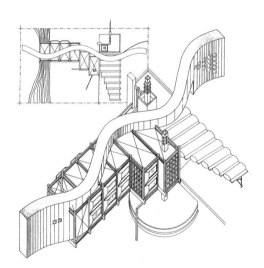

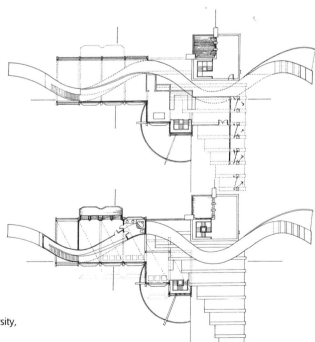

Drawing: Student project by John Crump
　　　　　Dwelling with a Bridge
Medium: Ink on Mylar
M. Saleh Uddin, Professor,
Savannah College of Art and Design, Savannah, GA; Southern University,
Baton Rouge, LA

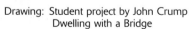

PLAN OBLIQUE HORIZONTAL CIRCLES

PLAN OBLIQUES—45°–45° AXES ANGLES

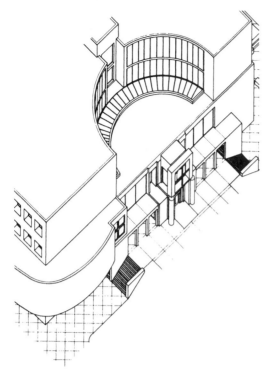

Drawing: Tallahassee City Hall, Tallahassee, Florida
Medium: Ink on tracing paper
24" × 36" (61 × 91.4 cm), Scale: 1/16"=1'0"
Courtesy of Heery International, Inc.

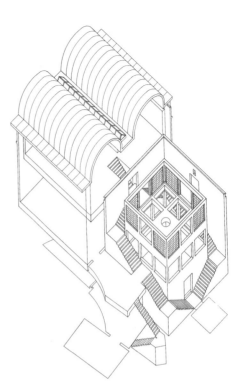

Drawing: Whanki Museum
        Seoul, Korea
18" × 24" (45.7 × 61 cm), Scale 1:500
Medium: Ink on vellum
Courtesy of Kyu Sung Woo, Architect

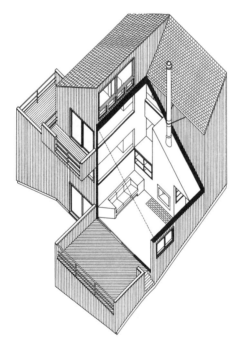

Drawing: Dattelbaum house
        Kezar Lake, Center Lovell, Maine
18" × 23" (45.7 × 58.4 cm), Scale: 1/4"=1'0"
Medium: Ink on Mylar
Courtesy of Solomon & Bauer Architects Inc.

Plan obliques are commonly drawn with axes angles of 30°–60°, 60°–30°, and 45°–45°. The plan in its true shape can be quickly transferred to construct the oblique drawings. The observer's vantage point is **higher** than in an isometric drawing. These plan obliques use axes angles of 45°–45°. Facade details show equally well on either receding axis. Roof configurations and interior spaces are also clearly seen. Partial roof cutaways help to focus on the interior spaces. Detail on a nonlinear facade will show especially well (upper left). Obliques lack the characteristic of size diminishment (as in a perspective) and thus have the advantage of retaining size, detail, and information.

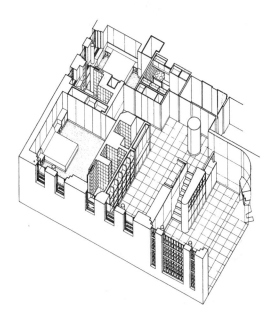

Drawing: Manhattan pied-a-terre, New York City
24" × 36" (61 × 91.4 cm), Scale: ¼" = 1'0"
Medium: Ink on Mylar
Courtesy of Gwathmey Siegel & Associates, Architects

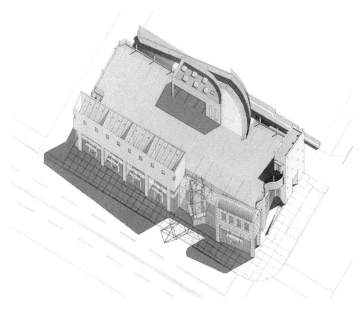

Drawing: Montana Collection
Santa Monica, California
24" × 36" (61 × 91.4 cm), Scale: ¼ = 1'0"
Medium: Ink on Mylar with Zipatone
Courtesy of Kanner Architects

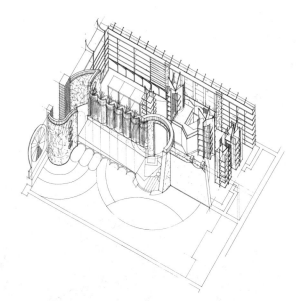

Drawing: Contemporary Arts Center
Bookstore and Artware
Cincinnati, Ohio
Medium: Pencil on vellum
24" × 36" (61 × 91.4 cm), Scale ½"=1'0"
Courtesy of Terry Brown Architect

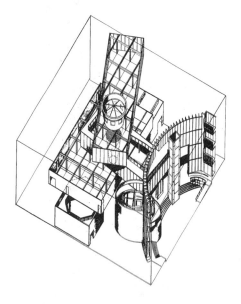

Drawing: Contemporary Arts Center
New Orleans, Louisiana
30" × 40" (76.2 × 101.6 cm), Scale: ¹⁄₁₆"=1'0"
Medium: Plastic lead on Mylar
Courtesy of Concordia Architects, New Orleans, Louisiana

PLAN OBLIQUES — 30°–60° AXES ANGLES

These plan obliques use axes angles of 30°–60°. This orientation allows the observer to clearly see interior spaces or roof configurations. Usually the 30° receding facade receives the most emphasis. However, if the facade is not linear, as with the New Orleans Arts Center, then a 60° receding axis can be the choice to show the more detailed facade.

PLAN OBLIQUES — 60°–30° AXES ANGLES

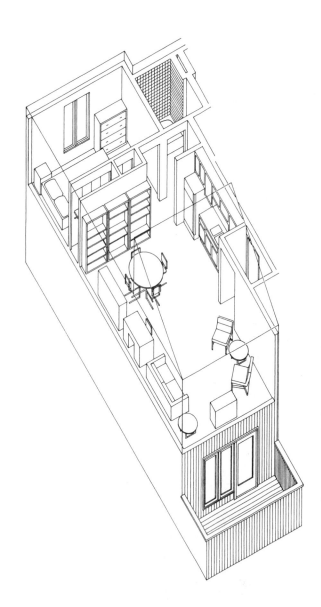

Drawing: Married Student Housing
University of Alaska
Fairbanks, Alaska
Medium: Ink
Courtesy of Hellmuth, Obata, and Kassabaum, Architects

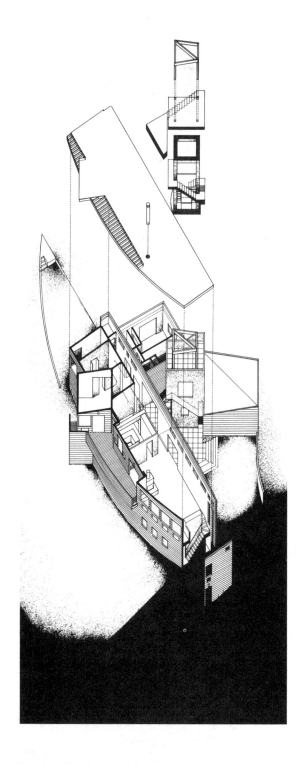

Drawing: Waldhauer residence
Woodside, California
20" × 48" (50.8 × 121.9 cm), Scale: ¼"=1'0"
Medium: India ink and airbrush on Mylar
Courtesy of House + House, Architects and Mark David
English, Inglese Architecture, Architectural Illustrator

These plan obliques use axes angles of 60°–30°. Normally the 30° receding facade is emphasized. However, note that much detail can be shown on the 60° receding facade if part of the facade is nonlinear. All built-in and movable furniture pieces retain their verticality and true heights (see p. 404. The 60°–30° axes angles allow the observer to clearly see the interior spaces when the roof and parts of both side elevations are removed.

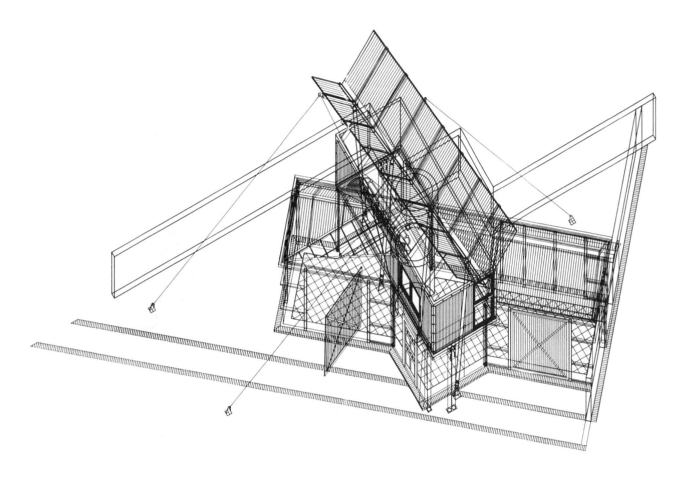

Drawing: Studio, The Ivy Villa, Pretoria, South Africa
400 × 300 mm (15.7" × 11.8"), Scale: 1:100
Medium: Ultimate CAD program
Drawn by Ian Thompson
Courtesy of Ora Joubert, Arhcitect

This drawing has one structure with axes angles of 9°–81° and another structure with axes angles of 60°–30°. The intersection of solid elements will always require two (dual) or more sets of plan oblique axes angles. Note that the structure with the 9°–81° orientation shows details on its 9° facade extremely well, whereas its 81° facade is barely visible. Also shown above are structural cables, which are not true-length in the plan oblique.

Drawing: House, Kumamoto, Japan
Courtesy of Terry Dwan for Studio
Citterio/Dwan, Architects

PLAN OBLIQUE DRAWINGS

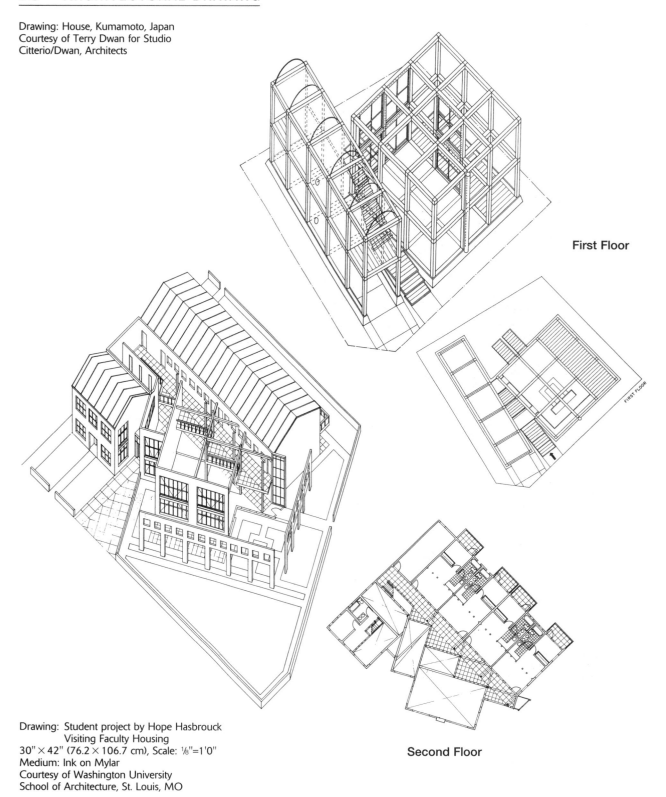

First Floor

Drawing: Student project by Hope Hasbrouck
                Visiting Faculty Housing
30" × 42" (76.2 × 106.7 cm), Scale: ⅛"=1'0"
Medium: Ink on Mylar
Courtesy of Washington University
School of Architecture, St. Louis, MO

Second Floor

These buildings require two sets of plan oblique axes angles: top (60°–30° and 45°–45°) and bottom (15°–75° and 45°–45°). The two axial directions are clearly seen on each building's floor plan. One set of plan oblique axes angles is most frequently seen. However, many designs require two or more sets.

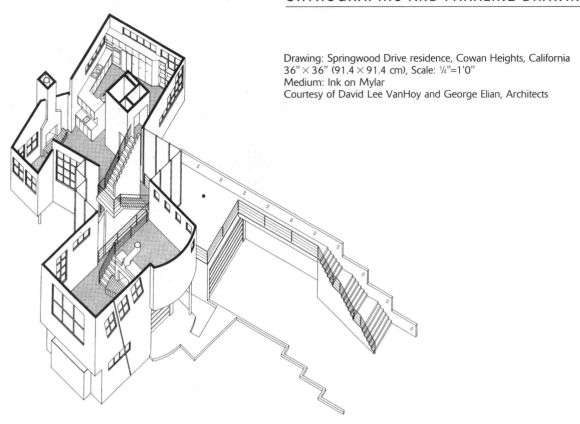

Drawing: Springwood Drive residence, Cowan Heights, California
36" × 36" (91.4 × 91.4 cm), Scale: ¼"=1'0"
Medium: Ink on Mylar
Courtesy of David Lee VanHoy and George Elian, Architects

The above example with the roof removed combines two axes of 45°–45° and 30°–60°. The example to the right has three axes (tri-axes angles).

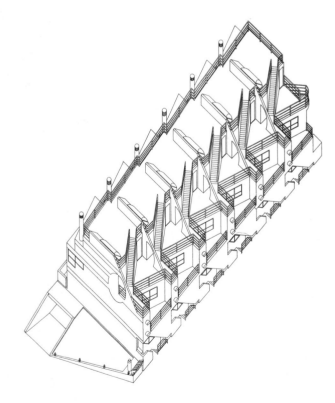

Drawing: 831 Pacific Street condominium
Santa Monica, California
24" × 42" (61 × 106.7 cm), Scale: ¼"=1'0"
Medium: Technical pens and ink
Courtesy of David Cooper, Architect of
A Design Group, Architects

DUAL AXES AND TRI-AXES ANGLES

COMBINING SECTION CUTS

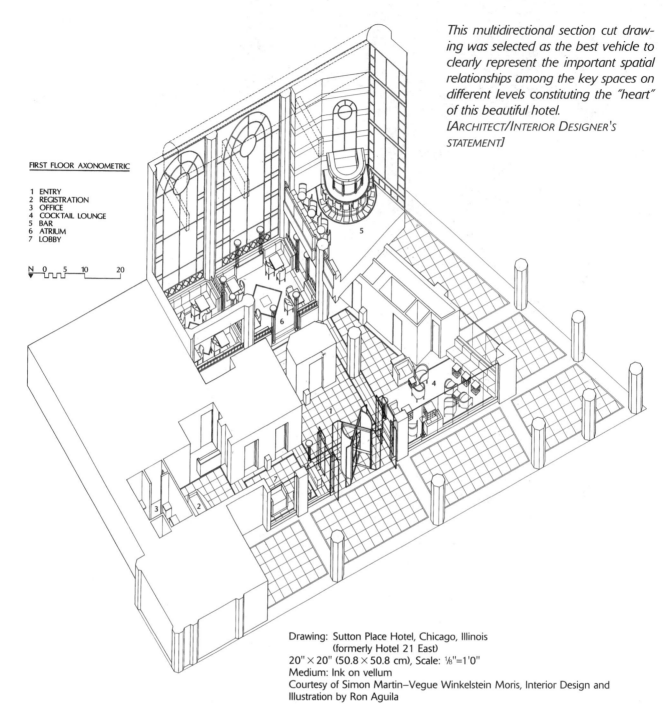

This multidirectional section cut drawing was selected as the best vehicle to clearly represent the important spatial relationships among the key spaces on different levels constituting the "heart" of this beautiful hotel.
[ARCHITECT/INTERIOR DESIGNER'S STATEMENT]

FIRST FLOOR AXONOMETRIC

1 ENTRY
2 REGISTRATION
3 OFFICE
4 COCKTAIL LOUNGE
5 BAR
6 ATRIUM
7 LOBBY

N 0 5 10 20

Drawing: Sutton Place Hotel, Chicago, Illinois
            (formerly Hotel 21 East)
20" × 20" (50.8 × 50.8 cm), Scale: ⅛"=1'0"
Medium: Ink on vellum
Courtesy of Simon Martin–Vegue Winkelstein Moris, Interior Design and
Illustration by Ron Aguila

The drawings on this and the facing page show how the anatomy of a building can be clearly revealed by combining a horizontal with a vertical section.

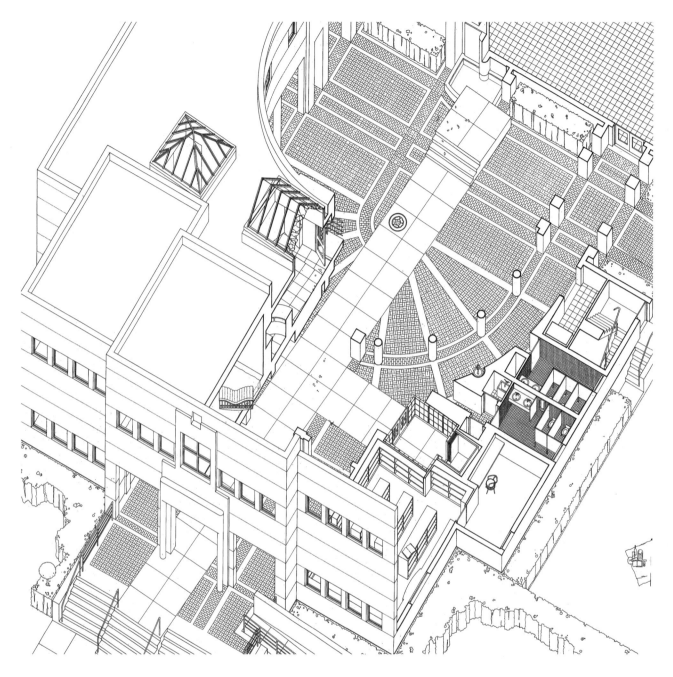

COMBINING SECTION CUTS

Drawing: Atlanta Botanical Garden Visitor's Center 1984, Atlanta, Georgia
30" × 30" (76.2 × 76.2 cm), Scale: ¼"=1'0"
Medium: Ink
Courtesy of Anthony Ames, Architect

Behind the facade in this oblique axonometric drawing, the building is dissected horizontally and vertically in order to show portions of the first-level plan and partial section through the building describing the relationship of the court to its adjacencies.
[ARCHITECT'S STATEMENT]

PLAN OBLIQUES—INCREMENTAL GROWTH

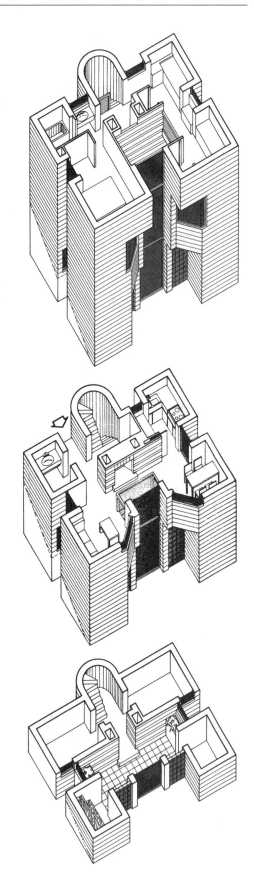

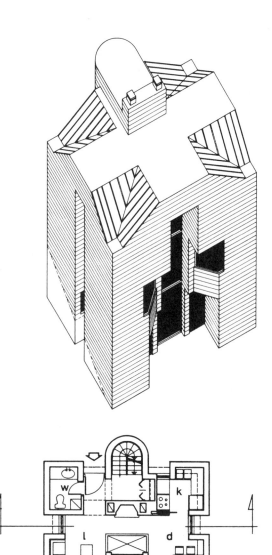

For multistory building types, the plan oblique can be effectively used in showing a **growth** (layering) sequence of floor levels. These drawings become an efficacious visual means of conveying how the entire building shell relates to the interior spaces.

Drawings: One-family Prototype House
Toronto, Ontario, Canada
Courtesy of G. Nino Rico and Giancarlo Garofalo
Reprinted from The Compact House Book, edited by Don Metz
with permission of Storey Communications/Garden Way Publishing,
Pownal, VT.

Plan obliques illustrating incremental growth can clarify details in plan view cuts taken at different locations. Axes angles of 45°–45° were used in the example to the right, whereas 60°–30° was used in the example on the facing page.

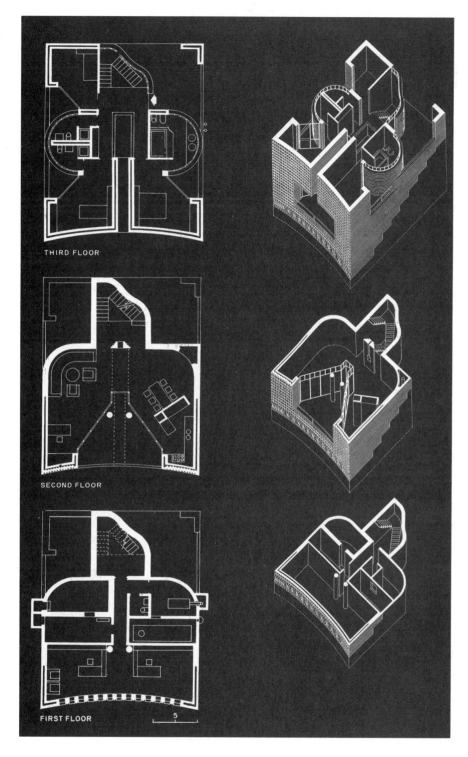

THIRD FLOOR

SECOND FLOOR

FIRST FLOOR   5

Drawings: Posteria residence
Morbio Superiore, Switzerland
Courtesy of Mario Botta, Architect, Lugano,
Switzerland

PLAN OBLIQUES—INCREMENTAL GROWTH

PLAN OBLIQUES—NONVERTICAL Z AXIS

A variation to the typical plan oblique is one in which the Z axis thrusts the vertical planes upward (most commonly at 45° or 60°) from the horizontal. This gives the observer a vantage point that is almost directly **overhead**. This method has the advantage of revealing more of the important horizontal planes. However, distortion appears greater than the typical plan oblique.

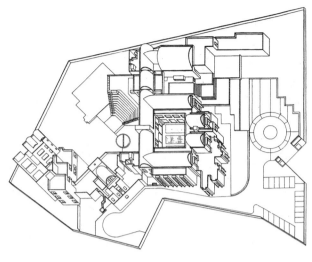

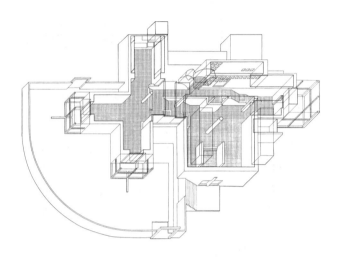

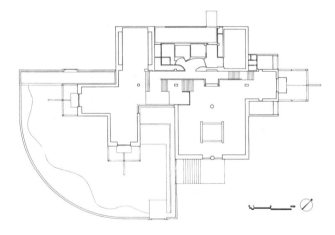

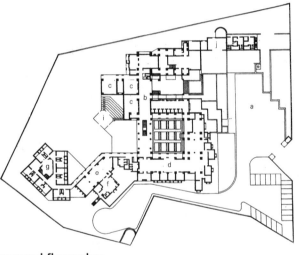

ground floor plan

Drawing: Gandhi Labour Institute
Ahmedabad, Gujrat, India
Courtesy of B.V. Doshi, Architect

Drawings: Iwasaki Art Museum
Kagoshima Prefecture, Kyushu, Japan
Axon: 59 × 43 cm (23.2" × 16.9"), Plan: 72 × 50 cm (28.3" × 19.7"), Scale: 1:100
Medium: Ink on vellum
Courtesy of Fumihiko Maki and Associates, Architects

The plan oblique with a plan sectional cut (left) shows the retention of the plan geometric configuration more so than the plan oblique (above), which displays a site plan view of the roof configuration.

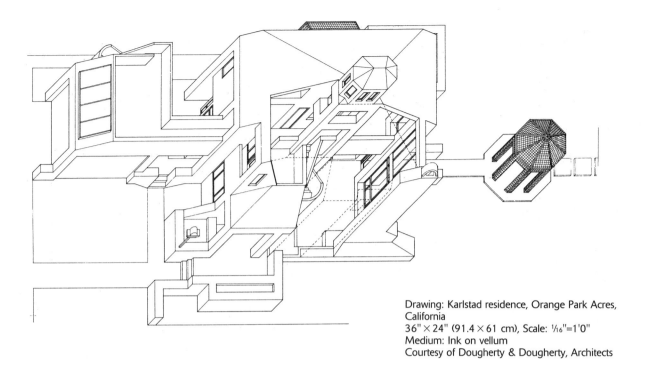

Drawing: Karlstad residence, Orange Park Acres, California
36" × 24" (91.4 × 61 cm), Scale: ¹⁄₁₆"=1'0"
Medium: Ink on vellum
Courtesy of Dougherty & Dougherty, Architects

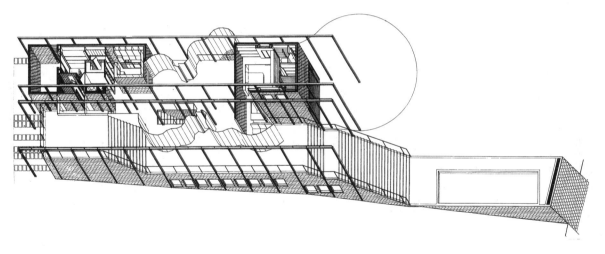

Drawing: Casa Canovelles, Granollers (Barcelona), Spain
Courtesy of MBM Arquitectes
Josep Martorell, Oriol Bohigas, David MacKay, Albert Puigdomènech

PLAN OBLIQUES—NONVERTICAL Z AXIS

The nonvertical *Z* axis can be swung either left or right of the vertical direction. These examples show that vantage points from either direction are equally effective: the choice is based on the viewing information one wishes to convey.

ELEVATION OBLIQUES: A COMPARISON

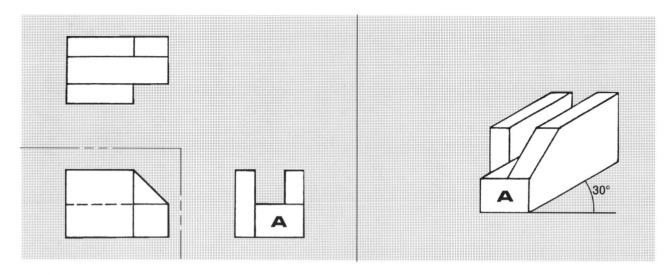

In an **elevation oblique** a chosen elevation view is seen as **true size** and **true shape.** Elevation surface A is used in this example. It is easy to draw elements like true shape circles or curves on true shape surfaces (4 is 2 with a surface modification). The receding lines are usually drawn at 30°, 45°, or 60° angles from the horizontal. Measure the "notated" oblique angle from due north. For example 1, this would be 90° minus 30° = 60°. The next two notations are the elevation scale and the receding line scale. For example 1, this would be 1:1.

1. 60° — 1:1   2. 45° — 1:1   3. 30° — 1:1   4. 45° — 1:1   5. 45° — 1:⅔   6. 45° — 1:½

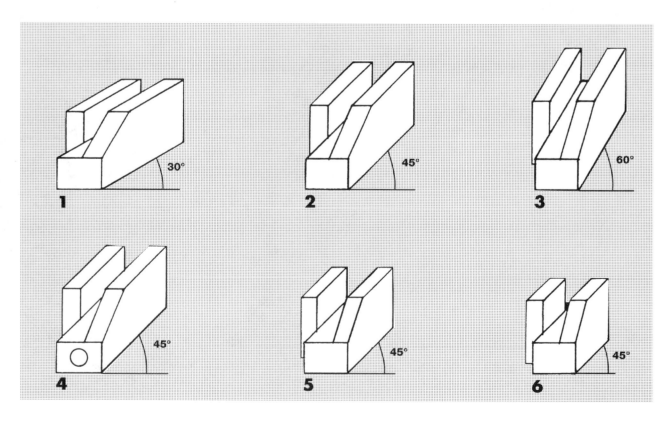

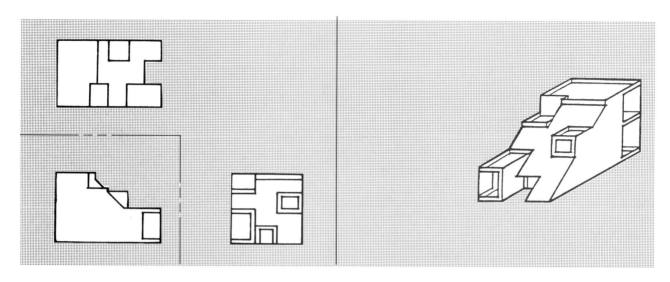

The building form shown in this example has a similar geometric configuration to the example shown on the opposite page. Note that all surfaces parallel to the vertical front elevation plane retain their true size and true shape. It is common practice to show the elevation with the most irregular form as the frontal elevation. The direction of the receding lines and the scale ratio of each drawing corresponds to the six drawings on the previous page.

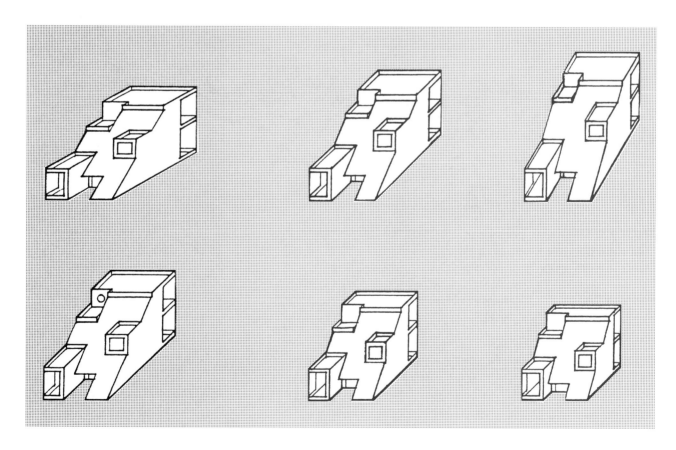

ELEVATION OBLIQUES: A COMPARISON

Drawing: Villa dall'Ava
Paris, France
Courtesy of Office for Metropolitan
Architecture (OMA)

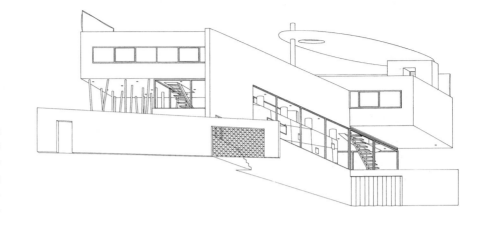

This elevation oblique of a house recedes down to the right. The result is a worm's-eye view looking up. Note that one can easily see interior details through the receding facade.

Drawing: Boathouse, St. Andrew's School
Middletown, Delaware
18" × 6" (45.7 × 15.2 cm), Scale: ⅛"=1'0"
Medium: Technical pen
Drawing by Kim Haskell
Courtesy of Richard Conway Meyer, Architect

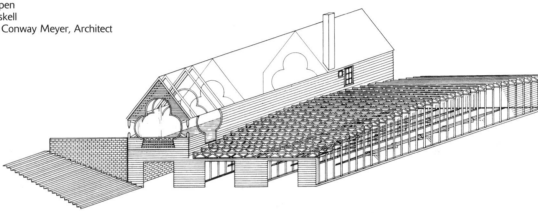

In most cases, elevation obliques recede up to the right or up to the left at a selected angle. Regular or irregular curvilinear forms are commonly seen in the true size elevation. It is sometimes necessary to use a cutaway wall or a transparent oblique to reveal interior spaces.

Drawing: GIADA, Inc., New York City
Scale: 1"=5'0"
Medium: Pen and ink
Courtesy of Steven Holl Architects

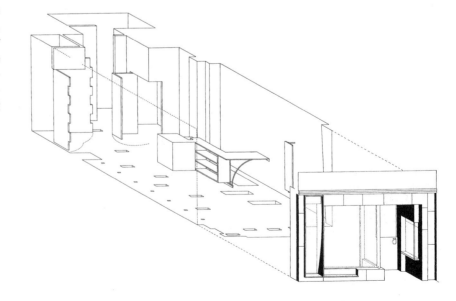

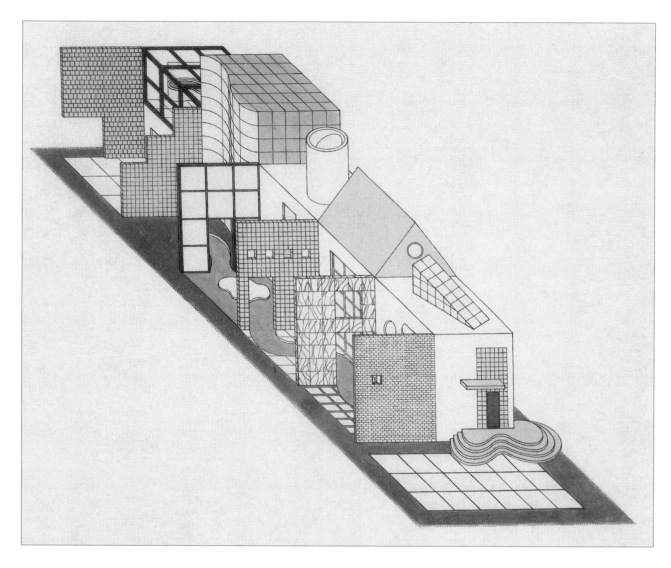

Drawing: Maba House, Houston, Texas
36" × 24" (91.4 × 61 cm)
Medium: Ink on Mylar
Courtesy of Arquitectonica International Corporation

This view was chosen because it best represented the whole house as a series of smaller cubes. The rendering was executed in 1982 on Mylar which was colored on the back. At that time this was typical of Arquitectonica's early visualization techniques. The design of the house was conceived as a series of five little houses, each with its own roof/light feature, court with walls, and different aspects of a continuous pool. The five units provide varied experiences in terms of texture, color and light. The fenestrations vary and entreat light differently within each cubic space. The courtyard of each house is varied and represents a totally unique experience within each. The water element is the only continuous element running through the various cubes.
[ARCHITECT'S STATEMENT]

This elevation oblique has its ground plane receding 45° to the left.

ELEVATION OBLIQUES: BUILDING EXAMPLE

USING THE ELEVATION OBLIQUE

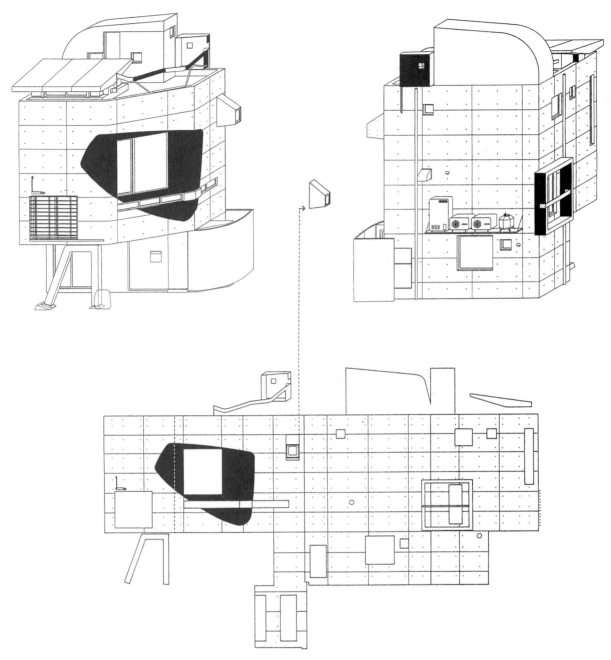

Drawings: Suzuki House, Tokyo, Japan
22 × 28 cm (8.7" × 11"), Scale: 1:30 (Japanese scale)
Medium: Ink on trace
Courtesy of Architekturbüro Bolles–Wilson + Partner

The elevation obliques above are geometrically correct in one elevation, preferable to axonometrics where the plan is true. But elevations do not show the building as experienced. In the fold out, the facade is one continuous pattern of concrete shuttering.
[ARCHITECT'S STATEMENT]

These two elevation obliques show all sides of this building, which also has its skin elevation completely unwrapped and laid out flat.

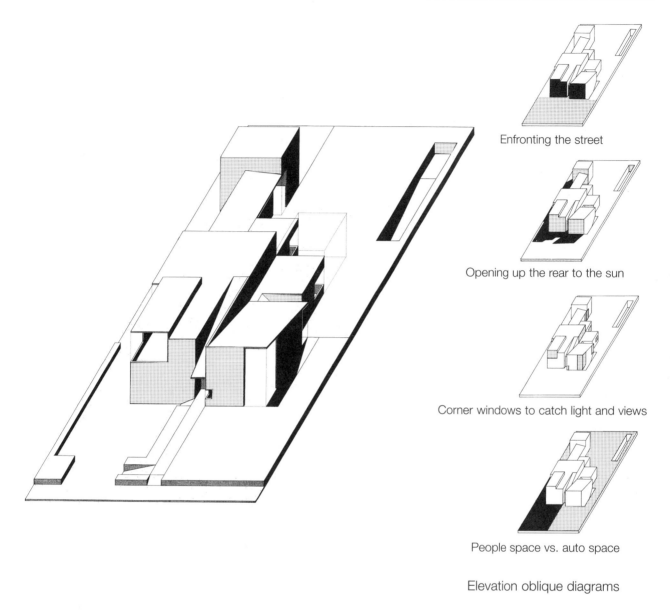

Enfronting the street

Opening up the rear to the sun

Corner windows to catch light and views

People space vs. auto space

Elevation oblique diagrams

Drawing: Adelman/Llanos residence, Santa Monica, California
Medium: Ink
Courtesy of Mack Architects, Mark Mack, principal

USING THE ELEVATION OBLIQUE

Elevation obliques can be very effective in showing how the building design responds to various design parameters. This example shows a simple form repeated five times with an upward receding angle of 60° for the
purpose of diagramming design concepts. Note the use of gray tone and black to express the parameters. The
largest diagram expresses rooms as volume. In this drawing vertical planes were toned black or gray to accentuate building components. Artificial toning can give the needed planar contrast to help enhance the understanding of a design, especially in cases where material texture is absent or not shown. (see pp. 114, 118).

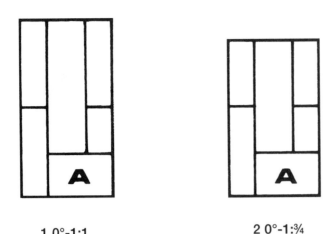

1 0°-1:1   **2 0°-1:¾**

In examples **1** and **2**, the front elevation remains true size. Example **2** shows that the plan dimension is sometimes reduced from true length to give a more realistic (foreshortened) view. This reduction can range from very little to as much as 25%. Most architects and designers, however, tend to maintain a true size plan. Both examples below as well as the drawings to the left can be categorized as a **planometric** since their elevations and roof plans are true size and true shape. A planometric results when either the roof plan or floor plan (see facing page) has one of its sides parallel to the picture plane.

THE PLANOMETRIC

Drawing: Pond Place, London, England
Medium: Ink
Courtesy of Troughton McAslan Architects

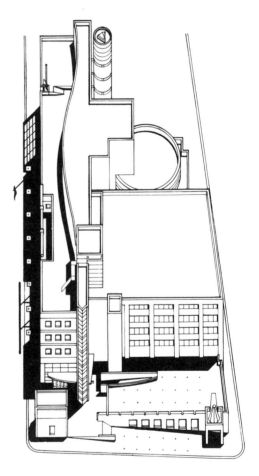

Drawing: Eugenio Maria de Hostos
          Community College, New York City
Medium: Ink on Mylar
20" × 30" (50.8 × 76.2 cm), Scale: ⅛"=1'0"
Courtesy of Bartholomew Voorsanger FAIA

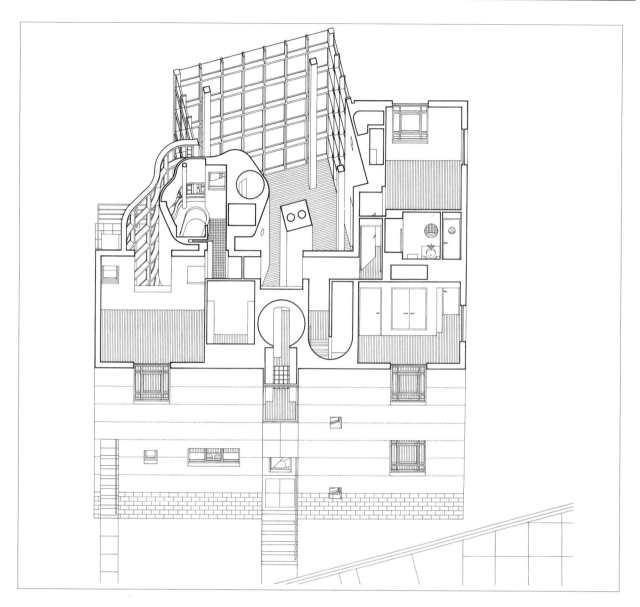

Drawing: Martinelli residence, Roxbury, Connecticut 1989
Medium: Ink
Courtesy of Anthony Ames, Architect

THE PLANOMETRIC

The roof is removed from the building in this frontal axonometric drawing in order to illustrate the room locations on the second floor and their relationship to the double height living and dining space with the cloud like element that encloses the master bathroom.
[ARCHITECT'S STATEMENT]

As with the drawings shown on the previous page, this planometric does not give an illusion of the third dimension. The planometric allows us to simultaneously see vertical dimensions and fenestration patterns along with the roof structure configuration or plan layout.

MULTIOBLIQUE COMBINATIONS

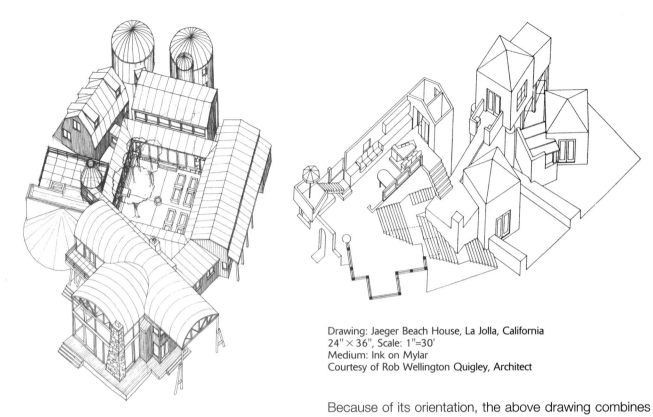

Drawing: Residence, Sun Valley, Idaho
24" × 30" (61 × 76.2 cm), Scale: ⅛"=1'0"
Medium: Pencil on vellum
Courtesy of Frederick Fisher, Architect

Drawing: Jaeger Beach House, La Jolla, California
24" × 36", Scale: 1"=30'
Medium: Ink on Mylar
Courtesy of Rob Wellington Quigley, Architect

Because of its orientation, the above drawing combines plan obliques with a planometric (elevation oblique).

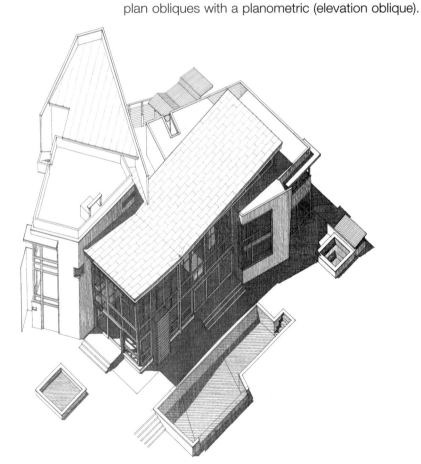

Drawing: Family co-operative
          Barnegat Light,
          New Jersey
Medium: Ink on Mylar
Courtesy of Brian Healy and
Michael Ryan, Architects

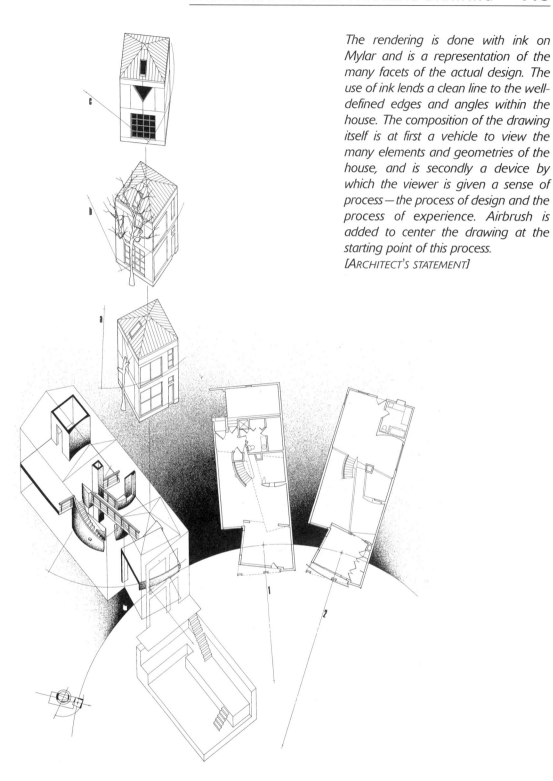

The rendering is done with ink on Mylar and is a representation of the many facets of the actual design. The use of ink lends a clean line to the well-defined edges and angles within the house. The composition of the drawing itself is at first a vehicle to view the many elements and geometries of the house, and is secondly a device by which the viewer is given a sense of process—the process of design and the process of experience. Airbrush is added to center the drawing at the starting point of this process.
[ARCHITECT'S STATEMENT]

MULTIOBLIQUE COMBINATIONS

Drawing: Exploded Axonometric and Plan Composite
            Chasen residence, San Francisco, California
Medium: India ink on Mylar, 30" × 52" (76.2 × 132.1 cm)
Scale: ³⁄₁₆"=1'0"
Courtesy of House + House Architects, San Francisco
Michael Baushke, Architectural Illustrator

THE EXPLODED VIEW

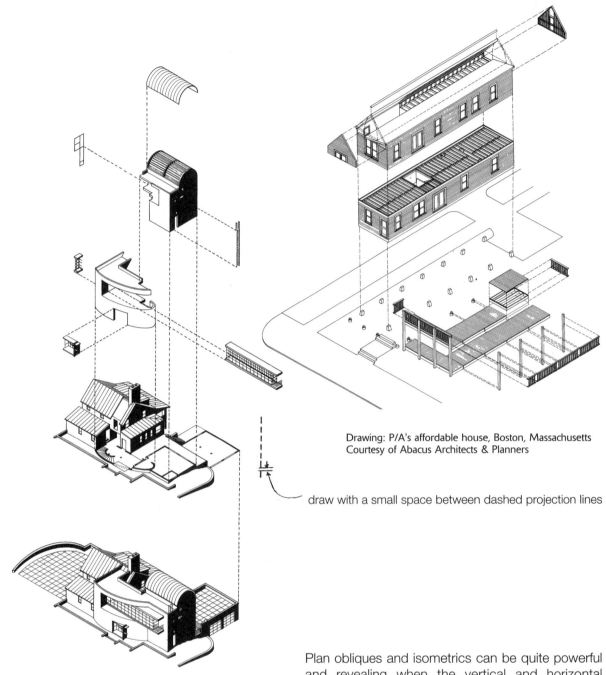

Drawing: P/A's affordable house, Boston, Massachusetts
Courtesy of Abacus Architects & Planners

draw with a small space between dashed projection lines

Drawing: Gorman residence, New Canaan, Connecticut
24" × 36" (61 × 91.4 cm), Scale: ¹⁄₁₆"=1'0"
Medium: Pen and ink
Courtesy of Hariri & Hariri Design, Architects

Plan obliques and isometrics can be quite powerful and revealing when the vertical and horizontal dimensions are expanded by either the use of dashed lines or light solid projection lines. These **exploded views** illustrate how structural components relate to one another. If possible, horizontally or vertically exploded elements should not overlap. **Expanded views** (opposite page) are exploded in one direction only as shown with the numerous roof removals on the previous pages.

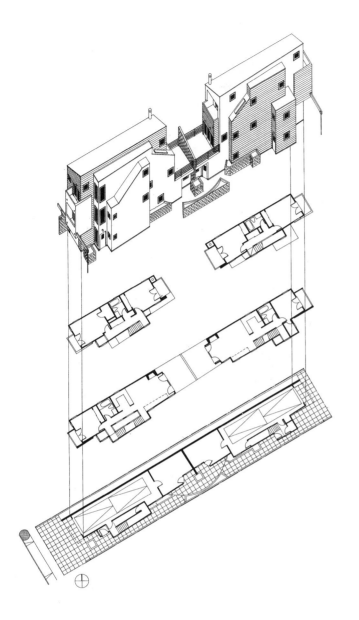

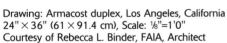

Drawing: Armacost duplex, Los Angeles, California
24" × 36" (61 × 91.4 cm), Scale: 1/8"=1'0"
Courtesy of Rebecca L. Binder, FAIA, Architect

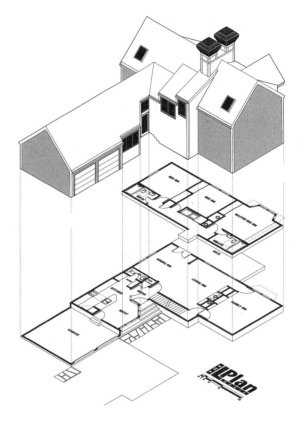

Drawing: House, Connecticut
8.5" × 11" (21.6 × 27.9 cm), Scale: 1/16"=1'0"
Originally drawn at 1/4"=1'0"
Medium: Macintosh computer in Power Draw
Courtesy of Robert T. Coolidge, AIA, Architect

THE EXPANDED VIEW

The concept of the expanded view in both plan obliques and isometrics is frequently applied to buildings with two or more floors. Stacked floors usually exhibit similar geometric configurations. These examples illustrate how the floor plans can be removed from the building shell to help visualize the vertical relationship of all levels in conjunction with the exterior form.

THE EXPANDED VIEW

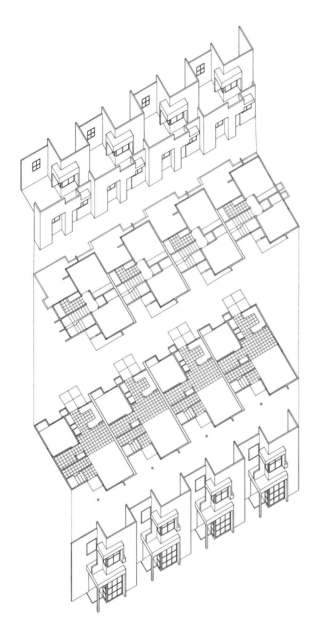

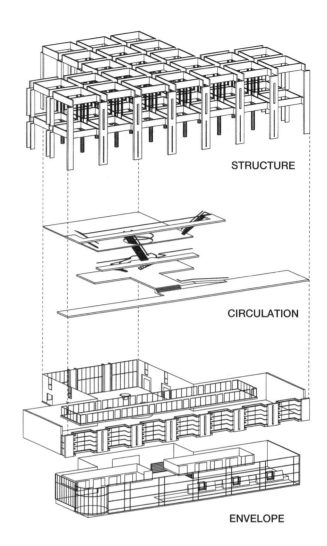

STRUCTURE

CIRCULATION

ENVELOPE

Dimetric of components

The front and rear elevations below and above the floor plans help to project the three-dimensional richness of the facade from the two-dimensional floor plans.
[ARCHITECT'S STATEMENT]

This expanded view uses a paraline axonometric in the form of a dimetric. The lower angle of view permits one to see the linking circulation elements between floors.

Drawing: Cabrillo Village, Saticoy, California
24" × 36" (61 × 91.4 cm), Scale: ⅛"=1'0"
Medium: Ink
Courtesy of John V. Mutlow, FAIA, Architects

Drawing: Library, Toronto, Canada
Medium: Ink
Courtesy of A.J. Diamond, Donald Schmitt, Architects

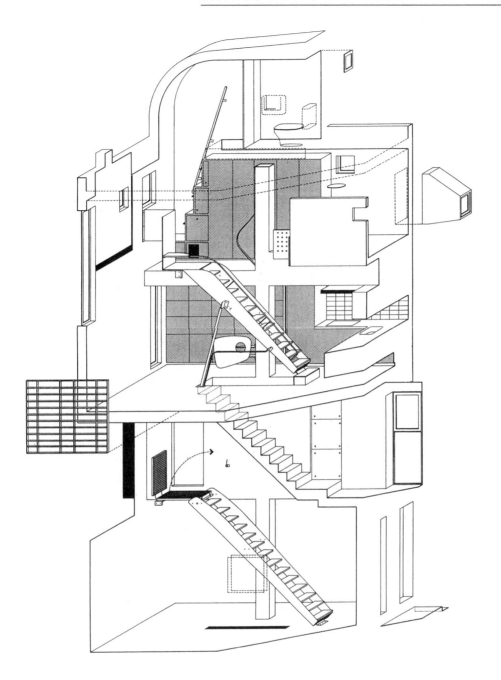

Drawings: Suzuki House, Tokyo, Japan
22 × 28 cm (8.7" × 11"), Scale: 1:30 (Japanese scale)
Medium: Ink on trace
Courtesy of Architekturbüro Bolles–Wilson + Partner

THE EXPLODED VIEW

The space of the house at all levels is visible on one projection. The central stair is understood as the connecting sequence…as in Japanese painting what is not shown is as important as what is shown.
[Architect's statement]

Both exploded and expanded views are excellent tools for examining the way details are put together whether they are small structural components or large building elements. This is an interior elevation oblique with exploded parts.

EXPANDED ELEVATION OBLIQUE

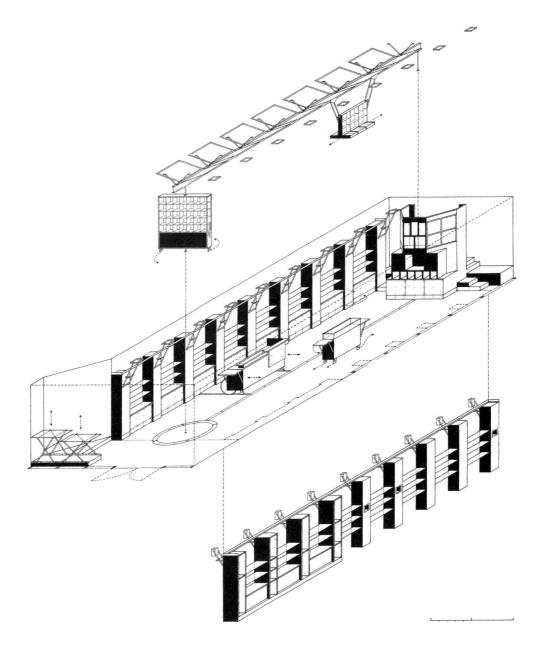

Drawing: Techsis Retail Store, San Francisco, California
17" × 22" (43.2 × 55.9 cm), Scale: ¼"=1'0"
Medium: Ink on Mylar
Courtesy of Jensen + Macy Architects

The elevation oblique was chosen because it gives more emphasis to the vertical planes (the display fixtures) than the plan oblique which emphasizes plan relationships. This drawing type has an analytical quality allowing one to understand space/object relationships not graspable from the single fixed vantage point of the perspective. The extension above and below of parts of the drawing allows a reading of the separate components of the store in the composition. [ARCHITECT'S STATEMENT]

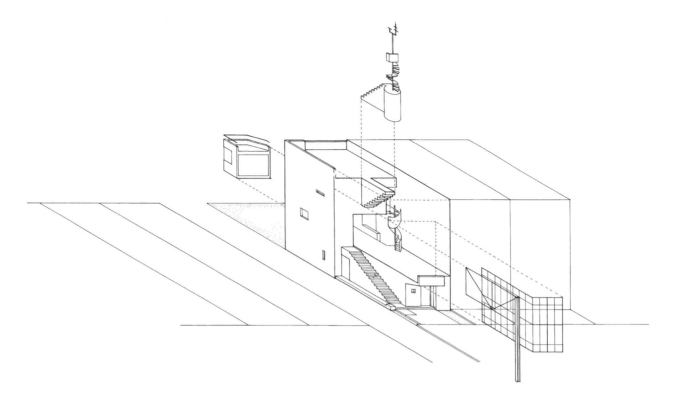

Drawing: Ruskin Square House, Seaside, Florida
10" × 8" (25.4 × 20.3 cm), Scale: ¹⁄₁₆"=1'0"
Medium: Pen and ink
Courtesy of Alexander Gorlin, Architect

This drawing projection was chosen to display a number of aspects of the project at the same time, and first, to locate the townhouse on its site, as part of an urban block on the pedestrian plaza Ruskin Place in Seaside, Florida and then, to articulate and isolate the distinct elements of the design by pulling them apart. This allows one to see the relationship between the stairs, the promenade architecturale, that are threaded through the house, from the base of the roof and beyond to the "crow's nest" where one can view the horizon of the Gulf of Mexico.
[ARCHITECT'S STATEMENT]

EXPLODED ELEVATION OBLIQUE

UP VIEWS

These dramatic worm's-eye views permit the viewer to peer upward into the buildings. This method was first developed and utilized by August Choisy (19th century). In design drawings it is sometimes necessary to show the relationship between the ceiling or the soffit and the walls. An excellent example of this type of drawing showing the resolution of wall to roof structure is shown on p. 595. The disadvantage of this type of drawing is that they are sometimes very difficult to interpret, especially for beginning students and the layperson.

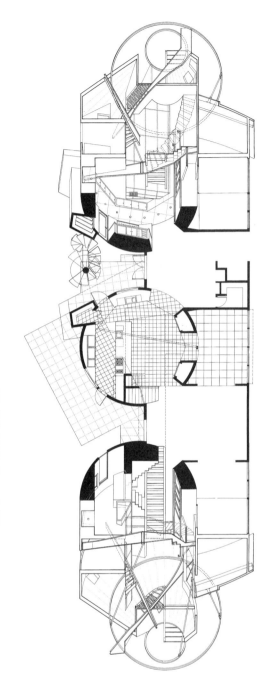

Split worm's-eye axonometric

Drawing: Lawson/Westen House, Los Angeles, California
Medium: Ink on Mylar
Courtesy of Eric Owen Moss, Architects

Drawing: Student project by Colin Alley
        Community Center
Medium: Ink on Mylar
Courtesy of Washington University
School of Architecture, St. Louis, MO

This drawing simultaneously allows one to understand the building's form and organization while giving clues as to how the designers conceived the building: a modest shell which bends to accommodate and encourage movement and circulation; a pure cylinder at the center of the mass as a primal gathering place; and a peaked conical roof capping the cylinder as a distinguishing image at the center of a four building residential village.
[ARCHITECT'S STATEMENTS]

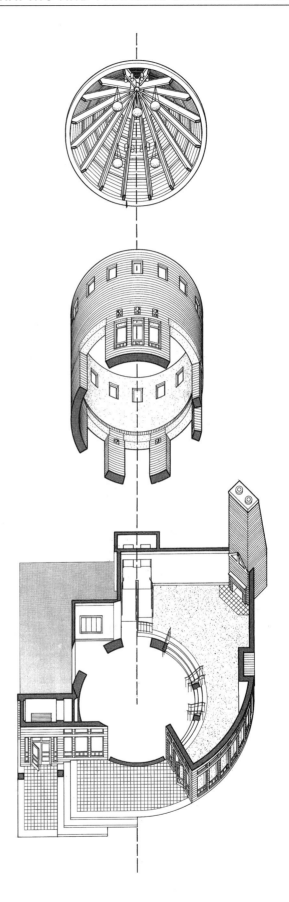

This drawing combines a plan oblique down view with plan oblique up views. Its advantage is that it allows us to simultaneously understand the total geometric configuration of a design.

Drawing: Bates College Social/Study Center
           (Residential Halls project) Lewiston, Maine
12" × 30" (30.5 × 76.2 cm), Scale: ¼"=1'0"
Medium: Ink on Mylar
Courtesy of William Rawn Associates,
Architects, Inc. Boston, MA

SIMULTANEOUS UP AND DOWN VIEWS

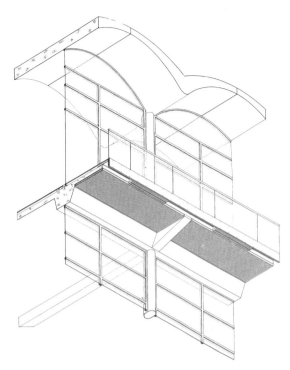

Detail of balcony edge

Drawing: Lycee Polyvalent de Fréjus
Fréjus School, Fréjus, France
418 × 595 mm (16.5" × 23.4")
Medium: Ink on film
Drawn by Keith Allen
Courtesy of Sir Norman Foster and Partners

UP VIEWS

Axonometric up views in the form of isometrics allow one to see more detail between floor levels than would be seen in a plan oblique up view. Note the isometric curvilinear form above and the horizontal and vertical isometric circles shown to the right.

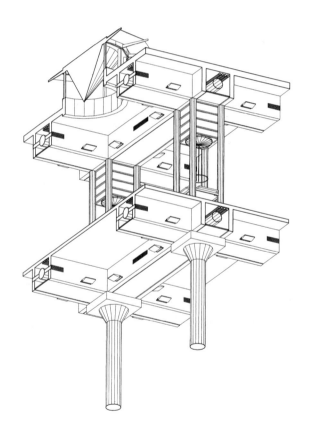

Isometric of typical bay

Drawing: Richmond Hill Library, Toronto, Canada
Courtesy of A.J Diamond, Donald Schmitt, Architects

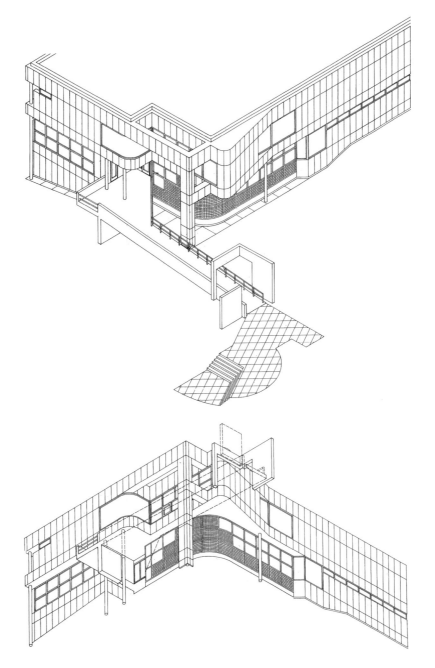

Drawings: Postindustrial factory
Dorval, Quebec, Canada
30" × 48" (76.2 × 121.9 cm), Scale: ⅛"=1'0"
Medium: Ink on Mylar
Courtesy of Michael Fieldman & Partners, Architects

A pair of axonometric views—one aerial, the other worm's eye—were used to describe a complex 3D corner entrance. Together they convey the spatial quality of the design.
[ARCHITECT'S STATEMENT]

SIMULTANEOUS UP AND DOWN VIEWS

5

Representational Sketching

Sketches of the built environment are analytical drawings that generally convey an overall image. We do these sketches to gain a greater understanding of the nature of the urban landscape. Those sketches must be executed quickly and accurately. Geometric shapes are the foundation for all derived form. Environmental form and composition is an aggregate of simple and complex forms. These forms must be graphically expressed in a visually appealing manner, whether you sketch from "life" or from your imagination.

The intent of this chapter is to cover the basic aspects of freehand descriptive sketching such as types of sketching tools, line, shape, proportion, and values, as well as to examine how to observe and depict encountered environmental elements. Another goal is to hone one's ability to sketch a subject in such a way as to describe it through the utilization of line, and volume, as well as proportional and perspective relationships.

Representational Sketching

Topic

Contour Drawing

References

Betti, C., and T. Sale. 1986. Drawing: A Contemporary Approach, 3rd ed. New York: Holt, Rinehart and Winston.

Ching, F. D. K. 1996. Architectural Graphics, 3rd ed. New York: Van Nostrand Reinhold.

Ching, F.D.K. 1990. Drawing: A Creative Process. New York: Van Nostrand Reinhold. (42–43, 51–51)

Dodson, B. 1990. Keys to Drawing. Cincinnati: OH: Northern Light Books.

Porter, T. and Goodman, S. 1988. Designer Primer. New York: Charles Scribner's sons. (52–53)

Topic

Stroke Character

Reference

Pencil Sketching (Wang 1977, 18–28, 75–81).

Drawing: A Creative Process (Ching 1990, 22–25).

Topic

Vegetation

Reference

Pencil Sketching (Wang 1977, 44–56).

Topic

Drawing Methods

References

Crowe and Laseau 1984. Visual Notes for Architects and Designers. New York: Van Nostrand Reinhold.

Goldstein, N. 1989. Design and Composition. Prentice Hall.

Hanks and Belliston 1977. Draw. Los Altos, CA: William Kaufmann, Inc. (33–136)

Mendelowitz, D. 1993. Guide to Drawing. Harcourt brace Jovanovich.

Topics

Human Figures, Sighting

References

Pencil Sketching (Wang 1977, 82–88).

Bridgman's Complete Guide to Drawing from Life (Bridgman, 1992).

Topic

Sketching with Markers

References

Sketching with Markers (Wang 1993).

Architectural Sketching in Markers (Linton and Strickfaden 1991).

Topic

Buildings / Travel Sketches

References

Drawn from the Source—The Travel sketches of Louis I. Kahn (Johnson and Lewis 1996).

Pencil Sketching (Wang 1977, 70–74)

The Sketch (Oliver 1979, 83–130)

Architectural Sketching and Rendering (Kliment 1984, 39–87, 105–113).

Designer Primer (Porter and Goodman 1988, 60–68).

Architectural Visions: The Drawings of Hugh Ferriss (Leich 1980).

Cross References

For p. 131	See pp. 84, 465
For p. 134	See pp. 371, 378, 379
For p. 135	See pp. 412, 422
For p. 139	See pp. 370, 371, 376
For pp. 146–151	See pp. 398–401
For pp. 152–153	See pp. 392–397
For pp. 154–155	See pp. 406–407
For pp. 174–175	See pp. 452–453

Drawing from life is essential to the development of the hand/eye/brain "loop." The more one draws, the more one becomes aware of the world in terms of vision. The more conscious the architects, artists, and designers are, the more formidable their work will be. Often, when students begin to draw, they are anxious that what is drawn will not "be the right shape"; in other words, it will not have the correct proportions. One of the most fundamental tools for controlling proportion is called **sighting** (explained on pages 142 and 143). This method of using a drawing instrument held at arm's length as a measuring device (essentially simulating a picture plane) is highly effective in helping the beginner to make objects in the drawing "the right shape," as well as controlling distances and relative sizes in general. Looking and recording reality with the aid of sighting will strengthen the visual sense and bring confidence to the drawing process.

Drawing is a process that progresses from seeing to visualizing and finally to expressing. The ability to see gives us the raw material for our perceptions and ultimately for what we draw. Visual information seen by the eye is processed, manipulated, and filtered by the mind in its active search for structure and meaning. The mind's eye creates the images we see and eventually tries to express them in the form of a drawn image. Our ability to express and communicate relies on our ability to draw.

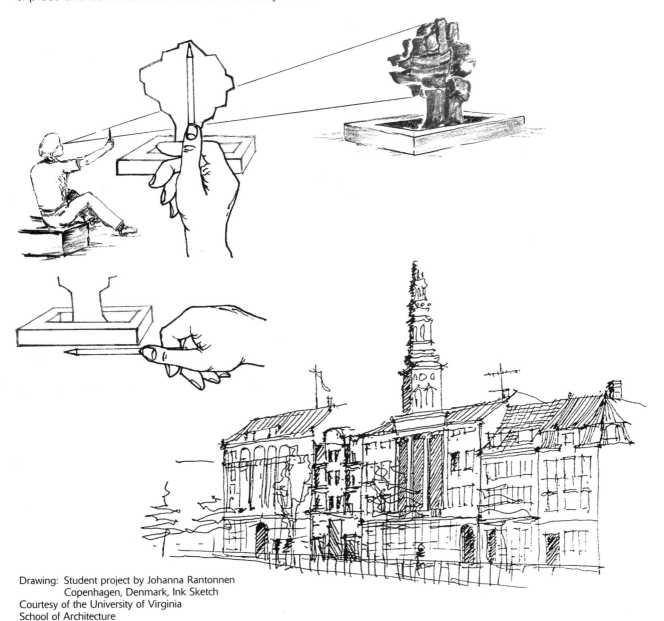

Drawing: Student project by Johanna Rantonnen
Copenhagen, Denmark, Ink Sketch
Courtesy of the University of Virginia
School of Architecture

INTRODUCTION

As an introduction to sketching, the scope of this chapter will cover pencils, pens, and markers in terms of black and white and shades of gray only. Utilize the excellent bibliography to do your own investigation into the significant area of color sketching. Some of the many quality sketching pencils are shown on this page. In addition experiment with charcoal sticks and Conté pencils. Also use different kinds of sketching paper. Beginners normally use inexpensive newsprint paper as their first drawing surface. Smooth (fine grain) sketching paper and coarse (textured) sketching paper are other popular surfaces.

GENERAL'S Sketching Pencil U.S.A. 531-4B

CARBONE Conté A PARIS FRANCE 722 2B

EF Eberhard Faber DESIGN™ EBONY JET BLACK EXTRA SMOOTH 6325

Berol DRAUGHTING 314

The selection of paper may be based on reprography. If your sketches or drawings are going to be reproduced as prints (black, blue, or sepia ozalid), you must use transparent paper. If they are to be reproduced using photographic or photocopying methods, you must use opaque paper.

Soft lead sketching pencils can have round or flat leads. A flat sketching pencil can be thick (carpenter's pencil) or medium thick (chisel pencil). Both must be sharpened by hand. Flat sketching pencils are mainly used in three degreees, 2B, 4B, and 6B. They are used commonly for covering large areas quickly such as tonal indications for brick, stone, and wood. Conté pencils or sticks come in three grades of black, in four different colors, and in soft, medium, and hard. Both Conté and Ebony pencils give smooth lines. The Ebony pencil's soft core is slightly wider than a typical pencil. A good general-purpose sketching pencil with a soft lead is Berol Draughting 314. An all purpose mechanical leadholder clutch freehand sketching pencil can adapt its lead to almost any shape and is ideal for rapidly sketching over large areas. Other excellent brands include Derwent and Mars.

Sketch: Student project by Wan Othman
Glass Study
Medium: Graphite pencil
Courtesy of Washington
University School of Architecture, St. Louis, MO

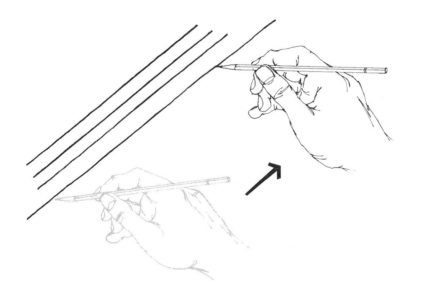

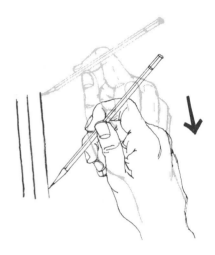

PENCIL STROKES

The quality of a freehand pencil stroke is determined by the hardness grade of the pencil lead, the character of the sharpened point, the amount of pressure applied, and the type of paper used. Compare parallel lines drawn on both smooth and rough sketching paper. Softer pencils work better with smoother paper, harder pencils with coarser paper. Architectural pencil sketching is most commonly done with grades such as HB, B, and 2B, though softer leads are not uncommon. Graphite and charcoal pencils can yield variable line widths and tone. Variable tone and value cannot be acheived when sketching with pens and markers. Lighting conditions resulting in shades and shadows are most accurately represented by using soft lead pencils, charcoal pencils, or Conté crayons. Fixative sprays prevent pencil work from smudging.

In the above illustration, the side of the little finger is resting down on the drawing surface. The pencil should be held in a relaxed position; too tight a grip will cause hand fatigue. A wrist and arm movement will produce longer strokes. Use the wrist, elbow, and shoulders as pivot points. Attempt to master the control of sketching straight lines, curved lines, circular spirals, and circles. When sketching, use the whole page (draw big).

PENS AND MARKERS

Using a pen or a marker as a communication tool allows the architect/designer to express a wide range of images, whether they be representational like the hotel courtyard and the Austrian street scene or conceptual as with the Lloyds of London sketch.

Sketch: The Garden Court of the Palace Hotel
             San Francisco, California
Medium: Ink pen
Sketch by Charles Moore, Architect
Courtesy of Saul Weingarten, Executor, Estate of Charles Moore and
the Department of Architecture, UCLA School of Art and Architecture

In addition to pencils, line and tone can be produced by a variety of pens and markers. Markers are available in a variety of halftones; but because of quick drying, mixing tones is difficult. The tips of markers vary in size from fine to broad and vary in shape from pointed to chisel shapes. Finer tips generate more detailed fine lines, whereas broader tips generate wider lines and solid tones. Technical pens are commonly used for precise mechanical lines. Razor-point pens, cartridge pens, and fountain pens can generate loose sketching lines that are permanent. Fountain pens become quite versatile in their application of line weight simply by adjusting the finger pressure.

Sketch: Lloyds of London, London, England
11.75" × 16.5" (29.8 × 41.9 cm)
Medium: Brown felt-tipped marker
Courtesy of Richard Rogers Partnership, Architects

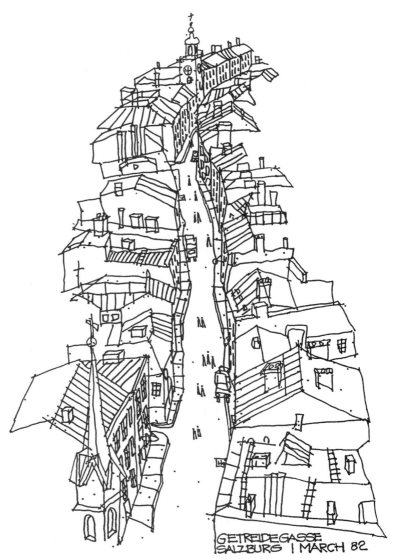

Drawing: Street scene, Salzburg, Austria
7" × 10" (17.8 × 25.4 cm)
Medium: Felt-tipped pen on paper
Courtesy of Steven House, Architect, San Francisco

Felt-tipped markers give a quick, loose, and very effective transparent (similar to watercolor) method of presentation when time is a critical factor. The advantage of a marker is that it very seldom smudges. It also comes in a great variety of premixed colors in addition to black and gray. Markers are more suitable to smoother, harder, and heavier grades of paper. Pencils and colored pencils best accommodate medium weight textured paper.

Ballpoint pens and rollerball pens can generate a variety of line widths. Ballpoints are just one of the many kinds of pen tips; others include felt-tipped, fiber-tipped, and roller-tipped. In general, all types of pens give steady, fluid, smooth-flowing lines without the need to apply pressure as one needs to do with a pencil.

Pens and markers are perhaps best suited to drawing conceptual ideas (see chapter on conceptual sketching). These tools give one the ability to "loosen up" to avoid inhibitions in the design-drawing process. See the bibliography for books on sketching with pens and markers.

BALL POINT PENS AND FELT-TIPPED MARKERS

PENCIL STROKES

Sketch: Texas Seaport Museum, Galveston, Texas
Medium: Ebony pencil on paper, 1991
Courtesy of David G. Woodcock, FAIA, RIBA
Professor of Architecture
Texas A & M University, Department of Architecture

The darkness quality of an Ebony pencil means that less applied pressure is needed when sketching. It can smoothly render any line width with its soft graphite and is acceptable for most slightly toothed paper surfaces.

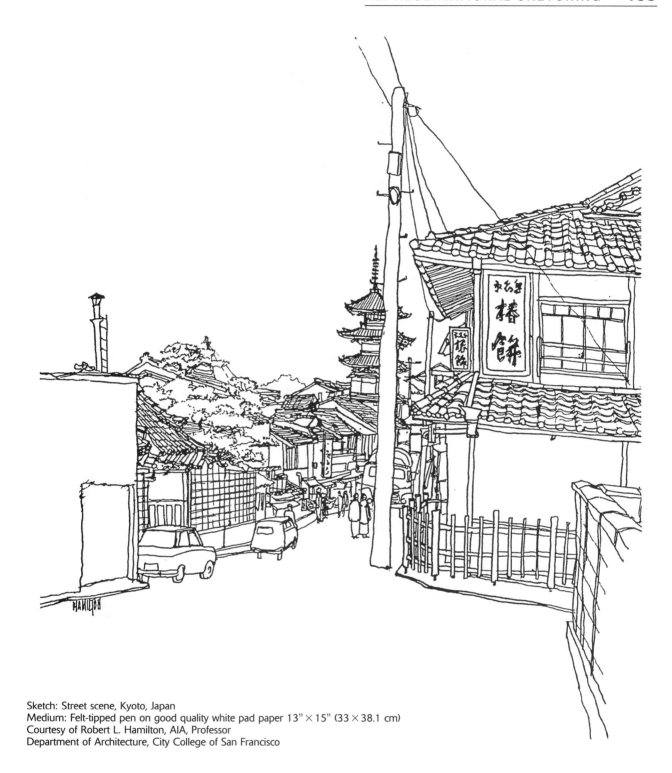

Sketch: Street scene, Kyoto, Japan
Medium: Felt-tipped pen on good quality white pad paper 13" × 15" (33 × 38.1 cm)
Courtesy of Robert L. Hamilton, AIA, Professor
Department of Architecture, City College of San Francisco

PEN STROKES

Like pencils, pens are a convenient medium when one is quickly sketching in a new unfamiliar place. They do not require extra setup time as, for example, with watercolors. Graphite and ink differ in that ink is more permanent: Every mark and stroke is critical in the development of any drawing done with a pen. Pen strokes emphasize line work and the interrelationship of the compositional shapes. Street scenes in the cityscape are always popular travel sketches. Enliven building sketches by adding visible accessories like vegetation, people, and vehicular traffic in their proper scale.

Sketch: Pomodoro showroom, New York City
35" × 24" (94.1 × 61 cm)
Medium: Black ink marker and sepia grease pencil
Courtesy of FTL Architects, PC

Lines in architectural sketches can be very disciplined like the sketch to the right, or they can be very loose like the sketches below. Both approaches convey a different character to each sketch. All these sketches were done with pen and ink. With this medium, the controlled cumulative effects of the strokes are the most critical.

Pen strokes often describe simultaneously different drawing elements. For example, form and volume in the Barcelona sketch combine with value and texture. Line weight (the thickness or thinness of a line) can express the "quality" of line. This quality may have the express purpose of conveying form and/or shadow. In representational sketches, lines guide the eye by delineating shapes and enclosing spaces. In drafting, lines are drawn accurately to give a hardline representation of buildings. In conceptual sketches, lines are drawn freely and with rhythmic strokes.

Church of Sagrada Familia
Medium: Pen and ink, 10" × 12" (25.4 × 30.5 cm)
Antonio Gaudi, Architect

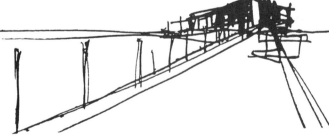

Medium: Felt-tipped pen on bond paper 3" × 7" (7.6 × 17.8 cm)

Sketches (above, middle, and right): Barcelona, Spain
Student projects respectively by Susan Pruchnicki, Kathryn Korn, Rosalino Figureras
Courtesy of Washington University School of Architecture, St. Louis, MO

STROKE CHARACTER

Sketches: Student project by Corvin Matei 18" × 18" (45.7 × 45.7 cm)
Courtesy of the University of Texas at Arlington
School of Architecture

Experimental train station for the D.A.R.T.
(Dallas Rapid Transit Systems)
Medium: 2B pencil on Strathmore paper

The drawing above shows precise controlled strokes of tone value within a mechanically constructed three-point perspective. Subtle tone values achieved with pencil are much more difficult to achieve with ink pens (facing page). The drawing fades from its detailed central image. Where there is less detail, there is a hint as to how the image might continue. This type of sketch is termed a vignette (see pp. 153, 159, 161, 164, and 175).

A soft 2B pencil was used to emphasize the parts of the drawing that are important in order to understand the spatial architecture. It has an unfinished look.
[ARCHITECTURE STUDENT'S STATEMENT]

STROKE CHARACTER

These two facing pages show a difference in stroke character based on the drawing instrument used. Felt-tipped or fiber-tipped markers and fountain pens usually encourage "looseness" in the hand and arm strokes, resulting in a more representational sketch (San Francisco sketches) rather than a detailed copy sketch of what we see. A fine-point technical pen or a fine-tipped marker encourages more detail and a copy quality (Rome sketches).

Sketch: The Vedanta Society building, San Francisco, California
Medium: Ink pen
Sketch by Charles Moore, Architect
Courtesy of Saul Weingarten, Executor, Estate of Charles Moore and the Department of Architecture, UCLA School of Art and Architecture

Sketch: Palace of Fine Arts San Francisco, California
Bernard Maybeck, Architect
Medium: Ink pen
Sketch by Charles Moore, Architect
Courtesy of Saul Weingarten, Executor,
Estate of Charles Moore and the Department of Architecture,
UCLA School of Art and Architecture

STROKE CHARACTER

Sketches: Student project by Corvin Matei, Rome, Italy
Medium: Ink on Strathmore paper, 6" × 9" (15.2 × 22.9 cm)
Courtesy of the University of Texas at Arlington
School of Architecture

STROKE CHARACTER

These are simple **contour** drawings executed with a great economy of line. As minimal as they are, they clearly define positive and negative qualities of space. The stroke character of a contour line can create an immense range of possibilites with respect to the viewer's sense of form, space, and light in the drawing context.

Drawing allows me to express the essence of a particular and dear quality of my design. This may be a play of light or color, a form or forms, a unique perspective, or most often, the relationship of my building with the sky. [ARCHITECT'S STATEMENT]

Sketch: Boyer Center for Molecular Medicine, New Haven, Connecticut
Medium: Pen and ink
6.25" × 9" (15.9 × 22.9 cm)
Courtesy of Cesar Pelli, Architect, Cesar Pelli & Associates

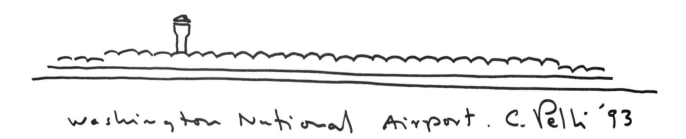

Sketch: New North Terminal Washington National Airport, Washington, D.C.
Medium: Pen and ink
Courtesy of Cesar Pelli, Architect, Cesar Pelli & Associates

Drawing: Petronas Towers, Kuala Lumpur, Malaysia
Medium: Oil pastels on acid-free vellum 9.5" × 12" (24.1 × 30.5 cm)
Courtesy of Cesar Pelli, Architect, Cesar Pelli & Associates

STROKE CHARACTER

These rapidly sketched strokes give the soft delicate quality commonly found when pastels are used. Pastels lend themselves to compostions that are not very detailed, such as this value study. Value refers to the lightness or darkness of a surface. In this representational sketch, there is a high value contrast in the sense that an extremely light color (building form or figure) is placed adjacent to an extremely dark color (sky or background). A low value contrast occurs when either two (or more) light values or two (or more) dark values are placed next to each other. In the above example, this phenomenon begins to occur as the sky gradually becomes lighter toward the horizon to almost merge in value with the value of the base of the towers. Classic examples of this kind of value transition can be seen in the 1920's and 1930's work of Hugh Ferriss (see bibliography). Architect Cesar Pelli is well known for using layered diagonal line strokes to control value and density. This expressive technique allows for qualities such as light and shadow, volume, surface, reflections, and transparency to appear.

Drawing is the essence of description.
Drawing connects the eye and the hand to define the world, both seen and unseen.
[ARCHITECT'S STATEMENT]

REPRESENTATIONAL SKETCHING

Representational sketching utilizes many basic elements, such as line, value, texture, the massing of shapes and volumes, scale, and color (if color is used). A noncolored pencil or an ink pen will result in a monochromatic sketch. Working in any medium, one consciously manipulates either one element or any combination of the elements to produce a desired final composition. Sketches should exhibit a creative richness regardless of the technique and medium used. The goal of representational sketching should go far beyond accurately imitating what one sees.

Sketches: Manhattan, Function and Form
Medium: Pen and ink
9" × 10" (22.9 × 25.4 cm)
Courtesy of Hugh Hardy, FAIA; Hardy Holzman Pfeiffer Associates

TOWN PLAZA

Sketch: Alabang Town Center, Alabang, Philippines
Medium: Felt-tipped pen on vellum
Courtesy of Architecture International and TAC, The Architects Collaborative,
Ayala Land, Inc., and GF and Partners, Architects, Co.
Renderer: Lawrence Ko Leong

MEDIA TO REPRESENT SKETCHES

The choice of medium will affect a sketch's character. Establish the character or feeling by deciding which words would best describe your subject or your design. Will the word and feeling be formal or informal, soft or slick, etc.? Graphite, ink, and watercolor are just a few of the possible media that one can use in communicating architectural sketches. In just the area of color media, there are many choices in addition to watercolor such as colored pencils, colored markers, oil pastels, etc. Work with the medium that you feel most at ease with. Be alert to other evolving media such as computers or computers combined with manual methods (mixed media).

SIGHTING

Drawing: Sacramento State Office Building, Sacramento, California
Fisher–Friedman Associates, San Francisco, CA

To properly establish accurate proportions in transferring what we see to our drawing pad, we must accurately compare relative lengths, widths, and angles.

1. Observe the subject/scene that you would like to draw.
2. Close one eye, hold your head still, and extend your arm to arm's length.
3. Using a pencil or pen, make a basic unit length measurement on any part of the viewed scene which will be the distance from your drawing instrument tip to the top of your thumb.

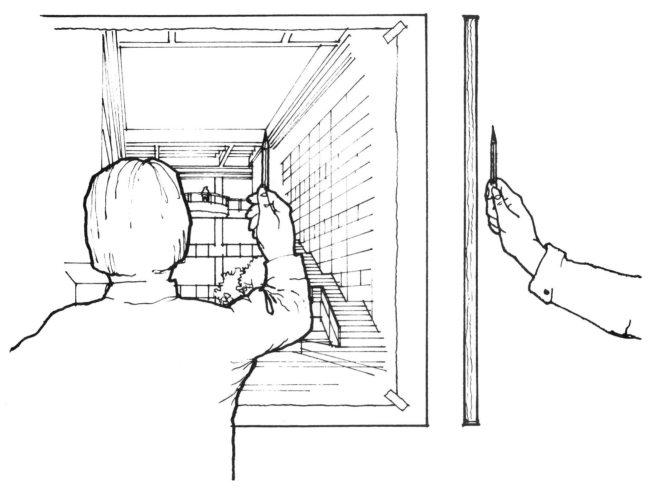

Drawing: Sacramento State Office Building, Sacramento, California
Fisher–Friedman Associates, San Francisco, CA

SIGHTING

4. Other lengths and widths can now be measured based on the smaller unit length. All of these distances must reference the basic unit in terms of relative size.
5. The drawing instrument must coincide and be aligned with any angled line to properly transfer a similar angle to the drawing pad. Measure the angle with respect to a horizontal and vertical reference which corresponds to the edges of your pad.

Remember:

- that the plane your eyes are in must always be parallel to your drawing instrument plane.
- to keep your drawing pad perpendicular to your line of sight so that your drawing instrument can lie in the same plane regardless of its orientation.

BLOCKING OUT AND CONSTRUCTION LINES

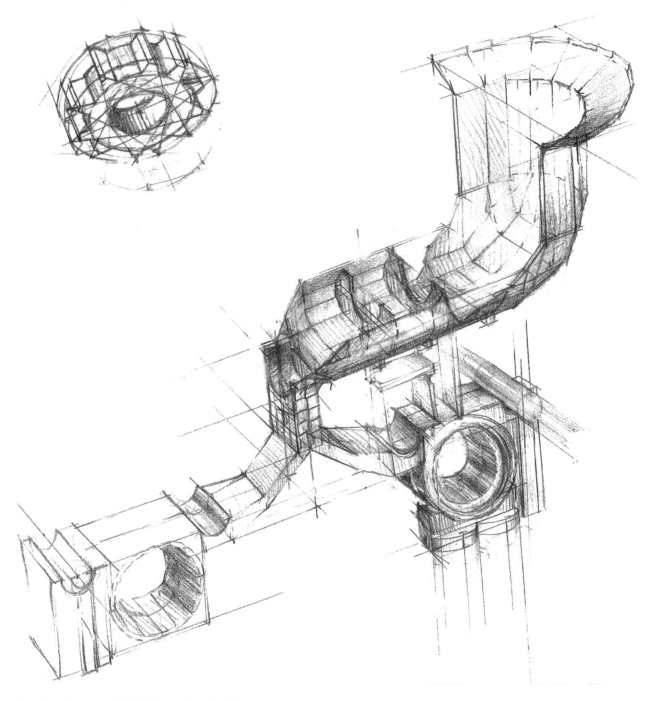

Drawing: Courtesy of Dick Davison, Associate Professor
Medium: HB graphite pencil on Strahmore 400, 18" × 18" (45.7 × 45.7 cm)
Texas A & M University, School of Architecture

Objects in a composition should always be blocked out within a geometric envelope. Two dimensionally, the shape can be either a triangle, a circle, a square, or a polygon. Three dimensionally, the basic element can be a cube, a sphere, or a polygon (3D). **Blocking out** helps to compose a drawing and gives us a clue as to what the end product will look like. Once an accurate composition is drawn, line weights can be adjusted or values applied to complete and finalize the drawing. An HB pencil has a lead that is in the transition zone between hard and soft. An HB pencil can achieve nice soft tone values halfway between white and black on a value chart (scale).

With any object, always begin to set up the proportions by using **construction lines.** These lightly drawn lines should envelop the object. The use of these lines is especially important with objects that are composed of nonlinear forms as shown above. On cylindrical or rounded shapes, be sure to locate the main central axis spine first. Long construction lines are most effectively drawn by holding the pencil beneath the hand with thumb and fingers.

Drawing: Courtesy of Dick Davison, Associate Professor
Medium: HB graphite pencil on Strathmore 400, 18" × 18" (45.7 × 45.7 cm)
Texas A & M University, School of Architecture

BLOCKING OUT AND CONSTRUCTION LINES

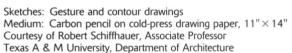

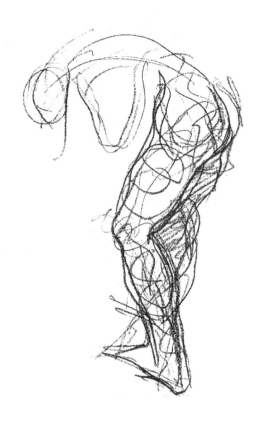

LIFE DRAWING

Sketches: Gesture and contour drawings
Medium: Carbon pencil on cold-press drawing paper, 11" × 14"
Courtesy of Robert Schiffhauer, Associate Professor
Texas A & M University, Department of Architecture

Gesture drawings are quick proportion and form studies which help to develop rapid hand–eye coordination. Contour drawings are more time-consuming and precise in nature.

The human figure is an excellent subject for both gesture and contour drawings. The human body is basically a composite of modified geometric solids. Note the cubic, conical, cylindrical, spherical, rectilinear, and wedge volumes in the human figure above.

The artistic discipline of **life drawing** has been an adjunct to most architecture programs. Freehand representational sketching of the human body combines the intuitive fluidity of art with the geometric structural precision of architecture (see pp. 398–401).

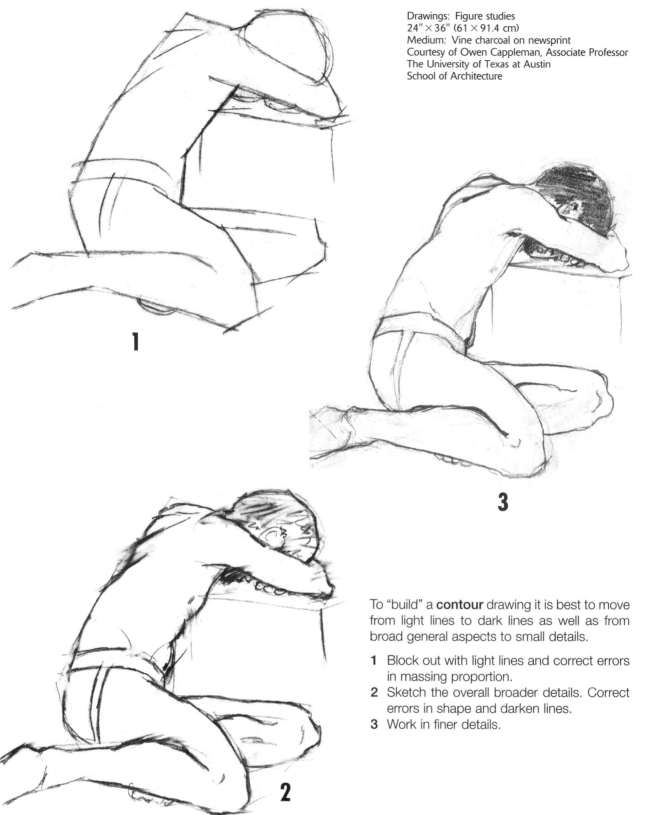

Drawings: Figure studies
24" × 36" (61 × 91.4 cm)
Medium: Vine charcoal on newsprint
Courtesy of Owen Cappleman, Associate Professor
The University of Texas at Austin
School of Architecture

LIFE DRAWING

To "build" a **contour** drawing it is best to move from light lines to dark lines as well as from broad general aspects to small details.

1 Block out with light lines and correct errors in massing proportion.
2 Sketch the overall broader details. Correct errors in shape and darken lines.
3 Work in finer details.

By studying the proportions of the human body, we broaden our knowledge and understanding of how people physically fit with respect to the environment. This study is called **anthropometrics.**

BLIND CONTOURS

VIOLIN

Blind contours (clockwise from left):
Student projects courtesy of Brian Blanchard
(Texas A & M University)
Dennis Martin, Amaza Lai Cheng Lam (City
College of San Francisco)

In the making of contour drawings, of which there are several varieties, the draftsman, artist, or architect attempts to use line in such a way as to express the essential form of the subject. In a good contour drawing, the line appears to wrap or traverse invisible volumes so that, as the eye follows the lines, the three dimensionality of the subject becomes apparent. One approach is to draw the subject "blind," that is, while looking only at the subject. The drawer attempts to supplant pencil with eye and "track" the surface of the subject. Concentrating and focusing on the subject allows one to be "loose" and relaxed as one explores the potential of the free-flowing contour line.

BLIND CONTOURS

It is best for blind drawings to be done quickly with the least amount of conscious thought. This results in contour lines that are more sensitive although not proportionally accurate. Note the concentrated small areas of dark tone in which many changes of line direction took place. This is the result of exaggerated and distorted lines, common characteristics of blind contour drawings. Blind drawings usually correspond very closely to one's visual perception.

Blind contours (clockwise from left):
Medium: Pencil
Student projects courtesy of
Ebby Chu (City College of San Francisco)
Jennifer Sobieraj (Texas A & M University)
Dennis Martin (City College of San Francisco)

LIFE DRAWING

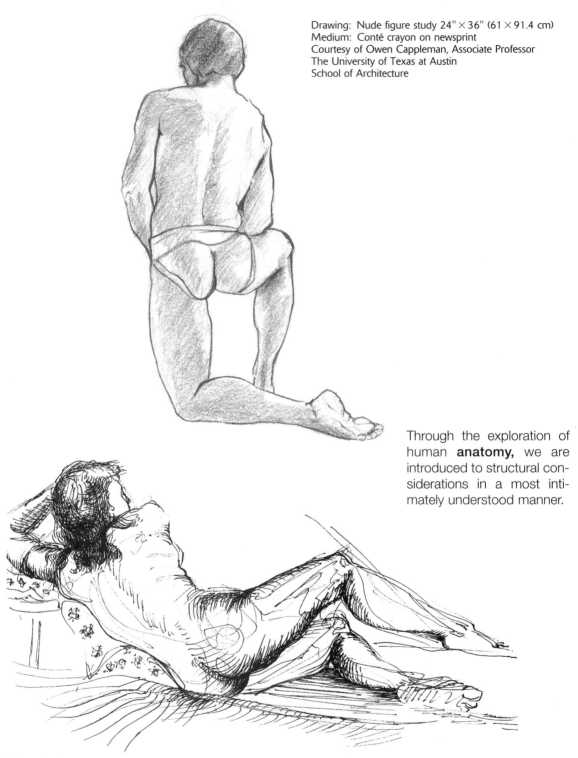

Drawing: Nude figure study 24" × 36" (61 × 91.4 cm)
Medium: Conté crayon on newsprint
Courtesy of Owen Cappleman, Associate Professor
The University of Texas at Austin
School of Architecture

Through the exploration of human **anatomy,** we are introduced to structural considerations in a most intimately understood manner.

Drawing: Nude figure study
Medium: Pen and ink on an all-purpose paper
Courtesy of Robert Schiffhauer, Associate Professor
Texas A & M University, Department of Architecture

Develop an awareness in the differences between the structural anatomy of the human female and male. For example, males are usually characterized by broad shoulders and narrow hips; females, on the other hand, are characterized by narrow shoulders and wide hips.

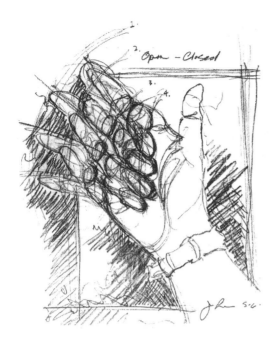

Drawing: Open and closed hand
Medium: Ink on trace 7.5" × 7.5" (19.1 × 19.1 cm)
Courtesy of Jerry W. Lum, Professor
City College of San Francisco
Department of Architecture

Study patterns of human body movement. A sequence of individual images can represent movement.

Drawing: Student project by John Rubins
        Head study
Medium: Ink
Courtesy of Washington University
School of Architecture, St. Louis, MO

LIFE DRAWING

Drawing: Student project by Wendy Cronk
        Figure study
Medium: Charcoal plus india ink wash
Courtesy of Washington University
School of Architecture, St. Louis, MO

All parts of the human body are composed of many wonderful contours. The human face is a good example. An excellent compositional exercise is to reverse the positive and negative spaces (figure and ground), as shown above. The negative space is filled in with a drawing medium such as ink or pencil. Note that the perception of the meaning of the black shadow areas makes sense only when the drawing is viewed right side up.

Drawing: Triton Museum of Art, Santa Clara, California
Courtesy of Barcelon & Jang, Architecture

A large massing of trees can be loosely rendered and their foliage made highly suggestive. Often groups of trees have a wall-like effect. Landscaping vegetation such as trees, plants, and shrubs should always be complementary and secondary to the architecture to which they are adjacent.

SKETCHING TREES

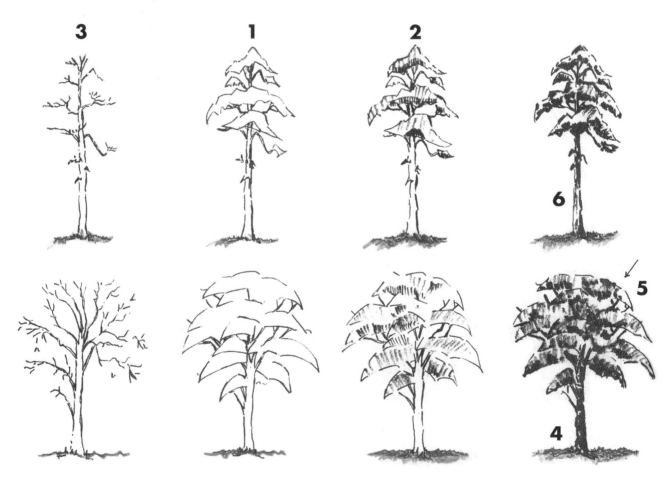

Each tree has a character of its own. When sketching or fabricating trees, one should always be aware of (**1**) the overall silhouette or shape (tall or short; bulky or thin), which is affected by gravity and wind; (**2**) the massing and pattern of the foliage; (**3**) the direction and pattern of growth on the branches, which is a clue to the tree form; (**4**) the manner in which the trunk flares or tapers off; (**5**) how the direction of light hits and penetrates various canopy shapes, producing shades and shadows; and (**6**) the texture of the bark. For pencil work, use 2B and HB for dark values and use 2H and 4H for contour lines and light values.

Sketch: Hillside residences, San Francisco, California
Sketch by Charles Moore, Architect
Courtesy of Saul Weingarten, Executor, Estate of Charles
Moore and the Department of Architecture, UCLA
School of Art and Architecture

When you are doing rapid sketch studies at a site, the time factor often dictates that you may not have enough time to draw all the tree details (branches, leaves, etc.). In such situations, your objective should be to give a representational feeling of the essence of a tree or some other landscape vegetation. Freehand trees can be abstractly simplistic. These quickly sketched suggestive trees are very effective. Sometimes it is what we leave out rather than what we put in a sketch that makes it highly expressive.

Sketch: Saitama Sports Arena Competition
Design offices: Takenaka Corporation, Tokyo, Japan
                         Cesar Pelli, Tokyo, Japan
17" × 11" (43.2 × 27.9 cm)
Medium: Prismacolor pencil
Courtesy of Lawrence Ko Leong, Architectural Illustrator

SKETCHING TREES

Drawing method: This was one of about 40 vignettes sketches done with the use of "eye-balling" a scale model, and using Prismacolor pencils. I used a light beige-rose pencil to outline the building, plaza, and entourage and used a soft blend of greens to maintain transparency and the canopy effect of foliage. A few bright spots of color were used to highlight the people and give liveliness to the composition.
[ARCHITECTURAL ILLUSTRATOR'S STATEMENT]

Sketch: Downtown Stockton, California
Courtesy of AIA and The Regional/Urban Design Assistance Team and Janice Filip, Architects

SKETCHING CARS

Approximately, cars range in length from 14' (4.27 m) to 20' (6.1 m) and in width from 5.8' (1.77 m) to 6.3' (1.92 m). Tires range from 22" (55.9 cm) to 28" (71.12 cm) in diameter.

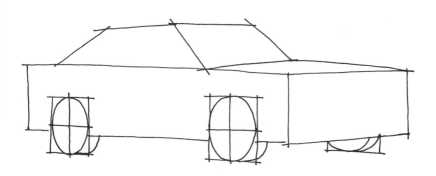

A car or any type of moving vehicle should be enclosed in an envelope of simple geometric shapes such as a truncated pyramid, rectangular solids, and cylindrical elements. Graphite is the ideal medium for layout work.

After the basic volume and form are developed with light construction lines, structural details should be sketched with a contour outline technique. Only major details should be added, like headlights and bumpers to keep it simple. The drawing can be finalized with pencil or any other rendering medium (see pp. 406–407).

Drawing: Sybase Hollis Street Campus, San Francisco, California
Robinson Mills & Williams, Architects
18" × 12" (30.5 × 45.7 cm)
Medium: Sketch watercolor on mounted presentation blackline print of pencil drawing.
Courtesy of Al Forster, Architectural Illustrator

Cars in perspective should always be in scale with the rest of the drawing and secondary to major building elements. Contour outline cars are usually adequate for most architectural drawings. Add details and shaded tones in accordance with the complexity of the rendering. Keep in mind that the roofs of cars are slightly below the eye-level line. Also, add visual interest by showing cars turning as well as moving in both directions.

SKETCHING CARS

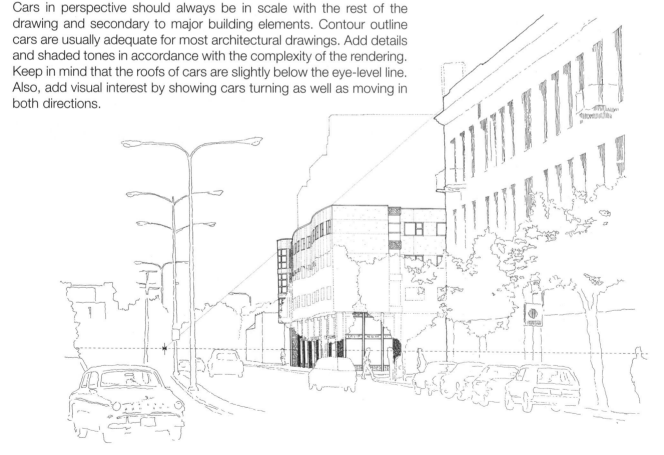

Drawing: Studio Durant (unbuilt), Berkeley, California
Medium: Computer-generated plot
Courtesy of David Baker Associates, Architects

SKETCHING BOATS

GALVESTON, TEXAS

Sketch: Shrimp fleet and bay, from Pier 19, Galveston, Texas
Medium: Ebony pencil on paper, 1990, 9" × 12" (22.9 × 30.5 cm)
Courtesy of David G. Woodcock, FAIA, RIBA
Professor of Architecture
Texas A & M University, Department of Architecture

Boats are similar to moving vehicles in the sense that they can be skeletally set up as a rectilinear box with shaped ends and a specific center line. As an architectural subject, they are commonly seen as an additional feature near harbor buildings and vacation resorts.

SKETCHING BUILDINGS

Sketch: Student project by Leigh Stringer
Movie theater
Medium: Pen and ink
Courtesy of Washington University
School of Architecture, St. Louis, MO

All objects can be broken down into simple **geometric solids.** For example, trees are basically spheres on cylinders. Buildings are usually a combination of rectangular solids, cylindrical solids, spherical solids, and planar elements. On close observation of building forms, we see that line is in reality the joining of two surfaces or a darker surface against a lighter surface. The sketch on the left shows the buildup of line within an enclosed space to simulate texture or tonal value.

Drawing: Industrial facade, San Pedro, California
23" × 17" (58.4 × 43.2 cm)
Medium: Oil paint
Courtesy of Kanner Architects
Painting by Stephen Kanner

Sketch with rough thumbnail vignette: Iglesia de San
Francisco, Javier, Cuatitlan, Mexico
5" × 8" (12.7 × 20.3 cm)
Medium: Black Pentel felt tip, semi-dry
Courtesy of Lawrence Ko Leong, Architectural Illustrator

SKETCHING BUILDINGS

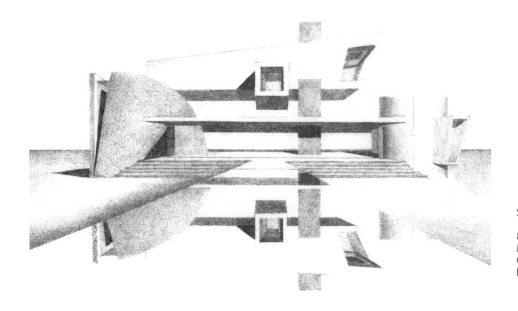

Sketch: House in Palm Springs II,
Palm Springs, California
8" × 5" (20.3 × 12.7 cm)
Medium: Prismacolor
Courtesy of Kanner Architects
Drawing by Stephen Kanner

*To create my drawings I lay the paper on glass, because it has a true, hard surface, and I draw and shade with the side
of the sharpened point of a No. 2, soft, Ticonderoga pencil. The way to get an even texture is to squint or look oblique-
ly, never directly, at one's work. To achieve hard edges, I draw against a straightedge* (see p. 171).
[ARCHITECT'S STATEMENT]

Drawing: Beverly Hills Civic Center Competition, Beverly Hills, California
Sketch by Charles Moore, Architect and Bill Hersey, Architectural Illustrator
Courtesy of Saul Weingarten, Executor, Estate of Charles Moore
and the Department of Architecture, UCLA School of Art and Architecture

As shown on the previous page, building sketches can be done using hard edges; the above sketch was done in a similar manner. Compare this with the loose lines in the soft edges shown below.

Sketch: Cottages at Longborough, Cotswolds, England
Medium: Uniball pen on paper 1992
Courtesy of David G. Woodcock, FAIA, RIBA
Professor of Architecture
Texas A & M University, Department of Architecture

SKETCHING BUILDINGS

A study of a drawing technique called "perspective" (see Chapter 6) in conjunction with this chapter will help you understand why the contours you draw instinctively in your representational sketches appear the way they are. We have seen that sighting skills give you an understanding of proportions seen in the viewed space. The theories of perspective will accurately verify these proportions. The sketch to the right is another good example of a sketch vignette. The continuation of the buildings are left to your imagination.

Sketch: Le Jardin Nelson, Montreal, Canada
Medium: Ebony pencil on paper, 1993, 9" × 12"
(22.9 × 30.5 cm)

Sketch: Galveston homes, Galveston Texas
Medium: Ebony pencil on paper, 1993, 9" × 12"
(22.9 × 30.5 cm)
Courtesy of David G. Woodcock, FAIA, RIBA
Professor of Architecture, Texas A & M University,
Department of Architecture

Drawing on site is always a challenge for me, and I rarely spend more than twenty minutes on each sketch. As an architect my objective is to learn more about the subject, so I focus a lot of attention on form and materials. Ebony pencil allows me to explore shade and shadow quickly, and by keeping at least two pencils with sharp points I can still pick out critical details.
[ARCHITECT'S STATEMENT]

SKETCHING BUILDINGS

Sketch: Student project by Margaret Stanton
Pencil sketch of Vicenza, Italy
Courtesy of the University of Virginia School of Architecture

On-the-spot representational sketching done when traveling gives you a chance to fill your sketchbook with interesting subjects. The urban landscape is filled with exciting visual surprises whether it be street scenes within a cityscape or mountainous roads in a rural village or panoramic beach views along a waterfront. Special events may be occurring and your goal may be to capture a sense of place and time. Unusual and interesting views should be sought. Perspective angles can vary from traditional ground eye-level views to bird's-eye or worm's-eye views.

Sketch: Student project by Behan Cagri, Ink sketch on vellum of Istanbul, Turkey
30" × 18" (76.2 × 45.7 cm)
Courtesy of the University of Maryland School of Architecture

After the shape and proportions of an architectural subject are sketched, focus in and concentrate on the surface material textures of the structure or the building.

TRAVEL SKETCHING

Charcoal is a good medium for deemphasizing details. You have to work with broad strokes so you can't be too fussy about details. Charcoal comes in both sticks and pencil forms and in a variety of grades. The long edge of the stick form is excellent for shading large areas.

Sketched images of China, Mexico, and Israel (clockwise from left): Project by student James Ke, City College of San Francisco, Department of Architecture
Medium: Charcoal, 3" × 4" (7.62 × 10.2 cm)
Lawrence Ko Leong, Architectural Illustrator
Medium: Pentel felt-tipped pen, 5" × 5" (12.7 × 12.7 cm)
Brian Kelly, Architect, Associate Professor, University of Maryland
Medium: Ink, 4" × 3" (10.2 × 7.6 cm)

TRAVEL SKETCHING

Sketch: Street scene, Miranda, Italy
Medium: Felt-tipped pen on paper, 8" × 10" (20.3 × 25.4 cm)
Courtesy of Steven House, Architect, San Francisco

Sketch: Roofscape, Macau
5" × 7" (12.7 × 17.8 cm)
Medium: Pentel felt-tipped pen
Courtesy of Lawrence Ko Leong, Architectural Illustrator

Sketch: European travel sketch
Medium: Ink on paper
Courtesy of Lawrence Halprin, Landscape Architect

Sometimes the time factor will influence the character of the sketch. Detailed sketches like the Miranda, Italy, scene may need a couple of hours of your time, whereas the sketch to the left was rapidly done in a short amount of time. Small thumbnail, rapid sketches (vignettes) are needed when many studies of the same locale are required. A quick sketch lacking detail can be highly expressive.

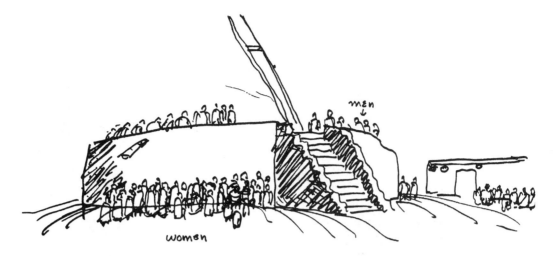

Drawings: Santo Domingo pueblo, Santa Fe, New Mexico
Medium: Ink on paper 8½" × 11" (21.6 × 27.9 cm)
Courtesy of Lawrence Halprin, Landscape Architect

Kiva at the
East end of the
plaza —
one clan around &
into the Kiva after
they finished the
CORN Dance
Monday Dec 28-80

Sketching and drawing are ways for me to have a dialogue with what I see and experience. In this interaction, I reveal my feelings about the world and my involvement with things and places and people. Sketches can influence my reactions of the moment and then lie dormant for future influences.
[LANDSCAPE ARCHITECT'S STATEMENT]

TRAVEL SKETCHING

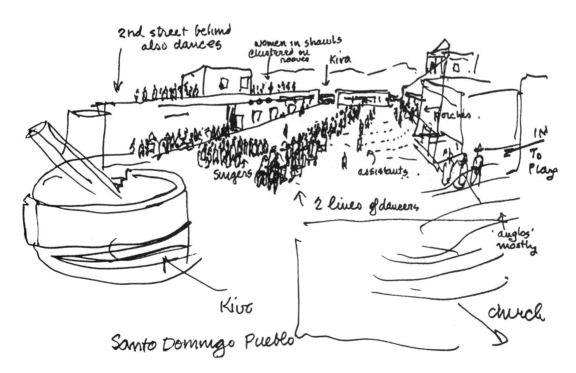

Another good habit is to write notes to yourself about your observations. It will help you recall activity highlights or important features in your sketches.

TRAVEL SKETCHING

Sketches: Taxco, Mexico, 8" × 10" (20.3 × 25.4 cm)
Medium: Grey felt-tipped pen and watercolor on paper
Courtesy of Steven House, Architect, San Francisco

Travel sketching enables me to record the essence of time and place…with just a few lines a special moment can be captured forever.
[ARCHITECT'S STATEMENT]

The examples above and on the facing page are serial sketches based on a visual progression or sequence through a site. Sketches done in this manner can function as a coherent group.

Sketches: Lefkes Paro, Greece
Medium: Felt-tipped pen on paper, 8" × 10" (20.3 × 25.4 cm)
Courtesy of Steven House, Architect, San Francisco

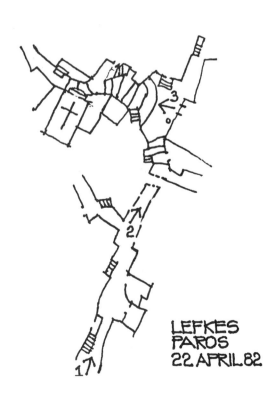

TRAVEL SKETCHING

TRAVEL SKETCHING

Sketch: Resort Hotel, Mexico
Design Office: Sandy & Babcock, San Francisco
17" × 11" (43.2 × 27.9 cm)
Medium: Black Prismacolor and thin Pilot razorpoint Pentel
Shading was built up with a single line thickness
Courtesy of Lawrence Ko Leong, Architectural Illustrator

Sketch: Central Park Boat Basin, New York City, 1991
Medium: Pencil, 1991, 7" × 4" (17.8 × 10.2 cm)
Courtesy of Stephen W. Parker, Architect

Sketch: Abbey of San Galgano, Montesiepi, Italy
Medium: Ebony pencil on paper 1987, 12" × 9" (30.5 × 22.9 cm)
Courtesy of David G. Woodcock, FAIA, RIBA
Professor of Architecture
Texas A & M University, Department of Architecture

TRAVEL SKETCHING

The vantage point selected can affect the character and feeling of a building subject. Choice of viewpoint must be carefully considered along with texture, lighting conditions, framing elements (like the foliage above), and the massing of forms. Studying the exact nature of light, shade, and shadow (Chapter 8) will help you understand lighting conditions as you sketch forms. Without any knowledge, your commonsense and logic must help you interpret, for example, why the lighting effects on the cylindrical and prismatic forms above are quite different.

TRAVEL SKETCHING

1816 HICKORY
ST. LOUIS, MISSOURI

SACRE COEURE
MONTMARTEE, PARIS
2 JULY 95

Sketch: Entry at 1816 Hickory
         Private residence, St. Louis, Missouri
3" × 9" (7.62 × 22.9 cm), 1992
Medium: Pencil
Courtesy of Stephen W. Parker, Architect

Sketch: Sacre Coeure Cathedral, Paris, France
4" × 9" (10.2 × 22.9 cm), 1995
Medium: Pencil
Courtesy of Stephen W. Parker, Architect

Travel sketching has always been one of the joys of my journeys—and afterwards a truer memory than what a photo can evoke in me. I strive to capture the spirit of the moment and all that defines the experience of being at a certain place, at a certain time, in a certain light, in a certain season. And all the lessons I learn, the discoveries I make with my pencil, are brought back to influence my professional artwork—opening my mind's eye to new possibilities.
[ARCHITECT'S STATEMENT]

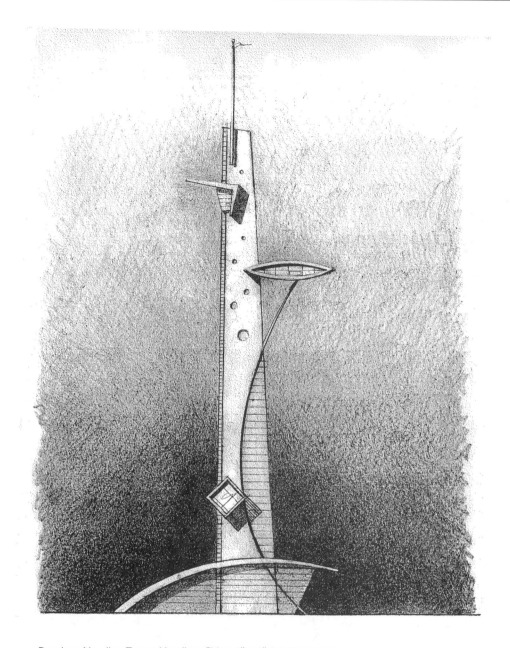

Drawing: Nan Jing Tower, Nan Jing, China, 5" × 8" (12.7 × 20.3 cm)
Medium: Pencil
Courtesy of Kanner Architects
Drawn by Stephen Kanner

Conceptual sketches (see Chapter 11) are typically loose and free in execution. However, as the above draw-ing of a high-rise tower shows, a conceptual sketch can convey much more than one might expect—even hav-ing the appearance of a hard-edge representational drawing (see p. 483). In truly efficient drawings, every line conveys information about form, light qualities, and volume of space. Detailing may be suggested and surface qualities alluded to. A good conceptual sketch often will suggest possibilities that were previously unconsidered. In other words, the sketch can dictate the direction of the subsequent design.

Architect Frank Lloyd Wright frequently did this kind of rendered freehand conceptual sketch (see p. 179) by strategically using a straightedge. The result was a polished and authoritative look.

CONCEPTUAL SKETCH/IMAGE QUALITY

STUDY SKETCHES

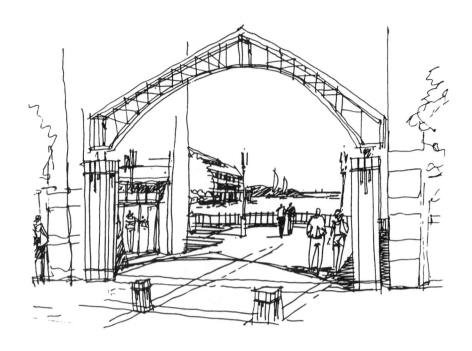

Access portal between bulkhead buildings, Piers 9–35.

Broadway View Corridor, looking east from Sansome Street

Sketches: Embarcadero Corridor Charette, San Francisco, California
Medium: Felt-tipped pen on trace, 11" × 8.5" (27.9 × 21.6 cm)
Courtesy of the San Francisco Chapter AIA, Drawn by Bruce Race, AIA

View from Pier 15 Bulkhead, looking north

View from the Ferrry Building, looking north

Sketches: Embarcadero Corridor Charette, San Francisco, California
Medium: Felt-tipped pen on trace, 11" × 8.5" (27.9 × 21.6 cm)
Courtesy of the San Francisco Chapter AIA, Drawn by Bruce Race, AIA

A **charette** (French word for cart) refers to an intense effort to complete an architectural project in a short peri-od of time. These quick sketches were done in response to a charette program developed by the Embarcadero Corridor Steering Committee.

STUDY SKETCHES

STUDY SKETCHES

Drawing: A study of the Central Glade, University of Califronia at Berkeley
Courtesy of Philip Enquist, Architect while with Skidmore, Owings & Merrill LLP

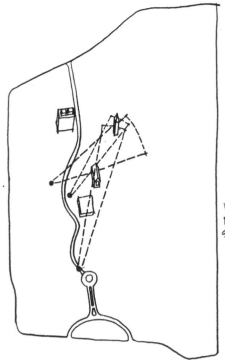

VIEWS OF BOTH DOE LIBRARY AND SATHER TOWER

Doe Library East Elevation

The time factor is especially critical when study sketches are needed for an evaluation of design parameters. These sketches demonstrate the use of a Berol 314 pencil to cover a large area quickly. They are from a "sketchbook" of ideas related to the restoration of the central glade area within the University of California at Berkeley campus for the purpose of improving and enhancing the existing views. The views are sketched from a variety of exterior vantage point locations.

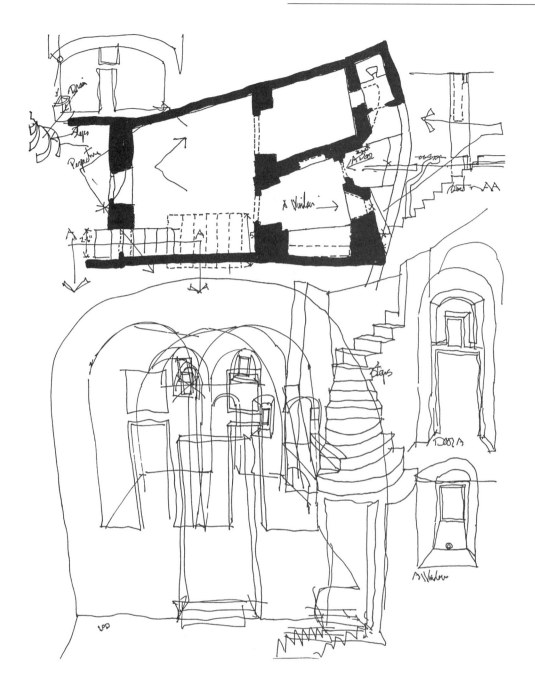

Drawing: House, Santorini, Greece
Pen & ink on paper, 8" × 10" (20.3 × 25.4 cm)
Courtesy of Steven House, Architect, San Francisco

Travel sketching can offer spontaneous opportunities to document the environment. By drawing a plan view along with a series of corresponding vignettes one can begin to capture the true essence of architectural space. These analytical studies can provide thoughtful insights into form and movement.
[ARCHITECT'S STATEMENT]

Multiple interior or exterior vantage points are common in study sketches. These superimposed sketches show a variety of perspective views taken inside a house with the direction of views indicated on the sketched plan. Travel sketches can sometimes be analytical studies.

6

Linear Perspective Drawing

Perspective drawings give the most realistic or life-like view of the built environment and the urban landscape. On a two-dimensional surface, pictorial views of three-dimensional forms can be represented in a visually believable manner using perspective methods.

Preliminary design drawings must clearly show form, scale, texture, light, shapes, shadows, and spatial order. Presentation design drawings take on a more precise character with these and related components. As a final step, they may be translated into perspective renderings to complement and enhance a presentation.

The intent of this chapter is to introduce the theory and methods of constructed architectural perspectives. It stresses the importance of visualizing in parallel (one point) or angular (two point) perspective from the plan and the elevation of an object. This, of course, comes with patience, perseverance, and, most of all, practice.

Linear Perspective Drawing

Through the years there have been many good books on this subject. These inlude: D'Amelio (Perspective Drawing Handbook, 1964), Coulin (Step-by-Step Perspective Drawing, 1966), Martin (Architectural Graphics, 1970, and Design Graphics, 1986), Hanks & Belliston (Rapid Viz, 1980), Forseth (Graphics for Architecture, 1980), Dines (Landscape Perspective Drawing, 1990) Helms (Perspective Drawing: A Step-by-Step Handbook, 1990) and Ward (Composition and Perspective, 1993).

Topics

Cone of Vision, Depth Judgement

References

Drawing: A Creative Process (Ching 1990): Perspective Measurements: 118–121.

Landscape Perspective Drawing (Dines 1990): One-Point Perspective: 22–27.

Topics

Diagonals, X, Y ,Z Axis

Topics

Station Point, Picture Plane, Horizon Line, Vanishing Points, Center of Vision, Vertical Measuring Line, X, Y, Z Axis, Mid Point, Perspective Field, Perspective Viewpoint, Perspective Set Up.

References

Rapid Viz (Hanks and Belliston 1980): Modeling: 16–19.
Sketching Cubes: 21–23.

Drawing: A Creative Process (Ching 1990): Sketching Cubes: 114.

Basic Perspective Drawing (Montague 1993): Modeling: 1–6.

Manual of Graphic Techniques 4 (Porter and Goodman 1985): Perspectives: 108–115.

Topic

One-point perspective using 45° diagonal lines

References

Architectural Graphics (Ching 1996): One-Point Perspective: 73–77.

Topics

Vertical Vanishing Lines, Diagonal Lines, Oblique Lines, Oblique Vanishing Points, Diagonal Vanishing Points, 45° Vanishing Points.

References

Basic Perspective Drawing (Montague 1993): Diagonal Vanishing Points: 80.

Graphics for Architecture (Forseth 1980): Diagonal Vanishing Points: 154–158.

Topic

One-point Office Method, Perspective charts

Reference

Designing and Drawing with Confidence (Lin 1993): 116–120, 124–134.

Topic

Three-point perspective

Reference

Basic Perspective (Gill 1989) Thames & Hudson: Chapter Six

Topics

Multiplying and Dividing, Circles

References

Rapid Viz (Hanks and Belliston 1980): Multiplying and Dividing: 122–123
Circles: 52.

Drawing a Creative Process (Ching 1990) Multiplying and Dividing: 122–123
Circles: 52

Basic Perspective Drawing (Montague 1993): Multiplying and Dividing: 69–72
Circles: 170.

Graphics for Architecture (Forseth 1980) Multiplying and Dividing: 168–169
Circles: 170

Architectural Graphics (Ching 1996): Multiplying and Dividing: 83
Circles: 84.

Perspective Drawing (Helms 1990): Multiplying and Dividing: 102–105, 109, 179, 218–222.
Circles: 182–183.

Cross References

For pp. 182–183   See pp. 264–267
                         See pp. 194–197, 268–271
For p. 192   See p. 258
For pp. 194–195   See p. 600
For pp. 209, 282–287   See pp. 408–419

Perspective is a method of depicting the manner in which objects appear to the human eye with respect to their relative positions and distance. The optic mechanism of seeing the urban landscape is done simultaneously with both eyes, and as a result we visually experience things three-dimensionally or spatially. The term "perspective" comes from the Latin *perspectare,* which means "to view through." The origin of linear perspective theory comes from the Renaissance. The perceptual schema of western philosophy and civilization values a drawing system that logically duplicates an individual's visual experience. Thus, linear perspective is considered "correct" in the sense that it values representation.

Architects use perspectives in both preliminary and final design stages. They utilize both drafting's traditional construction methods as well as new computer techniques to generate desired perspective views to aid in the design process. To fully appreciate perspective drawing it is important to understand the time-consuming manual procedures before embarking on quick methods that can be done by the computer.

In the preliminalry design stages, rough, freehand, perspective drawings are the norm. In the final presentation stages, perspectives are accurately constructed for the purposes of rendering them (see section on delineating and rendering entourage). In 1949, Frank Lloyd Wright did a rendered conceptual drawing (see p. 171) for his famous Guggenheim Museum in New York City. The rendering showed a tower in the background, which at the time was not built, with the original museum. The complete dream in a perspective rendering finally came to fruition with the completion of the tower addition in 1992.

Theories, definitions, and concepts (pp. 180–201) will be discussed before various step-by-step methods are explained.

INTRODUCTION

Frank Lloyd Wright
Solomon R. Guggenheim Museum (night rendering), ca. 1950–51.
37" × 26" (94 × 66 cm)
Medium: Tempera and black ink on composition board
Collection Peter Lawson–Johnston
Photograph by David Heald ©The Solomon R. Guggenheim Foundation, New York

DIMINUTION AND OVERLAPPING

Photo: Waterfront Pier
San Francisco, California

© Albert Lee

Whether we are viewing the environment or attempting to realistically depict what we see on a two-dimensional, flat drawing surface, we experience four major phenomena: (1) diminution, (2) overlapping, (3) convergence, and (4) foreshortening. **Diminution** occurs when equal-sized objects, such as the lamp posts above, appear to diminish in size with distance. This can be seen on the subsequent page where a fixed observer notices that columns and arches of equal size appear to diminish with distance. Photographs require the camera person to be viewing from a frozen position much like the singular vantage point of any perspective drawing. Thus, perspectives have a photo-like quality to their appearance.

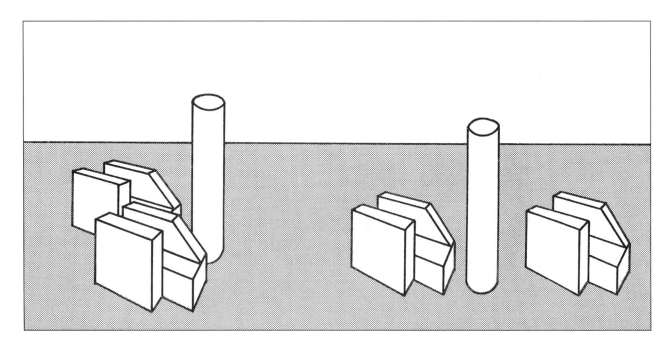

When we see objects **overlapping,** a sense of depth and space is achieved. Isolated objects give no sense of spatial depth.

Stanford University Quadrangle, Palo Alto, California
Shepley, Rutan and Coolidge, Architects

© Rendow Yee

These two photographs of a series of arches were taken at two different vantage point locations. The oblique angle at the left is not quite as sharp as the oblique angle shown below viewed behind the series of arches. In both cases the **convergence** of parallel lines occurs. For instance, the line that is tangent to all arches vanishes to the same point as the line that touches all the bases of the columns.

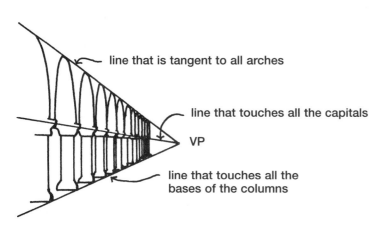

— line that is tangent to all arches

— line that touches all the capitals

VP

— line that touches all the bases of the columns

FORESHORTENED ARCHES

The three lines that converge above would be parallel if drawn in the true size view below.

TRUE-SIZE ARCHES

© Rendow Yee

In a head on view, there would be no illusion of perspective space since no convergence would be evident. The arches would be seen in their maximum or true size. At an oblique angle the arch size becomes **foreshortened** since it no longer is in its true size. The semi-circular arch becomes elliptical in all oblique angular positions.

CONVERGENCE AND FORESHORTENING

At the same time, all of us see objects from a different viewing angle since we cannot occupy the same physical space. However, once we abandon the physical space, another person can experience the same viewpoint. The eye-level line changes as the observer sits down, stands up, or stands on top of an object to view the chair. Notice the foreshortening of the legs of the chair as the observer moves higher and higher. The eye-level line is always at right angles to the observer's line of sight and theoretically considered to be located at an infinite distance.

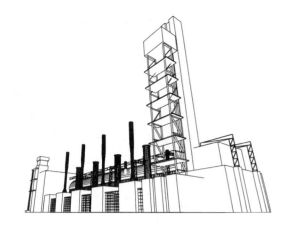

Worm's eye view at ground level with upward convergence

CAD Drawings (above and below)
Student projects by Bradford Winkeljohn
and Jordan Parnass
Excerpted from abstract, Columbia School of
Architecture Planning and Preservation (CSAPP)

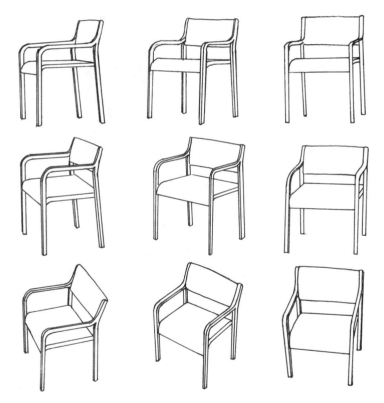

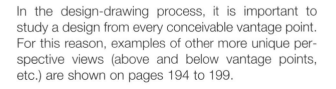

In the design-drawing process, it is important to study a design from every conceivable vantage point. For this reason, examples of other more unique perspective views (above and below vantage points, etc.) are shown on pages 194 to 199.

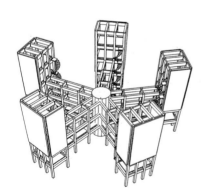

Bird's-eye view at a high angle

BIRD'S-EYE, EYE LEVEL, AND WORM'S-EYE VIEWS

For the most part, we view the urban environment at eye level in a standing position. The two views not at eye level are commonly termed worm's-eye and bird's-eye. Both are dramatic although unnatural views. A worm's-eye view can be at the ground level or below the ground plane as shown to the right.

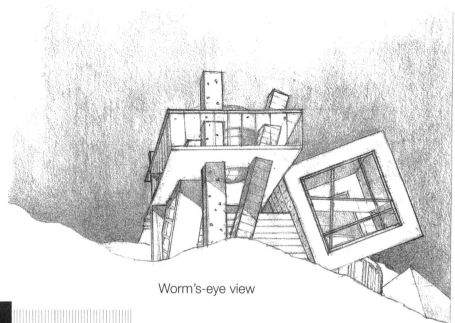

Worm's-eye view

Drawing: House in Hollywood Hills
          Los Angeles, California
8" × 5" (20.3 × 12.7 cm)
Medium: Pencil
Courtesy of Kanner Architects
Drawn by Stephen Kanner

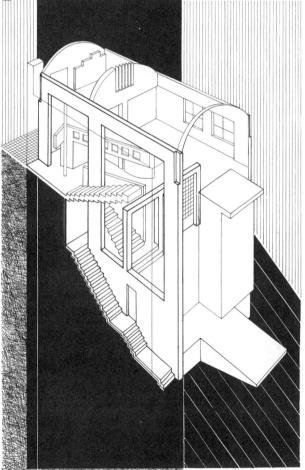

Bird's-eye view

Drawing: Shay House (1985), San Francisco, California
9.5" × 15.5" (24.1 × 39.4 cm), Scale: ⅜"=1'0"
Medium: Pen and ink
Courtesy of James Shay, AIA Architect

By stripping away exterior walls and casting the perspective as a "bird's-eye," the complex interior is communicated. The rendered areas around the building are read in plane rather than perspective, creating interesting ambiguity.
[ARCHITECT'S STATEMENT]

BIRD'S-EYE AND WORM'S-EYE VIEWS

Webster's Dictionary defines the term "cue" as a hint or intimation. We pick up visual cues all the time. The cues may not always be exactly how we see the physical environment. In general, what we see can be called "perspective" cues. The most fundamental and efficient types of drawing cues are those that employ lines to record the edges of surfaces as we experience them in reality. These are called perspective cues because they represent the relationships between the edges of surfaces at a particular point in time and space—they represent a particular perspective on the world. The perspective cues have been codified into three drawing systems: linear perspective, paraline perspective (used here to include axonometric and oblique systems), and orthographic perspective (multiview drawings). None of these is exactly how we see the world all the time. Each represents certain perceptual and cognitive realities—they represent some combination of what we see and what we know about things.

Linear Perspective Cues

Linear perspective is most acutely experienced in places where long rectangular surfaces begin near and recede into the distance, such as long, straight roads. The essential experience is that the parallel lines seem to come together in the distance. The edges of surfaces are represented by lines that follow the rules of lineal perspective and each has a line grammar. One-point perspectives have vertical lines, horizontal lines, and perspective lines (lines that go to vanishing points). Two-point perspectives have vertical lines and perspective lines. Three-point perspectives have only perspective lines.

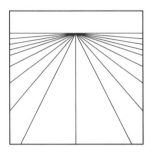 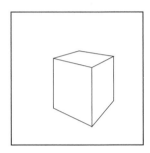

Diagrams and text: Courtesy of
William R. Benedict, Assistant Professor
California Polytechnic State University
College of Architecture & Environmental Design
San Luis Obispo, CA

Paraline Perspective Cues

The western perceptual schema is culturally biased toward linear perspective. To other cultures and in other times a paraline drawing looked more "correct" than one using linear perspective. When things are small relative to our visual field their edges and surfaces tend to retain their dimensions. The degree to which the edges vanish is so slight that our knowledge of their equality in length and angle can easily be more important than their adherence to the lineal perspective. Paraline systems codify this view of reality. The edges of surfaces are represented by lines that follow the rules of paraline drawing conventions. The edges of parallel surfaces remain parallel and retain direct measured relationships to each other and the thing being represented. Verticals remain vertical and the other axes slope at specified angles.

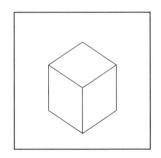

Orthographic Perspective Cues

Orthographic perspective is less acceptable to our eyes and requires experience with its conventions to be able to read it visually. It represents a single object with multiple drawings requiring the ability to assemble the drawings in your mind. We experience things in orthographic perspective when their surfaces are relatively flat and we are standing directly in front of and facing them. As we move away from an object our experience more closely corresponds to an orthographic drawing. The edges of surfaces are represented by lines that follow the rules of orthoghraphic drawing. Parallel edges remain parallel and retain direct measured relationships to each other and the thing being represented. Verticals remain vertical, horizontals remain horizontal, and the depth axis is represented by a point.

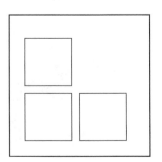

PERSPECTIVE CUES

Two of the most accurate mechanical methods for generating linear perspectives are shown in this chapter. They are the plan elevation (office) method and the measuring point method. **Linear perspective** drawing is a tool for the designer or delineator to make a reasonably accurate representation of a three-dimensional object on a two-dimensional surface (the drawing sheet). A linear perspective drawing is an image of an object projected upon an assumed plane (Picture Plane-PP) that is parallel to the observer's face or eyes. When used as a representational tool for the design–drawing process, it is of utmost importance not to misrepresent the physical appearance of buildings with inaccurate perspective representations. The following are the most commonly used terms in the vocabulary of perspective drawing techniques.

TERMS	ABBREVIATION	DEFINITION
Station Point	(SP)	• A vantage point location to view an object or group of objects; the location of the observer's eye.
Picture Plane	(PP)	• A stationary, transparent, two-dimensional, vertical plane or "window." This window receives a true-size image from the projection lines which converge to the station point. Perpendicular to the observer is the line of sight.
Line of Sight	(LS)	• An imaginary line that perpendicularly intersects the vertical picture plane as it is projected from the observer's eye (station point).
Horizon Line or Eye-Level Line	(HL)	• Represents the observer's eye level. The horizon line is recorded on the picture plane. It is the vanishing line for all horizontal lines and planes.
Ground Line	(GL)	• The line where the picture plane and the ground meet. The ground line lies within a ground plane from which vertical measurements are made.
Vanishing Point	(VPL, VPR, and VP_O)	• A point on the horizon line where any group of parallel horizontal lines converge in perspective. Groups of oblique (inclined) parallel lines vanish either above (sloping upward) or below (sloping downward) the horizon line. Parallel lines that are parallel to the picture plane do not converge.
Vertical Measuring Line	(VML)	• A vertical line within the picture plane. Vertical height dimensions are transferred from an elevation to this vertical true-length line in order to be projected into the perspective drawing.
Midpoint	(M)	• A point located on the horizon line that lies half way between the vanishing points in a two-point perspective.
Horizontal Measuring Line	(HML)	• A horizontal line lying in the picture plane, which therefore is a true-length line.

PERSPECTIVE GLOSSARY

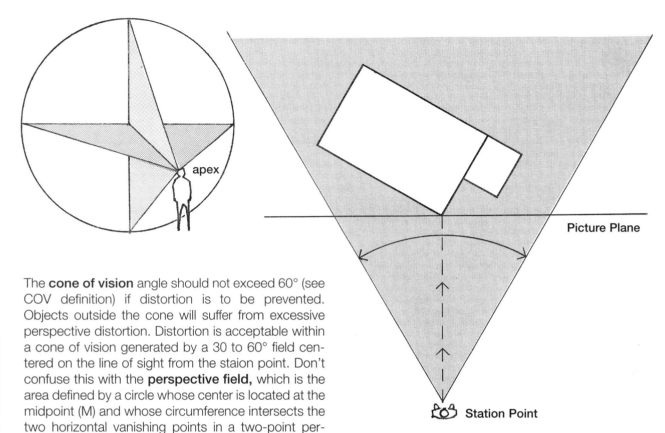

CONE OF VISION

The **cone of vision** angle should not exceed 60° (see COV definition) if distortion is to be prevented. Objects outside the cone will suffer from excessive perspective distortion. Distortion is acceptable within a cone of vision generated by a 30 to 60° field centered on the line of sight from the staion point. Don't confuse this with the **perspective field,** which is the area defined by a circle whose center is located at the midpoint (M) and whose circumference intersects the two horizontal vanishing points in a two-point perspective. The office method (see pp. 202–204, 248, 252–253) for drawing perspectives is based on the concept of the cone of vision. Perspectives not based on the cone of vision can be generated from a conventional architectural drawing—the building section (see pp. 256–259).

Visualize this as the base of a cone (circle in its true shape) that is perpendicular to the observer's center of vision line of sight. This circular area of the vertical picture plane can be seen in clear focus when the apex angle is less than 60°. The area viewed increases in size as the picture plane moves away from the station point.

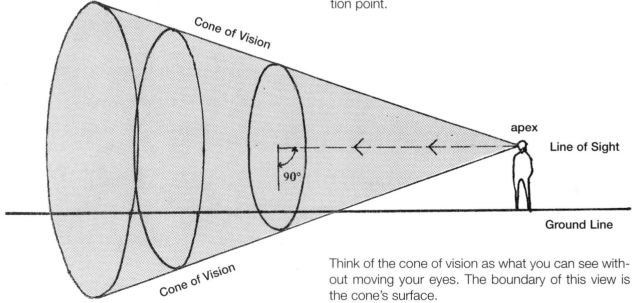

Think of the cone of vision as what you can see without moving your eyes. The boundary of this view is the cone's surface.

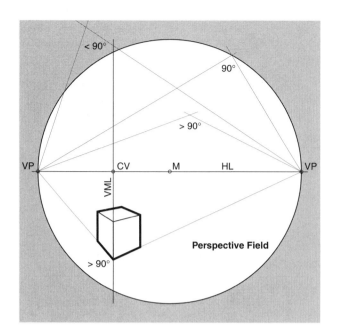

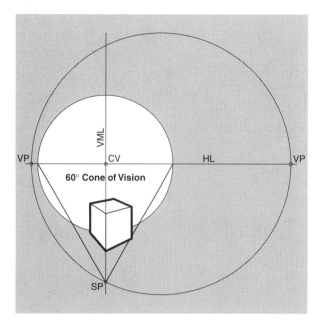

Acceptable Distortion

Linear perspective formalizes through geometry a system that attempts to represent three-dimensional reality on a two-dimensional surface—it attempts to place a portion of the visual field on a page. Because it is a closed system assuming a fixed, one-eyed observer it has limitations that must be respected if the goal is to accurately represent perceived visual reality—if the goal is for the drawing to look right. The cube that is drawn with its lead edge coinciding with the vertical measuring line (VML) (the line drawn through the center of vision) and centered vertically on the horizon line is the most accurate cube in the perspective. As the cubes move away from this location they progressively become more distorted. The question, therefore, is how far from this location does a perspective retain sufficient accuracy so as not to be visually disturbing—what are the limits within which the perspective looks right.

Cone of Vision

The cone of vision links the way our eyes work and the control of distortion within the perspective system. A 60° cone is one that extends 30° to either side of our line of sight. Distortion within the perspective system is acceptable within a cone of vision generated by a 30° to 60° field centered on the line of sight from the station point. A 30° cone is advisable for spheres and circles. The illustration simultaneously shows a 60° cone of vision in both plan and perspective. For any measuring point perspective setup the cone of vision can be constructed to establish the area within which a perspective will "look most correct."

Diagrams and text: Courtesy of
William R. Benedict, Assistant Professor
California Polytechnic State University
College of Architecture & Environmental Design
San Luis Obispo, CA

90° Horizontal Corner

The perspective field can be used to control the near internal angle of horizontal rectangles to 90° or greater. When the angle becomes less than 90° it does not look right. Any two lines intersecting at the circumference of the perspective field will create a 90° angle. Those intersecting beyond the circumference will create an angle of less than 90°, while those intersecting within the perspective field will create an angle of more than 90°. Therefore, the perspective field provides a guideline for establishing some limits within the linear perpsective system.

Measuring point methods for constructing perspectives (See pp. 232–247) are also related to the concept of the cone of vision.

CONE OF VISION/FIELD OF VIEW/ACCEPTABLE DISTORTION

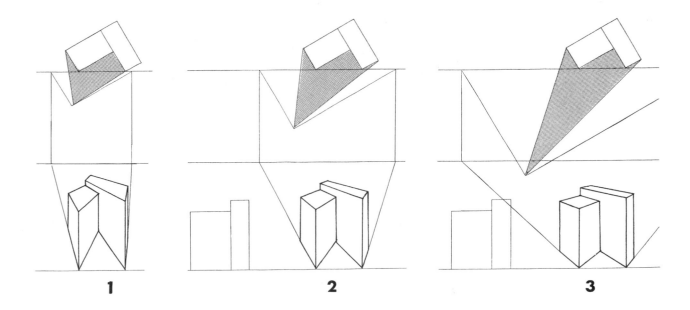

1 **2** **3**

DISTORTION

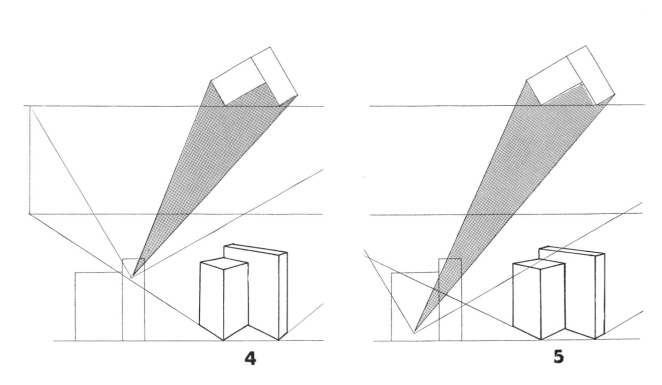

4 **5**

Perspective **distortion** is dependent on the spacing of vanishing points. A very close station point location with close vanishing points results in extreme convergence with a great amount of foreshortening (see **1** and **2**). A very distant station point results in minimal convergence with very little foreshortening. In the latter case, the base of the object becomes quite flat. A more natural pictorial view is obtained by spreading the vanishing points apart (see **4** and **5**). However, try not to spread them too far apart so that distorted "flatness" occurs. A good distance is three times the object height.

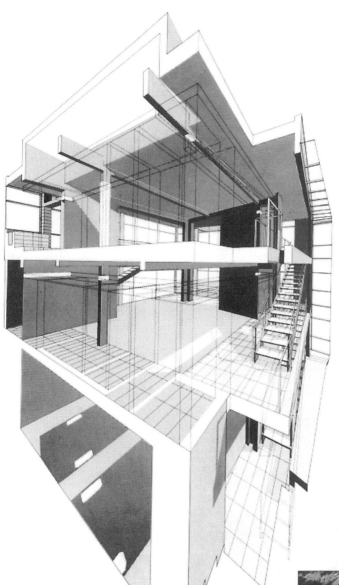

Drawing: Burnett House addition
          Lake Oswego, Oregon
24" × 36" (61 × 91.4 cm)
Medium: Ink on Mylar with Zipatone
Courtesy of David Rockwood Architects & Associates

This interior perspective shows a large amount of foreshortening with conditions similar to example **1** (opposite page). There is a point at which one reaches a state of distortion, with the vanishing points being too close with respect to the height (which relates to the cone of vision).

Example of extreme convergence

DISTORTION

This exterior perspective shows a small amount of foreshortening with conditions similar to example **5** on p. 188.

Example of a natural pictorial view

Drawing: Student Project by Steve Gambrel
          Seafarers' Church Institute
Courtesy of the University of Virginia School of Architecture

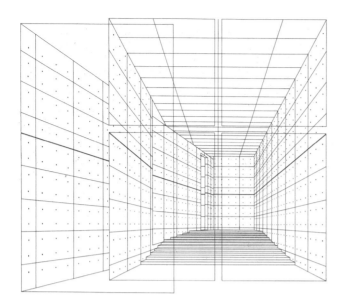

Drawing: Church of the Light
　　　　　Ibaraki, Japan
Medium: Ink, 594 × 420 mm (2.33" × 1.65")
Courtesy of Tadao Ando, Architect

This transparent interior perspective shows the wall with a cross slit behind the church's altar. The wall simulates a vertical picture plane through which one can capture the perspective view. An exception to the flat, two-dimensional picture plane is the spheroidal (similar to a sphere but not completely round) picture plane used with a fish-eye lens view (see p. 606).

THE PICTURE PLANE

Drawing: Student Project by Corvin Matei
　　　　　Vasari Museum, Florence, Italy
Medium: Ink on Mylar, 10" × 8" (25.4 × 20.3 cm)
Courtesy of the University of Texas at Arlington
School of Architecture

A window is a fixed transparent vertical plane. When we look through a window, our eyes receive images of the three-dimensional objects we see. This image is translated onto a two-dimensional plane (the window) at an infinite number of points when our lines of sight intersect the window. Thus, the window becomes **the picture plane.** This drawing shows the viewpoint of an observer looking through a window.

In this example of **parallel** (one-point) **perspective,** the image of the building form is projected on the picture plane. Vertical and horizontal lines retain verticality and horizontality in the image. Lines not parallel to this picture plane will converge to the vanishing point (VP). If the building form is **behind** the picture plane as illustrated in this drawing, it is projected **smaller** than true size on the picture plane. If **in front,** it is projected **larger** than true size.

The three major perspective types are one point, two point, and three point (referring to the number of vanishing points). A one point always has a plane parallel to the picture plane. Planes perpendicular to the picture plane vanish to one point.

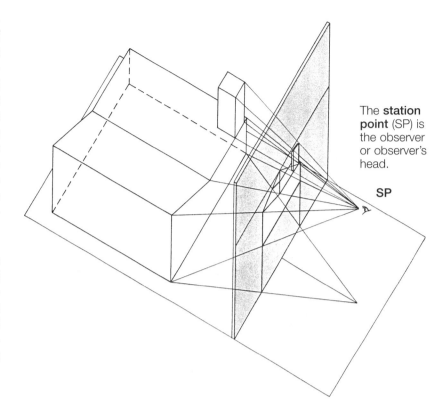

The **station point** (SP) is the observer or observer's head.

SP

Picture Plane

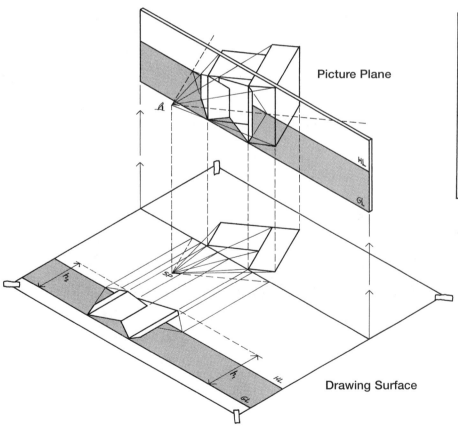

Drawing Surface

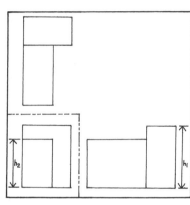

The **picture plane** is always perpendicular to the drawing surface and represented by a **line** on the drawing. Also on the drawing, the observer reduces to a dot and the building form to a two-dimensional plan view. True heights (h_1 and h_2) are always obtained from a set of orthographic drawings (plans and elevations). They are measured vertically from the ground line.

THE PICTURE PLANE

ONE-POINT PERSPECTIVE

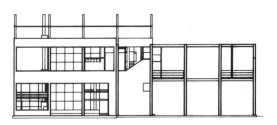

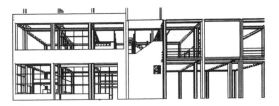

Drawings: Student project by Lois McGinnis and Michael Patrick
 Shelby's Lake House—A project in CAD
Courtesy of the University of Texas at Arlington
School of Architecture

The above one point seen at ground level is much more descriptive than its flat two-dimensional elevation.

Drawing   Chapel for Rose Hills Memorial Park
 Whittier, California
24" × 36" (61 × 91.4 cm), Scale: ¼"=1'0"
Medium: Pencil and ink
Courtesy of Fay Jones & Maurice Jennings, Architects
Drawn by Barry McNeill/Jones & Jennings

The three main types of perspectives are classified based on the drawing's primary vanishing points. Many drawings have secondary minor vanishing points. These building examples show that all horizontal lines that recede away from the observer's eye converge to **one** vanishing point. Therefore, they can be classified as **one-point** perspectives.

Drawing: Milam residence
 St. John's County, Florida
Medium: Ink on board,
33" × 30" (83.8 × 76.2 cm)
Courtesy of Paul Rudolph, Architect

These building examples show their dominant facades converging on left and right sides to **two** vanishing points on their respective horizon lines. Therefore, they can be classified as **two-point** perspectives.

Drawing: Student project by Leopoldo Chang
　　　　　　　 Poet's Hotel, New York
Medium: Ink on Mylar
Excerpted from Abstract, Columbia School of
Architecture Planning and Preservation (CSAAP)

Drawing: Studio Durant (unbuilt), Berkeley, California
Medium: Computer generated plot
(size dependent on size of plot)
Courtesy of David Baker Associates Architects

TWO-POINT PERSPECTIVE

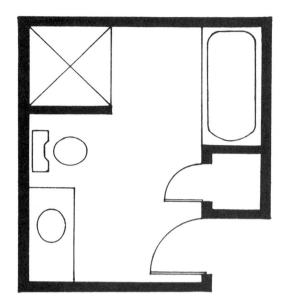
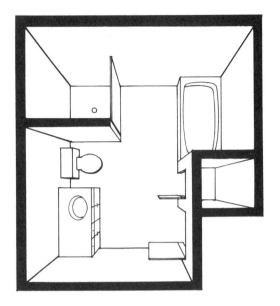

An unusual variation of the **one-point** perspective is a bird's-eye view with the line of sight perpendicular to the ground plane. This variation, which is achieved by transposing the positions of plan and elevation, is commonly used for small interior spaces and interior or exterior courtyard areas.

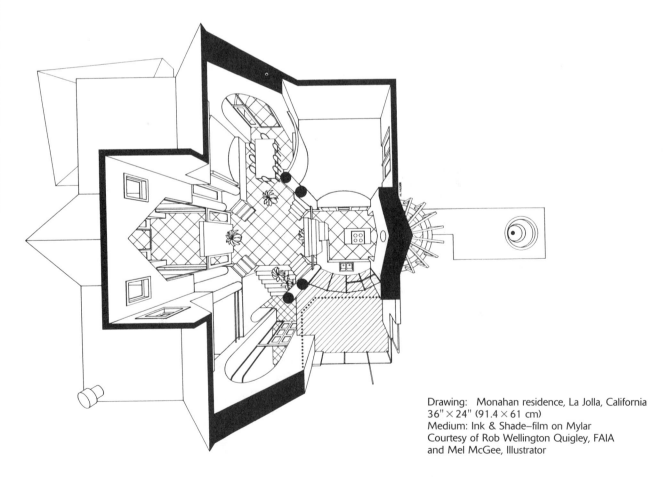

Drawing: Monahan residence, La Jolla, California
36" × 24" (91.4 × 61 cm)
Medium: Ink & Shade–film on Mylar
Courtesy of Rob Wellington Quigley, FAIA
and Mel McGee, Illustrator

Drawings: Freeport Hospital Health
Care Village, Kitchener, Ontario, Canada
Courtesy of NORR Partnership Ltd./
NORR Health Care Design Group

Drawing: New Hope Church, Duarte, California
24" × 36" (61 × 91.4 cm)
Medium: Ink on vellum
Courtesy of Rebecca L. Binder FAIA

ONE POINT FROM ABOVE

Interior views from above are very descriptive and hence quite informative, especially to a person (client) who may not completely understand an architectural plan. In most cases, they simulate a one-point perspective view that one would have if the roof or ceiling of a scale model were removed. Quick construction of the view can be achieved by placing the plan view so that it coincides with the picture plane. Vertical height lines through all corners of the plane are then drawn converging to one vanishing point in a relatively central location. Height lines are terminated where descriptively appropriate (typically where the plan section cut is taken). With the church on the right, there is no plan section cut and the curving of the roof elements gives a "fish-eye" lens effect (see p. 606).

ONE POINT FROM BELOW

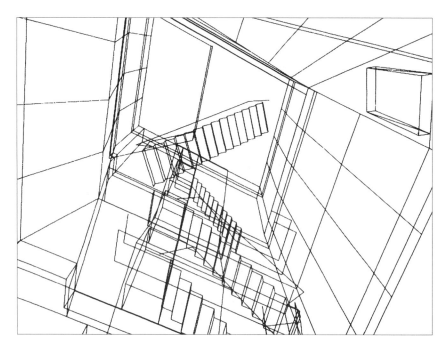

This computer-generated wire frame (see pp. 510–511) drawing is essentially a one-point perspective that has the sides of the structure tilted with respect to the edges of the picture plane and converging to other far distant vanishing points. The stairs also converge to other distant vanishing points.

View up through tower

Drawing: 3ER House, Venice, California
Medium: CAD
Courtesy of COOP HIMMELB(L)AU Architects
Wolf D. Prix, Helmut Swiczinsky & Partner

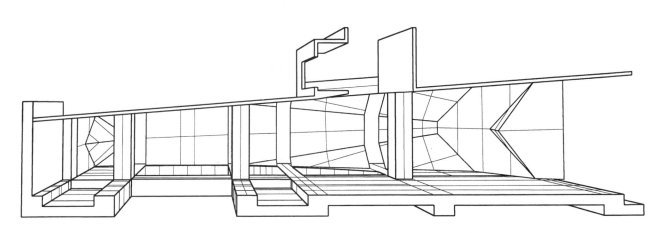

Drawing: Ackerman Student Union, UCLA
Medium: AutoCAD release 12
Courtesy of Rebecca L. Binder FAIA

The entry elements and circulation in this Remodel/Addition project are key to the establishment of a "new" whole. The ceilings are integral to the design, articulated in finished plywood. This floor view perspective offers a clear description of this northeast entry element.
[ARCHITECT'S STATMENT]

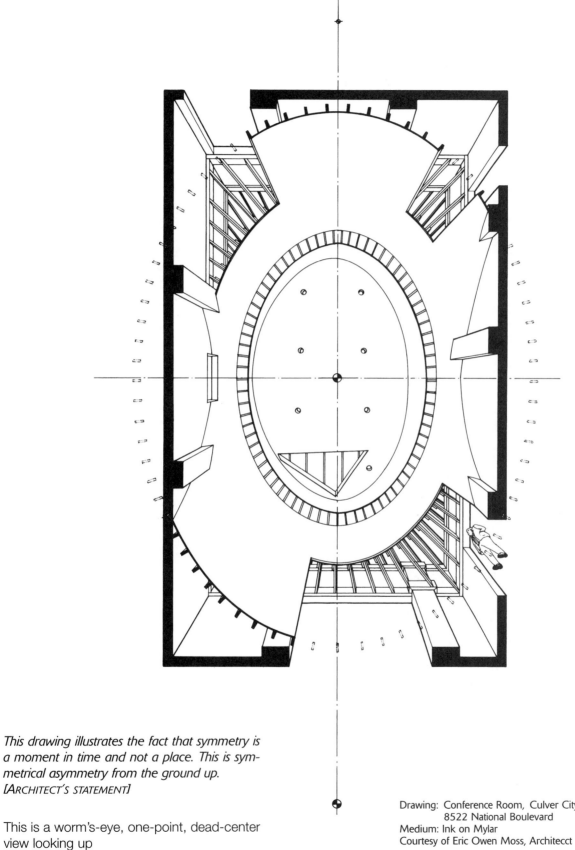

ONE POINT FROM BELOW

This drawing illustrates the fact that symmetry is a moment in time and not a place. This is symmetrical asymmetry from the ground up.
[ARCHITECT'S STATEMENT]

This is a worm's-eye, one-point, dead-center view looking up

Drawing: Conference Room, Culver City, California
8522 National Boulevard
Medium: Ink on Mylar
Courtesy of Eric Owen Moss, Architecct

When the lines of sight of our bird's-eye and worm's-eye views are parallel to an inclined plane, we are looking downhill and uphill. We see downhill and uphill perspective views in the natural landscape as well as in street scenes in the cityscape. Downhill and uphill views inside or outside a building's environment are characterized by stairs, escalators, or ramps.

LOOKING DOWNHILL AND UPHILL

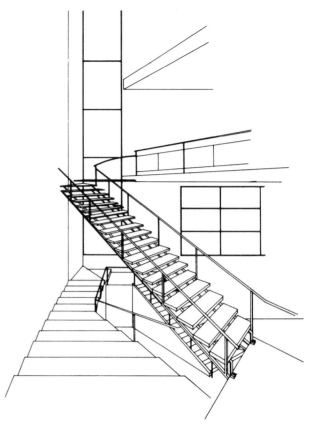

Drawing: Student project by Stacey Wenger
                Barcelona studio, Barcelona, Spain
Medium: Ink on Mylar
Courtesy of Washington University
School of Architecture, St. Louis, MO

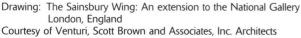

Drawing: The Sainsbury Wing: An extension to the National Gallery
               London, England
Courtesy of Venturi, Scott Brown and Associates, Inc. Architects

Vanishing trace line

False horizon line

Drawings: Student project by Thanh Do
San Francisco downhill and uphill views
Medium: Ink on vellum, 4" × 6" (10.2 × 15.2 cm)
Courtesy of the City College of San Francisco
Department of Architecture

©Winnie T. Leong

Photo: Great Wall of China near Beijing, China

Aligned vertically

False horizon line

Downhill and uphill views produce false horizon lines and result in oblique vanishing points. The observer's view is parallel to the sloping hills. The true horizon lines are where the vanishing point of all the horizontal lines on the building facade rests. The streetcar in the downhill view vanishes at a point on a false horizon line below the true horizon line. Likewise, the streetcar tracks in the uphill view vanish at a point on a false horizon line above the true horizon line. In both the downhill and the uphill situations, the different vanishing points align themselves vertically above and below each other.

LOOKING DOWNHILL AND UPHILL

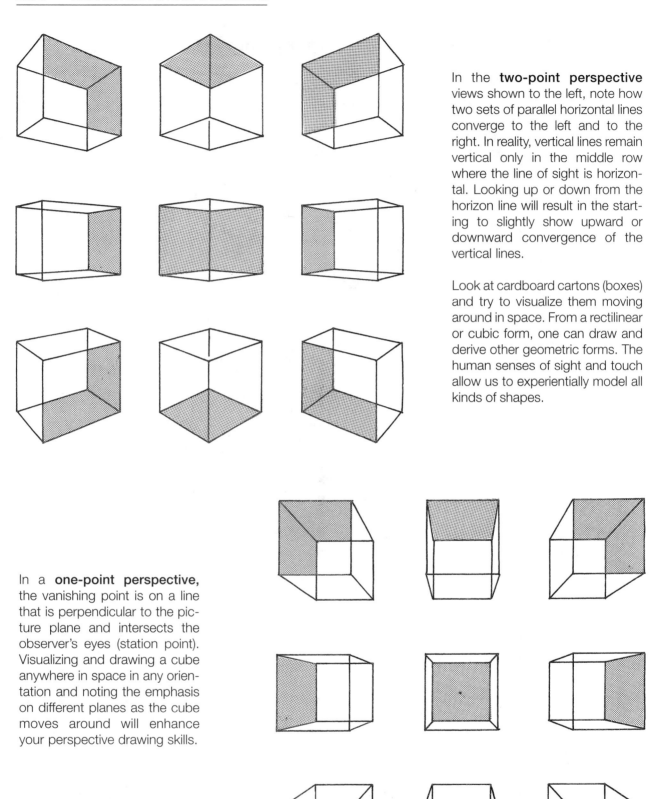

TWO-POINT AND ONE-POINT PERSPECTIVES

In the **two-point perspective** views shown to the left, note how two sets of parallel horizontal lines converge to the left and to the right. In reality, vertical lines remain vertical only in the middle row where the line of sight is horizontal. Looking up or down from the horizon line will result in the starting to slightly show upward or downward convergence of the vertical lines.

Look at cardboard cartons (boxes) and try to visualize them moving around in space. From a rectilinear or cubic form, one can draw and derive other geometric forms. The human senses of sight and touch allow us to experientially model all kinds of shapes.

In a **one-point perspective,** the vanishing point is on a line that is perpendicular to the picture plane and intersects the observer's eyes (station point). Visualizing and drawing a cube anywhere in space in any orientation and noting the emphasis on different planes as the cube moves around will enhance your perspective drawing skills.

Drawing: Theater Lobby
          Perry Community Education
          Village, Perry, Ohio
36" × 24" (91 × 61.4 cm)
Medium: Ink on Mylar
Courtesy of Perkins & Will, Architects

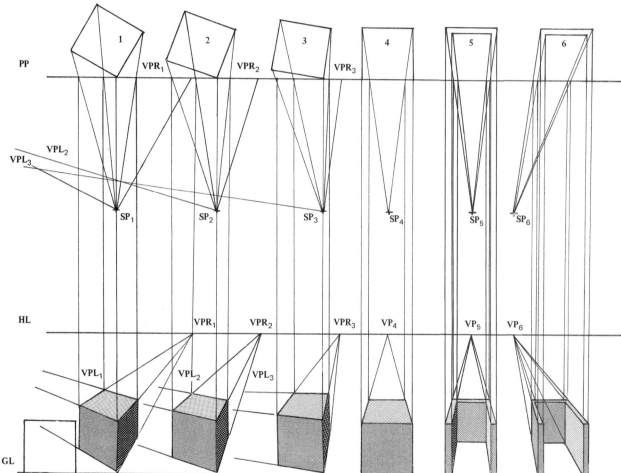

It is generally easier to learn how to construct a two-point perspective before attempting a one-point perspective. A one-point perspective can be termed a special case of a two-point perspective in which the plan view is not rotated and one set of lines are either parallel or coincident with the picture plane. Note how the cube transforms from a two-point perspective image (**1–3**) to a one-point perspective image (**4**). The open cube is also shown in one-point perspective variations (**5** and **6**). In one-point perspective, the plan view must be placed parallel to the picture plane so that the profile and the ground plane can project to the one vanishing point.

The example at the top of this page shows characteristics of both one- and two-point perspectives. Also note the tilted ellipses (see p. 275).

TWO-POINT AND ONE-POINT PERSPECTIVES

The first method (known as "office or "common") that we will examine for constructing an accurate perspective is a traditional one. It is dependent on both the plan and the elevation.

(1) In the top or plan view, place the outline of the object or objects (buildings) with an arbitrary orientation angle Θ (based on the view desired).

(2) Arbitrarily locate the picture plane and the station point in the plan view to create a distortionless view. It is advantageous to have the corner of the object touch the picture plane since that would establish a convenient vertical measuring line.

In a preliminary design drawing, an overlay of the floor plan, roof plan, and elevation would be made with tracing paper. If possible, never draw on the original drawings (use prints).

PLAN/ELEVATION OFFICE METHOD

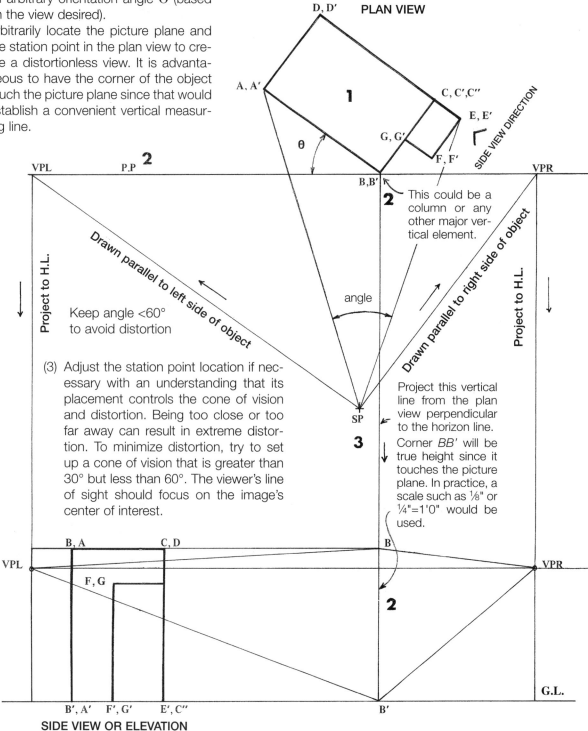

(3) Adjust the station point location if necessary with an understanding that its placement controls the cone of vision and distortion. Being too close or too far away can result in extreme distortion. To minimize distortion, try to set up a cone of vision that is greater than 30° but less than 60°. The viewer's line of sight should focus on the image's center of interest.

Keep angle <60° to avoid distortion

This could be a column or any other major vertical element.

Project this vertical line from the plan view perpendicular to the horizon line. Corner *BB'* will be true height since it touches the picture plane. In practice, a scale such as ⅛" or ¼"=1'0" would be used.

PLAN VIEW

Drawn parallel to left side of object

Drawn parallel to right side of object

SIDE VIEW OR ELEVATION

(4) Draw lines parallel to the sides of the object from the station point until they intersect the picture plane. At these points drop vertical tracer lines until they inersect the horizon line established for the perspective. The intersection points become the vanishing points for the perspective.

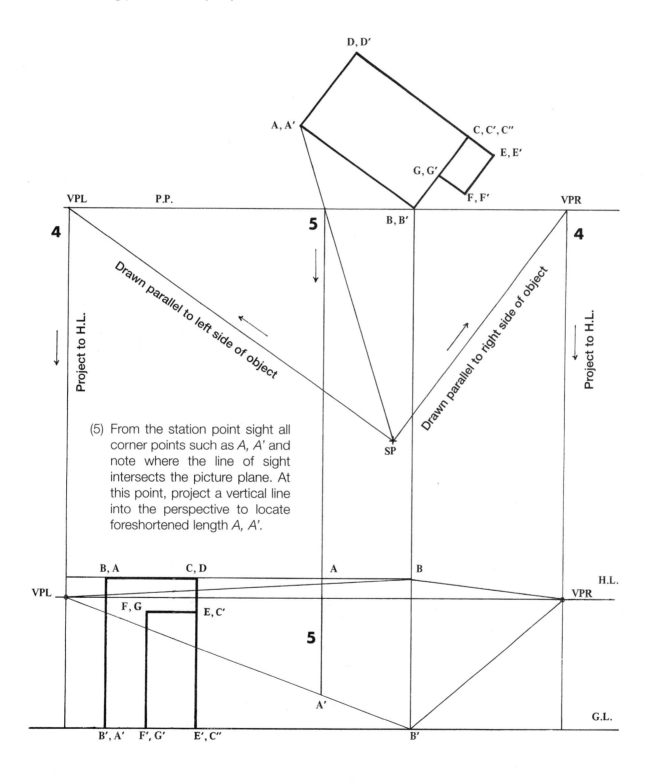

(5) From the station point sight all corner points such as *A, A'* and note where the line of sight intersects the picture plane. At this point, project a vertical line into the perspective to locate foreshortened length *A, A'*.

PLAN/ELEVATION OFFICE METHOD

(6) Project all sighting intersection points on the picture plane into the perspective in order to complete the perspective of the object. Hidden lines are optional.

PLAN/ELEVATION OFFICE METHOD

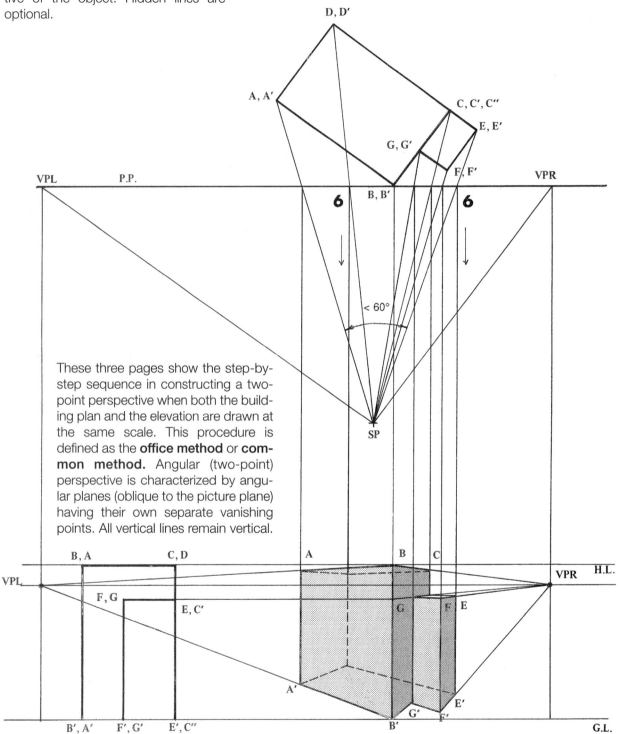

These three pages show the step-by-step sequence in constructing a two-point perspective when both the building plan and the elevation are drawn at the same scale. This procedure is defined as the **office method** or **common method.** Angular (two-point) perspective is characterized by angular planes (oblique to the picture plane) having their own separate vanishing points. All vertical lines remain vertical.

Drawing: Bogner Fashion House, Munich, West Germany
Medium: Ink
Courtesy of MACK-Mark Mack, Architect
Heino Stamm Planungsbüro; Bruckner & Partner, Associated Architects

APPLICATION: TWO-POINT PERSPECTIVE

This unique two-point cutaway sectional perspective (see pp. 258–259) has lines going to two vanishing points on a horizon line. Note that the basement level shows a partial perspective plan view. The two vanishing points on the previous page are more evenly spread apart from the observer's line of sight and the cone of vision than the vanishing points shown above. This is because the observer's line of sight is almost exactly at the corner of the object. In the above drawing the vanishing points are quite unevenly spread apart since the front facade is almost parallel to the observer's face and the sectional cut surface is almost perpendicular to the observer's face (foreshortens).

(1) Label each block element and find the vanishing points for each. This particular example has six vanishing points.

(2) Drop true-height tracer lines (circled points) from where the object touches the picture plane. Transfer corresponding true heights from the elevation.

(3) Draw lines from the top and the bottom of the true-height lines to the appropriate vanishing points.

(4) From the station point, sight all object corners and follow appropriate procedures to complete the perspective view.

MULTIPLE HORIZON LINE VANISHING POINTS

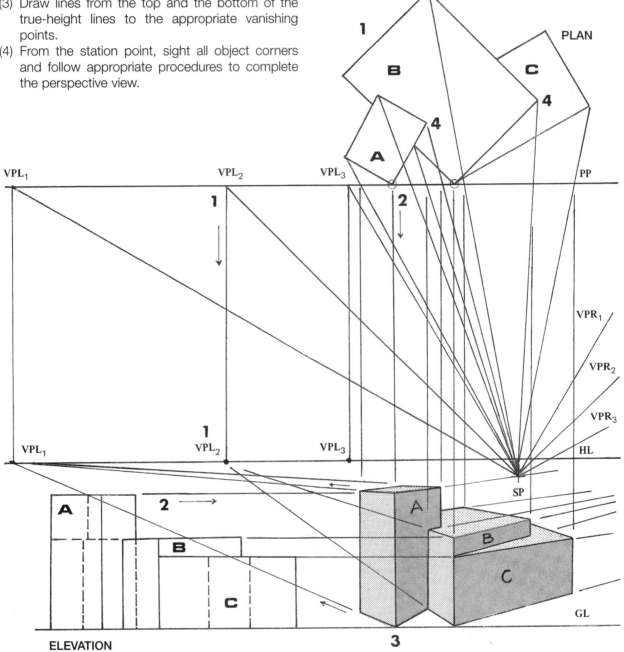

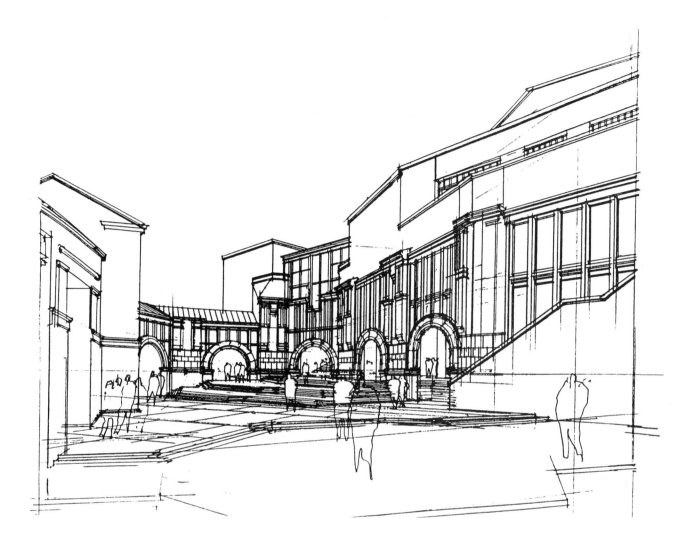

Drawing: California Center for the Arts, Escondido, California
          Moore Ruble Yudell Architects
Courtesy of Al Foster, Architectural Illustrator

The blockout began as if there was just one ground plane. Plaza levels were added or (as in foreground) subtracted from the ground plane and the figures in the final drawing were placed below or above the horizon line on their proper plaza levels. In a complicated drawing like this one with multiple levels, vanishing points, and detail, it is easier to disguise certain inevitable errors than it is in a very simple drawing.
[Architectural illustrator's statement]

This entry plaza is partially enclosed by wall planes that have multiple vanishing points on the horizon line.

MULTIPLE HORIZON LINE VANISHING POINTS

(1) Project extension lines from the left and right sides of the object to the picture plane and drop vertically to the ground line.

OBJECT/PP RELATIONSHIP

Drawing: Lotus Mansion
Shanghai, China
16.75" × 22" (42.5 × 55.9 cm)
Medium: Watercolor by brush and airbrush
on watercolor paper—linework is in pen and ink
Courtesy of Vitols Associates, Architects/Planners
Rendered by Thomas Wells Schaller of
Schaller Architectural Illustrations

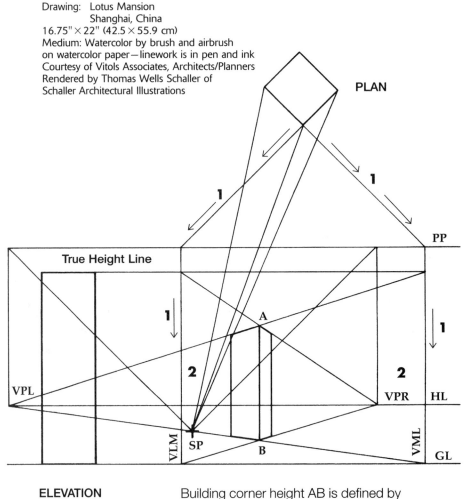

ELEVATION

Building corner height AB is defined by the intersecting perspective planes.

(2) Project the perspective planes back to VPR and VPL for both sides.

Objects that are behind the picture plane usually fall well within the cone of vision and show no distortion. The high-rise illustration was drawn with a greater degree of convergence to the left vanishing point than the example diagram to the right. Nevertheless, the view is well within the cone of vision. To find all the vanishing points when an object does not touch the picture plane, always construct (or trace) the plan view and note all the planar elements and their angles relative to the picture plane. Draw light construction lines parallel to all these planar elements regardless if they are on the left or right side of the building. Drop these projection lines vertically from the picture plane to the horizon line. Relative to the station point, all left-side planar elements go to left vanishing points and all right-side planar elements go to right vanishing points.

Drawing: Student project by A. Zainie Zainul
Medium: Ink on Mylar
Courtesy of Washington University
School of Architecture, St. Louis, MO

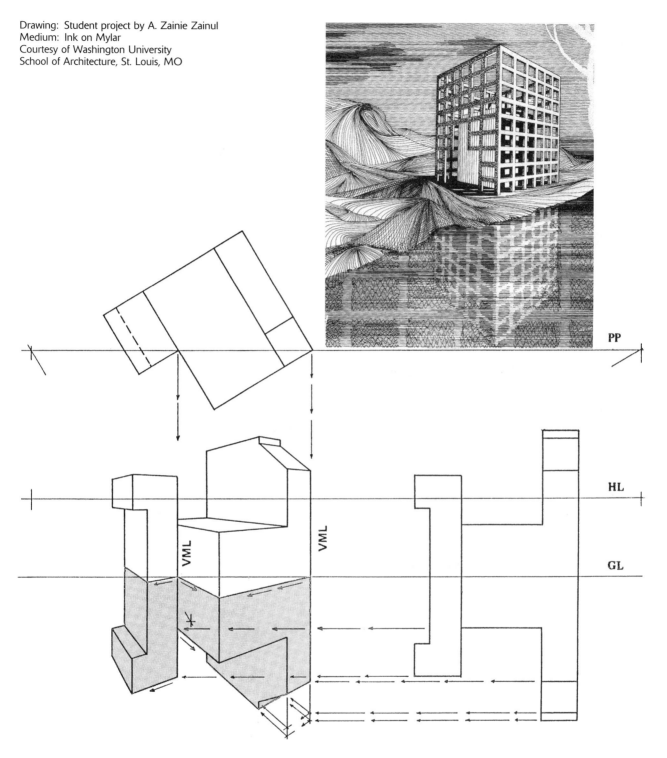

OBJECT/PP RELATIONSHIP

Objects completely in front of the picture plane will have distorted perspective image because they begin to fall outside the cone of vision. However, partial penetration of the picture plane by an object is usually visually acceptable, as shown above. Use all **vertical measuring lines** (VML) that touch the picture plane to project construction lines into the volume in front of the picture plane. The schematic example shown has a reflection (see pages on reflections) that also falls partially in front of the picture plane.

You can manipulate a perspective image by changing certain variables. These include moving the picture plane, changing the orientation, changing the station point location with respect to the object, and moving the horizon line up and down.

PICTORIAL EFFECT: VARIABLE S.P. HT. AND H.L.

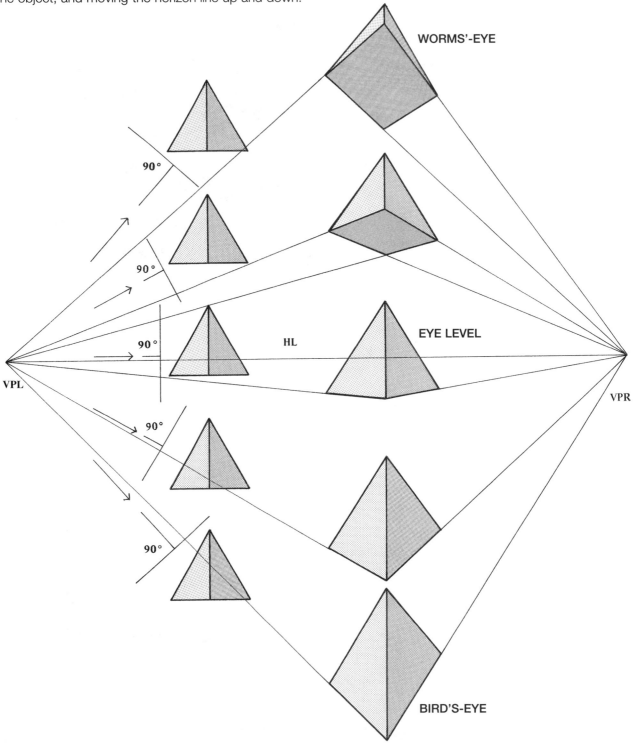

In this example, the picture plane, the orientation, and the station point location remain fixed. The horizon line with respect to the ground plane moves up and down.

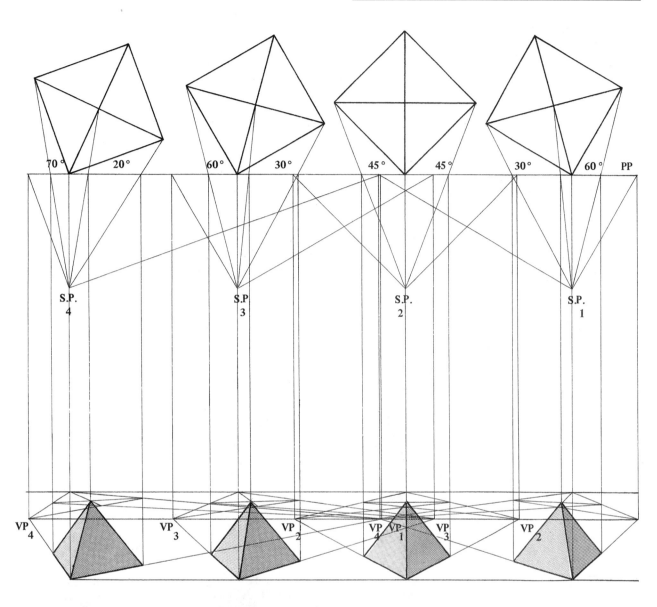

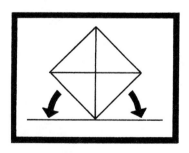

Each **orientation** change produces a new set of angles with respect to the picture plane.

In this example, the picture plane, the station point location, and the horizon line remain fixed. The orientation changes.

PICTORIAL EFFECT: VARIABLE ORIENTATION

Note that increasing the distance from the picture plane to the station point (P.P.$_4$ to P.P.$_1$) causes a progressive enlargement of the perspective image.

PICTORIAL EFFECT: VARIABLE PICTURE PLANE

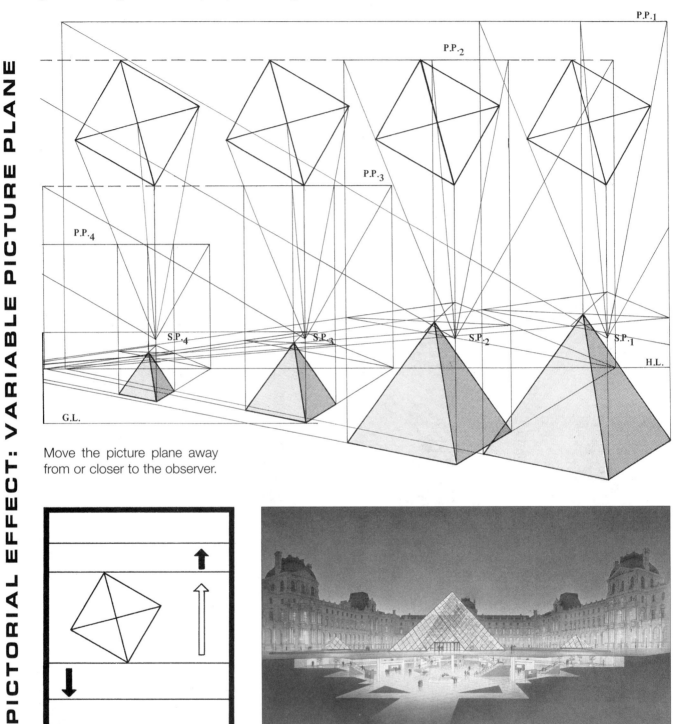

Move the picture plane away from or closer to the observer.

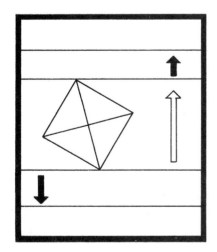

In this example, the station point location, the horizon line, and the orientation remain fixed. The **picture plane** location changes.

The Pyramid at Le Grand Louvre
Pei Cobb Freed & Partners / Michel Macary Architects
Courtesy of Lee Dunnete, Architectural Illustrator

Note that increasing the station point distance to the object (S.P.₄ to S.P.₁) causes a decrease in foreshortening due to the two vanishing points progressively moving away from each other.

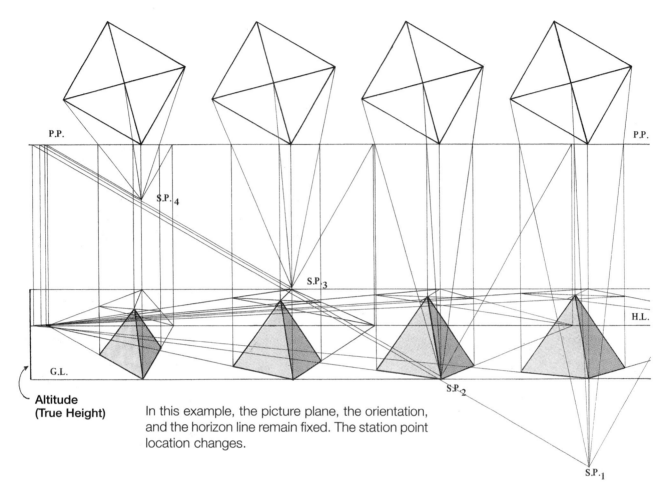

P.P.

P.P.

S.P.₄

S.P.₃

S.P.₂

S.P.₁

H.L.

G.L.

Altitude
(True Height)

In this example, the picture plane, the orientation, and the horizon line remain fixed. The station point location changes.

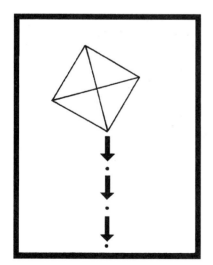

The **observer moves** from near to far away from the viewed object.

PICTORIAL EFFECT: VARIABLE STATION POINT

Drawing: Student project by Jennifer Kinkead
Bicycle factory, Mexico
Medium: Ink on Mylar
Excerpted from Abstract, Columbia School of Architecture
Planning and Preservation (CSAPP)

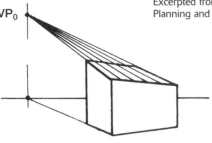

OBLIQUE VANISHING POINTS

It is quite common to find a series of **oblique** (also termed sloping and inclined) edges that are parallel in building forms. In such cases an oblique vanishing point (VP_O) expedites perspective construction.

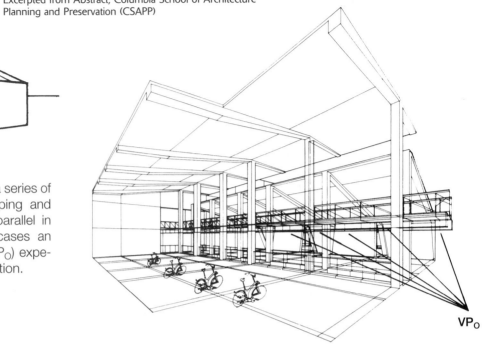

VP_O = oblique vanishing point

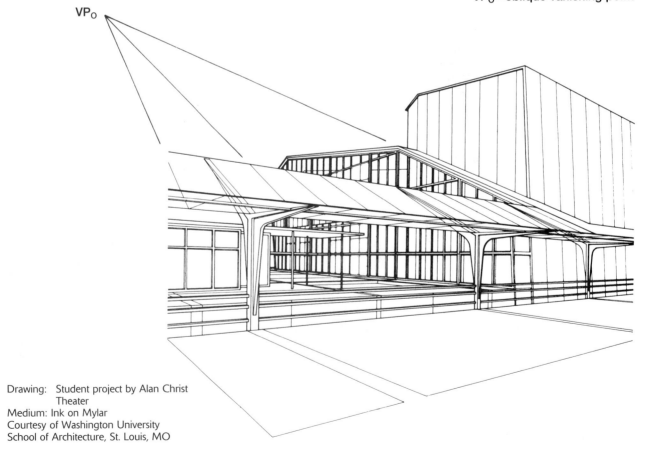

Drawing: Student project by Alan Christ
Theater
Medium: Ink on Mylar
Courtesy of Washington University
School of Architecture, St. Louis, MO

Drawing: Glass–Kline residence
New Paltz, New York
14" × 17" (35.6 × 43.2 cm)
Medium: Ink on vellum
Courtesy of Taeg Nishimoto &
allied architects

This interior perspective has structural ceiling elements that have oblique vanishing points both down to the right and down to the left.

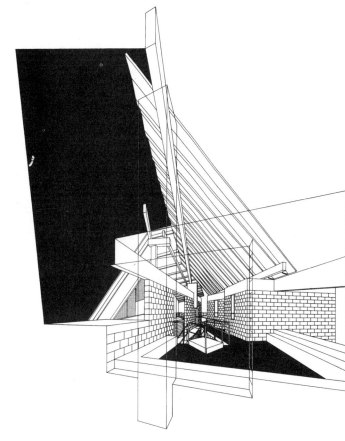

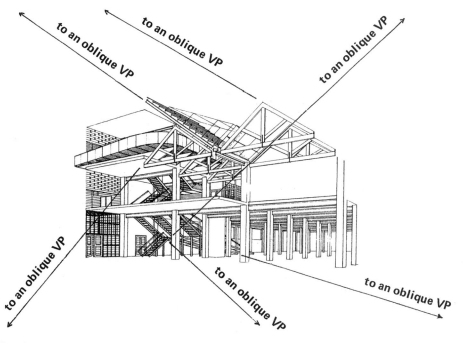

OBLIQUE VANISHING POINTS

Edges that are **parallel** in an inclined plane converge to a **common** vanishing point. This vanishing point is not on the eye-level line. The vanishing points for a building's **oblique** lines either fall above or below its eye-level vanishing points. The process of determining the proper direction is discussed on the next two pages.

Drawing: La Llauna School, Badalona, Spain
Medium: Ink on Mylar
Courtesy of Enric Miralles & Carme Pinós, Architects

The perspective of this building has numerous inclined lines and planes and consequently many oblique vanishing points. Sloping lines in perspective are a common occurrence with staircases and ramps.

OBLIQUE VANISHING POINTS: LEFT SIDE

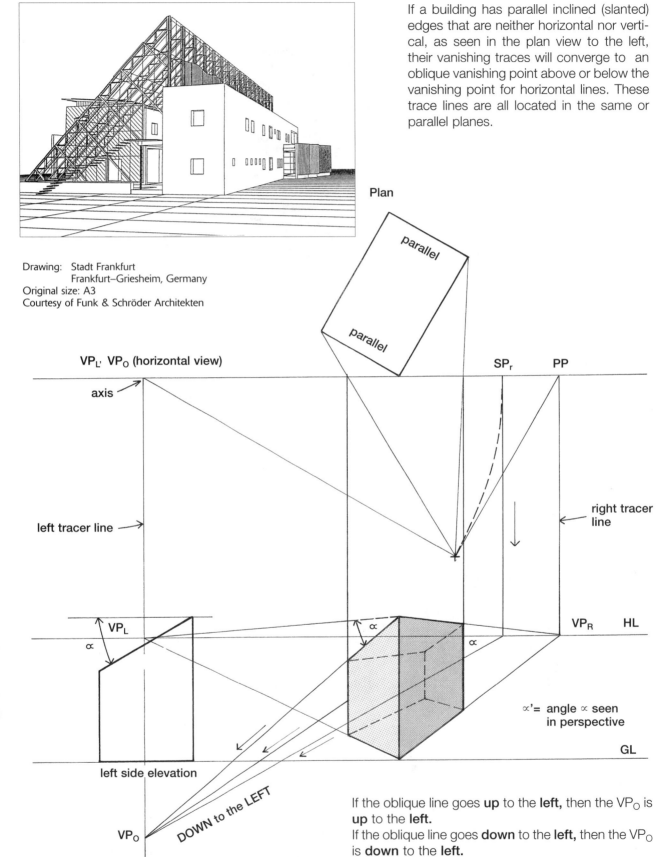

Drawing: Stadt Frankfurt
            Frankfurt–Griesheim, Germany
Original size: A3
Courtesy of Funk & Schröder Architekten

If a building has parallel inclined (slanted) edges that are neither horizontal nor vertical, as seen in the plan view to the left, their vanishing traces will converge to an oblique vanishing point above or below the vanishing point for horizontal lines. These trace lines are all located in the same or parallel planes.

Plan

parallel

parallel

VP_L, VP_O (horizontal view)

SP_r PP

axis

left tracer line

right tracer line

VP_L

α

α

α

VP_R HL

α

α'= angle α seen in perspective

GL

left side elevation

DOWN to the LEFT

VP_O

If the oblique line goes **up** to the **left,** then the VP_O is **up** to the **left.**
If the oblique line goes **down** to the **left,** then the VP_O is **down** to the **left.**

ΔABC is proportional to ΔSP_r, VP_R, VP_O where r means rotated.

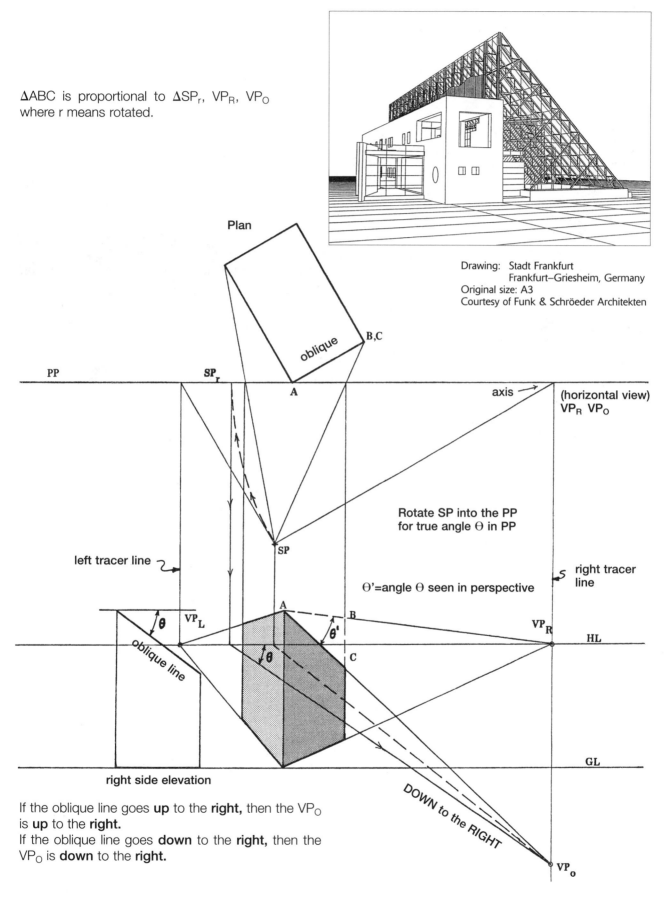

Drawing: Stadt Frankfurt
               Frankfurt–Griesheim, Germany
Original size: A3
Courtesy of Funk & Schröeder Architekten

Plan

PP

SP_r

B,C

oblique

A

axis →

(horizontal view)
VP_R VP_O

Rotate SP into the PP
for true angle Θ in PP

SP

left tracer line

Θ'=angle Θ seen in perspective

right tracer
line

A

B

VP_L

θ

VP_R

HL

oblique line

θ'

θ

C

VP_R

GL

right side elevation

DOWN to the RIGHT

VP_o

If the oblique line goes **up** to the **right,** then the VP_O is **up** to the **right.**
If the oblique line goes **down** to the **right,** then the VP_O is **down** to the **right.**

OBLIQUE VANISHING POINTS: RIGHT SIDE

MULTIPLYING, DIVIDING, AND TRANSFERRING

Drawing: Perry Community Education Village, Perry, Ohio
Medium: Ink on Mylar, 36" × 24" (91.4 × 61 cm)
Courtesy of Perkins & Will Architects

The plan/elevation method (for both two- and one-point) is just one of many ways to generate mechanical perspective drawings. In the future, new methods will always be emerging; and it is important not to be afraid to experiment with them. The balance of this chapter will, for the most part, discuss other methods.

Once an initial cube has been constructed, concepts and techniques for **multiplying, dividing,** and **transferring** dimensions in perspective space can be employed. These techniques support the development of a perspective without adding to its constructional framework. They build and reinforce an understanding of the perspective structure and the relationships between things within it regardless of the generated perspective method used. They do not require drawing space beyond the perspective itself and they can be applied to any part of any existing perspective. Armed with this set of concepts and strategies for their employment, anything can be accurately drawn in perspective.

The application of the multiplying, dividing, and transferring techniques is of particular importance because it provides the means for linking sketching with the computer (see chapter on 3D modeling). The ability to quickly and accurately sketch within and to extend a computer-generated perspective supports the exploration of alternatives and the development of presentation drawings. It allows three-dimensional modeling programs to be used to create simpler and more efficient mass models for generated perspective frameworks that can also be elaborated on by hand.

Diagram (p. 219) and text (pp. 218–219): Courtesy
of William R. Benedict, Assistant Professor
California Polytechnic State University
School of Architecture, San Luis Obispo, CA

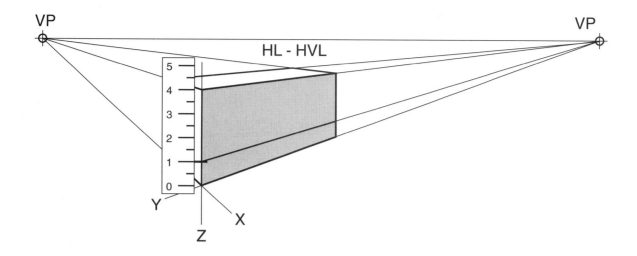

X, Y, & Z **Axes:** The axes of the Cartesian coordinate system that are parallel to the three sets of parallel edges of a cube or any rectangular object or rectangular space. Moving through perspective space can be visualized as moving successively along the axes to arrive at the desired location. The *Z* axis is parallel to the picture plane; therefore, all lines parallel to it will retain their true orientation, that is drawn as vertical lines.

Dividing by Measuring

A common need in drawing is to give a line some scale and establish dimensions along it. You may have a line of some length that you wish to call a specific dimension (give a specific scale), say four feet, and then establish a point on the line that is one foot from one end.

Three techniques can be used: Direct Measurement, Vanished Transfer, and Parallel Transfer. All three techniques are intended to give a line scale and locate specific dimensions. Once this has occurred, other techniques must be used to move the dimensions within the drawing. Direct measurement, parallel transfer and a variation of parallel transfer with vertical and horizontal lines will be discussed.

Direct Measurement

This technique involves directly measuring the line. It is used when establishing dimensions through visual judgment or direct measurement with a scale. Direct measurement with the eye involves making visual judgments that proportionally divide the line. For example, if the line is assumed to be four feet long and a one-foot increment is needed, then you can visually divide the line in half and then half again to locate one foot. This works very well because we can accurately judge the middle of things. With practice you can also divide a line into thirds or fifths. By combining judgments of halves, thirds, and fifths, you can easily and accurately use your eye to establish dimensions in a drawing.

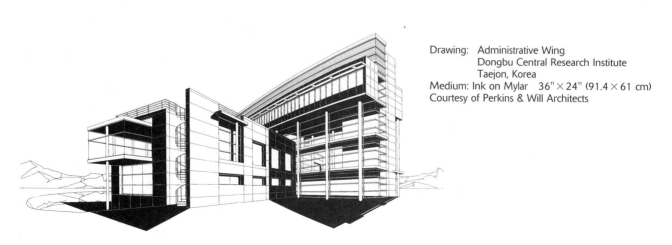

Drawing: Administrative Wing
Dongbu Central Research Institute
Taejon, Korea
Medium: Ink on Mylar 36" × 24" (91.4 × 61 cm)
Courtesy of Perkins & Will Architects

DIRECT MEASUREMENT

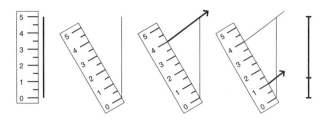

Parallel Transfer

The existing line that you want to make four feet may be of a dimension that is not readily divisible by four. Identify the line that is parallel to the picture plane that you want to make equal to the desired dimension (e.g., four feet).

Choose a scale that is reasonably close to the actual length of the line. Align the zero mark on the scale to one end of the line to be dimensioned. Angle the scale away from the line. Mark the desired dimensions along the edge of the scale including the one that designates the full length of the line (e.g., four feet).

Draw a line from the full-length dimension along the scale to the end of the line you want to dimension. The angle of this line will be used to transfer all other dimensions from the scale to the line. Draw lines that are parallel to the line created in the preceding step between all dimensions along the scale and the line you are dimensioning (e.g., one foot). You have proportionally dimensioned the base line and can proceed with the drawing construction using other techniques.

PARALLEL TRANSFER

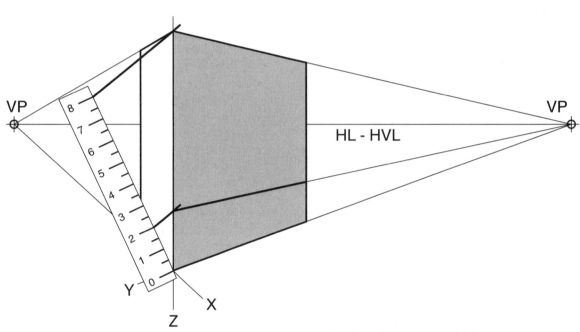

Vertical and Horizontal Lines

The technique translates directly to any line that is parallel to the picture plane, such as those that are vertical and horizontal. The perspective example to the above left shows the technique being used for a vertical edge—a condition that occurs in both one- and two-point perspectives.

Diagrams and text (both pages): Courtesy of William R. Benedict, Assistant Professor California Polytechnic State University School of Architecture, San Luis Obispo, CA

Multiplying by Measuring

The assumption is that you have a visually and proportionally correct square and wish to generate additional squares above or below.

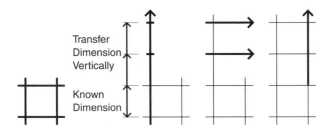

Draw or identify the base square whose vertical edges are parallel to the picture plane. All edges are parallel in orthoghraphic drawings.

Extend a vertical edge of the base square to function as a measuring line. Transfer the height of the base square (the known dimension) along this edge. You can transfer dimensions above and/or below the base square as many times as needed.

Principle: Vertical lines in both one- and two-point perspectives represent edges that are parallel to the picture plane—they do not vanish. This means that a dimension or portion of the dimension (½, ¼, etc.) established on any vertical line within a perspective can be transferred vertically along that line.

Draw horizontal lines through these points (orthographic) or lines that go to the vanishing point for the plane (perspective).

Principle: Sets of parallel horizontal lines not parallel to the picture plane in both one- and two-point perspectives vanish to a common vanishing point on the horizon line. This means that dimensions can be transferred horizontally between vertical lines on the same plane by using the vanishing point for horizontal lines for that plane.

Extend the remaining vertical edge to complete the additional squares.

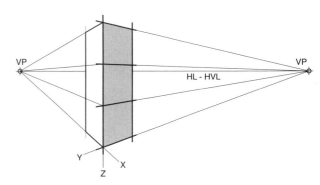

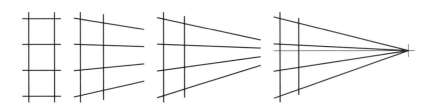

Drawing: Student project by
        Gorran Tsui
Torre de Telecomunicacions de Montjuïc
Barcelona, Spain, 1992
Santiago Calatrava, Architect
4.5" × 7" (11.4 × 17.8 cm)
Medium: Ink on vellum
Courtesy of the Department of Architecture
City College of San Francisco

MULTIPLYING BY MEASURING

DIVIDING/OBLIQUE GRID

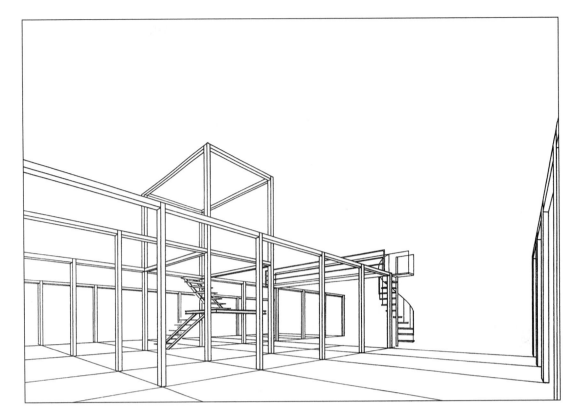

Drawing: T residence, Hayama, Kanagawa, Japan
Courtesy of Iida Archiship Studio

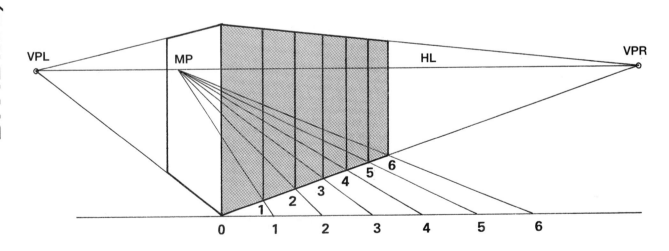

The above method shows an auxiliary vanishing point (also defined as a measuring point, MP) that is generated by a particular station point in the measuring point system (see pages on measuring points). A vertical building facade (exterior face) can be divided with proper projected depths using this concept (see pp. 230–231).

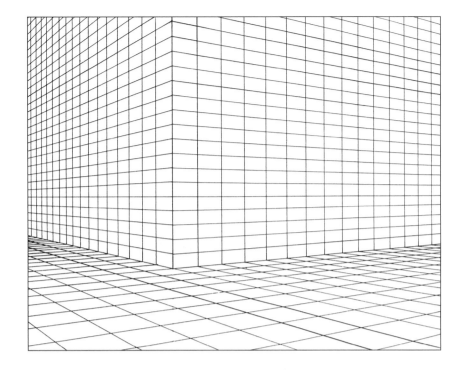

Perspective charts that are available commercially save time and space, especially when a large layout is required (residential layouts may need five feet or more). The time factor is reduced immensely, especially when generating many similar images. Nice features of perspective charts are (1) that the scale of the grid lines is flexible to suit the size of the structure being drawn and (2) that the observer's relationship to the horizon line (bird's-eye, worm's-eye, eye level, etc.) can always be adjusted. The major undesirable features are the restricted freedom in selecting the station point position and the picture plane placement. Charts that are made for both two-point and one-point perspectives are divided into two categories: those with a relatively high horizon line and those with a relatively low horizon line.

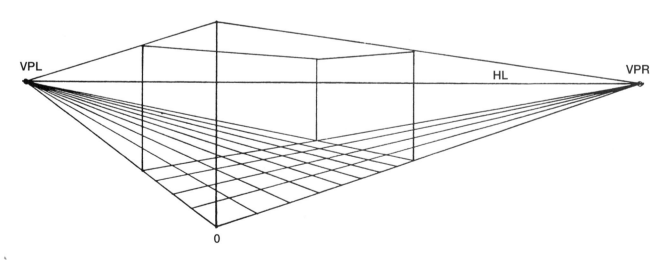

A perspective plan can be divided by using the two vanished lines from corner point 0. The result is a two-point perspective grid. A two-point perspective grid is useful for drawing either exterior or interior perspectives. The grid can be used to accurately locate elements in the urban landscape. The grid can also position scale elements like furniture and human figures in their accurate relative positions (see p. 396).

OBLIQUE GRID CHARTS

GRID IN OBLIQUE PERSPECTIVE

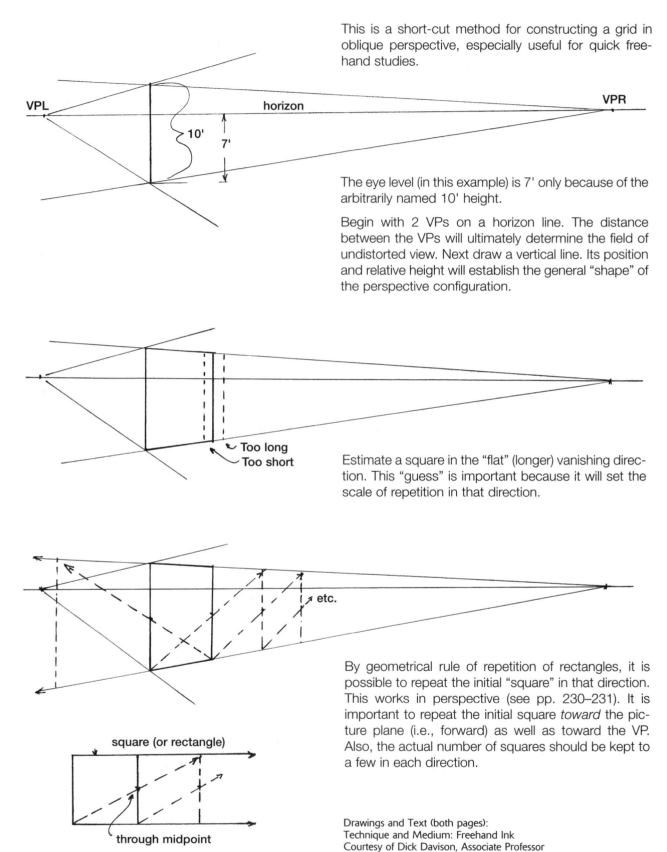

This is a short-cut method for constructing a grid in oblique perspective, especially useful for quick free-hand studies.

The eye level (in this example) is 7' only because of the arbitrarily named 10' height.

Begin with 2 VPs on a horizon line. The distance between the VPs will ultimately determine the field of undistorted view. Next draw a vertical line. Its position and relative height will establish the general "shape" of the perspective configuration.

Estimate a square in the "flat" (longer) vanishing direction. This "guess" is important because it will set the scale of repetition in that direction.

By geometrical rule of repetition of rectangles, it is possible to repeat the initial "square" in that direction. This works in perspective (see pp. 230–231). It is important to repeat the initial square *toward* the picture plane (i.e., forward) as well as toward the VP. Also, the actual number of squares should be kept to a few in each direction.

Drawings and Text (both pages):
Technique and Medium: Freehand Ink
Courtesy of Dick Davison, Associate Professor
Texas A & M University
Department of Architecture

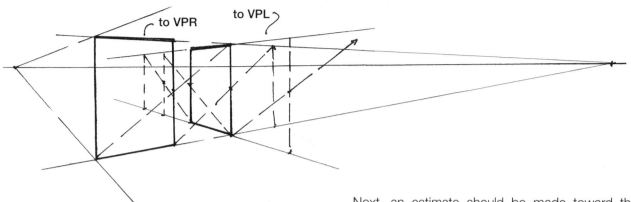

to VPR   to VPL

Next, an estimate should be made toward the "short" VP. It may be easier to make the estimate from the second or third cube so as to get a "flatter" look as the estimate is made in that direction.

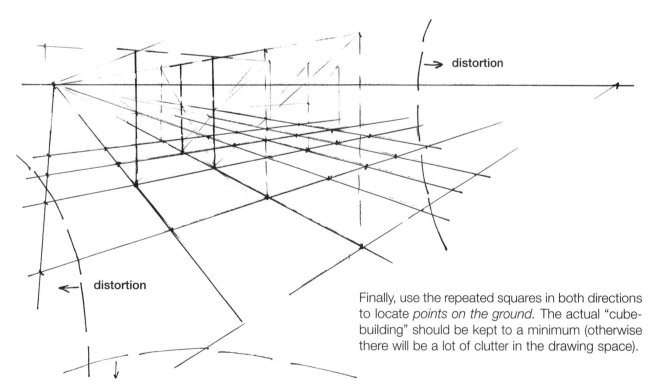

→ distortion

← distortion

Finally, use the repeated squares in both directions to locate *points on the ground*. The actual "cube-building" should be kept to a minimum (otherwise there will be a lot of clutter in the drawing space).

This will produce a two-point *measurable* grid.

The grid can be subdivided and/or repeated indefinitely with the same geometry as long as the distortion is minimal (which is a function of VP spacing).

GRID IN OBLIQUE PERSPECTIVE

TRANSFERRING WITH THE DIAGONAL

Transferring with the Diagonal

Suppose that you have a visually and proportionally correct square with dimensions located on one side that you want to transfer to an adjacent side.

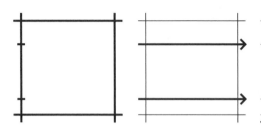

Draw or identify the base square and the dimensions. The vertical edges are parallel to the picture plane. All edges are parallel in orthographic drawings. Extend the dimensions across the square. Draw one of the diagonals of the square. Draw lines that intersect with the sides of the square through the intersections of the diagonal and dimension lines.

Principle: A 45° line drawn through the intersection of two perpendicular lines will transfer dimensions from one line to the other. The diagonal you choose to draw will control the side to which a dimension is transferred. This technique has slightly different results when used in a square as illustrated and than when used in other rectangles. The diagonal of a square will transfer the exact dimensions (2' to 2') while the diagonal of a rectangle will transfer only proportions (¼ to ¼) .

Diagrams and text (both pages): Courtesy of William R. Benedict, Assistant Professor California Polytechnic State University College of Architecture & Environmental Design San Luis Obispo, CA

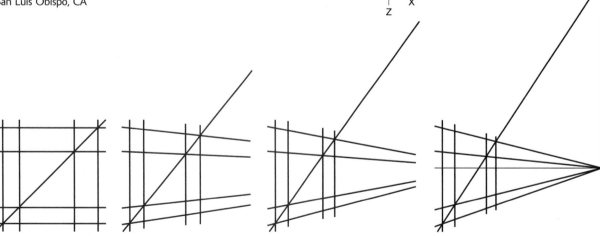

Multiplying by Measuring Plus the Diagonal

Suppose that you have a visually and proportionally correct square and wish to generate additional squares to one or more sides. The strategy combines the vertical transfer of dimensions introduced in Multiplying by Measuring with the diagonal of a square.

As the illustrations show, the diagonal can be further extended to intersect a vertical line (VVL) drawn through the vanishing point (VP) for the horizontal lines. This creates a diagonal vanishing point (DVP) to which all parallel diagonals will converge. You do not need to create the diagonal vanishing point to use this technique. The diagonal vanishing points may be above or below or to either side of a VP.

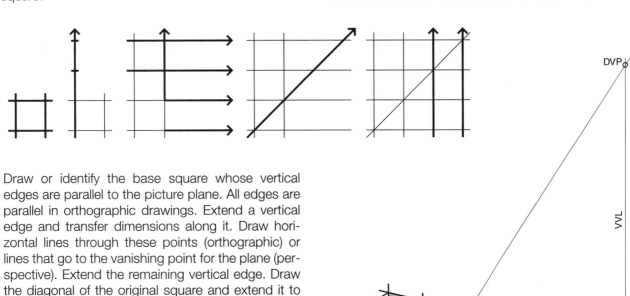

Draw or identify the base square whose vertical edges are parallel to the picture plane. All edges are parallel in orthographic drawings. Extend a vertical edge and transfer dimensions along it. Draw horizontal lines through these points (orthographic) or lines that go to the vanishing point for the plane (perspective). Extend the remaining vertical edge. Draw the diagonal of the original square and extend it to cross all horizontal or vanished lines.

Principle: A diagonal line crossing a set of equally spaced parallel lines produces intersections that can be used to define another equally spaced set of parallel lines. If the diagonal is at 45°, and the sets of lines are perpendicular to each other, a square grid is produced as shown in the illustrations. Draw vertical lines through each intersection of the diagonal with a horizontal or vanished line to complete the additional squares.

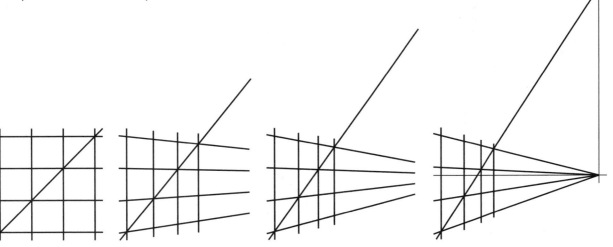

Multiplying With the Diagonal

Suppose that you have a visually and proportionally correct square and wish to generate additional squares to either side, above or below.

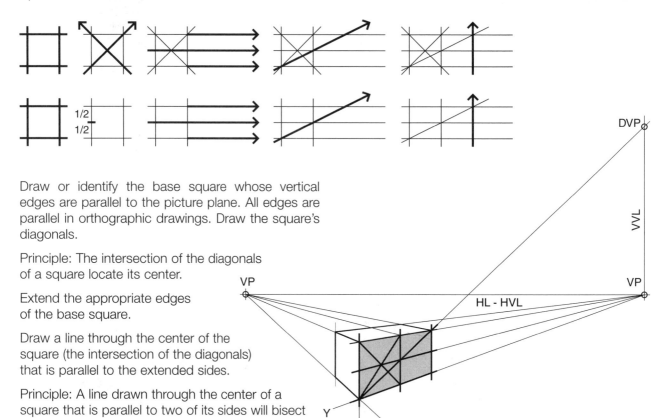

Draw or identify the base square whose vertical edges are parallel to the picture plane. All edges are parallel in orthographic drawings. Draw the square's diagonals.

Principle: The intersection of the diagonals of a square locate its center.

Extend the appropriate edges of the base square.

Draw a line through the center of the square (the intersection of the diagonals) that is parallel to the extended sides.

Principle: A line drawn through the center of a square that is parallel to two of its sides will bisect the other two sides.

Alternative (bottom illustration): Sometimes it is faster to divide a vertical edge with a scale or by visual judgment. In this case, draw a line through the center of the side that is parallel to the extended sides.

Draw a line from one corner of the square through the center of an opposite side. Extend this line until it intersects one of the extended sides. This line is now the diagonal of a rectangle that is twice as wide as the original square.

Draw a line through the intersection of the line just completed and the side of the square to define the new square.

As the illlustrations show, the diagonal of the double-wide rectangle can be further extended to intersect a vertical line (VVL) drawn through the vanishing point for the horizontal lines. This creates a diagonal vanishing point (DVP) to which all similar diagonals will converge. You do not need to create the diagonal vanishing point to use this technique.

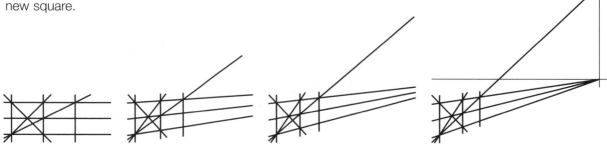

Dividing With the Diagonal

It is a good strategy to draw the largest inclusive form possible as a first step in constructing a perspective and then to subdivide that form to locate smaller elements. This technique assumes that you have a visually and proportionally correct square and wish to divide it into halves, quarters, eights, etc.

As the illustrations show, the diagonals can be further extended to intersect a vertical line (VVL) drawn through the vanishing point (VP) for the horizontal lines. This creates a diagonal vanishing point (DVP). You do not need to create the diagonal vanishing point to use this technique. The diagonal vanishing points may be above or below or to either side of a VP.

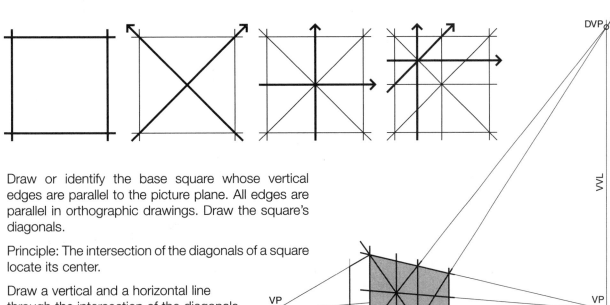

Draw or identify the base square whose vertical edges are parallel to the picture plane. All edges are parallel in orthographic drawings. Draw the square's diagonals.

Principle: The intersection of the diagonals of a square locate its center.

Draw a vertical and a horizontal line through the intersection of the diagonals. In perspective the horizontal line vanishes to the vanishing point for horizontal lines on that surface.

Principle: A line drawn through the center of a square that is parallel to two of its sides will bisect the other two sides.

The vertical and horizontal lines have defined four smaller squares that have the same proportions as the original but are one-quarter the size. This process can be repeated within each progressively smaller square until the desired subdivision is produced. Each subdivdsion halves the square (e.g., a twelve-foot square becomes four six-foot squares.

Diagrams and text (both pages): Courtesy of William R. Benedict, Assistant Professor California Polytechnic State University College of Architecture & Environmental Design San Luis Obispo, CA

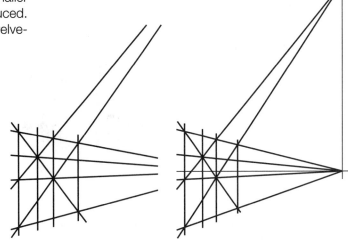

DIVIDING WITH THE DIAGONAL

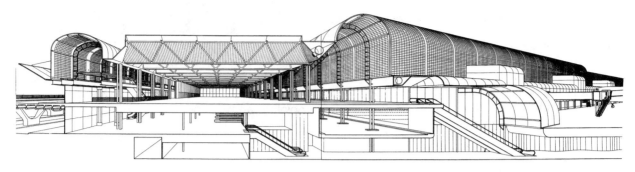

Drawing (above): United Airlines Terminal
Chicago, Illinois
34" × 22" (86.4 × 55.9 cm)
Medium: Sepia ink on 1000H paper
Courtesy of Murphy/Jahn, Architects
with A. Epstein & Sons, Architects

Drawing (left): Storrow Drive, Boston, Massachusetts
Medium: Ink on Mylar
Courtesy of Koetter Kim & Associates, Inc.
Architects and Urban Designers

The principles for multiplying and dividing with diagonals are frequently used on the fenestration of buildings in terms of distributing elements along a plane.

In building structures of great lengths (institutional, commercial, etc.), it is common to have **equally** spaced repetitious elements. Perspective construction can be expedited by the use of **diagonals;** this is possible because all diagonals of squares and rectangles intersect in the exact center of the figure (see pp. 228–229).

PROJECTED DEPTHS USING DIAGONALS

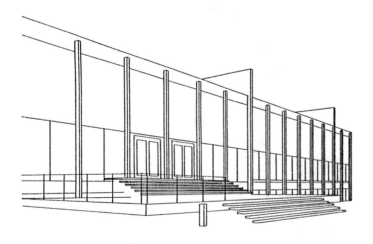

Drawing: Crown Hall, Illinois Institute of Technology, Chicago, Illinois
Ludwig Mies Van der Rohe, Architect

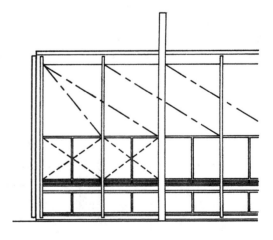

TYPICAL PARTIAL ELEVATION

(1) Decide on the spacing between two primary window mullions, *a* and *b.*
(2) Draw diagonals between *a* and *b* to determine the mullion midline bisector.
(3) Locate mullion *c'c* by drawing a line from *a'* through the midpoint of *b'b.*

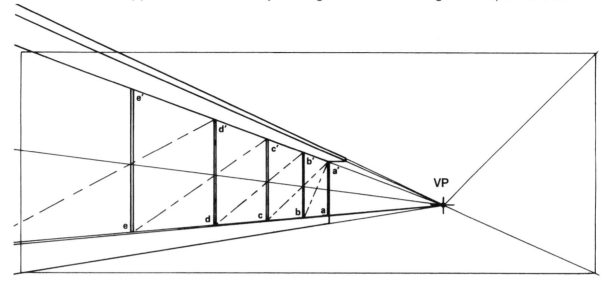

(4) Repeat the procedure in step 3 to locate *d'd* starting from *b',* *e'e* starting from *c',* etc.
(5) Locate secondary window mullions 1'1, 2'2, 3'3, etc., by drawing diagonals between the primary window mullions.

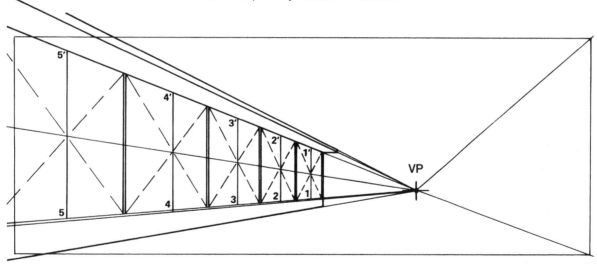

NOTATION — · — · — · — · — **Diagonal lines locating primary window mullions.**

— — — — — — — — — **Diagonal lines locating secondary window mullions.**

Follow steps 1 through 5 to accurately locate equally spaced lines in perspective. In both one-point (above example) and two-point perspectives, it is frequently necessary to repeat lines that are equally spaced. For example, window mullions seen in both exterior or interior perspective views are often equally spaced. Many other elements that are seen in our urban landscape are equally spaced, such as lampposts, parking meters, telephone poles, building types with repetitious units, columns in a colonnade, and sidewalk units. **Diagonals** provide the best method of determining projected depths in perspective.

PROJECTED DEPTHS USING DIAGONALS

Diagrams and text (both pages): Courtesy
of William R. Benedict, Assistant Professor
California Polytechnic State University
College of Architecture & Environmental Design
San Luis Obispo, CA

DIAGONAL VANISHING POINTS

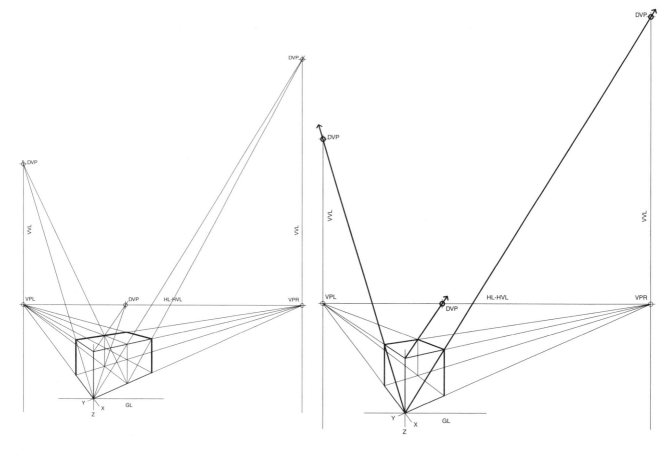

The techniques of multiplying, dividing, and transferring discussed on pp. 226 to 229 become especially applicable as methods for constructing two-point perspectives. These techniques have the advantage of requiring fewer construction lines than the plan-elevation cone of vision method.

Diagonal Vanishing Points

Draw and extend the diagonals of the visible faces of the cube until they intersect with their respective vanishing lines. Label the diagonal vanishing points (DVP). There are two possible diagonal vanishing points for each square face. One will be above and one below the horizon line on the vertical vanishing lines. The illustrations show only one set to save space and we usually draw only one for the same rea-

son. The decision to draw one or the other or both depends on what is useful in constructing a specific perspective.

The illustration to the left shows that the diagonals of the opposite faces of the cube go to the same vanishing point because they are parallel and therefore their diagonals are parallel. All parallel lines go to the same vanishing point. The use of the diagonal to generate (multiply) a new cube is also illustrated.
If you become confused as to which diagonal vanishing point to use, then find the vanishing point for horizontal lines on the same plane. The vanishing line for the diagonals will pass through the vanishing point for the horizontal lines on the plane.

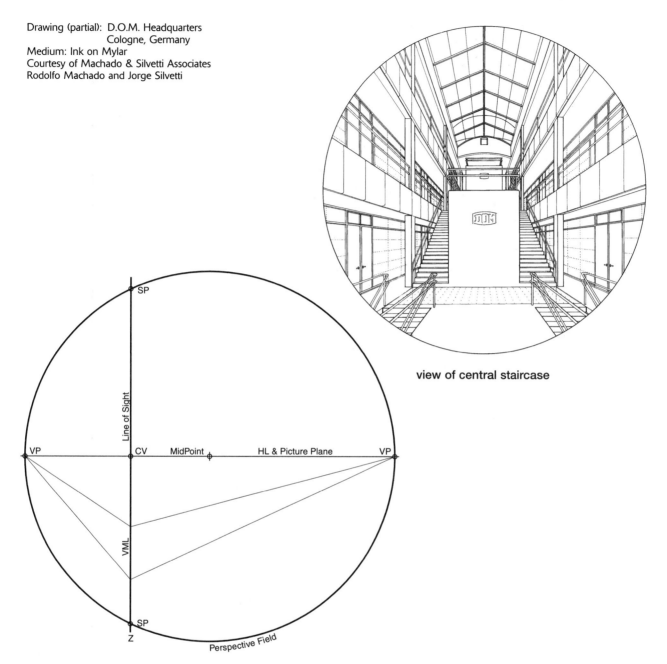

Drawing (partial): D.O.M. Headquarters
Cologne, Germany
Medium: Ink on Mylar
Courtesy of Machado & Silvetti Associates
Rodolfo Machado and Jorge Silvetti

view of central staircase

Midpoint and Perspective Field of View

Locate the midpoint between the two vanishing points and use it to draw a circle that passes through the two vanishing points—use it to construct the perspective field of view. The intersection of the perspective field and the vertical line through the center of vision (the line of sight) locates the station point (SP).

The perspective field of view is the interface between our visual experience of the world and the geometry of the linear perspective. The vanishing points for the horizontal edges of an object within our visual field can fall anywhere along the perceived horizon line from directly in front of us to the limits of our peripheral vision. The perspective field of view encompasses the two vanishing points for a specific rectilinear object within our visual field or the one vanishing point in a one-point perspective as shown above.

Center of Vision (CV): The point created by the orthogonal (90°) intersection of the line of sight and the horizon line on the picture plane. The CV in the example above is near the circle's center.

Diagrams and text (both pages): Courtesy
of William R. Benedict, Assistant Professor
California Polytechnic State University
College of Architecture & Environmental Design
San Luis Obispo, CA

VERTICAL VANISHING LINES

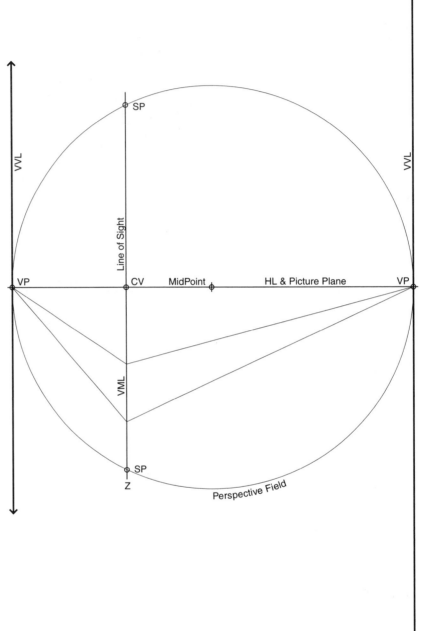

Vertical Vanishing Lines

Vertical vanishing lines (VVL) must be drawn through both vanishing points (VP). These are the vanishing lines for all planes and lines parallel to the vertical faces of the cube. We now have the information necessary to locate the 45° diagonal vanishing points for the two vertical surfaces of the cube or any surfaces parallel to them. The 45° diagonal vanishing points are the points to which the two sets of 45° lines lying on a particular plane will vanish. They are located on the vanishing line for the plane.

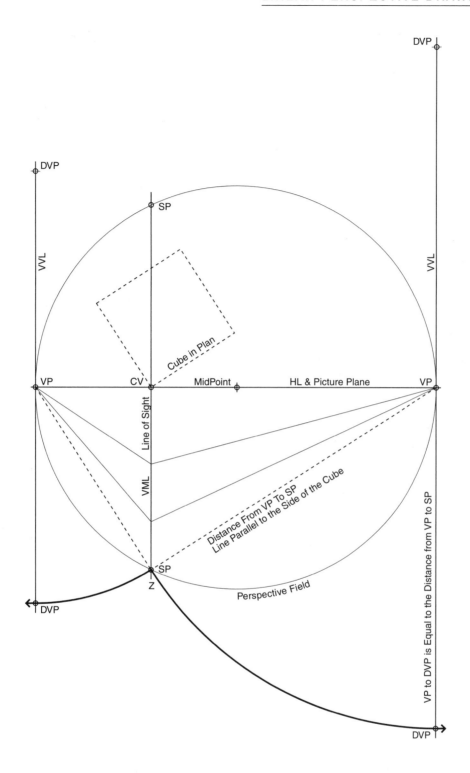

Constructing Diagonal Vanishing Points

Transfer the distance from each VP to the SP to the vertical vanishing line passing through the respective VP. This can be done with a compass, as shown in the illustration, or with a scale. The 45° diagonal vanishing points can be generated for each plane—one will be above and one below their respective vanishing points. One diagonal vanishing point for each plane is often all that is necessary for construction, as indicated in the illustration.

Diagrams and text (both pages): Courtesy
of William R. Benedict, Assistant Professor
California Polytechnic State University
College of Architecture & Environmental Design
San Luis Obispo, CA

CONSTRUCTING CUBE FACES

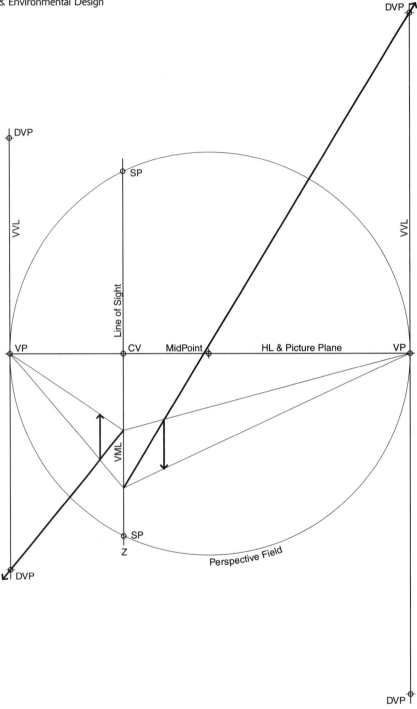

Constructing Cube Faces

Draw lines from the DVPs to one end of the known vertical edge of the cube. Use the DVP that is above or below the VP for horizontal lines on the same plane. The diagonal lines are 45° lines and therefore their intersection with a vanishing edge transfers the length of the vertical edge to the horizontal—it defines a square on each surface. Draw vertical lines through the intersections to establish the vertical faces of the cube.

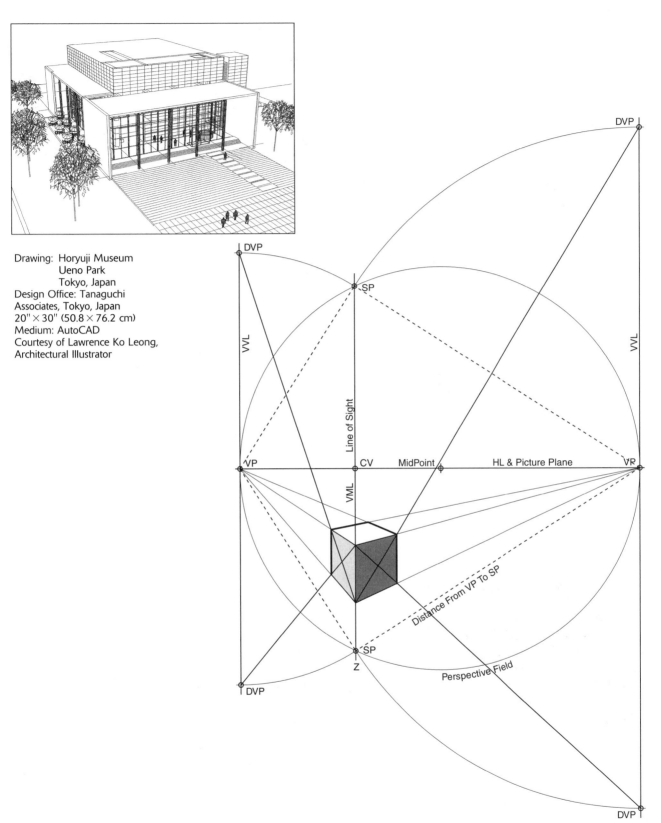

Drawing: Horyuji Museum
                Ueno Park
                Tokyo, Japan
Design Office: Tanaguchi
Associates, Tokyo, Japan
20" × 30" (50.8 × 76.2 cm)
Medium: AutoCAD
Courtesy of Lawrence Ko Leong,
Architectural Illustrator

CUBE COMPLETION

Cube Completion

Vanish lines to define the top face of the cube and add line weight and value to complete the cube. Additional cubes can be generated using the diagonal.

MEASURING POINTS

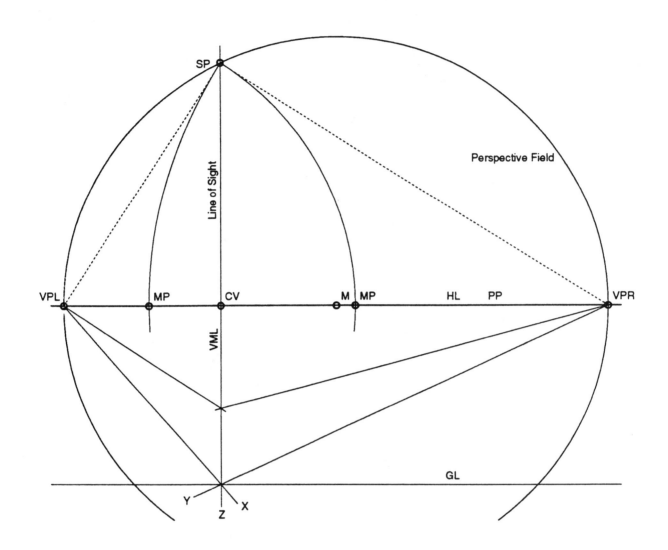

Cubes as well as other geometric forms can be constructed simply using **measuring points**. Measuring points (MP) are the points used to transfer scaled dimensions from the horizontal measuring line to lines vanishing through the intersection of the horizontal and vertical measuring lines. Proportional sizes can be transferred with the measuring points from any horizontal line to vanished lines passing through the intersection of that horizontal line and a vertical line. Measuring points offer an additional way of introducing dimensions into a perspective. The process begins with the construction of the horizon line, ground line, vanishing points, midpoint, and the perspective field of view, etc. Transfer the distances from the VPR to SP and VPL to SP down to the horizon line. This can be done with a compass as shown in the illustration or with a scale. The points on the horizon line resulting from this transfer are the measuring points for the perspective setup.

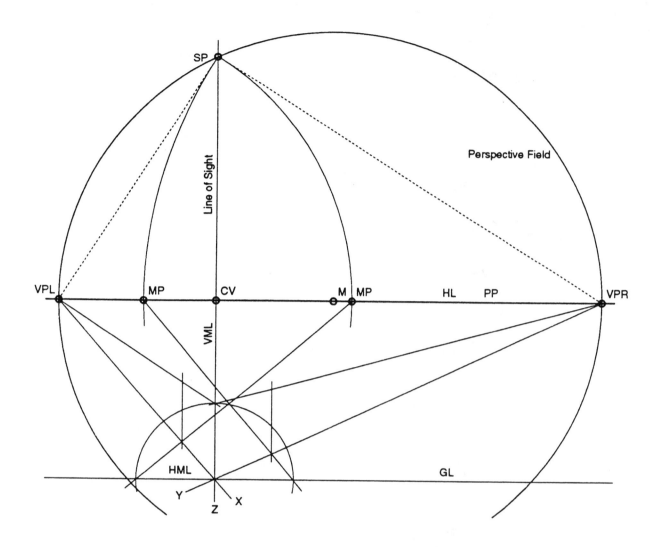

Entering Dimensions

Enter the horizontal dimensions that you want to transfer into the perspective. The dimensions are entered on a horizontal measuring line (HML). In the example, an arc is used to transfer the height of the cube to either side of its existing lead edge and vertical measuring line.

A horizontal measuring line (HML) may be located anywhere along any vertical line within the perspective. The only requirements are that the vertical line can be used to establish the measurement scale or is a vertical measuring line (VML) and that a pair of lines parallel to the *X* and *Y* axes be drawn through the intersection of the vertical line and the horizontal measuring line.

Constructing Cube Faces

The measuring points are now used to transfer the dimensions from the horizontal measuring line to the *X* and *Y* axes or lines parallel to them. The intersection of the line drawn from the dimension on the HML to the appropriate MP with the axis transfers the dimension into the perspective. Draw a vertical line through the intersections to define the two faces.

Note: When transferring a dimension back into the perspective—when making it smaller—you use the MP on the opposite side of the vertical line. When transferring it forward—making it bigger—you use the MP on the same side.

Diagrams and text (both pages): Courtesy
of William R. Benedict, Assistant Professor
California Polytechnic State University
College of Architecture & Environmental Design
San Luis Obispo, CA

MEASURING POINT SYSTEM

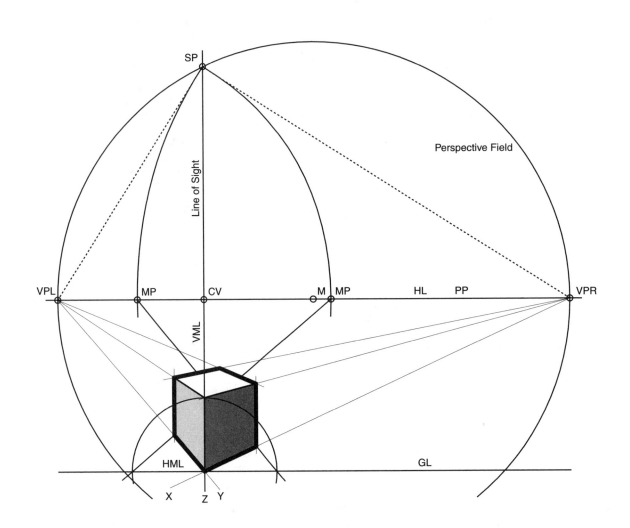

Cube Completion

Vanish lines to define the top surface of the cube and add line weight and value to complete the cube. This approach brings together the two halves of the measuring point system—the diagonal vanishing points and the measuring points. Once the initial volume is established, any combination of vanishing points and dividing, multiplying, and transferring techniques can be employed along with the measuring points to develop the perspective. The goal is to make choices that complete the drawing as efficiently as possible.

This illustration brings together the basic elements of the measuring point system. Notice, as stated earlier, that the arc defining the diagonal vanishing points is the same one that defines the measuring points. The complexity of the drawing makes a good case for introducing the concepts in some systematic and gradual manner to avoid being caught in the web of lines and concepts.

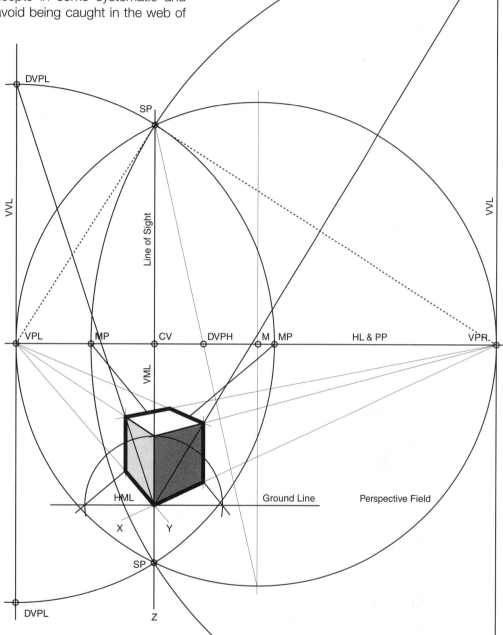

MEASURING POINT SYSTEM

The link between the diagonal vanishing points and the measuring points is that they are both established with the same dimension. You can employ the diagonal vanishing points, measuring points, and multiplication, division, and transfer techniques in any perspective construction. The choice as to which to use should depend on the strategy that will produce the desired results with the greatest efficiency.

MEASURING POINTS AND OBLIQUE LINES

The vertical lines in the diagram below are parallel. In reality, these lines would begin to converge to a third vanishing point far below the horizon line, as seen in the illustration to the right (see pp. 270–273).

Drawing: National Audubon
Society's National
Headquarters, New York City
9" × 13" (22.9 × 33 cm)
Medium: Wax-based pencil
Courtesy of Paul Sevenson Oles,
Architectural Illustrator
Croxton Collaborative Architects

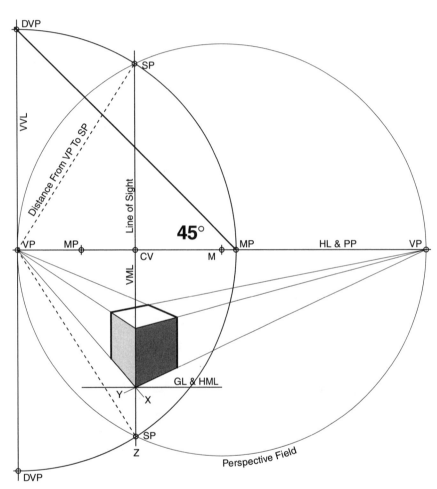

Measuring Points and Oblique Lines

If you combine and examine the construction process for determining the location of the diagonal vanishing points for the faces of the cube and its measuring points you will realize that a 45° line will connect the corresponding MPs and DVPs. This means that if the location of the measuring points is known you can construct the 45° diagonal vanishing point by drawing the vertical vanishing lines and then extending 45° lines through the measuring points until they intersect their respective vertical vanishing lines (the one farther away).

The construction of the measuring points is necessary before this technique can be employed. The concept works for sloped planes whose edges are parallel to the X or Y axis. The vanishing point for the inclined edges or lines can be found by drawing a line at the corresponding slope through the appropriate measuring point until it intersects with the corresponding vertical vanishing line.

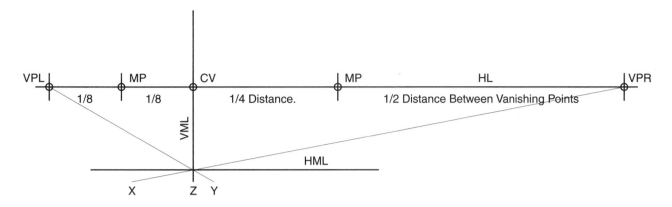

Measuring Points-30°/60° Shortcut

One of the liabilities of the measuring point system is the space and scale of instruments required to construct the framework—especially the diagonal vanishing points. This can be overcome by making a small drawing of the setup to establish the relative dimensions within the framework and then enlarging it proportionally to support the actual construction of the perspective.

The 30°/60° setup provides another way around the problem. Perspectives in which the plan is oriented in a 30°/60° relationship to the picture plane are common and produce a simple set of geometric relationships between the vanishing points, measuring points, and center of the drawing above. By drawing the horizon line, establishing the vanishing points, and subdividing the distance between them accordingly you can quickly generate the full component of information necessary to construct an accurate perspective framework at any scale. The process simply divides the distance between the vanishing points into successively smaller halves.

Remember that the distance from a vanishing point to the farther measuring point is equal to the distance from that vanishing point to the diagonal vanishing points above and below it on the vertical vanishing line.

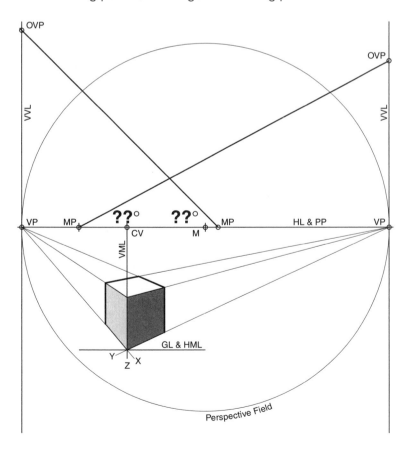

Diagrams and text: Courtesy of
William R. Benedict, Assistant Professor
California Polytechnic State University
College of Architecture & Environmental Design
San Luis Obispo, CA

MEASURING POINTS—30°/60° SHORTCUT

Diagrams and text (both pages): Courtesy
of William R. Benedict, Assistant Professor
California Polytechnic State University
College of Architecture & Environmental Design
San Luis Obispo, CA

ESTABLISHING SCALE IN TWO-POINT PERSPECTIVES *(vertical, left margin)*

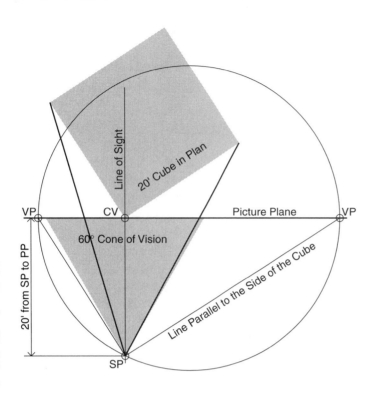

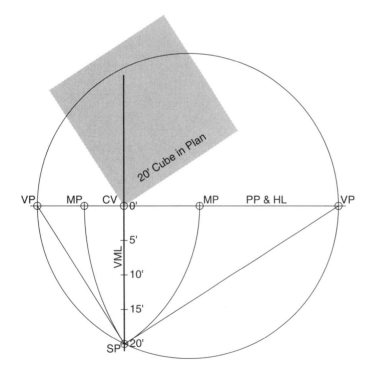

ESTABLISHING SCALE IN TWO-POINT PERSPECTIVES

When the measuring point method is used to construct a perspective using a plan drawing, the scale of the perspective is established by the scale used to construct the drawing (plan, picture plane [PP], center of vision [CV], station point [SP], etc.). The goal is to make the perspective as large as possible while keeping the image projected on the picture plane within a 60° cone of vision. The problem comes when we want to draw a perspective without or before there is a plan. The question is: What rule of thumb can be used to develop a two-point perspective framework for sketching given only the general dimensions of the form or space? The rule of thumb can be found in the illustration to the left. Notice that when the distance from the station point to the picture plane is equal to the horizontal dimension of the subject, the projected image just fits within the 60° cone of vision. This 1:1 relationship is the same one noted in the section on one-point perspective. The 1:1 relationship means that to draw a perspective of a 20' wide object, the station point is located 20' back from the picture plane, assuming that the object also touches the picture plane as shown. More generally, the greatest horizontal dimension of the subject establishes the distance from the station point to the picture plane and produces a perspective that will fall within a zone of acceptable distortion.

Basic Setup

Draw a horizon line (HL) and vanishing points (VP) and locate the center of vision (CV), station point (SP), and measuring points (MP). The location of the vanishing points is arbitrarily established to fit on the sheet of paper being used—the layout has no inherent scale. Given the 1:1 ratio as a guide, scale can be introduced by making the distance from the station point to the picture plane equal to the greatest horizontal dimension of the object being drawn (20' in the example). The distance between the SP and the PP is proportionally divided along the VML to create a scale for the drawing.

Ground Line and Dimensions

The proportional scale created along the VML is used to locate the ground line (GL), which is also a horizontal measuring line (HML). In the example, the ground line is located 5 feet below the horizon line to create an eye-level perspective. The scale created on the VML is then transferred along the VML and HML to locate the needed dimensions.

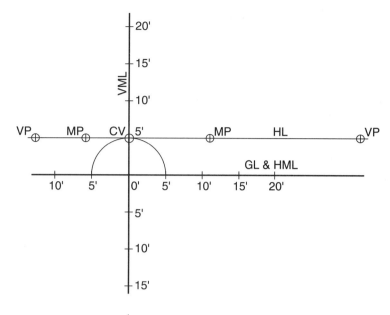

Perspective Construction

Once the dimensions have been established, the perspective can be developed using the measuring point and other construction techniques previously discussed. The resultant drawing will fall within an acceptable zone of distortion. Note that the cube extends vertically beyond the 60° cone of vision for an eye level perspective and, therefore, if the subject is significantly taller than it is wide, then its height should be used to establish the scale. The 1:1 rule of thumb must be adjusted in response to the subject and the desired communication.

Note: The passing of the vertical edges of the cube through the measuring points is coincidental.

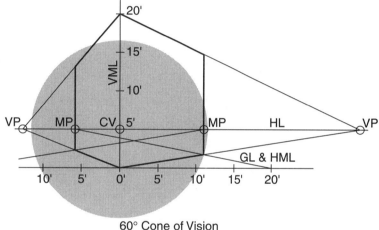

60° Cone of Vision

The Hypotenuse

The points identified as SP, CV, and VP define two right triangles whose hypotenuse is VP-SP (see gray triangle). The hypotenuse establishes a proportional relationship between the two other sides of a triangle. Therefore, if a line parallel to the hypotenuse is drawn through the center point of one side it will pass through the center of the other side as illustrated. This is important because it will allow the establishment of scale in some two-point perspectives without requiring us to locate the station point.

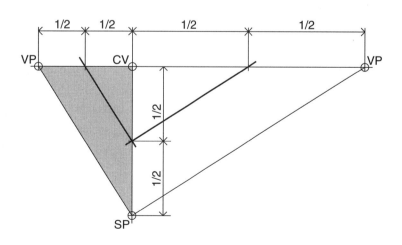

ESTABLISHING SCALE IN TWO-POINT PERSPECTIVES

Drawing: Boston Ballet Building
Boston, Massachusetts
Medium: Watercolor
Architect: Graham Gund Architect

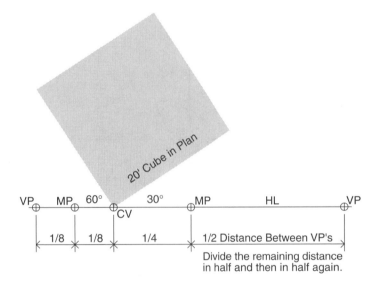

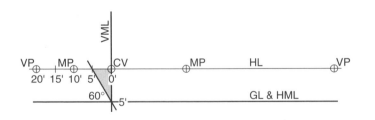

Divide the remaining distance in half and then in half again.

30°/60° Shortcut Perspective

Draw a horizon line and locate the vanishing points to fit on the sheet of paper being used. Locate the measuring points and center of vision for a 30/60° perspective using the proportions as illustrated and described in the section on the 30/60° shortcut method.

Establishing and Transferring the Scale

Given this approach, there is no station point or line that connects it to the picture plane. In its place the distance from a vanishing point to the center of vision will be used. Given the 1:1 ratio, scale can be introduced by making the distance from a vanishing point to the center of vision equal to the greatest horizontal dimension of the object being drawn (20' in the example). The distance is then proportionally divided to produce useful dimensions (e.g., the distance from the horizon line to the ground line). Next the dimension must be transferred to the vertical measuring line that passes through the center of vision. This is accomplished by drawing a line parallel to the hypotenuse of the corresponding SP, CV, VP triangle through the known dimension so that it intersects the vertical measuring line. For a 30/60° perspective the hypotenuse will be at either 30° or 60° (the 60° triangle is being used in the example). In the illustration, a five-foot distance is being transferred to locate the ground line and establish an eye-level perspective.

Diagrams and text (both pages): Courtesy of William R. Benedict, Assistant Professor California Polytechnic State University College of Architecture & Environmental Design San Luis Obispo, CA

Drawing: Scripps Memorial Hospital
        View of Entrance
        Chula Vista, California
23" × 24" (58.2 × 61 cm)
Medium: Ink on Mylar
Courtesy of Perkins & Will
Associate Architect James A. Leary
Architecture & Planning

Dimensions

The dimensions transferred to the vertical measuring line establish a scale for the drawing. These dimensions can then be transferred along the vertical and horizontal measuring lines to locate the needed dimensions.

Perspective Construction

Once the dimensions have been established, the perspective can be developed using the measuring point and other construction techniques previously discussed. If it is desirable to have the perspective fall more completely within the cone of vision, then the controlling dimension is set to something greater than the width of the subject (e.g., 30 feet).

A standard 6' figure is excellent for sizing objects in a perspective. In the subsequent chapter on perspective view development, note that all the views start with a horizon line and a scale figure that seems appropriate to begin the blockout of the drawing. There is no "scale" other than the assumed 6' figure.

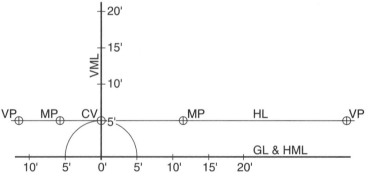

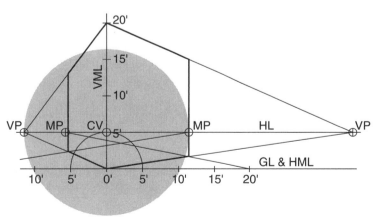

60° Cone of Vision

ESTABLISHING SCALE IN TWO-POINT PERSPECTIVES

TWO-POINT INTERIOR – OFFICE METHOD

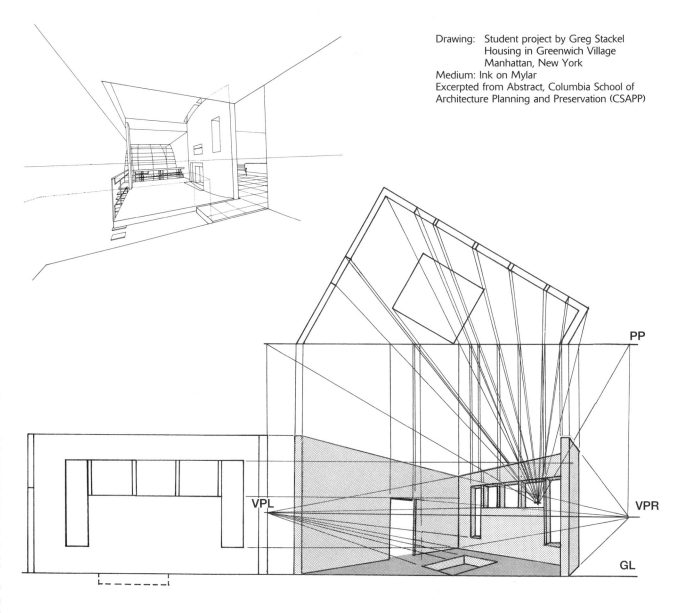

Drawing: Student project by Greg Stackel
Housing in Greenwich Village
Manhattan, New York
Medium: Ink on Mylar
Excerpted from Abstract, Columbia School of
Architecture Planning and Preservation (CSAPP)

Let's examine the perspective plan-elevation method (pp. 202–204) again. These perspectives are commonly constructed for both two-point exterior and interior perspectives. The method is basically the same in both cases. This method can also be applied to exterior and interior one-point perspectives. Choose a station point that best describes the important interior elements and the feeling you would like to convey. Frank Lloyd Wright favored the two-point interior view, which is essentially a one-point made slightly oblique to the picture plane, resulting in a very long second vanishing point (see p. 397). Also avoid placing the eye-level horizon line in a position where it coincides with any horizontal structural element (i.e., the window sill shown above).

(1) Select locations of SP, HL, and PP based on the perspective desired.
(2) Select a PP that will cut both walls of an interior space and will intersect corners of important or major interior elements.
(3) Construct the appropriate parallel lines to find vanishing points.
(4) Transfer true heights from the elevation view to vertical tracers from the interior wall intersections.
(5) Converge the wall planes to their appropriate vanishing points and subsequently construct the details of the interior space.

Compare this method to the one-point procedure (pp. 252–253, 260–261).

Drawing: Student Project
           by Quincey Nixon
Ferry Terminal, New York City
Medium: Ink on Mylar
Excerpted from Abstract, Columbia
School of Architecture Planning and
Preservation (CSAPP)

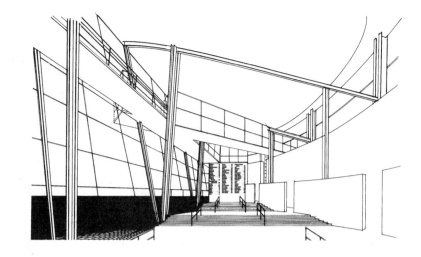

The station point location for this interior perspective produces an angle of view that puts equal emphasis on both left and right walls.

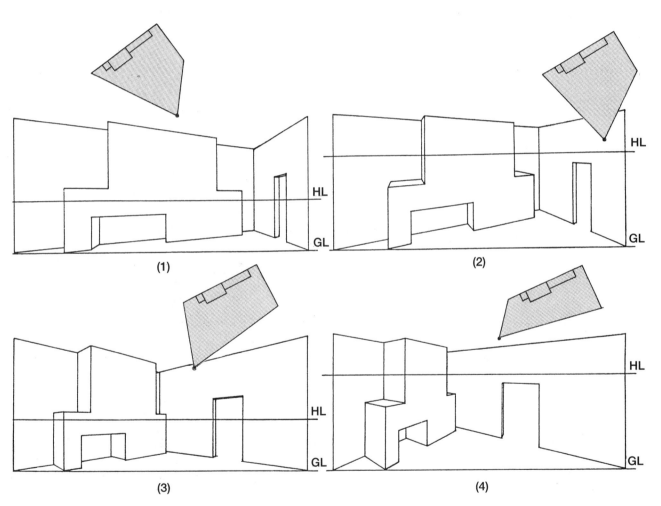

(1)

(2)

(3)

(4)

TWO-POINT INTERIOR—PICTORIAL EFFECT

In any interior perspective, visual emphasis on the left or right wall is governed by the **variable station point.** The station point also dictates whether the wall vanishing points fall within or out of the drawing. Note how the images of the fireplace and the door change as one moves from being close to the wall with the door (**1**) to being close to the fireplace wall (**4**). Also note that the higher horizon line in (**2**) and (**4**) allows the viewer to see more floor and less ceiling (above normal eye level).

TWO-POINT INTERIOR—EXAMPLES

These interior two-point perspectives have a greater sense of **enclosure** than the interior on the previous page simply because a **third** wall or third side is included. This third element has its own vanishing point.

Drawing: Master Bath
           Westview Grande Condominium
           Indian Shores, Florida
5" × 4" (12.7 × 10.2 cm)
Medium: Computer imaging; Macintosh system using Strata Studio Pro and Adobe Photoshop. Completely computer generated.
Courtesy of Robert L. Montry,
Media IV Design & Marketing Services, Inc., Largo, FL

Drawing: Seagram Museum
         Waterloo, Ontario, Canada
Courtesy of Barton Myers Associates Architects/Planner

Drawing: Carnegie Mellon Research Institute
Pittsburgh, Pennsylvania
Courtesy of Peter D. Eisenman, FAIA
of Eisenman Architects

The interior to the left is primarily a one-point perspective. It is modified by an additional wall element which has its own vanishing point. The lobby below has essentially only one vanishing point, but the interior corridor in the background is curvilinear and has multiple vanishing points. These drawings can be called **modified one-points** in the sense that they have one vanishing point in the picture area even though the total drawing is a multipoint perspective.

Drawing: GSA-IRS
Competition project
original size: 18" × 17" (45.7 × 43.2 cm) (approx.)
Scale used: ⅛" and ¼"=1'0"
Medium: Pen and ink with colored pencil on vellum paper
Perkins & Will Architects
Courtesy of Manuel Avila, Architectural Illustrator

INTERIOR EXAMPLES

In a one-point persective, a group of lines will vanish to one point and this group will not be parallel to the picture plane. All vertical lines remain vertical and all horizontal lines remain horizontal in the constructed perspective. The plan and the elevation of the room should always be traced to obtain exact dimensions.

ONE-POINT INTERIOR—OFFICE METHOD

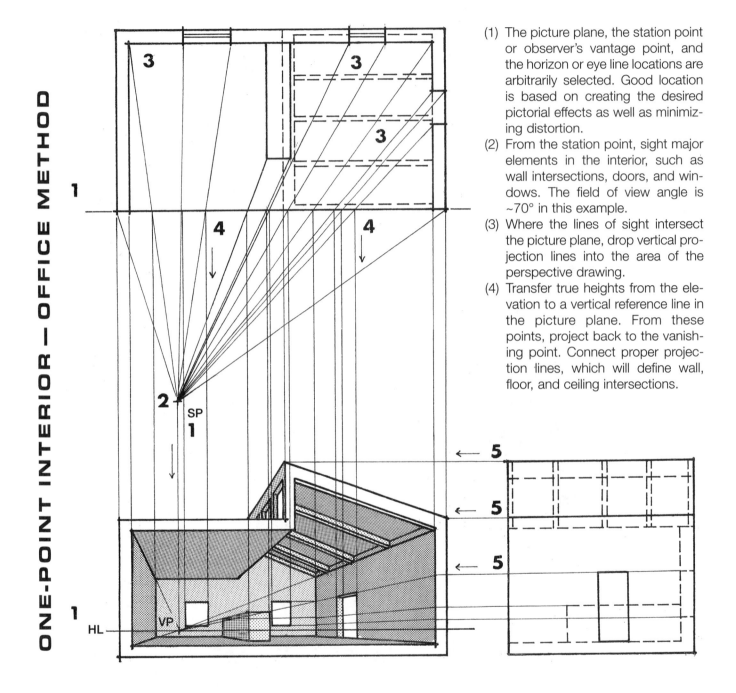

(1) The picture plane, the station point or observer's vantage point, and the horizon or eye line locations are arbitrarily selected. Good location is based on creating the desired pictorial effects as well as minimizing distortion.

(2) From the station point, sight major elements in the interior, such as wall intersections, doors, and windows. The field of view angle is ~70° in this example.

(3) Where the lines of sight intersect the picture plane, drop vertical projection lines into the area of the perspective drawing.

(4) Transfer true heights from the elevation to a vertical reference line in the picture plane. From these points, project back to the vanishing point. Connect proper projection lines, which will define wall, floor, and ceiling intersections.

As with two-point perspectives, the **office** or **common method** is frequently used for one-point perspectives. A one-point is always characterized by at least one plane within the object being parallel to the picture plane. This plane or these planes are always perpendicular to the line of sight of the observer. The picture plane makes a sectional cut through the building or object. See discussion on pages 256–259.

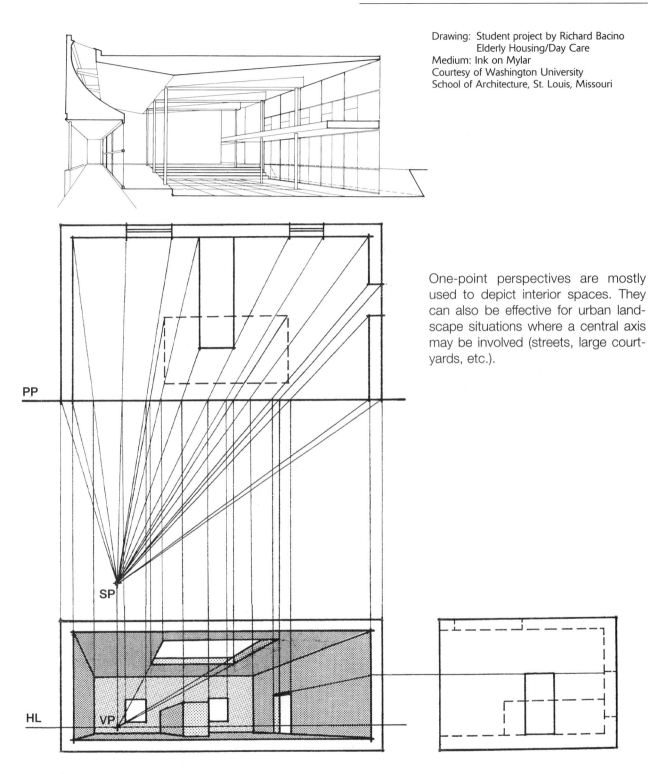

Drawing: Student project by Richard Bacino
Elderly Housing/Day Care
Medium: Ink on Mylar
Courtesy of Washington University
School of Architecture, St. Louis, Missouri

One-point perspectives are mostly used to depict interior spaces. They can also be effective for urban land-scape situations where a central axis may be involved (streets, large court-yards, etc.).

ONE-POINT INTERIOR – OFFICE METHOD

The placement of the vanishing point will govern what one sees in the interior space. If the Vanishing Point is high, very little ceiling will show; much of the floor will show. If the Vanishing Point is near the center, an equal amount of ceiling and floor will show. If the Vanishing Point is low, much of the ceiling and very little of the floor will show. Moving the Vanishing Point to the right or to the left on the back wall has a similar effect on the side walls; that is, if near the left, more of the right wall will show, and if near the right, more of the left wall will show.

GRID IN PARALLEL PERSPECTIVE

Drawing: Kiahuna Resort, Kauai, Hawaii
Medium: Ink on Mylar, 14" × 11" (35.6 × 27.9 cm)
Bull Stockwell & Allen Architects
Courtesy of Chun/Ishimaru & Assoc.

Design professionals frequently study interior space usage. An efficient method for locating interior furniture within a plan grid setting is the **measuring line and point method.** This method has the advantage of not needing a plan and elevation as in the office method; it also has the advantage of allowing one to start with the approximate size of perspective one desires. The primary goal of this method is to divide a line in perspective into equal or unequal parts. True heights are measured in the picture plane and projected back along the walls. True widths are similarly projected back on the floor. Chairs, tables, and lighting elements can quickly be positioned (see opposite page) and the drawing susequently rendered as shown above.

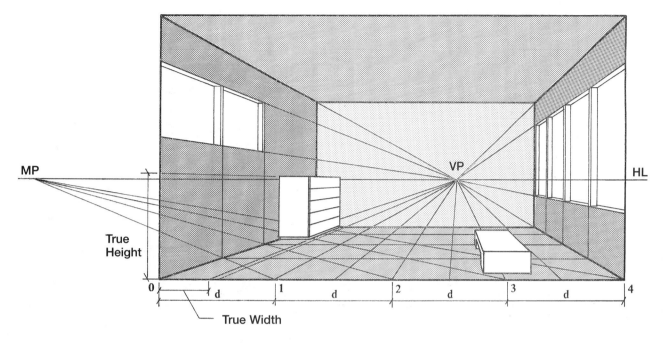

These steps explain how to generate a grid in parallel perspective. Acute perspective foreshortening will occur if one moves the measuring point too close to the vanishing point along the horizon line. A general rule is to keep the width of the drawing smaller than the distance between the measuring point and the vanishing points. The drawing above slightly violates this rule but still is within the limits of a correctly foreshortened perspective.

(1) A horizontal line is drawn through point **0**, which in this case is a part of the room interior.
(2) Decide on the relative depth locations of elements (mullions) in the perspective. Select a measuring point (MP) on the horizon line and connect to outside point **4**.
(3) The measuring line at the ground line where the section cut is taken is divided into *n* equal increments *(d)*, the number *n* being based on how many mullions or other interior elements need to be spaced in perspective (in this case, four).
(4) Horizontal lines can be located in perspective at the intersection of the measuring-point diagonals and the line from *0* to the vanishing point.
(5) Complete the grid by generating vanishing parallels from points **1**, **2**, **3**, and **4** to the vanishing point.
(6) The diagonal line from **0** can also be divided unequally using the same principles in order to locate furniture or other interior elements.

The addition of wall, floor, and ceiling thicknesses to the plan grid measuring point drawing on page 255 would create a section cut, with the picture plane exhibiting a three-dimensional space called a perspective section. As with measuring point methods, no projection from a plan veiw is needed and thus excess drawing space is not needed. Construction is easier.

CONSTRUCTING A PERSPECTIVE SECTION

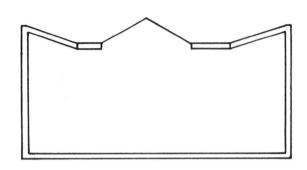

(1) Determine where the section will be taken.

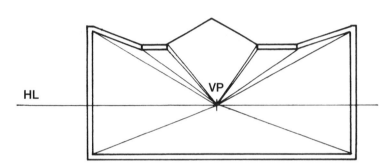

(2) Establish the locations of the horizon line and the vanishing point. Project vanishing corner lines from the sectional corners.

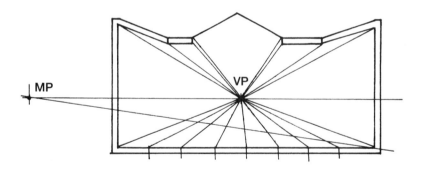

(3) Mark equal increments along the sectional floor line. Select an arbitrary measuring point (MP). The farther away the measuring point is placed from the vanishing point on the horizon line, the less the distortion. Draw a diagonal line from the measuring point to the farthest lower corner.

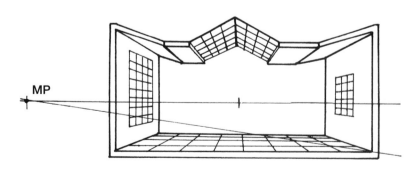

(4) At the intersections of the diagonal line and the receding floor plane lines, construct horizontal lines that divide the floor, wall, and ceiling in perspective.

Generating a perspective from a building section sometimes has the drawback of exaggerating the apparent length of spaces (see p. 258).

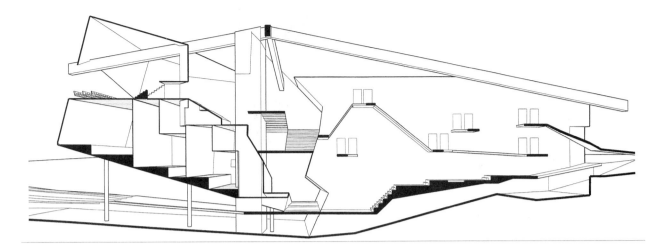

Drawing: Wagrammer Strasse, Vienna, Austria
Medium: Computer-generated
Courtesy of Eric Owen Moss Architects

The perspective view above has a shallow depth of field. The perspective view (right) creates its own frame with a profile line which defines the section plane. Perspective sections are useful in making the often difficult to read section more communicative. Note that the vanishing point is placed within the major space. Avoid placing the vanishing point in smaller secondary spaces like the basement level shown to the right.

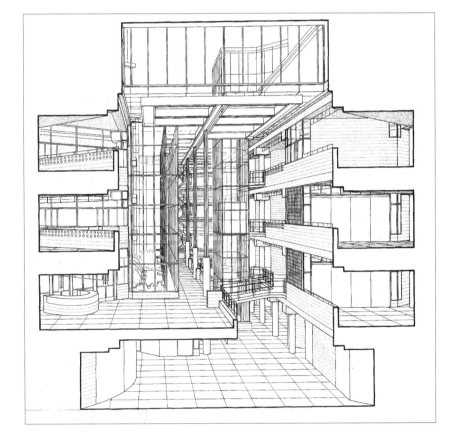

Drawing: Ministry of Social Welfare and Employment
                The Hague, The Netherlands
Medium: Ink on calque, 80 × 81 cm (31.5" × 31.9")
Drawn by R. Rietveld
Courtesy of Herman Hertzberger, Architect

PERSPECTIVE SECTIONS

Competition Drawing: U.S. Embassy, Berlin, Germany
Garden Area
Courtesy of Bohlin Cywinski Jackson
Joint venture with Sverdrup Facilities

PERSPECTIVE SECTIONS

Drawing: J. B. Speed Art Museum addition
Louisville, Kentucky
Courtesy of GBQC Architects

Drawing: Class of 1927/Clapp Hall
Princeton University, Princeton, New Jersey
Medium: Ink on Mylar, 24" × 24" (61 cm × 61 cm)
Courtesy of Koetter, Kim & Associates, Inc.
Architects and Urban Designers

A **perspective section** adds a dramatic effect to the two-dimensional section. The receding third dimension reveals the pictorial quality of the interior spaces. The sectional perspective is more commonly seen as a one-point perspective. A two-point sectional perspective as shown to the left is also possible but not frequently used. Emphasis should always be placed on the interior details of the cut spaces as opposed to the structural details within the sectional cuts.

The pictorial or "real" view quality is a perspective section's strength; its weakness is that it does not convey the overall organization of spaces as well as in a plan oblique (axonometric).

Drawing: Residential/Commercial building, Seaside, Florida
30" × 24" (76.2 × 61 cm)
Medium: Prismacolor on blueprint paper
Courtesy of Machado and Silvetti Associates
Rodolfo Machado and Jorge Silvetti

As with shadows cast within the section view (p. 343), shadows cast in perspective sections as shown to the left and in the Berlin U.S. Embassy (facing page) add depth and a three-dimensional quality.

PERSPECTIVE SECTIONS

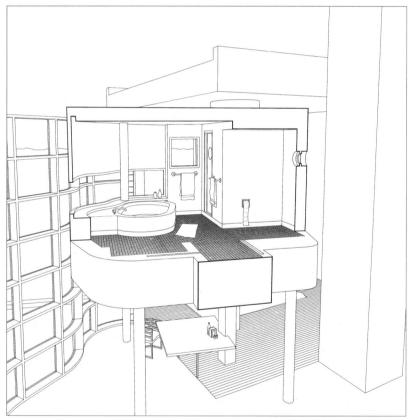

Drawing: Martinelli residence, Roxbury, Connecticut, 1989
Medium: Ink, 24" × 24" (61 × 61 cm)
Courtesy of Anthony Ames, Architect

Horizontal and vertical cuts are made in the master bathroom in this perspective drawing showing its location in a cloud like form on columns, hovering above the dining area.
[ARCHITECT'S STATEMENT]

Perspective sections delineate the structural profile of a building. If the purpose of the section is to show spatial relationships, then keep accessories (people, furniture, etc.) to a minimum.

PLAN/ELEVATION—ONE-POINT

Drawing: Museum of Modern Art, Frankfurt, Germany
Medium: Ink
Courtesy of Hans Hollein, Architekt

Other than the use of the measuring point method and the perspective section method, a grid in parallel perpsective can be constructed using a plan view and elevation heights. In this example, you are given rectilinear slabs and a circular pond drawn to a specific scale (scale and heights not shown).

(1) Draw both the plan grid and the perspective grid. Construct lines to the vanishing point to see how grid lines in plan converge in perspective.
(2) Find where the objects in plan intersect the picture plane.
(3) Establish a section image and project through the critical points to the vanishing points. Find corner points of objects by sighting corresponding plan points *(a)*.
(4) Draw the completed perspective image of the first plan object selected (in this case a rectilinear slab).

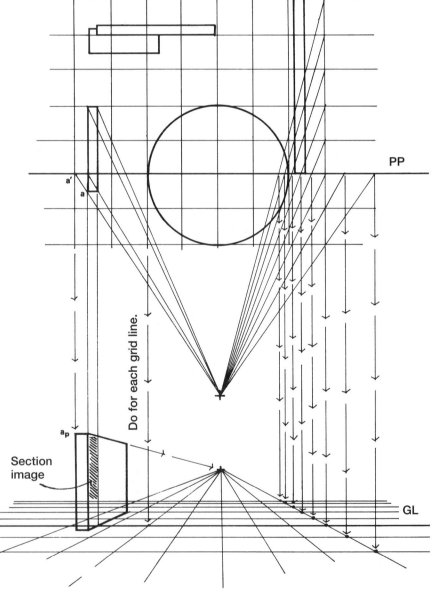

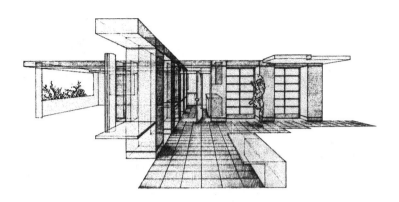

Drawing: The Rittenhouse square apartment
Philadelphia, Pennsylvania
Medium: Ink
Courtesy of Wesley Wei, AIA, Wesley Wei Architects

(5) Follow the same procedure to complete the other rectilinear objects in the perspective.

(6) For the pond, enclose the circle within a square. Divide the circle into quarter circles. Sight critical points *k, l, m,* and *n* and project picture plane intersections into the perspective image of these same points. Use a french curve and construct the pond (takes the form of an ellipse).

Hand-drafted grids are useful for constructing both one- and two-point perspectives. With the development of perspective charts and especially computer-aided drafting, the time factor for construction has been reduced immensely.

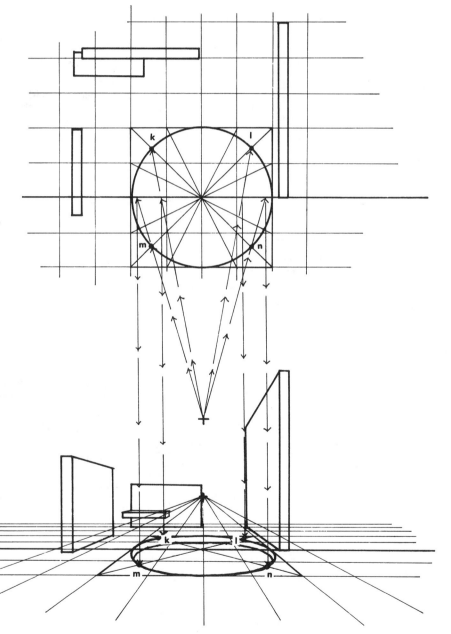

PLAN/ELEVATION—ONE POINT

Drawing: Student project by Howard Fineman
            Augusta City Hall
Medium: Ink on Mylar
Courtesy of Washington University School of Architecture,
St. Louis, MO

GRID IN PARALLEL PERSPECTIVE

Plan view of grid

1$_{PL}$ 2$_{PL}$ **PP**

45° diagonal line

SP

VP

2$_P$

1$_P$ HL

GL

The above interior one-point places a strong visual emphasis on the left wall and the ceiling. This is because the observer is closer to the right wall. The location of the horizon line can be manipulated to emphasize either the ceiling or the floor. The manipulation zone ranges approximately from 4' to 6' above the ground. Depth enhancement is achieved by adding scaled figures.

Notation for diagram (left):

1$_{PL}$–plan view point 1
2$_{PL}$–plan view point 2
1$_P$–perspective view pt. 1
2$_P$–perspective view pt. 2

This quick procedure simply utilizes 45° diagonal plan lines from the station point. This results in an equilateral (45°) triangle. The length of the bisector from the station point will always be equal to the distance from points **1** or **2** to the picture plane intersection point. The diagonal line in perspective passes through the lower left or right corners of the picture plane. Its intersection with converging vanishing lines on the ground plane produces all the needed horizontal grid lines in perspective.

Drawing: Triton Museum of Art, Santa Clara,
California
14.5" × 9' (36.8 × 22.9 cm)
Medium: Pencil on vellum
Courtesy of Rosekrans and Broder Inc., Architects

This one-point has an excellent field of view. Don't be afraid to step back when attempting to depict an interior space; most problems in distortion come from being too close to the picture plane. With interior one-points it is essential to give the feeling that you are part of the viewed space. This requires good judgment in cropping interior features on the ground plane (see pp. 396 and 343).

Using 45° diagonals, what will happen when the station point is moved? The station point location will affect the corresponding point location on the horizon line (and thus the picture plane).

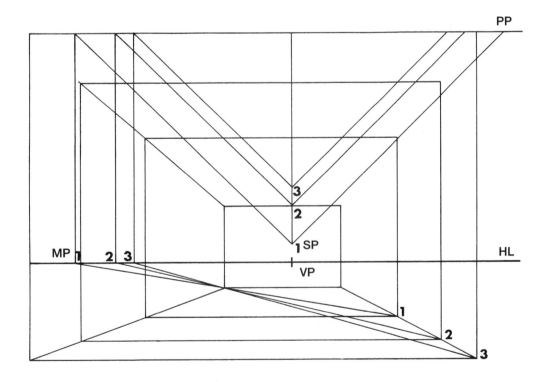

The placement of the points **1**, **2**, and **3** along the horizon line controls perspective distortion of the grid. The farther the point is moved away from the vanishing point (and thus, the picture plane), the less the distortion will be. The field of view also changes as one moves farther away. The observer's view is a much larger area and thus the cone of vision is much greater. Even though the 45° VP is a direct function of the station point distance from the picture plane, it is nevertheless variable, even arbitrary within limits in a one-point perspective.

VARIABLE STATION POINT IN PARALLEL PERSPECTIVE

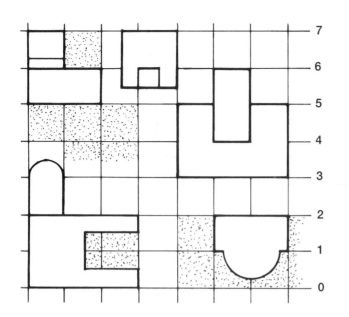

Technically, the terms "bird's-eye" and "aerial" are synonymous.

A grid procedure for bird's-eye perspectives is advantageous when the building complex or urban landscape is in a predominantly regular arrangement. After transposing the elements from plan grid to perspective grid, structural forms can be "eyeballed" and sketched using appropriate heights. The plan grid and perspective grid can be at different scales, but the total number of grid lines must correspond. Relate the plan shown at the left to the selected aerial perspective view shown below. Note that the eight (0 to 7) grid lines correspond.

Foreground building details show better with a low angle of view. A higher angle of view shows orientation and traffic patterns better. The goals and purpose of your illustration will determine the proper station point location.

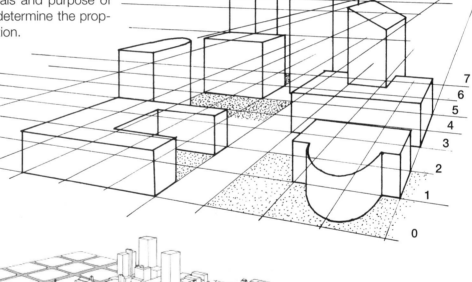

Drawing: Masterplan concept
Phoenix Municipal
Government Center
Phoenix, Arizona
Courtesy of John Schreier,
Barton Myers
Associates, Architects

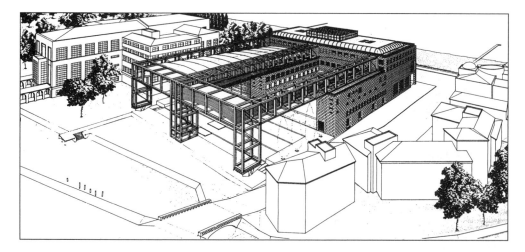

Drawing: A Film Palace
Venice, Italy
Courtesy of Oswald Mathias
Ungers, Architect

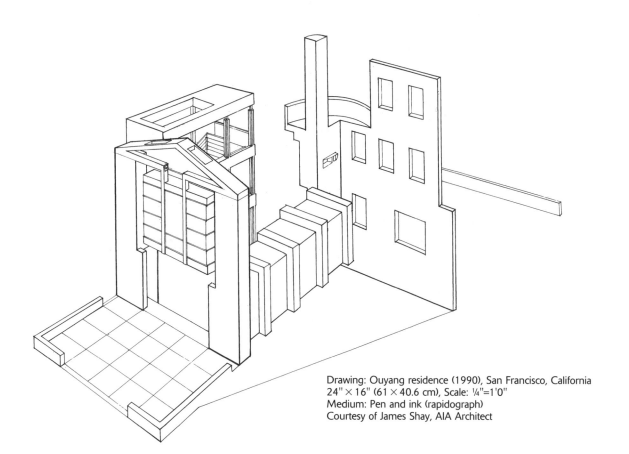

Drawing: Ouyang residence (1990), San Francisco, California
24" × 16" (61 × 40.6 cm), Scale: ¼"=1'0"
Medium: Pen and ink (rapidograph)
Courtesy of James Shay, AIA Architect

BIRD'S-EYE EXAMPLES

This is drawn to show important parts of the house without showing the entire building. This enables the architect to clearly communicate what he or she regards as most important.
[ARCHITECT'S STATEMENT]

Most bird'-eye view perspectives that are slightly above roof level are characterizd by a horizon line that is in the range of 40 to 80 feet above the ground plane. It has the advantage over an eye-level view perspective of revealing the surrounding landscape (trees, group of buildings, townscape, etc.) as well as unexpected roof line details.

CITYSCAPE BIRD'S-EYE VIEW PERSPECTIVE

Drawing: First Street Plaza, Los Angeles, California
Courtesy of First Street Plaza Partners
and TAC, The Architects Collaborative
Renderer: Jim Arp

Large-scale bird's-eye views are frequently used by not only architects but also landscape architects, city planners, urban designers, environmental analysts, and site engineers. In comparing the above bird's-eye perspective to the bird's-eye plan oblique (axonometric) on the facing page, note that the perspective has the advantage of revealing more building facade, whereas the plan oblique has the advantage of showing more of the pedestrian streetscape and the open spaces between buildings.

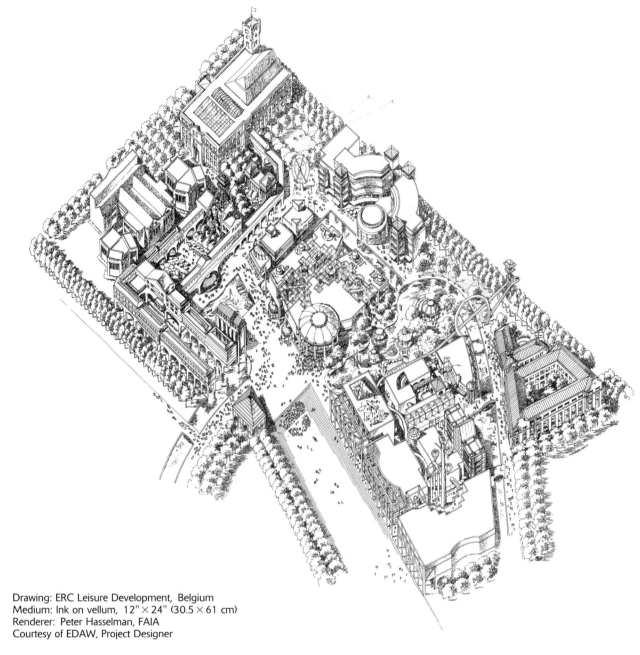

Drawing: ERC Leisure Development, Belgium
Medium: Ink on vellum, 12" × 24" (30.5 × 61 cm)
Renderer: Peter Hasselman, FAIA
Courtesy of EDAW, Project Designer

Bird's-eye plan obliques are similar to steep angled perspectives. Landscaping patterns as well as vehicular and pedestrian circulation patterns usually are more easily visible with an oblique view.

CITYSCAPE BIRD'S-EYE VIEW PLAN OBLIQUE

LOOKING UP AND LOOKING DOWN

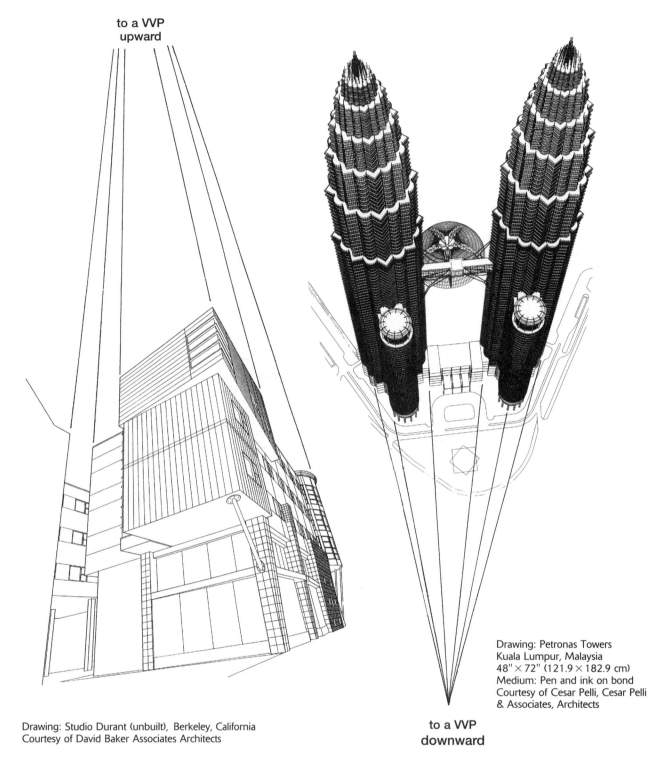

to a VVP
upward

Drawing: Studio Durant (unbuilt), Berkeley, California
Courtesy of David Baker Associates Architects

Drawing: Petronas Towers
Kuala Lumpur, Malaysia
48" × 72" (121.9 × 182.9 cm)
Medium: Pen and ink on bond
Courtesy of Cesar Pelli, Cesar Pelli
& Associates, Architects

to a VVP
downward

Looking up results in an upward convergence of vertical lines; looking down results in downward convergence of vertical lines. A view with upward or downward convergence has the characteristic of a tipped picture plane. The picture plane is inclined at an angle to the ground plane and not perpendicular as with one- and two-point perspectives. The vertical vanishing points above and below are usually placed closer to the ground plane than they normally would be in order to exaggerate the soaring or plunging feeling. See the discussion on three-point perspectives on the subsequent pages.

Any object seen in a three-point perspective is characterized by projection lines, which are extensions of vertical lines in the object converging to a vertical vanishing point (VVP). Note that the ski resort is actually a more than three- (multi) point perspective due to other horizontal lines vanshing left or right (see below).

**to a VVP
upward**

upward convergence

Drawing: Ski Resort
              Avoriaz, France
Courtesy of Jacques LABRO et
Jean-Jacques ORZONI, Architectes

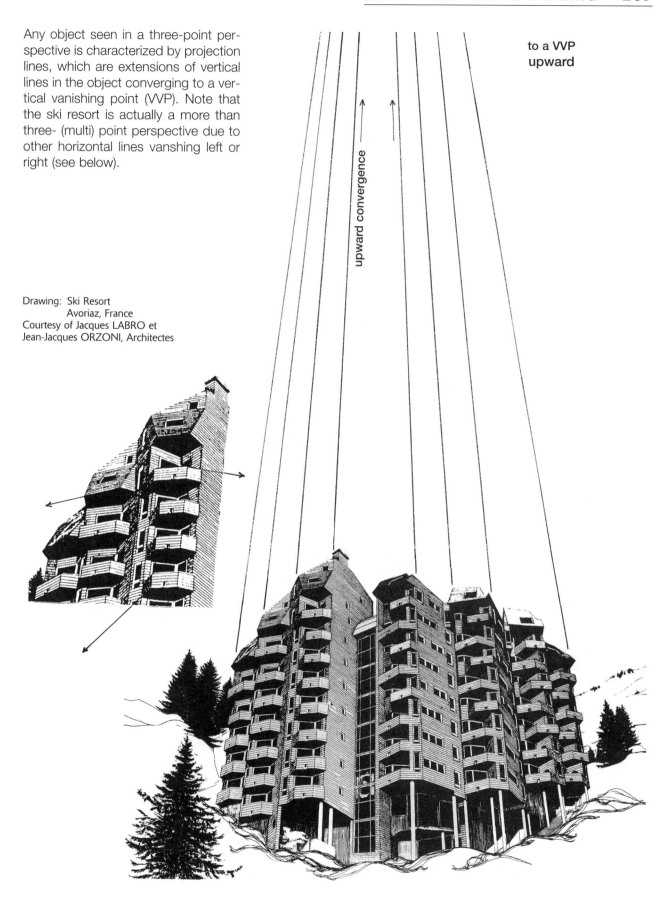

LOOKING UP

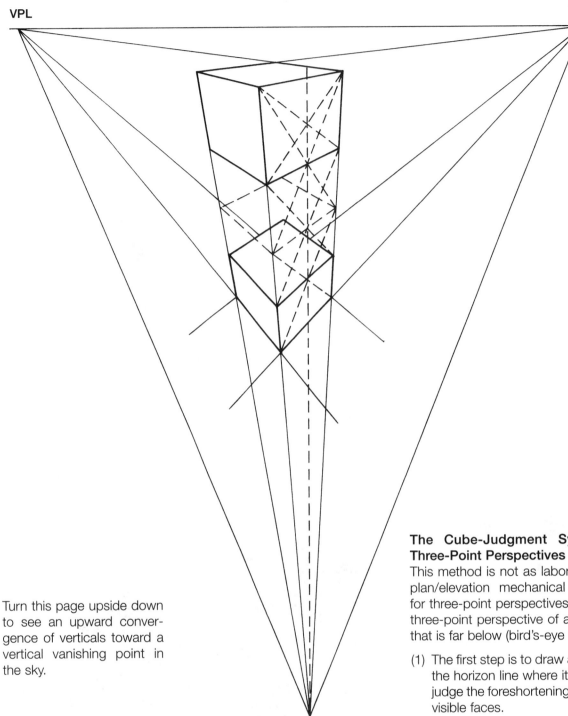

VPL

VPR

THREE-POINT PERSPECTIVE

Turn this page upside down to see an upward convergence of verticals toward a vertical vanishing point in the sky.

VPB (bottom or below)
This is arbitrarily placed.

Diagram and text: Courtesy of Dik Vrooman, Professor
Texas A & M University
Department of Architecture

The Cube-Judgment System for Three-Point Perspectives

This method is not as laborious as the plan/elevation mechanical procedure for three-point perspectives. To draw a three-point perspective of a cube form that is far below (bird's-eye view):

(1) The first step is to draw a cube near the horizon line where it is easier to judge the foreshortening of all three visible faces.

(2) Using diagonals, extend the cube module system downward to draw the correct perspective of the cube on the ground.

(3) Also using diagonals, you can extend this system laterally.

(4) Building design shapes that are other than cubes are measured from these cubes.

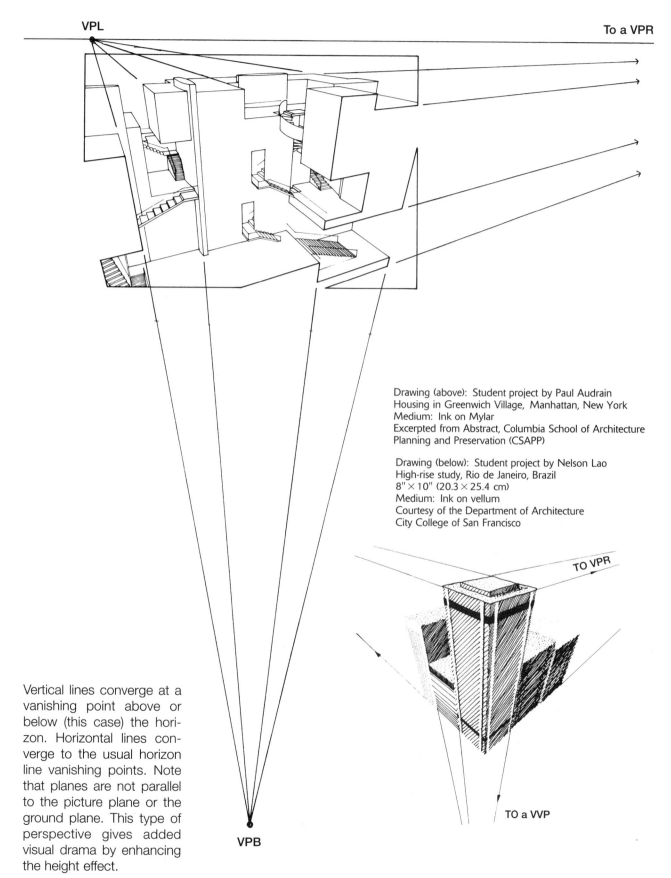

VPL

To a VPR

Drawing (above): Student project by Paul Audrain
Housing in Greenwich Village, Manhattan, New York
Medium: Ink on Mylar
Excerpted from Abstract, Columbia School of Architecture
Planning and Preservation (CSAPP)

Drawing (below): Student project by Nelson Lao
High-rise study, Rio de Janeiro, Brazil
8" × 10" (20.3 × 25.4 cm)
Medium: Ink on vellum
Courtesy of the Department of Architecture
City College of San Francisco

TO VPR

TO a VVP

Vertical lines converge at a vanishing point above or below (this case) the horizon. Horizontal lines converge to the usual horizon line vanishing points. Note that planes are not parallel to the picture plane or the ground plane. This type of perspective gives added visual drama by enhancing the height effect.

VPB

THREE-POINT PERSPECTIVE

THREE-POINT PERSPECTIVE

This method of construction produces an accurately measured three-point perspective drawing. The principle is based on the measured two-point perspective method: the image generated on a picture plane by projecting lines from the object to a single eye point. In three-point perspective, in addition, the picture plane will be tilted at an angle, similarly as one would tilt a camera to photograph a tall object. When the picture plane (and the camera) are tilted, the lines in the vertical direction will converge as well. The principle is illustrated in the diagram below. Using a scale for the perspective layout allows control of the image. In the example 1"=50' scale was used.

(1) Determine the distance of the observer (the eyepoint E) from the picture plane. A larger distance will produce a smaller but less distorted image. This distance is the radius of the circle drawn.

(2) To generate the vanishing point for the vertical lines (VVP), the eye point (E) must be rotated around the centerline (CL) from the center of the circle (C) into the surface of the picture plane. The point received (EV) will be used for generating measurements in the vertical direction.

(3) Determine the tilting of the picture plane. A larger angle produces a closer vanishing point. In the example, the angle is 20°. Draw a line (h) with the angle from EV. The intersection with the center line (CL) gives the location of the horizon line. Perpendicular to the line h draw a line (v). The intersection with the center line (CL) will give the vanishing point (VVP) for the vertical lines. Note that the tilted picture plane is the surface of the paper; thus the vertical and horizontal lines (h and v) must be drawn tilted instead.

(4) Rotate the EV eyepoint around point H into the center line (CL) to generate the eyepoint (EH). This point will be used to construct the perspective in the horizontal direction.

(5) Determine the distance of the base plane from the horizontal plane. In the example it is 60'. In this perspective, the base plane was selected at the top of the object to reduce the drawing size. The base line (BL), intersection of the base plane and the picture plane, is drawn in scale 60' below the horizon line (HL).

(6) Position the plan on the base plane. Here the object was placed behind the picture plane with one corner touching it. From EH we can construct the vanishing point (HVP) by drawing parallel lines with corresponding sides and intersecting with the horizon line (HL).

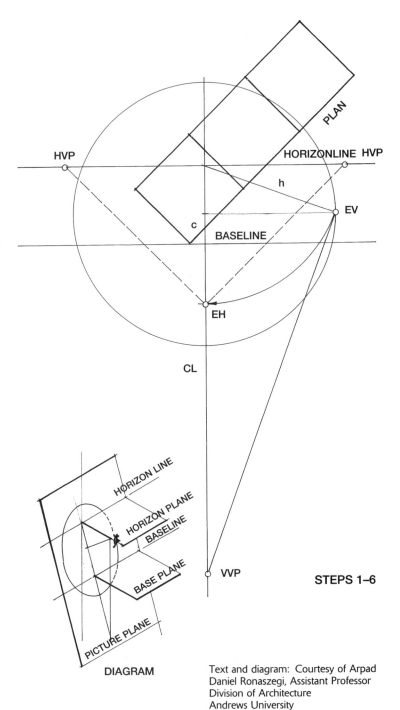

DIAGRAM

STEPS 1–6

Text and diagram: Courtesy of Arpad Daniel Ronaszegi, Assistant Professor Division of Architecture Andrews University

(7) Construct the perpsective image of the plan by connecting lines to the appropriate horizontal vanishing points (HVP). The length of the lines will be measured by connecting points to the eyepoint (EH) and intersecting them with the corresponding lines.

(8) The image of vertical lines can be constructed by connecting points from the plan image to the vertical vanishing point (VVP).

(9) The heights in the vertical direction will be generated from the vertical measuring line (vml). Draw a parallel line with the line *v* starting from the point where the plan touches the picture plane (BL on the drawing). On the line generated (vml) the actual heights can be measured out. In this example, the elevation is drawn orthogonal to the vml and then projected onto it.

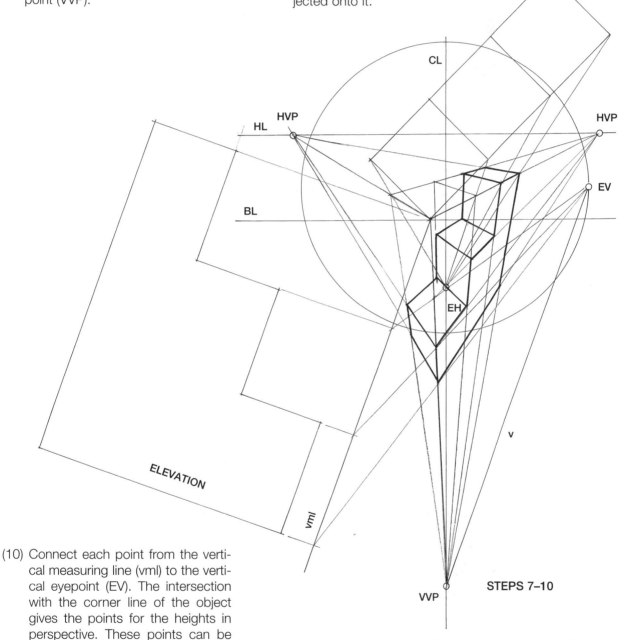

THREE-POINT PERSPECTIVE

STEPS 7–10

(10) Connect each point from the vertical measuring line (vml) to the vertical eyepoint (EV). The intersection with the corner line of the object gives the points for the heights in perspective. These points can be connected to the appropriate HVP points to finish the construction of the image.

Text and diagram: Courtesy of Arpad Daniel Ronaszegi, Assistant Professor Division of Architecture Andrews University

Drawing: Residence, Palm Springs, California
8" × 5" (20.3 × 12.7 cm)
Medium: Prismacolor
Courtesy of Kanner Architects
Drawing by Stephen Kanner

CIRCLES IN PERSPECTIVE

Circles in perspective take the form of an **ellipse.** We see this form not only in architectural subjects but also in everyday things such as bottles, dishware, pots, waste containers, coins, and wheels for transportation. Architecturally, **vertical circles** are commonly part of arches, semicircular windows, and circular vertical cylindrical forms.

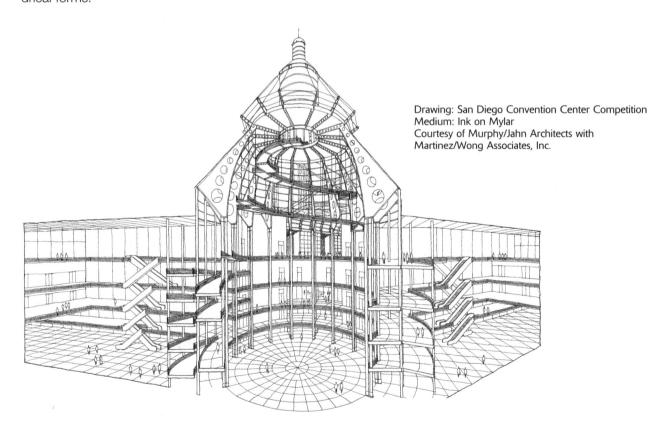

Drawing: San Diego Convention Center Competition
Medium: Ink on Mylar
Courtesy of Murphy/Jahn Architects with
Martinez/Wong Associates, Inc.

Horizontal circles are commonly part of semicircular or circular skylights and semicircular or circular horizontal cylindrical forms (e.g., rotundas).

Visualize a circle such as a bicycle wheel. The wheel below can take the form of a **horizontal** circle as it rotates about its diameter. This diameter can be described as major (longest true length). The minor diameter (axis) is perpendicular and foreshortened and becomes progressively smaller. Or the wheel can take the form of a **vertical** circle as it rotates about its diameter. The minor diameter (axis) is perpendicular and becomes progressively smaller as in the first case.

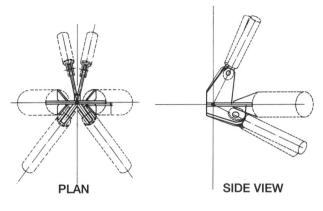

PLAN   SIDE VIEW

Drawing: Stuctural connection details
Sydney Football Stadium, Sydney, Australia
Medium: CADD, Scale:1:10
Courtesy of Cox Richardson
Architects and Planners
Ove Arup, Structural Engineer

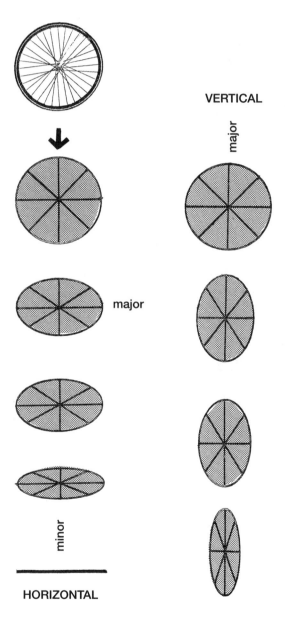

VERTICAL

major

major

minor

HORIZONTAL

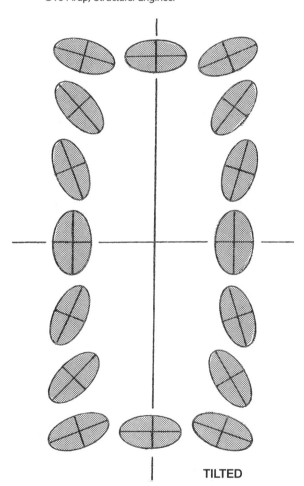

TILTED

CIRCLES IN PERSPECTVE

The above diagram illustrates how a circle seen in perspective as an ellipse will change in orientation from a horizontal to a vertical condition for the major axis. The intermediate conditions result in **tilted ellipses,** the degree of which depends on the inclination of the axes relative to the observer's position.

VERTICAL CIRCLE IN PERSPECTIVE

Drawing Perspective Circles

To draw a circle or a portion of a circle accurately in perspective requires that you first draw its circumscribing square. With experience and practice the square will provide all the reference that is needed for quick sketches. However, as accuracy requirements and circle size increase, so does the need to construct additional points of reference to assist in constructing the circle. The following sections describe the four-, eight-, and twelve-point techniques for constructing circles.

The Four-Point Perspective Circle

The four-point technique locates the points of tangency between the circle and square.

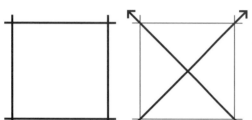

Draw or identify the square that circumscribes the circle. Draw the diagonals of the square to locate its center. Draw vertical and horizontal lines through the center point of the square. The intersection of these lines with the sides of the square will locate the midpoints of the respective sides that are also the tangent points for the circle and square. Draw a smooth curve that connects the four points to create a circle in perspective. Visually adjust the circle until it looks correct.

Note that the highest and lowest points of the circle are to the near side of their respective tangent points.

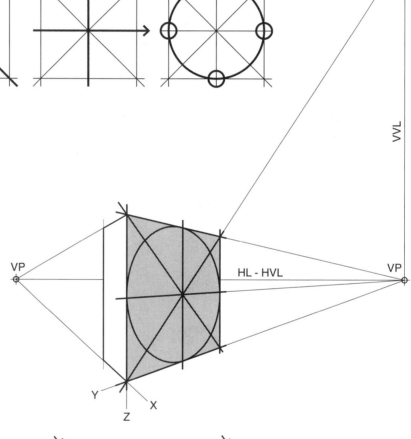

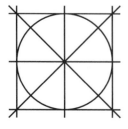
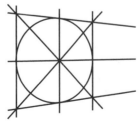
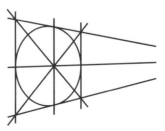
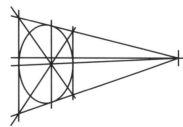

The Eight-Point Perspective Circle

The eight-point technique builds directly on the four-point system with a visual approximation that provides four more points.

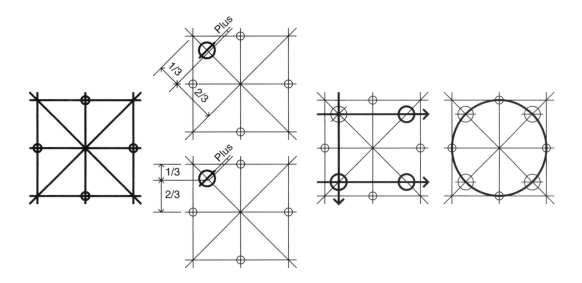

Follow the four-point procedure to locate the first four points. The diagonals used in this process are now divided to locate the additional points.

Divide the near half of one of the diagonals into thirds to locate the two-thirds point as shown. This can be done either directly along the diagonal or along the corresponding half of the square's side. If you use the square's side you must transfer the two-thirds mark to the diagonal.

Mark a point just beyond the two-thirds point of the diagonal. This locates the point at which the circle will intersect the diagonal.

Transfer this point to the other diagonals with lines that are parallel to the respective sides. This locates the other three points, giving you eight to guide your circle construction.

Draw a smooth curve that connects the eight points to create a circle. Visually adjust the circle until it looks correct.

Drawing (partial): The Peninsula Regent, San Mateo, California
Medium: Ink on Mylar, 16" × 24" (40.6 × 61 cm)
Peter Szasz, Architectural Illustrator
Courtesy of Backen Arrigoni & Ross, Inc.
Architecture, Planning & Interior Design

VERTICAL CIRCLE IN PERSPECTIVE

VERTICAL CIRCLE IN PERSPECTIVE

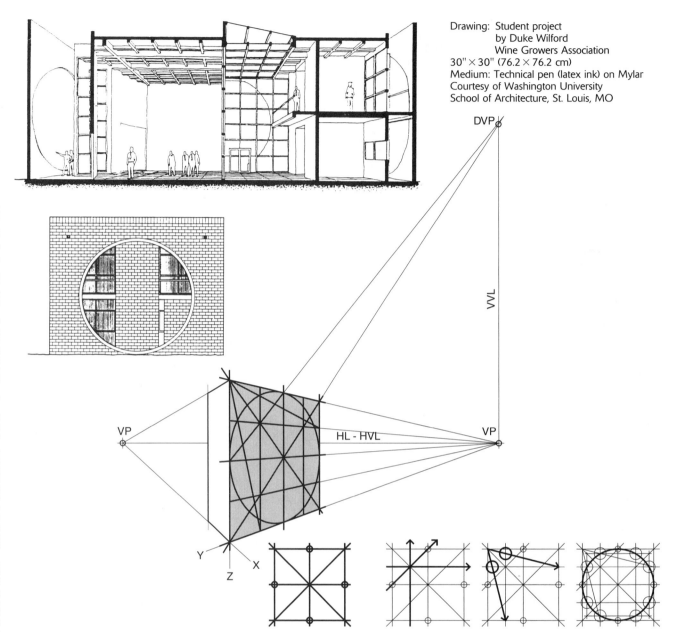

Drawing: Student project
by Duke Wilford
Wine Growers Association
30" × 30" (76.2 × 76.2 cm)
Medium: Technical pen (latex ink) on Mylar
Courtesy of Washington University
School of Architecture, St. Louis, MO

The TWELVE-POINT Perspective Circle

Follow the four-point procedure to locate the first four points.

Draw a diagonal through a near quarter of the original square to find its center. Draw vertical and horizontal lines through this point.

Draw lines from the corner of the original square to the one-quarter points on the opposite sides as shown. The intersection of these lines with the nearest horizontal or vertical one-quarter line defines two new points on the circle.

Use transfer techniques to create the other vertical and horizontal lines and then transfer the location of the two new points on the circle to the appropriate lines. This locates the other six new points and provides twelve to guide circle construction. Draw a smooth curve that connects the eight points to create a circle. Visually adjust the circle until it looks correct.

Diagrams and text: Courtesy of William R. Benedict, Assistant Professor
California Polytechnic State University School of Architecture
San Luis Obispo, CA

The **twelve-point** procedure is equally effective in constructing a horizontal perspective circle. It can also be used to construct an isometric circle. (See construction of isometric circles on p. 84).

Drawing: The Getty Center Museum
Entry Rotunda, Los Angeles,
California
42" × 42" (106.7 × 106.7 cm)
Medium: Ink on Mylar
Courtesy of Richard Meier &
Partners, Architects

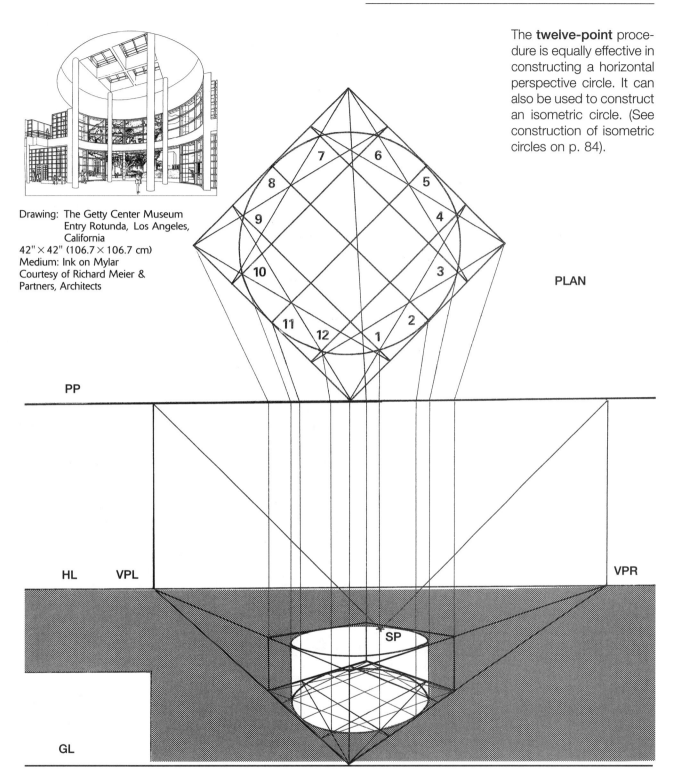

PLAN

PP

HL   VPL   VPR

SP

GL

ELEVATION

HORIZONTAL CIRCLE IN PERSPECTIVE

The **twelve-point** perspective circle

(1) Divide the encompassing square into sixteen squares of equal size.
(2) Project lines from the four major corners to the farthest corner of the smaller squares.
(3) Intersection points (8) for the circle occur at the first intersection of the two lines.
(4) The other four points are the tangent points. Carefully draw the elliptical curve connecting the twelve points.

Noncircular curvilinear forms in architecture can be elliptical in nature or even undulating (wave-like continuum), as seen in the work of Alvar Aalto.

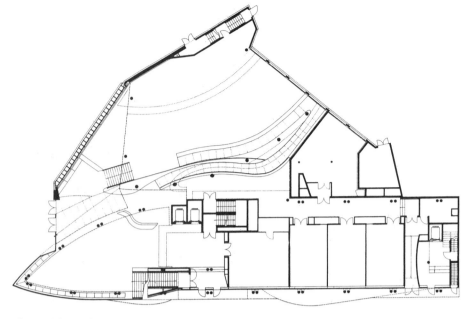

Ground floor plan

NONCIRCULAR CURVES IN PERSPECTIVE

Interior perspective: Entrance Hall

Noncircular curvilinear horizontal or vertical forms can be plotted by using a similar point-by-point technique as shown with perspective circles. Contemporary graphic strategies dictate that its expeditious accurate plotting be computer-generated or approximated by "eye" using freehand techniques. These curves in the horizontal plane are much easier to draw in plan obliques since they are seen in true shape and true size.

Drawings: Maison du Sport Français
Paris, France
Courtesy of Atelier Henri Gaudin,
Architect

Drawing: Student project by Cort Morgan
             Film Institute in Vicenza, Italy
Medium: Ink on Mylar
Courtesy of the University of Texas at Arlington
School of Architecture

Drawing (partial): The Getty Center for the History of Art and
                  the Humanities, Los Angeles, California
Medium: Ink on Mylar
Courtesy of Richard Meier & Partners, Architects
Reprinted from The Getty Center Design Process
with permission of The J. Paul Getty Trust

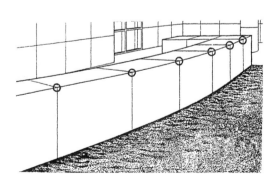

NONCIRCULAR CURVES IN PERSPECTIVE

Plot a series of points using a plan grid to determine the proper curvature.

THE PHYSICS OF REFLECTIONS

© Rendow Yee

Oakland Museum Pool Structure, Oakland, California
Oakland Museum
Kevin Roche, John Dinkeloo, and Associates, Architects

In most cases, a reflecting surface causes a visually interesting and appealing phenomenon. One associates reflections in architecture with the more predominant reflecting surfaces. These could be water, glass window panes, glass mirrors, wet pavement, and materials with a shiny surface, such as polished granite. Light causes the phenomenon of reflections. A **reflecting surface** results in an **extension** of any viewed perspective. The rendering of reflections (pp. 408–419) helps one understand a building within its contextual setting. The analytical drawing of the sculpture and its reflection is the idealistic case of the reflected inverted object being identical to the size of the object itself. In reality, when one observes a horizontally reflected object, the perspective seen of the object does not give an exact mirror image of the reflected perspective of the object. This is due to the fact that the observer's eye level is always above the ground (reflecting surface) line. This results in different distances between the eye and any point and its corresponding reflected point on the inverted image.

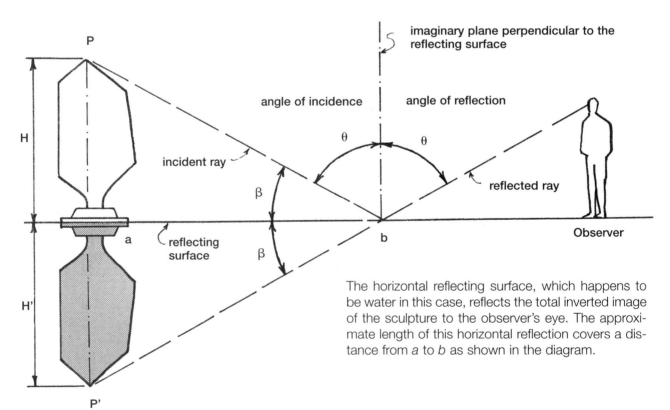

The horizontal reflecting surface, which happens to be water in this case, reflects the total inverted image of the sculpture to the observer's eye. The approximate length of this horizontal reflection covers a distance from *a* to *b* as shown in the diagram.

Building Touching the Reflective Surface

(1) Construct the perspective of the building.

(2) Extend all vertical lines into the reflection. The reflected lengths will be equal to the existing building verticals *(aa'= aa")*.

(3) Horizontal lines in the reflection vanish to the same vanishing points as their corresponding horizontal lines in the existing building.

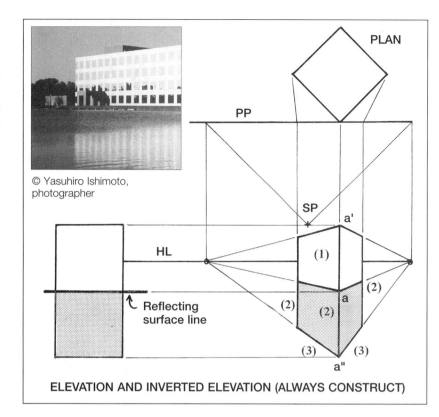

© Yasuhiro Ishimoto, photographer

Photo: Team Disney Building
      Lake Buena Vista, Florida
Courtesy of Arata Isozaki &
Associates, Architects

ELEVATION AND INVERTED ELEVATION (ALWAYS CONSTRUCT)

Building Not Touching the Reflective Surface

(1) Construct the perspective of the building.

(2) The reflecting surface does not extend under the building; therefore, parts of the reflection will be concealed. Construct the projection of the building onto the plane of the reflecting surface. The verticals are measured to the plane of the reflecting surface.

(3) These vertical distances are duplicated to construct the reflection.

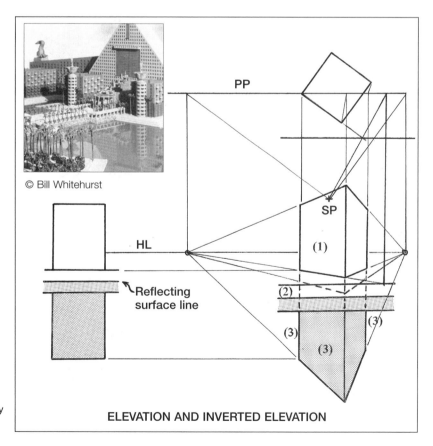

© Bill Whitehurst

Photo: Dolphin and Swan Convention Hotels
      Orlando, Florida
Photo by Bill Whitehurst, courtesy of Michael
Graves, Architect, and Courtesy of Tishman Realty
& Construction Company

ELEVATION AND INVERTED ELEVATION

REFLECTIONS IN PERSPECTIVE

REFLECTIONS IN PERSPECTIVE

If a building has **parallel inclined** edges as seen in the plan view to the right, the vanishing trace lines will converge to an oblique vanishing point above or below the vanishing point for horizontal lines. These trace lines are all located in the same or parallel planes.

Line *AB* is part of an inclined surface which has its own vanishing point oblique. Its reflected image *(A'B')* vanishes at an oblique vanishing point that is an equal distance above the HL as its nonreflected counterpart VP_O is below.

Horizontal reflections in perspective are always seen with the horizon line **higher** than the reflecting surface line, resulting in the reflected lines always sloping at a **sharper angle** than those of the building itself.

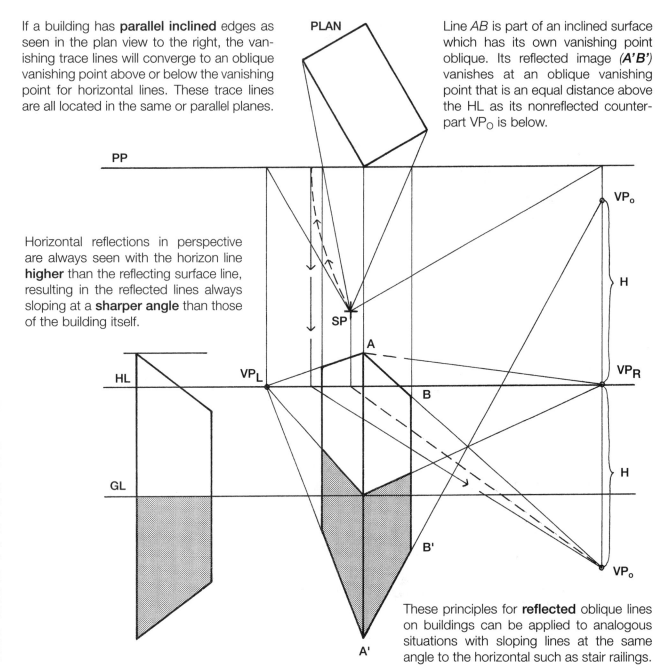

PLAN

PP

VP_O

H

SP

A

VP_L

VP_R

B

H

B'

A'

VP_O

HL

GL

These principles for **reflected** oblique lines on buildings can be applied to analogous situations with sloping lines at the same angle to the horizontal such as stair railings.

Drawing: Kitakyushu International Conference Center
Kitakyushu, Fukuoka, Japan
Courtesy of Arata Isozaki & Associates, Architects
Drawn by Arata Isozaki

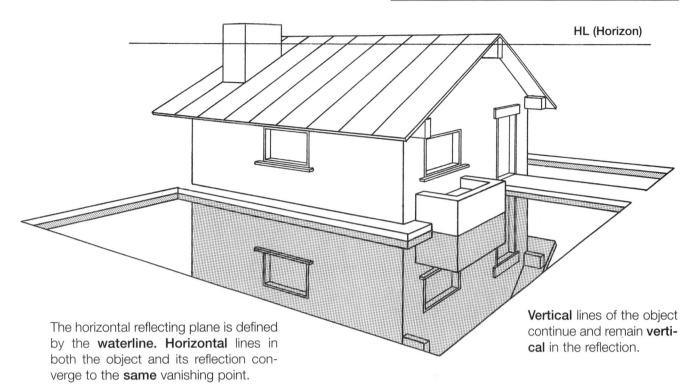

HL (Horizon)

The horizontal reflecting plane is defined by the **waterline. Horizontal** lines in both the object and its reflection converge to the **same** vanishing point.

Vertical lines of the object continue and remain **vertical** in the reflection.

Artificial reflecting pools commonly display **partial** reflections due to the pool's enclosing elements. Natural bodies of water display almost total reflections. The bottom of the reflected image above is concealed by the area around the pool's edge, whereas the top of the reflected image is hidden by the pool's deck in the photo below.

Photo: Sklar House
      Westchester County, New York
Courtesy of Christohper H.L. Owen, Architect
and Norman McGrath, Photographer

© Norman McGrath, Photographer

The soft light of a late fall day established the mood of this photograph. The selection of a low viewpoint captures an almost complete reflection of the house and emphasizes the strong geometry of the design. A strong conscious effort was made to establish the sympathetic relationship of the house setting with freshly fallen leaves around and on the pool surface. Some photographers might have "cleaned up," producing a stiffer more formal result. Recognizing and taking advantage of unpredictable circumstances such as those shown here can produce images that are both aesthetic and informative. A 4 × 5 view camera with a wide-angle lens was used to produce this photograph.
[ARCHITECTURAL PHOTOGRAPHER'S STATEMENT]

REFLECTIONS IN WATER

REFLECTIONS IN PERSPECTIVE

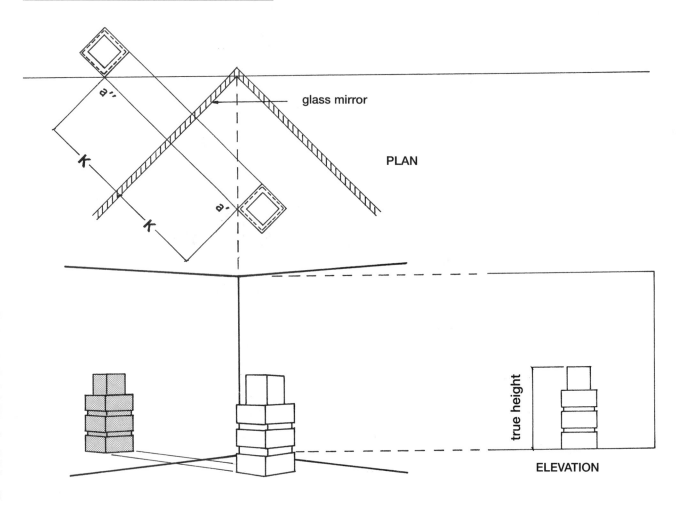

glass mirror

PLAN

true height

ELEVATION

Drawing: Pico Partners, San Clemente, California
Courtesy of Architect: ARC-ID CORPORATION
Renderer: Robert J. Reynolds

It is common to have either interior perspective views or urban landscape perspective views where vertical reflecting surfaces (such as a mirror in this case and a building facade in the case study on the subsequent page) give an added dimension to the perspective. The added dimension for a mirror is the optic expansion of a small interior space. This enlargement seen in the mirror usually shows parts of the room not seen from the perspective vantage point. For vertical reflections, the most important principles to remember are:

- All points such as *a'* in front of a reflecting surface are reflected back an **equal distance** *(K)* to its reflected image *a"*.
- A point *a'* and its corresponding reflected image *a"* always lie on a line **perpendicular** to the reflecting surface.
- The object and its reflected image follow the same rules for perspective construction.

This aerial shows buildings being reflected into other buildings in a three-point perspective.

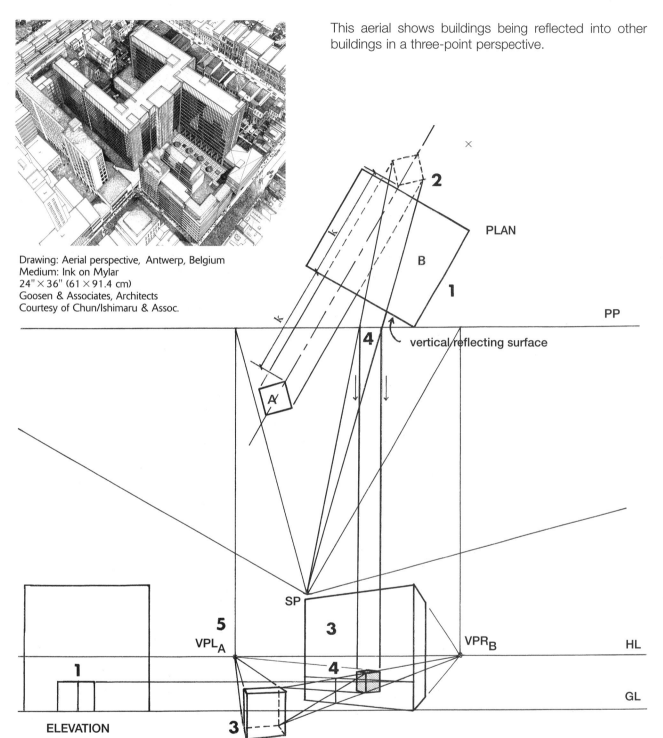

Drawing: Aerial perspective, Antwerp, Belgium
Medium: Ink on Mylar
24" × 36" (61 × 91.4 cm)
Goosen & Associates, Architects
Courtesy of Chun/Ishimaru & Assoc.

VERTICAL REFLECTING SURFACE

Step-by-step Procedure for a Vertical Reflecting Surface in a Two-Point Perspective

(1) Construct plan and elevation views of the buildings (A and B) involved.

(2) Construct the plan view of the building (A) reflected in a reverse image an equal distance (k) beyond the reflecting surface.

(3) Construct a two-point perspective of the reflecting surface and the building (B) being reflected.

(4) Construct the reflected reverse image by first finding an image height on the reflecting surface and then using projecting rays from the SP through the PP and down into the perspective view.

(5) The reflected reverse image of the building uses the same set of vanishing points as the building itself.

7

Perspective View Development

Once the theory of linear perspective drawing is understood, one can learn how to develop perspective views (from the rough to the finished form). In the profession of architectural illustration this requires an understanding of the design of the project being illustrated as well as skills in managing the balance, composition, and arrangement of all the many elements in the drawing.

The intent of this chapter is to show the process of view development by using actual examples of sketches and drawings from working architectural illustrators.

Perspective View Development

Topic

Perspective View Development

References

Drawing Techniques For Designers: Advocating Line and Tone Drawing (Lockhard 1991) Pepper Publishing

Topic

Non-mechanical perspective transfer alternative methods

References

Designing and Drawing with Confidence (Lin 1993) Van Nostrand Reinhold (136–138).

Architectural Delineation: A Photographic Approach to Presentation (Burden 1971) McGraw Hill.

Cross References

Chapter 6—Linear Perspective Drawing
Chapter 8—Light, Shade, and Shadow
Chapter 9—Delineating and Rendering Entourage

INTRODUCTION

Step 1

Drawing: Peek & Cloppenburg Deparment Store Competition
Winner, Leipzig, Germany
Moore, Ruble, Yudell, Architects
14" × 17" (35.6 × 43.2 cm)
Medium: Full watercolor over pencil line transfer
Courtesy of Al Forster, Architectural Illustrator

The process of doing a rough layout to a line tranfer rendering is shown on this and the following two pages. The architectural illustrator must decide "how best to view the project" so that the architect's client will accept the design concept.

VIEW DEVELOPMENT — ROUGH LAYOUT

Step 2

Drawing: Peek & Cloppenburg Department Store Competition Winner, Leipzig, Germany
Moore, Ruble, Yudell, Architects
14" × 17" (35.6 × 43.2 cm)
Medium: Full watercolor over pencil line transfer
Courtesy of Al Forster, Architectural Illustrator

The project site was a narrow street/mall. The rough layout was done to determine the view and the relationship to the background building. The view of the final line transfer was done from a photograph supplied by the client to each competitor so that each scheme could be compared from the same fixed station point. Note the actual amount of background building that shows versus the perceived amount of the building that shows in the rough layout.
[ARCHITECTURAL ILLUSTRATOR'S STATEMENT]

VIEW DEVELOPMENT — LINE TRANSFER

Step 3

Drawing: Peek & Cloppenburg Department Store Competition Winner, Leipzig, Germany
Moore, Ruble, Yudell, Architects
14" × 17" (35.6 × 43.2 cm)
Medium: Full watercolor over pencil line transfer
Courtesy of Al Forster, Architectural Illustrator

VIEW DEVELOPMENT – ROUGH LAYOUT

Step 1

Step 2

Step 3

Drawing: Sybase Hollis Street Campus, San Francisco, California
                  Robinson Mills & Williams
18" × 12" (45.7 × 30.5 cm)
Medium: Sketch watercolor on mounted presentation blackline
print of pencil drawing
Courtesy of Al Forster, Architectural Illustrator

Step 1: At the time of a rough blockout, human figures, cars, and tree forms are sketched in for scale, depth, and possible (or actual) placement (see facing page).
Step 2: An entourage tracing paper overlay is used for clean figures, cars, etc. . . . can be done directly onto rough blockout (step 1).
Step 3: A final line sketch or pencil transfer incorporates building and entourage together. More tree detail is now added as well as (small) distant, hand-drawn figures not necessarily on the entourage overlay. (See p. 247 for a discussion of scale.)
[ARCHITECTURAL ILLUSTRATOR'S STATEMENT]

VIEW DEVELOPMENT—LINE TRANSFER

VIEW DEVELOPMENT — ROUGH LAYOUT

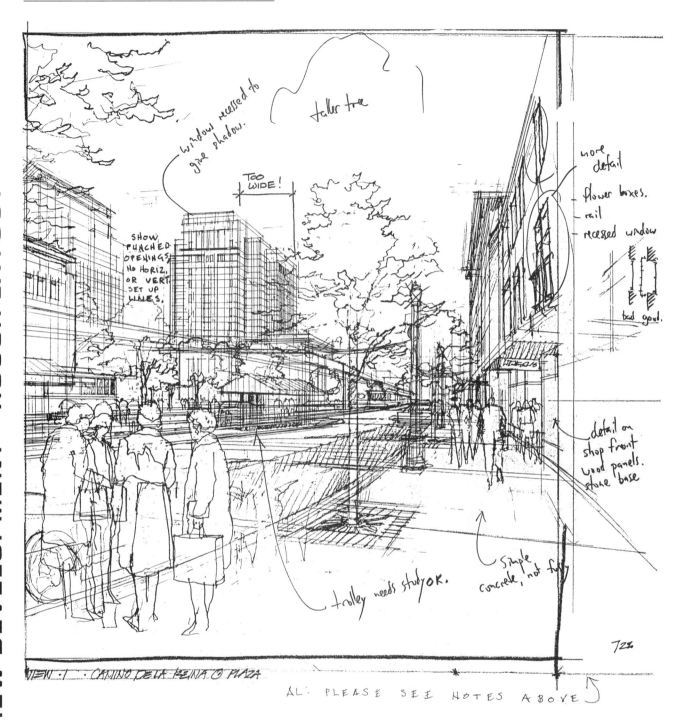

Drawing: Concept study, Riverwalk, Mixed use project, San Diego, California
14" × 17" (35.6 × 43.2 cm)
Medium: Full watercolor over pencil line transfer
Robert AM Stern with Fehlman LaBarre Architects
Courtesy of Al Forster, Architectural Illustrator

Written comments on the rough layout allow on the spot corrections, refinements, and adjustments and provide a record that can become a legal document for disputes that might arise later.
[ARCHITECTURAL ILLUSTRATOR'S STATEMENT]

Drawing: Concept study, Riverwalk, Mixed use project, San Diego, California
14" × 17" (35.6 × 43.2 cm)
Medium: Full watercolor over pencil line transfer
Robert AM Stern with Fehlman LaBarre Architects
Courtesy of Al Forster, Architectural Illustrator

Compare the development of individual parts and pieces of the drawing in the before and after examples as well as the illustrator's response to actual comments.
[ARCHITECTURAL ILLUSTRATOR'S STATEMENT]

Within a perspective layout the architect/designer/renderer can experiment by adding accessories such as cars, trees, and human figures (see chapter on delineating and rendering entourage for a more detailed coverage of perspective accessories). Even with the most recent computer-generated drawing techniques, accessories such as trees and people are very time-consuming to generate. Therefore, it is of utmost importance that students and design professionals develop good freehand techniques to draw accessories.

VIEW DEVELOPMENT—ROUGH LAYOUT

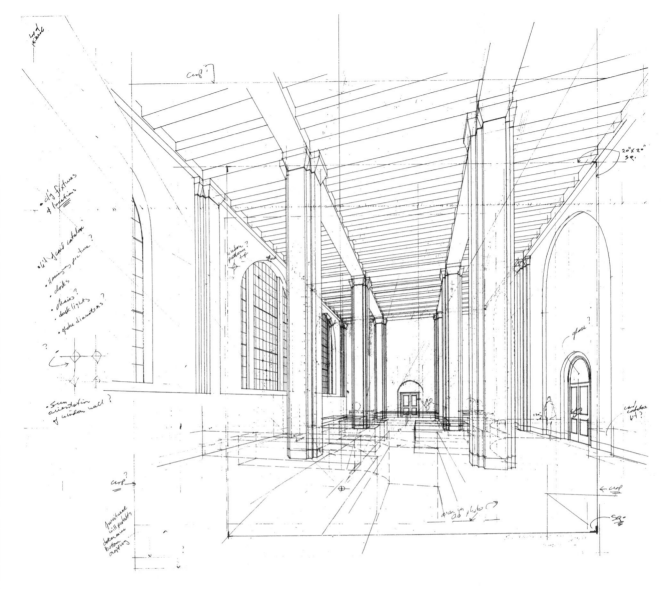

Drawings: Perspective layout setup (above) and finished rendering (facing page)
　　　　　Stanford University Green library–West Seismic Reconstruction Project, Palo Alto, California
Courtesy of TAC, The Architects Collaborative, Inc., and Mark Pechenik, Renderer

The advantage of a constructed perspective layout is that before the renderer finalizes tone and values, he or she can experiment with additions, deletions, and corrections to apparent distortions. Also tonal values and color can be applied to varying degrees with overlays to help determine how to finalize the rendering.

Medium: Black Prismacolor on vellum shot onto museum board and colored with Prismacolors

An 8" × 10" (20.3 × 25.4 cm) continuous tone negative was made and photographically enlarged to the 22" × 22" (55.9 × 55.9 cm) original size. Before colors were applied, it was drymounted on the board.

REFLECTION SET UP

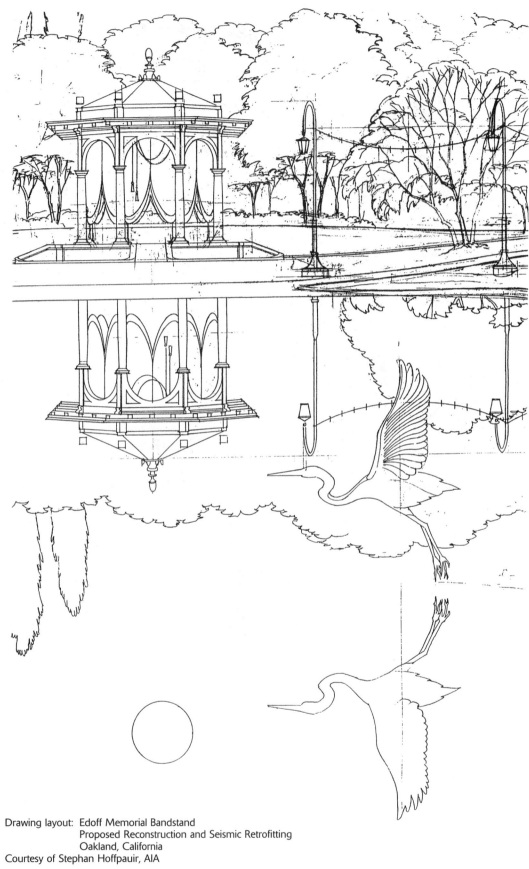

Drawing layout: Edoff Memorial Bandstand
Proposed Reconstruction and Seismic Retrofitting
Oakland, California
Courtesy of Stephan Hoffpauir, AIA

When there is very little air movement, reflections on a body of water become very sharp. In such instances a building at the water's edge will look almost as though it is being reflected in a mirror. The mood created under these conditions is one of placid tranquility.

To recreate this effect in an illustration, one simply draws the building upside down. The reflection of the building should be rendered slightly darker than the building itself, and the vertical lines made somewhat wavy. This technique is particularly successful in elevations and has the advantage of being both easy and dramatic. [ARCHITECTURAL ILLUSTRATOR'S STATEMENT]

The circle that was constructed in the water (facing page) was to be a reflection of the moon. As the renderer was completing the watercolor composition, he decided to omit it.

Drawing: Edoff Memorial Bandstand
　　　　 Proposed Reconstruction and Seismic
　　　　 Retrofitting
　　　　 Oakland, California
Medium: Watercolor (12" × 21") (30.5 × 53.3 cm)
Courtesy of Stephan Hoffpauir, AIA

FINISHED RENDERING

VIEW DEVELOPMENT—LINE TRANSFER

This layout was developed thanks to the use of computer-generated images, which helped us get the best angle. The collaboration with architects was very important in finding and deciding the view to develop. Our intention was to create a very attractive and slender building that sits next to the harbor. By extending down the bottom of the drawing to include water reflections and doing the illustration at nighttime to get more contrast, the overall view of the project is presented in a more dramatic way.
[ARCHITECTURAL ILLUSTRATOR'S STATEMENT]

This view in the preliminary studies did not include the extension of water, because we wanted to emphasize the brightness of the building at dusk. However, to achieve a more vertical feeling, reflections in the water were added to expand the lightness of the tower. The water was done in colored pencil to create the dark reflections and in pastels to bring the light reflections up.
[ARCHITECTURAL ILLUSTRATOR'S STATEMENT]

FINISHED RENDERING

Drawing: Shekou Harbor Building, China
Medium: Ink, colored pencil, pastel, and airbrush
Loebl, Scholossman and Hackl, Architects; in conjunction with the
Shenzen University Institute of Architectural Design
Courtesy of Manuel Avila Associates, Architectural Illustrator

VIEW DEVELOPMENT — LINE TRANSFER

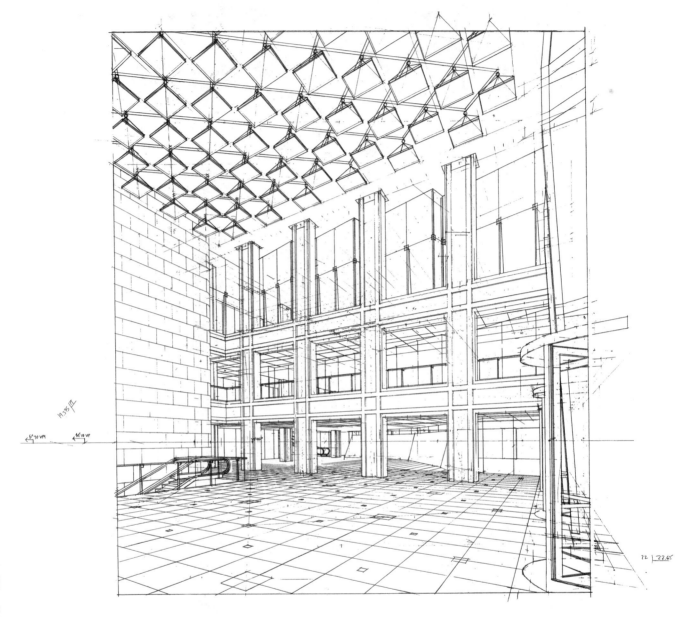

Drawing: Sears Tower Renovation Project, Chicago, Illinois
DeStefano & Partners, Architects
Courtesy of Manuel Avila Associates, Architectural Illustrator

To establish the proportions and the size of the new enlarged interior space (original space consisted of only two floors instead of three) we set ourselves as close to the entrance wall as we could to show the full extension of the room with all the new floor materials, new clad columns, and glass walls. We always try to show three sides of the room to feel enclosement. Although we only partially see the entrance wall, we will emphasize its presence with the sunlight coming in.
[ARCHITECTURAL ILLUSTRATOR'S STATEMENT]

Drawing: Sears Tower Renovation Project, Chicago, Illinois
DeStefano & Partners, Architects
Courtesy of Manuel Avila Associates, Architectural Illustrator

In this interior, the technique of shadows flooding the space was used to establish different level contrasts, because the materials used were basically light. The different levels of contrast in shadows and reflections were achieved first by the use of pen and ink followed by the use of colored pencil to saturate and emphasize forms. To make the illustration more complete, people were done very carefully and detailed to bring more reality to the floor activity.
[ARCHITECTURAL ILLUSTRATOR'S STATEMENT]

FINISHED RENDERING

VIEW DEVELOPMENT — LINE TRANSFER

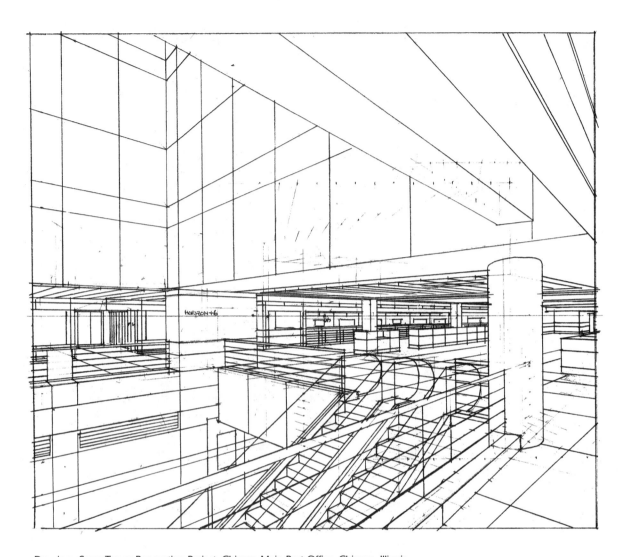

Drawing: Sears Tower Renovation Project, Chicago Main Post Office, Chicago, Illinois
Medium: Pen and ink
Courtesy of Knight Architects Engineers Planners, Inc.
Courtesy of Manuel Avila Associates, Architectural Illustrator

After providing a series of different preliminary layouts to find out which was the most compelling and descriptive space view, this one was chosen to be developed. All the details and design elements were then drawn in collaboration with the architects, so all the correct information is included. The completion of the layout was done technically by hand. By the time the illustrator was ready to draw the final black and white illustration, the layout was completed and ready to be rendered.
[ARCHITECTURAL ILLUSTRATOR'S STATEMENT]

FINISHED RENDERING

Drawing: Sears Tower Renovation Project, Chicago Main Post Office,
Chicago, Illinois
Original size: (approx.) 24" × 20½" (61 × 52.1 cm), Scale used: ¼"=1'0"
Medium: Pen and ink
Courtesy of Knight Architects Engineer Planners, Inc.
Courtesy of Manuel Avila Associates, Architectural Illustrator

After the layout is completed, the rendering is done in pen and black ink. The focus of the drawing is, first of all, to show the main floor amenities; second, to show how busy the space is: people moving, buying stamps, using mail boxes, etc.; and finally, to pay attention to the multistoried lobby that precedes the main floor.
[ARCHITECTURAL ILLUSTRATOR'S STATEMENT]

8

Light, Shade, and Shadow

Light allows us to have vision. With light we can structure and put order into the environment. It enhances our senses for experiencing architecture as we move through space over a period of time. A thorough knowledge and understanding of light and the application of shades and shadows to your presentations of the built environment helps to further client/architect understanding during the design process. Shadows accent orthographic (particularly elevations and site plans), paraline, and perspective drawings, adding a sense of clarity and substance to the represented forms.

The intent of this chapter is to develop your ability to draw and construct shades and shadows in plan, elevation, paraline, and perspective drawings.

Light, Shade, and Shadow

Topics

Casting Edge, Vertical Casting Edge, Altitude and Azimuth, Sun's Bearing, Sun Bearing Vanishing Point, Sun's Ray, Sun Ray Vanishing Point, Sun Ray Triangle, Horizontal Casting Edge, Shadows in Plan

References:

Rapid Viz (Hanks and Belliston 1980): Shadow Casting: 66–67.

Drawing a Creative Process (Ching 1990):Shadow Casting: 130–133.

Design Drawing (Lockard 1982): Shadow Casting: 127–160.

Basic Perspective Drawing (Montague 1993): Shadow Casting: 126–133.

Graphics for Architecture (Forseth 1980): Shadow Casting: 130–134.

Architectural Graphics (Ching 1996): Shadow Casting: 112–126.

Perspective Drawing (Helms 1990): Shadow Casting: 240–296.

Manual of Graphic Techniques 4 (Porter and Goodman 1985): Shadow Casting: 22–27.

Photographic Perspective Drawing Techniques (Leach 1990): Shadow Casting: 85–107.

Cross References

For p. 312   See pp. 420, 421
For p. 315   See p. 459
For p. 316   See p. 376
For p. 326   See p. 338

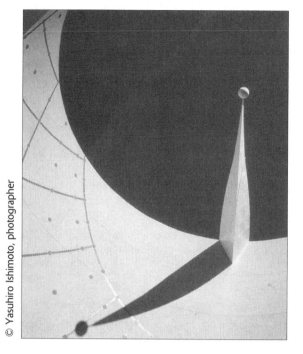

Photo: Stylus in sundial courtyard
Team Disney Building, Lake Buena Vista, Florida
Courtesy of Arata Isozaki and Associates, Architects

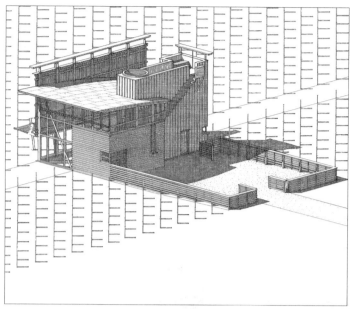

Drawing: A small lodge, Saint Helena, California
Medium: Ink on Mylar, 30" × 30"
(76.2 × 76.2 cm), Scale: ¼"=1'0"
Courtesy of Brian Healy Architects

INTRODUCTION

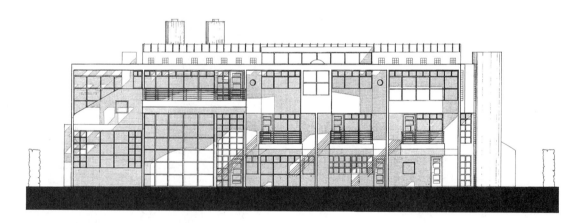

Drawing: Meyer residence, Malibu, California
Medium: Ink on Mylar
Courtesy of Gwathmey Siegel & Associates, Architects

During the daytime hours, our constant companion, whether we are aware of it or not, is our shadow (see p. 199). Shade on that part of our body not receiving direct light is also constantly with us. We perceive shades and shadows on both animate and inanimate objects. Empirically, most of us can generally sense why an object's shadow takes on a certain geometric configuration. However, that shadow sense is inadequate for architectural students, architectural illustrators, and architects. To properly convey a design concept, it is imperative that we learn how to construct precise shadow drawings.

Four terms can appropriately describe our timeless response to and interpretation of shadows: (1) mysterious, (2) vague, (3) dramatic, and (4) dimensional. Dimensional refers to a shadow's unique property of delineating form and scale in the urban landscape. Shades and shadows were of utmost importance in providing depth to the facades for front elevations during the early periods of architecture. The added illusion of depth was aesthetically pleasing. It clarified overlapping elements on the facade to the layperson. Knowing how to delineate and draw shades and shadows helps us to better understand spatial concepts in our designs. *Sciagraphy* is the science of shade and shadow graphics and is an indispensable tool for architects, designers, and delineators. Sciagraphy provides a tool for obtaining a finished and realistic appearance to any drawing.

The illustration below left emulates the work of the professional renderer Hugh Ferriss. It is rendered to give form to a lighting quality that has mystery and drama. The other illustration typifies the meticulous delineation techniques that were instilled by the 19th century École de Beaux Arts. Light, shade, and shadow are purposely articulated to create artificial lighting effects for compositions of classical details. Shadows play an important role in conceptual design-development stages of contemporary graphic strategies. Fenestration patterns on conceptual elevations are visually articulated and enhanced by the use of shadows. These studies of the interplay of solids, voids, and inclined planes give a surface modulation to make interrelated parts understandable.

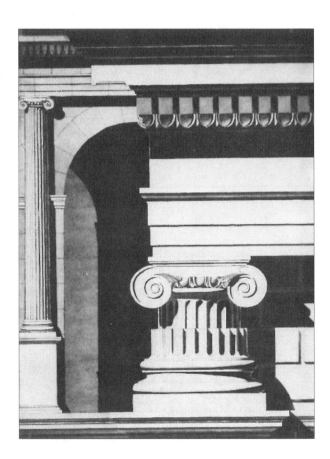

Drawing: Student project by Ed Yeomans
             Rudder Tower
Medium: Charcoal 18" × 24" (45.7 × 61 cm)
Courtesy of Texas A & M University
Department of Architecture

Drawing: Student project by Eberhard Lenz
             Classical details
Medium: Ink wash, 18.5" × 25.5" (47 × 64.8 cm)
Courtesy of Washington University
School of Architecture, St. Louis, MO

The application of sciagraphy is of great importance to the design professional. Light, shade, and shadow define form and space. The **shadows** indicate the shape of the object casting the shadow and can in many ways indicate the texture of the surface receiving the shadow. When **light** rays are intercepted by an object, the portion on the light side will be illuminated, while the portion opposite the light side will be protected from the light rays. This shielded portion can be defined as **shade.** The boundary line that separates light from shade determines the **shadow line** on a receiving surface. The boundary of the shadow line determines the dark area "casted" onto the surface on which the object rests and receives the cast **shadow.** To produce a shadow, three conditions are required:

(1) A **light source**
(2) An **object** to cast the shadow line, or to intercept the light ray
(3) A **surface** to receive the shadow line and shadow

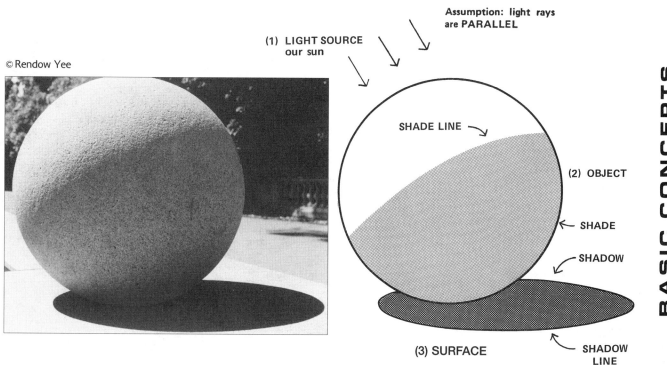

© Rendow Yee

BASIC CONCEPTS

Due to the enormous distance of the earth from the sun, the light rays from the sun are considered to be parallel (In reality the rays are diverging). This condition can be contrasted with artifical light, which gives radiating rays of light due to the proximity of the light source. The photograph of the spherical solid above shows that human perception sees shade and shadow to be approximately the same value intensity or darkness. When sketching, the gradual transition in tone from shade to light seen in the photo is described as a "soft-edge" area. A sharply defined border such as the edge of the shade area is described as "hard edge." In architectural drawings shadow is always shown darker than shade regardless of the sketching or rendering medium.

SOLAR ANGLE DIAGRAMS

The direction of solar rays are identifed by two angles described as **bearing** and **azimuth.** Both bearing and azimuth are measured only in the plan view. The bearing acute angle of an inclined line is always measured in degrees.

Altitude is the angle between the sun's position in the sky vault and the earth's horizontal plane for a given latitude.

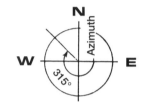

Example
N 45°W is a bearing
or
315° azimuth

Light rays are notated by their **bearing** relative to due north or south, and their **azimuth** is measured clockwise from due north.

Azimuth is the angle between the sun's bearing and a horizontal line that is in a plane perpendicular to the horizonal plane of the earth's surface.

Latitude is the angular distance north or south from the equator measured in degrees on the meridian of a point. **Longitude** is the angular distance east or west, between the meridian of a particular place and that of Greenwich, England, expressed in degrees.

WINTER SUNSET

SUMMER SUNSET

WINTER SUNRISE

SUMMER SUNRISE

SAN FRANCISCO BAY AREA
38° LATITUDE
122° LONGITUDE

Sun path diagram: Courtesy of Thomas L. Turman, Professor
Medium: Ink (freehand)
11"×8½" (27.9 × 21.6 cm)
Laney College Department of Architecture

One of the most important factors in architectural design is natural sunlight. How the sun moves across the sky for different locations affects how architects design. Architects are concerned about radiant heat energy as well as the design of shading devices for buildings.

Solstice is defined as either of the two times a year when the sun is at its greatest distance from the celestial equator. The summer solstice is about 21 June and the winter solstice is about 21 December. In North America, which is in the northern hemisphere, 21 June marks the sun's highest point in the sky and thus the longest solar day, whereas 21 December marks the sun's lowest point in the sky and thus the shortest solar day. A solar day is from 12 o'clock noon to 12 o'clock noon. The simple diagram above is for the San Francisco Bay Area in the United States of America.

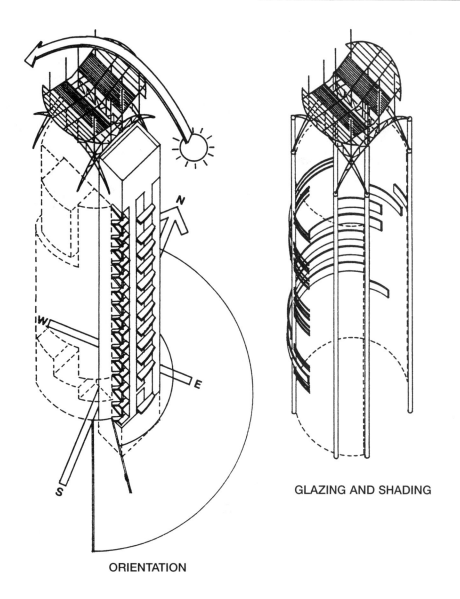

ORIENTATION

GLAZING AND SHADING

Drawing: Menara Mesiniaga (IBM Tower)
Selangor, Malaysia
T. R. Hamzah & Yeang, Architect

SOLAR ANGLE DIAGRAMS

Tall buildings are more exposed to the full impact of the sun and heat than low-rise structures. Office towers throughout the world do not adapt to their local climates. Rather they fight it using the 20th century's arsenal of mechanical systems such as air conditioning, artificial light, and heating.
[ARCHITECT'S STATEMENT]

Perspective solar angle diagrams are the most difficult and most complex of all shadow diagrams for the beginner. For this reason, this chapter progressively examines shadow constructions starting with prismatic forms in orthographic views. It then focuses on common construction situations in elevations such as overhangs, canopies, colonnades, arcades, stairs, niches, dormers, and inclines. This is followed by a study of paraline shadow constructions, and, finally, perspective shadow constructions. Techniques for using shades and shadows to accentuate architectural form and space are explored in the subsequent chapter on delineating and rendering entourage.

Drawing: West Adams Place, Los Angeles, California
Medium: Ink, 36" × 24" (91.4 × 61 cm)
Courtesy of John V. Mutlow FAIA, Architects and
Iraj Yamin Esfandiary, Illustrator

These building solids cast shadows and show shade with a line hatching technique (shadow darker than shade). The foreground road has the heaviest hatching.

SHADOW PRINCIPLES

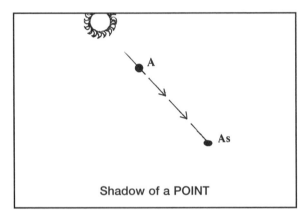

Shadow of a POINT

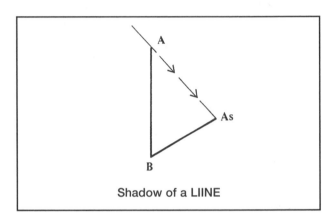

Shadow of a LIINE

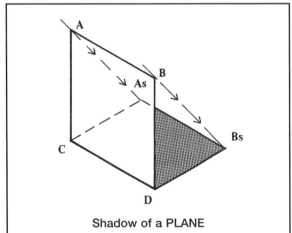

Shadow of a PLANE

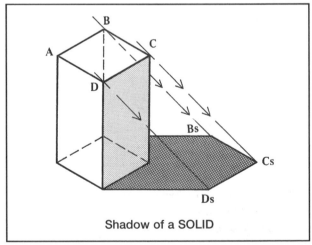

Shadow of a SOLID

Shadow development can be analyzed by studying shadow progressions from points to lines to planes and finally to solids. Begin by studying point shadows, since a finite series of points will ultimately

(1) Determine shadows of **lines** (lines being composed of points)
(2) Determine shadows of **planes** (planes being composed of lines)
(3) Determine shadows of **solids** (solids being composed of planes)

The shadow of a line, a plane, or a solid is most efficiently determined by locating the shadows of the **critical** points of the line, plane, or solid.

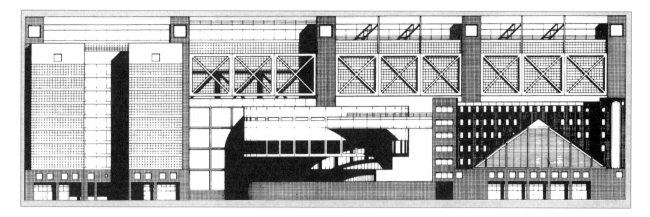

Drawing: City Hall
Missisauga, Ontario, Canada
48" × 30" (121.9 × 76.2 cm), Scale: ⅛"=1'0"
Medium: Ink on Mylar
Courtesy of Michael Fieldman and Partners

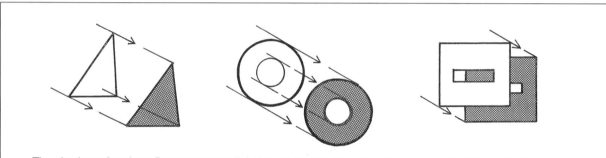

The shadow of a plane figure on a parallel plane is identical in size, shape, and orientation with the figure. The more distant the parallel plane (triangle and donut), the more shadow will show.

For architectural graphics a 45° angle light ray direction from the left in plan and in elevation is conventionally used. In cubic form this can be represented by the diagonal of a cube with a slope of 35°15'52" (θ). Also commonly used is a 45° angle light ray direction from the right. Note that the **slope** angle of the light ray is the inclination relative to the horizontal plane.

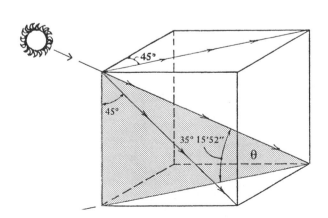

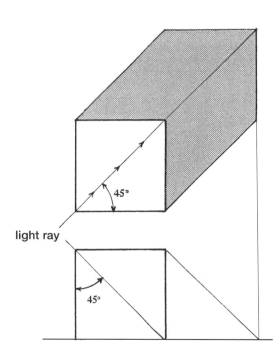

light ray

SHADOW PRINCIPLES

Drawing: Erectheum house, San Francisco, California
12" × 20" (30.5 × 50.8 cm), Scale: ¼"=1'0"
Medium: Pencil, Prismacolor, pastel, Zipatone
Courtesy of Kotas/Pantaleoni, Architects
Mr. Jeremy Kotas

RECTILINEAR FORMS

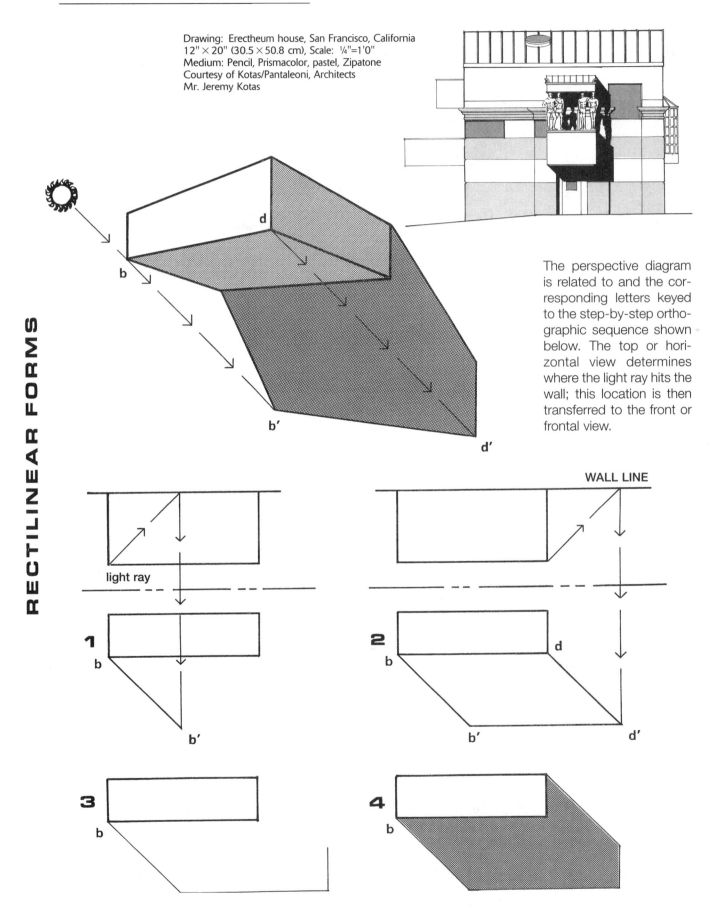

The perspective diagram is related to and the corresponding letters keyed to the step-by-step orthographic sequence shown below. The top or horizontal view determines where the light ray hits the wall; this location is then transferred to the front or frontal view.

light ray

WALL LINE

1

2

3

4

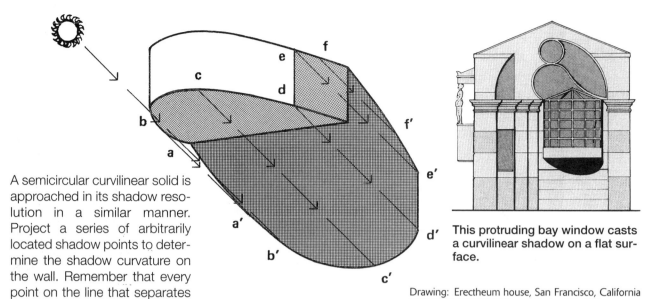

A semicircular curvilinear solid is approached in its shadow resolution in a similar manner. Project a series of arbitrarily located shadow points to determine the shadow curvature on the wall. Remember that every point on the line that separates light from shade **(shade line)** will cast a shadow point on the **shadow line.**

This protruding bay window casts a curvilinear shadow on a flat surface.

Drawing: Erectheum house, San Francisco, California
12" × 20" (30.5 × 50.8 cm), Scale: ¼"=1'0"
Medium: Pencil, Prismacolor, pastel, Zipatone
Courtesy of Kotas/Pantaleoni, Architects
Mr. Jeremy Kotas

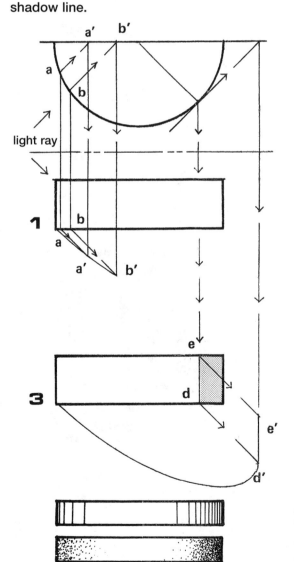

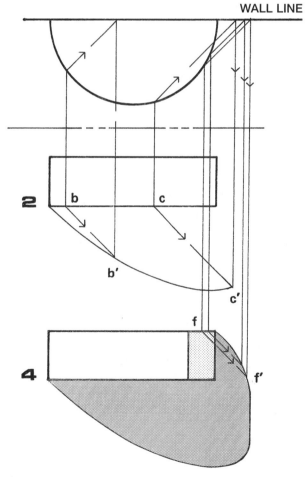

A cylindrical or curvilinear surface always appears flat in the front elevation. Alternatives to a uniform shade value to create a feeling of depth are to use a series of unequally spaced fine lines or increasing dot density (see p. 55).

CURVILINEAR FORMS

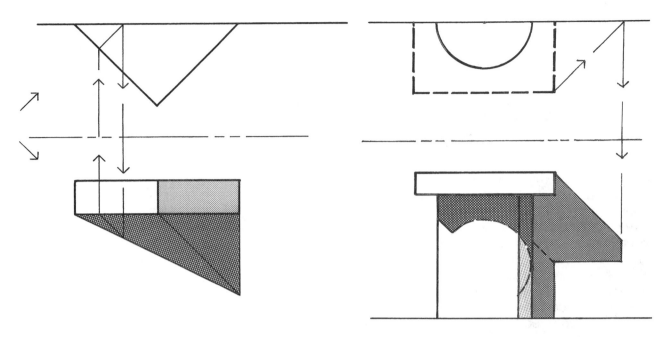

The study of wall condition shadows for various geometric forms, such as the previously described rectilinear and curvilinear forms and the variety shown on this page, provides the necesary framework for the analogous situations encountered in site plan and roof plan shadows. This analogy becomes apparent by turning any wall condition drawing upside down and realizing that the "wall line" is now the "ground line" and the "wall object" is now the object seen in the plan view.

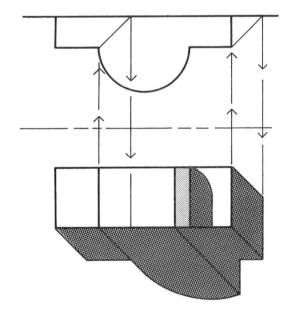

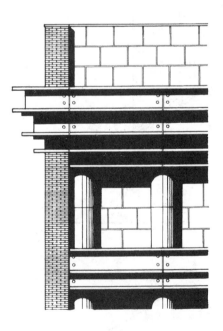

Partial elevation: Hotel Il Palazzo
Fukuoka, Japan
18" × 24" (45.7 × 61 cm), Scale: 1:50 m
Medium: Black ink on Mylar
Courtesy of Aldo Rossi, Studio di Architettura
New York, Architect

ELEVATION VIEW SHADOWS

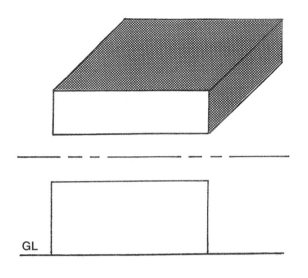

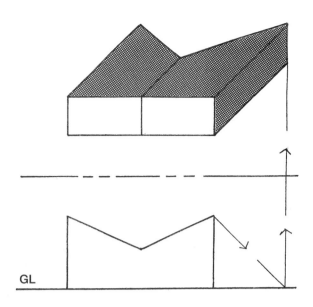

These drawings illustrate the analogy between wall elevation shadows and site/roof plan shadows. The height of the solid forms above the "ground line" determines the length of the shadow cast in the plan view. Note that by simply turning the drawing upside down and switching the plan and elevation views, wall elevation conditions result.

Drawing: Town Square, four houses and chapel
                  Port Ludlow, Washington
Scale: 1"=40'0"
Medium: Pen and ink
Courtesy of Steven Holl Architects

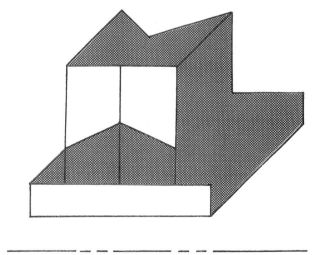

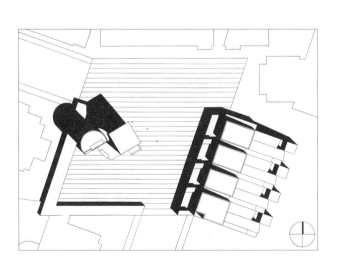

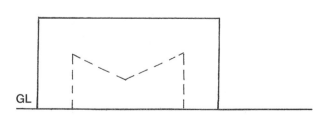

PLAN VIEW SHADOWS

SINGULAR FORMS COMBINED

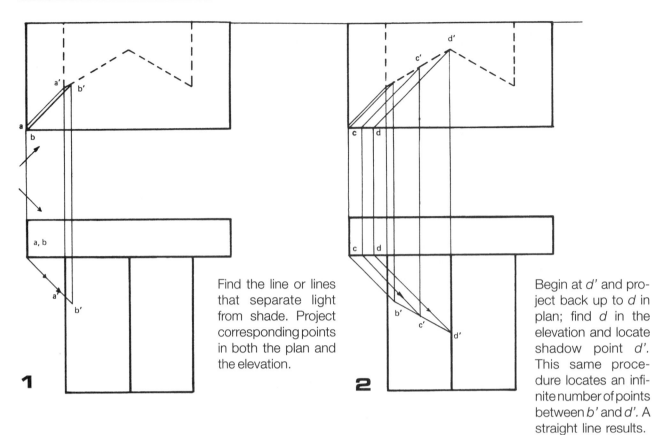

1 Find the line or lines that separate light from shade. Project corresponding points in both the plan and the elevation.

2 Begin at *d'* and project back up to *d* in plan; find *d* in the elevation and locate shadow point *d'*. This same procedure locates an infinite number of points between *b'* and *d'*. A straight line results.

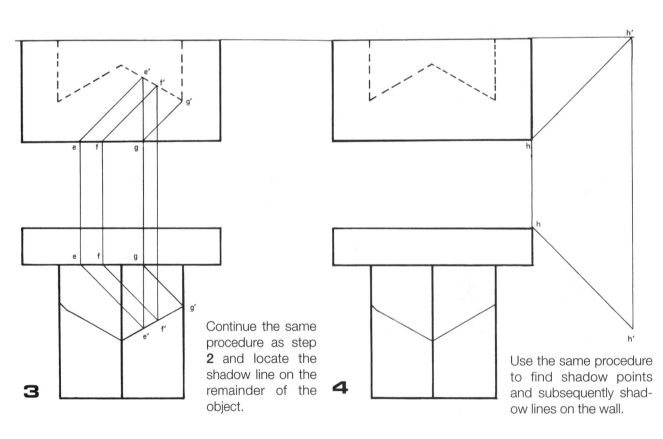

3 Continue the same procedure as step **2** and locate the shadow line on the remainder of the object.

4 Use the same procedure to find shadow points and subsequently shadow lines on the wall.

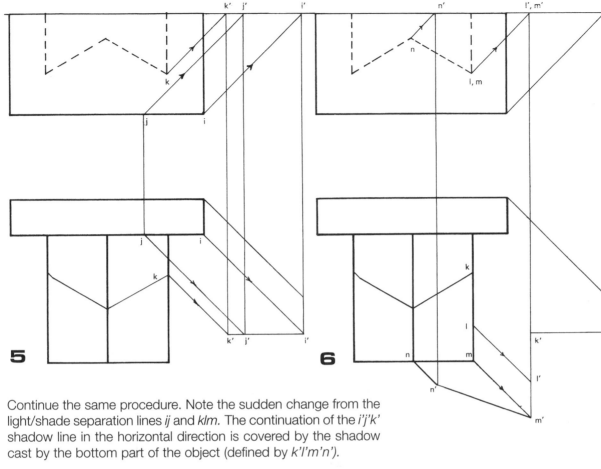

5

6

Continue the same procedure. Note the sudden change from the light/shade separation lines *ij* and *klm.* The continuation of the *i'j'k'* shadow line in the horizontal direction is covered by the shadow cast by the bottom part of the object (defined by *k'l'm'n'*).

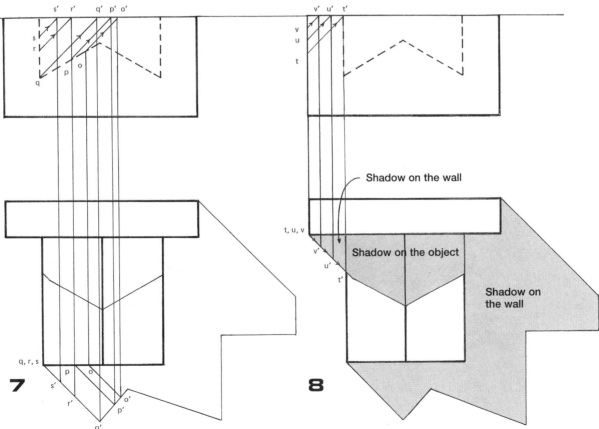

7

8

Shadow on the wall

Shadow on the object

Shadow on the wall

S I N G U L A R   F O R M S   C O M B I N E D

SINGULAR FORMS COMBINED

wall treatments

30° zigzag

45° zigzag

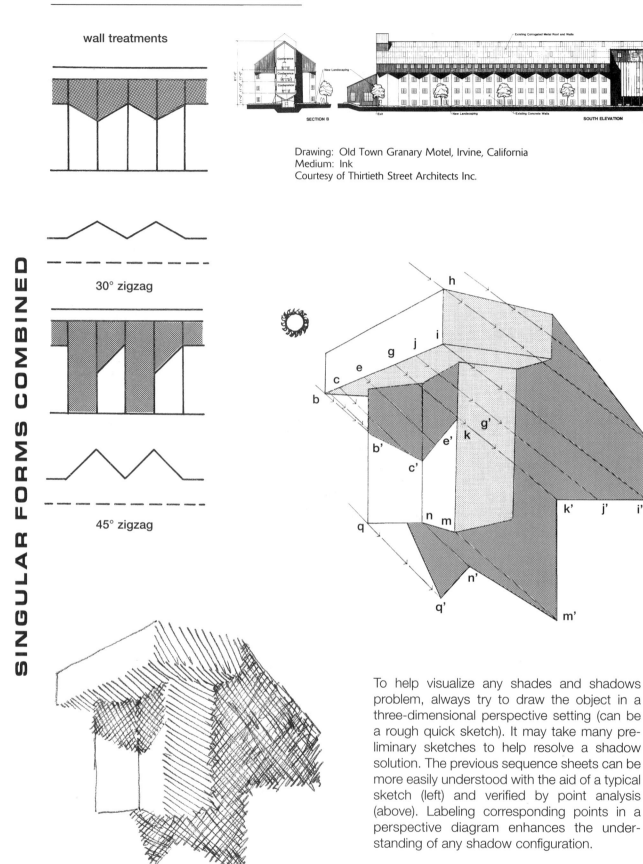

Drawing: Old Town Granary Motel, Irvine, California
Medium: Ink
Courtesy of Thirtieth Street Architects Inc.

SECTION B

SOUTH ELEVATION

To help visualize any shades and shadows problem, always try to draw the object in a three-dimensional perspective setting (can be a rough quick sketch). It may take many preliminary sketches to help resolve a shadow solution. The previous sequence sheets can be more easily understood with the aid of a typical sketch (left) and verified by point analysis (above). Labeling corresponding points in a perspective diagram enhances the understanding of any shadow configuration.

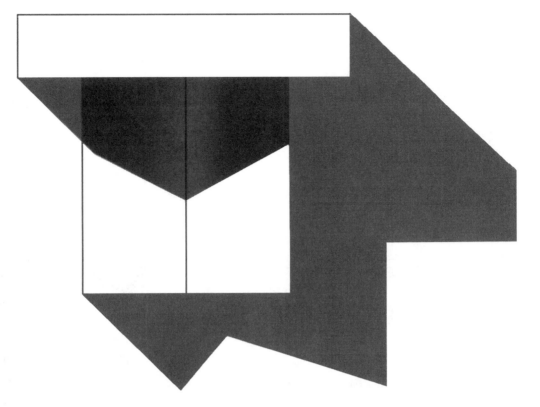

Airbrush rendering: Student project by Steven Toy
Courtesy of the City College of San Francisco
Department of Architecture

The above rendering of the wall elements example shown in the sequence diagrams on the previous pages was done with an airbrush to display the tone intensity on various surfaces for the shadow cast. Airbrush renderings are extremely time-consuming and the equipment is expensive. For these reasons, it is not a favorite technique among architectural design professionals. Hybrid sprayers, which combine marker and airbrush characteristics, are more popular and highly efficient.

An airbrush instrument sprays paint to cover large areas of flat color or gradations of color using compressed air. Note that the contrast is greater on surfaces closer to the observer's eye. This is because the surface appears brighter when it is closer to the observer's eye, whereas in reality the difference may be insignificant. The illustration to the right shows this concept as receding surfaces are rendered with less contrast. In professional practice, this difference in the rendition of value for receding plan or elevation surfaces is seldom shown. Thus, with a uniform shadow value, the ability to visualize surface changes becomes imperative. Attempt to exercise this ability on the building examples on the subsequent pages.

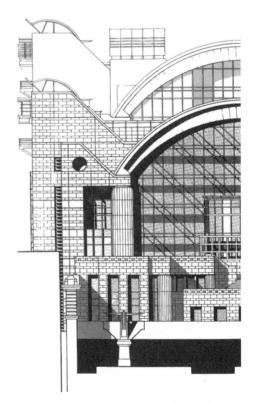

Drawing: Embankment Place, London, England
Medium: Letratone
Courtesy of the Terry Farrell & Partners, Architects

SHADOW INTENSITY ON RECEDING SURFACES

Drawing: Parkview Commons, San Francisco, California
36" × 24" (91.4 × 61 cm), Scale: ⅛"=1'0"
Medium: Ink on Canson paper
Courtesy of David Baker Architects

SOLID OVERHANG SHADOWS

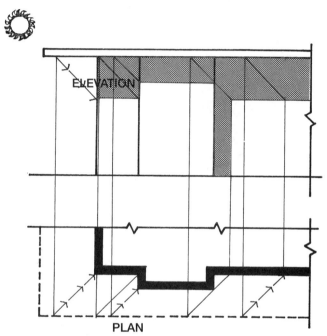

ELEVATION

PLAN

FLAT OVERHANG PARALLEL TO WALL

FLAT OVERHANG OBLIQUE TO WALL

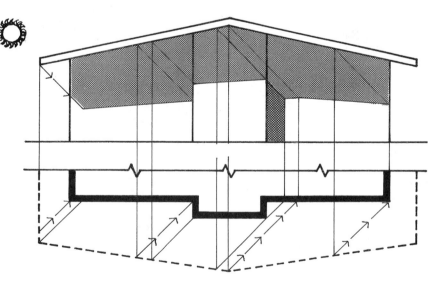

INCLINED OVERHANG OBLIQUE TO WALL

It is common to encounter buildings that have either flat or inclined solid overhangs. The edge casting the shadow line on the vertical wall can be either parallel or oblique to the wall. The previous shadow casting principles for objects on a vertical wall apply for overhangs. Use the plan view to transfer critical points into the elevation. Notice that if the angle of the light ray with respect to the ground line becomes steeper, the length of the resulting shadow will become longer.

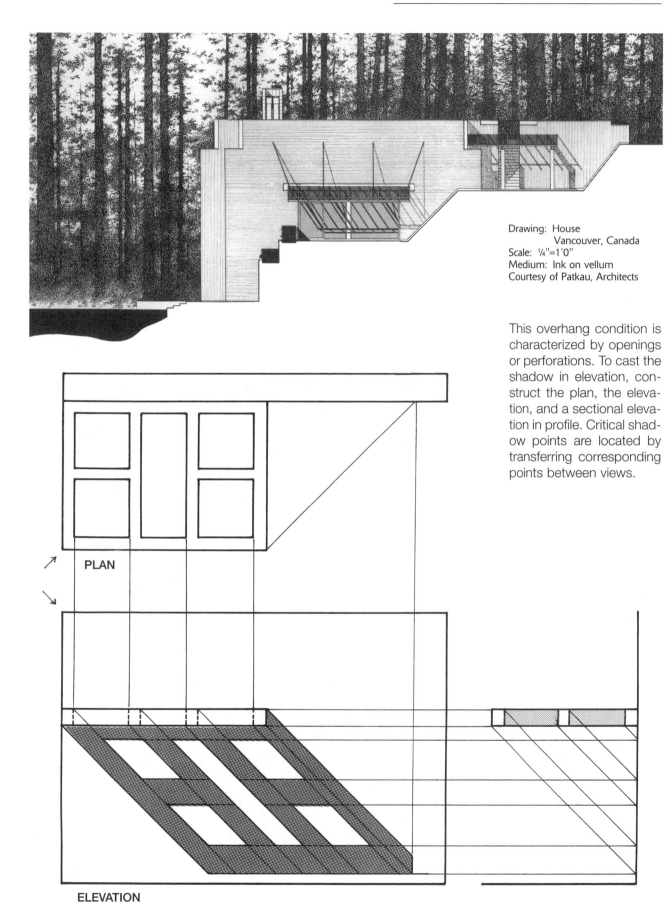

Drawing: House
          Vancouver, Canada
Scale: ¼"=1'0"
Medium: Ink on vellum
Courtesy of Patkau, Architects

This overhang condition is characterized by openings or perforations. To cast the shadow in elevation, construct the plan, the elevation, and a sectional elevation in profile. Critical shadow points are located by transferring corresponding points between views.

PLAN

ELEVATION

PERFORATED OVERHANG SHADOWS

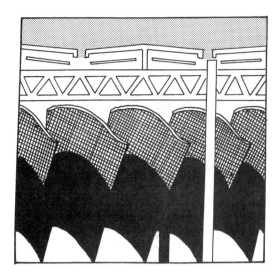

Drawing: Student project by Gorran Tsui
2.5" × 2.5" (6.4 × 6.4 cm)
Medium: Ink and Zipatone on vellum
The Menil Collection Museum, Houston, Texas
Courtesy of Renzo Piano Architect, Piano & Fitzgerald, Houston
and the City College of San Francisco Department of Architecture
Structural Consultant: Ove Arup

CANOPY SHADOWS

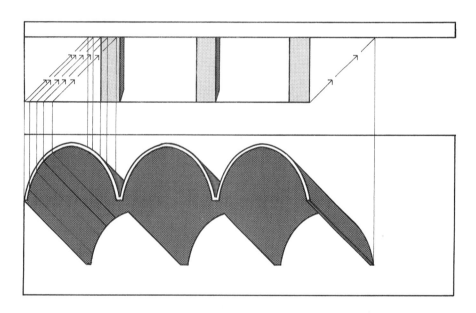

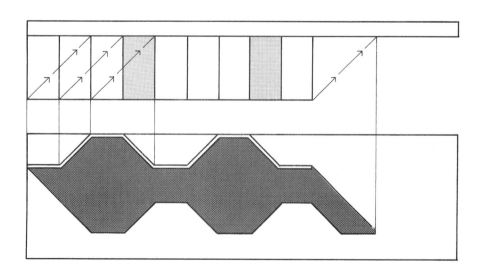

The principle of the shadow of a plane figure casting on a parallel plane is demonstrated on these two facing pages. The bottom edges of the canopies cause a wall shadow line that has the same orientation and configuration as the canopy forms. Likewise, the same geometric shapes of the arcade and the colonnade are cast and seen on the recessed wall shadows. The repetition of geometric forms in all cases gives a shadow rhythm on the receiving surfaces. Note the shade on the underside of the sinuously curved roof canopy (upper left).

Drawing: San Francisco
Waldorf School
36" × 24" (91.4 × ±61 cm),
Scale: ¼"=1'0"
Medium: Ink on Mylar
Courtesy of Tanner Leddy
Maytum Stacy, Architects

Drawing: Texas Rangers Ballpark, Arlington, Texas
24" × 18" (61 × 45.7 cm), Scale: ¼"=1'0"
Medium: Watercolor and pencil on mounted bristol paper
Courtesy of David M. Schwarz/Architectural Services

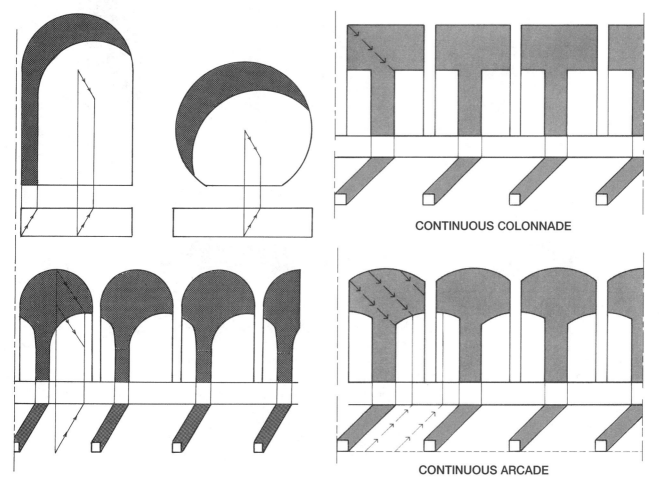

CONTINUOUS COLONNADE

CONTINUOUS ARCADE

COLONNADE AND ARCADE SHADOWS

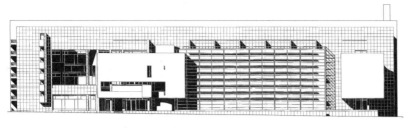

Drawing: Museum of Contemporary Art
Barcelona, Spain
36" × 48" (91.4 × 121.9 cm)
Medium: Ink on Mylar
Courtesy of Richard Meier
& Partners, Architects

NONOVERLAPPING SHADOWS

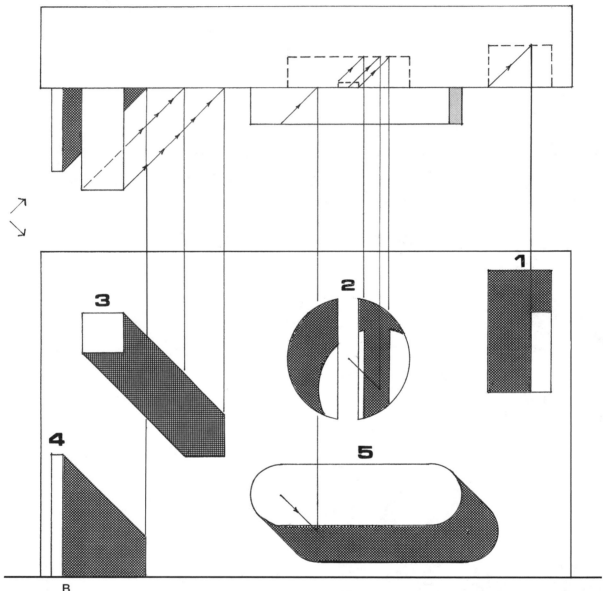

In the wall of shadows shown above, the light source is coming from the left at 45° (see direction arrows in the elevation and the plan views). When we apply the general rule that shadows of plane figures on parallel planes cause shadows of the same size, shape, and orientation, the shadow configurations seen in conditions **1** and **2** become readily apparent and are easily understood. When edges are perpendicular to a vertical wall as in condition **3** and the top edge of condition **4**, the shadow line produced is in the sunlight-bearing direction. Likewise edge AB is perpendicular to the horizontal ground surface, and the shadow line produced on the ground is in the sunlight-bearing direction (plan view) as well as parallel to edge AB when it is intercepted by the vertical wall (elevation view). Condition **5** follows the aforementioned rules.

Photo: Renault Factory (partial elevation), northern Mexico
Courtesy of Legorreta Arquitectos—Ricardo Legorreta,
Victor Legorreta, Noe Castro

This photograph was taken early in the morning in order to obtain hard shadows. Facade details were taken with a 200-mm telefoto lens. I used a Minolta camera with a polarizing filter.
[ARCHITECTURAL PHOTOGRAPHER'S STATEMENT]

OVERLAPPING SHADOWS

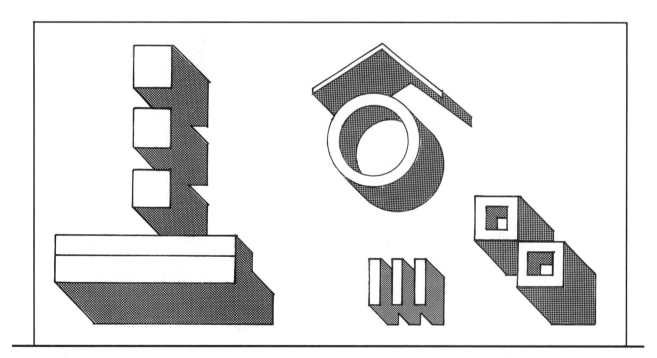

Drawing: Student project by William Xie and Daniel Orona
          Design of a sculptural wall of shadows
Courtesy of the City College of San Francisco
Department of Architecture

When casting shadows of protruding elements that are in close proximity to each other, it is common to find shadows that are interrupted before they hit the major receiving surface. The shadow lines that we do not see sneak across the lighted surface closest to their neighbor.

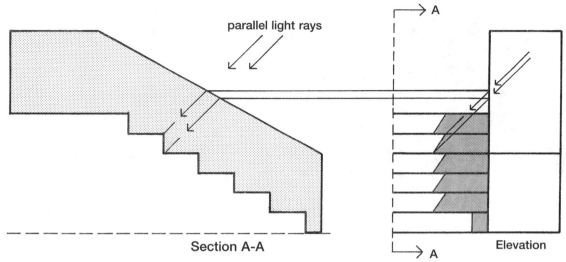

Section A-A

Elevation

Project corresponding points to find the shadow line of an oblique line on the steps above.

Light rays maintain a parallel condition regardless of the geometric configuration of the receiving surface. See condition *A* in both elevation and plan below. A horizontal edge is seen as a point in the elevation **1**. It causes shadow line *A* seen in elevation.

Section B-B

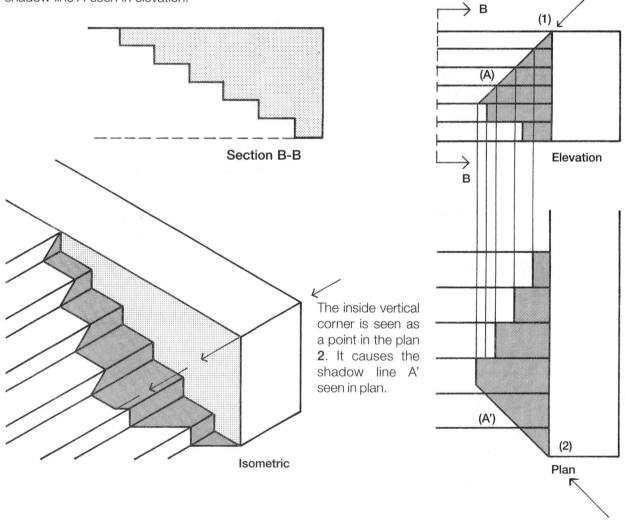

The inside vertical corner is seen as a point in the plan **2**. It causes the shadow line A' seen in plan.

Isometric

Elevation

Plan

STAIRWAY SHADOWS

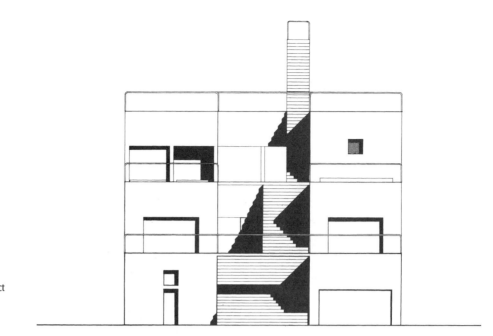

Drawing: Les Echelles
        House for a musician
        Mallorca, Spain
12" × 12" (30.5 × 30.5 cm)
Medium: Ink on Mylar
Courtesy of Diana Agrest, Architect

STAIRWAY SHADOWS

Sometimes stairway configurations
protrude from a vertical surface.

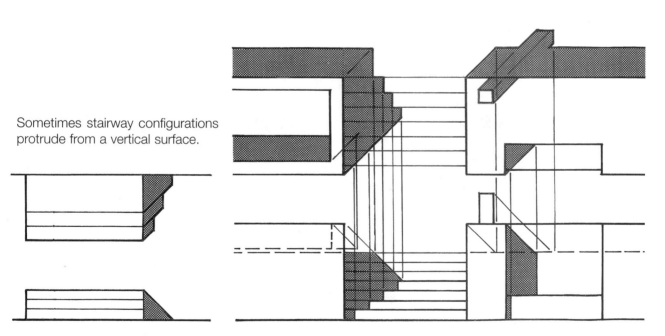

Note that the elevation shadows on the stairway take the same configuration (see facing page) regardless of the direction of the sun's rays.

CYLINDRICAL FORMS AND NICHES

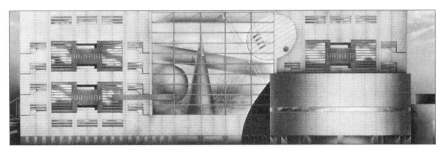

Triangular and trapezoidal niches and cylindrical forms produce interesting shadows. The protruding element on this facade is slightly larger than a semi-cylinder, producing a shadow that begins in a hidden position, as seen in the frontal elevation.

Drawing: Kunibiki Messe, Matsue, Shimane, Japan
48.6" × 33.1" (118.9 × 84.1 cm)
Medium: Airbrush
Courtesy of Shin Takamatsu
Architect & Associates, Kyoto

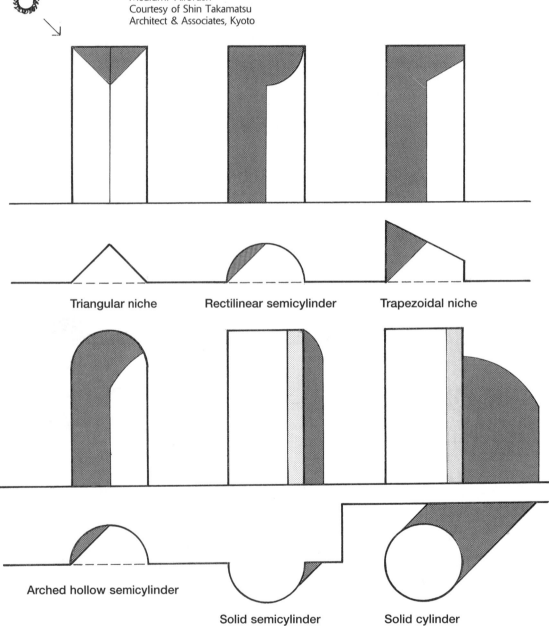

Triangular niche   Rectilinear semicylinder   Trapezoidal niche

Arched hollow semicylinder

Solid semicylinder   Solid cylinder

Shadow designs (two facing pages): Courtesy of Ann Cederna,
Associate Professor
Original medium: Pencil, 8½" × 11" (21.6 × 27.9 cm)
The Catholic University of America School of Architecture & Planning

Rectilinear niches and overhangs also produce interesting shadows. Overhangs in this example cast shadows on both flat and curvilinear surfaces. The curvilinear shape beneath the flat facade results in a curvilinear shadow line.

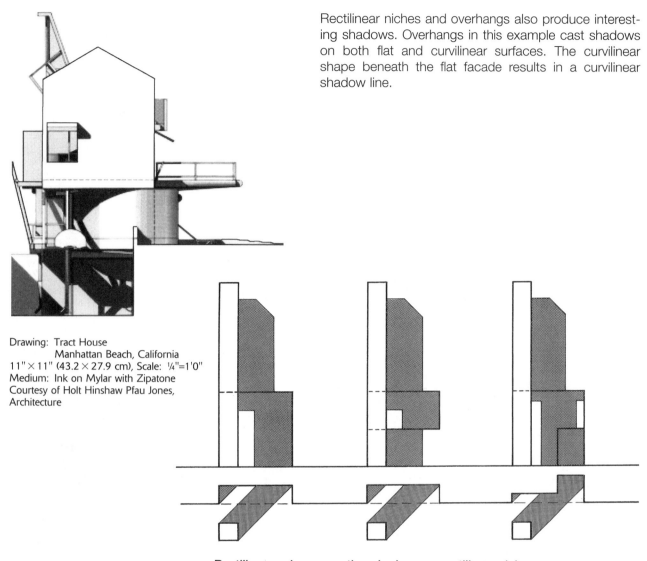

Drawing: Tract House
        Manhattan Beach, California
11" × 11" (43.2 × 27.9 cm), Scale: ¼"=1'0"
Medium: Ink on Mylar with Zipatone
Courtesy of Holt Hinshaw Pfau Jones,
Architecture

Rectilinear columns casting shadows on rectilinear niches

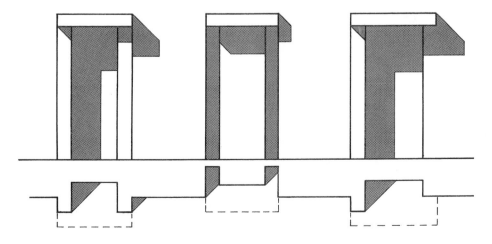

Overhangs casting shadows on rectilinear wall recessions and protrusions

OVERHANGS AND NICHES

PROJECTION USING CORRESPONDING POINTS

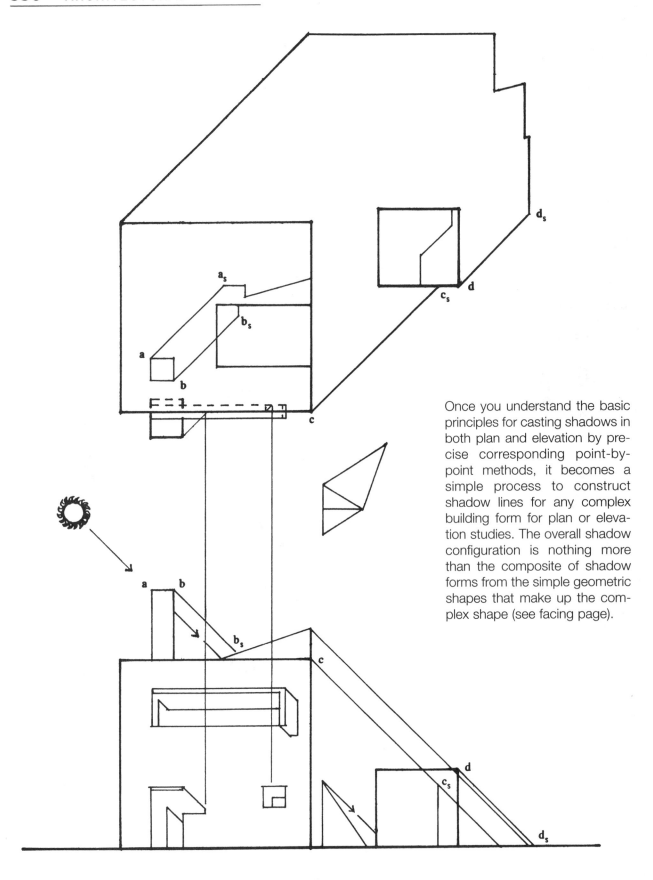

Once you understand the basic principles for casting shadows in both plan and elevation by precise corresponding point-by-point methods, it becomes a simple process to construct shadow lines for any complex building form for plan or elevation studies. The overall shadow configuration is nothing more than the composite of shadow forms from the simple geometric shapes that make up the complex shape (see facing page).

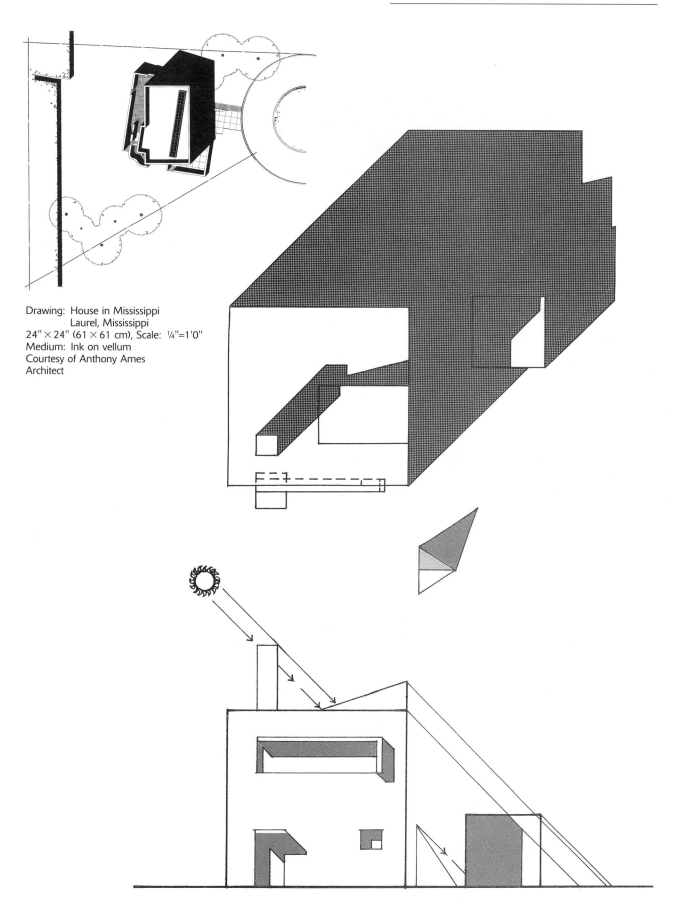

Drawing: House in Mississippi
Laurel, Mississippi
24" × 24" (61 × 61 cm), Scale: ¼"=1'0"
Medium: Ink on vellum
Courtesy of Anthony Ames
Architect

SHADOWS IN PLAN AND IN ELEVATION

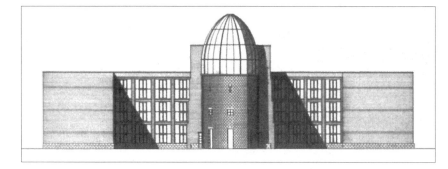

Drawing: Bonnefanten Museum
Maastrich, Holland
Medium: Black and red ink on vellum
Courtesy of Aldo Rossi, Architect
with Etienne Van Sloun & Gregor Ramaekers

Intersecting 90° exterior walls (above) produce a continuous shadow line. Intersecting exterior walls at uneven heights produce a broken shadow line. If a cylindrical form has a shaded side as above, the shaded area cannot have any shadow fall on it.

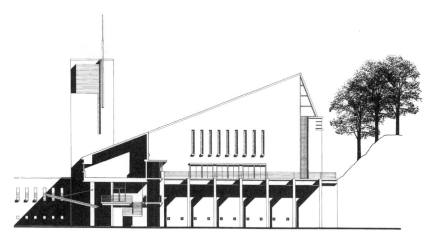

Drawing: Singapore American School, Singapore
Medium: Ink on Mylar, 36" × 24" (91 × 61.4 cm)
Courtesy of Perkins & Will Architects

The form displacement and composition of the fenestration on building facades cannot be rendered without shadows. Shadows give us clues as to how a facade articulates. For example, the wider the shadow on its receiving surface, the more the protruding element that casts the shadow on the surface will extend outward. Shadows on elevations are an effective means of showing the massing and character of protruding and recessed elements. All of these examples with deeply casted shadows illustrate how two-dimensional elevations can be given a three-dimensional feeling and quality.

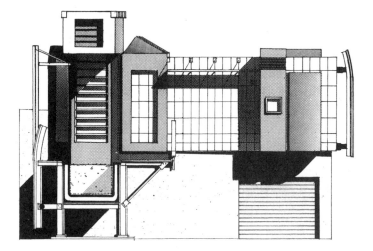

Drawing: Private studio, Venice, California
10" × 8" (25.4 × 20.3 cm), Scale: ⅛"=1'0"
Medium: Vellum, ink, and Zipatone
Courtesy of William Adams Architect

The purpose of elevation shadows in presentation drawings is to provide contrast in order to suggest a third dimension. In practice the designer or delineator has the liberty to choose the sunlight direction and is not required to keep the standard 45° light ray from the top behind the left shoulder convention. One should select the sun's position in a manner that would accentuate the architectural design.

SHADOWS IN ELEVATION — BUILDING EXAMPLES

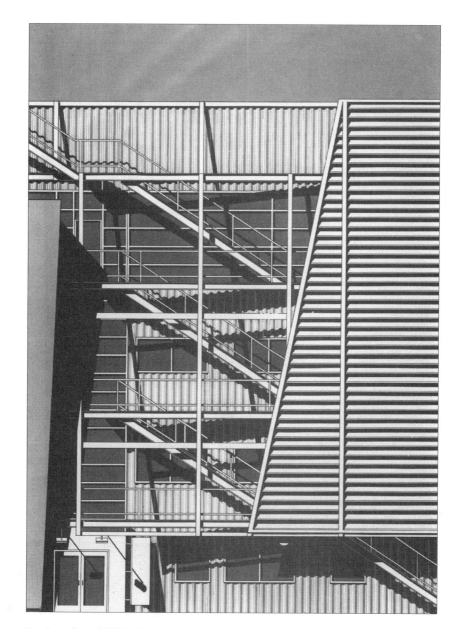

Drawing: Central Chiller Plant and Cogeneration Facility, UCLA
          North elevation detail
24" × 30" (61 × 76.2 cm), Scale: ½"=1'0"
Medium: Ink on Mylar and Zipatone
Courtesy of Holt Hinshaw Pfau Jones Architecture

This north elevation has no true solar orientation. In order to create a convincing portrayal of the complex building planes, therefore, the shade and shadow was constructed intuitively, to best illuminate the juxtaposition of the orthogonal and nonorthogonal geometries.
[ARCHITECT'S STATEMENT BY PAUL C. HOLT]

The tight composition of this drawing allows it to be read both as a representation of three-dimensional space as well as an abstract two-dimensional composition. Due to the fact that the corrugated receiving surface slopes away from the viewer, the cast shadows rake across it, introducing a secondary geometry to this otherwise orthogonal composition. Moreover, they afford a greater sense of depth to a drawing format which traditionally tends to compress space.
[ARCHITECT'S STATEMENT BY WES JONES]

SHADOWS IN ELEVATION — BUILDING EXAMPLE

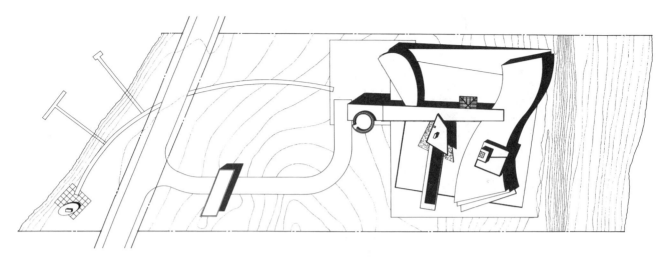

Drawing: Worrel residence, Hillsborough, Florida
36" × 24" (91.4 × 61 cm)
Medium: Ink on vellum
Courtesy of Arquitectonica

When there are many elements in a site plan, as shown in these examples, the resolution of their proper shadow lengths will require both the plan and the elevation (height) of each element. Note that the procedure is analogous to resolving shadow lengths for wall elements seen in elevation.

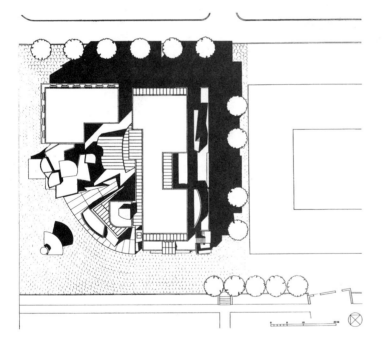

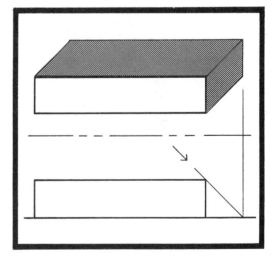

Drawing: American Center, Bercy Park, Paris, France
30" × 40" (76.2 × 101.6 cm)
Medium: Ink on Mylar
Courtesy of Frank O. Gehry & Associates, Architects

SHADOWS ON ROOF AND SITE PLANS

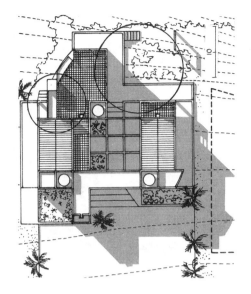

Drawing: Lohmann House
        Akumal, Yucatan, Mexico
16" × 24" (40.6 × 61 cm), Scale: 1:100
Medium: Ink and Zipatone
Courtesy of George C. T. Woo, Architect, FAIA

Drawing: The Church of St. Therese
        Wilson, North Carolina
9.5" × 7" (24.1 × 17.8 cm), Scale: 1"=20'0"
Medium: Ink on Mylar
Courtesy of Allen, Harbinson &
Associates, Architect

Circled situations in the above left site plan adhere to the following principles: In the plan view light rays and shadow lines cast by vertical light/shade lines maintain **parallelity** regardless of the geometric configuration of the receiving surfaces. The shadow line retains continuity in a straight line when it strikes the receiving geometric forms. The shadows of all the posts in the drawing to the right are parallel to each other as well as parallel to the shadows of the other structural elements, following the parallelity principle.

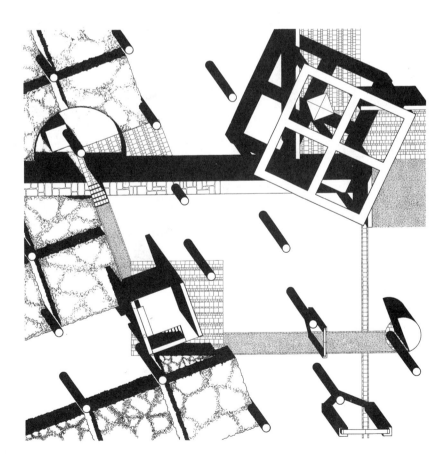

Drawing: Student project by Stephen Roberts
        and Doug Lincer
        Garden Intervention
Medium: Ink on Mylar
Courtesy of the University of Texas at
Arlington School of Architecture

SHADOWS ON ROOF PLANS AND SITE PLANS

SHADOWS CAST WITHIN THE PLAN VIEW

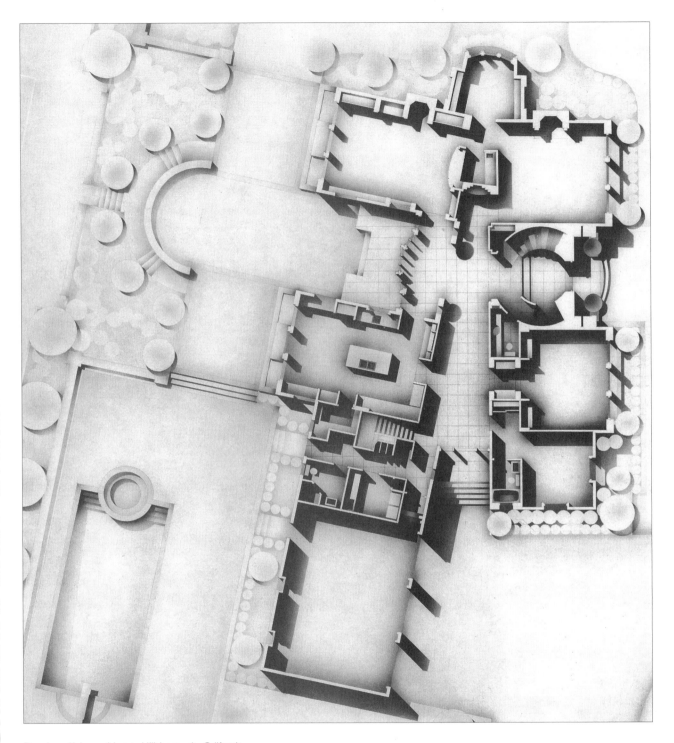

Drawing: Kahn residence, Hillsborough, California
24" × 30" (61 × 76.2 cm), Scale: ¼"=1'0"
Medium: Airbrush using acrylic inks over latex paint on masonite board
Courtesy of House + House, Architects, San Francisco
Mark David English, Inglese Architecture, Architectural Illustrator

This drawing shows shadows cast in the plan view by vertical elements cut in plan. The purpose is to make the drawing "read" better by accentuating the heights of the elements (walls, columns etc.) to give a greater feeling of depth and to eliminate the flatness of the plan view.

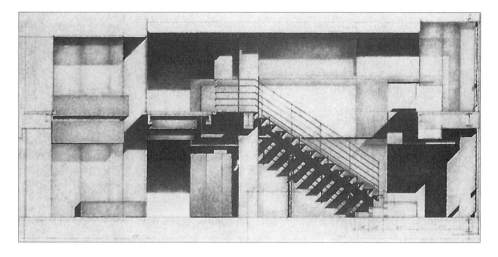

Drawing: The Stainless Steel Apartment, Chicago, Illinois
36" × 24" (91.4 × 61 cm), Scale: ½"=1'0"
Medium: Colored pencil
Courtesy of Krueck & Sexton, Architects
and Ludwig Mies Van der Rohe, Building Architect

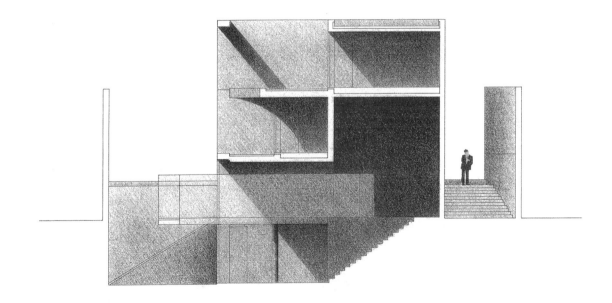

Drawing: I Gallery, Tokyo, Japan
429 × 297 mm (16.9" × 11.7"), Scale: 1:100
Medium: Colored pencil on the copy of the inked drawing
Courtesy of Tadao Ando, Architect

These drawings show shadows cast in a cut section. All elements that protrude (i.e., wall, floor, roof, stairs, built-in furniture, etc.) will cast a shadow. This allows a normally flat two-dimensional section to "punch out."

SHADOWS CAST WITHIN THE SECTION

Drawing: Villa Gables
Meersbusch near Dusseldorf, Germany
Southwest facade 15" × 9" (381. × 22.9 cm), Scale: 1:50
Medium: Colored pencil on yellow tracing paper
Courtesy of Michael Graves, Architect
Photo credit: Marek Bulaj

The representational style that Architect Michael Graves uses in his soft colored pencil conceptual sketches is characterized by predominantly frontal views such as elevations, plans, and projections (see Bibliography).

SHADOWS ON INCLINED SURFACES

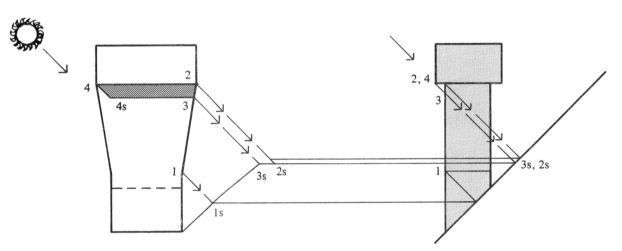

Chimneys are commonly seen casting shadows on a roof plane that is inclined. Most chimney shapes are rectilinear; this example shows a slight variation. With two or more elevations, you can project shadow construction lines from one to the other to determine the proper shadow configuration. Always label the critical points in all views and be systematic in your convention.

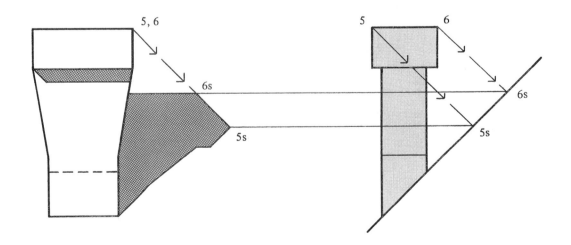

Drawing: Villa Gables
Meerbusch near Dusseldorf, Germany
Northwest facade 14" × 9" (35.6 × 22.9 cm), Scale: 1:50
Medium: Colored pencil on yellow tracing paper
Courtesy of Michael Graves, Architect
Photo credit: Marek Bulaj

A dormer is characterized by a projection that extends above a wall and intersects a sloping roof. Windows on its front vertical face provide light, ventilation, and attic space. These two examples show typical shade and shadow conditions.

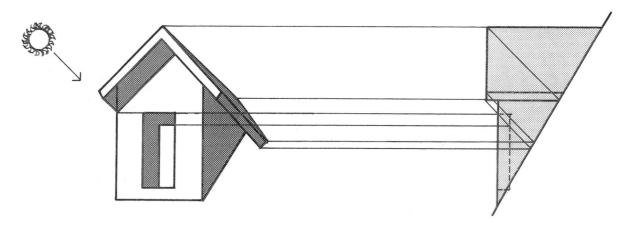

Dormers exhibit a combination of shadows on vertical and inclined surfaces seen in elevation. The profile of the side elevation of the dormer that is seen in shade will cast critical points on the sloping roof. These points are horizontally projected back into the front elevation in order to locate the same critical points seen in the front elevation view.

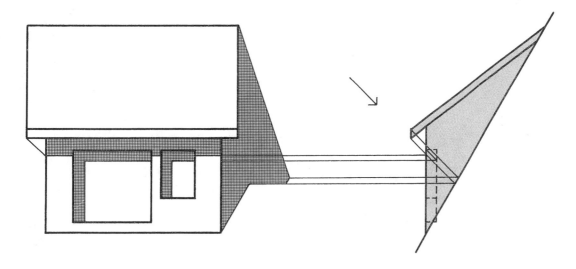

SHADOWS ON INCLINED SURFACES

Since the sun's light rays are assumed to be **parallel,** they cause vertical (parallel) object lines to cast **parallel shadow lines** on flat or inclined surfaces. This is always true for shadow lines seen either in the plan view or in the elevation view (see example to the right).

SHADOWS ON INCLINED SURFACES

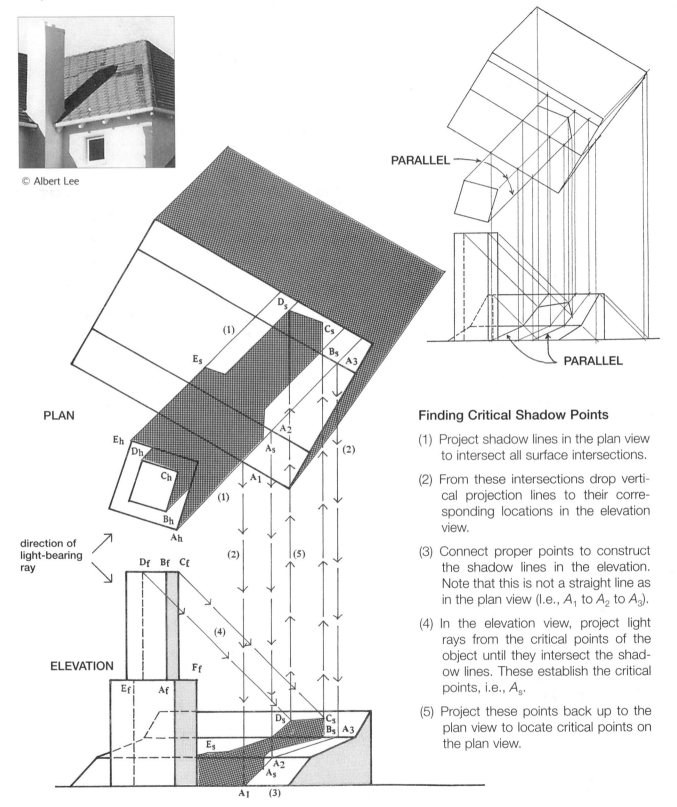

© Albert Lee

Finding Critical Shadow Points

(1) Project shadow lines in the plan view to intersect all surface intersections.

(2) From these intersections drop vertical projection lines to their corresponding locations in the elevation view.

(3) Connect proper points to construct the shadow lines in the elevation. Note that this is not a straight line as in the plan view (I.e., A_1 to A_2 to A_3).

(4) In the elevation view, project light rays from the critical points of the object until they intersect the shadow lines. These establish the critical points, i.e., A_s.

(5) Project these points back up to the plan view to locate critical points on the plan view.

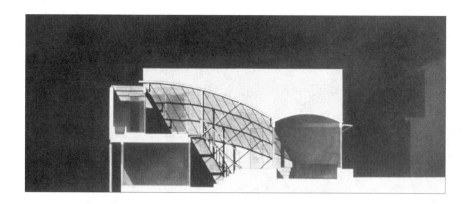

This curvilinear roof fenestration casts a strong shadow in the sectional elevation. This is another nice example of shadows cast within the section.

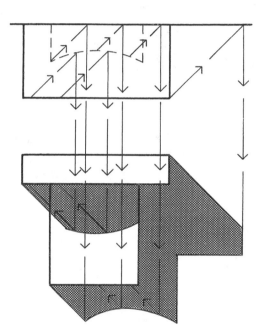

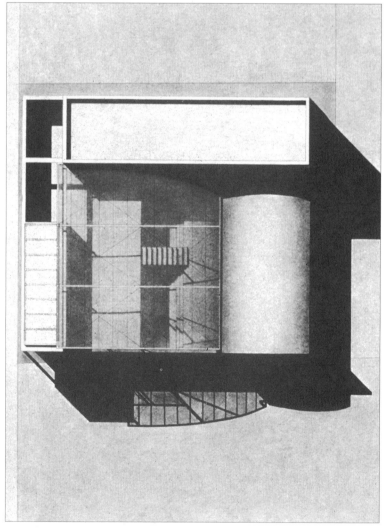

Curvilinear surfaces differ from inclined surfaces in the sense that a series of points, rather than just end points, are needed. Shadow lines on a curvilinear surface cast by a horizontal line can be determined by plotting arbitrary points. Likewise, the same procedure applies for a curvilinear line casting a shadow line on a horizontal surface.

Drawings: Sugita House, Katsushika-ku, Tokyo, Japan
9.88" × 13.88" (25.1 × 35.3 cm), Scale: $\frac{1}{30}$"=1'0"
Medium: Charcoal
Courtesy of Riken Yamamoto & Field Shop, Architects
Drawing by Monica Shanley

SHADOWS ON CURVILINEAR SURFACES

ISOMETRIC PARALINE SHADOWS

45° Light ray condition
Paraline conditions exhibit light rays parallel to the picture plane.

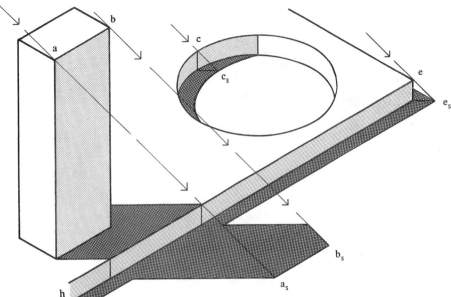

Drawing: Faculty Housing
The Rockefeller
University
Pocantico Hills, New York
Partial drawing is shown
30" × 48" (76.2 × 121.9 cm)
Scale: ⅛"=1'0"
Medium: Oil paint and colored
pencil on black line diazo print
Courtesy of Michael Fieldman
& Partners, Architects

Critical paraline shadow points are determined by constructing triangular planes parallel to the picture plane. A vertical drop or rise (h) in the horizontal surface connects paraline shadows on different horizontal surfaces. A drop in a horizontal receiving surface always results in a longer shadow. A rise in a horizontal receiving surface always results in a shorter shadow.

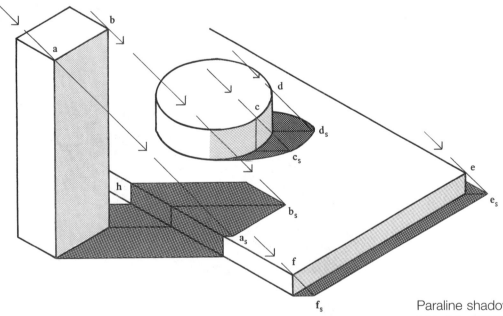

Paraline shadows of cylindrical forms can be determined by finding and plotting a series of arbitrary points (c and d) on the light/shade boundary.

45° Light ray condition
Paraline conditions exhibit light rays parallel to the picture plane.

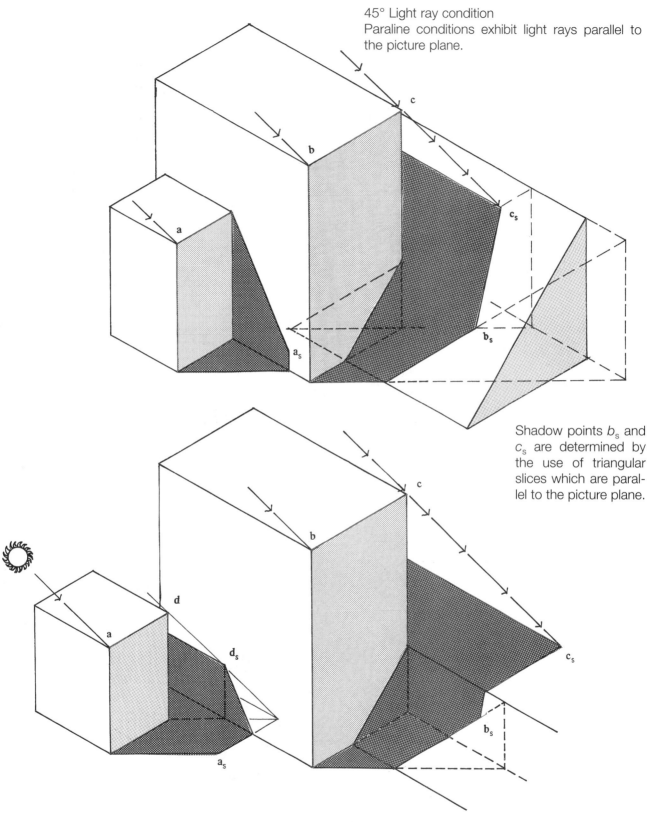

Shadow points b_s and c_s are determined by the use of triangular slices which are parallel to the picture plane.

ISOMETRIC PARALINE SHADOWS

For separate blocks, to determine the shadow on the vertical wall, it is best to cast a shadow on the ground assuming there is no wall. Then project horizontal and vertical trace lines until they intersect the light-bearing rays.

PLAN OBLIQUE PARALINE SHADOWS

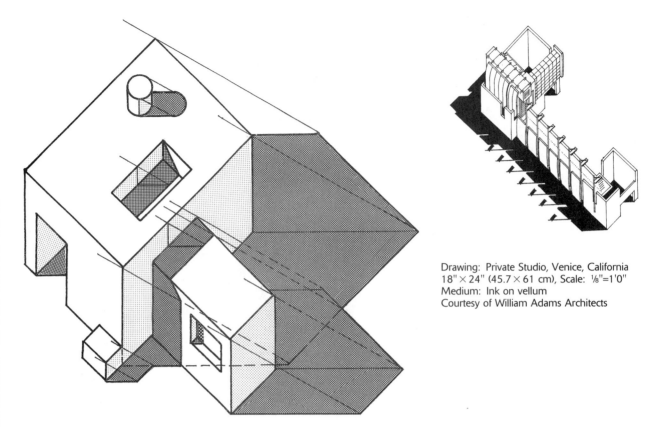

Drawing: Private Studio, Venice, California
18" × 24" (45.7 × 61 cm), Scale: ⅛"=1'0"
Medium: Ink on vellum
Courtesy of William Adams Architects

These plan oblique (45-45°) drawings exhibit shadows cast from light rays that are parallel to the picture plane. Critical shadow points on the ground are determined by the intersection of sloping light rays from a casting edge (height or altitude) and the bearing line on the ground. In the above example, the small building elements intercept the light rays cast by vertical and horizontal casting edges of the large building element. This results in a shadow line that climbs across the small element.

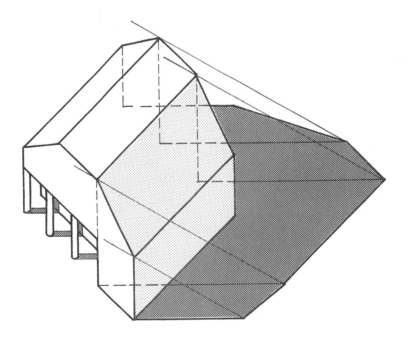

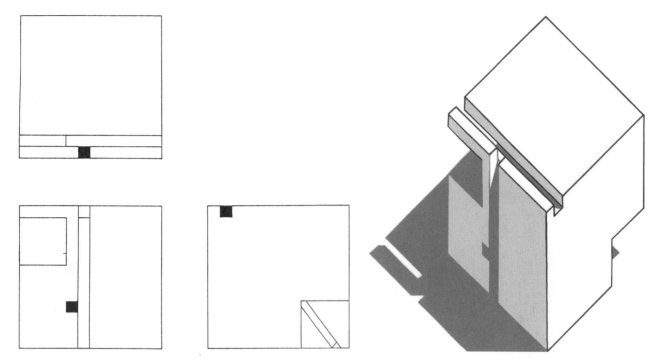

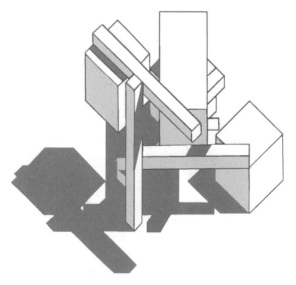

Drawing: Student project by Andrew Von Mauer, Solid void relationship investigation
Medium: Ink on Mylar, 17" × 11" (43.2 × 27.9 cm), Scale: Full-size after model
Courtesy of Andrews University, Division of Architecture, 1st year Graphics Studio
Studio Professor: Arpad Daniel Ronaszegi, Assistant: Tom Lowing

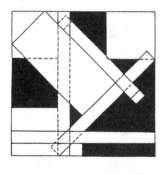

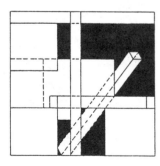

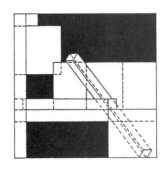

Drawing: Student project by Andrew Von Mauer, Solid void relationship investigation
Medium: Ink on Mylar, 17" × 11" (43.2 × 27.9 cm), Scale: Full-size after model
Courtesy of Andrews University, Division of Architecture, 1st year Graphics Studio
Studio Professor: Arpad Daniel Ronaszegi, Assistant: Tom Lowing

PLAN OBLIQUE PARALINE SHADOWS

PARALINE SHADOWS

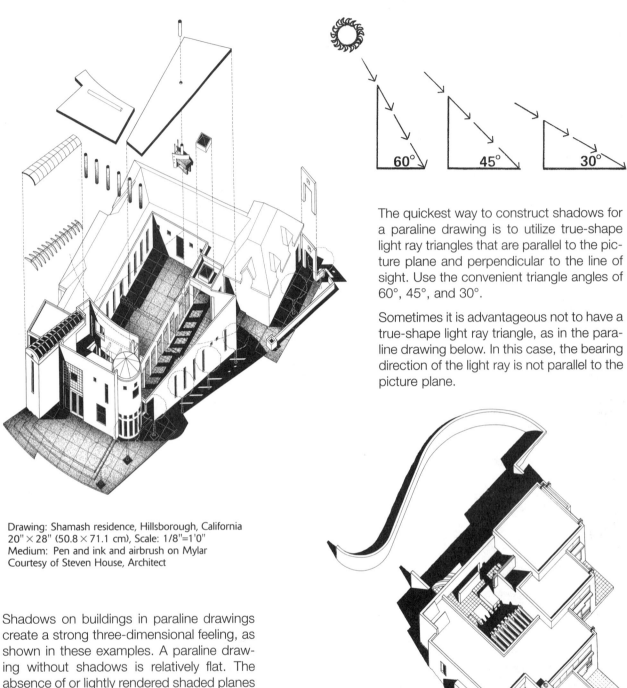

The quickest way to construct shadows for a paraline drawing is to utilize true-shape light ray triangles that are parallel to the picture plane and perpendicular to the line of sight. Use the convenient triangle angles of 60°, 45°, and 30°.

Sometimes it is advantageous not to have a true-shape light ray triangle, as in the paraline drawing below. In this case, the bearing direction of the light ray is not parallel to the picture plane.

Drawing: Shamash residence, Hillsborough, California
20" × 28" (50.8 × 71.1 cm), Scale: 1/8"=1'0"
Medium: Pen and ink and airbrush on Mylar
Courtesy of Steven House, Architect

Shadows on buildings in paraline drawings create a strong three-dimensional feeling, as shown in these examples. A paraline drawing without shadows is relatively flat. The absence of or lightly rendered shaded planes are permissible when fenestration detail must be clear (see above). Always choose a convenient angle (45 or 60°) and direction for the slope of the light rays. Complex configurations can best be resolved by a series of shadow point casting triangles.

Drawing: Kress residence, Albuquerque, New Mexico
20" × 30" (50.8 × 76.2 cm), Scale: ¼"=1'0"
Medium: Ink on vellum
Courtesy of Robert W. Peters FAIA,
Alianza Arquitectos/An Architect's Alliance

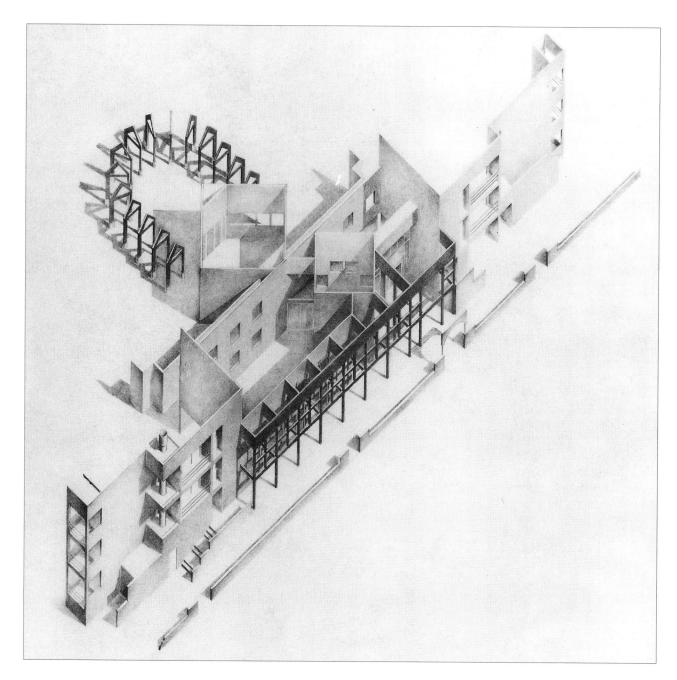

Drawing: Verdugo Hacienda Elderly Housing, Sunland, Tujunga, California
24" × 24" (61 × 61 cm), Scale: ⅛"=1'0"
Medium: Ink and colored pencil
Courtesy of John V. Mutlow FAIA, Architects

To articulate the basic premise of this courtyard building, only the important public spaces and enclosure planes were selected for delineation. The brisesoleil shades the south-facing front elevation and the rotating volumes connect the off-center enclosure to the axial coutyard and lanai. The shadows were then cast in order to best articulate the building form and movement sequence.
[ARCHITECT'S STATEMENT]

This drawing also does not use a true shape light ray triangle. Note the use of nice soft shadows.

SHADOW AND SUN'S RAYS VANISHING POINTS

Select the location of the vanishing point of the sun's rays on the vertical tracer line. The vanishing point of the shadow will also fall on this line. Note that the small triangle (ABC) and the large triangle are similar.

VP$_S$ or VPS is the vanishing point of the shadow.

VP$_{SR}$ or VPSR is the vanishing point of the sun's rays.

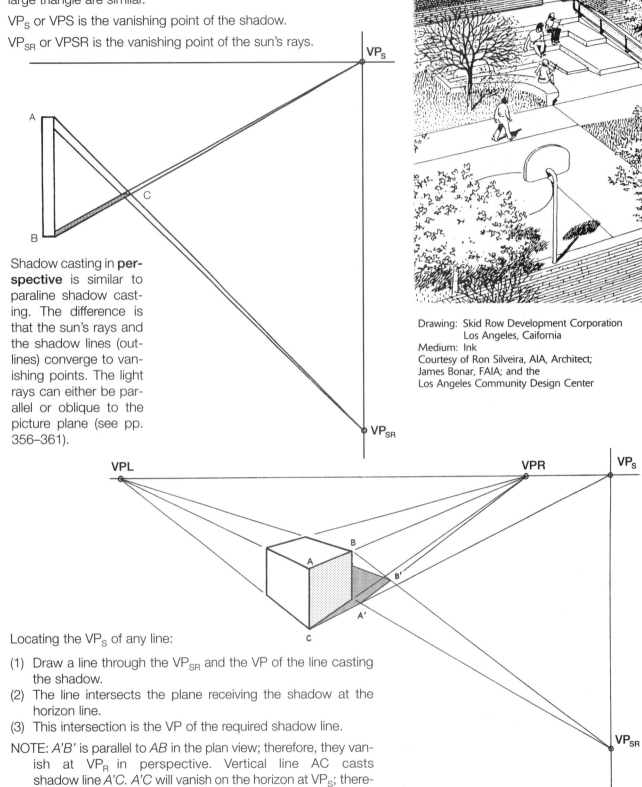

Drawing: Skid Row Development Corporation
         Los Angeles, Caifornia
Medium: Ink
Courtesy of Ron Silveira, AIA, Architect;
James Bonar, FAIA; and the
Los Angeles Community Design Center

Shadow casting in **perspective** is similar to paraline shadow casting. The difference is that the sun's rays and the shadow lines (outlines) converge to vanishing points. The light rays can either be parallel or oblique to the picture plane (see pp. 356–361).

Locating the VP$_S$ of any line:

(1) Draw a line through the VP$_{SR}$ and the VP of the line casting the shadow.

(2) The line intersects the plane receiving the shadow at the horizon line.

(3) This intersection is the VP of the required shadow line.

NOTE: A'B' is parallel to AB in the plan view; therefore, they vanish at VP$_R$ in perspective. Vertical line AC casts shadow line A'C. A'C will vanish on the horizon at VP$_S$; therefore, all vertical lines will cast shadows that vanish at VP$_S$.

Photo: Notre Dame Catholic Church, Kerrville, Texas
Courtesy of Tapley/Lunow Architects,
Gerald Moorhead FAIA

Shadows Cast on a Combination of Horizontal and Vertical Surfaces

(1) Vertical light/shade line *ab* casts shadow line ab_s on the ground and this line vanishes at the VPS.

(2) Vertical light/shade line *bc* casts shadow line $b_s c_s$. This is a case of a vertical line casting a shadow line on a vertical surface.

(3) Horizontal light/shade line *cd* casts shadow line $c_s d_s$, which vanishes at the intersection of the line through the VPSR and the VPR and the vertical traces through the VPL.

(4) Vertical light/shade line *de* casts shadow line $d_s e_s$ following the principle stated in step 2.

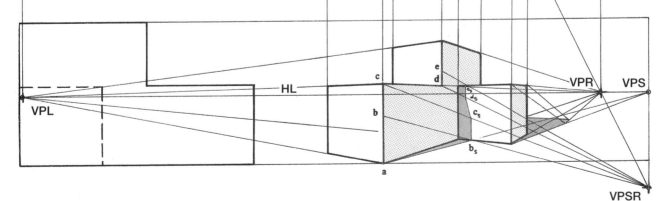

PP

HL

VPL

SP

VPR   VPS

VPSR

a *b* *c* *d* *e* b_s c_s d_s

PERSPECTIVE SHADOWS ON INTERSECTING SURFACES

PERSPECTIVE SHADES AND SHADOWS

Photo (right): Newport Center/Fashion Island
Newport Beach, California
Courtesy of the SWA Group

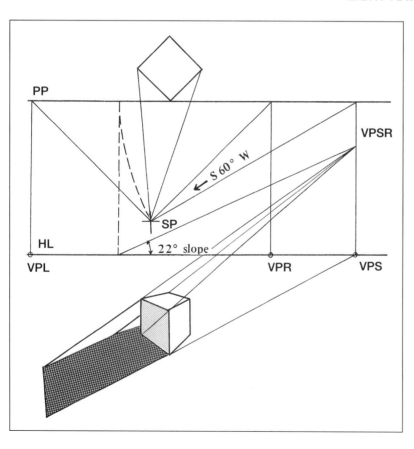

LIGHT RAYS PARALLEL TO THE PICTURE PLANE

Light rays **parallel** to the picture plane can be cast at any convenient angle, such as 45°, depending on the effect desired. A **vertical line** casts a shadow line that is **parallel** to the HL and the PP in the direction of the bearing of the light rays. Lines **parallel** to the ground plane cast shadow lines that are **parallel** to the line casting the shadow line.

LIGHT RAYS OBLIQUE TO THE PICTURE PLANE

Given conditions:
Bearing of light rays = S 60° W
slope = 22°

Note that the VPSR is **above** the HL.

The vanishing point of the sun's rays (VPSR) is located by **rotating** the bearing line into the PP and dropping a vertical to locate the corresponding point on the HL. From this point the slope of the light ray is drawn until it intercepts the vertical tracer line drawn from the penetration point on the PP by the bearing of the light rays. The vanishing point of the shadow (VPS) lies at the intersection of this vertical tracer and the HL.

BEARING—the direction of the line (in this case a light ray) relative to due north or south. It is always measured in the plan view and expressed in degrees.

SLOPE— the slope angle of a line measured in the elevation view relative to the horizon line and expressed in degrees.

View from west

View from northwest

Drawing: High Sierra Meadow's Edge Cabin
Medium: CAD
Courtesy of Jones, Partners: Architecture

PERSPECTIVE SHADES AND SHADOWS

PERSPECTIVE SHADES AND SHADOWS

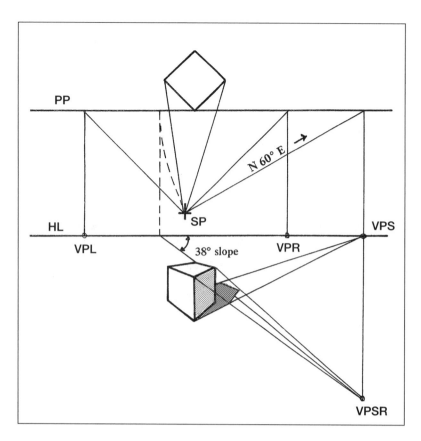

PP

HL

VPL

SP

VPR

VPS

38° slope

N 60° E

VPSR

Light rays oblique to the picture plane

Given conditions:

Bearing of light rays = N 60° E
Slope = 38°

Note that the VPSR is **below** the HL.

Photo: Bollard, Alcoa Building Plaza
(Maritime Plaza)
San Francisco, California
Courtesy of the SWA Group

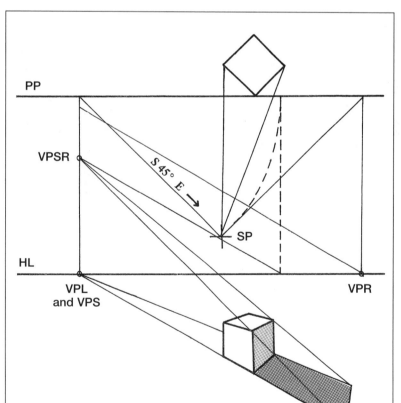

PP

VPSR

S 45° E

SP

HL

VPL
and VPS

VPR

Light rays oblique to the picture plane

Given conditions:

Bearing of light rays = S 45° E
Slope = 30°

Note that the VPSR is **above** the HL.

Photo: Garden Area of Pitney Bowes
World Headquarters
Stamford, Connecticut
Courtesy of I. M. Pei & Partners, Architects
© 1987 Steve Rosenthal

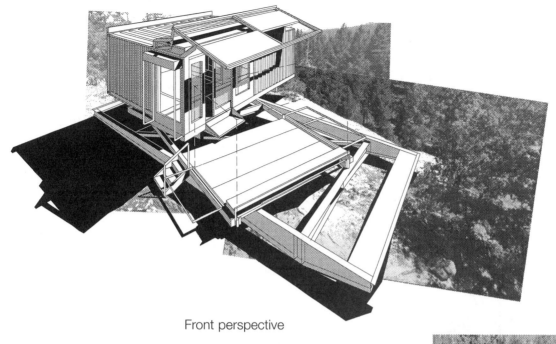

Front perspective

Rear perspective

PERSPECTIVE SHADES AND SHADOWS

Drawings: High Sierras Guest Cabin
Medium: CAD
Courtesy of Jones, Partners: Architecture

Integral to this project is the contrasting nature of human-generated systems [as represented by the modular container element] and naturally generated systems [the site environs]. The juxtaposition of hardline, shadowed rendering with scanned photographic information underscores this dichotomy. The representation of shade and shadow provides a link between these two graphic modes.
[ARCHITECT'S STATEMENT]

PERSPECTIVE SHADOWS ON SURFACES

Light rays are parallel to the picture plane for these two perspective conditions. Triangular slice *rst* is in a plane that is parallel to the picture plane. Its location is determned by horizontal line *qrt*. Line *rs* determines the locus for piercing points for a variety of light ray angles.

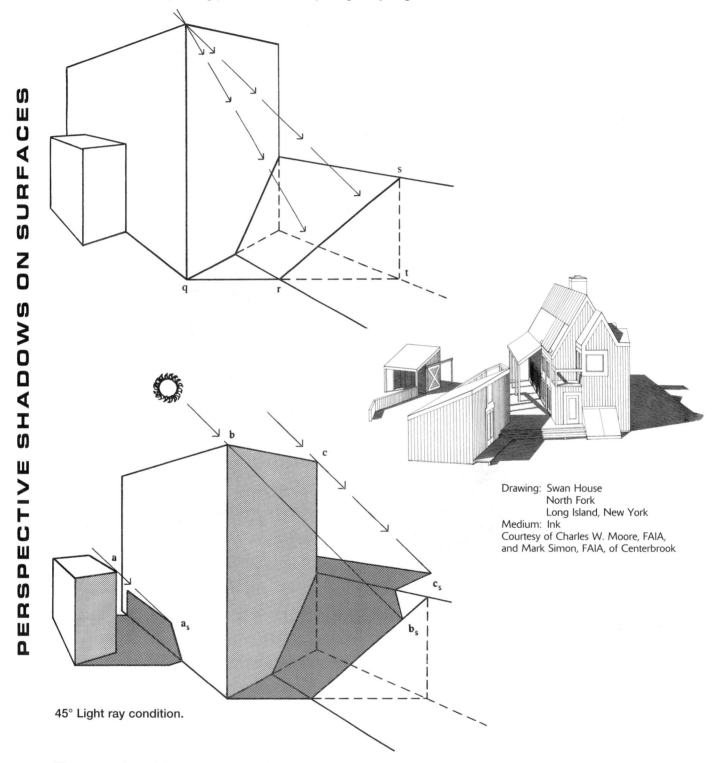

45° Light ray condition.

Drawing: Swan House
North Fork
Long Island, New York
Medium: Ink
Courtesy of Charles W. Moore, FAIA,
and Mark Simon, FAIA, of Centerbrook

The separation of the two block forms causes shadows to be cast on both horizontal and vertical surfaces similar to the two building elements of the Swan House.

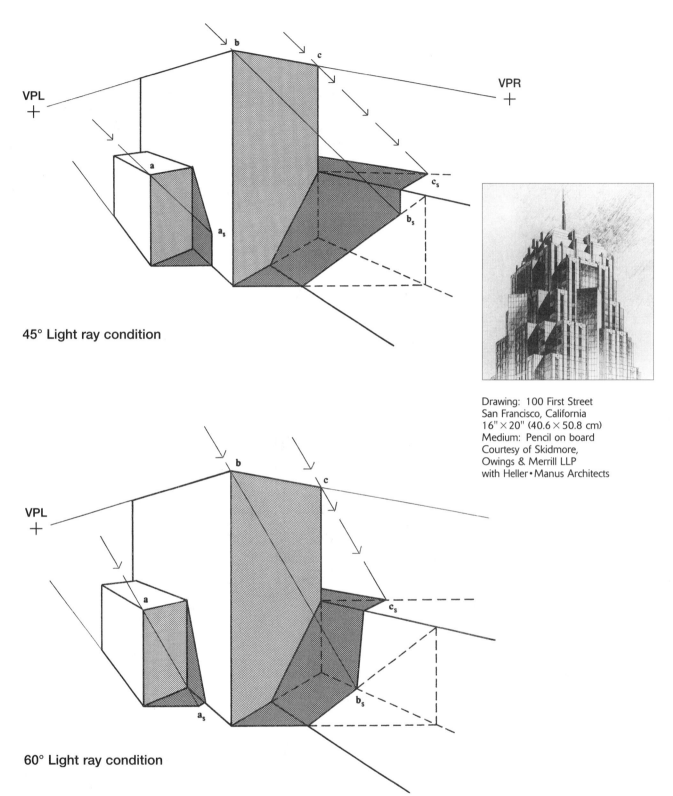

VPL

VPR

45° Light ray condition

Drawing: 100 First Street
San Francisco, California
16" × 20" (40.6 × 50.8 cm)
Medium: Pencil on board
Courtesy of Skidmore,
Owings & Merrill LLP
with Heller • Manus Architects

VPL

60° Light ray condition

PERSPECTIVE SHADOWS ON SURFACES

As on the previous page, light rays for these two perspective conditions are parallel to the picture plane, and they are also parallel to each other. To determine the critical shadow piercing point on the sloping surface (b_s), set up a triangular slice (dashed lines) that is parallel to the picture plane. Critical point c_s also lies in a plane that is parallel to the picture plane.

As the sun moves during the daytime, the solar angle changes, causing the perspective shadow of a dormer on an inclined roof to have an infinite number of positions as it moves across the sloping roof. Two conditions on opposite uphill sides of a dormer are shown on this and the facing page.

Dormer shadows sloping uphill are always shorter than they would be on a horizontal surface regardless of the light ray direction. When sloping downhill, they are always longer than on a horizontal plane.

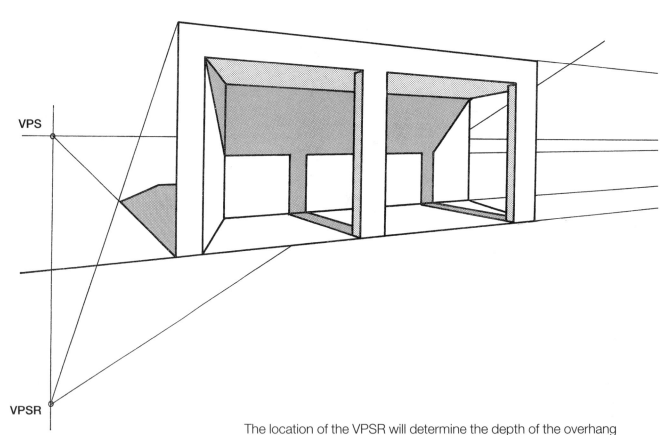

The location of the VPSR will determine the depth of the overhang shadow on the back wall. A vertical line through the VPSR will determine the VPS on the horizon line. The columns cast shadows on the ground whose edges vanish at the VPS. Then the shadow vertically creeps up the back wall and connects to the overhang shadow.

PERSPECTIVE SHADOWS OF DORMER AND OVERHANG

Drawing: Private house, Wilmington, North Carolina
24" × 36" (61 × 91.4 cm), Scale (site plan): 1"=20'0"
Medium: Ink on Mylar
Courtesy of Gerald Allen & Jeffrey Harbinson, Architects, P.C.

Three-dimensional objects can be understood, for the most part, by the result of how they mold shadow and light. The house in the drawing above uses no lines to define its form. Instead, its image is entirely a result of the shadows that it casts.
[ARCHITECT'S STATEMENT]

PERSPECTIVE SHADOWS OF DORMER AND OVERHANG

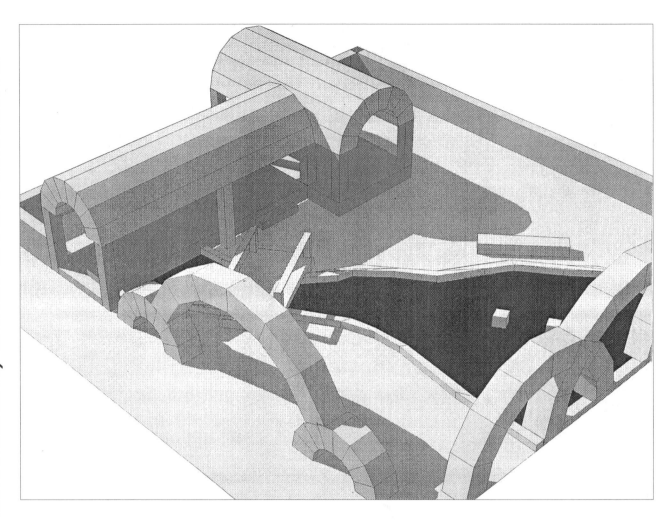

Drawings: Student project by Jeremy McFarland
　　　　　 Bird's-eye and pedestrian views
　　　　　 (opposite) of a building complex
Studio Professor: Dick Davison
Courtesy of Texas A & M University
Department of Architecture

Drawings done on Silicon Graphics Indigo
computers using Alias Upfront software

An understanding of shadow constructions is important for anyone involved in creating two-dimensional images that are meant to be realistic or believable as three-dimensional concepts. After the manual methods of perspective and shadow construction are understood, the time-saving computer-generated image can be fully appreciated. Most computer programs that offer perspective can create shadows for any possible shadow-casting scenario.

These pages represent a project that involved the design of a pavilion within a 100' square space. The modeling capability of the computer software makes it possible to create quick views within the space (as in the above perspective through the arch). The shadow configuration is, of course, also in perspective. Computer-generated shadow constructions will generally give the same added sense of realness that hand-drawn shadows offer. However, a truly practiced eye will be able to render nuances of light and shadow that will not be found in the more "automatic" CADD renditions.
[STUDIO PROFESSOR'S STATEMENT]

"Nuances of light and shadow" as they are applied in order to articulate form and express depth will be examined in the next chapter.

PERSPECTIVE SHADOWS/COMPUTER IMAGING

9

Delineating and Rendering Entourage

The major communicative drawings (plan, elevation, section, paralines, and perspectives) are part of a presentation package. It is of utmost importance to accentuate these drawings by the use of contrast so that they "read" for the prospective client. This process of delineating and rendering is critical in the presentation phase of a design project. Contrast must be properly balanced for a presentation to be clear; thus, different shades of dark values must be played against various degrees of light values. The amount of rendered contrast is based on the contextual relationship of the adjacent forms.

The intent of this chapter is to introduce techniques of delineation and rendering as applied to contextual elements (or, to use the Beaux Arts term, "entourage") such as landscaping, human figures, furniture, cars, and building materials.

Delineating and Rendering Entourage

Resources

The following books are good resources to help one understand the graphic language concepts.

Cheatham, Frank R., Jane Hart Cheatham and Sheryl Haler Owens. 1987. Design Concepts and Applications. Second edition, Englewood Cliffs, NJ: Prentice-Hall, Inc.

Ching, Francis D.K. 1990. Drawing: A Creative Process. New York: Van Nostrand Reinhold Co.

Ching, Francis D.K. 1996. Architectural Graphics. Third edition, New York: Van Nostrand Reinhold.

Cooper, Douglas. 1992. Drawing and Perceiving. Second edition, New York: Van Nostrand Reinhold Co.

Forseth, Kevin. 1991. Rendering The Visual Field. New York: Van Nostrand Reinhold.

Gill, Robert W. 1980. Creative Perspective. London: Thames & Hudson.

Lin, Mike. 1993. Designing and Drawing with Confidence. New York: Van Nostrand Reinhold.

Lockard, William Kirby. 1982. Design Drawing. Revised edition, Tucson, AZ: Pepper Publishing.

Myers, Jack F. 1989. The Language of Visual Art: Perception as a Basis for Design. Forth Worth, TX: Holt, Rinehart and Winston, Inc.

Oles, Paul S. 1979. Architectural Illustration: The Value Delineation Process. New York: Van Nostrand Reinhold.

Petrie, Ferdinard. 1992. Drawing Landscapes in Pencils. New York: Guptill Pub.

Shen, J. and Walker, T.D. 1992. Sketching and Rendering for Design Presentations. New York: Van Nostrand Reinhold.

Wallschlaeger, Charles and Cynthia Busic-Snyder. 1992. Basic Visual Concepts and Principles for Artists, Architects, and Designers. Dubuque, IA: Wm. C. Brown Publishers.

Topic

Contour & Form Language

References

Architectural Graphics (Ching 1996, 92–93).

Drawing: A Creative Process (Ching 1990, 44–45).

Design Drawing (Lockard 1982, 82, 86).

Topic

Basic Value Languages

References

Architectural Graphics (Ching 1990, 94–107).

Drawing: A Creative Process (Ching 1990, 48, 78–83).

Design Drawing (Lockard 1982, 83).

Topic

Rendering Human Figures

References

Drawing as a Means to Architecture (Lockard 1977, 60–63).

Drawing: A Creative Process (Ching 1990, 174–175).

Architectural Graphics (Ching 1996, 128–130).

Entourage A Tracing File (Burden 1981, 12–137).

Topic

Rendering Entourage (other than people)

References

Architectural Drawing (Porter 1990, 58–87).

Manual of Graphic Techniques 4 (Porter and Goodman 1985, 20–21, 40–47, 52–53, 96–97, 120–121).

Architectural Illustration Inside and Out (Lorenz and Lizak 1988, 23–40).

Design Communication for Landscape Architects (Wester 1990).

Drawing as a Means to Architecture (Lockard 1977).

A Graphic Vocabulary for Architectural Presentation (White 1972).

Designing and Drawing with Confidence. (Lin 1993, 79–90).

Plan and Section Drawing (Wang 1979, 34–43, 50–51, 68–86).

Cross References

For p. 372   See p. 339
For p. 379   See p. 416
For p. 389   See p. 90
For p. 394   See p. 403
For p. 396   See p. 400
For p. 406   See p. 589

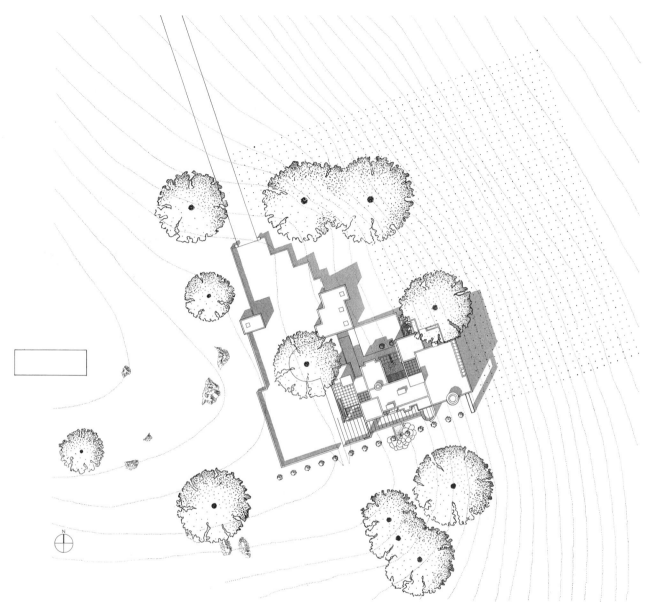

Drawing: Private Residence, Healdsburg, California
24" × 36" (61 × 91.4 cm), Scale: ⅛"=1'0"
Medium: Ink on Mylar
Courtesy of Sandy & Babcock, Inc.
Architecture & Planning

SITE PLAN

In the section on drawing conventions, the page on plan view wall indications showed the same plan drawn with and without surrounding landscaping. With the dark field caused by values to the surrounding contextual environment, the plan's figure–ground/light–dark/positive–negative areas give better depth because of **contrast.** Contrast in architectural drawings is achieved by **rendering.** Rendering is the application of artistic delineation to site plans, perspectives, elevations, and other architectural drawings. Landscaping symbols and material symbols in these drawings are delineated and rendered. **Rendu** is a French word that means "the coloring of a drawing" or "the finished project" or "the delivery of a project." The objective of rendering is either to further client understanding of the proposed design or for publicity and promotion. This section covers only a brief introduction to this complex topic. Refer to the bibliography for many excellent sources in this subject area. This chapter does not cover color techniques in rendering.

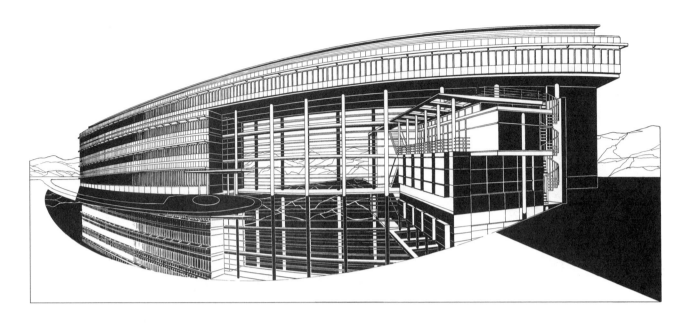

Drawing: Dongbu Central Research Institute, Taejon, Korea, view from south
Medium: Ink on Mylar, 36" × 24" (91.4 × 61 cm)
Courtesy of Perkins & Will Architects

VALUE TYPES

Diagrams and text: Courtesy of William R. Benedict, Assistant Professor
California Polytechnic State University College of Architecture and
Environmental Design, San Luis Obispo, California

Basic Value Types

A value is any technique that directly describes a surface rather than its edges. The edges are made visible by the limits of and/or a sharp change in value. A value (sometimes called a tonal value or tone in drawing) can be a continuous value or created by lines. A continuous value is even, small in scale and fine in implied texture. A value of lines is one whose texture is significant in scale and composed of individual marks that retain their identity within the value. These marks include stippling, lines, cross hatching, scrubbing, scrubbing over texture, and scribbling. The classification of a value as one or the other is dependent on the media and application technique employed.

The role of value in a drawing includes describing the area of a surface, the gradations produced by the surface's texture, the orientation of the surface to the light source, and the surfaces's attributes—materiality, texture, uniformity, reflectance, transparency, color, value, etc. In representing these qualities, the scale, coarseness, form, value, and hue of the value can be manipulated. Gradations are value changes on a surface or form.

2H, H, HB, and 4B pencils (left to right)

Ink pen on all four scales

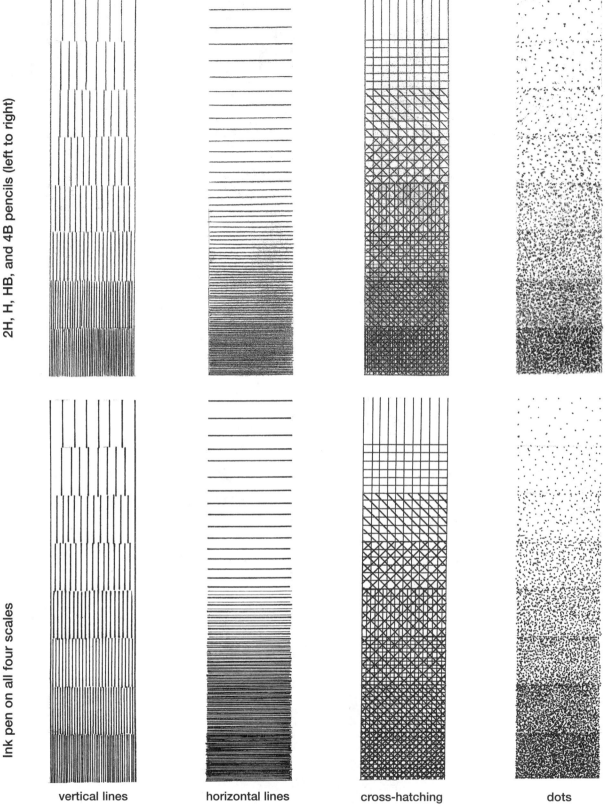

vertical lines horizontal lines cross-hatching dots

The use of dots is also termed "stippling" (see pointillism, p. 426)

VALUE SCALES USING VALUE GRADING TECHNIQUES

The above scales show four methods to render value using pencil or ink pen. Other value-producing media are ink wash, watercolor wash, markers, and dry transfer Zipatone.

CONTOUR LANGUAGE

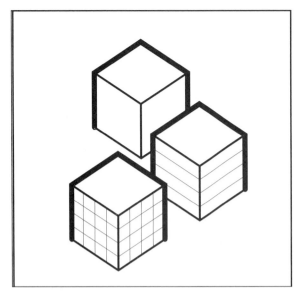

Contour and Form

The contour form language relates line weight choices to the aspect of the form that they are representing. The language defines primary, secondary, and tertiary edge conditions to define a language that uses a vocabulary of three different line weights, with the grammar defining primary contours as heavy, secondary contours as medium, and tertiary contours as light.

Primary Contours

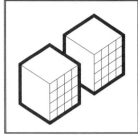

Primary contours define the outermost extremities of a form —they record the outline or profile of an object. They are edges formed by the meeting of two surfaces when only one surface can be seen. They respond to and record all edge textures and irregularities. Drawing only the profile of an object tends to flatten the object.

Secondary Contours

Secondary contours describe the edges of surfaces when both surfaces are visible. They respond to and record all edge textures and irregularities.

Tertiary Contours

Tertiary contours describe changes in the uniformity of a surface or plane. They respond to and record linear markings on a surface and the edges of values, shadows, textures, and colors. Tertiary contours disclose the volume of an object. They are plastic and emphasize the three-dimensionality of the object.

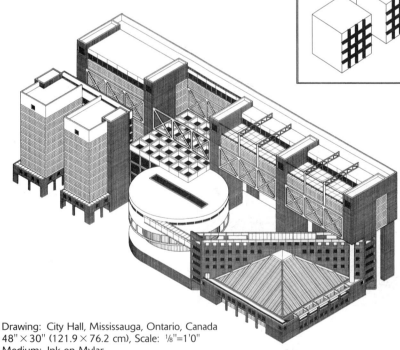

Drawing: City Hall, Mississauga, Ontario, Canada
48" × 30" (121.9 × 76.2 cm), Scale: ⅛"=1'0"
Medium: Ink on Mylar
Courtesy of Michael Fieldman & Partners, Architects

Software: Aldus "Freehand"

Diagrams and text (both pages): Courtesy of William R. Benedict, Assistant Professor California Polytechnic State University College of Architecture & Environmental Design San Luis Obispo, California

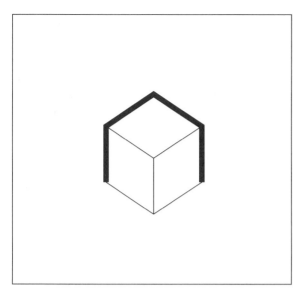

Spatial Profiling

Edges are perceived under two conditions: when both surfaces defining the edge are visible and when only one surface is visible. Lighter lines indicate an edge between two planes when both can be seen. Heavier lines—profile lines—indicate an edge between two planes where only one plane can be seen. To one side of a profile edge you are looking through space to some distant surface. The greatest spatial differential—the heaviest profile line—occurs at the edge between the object and the sky and earth (its environment or background). Lines become heavier as the distance between the edge they represent and the surface against which the edge is seen increases.

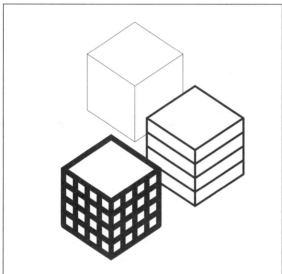

Contours and Distance

A heavy black line on a white sheet of paper reads as closer than a light line due to its size and our experience with the effect of aerial perspective on contrast. A thin black line appears as lighter in value than a thick black line because it has less surface area with which to communicate its value. From these cues we can establish a language that says that the closest contours are the heaviest and weight decreases with distance. Lines of varying distance can taper. The illustration categorizes all the lines of a cube as the same but the language can be much subtler by further varying the line weights within each cube.

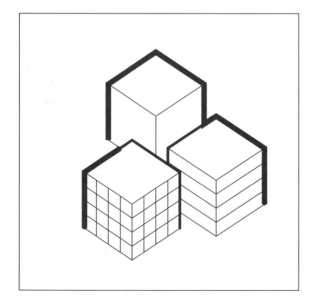

Contours and Depth

Primary contours record edges where one of their defining surfaces can be seen. Therefore, to one side of the contour is the surface that the contour is defining, and to the other there is some distance or depth of space until another surface is encountered. The greater the depth, the heavier the contour line. This language is a development of the spatial profiling cues.

CONTOUR LANGUAGE

VALUE LANGUAGE

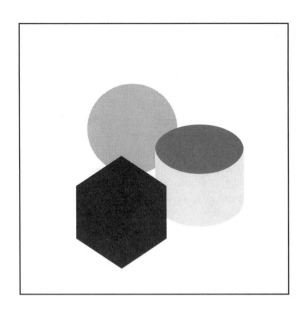

Value and Color

Value directly represents the color of the surface. Whatever color (value, hue, chroma) that a surface possesses is represented in the drawing. If the surface is dark red, the surface is drawn dark red. Issues of relative illumination and orientation of the surface are not considered. The liability of this language is that it tends to flatten and disguise form, as indicated in the illustration.

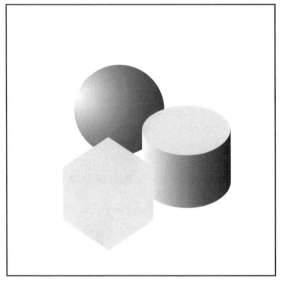

Value and Form

Value can delineate form by defining and differentiating surfaces. The simplest value and form language represents flat surfaces with uniform values and curved surfaces with tonal gradations. As in the value and color language, issues of relative illumination and orientation of the surface are not considered, and the liability of the language is that it can flatten and disguise form, as indicated in the illustration.

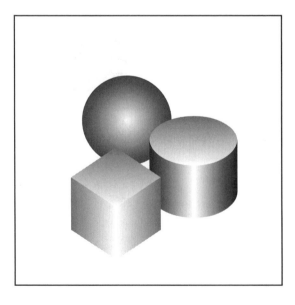

Value and Texture

If a surface has some perceivable textural qualities, then value can represent the surface's textural gradients. A surface that is directly facing the observer has a uniform textural gradient and is represented by a uniform value. A surface that is oblique to the observer has a varying textural gradient and is represented by a gradation that goes from light to dark as it moves away from the observer. A textured surface will also appear darker as it turns away from the observer—as it moves from perpendicular to parallel to the observer's line of sight.

Diagrams and text: Courtesy of William R. Benedict, Assistant Professor
California Polytechnic State University College of Architecture & Environmental Design, San Luis Obispo, California

Value and Orientation

Using value to represent orientation requires the assumption of a light source. A surface's value corresponds to its orientation to the light source. In this example, flat surfaces are represented by uniform values. The values are then adjusted to represent the surface's orientation to the assumed light source. The surfaces most directly facing the source are the lightest, and the surface facing most directly away from the source is darkest. Surfaces with the same orientation receive the same value no matter where they are within the drawing.

Value and Shadow

This language builds on the orientation language. The orientation of the surfaces to the light source must be established before shadows can be cast. Once the orientation is established, shadows are cast and values are adjusted for reflected light. The example shows all values as flat or even. In reality, bounced light modifies the values.

Value and Distance

Value is also affected by the aerial cues of contrast and blueness. The closest cubes will have the greatest contrast within themselves and with the environment, while those farther away will have less. Furthermore, as the cubes get farther away, they move toward a middle gray because of the intervening atmosphere.

VALUE LANGUAGE

SUN/SHADE/SHADOW/VALUE LANGUAGE

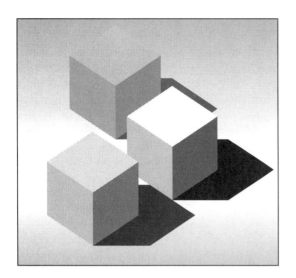

Sun, Shade, and Shadow

This language employs an abbreviated vocabulary and grammar. The vocabulary consists of only three continuous values and responds to three formal conditions. The surfaces that are in direct sunlight are to be white, those that are in shade are to be gray, and those that are in shadow are to be black. This language tends to abstract reality and create strong graphic images with sharp contrast. It is useful in compositional and massing studies.

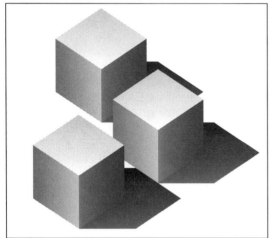

Orientation, Shadow, and Texture

In this combination the orientation and shadow languages have been enriched to include gradations created by the surface's textures. The textural gradations cause the surfaces to get darker as they move away from the viewer. This is true for all surfaces not parallel to the face of the viewer. The greater the angle, the more dramatic the gradation.

Value and Expression

The technique used, media, key (value or tonal range), and distribution of values within a drawing can support different moods—freehand is different from drafted, pen is different from pencil, high key is different from low key, and variegated is different from uniform. Each combination will create a different mood.

A high key drawing is one in which all the values are at the light end of the value scale, while a low key drawing is the opposite.

The scale and shape of the marks—the style or techniques used to create the values—also influence the expression of the drawing as well as communicate additional meaning. The example below feels very different from the previous drawings.

Created in Fractal Design Painter

Diagrams and text: Courtesy of William R. Benedict, Assistant Professor
California Polytechnic State University College of Architecture & Environmental Design, San Luis Obispo, California

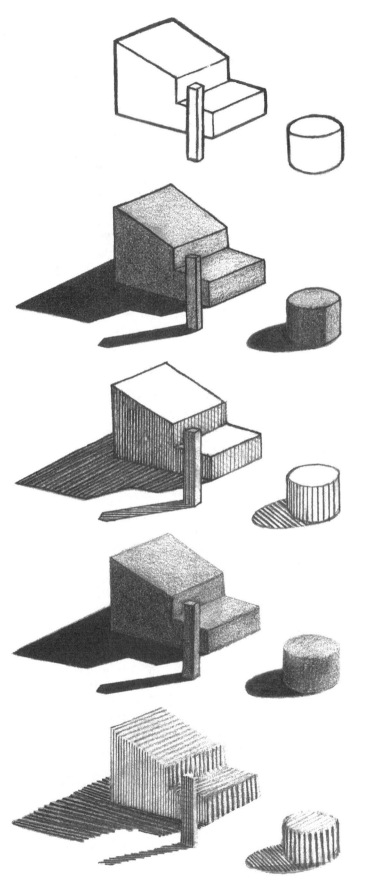

(1) **Line** with space-defining edges accented (profiled)

Profiling or silhouetting gives a needed contour to help define any form against negative space.

(2) **Line** with **value**

Shadow is rendered darker than shade. Silhouetting against negative space is normally not done.

(3) **Line** with **value** of **lines**

Planar edges are defined by both line and value of lines. Silhouetting against negative space is normally not done. For directional reinforcement, use vertical lines for vertical planes and horizontal or near horizontal lines for horizontal planes.

(4) **Value**

Planes rendered with different values of pure value define planar edges. Shadow is rendered darker than shade.

(5) **Value** of **lines**

Planar edges are defined, when two planes, each with a value of lines, meet. A flat plane uses evenly spaced lines. A curvilinear form uses unevenly spaced lines (see p. 319).

SUN/SHADE/SHADOW/VALUE LANGUAGE

Stippling is used to build up shade and value. Its objective of modeling form is the same as that of the linear technique of cross-hatching (see p. 371). By varying the size and spacing of dots, one can create tone values and model form. Although quite time-consuming, this method gives excellent control over gradations and produces a copy-like quality. Note the stippling for the sky area in the villa rendering and on the building exterior on the facing page.

Hatching is the use of lines in a tonal arrangement in order to portray surface or form. It can describe light, space, and material as an abstraction of reality (see sky and glass on p. 413).

Rendering: Fhilothei Villa, Greece
24" × 36" (61 × 91.4 cm), Scale: ⅛"=1'0"
Courtesy of Hugh Newell Jacobson, FAIA, Architect, and Stephen S. Evanusa, Architect

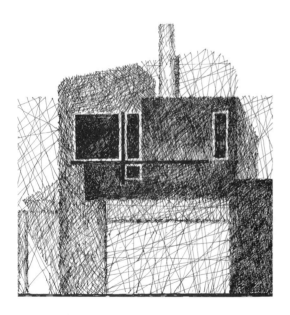

Drawing: Van Kirk House (1991), San Francisco, California
7.5" × 7.5" (19.1 × 19.1 cm), Scale: ¼"=1'0"
Medium: Pen and ink
Courtesy of James Shay, AIA Architect

This style of rendering communicates visual tonal values very effectively. The high contrast achieved creates a lot of visual "snap."
[ARCHITECT'S STATEMENT]

Pen and ink is an excellent medium for producing a variety of stroke patterns. These illustrations show the use of straight lines, cross-hatched lines, and dots to give excellent tonal values. Regardless of the technique, the density of tone produced gives the needed contrast. Different stroke techniques are often used in combination to depict shape clusters. The number of techniques that should be employed is dependent on how much detail and precision one wants. Spontaneous loose, imprecise strokes are more suggestive and symbolic.

Drawing: Student project by Richard Tsai
               Interior study
Medium: Ink on Mylar
Courtesy of Washington University
School of Architecture, St. Louis, MO

The rendering to the right is an exercise using dots or very short strokes with the objective of creating a line drawing. Only dots of varying intensity and dimension were used. The effect of lines is created with dots only. The student begins this exercise by carefully studying shade and shadow conditions on the building.

Drawing: Student project by Roosevelt Sanders
Medium: Ink on Mylar
M. Saleh Uddin, Professor, Savannah College of Art and Design,
Savannah, GA; Southern University, Baton Rouge, LA

APPLICATION OF VALUE SCALES AND TONING TECHNIQUES

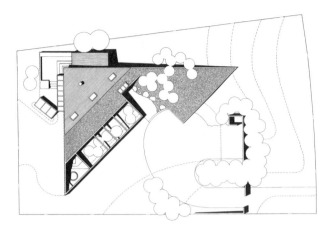

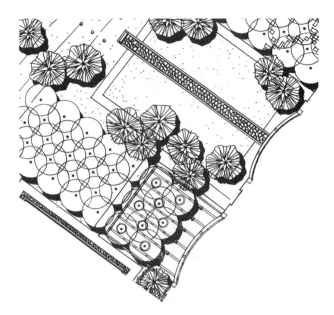

Drawing: Brugler residence, The Sea Ranch, California
20" × 15" (50.8 × 38.1 cm), Scale: ⅛"=1'0"
Medium: Rapidograph ink pen
Courtesy of Obie G. Bowman, Architect AIA

TREES IN PLAN

There are numerous ways to depict an abstract rendered tree in plan. The nature and quantity of abstract detail is dependent on the scale and objective of the drawing. Different types of plan trees can be interchanged. Deciduous and coniferous trees are commonly rendered. Coniferous trees (below middle) are delineated with radiating bicycle spoke-like lines. Sometimes smaller trees and shrubs are clustered as a group with one continuous outline.

Drawing: Takamiya
         Country Club
         Hiroshima, Japan
Medium: Pencil
ED2 International Architects
Courtesy of the SWA Group

Note the range of the plan tree types above from a simple circle to more elaborate forms. Ground textures can give a value contrast that causes the trees to have distinct edges. Trees, ground textures, and other plan entourage should always complement and be secondary to the architectural building elements to which they are adjacent. Site plan entourage provides vital field–background (dark–light) tonal contrast to give added drawing depth.

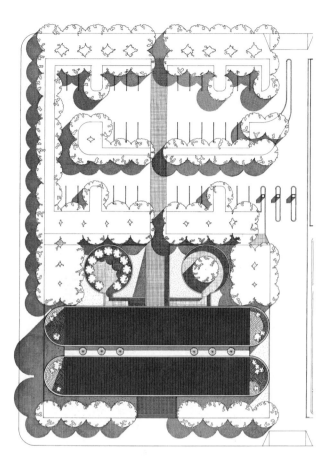

Drawing: Savings Association Headquarters
         Denver, Colorado
24" × 32" (61 × 81.3 cm), Scale: ¹/₁₀"=1'0"
Medium: Ink on vellum with pressure-applied screens (Zipatone)
Courtesy of James Ream FAIA, San Francisco, California

The trees shown in both of these rendered site plans nicely complement the building forms that they are near. Note the added depth that is given to both site plans by the use of cast shadow. Circular trees cast circular shadows. Draw with a circle template. A sense of depth can be achieved by a slight displacement of one circle forming two intersecting circles. When circular shadows are cast as a whole group (left), they are every effective. Trees can overlap ground textures and landscaping elements to give added depth (below).

Trees in a plan fall into two categories: (1) sectional trees, as shown on the previous page, in which a horizontal cut reveals branching, trunk size, and foliage (or no foliage); and (2) nonsectional trees (overhead view) in which shade on the foliage gives a three-dimensional effect.

Drawing: Amancio Ergina Village
         San Francisco, California
24" × 36" (61 × 91.4 cm), Scale: ¹/₁₆"=1'0"
Medium: Ink on vellum
Courtesy of Daniel Solomon FAIA

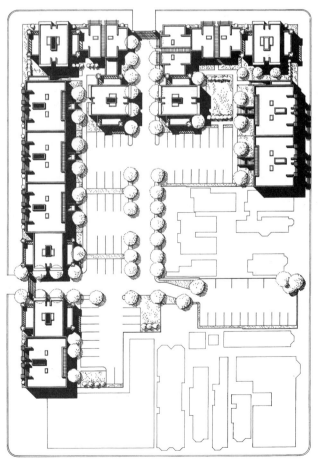

TREES IN PLAN

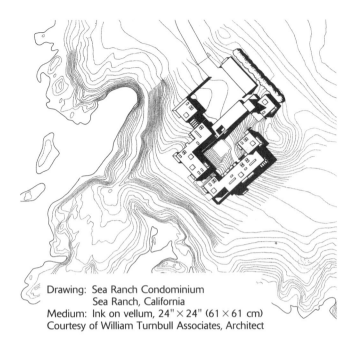

Drawing: Sea Ranch Condominium
         Sea Ranch, California
Medium: Ink on vellum, 24" × 24" (61 × 61 cm)
Courtesy of William Turnbull Associates, Architect

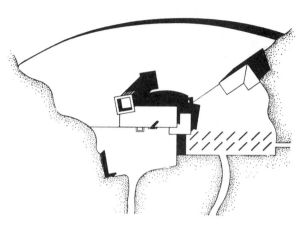

Drawing: Bargonetti, Kent, Connecticut
11" × 14" (27.9 × 35.6 cm), Scale: 1"=32'0"
Medium: Ink on Mylar
Courtesy of Steven Harris & Associates, Architect

There are many ways to indicate groundcover for soft areas such as grass. Clockwise from upper left: (1) contour lines; (2) dot clusters; and (3) short lines ordered into layers defining contours.

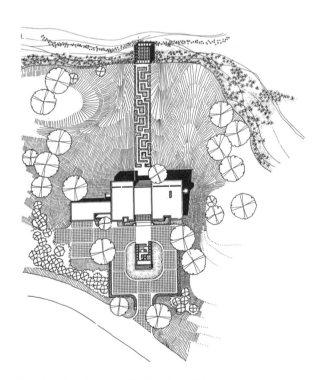

Drawing: Private house, Southeastern Michigan
20" × 30" (50.8 × 76.2 cm), Scale: 1"=30'0"
Medium: Ink on vellum
Courtesy of William Kessler and Associates Architects

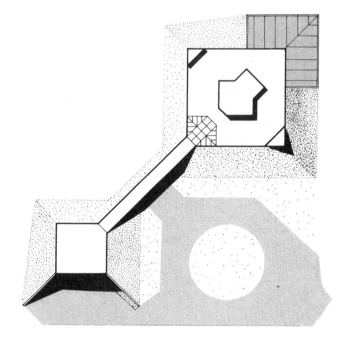

Drawing: Private residence, Gainsville, Florida
24" × 24" (61 × 61 cm), Scale: ⅛"=1'0"
Medium: Ink on Mylar film with Zipatone shading
Courtesy of William Morgan FAIA,
William Morgan Architects, P.A.

GROUND TEXTURES FOR SOFT AREAS

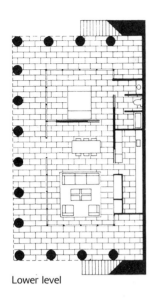
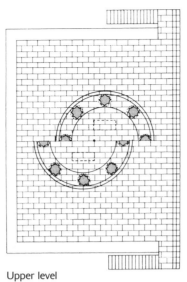

Lower level   Upper level

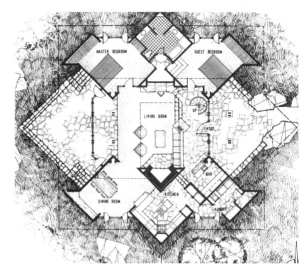

First Floor

Drawing: Two crypts near Athens, Greece
24" × 36" (61 × 91.4 cm), Scale: ⅛"=1'0"
Courtesy of Hugh Newell Jaobsen FAIA

Drawing: Davenport house, Evergreen, Colorado
18" × 24" (45.7 × 61 cm), Scale: ¼"=1'0"
Medium: Ink on vellum
Courtesy of Fay Jones + Maurice Jennings, Architects

Landscaping indication symbols for hard surfaces should be consistent with the interior floor material of the building they surround. These symbols provide a clue as to how the interior relates to its adjacent transitional spaces as well as to its external landscape/environment.

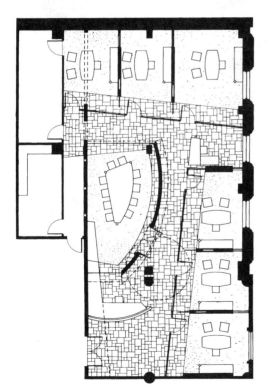

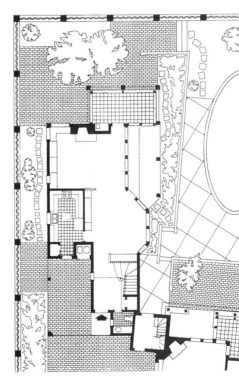

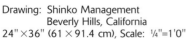

Drawing: Shinko Management
            Beverly Hills, California
24" × 36" (61 × 91.4 cm), Scale: ¼"=1'0"
Medium: Ink on Mylar
Courtesy of David Kellen, Architect

Drawing: Salasky/Sedel house, Virginia Beach, Virginia
30" × 40" (76.2 × 101.6 cm), Scale: ⅛"=1'0"
Medium: Ink on Mylar
Courtesy of B FIVE STUDIO

GROUND TEXTURES FOR HARD AREAS

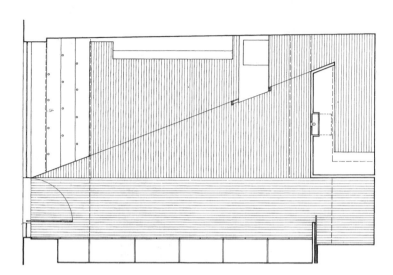

Drawing: Kinder Kind Shop I
          Repulse Bay, Hong Kong
14" × 10" (35.6 × 25.4 cm)
Medium: Ink on Mylar, Scale: 1:20
Courtesy of Tsao & McKown Architects

As with ground textures, the rendition of materials within the plan view helps to give depth by contrast to an otherwise flat two-dimensional plan. Major circulation areas can be quickly identified when defined with a uniform tone value (see below). Floorscape is normally the material symbol of the actual material seen presented in a simplified technique.

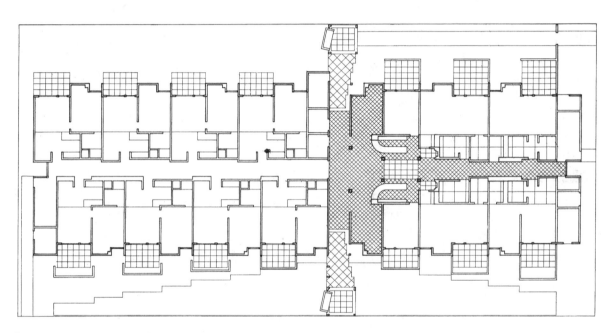

Drawing: Plymouth Place Housing, Stockton, California
Medium: Ink, 31" × 36" (78.7 × 91.4 cm), Scale: ⅛"=1'0"
Courtesy of John V. Mutlow, FAIA, Architects

The rendition of floor patterns in a two-dimensional plan assists in the understanding of the design intention of the project. The floorscape identifies the areas of public circulation space, the sequence of the public spaces and accentuates the principle elements, the major axis and the circulation. The variation in floor pattern intensity differentiates the inside space from the outside and the diagonal to the square pattern the public to the private.
[ARCHITECT'S STATEMENT]

Most ground floor plans show the relationship of the interior floorscape to the immediate exterior landscape. Thus, the surrounding area not occupied by the building plan should be rendered with a ground texture (See the Salasky/Sedel House on the previous page).

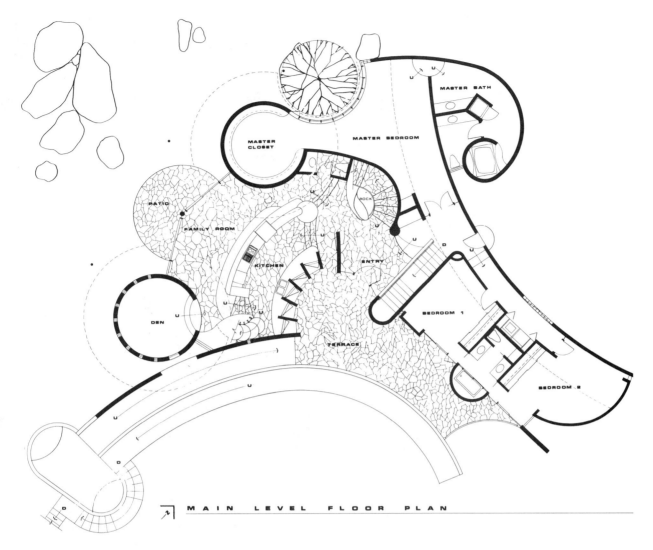

MAIN   LEVEL   FLOOR   PLAN

Drawing: Prince house, Albuquerque, New Mexico
24" × 36" (61 × 91.4 cm), Scale: ¼"=1'0"
Courtesy of Bart Prince, Architect

This drawing done in pencil on Mylar indicates the floor areas, which are to be finished in random slate stone. Note that the stone paving continues uninterrupted from the inside to the outside and over floor level changes thus integrating several areas and increasing the sense of space.
[ARCHITECT'S STATEMENT]

A better understanding of how to represent floorscape and the surrounding groundscape can be achieved by observing how artificial light and sunlight affects these materials. For example, make a careful study of interior floor materials as well as exterior masonry and cobblestone walks, concrete paving, rock/gravel beds, wooden decks, and patios. Practice rendering abstract graphic representations for all of these using both pen and pencil.

FLOOR SURFACE MATERIAL INDICATIONS

GROUND SURFACE INDICATIONS

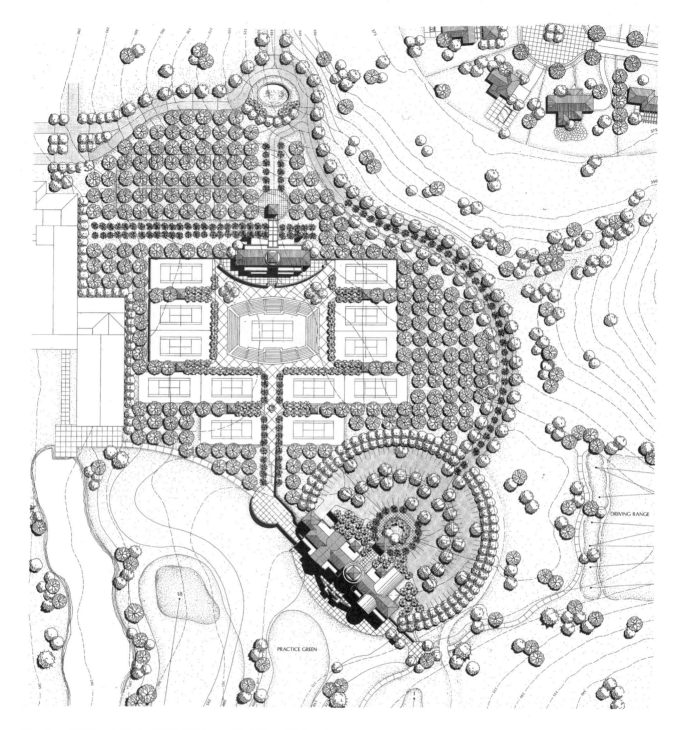

Drawing: ATP Tennis Center/ TPC Clubhouse, Black Mountain Ranch
San Diego County, California
30" × 42" (76.2 × 106.7 cm), Scale: 1"=40'
Medium: Ink on Mylar
Courtesy of Sandy & Babcock Inc., Architecture & Planning

As the size of a site plan becomes larger and larger, the amount of detail needed to indicate a tree in plan becomes less and less. Regardless of the scale, a value differentiation between the trees and the ground cover must be maintained.

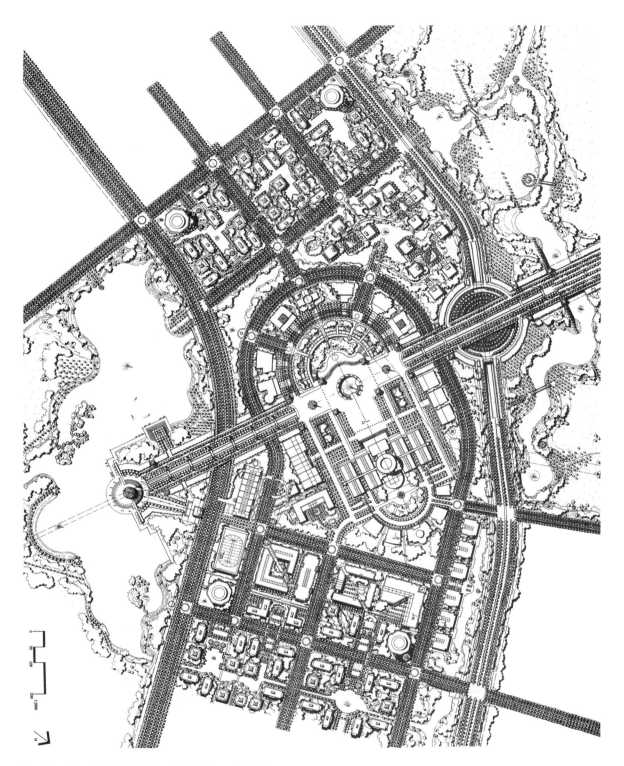

GROUND SURFACE INDICATIONS

Drawing: Shanghai Civic Center District, Shanghai, China
Medium: Pencil
36" × 48" (91.4 × 121.9 cm), Scale: 1:2000
Drawn by John L. Wong, Landscape Architect
Courtesy of The SWA Group

In this site plan, the trees no longer "read" as individual trees; but rather as a clustered group which produces a dense value and a circulation pattern.

ELEVATION MATERIAL SYMBOLS

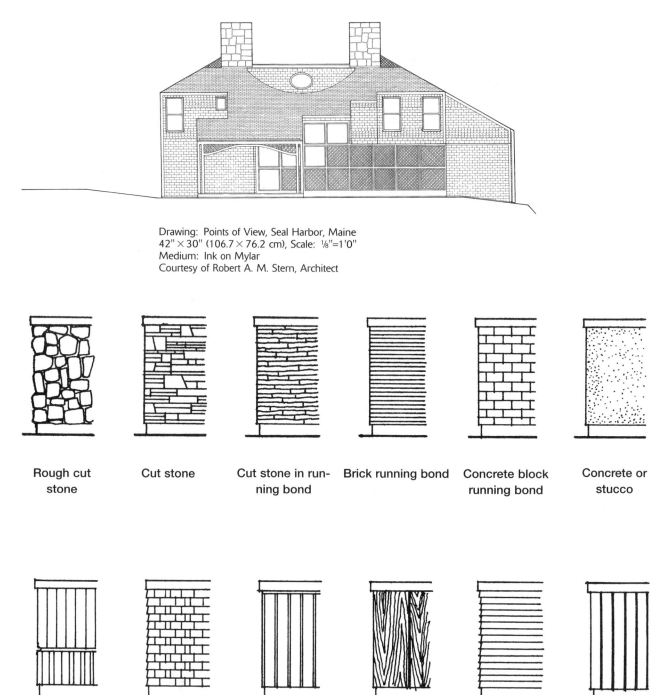

Drawing: Points of View, Seal Harbor, Maine
42" × 30" (106.7 × 76.2 cm), Scale: ⅛"=1'0"
Medium: Ink on Mylar
Courtesy of Robert A. M. Stern, Architect

Rough cut stone

Cut stone

Cut stone in running bond

Brick running bond

Concrete block running bond

Concrete or stucco

Concrete with board forms

Shingle siding

Board and batten- normal or reverse siding

Plywood

Lap siding

Vertical siding

As with floorscape, building elevations are commonly rendered with material symbols in order to accentuate their typical flatness and communicate building material choices. Generally, the materials are drawn simplified due to the small scales used. The material texture indication symbols above are selected examples. Material textures rendered on plan obliques and perspectives are, for the most part, similar to their corresponding elevation textures (see the many examples in this chapter).

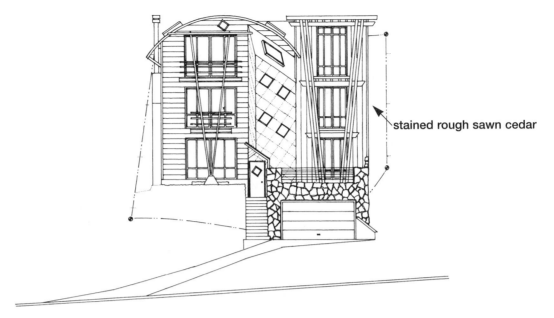

stained rough sawn cedar

ELEVATION MATERIAL SYMBOLS

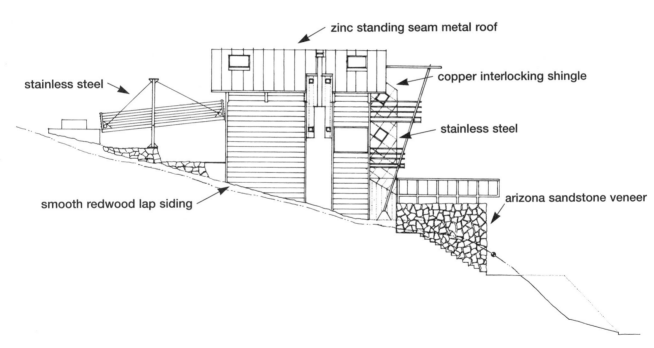

zinc standing seam metal roof

stainless steel

copper interlocking shingle

stainless steel

smooth redwood lap siding

arizona sandstone veneer

Drawing: Schuh Box (unbuilt), Hills above San Francisco Bay
Medium: Ink on trace
Courtesy of David Baker Associates Architects

Distinct natural-finish materials, such as copper, zinc, stainless steel, transparent stain on rough sawn cedar, smooth redwood, and Arizona sandstone, are used to code the distinct volumetric elements that compose this design.
[ARCHITECT'S STATEMENT]

Floor and elevation material symbols are commonly shown in pictorial drawings such as obliques, axonometrics, and perspectives. In this example, wall and floor material textures help enhance the powerful spatial quality that is created. In these two drawings, note the extensive use of material texture (porcelain enamel panels, concrete blocks, etc.) on both horizontal and vertical planes.

MATERIAL SYMBOLS

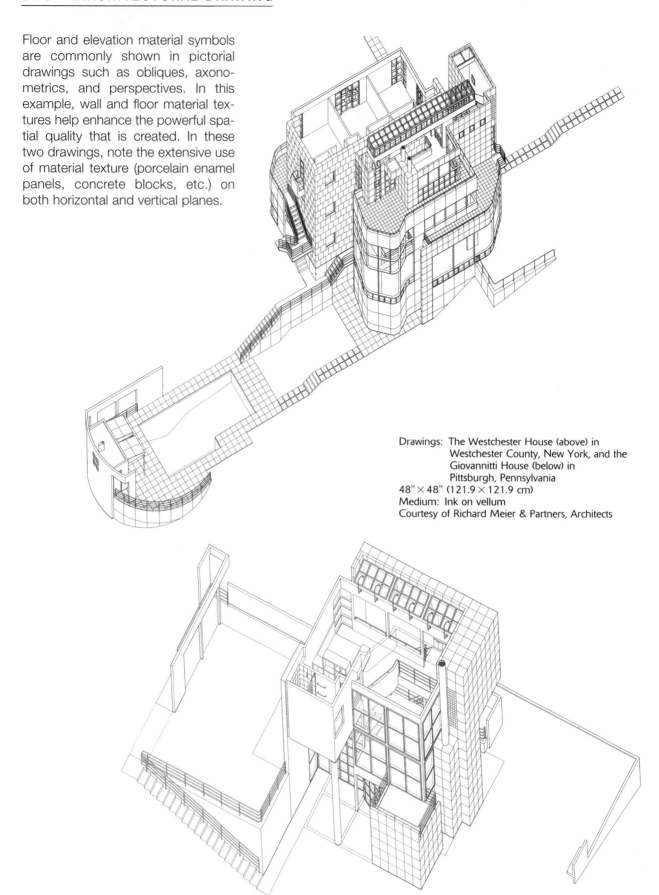

Drawings: The Westchester House (above) in Westchester County, New York, and the Giovannitti House (below) in Pittsburgh, Pennsylvania
48" × 48" (121.9 × 121.9 cm)
Medium: Ink on vellum
Courtesy of Richard Meier & Partners, Architects

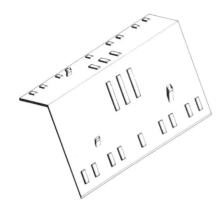

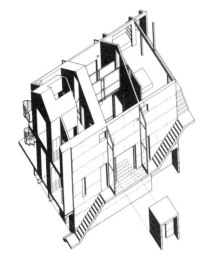

The exploded axonometric view was selected to express the conceptual basis of this design: the creation of a tectonic dialogue between past and present. A contemporary dwelling, articulated as a new wooden "box," is inserted within the old stone shell of a Pennsylvania barn. A family of other new elements, clad in metal and abstracted from nearby agrarian forms, engage the exterior of the stone shell at various places.
[ARCHITECT'S STATEMENT]

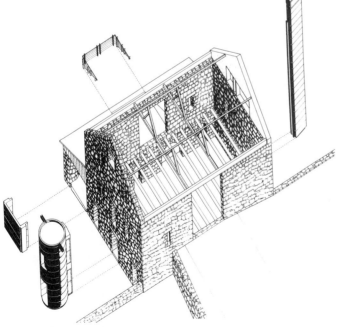

Drawing: Martin residence
          Kennett Square, Pennsylvania
20" × 48" (50.8 × 121.9 cm), Scale: ¼"=1'0"
Medium: Ink on Mylar
Courtesy of Tanner Leddy Maytum Stacy Architects

This exploded drawing of a design scheme of a "box inside a box" shows a small box faced with cherrywood inside a large rough stone shell. The material symbols on the walls are easily identifyable.

MATERIAL SYMBOLS

DELINEATING TREES

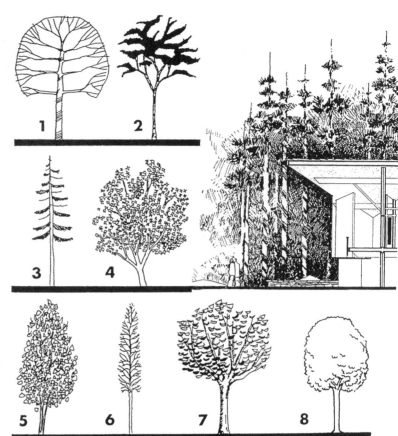

Drawing: The Moir Building
San Jose, California
Medium: Pentel on vellum
36" × 42" (91.4 × 106.7 cm)
Courtesy of Jerome King, AIA
Renderer: Barney Davidge Associates

Drawing (above right): Rendered trees
Davenport House, Evergreen, Colorado
18" × 24" (45.7 × 61 cm), Scale: ¼"=1'0"
Medium: Ink on vellum
Courtesy of Fay Jones + Maurice Jennings,
Architects

Rendered trees can show branching (3 and 6), branching with outline (1), partial texture with outline (8), full texture (2, 4, and 5), or full texture with shade (7). Texture with shade is based on directional sunlight. Trees form a parachute shape as they react to gravity.

Drawing: Foliage texture for foreground trees
Medium: Ink on vellum
Herbert Cuevas, AIA Architect
Courtesy of Brigette Nalley

Symbolic trees can be abstract or representational. They should always complement rather than compete with or overpower the human-built environment they are surrounding. Trees can be made darker (above right) or lighter than the building they are behind to give more contrast. Tracing excellent existing delineated tree examples will build up your graphic vocabulary for these symbols.

Drawing: The Peninsula Regent, San Mateo, California
Medium: Ink
24" × 24" (61 × 61 cm)
Courtesy of Backen Arrigoni & Ross, Inc.
Architecture, Planning & Interior Design
Peter Szasz, Architectural Illustrator

TREES IN PERSPECTIVE

Trees and other vegetation, human figures, furniture, moving vehicles, and ground textures are defined as **entourage** (French for surroundings) in an architectural rendering. These supporting elements should always complement the human-built environment and should not compete with it. Accurately drawn entourage also helps to give scale to the drawing.

The trees in this illustration and the subsequent page are quite detailed and realistic in appearance. When delineating abstract or realistic trees in perspective, you can create more visual interest to the composition by changing the height of the trees; and you can add more depth to the rendering by casting ground shadows (see p. 394).

FOREGROUND TREES

Drawing: Burnett residence, 17 Mile Drive, Pebble Beach, California
Medium: Pen and ink on Mylar, 36" × 24" (91.4 × 61 cm)
Simpson Gumpertz & Heger, Inc., Architects
Courtesy of Markus Lui & Associates, Architectural Illustrators

Foliage texture for foreground trees should exhibit more detail. The more highly detailed a symbolic tree, the more time-consuming it will be to draw. These foreground trees frame the building in the background. The sun is behind the observer causing casted ground shadows that are away from the observer. This location for the light source permits both sides of the building to be in sunlight. The foreground tree trunk bark texture and the foreground grass are both rendered darker than the background tree trunks and background grass.

BIRD'S-EYE VIEW TREES

Drawings: (above) Daly City Housing proposal, Daly City, California
Design Office: Sinclair Associates, San Mateo, California
(below) Santa Clara Housing Project, Santa Clara, California
Client: Santa Clara development
Both 20" × 30" (50.8 × 76.2 cm)
Courtesy of Lawrence Ko Leong, Architectural Illustrator

Drawing method: First, an AutoCAD wire-frame massing model was done to select a viewpoint and as a base for a black and white Prismacolor pencil hand drawing. A baseline print is made with intense colored pencil colors. The black and white version was done so the client could use it for monochrome copies. For both landscaping and building, "soft," short, even strokes were used to give a smooth, consistent look and feel.
[ARCHITECTURAL ILLUSTRATOR'S STATEMENT]

DELINEATING INTERIOR VEGETATION

Drawing: 1333 Broadway, Oakland, California
Medium: Pen and ink on Mylar, 36" × 24" (91.4 × 61 cm)
ED2 International, Richard Hom, Architects
Courtesy of Markus Lui & Associates, Architectural Illustrators

Interior vegetation should complement and not overpower interior architecture. The plant in the right foreground above increases the feeling of perspective depth in the interior space. The lower perspective on the facing page is a good example of a "fudged one-point" or a "soft two-point." A soft two-point is essentially a one-point view with a very long second vanishing point. The effect is basically a one-point, but is less "static" than a one-point. This very natural drawing type was a favorite of Frank Lloyd Wright (see bibliography).

Drawing: 12-Plex Motion Picture Theatre, Gateway Center, Arizona
Medium: Pen and ink on Mylar, 36"×24" (91.4×61 cm)
Vincent Raney, AIA, Architect
Courtesy of Markus Lui & Associates, Architectural Illustrators

Plant and shrub vegetation, like trees, can be simplistically symbolic or realistically detailed.

Drawing: Cheeca Lodge Resort, Islamadora, Florida
Medium: Pencil on vellum, 24"×13" (61×33 cm)
Courtesy of Simon Martin–Vegue Winkelstein Moris, Interior design and illustration by G. Lawrence Saber

DELINEATING EXTERIOR AND INTERIOR VEGETATION

DELINEATING HUMAN FIGURES

1/16"=1'0"

1/8"=1'0"

1/4"=1'0"

3/8"=1'0"

Keep in mind the following when using human figures:

- figures show the scale of a drawing.
- figures are secondary to the architecture.
- figures should not cover space defining intersections.
- figures should imply activity yet not be shown to be over-active
- figures should have simple details for clothes.
- grouped figures should show overlap (see pp. 400–401).

Drawing (partial): Walking figures
Medium: Ink
Courtesy of Chun/Ishimaru & Assoc.

Keep a reference clipping file of photographs and drawings of people in different poses singly as well as in groups. Use a Polaroid camera to freeze figure images for future referrals.

Grouped figures (2nd and 5th row left)
Medium: Ink
2nd row: Courtesy of Martin Liefhebbe, Barton Myers Associates, Architects
5th row: Courtesy of Chun/Ishimaru, Architectural Illustrators

1/2"=1'0"

The people in the drawing at right are abstract with little or no clothing detail. Abstract figures (either with contour outline or with gray shades) are usually adequate for most drawings. Clothing detail for figures is dependent on the scales, style, and intent of the drawing.

Drawing (partial): East Wing of the National Gallery of Art
Washington, D.C.
Entire original: 21" × 14" (53.3 × 35.6 cm)
Medium: Black Prismacolor on vellum
Pei, Cobb, Freed, and Partners, Architects
Courtesy of Paul Stevenson Oles FAIA, Renderer

Drawing (partial): Waterfront Development Plan
Asbury Park, New Jersey
Medium: Ink
Courtesy of Koetter, Kim & Associates, Inc.
Architects and Urban Designers

As the scale of the human figure increases in size, a simple form without clothing detail is no longer adequate. When adding clothing detail, keep it to a minimum so as not to distract from the architectural subject. The drawing to the right successfully keeps clothing detail to a minimum, as it adds important human scale for the background building. Avoid drawing extremes in clothing fashion, which, for the most part, tend to be "eye-catching."

Drawing: Renovation Santa Fe Depot, San Diego, California
Hanna/Olin Ltd. Landscape Architecture
16" × 24" (40.6 × 61 cm)
Medium: Full watercolor over pencil line transfer
Courtesy of Al Forster, Architectural Illustrator

DELINEATING HUMAN FIGURES

HUMAN FIGURES AND THE HORIZON LINE

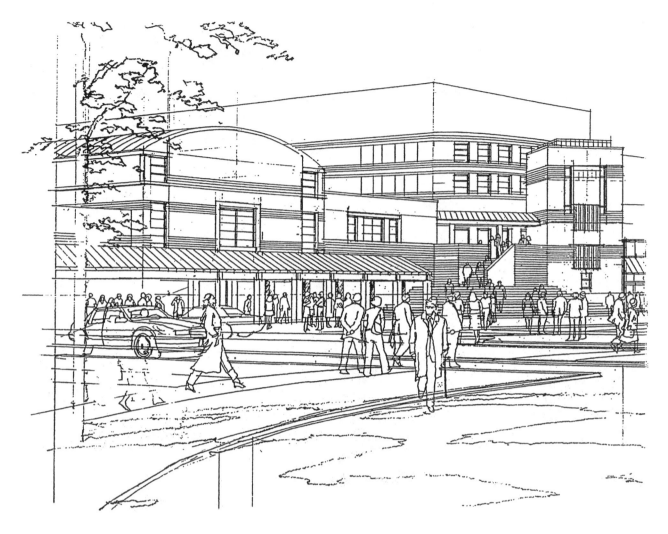

Drawing: Competition: University of Maryland Center for the Performing Arts. Winner.
Moore Ruble Yudell Architects
18" × 12" (45.7 × 30.5 cm)
Medium: Sketch watercolor on mounted presentation
blackline print of ink line drawing
Courtesy of Al Forster, Architectural Illustrator

In the perspective above, note that almost all of the human heads are on the observer's horizon line. It does not matter whether the figure is closer to or farther away from the observer. If the human figure is taller than the observer, then his or her eyes will be above the horizon line. Likewise, the same relationship is valid for a shorter human figure. On the facing page, the children standing have their heads below the horizon line. Figures on higher elevations (see staircase above) are far above the observer's eye level.

Drawing: Proposed NTC Navy Housing, San Diego, California
　　　　　　Fehlman Labarre Architecture & Planning
18" × 12" (45.7 × 30.5 cm)
Medium: Full watercolor over pencil line transfer
People overlay courtesy of Al Forster, Architectural Illustrator

Human figures should be well distributed in a perspective drawing in order to give a proper sense of depth. This distribution should be in three zones: the foreground, or the area nearest to the observer; the middle ground, or the area that has the observer's attention (building on facing page and playground structure above); and the background, or the area that is in back of that which has the observer's attention (smallest figures). When possible, carefully insert figures in the distinct areas of the foreground, the middle ground, and the background, whether they be single or in a group.

HUMAN FIGURES AND THE HORIZON LINE

Drawing: Vila Sheraton Senggigi
         Indonesia
17" × 11" (43.2 × 27.9 cm)
Medium: Felt pen, markers, and
pencil crayons on white
tracing paper
Courtesy of the Timothy Seow
Group Architects

Furniture must suit the style of the interior space. Sofas and chairs are commonly seen in groups of two or more.

DELINEATING FURNITURE

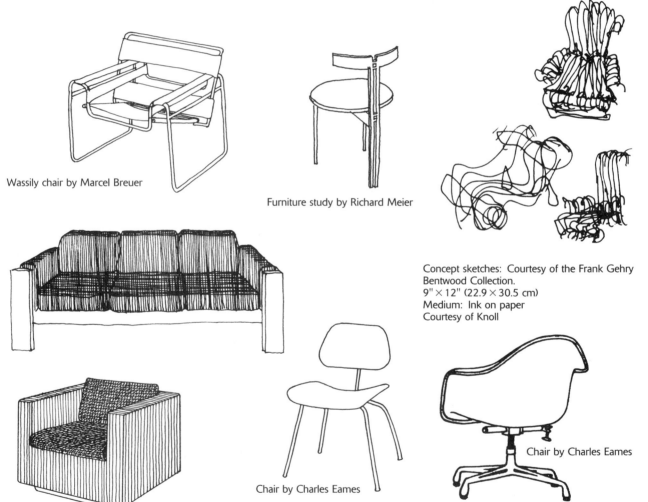

Wassily chair by Marcel Breuer

Furniture study by Richard Meier

Concept sketches: Courtesy of the Frank Gehry
Bentwood Collection.
9" × 12" (22.9 × 30.5 cm)
Medium: Ink on paper
Courtesy of Knoll

Chair by Charles Eames

Chair by Charles Eames

Chair by Charles Eames

Become familiar with good furniture design. Outstanding furniture has been designed by many noted architects, such as Alvar Aalto, Charles Eames, Frank Lloyd Wright, Eero Saarinen, Marcel Breuer, Richard Meier, and Frank Gehry. As with people and cars, keep a reference photo file.

Drawing: The Peninsula Regent, San Mateo, California
20" × 24" (50.8 × 61 cm)
Medium: Pencil on vellum
Courtesy of Backen Arrigoni & Ross, Inc.
Architecture, Planning and Interior Design
Jim Gillam, Architectural Illustrator

Furniture accessories, such as lighting elements, chairs, sofas, and tables, should complement the interior architecture and show how interior space is used. The size and scale of an interior space can be indicated when human figures are added with the furniture. Drawing properly scaled people in the interior space will help in drawing properly scaled furniture. It is easier to start with the scaled person first and then draw the piece of furniture on which he or she is sitting (see p. 397).

DELINEATING FURNITURE

FURNITURE AND FIGURES — PLAN OBLIQUE ACCESSORIES

Drawing: Arcadia Clinic
        Arcadia, California
Medium: Ink
Group Four Architecture, Research, and Planning
Courtesy of Robin Chiang, Architect and
Architectural Illustrator

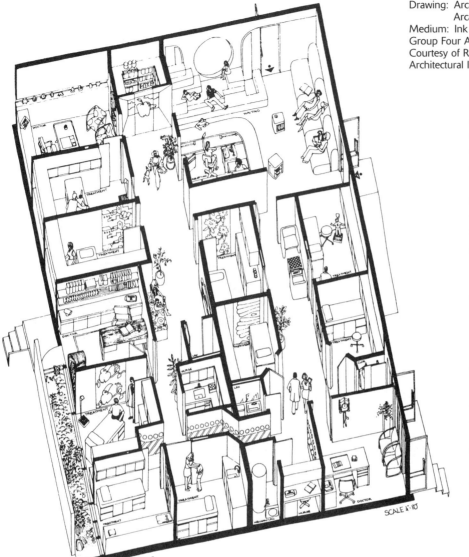

The projected drawing shown here depicts actual (to scale) room dimensions…including heights of walls and counters. As a preliminary sketch, this was an efficient method of presentation…giving an idea of the sorts of activities while allowing users to measure proposed scales. With one drawing, it was possible to convey information on a single sheet that was copied and distributed to fourteen users.
[ARCHITECT'S STATEMENT]

The plan oblique down view is the appropriate view when communicating interior accessories such as furnishings and examining how the walls meet the floor plane. Compare this with the up view on p. 599 where the walls meet the ceiling plane and ceiling structure.

PROPOSED PEDIATRICS

75°–15°

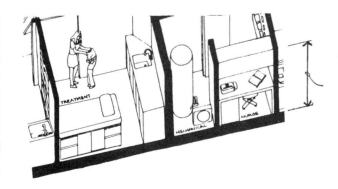

The height of the horizontal section (plan view) cut is usually taken slightly below the ceiling height (7' to 8'). This allows a clear view of important interior elements. People, plants, furniture, and columns retain verticality.

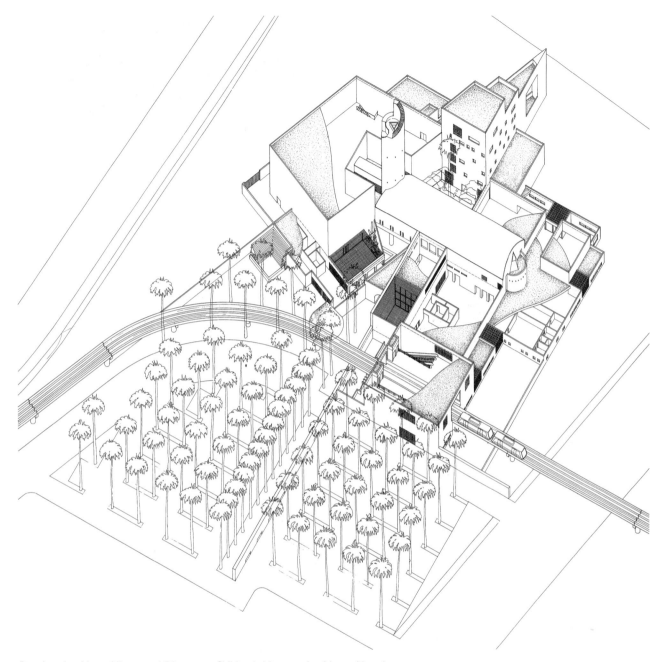

Drawing: Las Vegas Library and Discovery: Children's Museum, Las Vegas, Nevada
Medium: Ink, 30" × 42" (76.2 × 106.7 cm), Scale: approx 1"=80'
Courtesy of Antoine Predock, Architect

The fragility of both the desert and the communities that colonize it is apparent when one views Las Vegas, Nevada, from the air. This confluence of nature, fantasy, urbanization, and science underscores the complexities of the desert environment and the task of making architecture responsive to its many faces.
[ARCHITECT'S STATEMENT]

Trees retain their verticality in plan obliques. In this drawing, a group of trees complements the building complex. Also, moving vehicles (trains, cars, etc.) retain their verticality. The nice "partial roof removal" revealing technique allows the building to retain the feeling of a complete enclosure while at the same time permitting glimpses of the interior spaces.

TREES — PLAN OBLIQUE ACCESSORIES

DELINEATING CARS IN PLAN AND IN ELEVATION

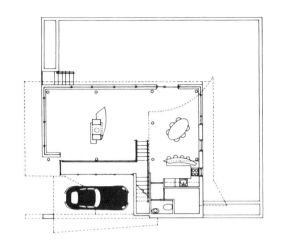

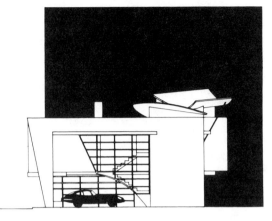

Drawings above: The Hague Villa Project
The Hague, The Netherlands
10" × 8" (25.4 × 20.3 cm), Scale: ¼"=1'0"
Medium: Pen and ink
Courtesy of Hariri & Hariri, Architects

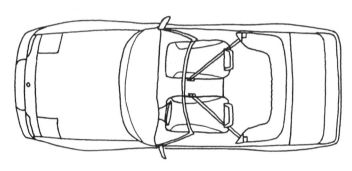

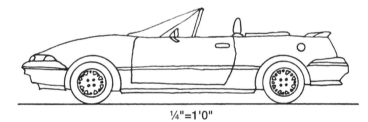

¼"=1'0"

Cars seen in the plan view are good scale indicators when placed on driveways and roadways on site plans. Likewise, cars seen in elevation, as with human figures, are good scale indicators for buildings. They can be symbolic as shown above or delineated with more detail.

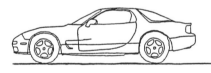  

⅛"=1'0"

¼"=1'0"

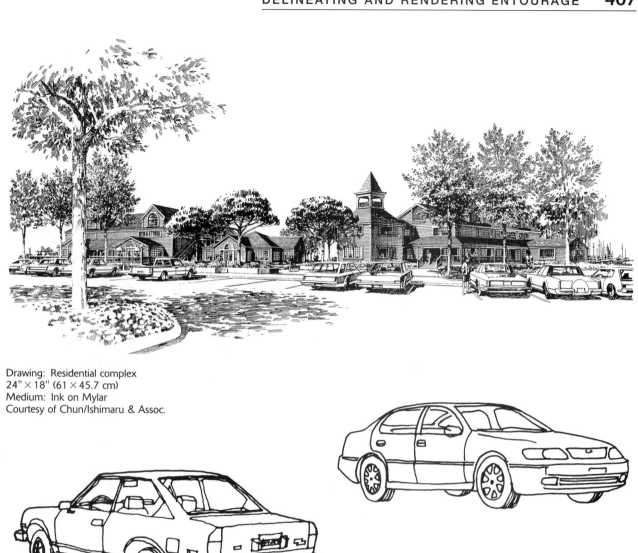

Drawing: Residential complex
24" × 18" (61 × 45.7 cm)
Medium: Ink on Mylar
Courtesy of Chun/Ishimaru & Assoc.

Car shapes in plan and in elevation are essentially rectangles. Cars in perspective can be simplified into rectangular boxes (see p. 154). Standing human figures are usually drawn in perspective with cars in order to indicate an appropriate scale.

As with people and landscaping entourage, cars should complement the architecture. Keep a reference file of photos and drawings for cars.

DELINEATING CARS IN PERSPECTIVE

RENDERING WATER REFLECTIONS

Drawing: Project, Japan
Courtesy of Projects International, Palo Alto
and Christopher Grubbs, Illustrator

Buildings or small structures in the urban landscape appear light in daylight and their reflections should be shown lighter than the value of the body of the water. The above example shows these elements reflected as pure white with minimal horizontal strokes within the white area. The dark part of the landscape (background trees) is reflected in the water with closely spaced short horizontal marks. The water reflections on both of these pages show slight agitation, with a general feeling of calmness and serenity. A horizontal reflection actually begins where the object reflected meets the reflecting surface. Part of the reflection may be concealed by a non-reflecting surface (see lower left steps).

Both water reflection drawings measure 8" × 5" and were drawn with a Uniball Micro pen on Clearprint. These images represent the first of a two-step process in which the drawings were copied and Prismacolor was applied to the copies for a color version.
[ARCHITECTURAL ILLUSTRATOR'S STATEMENT]

For the purposes of rendering, **water** can be depicted either as **still** or with **ripples.** Still water is best illustrated with precise parallel **horizontal** lines. These can be equally spaced or unequally spaced at increasing intervals depending on the nature of the body of water. Wave ripples have a convex and concave form that reflects objects at different angles. The resulting visual phenomenon is that of irregular stripes. Small **wavy** freehand lines produce the best results for agitated water. In this river scene, the darker value of the boats reflect darker than the background foliage. Also note the multiple directions for the wavy lines to represent agitated water.

Drawing: Saigon City, Vietnam
Courtesy of Skidmore, Owings, and Merrill, San Francisco
and Christopher Grubbs, Illustrator

Shifting reflective water surfaces tend to intimidate the artist. But water is just as tangible a material as brick. The first rule is not to overdraw the surface. This is best achieved by planning ahead. In the preliminary drawing, flip upside-down those elements that will best express reflections. Anticipate the scale change of big strokes (foreground waves) versus tiny strokes (distant waves). Since water surfaces are so varied and quick to change, it's very important to establish a specific instant of time or condition for your scene and to anticipate the graphic implications: Is there a breeze rippling the surface or is it glass? Is this a pond or an ocean?
[ARCHITECTURAL ILLUSTRATOR'S STATEMENT]

RENDERING WATER REFLECTIONS

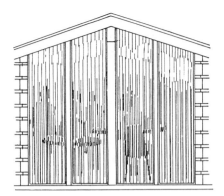

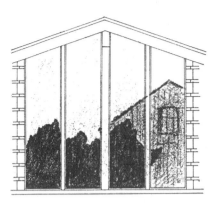

RENDERING GLASS REFLECTIONS

Most glass situations are reflective. A **nonreflective** situation results in a see-through transparency. Show human figures, vegetation, and furniture seen in the interior space to give a realistic effect. A **reflective** situation will show objects behind the observer, such as trees, buildings, vehicles, and the sky condition. A **partial reflective/partial transparent** situation shows objects (e.g., clouds) behind the observer as well as human figures and furniture within the space.

Drawing: New England Sunbox
          Methuen, Massachusetts
9" × 11" (22.9 × 27.9 cm)
Medium: Black Prismacolor on vellum
with watercolor paper underlay
Courtesy of Interface Architects
Illustration: Paul Stevenson Oles, FAIA

This drawing is a straightforward example of wax-based pencil on vellum with a watercolor paper underlay. The reflections in the glazing were carefully plotted, using a folded-tracing device. To do this, plan elements were traced which will be seen as reflected, then the tracing was folded 180° about the axis (in plan) of the reflecting surface (glass, in this case), and the perspective image was constructed beyond the glass in exactly the usual way. Deciding on tonal values for superimposed images (real and virtual) is a little tricky and requires some analysis; but intuitive judgments allow a reasonably convincing depiction of transparent and reflective glazing. [ARCHITECTURAL ILLUSTRATOR'S STATEMENT]

RENDERING GLASS REFLECTIONS

Drawing: Student project by Corvin Matei
               D.A.R.T. (Dallas Rapid Transit Systems)
18" × 18" (45.7 × 45.7 cm)
Medium: 2B pencil on Strathmore paper
Courtesy of the University of Texas at Arlington
School of Architecture

This drawing is an investigative study rather than a straightforward representation of a space. It tries to convey the differences and similarities between "virtual" and "real." This is done by assigning different textures only to the surfaces important to the study. The glass, which is the focus of this drawing, is assigned the darkest tone, while other unimportant areas are left blank. The sketches at the lower right are section and plan studies done simultaneously with the perspective; they become part of the study and help to better understand and develop the design of the piece.
[ARCHITECTURE STUDENT'S STATEMENT]

The reflection is typical of a night scene (dark exterior) and is caused by the artifical illumination inside the train. This is analogous to observed reflections on windows separating a dark interior from a sunlit exterior. In the daytime, a train traveller would experience completely transparent glass.

RENDERING GLASS REFLECTIONS

Drawing: San Franciso Ballet Building
Medium: Pencil 40" × 30" (101.6 × 76.2 cm)
Rendered by J. Poey
Courtesy of Beverly Willis, FAIA

This nicely rendered two-point perspective shows a combination of reflective glass on the windows at the top, and see-through, transparent glass on the windows below. One sees the interior ceiling lighting fixtures predominating over the balcony shadows. The Opera House building (left) is seen visible and "ghosted" over the part of the building that the Ballet Association would obscure. This shows reflective glass seen from an interior space. "Ghosting" is a technique that allows us to see the complete exterior shape of a building as well as building forms hidden behind or building shapes within the major building. It depends on subtle color shading changes that will not affect the building exterior in preference to the building interior or the hidden building beyond.

Drawings: Bank of Tokyo of California
            Headquarters Building
            San Francisco, California
Rendered by Carlos Diniz Associates
Visual Communication

For high-rise buildings with a predominantly glass facade, the sky and clouds generally will give reflections to the windows up high and the surrounding urban landscape will give reflections to the windows down below.

Hatching techniques can effectively indicate reflections in glass. A series of approximately parallel thin marks or lines are hand-drawn to simulate tone. Lines closely spaced give a dark tone or value; lines spaced farther apart give a light tone or value. **Hatching** or **cross-hatching** (crisscrossing hatched lines) makes a rendered surface seem more animated than if it were toned a solid shade. By using a cross-hatching technique to create tone density, the renderer has given the feeling of an overcast sky.

RENDERING GLASS REFLECTIONS

RENDERING GLASS REFLECTIONS

Drawing: "Ojo de dios" (Eye of God)
        Residence for P.S. Oles and Susan Thompson
        Projected Construction: 2000 A.D.
        Taos, New Mexico
Medium: Prismacolor on Strathmore, 14" × 11" (35.6 × 27.9 cm)
        Photo/rendering montage
Courtesy of Paul Stevenson Oles, FAIA

The station point from which the building perspective was plotted by computer and from which the site photograph was taken were carefully matched. Similarly, the building shadows were calculated by the computer to be those occurring at 12 noon on the winter solstice (in this latitude), and the site photograph was taken at that time. The building image was scaled and located in the site image by means of prepared markers located in the site when it was photographed. The final composite image was achieved by cutting out a building-shaped "window" in the rubber-cement-mounted photo, removing the piece, cleaning the exposed board, and completing the final wax pencil image of the building to match the contrast level and key of the surrounding photograph.
[ARCHITECTURAL ILLUSTRATOR'S STATEMENT]

Drawing: State of California Library and Court Annex, Sacramento, California
9" × 6.5" (22.9 × 16.5 cm)
Courtesy of TAC The Architects Collaborative and Christopher Grubbs, Renderer

RENDERING GLASS REFLECTIONS

This glass reflection was drawn with a 3B pencil lead base on Clearprint. This image represents the first of a two-step process in which the drawing was copied and Prismacolor applied to the copy for a color version. Before the artist resorts to the standard diagonal cross-hatching that is supposed to say "glass," he or she should go outside with a sketch pad and do some simple studies of how glass really looks under as many conditions as possible. What I learned from observation told me that the curved glass conditions in this drawing could feature "highlights" or glare. This is best expressed by simply not toning those areas at all but rather keeping them as light as possible.
[ARCHITECTURAL ILLUSTRATOR'S STATEMENT]

RENDERING POLISHED SURFACES

Drawing: New England Sunbox
                  Methuen, Massachusetts
Courtesy of Interface Architects
Illustration: Paul Stevenson Oles, FAIA

*The three horizontal shiny surfaces (floor, table, counter) are indicated as partially reflective by repeating the high-con-
trast patterns of the bright openings with their vertical edges and mullions. The nearer reflections become less precise
and contrasty because the angle of incident view is greater. The vertical smooth surface (picture glazing on the left) is
shown very brightly and precisely reflective because of the extremely raking angle of incident view.*
[ARCHITECTURAL ILLUSTRATOR'S STATEMENT]

Drawing: Dolby Building, San Francisco, California
18" × 24" (45.7 × 61 cm)
Medium: Ink on Mylar
Courtesy of Chun/Ishimaru & Assoc., Architectural Illustrators

The most important purpose of any rendering to us is the readability of the space. We will purposely manipulate shadows and reflections to further this end. In the final analysis, it is a matter of simple composition and the use of darks against lights and lights against darks…this is true for any medium. Interiors are more difficult to illustrate because there are so many options and choices of light sources. Exteriors are rather simple because once the light source direction is determined, it is just a matter of putting in lighted surfaces, shaded surfaces, and shadows.
[ARCHITECTURAL ILLUSTRATOR'S STATEMENT]

RENDERING POLISHED SURFACES

RENDERING REFLECTIONS ON WET PAVEMENT

Drawing: 1401 Broadway—Proposed restorations, alterations, and additions
Oakland, California
Medium: Graphite on vellum, 8" × 14" (20.3 × 35.6 cm)
Courtesy of Stephan Hoffpauir, AIA

Reflecting a building in wet pavement is a common trick used by architectural illustrators to add sparkle to an otherwise uninteresting part of a drawing. The effect is created by simply extending the vertical lines of the building, and perhaps a few horizontal ones as well, into the sidewalk and street. The reflection gradually fades away as it extends downward.
[ARCHITECTURAL ILLUSTRATOR'S STATEMENT]

Drawing: The Lytton Building, Palo Alto, California
          Korth Sunseri Architects
Medium: Watercolor, 20½" × 12" (52.1 × 30.5 cm)
Courtesy of Stephan Hoffpauir, AIA

The pavement in front of the building often occupies a significant portion of a perspective drawing. This seeming liability can be made into an asset through the use of reflections. In this example the reflections in the wet pavement are almost as detailed as the building and cars themselves and must be plotted as carefully as the rest of the drawing. While this technique is far more time-consuming than the previous example, the effect can be quite striking.
[ARCHITECTURAL ILLUSTRATOR'S STATEMENT]

This watercolor rendering shows the luminous quality of this medium. Watercolor receives high marks for its transparency. When applied, it can be fairly controlled, as shown above, or completely spontaneous and uncontrolled. Watercolor traditionally has been applied using soft sable brushes. Brushes are excellent tone blenders and can produce a wide range of strokes, from bold to fine. Water-soluble pencils are an excellent alternative to brushes. By adding water to pencil marks, one can produce a colored wash. Most watercolor papers are very receptive to all types of media, including pencil, charcoal, sanguine crayons, chalk, and pastels.

RENDERING REFLECTIONS ON WET PAVEMENT

RENDERING ARTIFICIAL LIGHTING IN INTERIORS

Drawing: Ahmanson Theatre
Renovation
Los Angeles,
California
24" × 24" (61 × 61 cm)
Medium: Pen and ink with
oil and acrylics
Ellerbe Becket, Architects
Courtesy of Art Zendarski,
Architectural Illustrator

The intent of the rendering was to meet two requirements. First, the drawing was needed to communicate the design renovation to the Music Center administrators. Second, the rendering, in conjunction with the new Music Center being designed by Frank Gehry, would be incorporated into a marketing package used for fund raisers seeking private and public donations to cover the cost of construction.

Expressing the architect's complex, unconventional design to first-time viewers posed quite a challenge. Numbers of study views were analyzed to capture just the right vantage point. The study views and initial perspective blockout were created by computer. To clearly and accurately depict the complexity of the ceiling acoustic forms and lighting design elements and also the additional balcony and box seating, I used the technique of pen and ink on vellum. The ink-line drawing was then transferred photographically onto photomural paper. Oils and acrylics were used to complete the rendering. Working in pen and ink also helped in meeting the marketing specifications that called for the rendering to provide both black and white and color reproduction capabilities.

The rendering was meticulously detailed to give a true and accurate portrayal. Also, the drawing needed to depict a level of excitement that would get potential investors enthusiastic about the project. The artificial lighting is a strong visual element used to build this excitement. The diagonal thrust of light from the ceiling onto the stage is a composition device that creates a sense of drama and focal point for the drawing while prominently featuring the new lighting design elements. The careful composition of the viewpoint that draws the viewer into the interior space, lighting, texture, the on-stage scene from the popular play Les Misérables and the animation of the people in the audience was all added to give the drawing a sense of reality.
[ARCHITECTURAL ILLUSTRATOR'S STATEMENT]

The purpose of this illustration was to portray the drama and monumental scale of the elliptical entrance rotunda. An exaggerated shaft of light emanating from the dome's oculus was chosen to achieve a dramatic quality, while the low station point emphasizes the monumental scale of the space.
[ARCHITECTURAL ILLUSTRATOR'S
STATEMENT]

The rendering of both artificial lighting and natural lighting helps to create an ambiance and a mood in interior spaces. Artificial exterior lighting (spotlights, etc.) can produce dramatic sky patterns and enliven a rendering (see Shekou Harbour Building, p. 303). The artificial interior lighting on the facing page helps to highlight the architectural design of the interior space. Natural solar lighting shown on this page functions in a similar manner.

Drawing: Federal Courthouse, St. Louis, Missouri
Medium: Pencil on vellum, 9½" × 20" (24.1 × 50.8 cm)
Architect: Hellmuth, Obata & Kassabaum, Inc.
Courtesy of Kenneth E. Miller, Architect, Architectural Illustrator

RENDERING NATURAL LIGHTING IN INTERIORS

PENCIL RENDERING

Sketches: Student project by Corvin Matei
Medium: 2B pencil on Strathmore paper
Courtesy of the University of Texas at Arlington
School of Architecture

"Forum America — Competition for a Virtual Building"
P/A Competition Grand Prize winner
15" × 20" (38.1 × 50.8 cm)

A 2B pencil is almost in the middle of the "soft" range for soft lead pencils. Pencil renderings, like this example, are usually done with HB, B, and 2B grades. these grades can give nice dense dark soft tones. Textured Strathmore paper of medium weight is very receptive to soft graphite pencils.

Drawing: Sydney Opera House, Sydney, Australia, Jorn Utzon, Architect
Medium: Prismacolor on Mylar, 7" × 5" (17.8 × 12.7 cm)
Courtesy of Paul Stevenson Oles, FAIA

COLORED PENCIL RENDERING

This drawng of an entirely existing building was based on one of several dozen photographs that I took in order to dis-cover the most interesting station point. The contours were traced directly onto Mylar from a 5" × 7" black and white print of the photograph. Then it was finished in tones and textures while observing paper prints of the photograph and after removing the photographic underlay. Mylar allowed the extremely high resolution necessary for this very small original drawng.
[ARCHITECTURAL ILLUSTRATOR'S STATEMENT]

Colored pencils are an excellent medium for architectural subjects. They are extremely versatile, although some-what time-consuming to apply. They are wonderful for both quick preliminary design studies and for final pre-sentations. The roof structure shown above shows nice value changes and lighting effects, both done easily with colored pencils. This medium takes to most kinds of paper and provides a wide range of color choices from bold solids to softer gradations. However, it is best to limit your palette to a few hues to get the best results. Colored pencils give a soft impressionistic feeling to a drawing in addition to showing the actual surface color.

PEN AND INK RENDERING

Drawing: Villa Syrigos, near Athens, Greece
36" × 24" (91.4 × 61 cm), Scale: ⅛"=1'0"
Medium: Ink on Mylar, Rapidograph pen
Courtesy of Hugh Newell Jacobsen, FAIA, Architect
and Stephen S. Evanusa, Architect

The careful study of shadows and reflections is an essential element in this rendering.
[ARCHITECTURAL ILLUSTRATOR'S STATEMENT]

Design development drawings, which are examined in detail in the subsequent two chapters, are more "developmental" and take less time to produce than rendered drawings which are made for final presentation to a client. Finalized rendered delineations can be (and often are) manipulated to obscure design flaws in order to increase the design's acceptability and marketability. Architects will frequently contract out renderings for their designs to specialists called "delineators" or "architectural illustrators." Their primary goal is to generate a drawing that will "sell" a design to a potential client.

Drawing: Villa Andropoulos, near Athens, Greece
36" × 24" (91.4 × 61 cm), Scale: ⅛"=1'0"
Medium: Ink on Mylar, rapidograph pen
Courtesy of Hugh Newell Jacobsen, FAIA, Architect
and Stephen S. Evanusa, Architect

The character of this drawing is derived by the interplay of two ink drawing line techniques: line and tone. The house is described by shade and shadow, drawn with a "stippled" texture; the surrounding rocky mountain by freehand contour. [DELINEATOR'S STATEMENT]

Note the long continuous contour lines on the hillsides in these two renderings. Regardless whether they are linear or curvilinear, they tend to have a deliberate feeling because of their length. When closely spaced, these lines can be very effective in describing the shape and overall form of a landscape.

PEN AND INK RENDERING

Drawing: Church perspective with an addition, Wilmington, North Carolina
Medium: Ink on Mylar
Courtesy of Gerald Allen and Jeffrey Harbinson, Architects, P.C.

The use of broken lines and dots to simulate line (the optical response to light) can be seen in a technique nick-named "pointillism" (see stippling—p. 378) after the French artists (Georges Seurat, etc.) who made similar experiments with light and vision. The linework used in this drawing is pointillism.

In a shadow cast drawing, the only things seen are those created by shadows. In this drawing, for example, shadows highlight the church steeple and the backside of the buttress; the viewer's imagination completes the drawing.
Since it is not possible to use the shadow cast method in drawing the church windows, this perspective presents two examples to resolve this situation. The stained glass windows are figurative pieces, drawn to show religious artifacts (angels, doves, etc.) in the windows. The clouds drawn in the clear glass window of the church addition capture the reflective nature of glass.
[ARCHITECT'S STATEMENT]

Drawing: Pedestrian streetscape
Medium: Pen and ink on Mylar, 24" × 36" (61 × 91.4 cm)
Courtesy of Markus Lui & Associates, Architectural Illustrator

PEN AND INK RENDERING

This rendering makes extensive use of dot tone density (stippling) with line to give value to the building structure and the entourage. Note the nicely delineated human figures and foreground palm trees as well as the cropping of the drawing to give the viewer a feeling that he or she is actually there.

10

Diagramming

Conceptual diagrams constitute a language in themselves. This abstract language must be understood and communicated properly among the design community. It is through graphic diagramming that one develops a design vocabulary. Elements like arrows, nodes, and other symbols help the beginner to use graphic techniques to explore ideas.

The intent of this chapter is to show professional examples of diagramming techniques and to examine how architects develop the most essential aspects of their design ideas through the use of diagrams.

Diagramming

Topic

Diagramming

References

Ching, Francis D.K. 1996. Architectural Graphics. Van Nostrand Reinhold. 158–163.

Lacy, Bill. 1991. 100 Contemporary Architects: Drawings and Sketches. Abrams.

Laseau, Paul. 1980. Graphic Thinking for Architects and Designers. Van Nostrand Reinhold.

Lin, Mike. 1993. Designing and Drawing with Confidence. Van Nostrand Reinhold. 149–157.

Porter, Tom. 1990. Architectural Drawing. Van Nostrand Reinhold. 112–119.

Porter, Tom and Goodman, Sue. 1988. Designer Primer. Charles Scribner's Sons. 95–101.

White, Edward T. 1985. Developing Baseline Skills for Architectural Diagramming. In Representation: Journal of Graphic Education. Vol 2, Issue 2, Summer 1985, edited by Kirby Lockard, Tucson, AZ.

White, Edward T. 1983. Site Analysis. Architectural Media Ltd.

White, Edward T. Space Adjacency Analysis. Architectural Media Ltd.

White, Edward T. Concept Source Book. Architectural Media Ltd.

Cross References

For p. 431   See p. 41
For pp. 434, 435, 446   See p. 482
For p. 441   See p. 499
For pp. 452–453   See p. 174
For p. 459   See p. 315

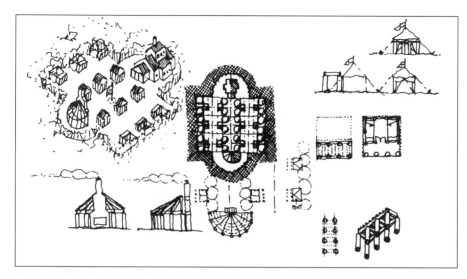

Preliminary schematic diagrams are frequently the seeds for the final design and ultimately the built project. They can take a two-dimensional or three-dimensional configuration, as shown in the Hoover Center. The diagrams below use a combination of point, line, and two-dimensional zone to explain the design concept.

Diagrams: Hoover Outdoor Education Center, Yorkville, Illinois
Medium: Felt-tipped pen on trace
Courtesy of Tigerman McCurry Architects

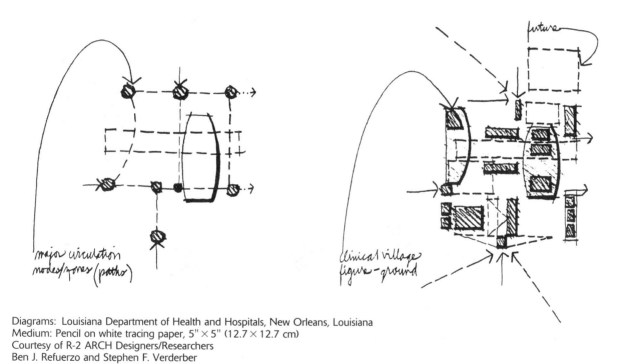

Diagrams: Louisiana Department of Health and Hospitals, New Orleans, Louisiana
Medium: Pencil on white tracing paper, 5" × 5" (12.7 × 12.7 cm)
Courtesy of R-2 ARCH Designers/Researchers
Ben J. Refuerzo and Stephen F. Verderber

INTRODUCTION

Once an architecture student's freehand graphics skills are honed, he or she will begin to appreciate the potential of this skill not only in drawing contextual elements (people, vegetation, cars, etc.) but also in drawing **conceptual diagrams.** The students are immediately confronted with developing sketches on "flimsy" (tracing paper) as part of the design process in a design studio project. Beginning with the first course in architectural design, students will be faced throughout their academic careers and professional lives with the task of developing numerous alternative ideas or schemes for each design problem. The ability to do quick freehand graphics in the form of scribbles and doodles is imperative. These **graphic diagrams** help us to explore alternative solutions and encourage **visualization** and **visual thinking.**

BASIC DIAGRAM SYMBOLS AND TYPES

point   point becomes line   line

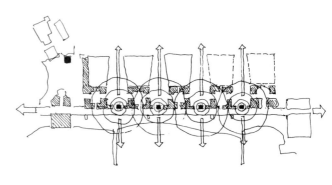

Diagram: Waterfront Development Plan
Asbury Park, New Jersey
Medium: Ink on trace, 6" × 3" (15.2 × 7.6 cm)
Courtesy of Koetter, Kim & Associates, Inc.
Architects and Urban Designers

Graphic diagrams can be two dimensional or three dimensional in their abstract communication of a design scheme. Through point, line, symbol, and zone diagrams, a building's organization can be represented in terms of user movement (circulation), space usage (zoning), site plan and site section analysis, structural analysis, and volumetric enclosure (geometric configuration).

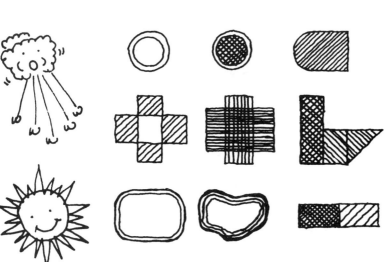

Pictorial symbol   Two-dimensional zone diagrams

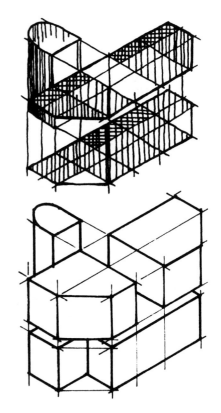

Three-dimensional zone and volume diagrams

The students hear a new vocabulary in the design studio. Terms like bubble diagram, schematics, flow, circulation, zoning, hierarchy, and metaphor become commonplace. The many new terms of this studio language, coupled with incessant demands for an abundance of ideas, sometimes overwhelms beginning students. An understanding of the language comes with reading architectural literature.

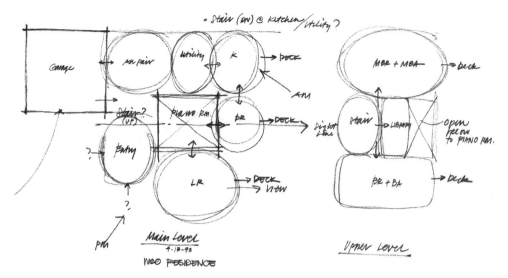

Sketch: Woo residence, Oakland, California
Medium: HB pencil
Courtesy of Kenzo Handa, Architect

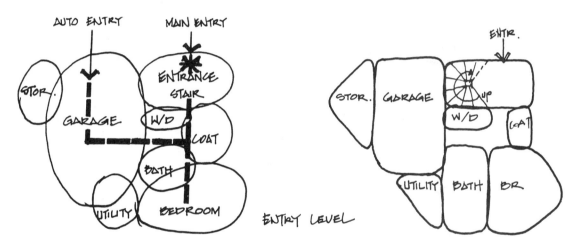

Bubble (can be any shape) diagrams relate interior spaces to each other as well as their relationship to external site determinants. Circulation linkages can quickly be analyzed and evaluated.

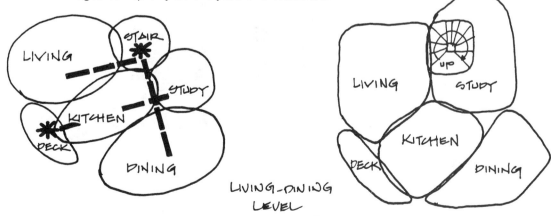

With an area program, it is important to set up functional zone adjacencies. Its intent is more informational.

SITE PLAN AS DIAGRAM

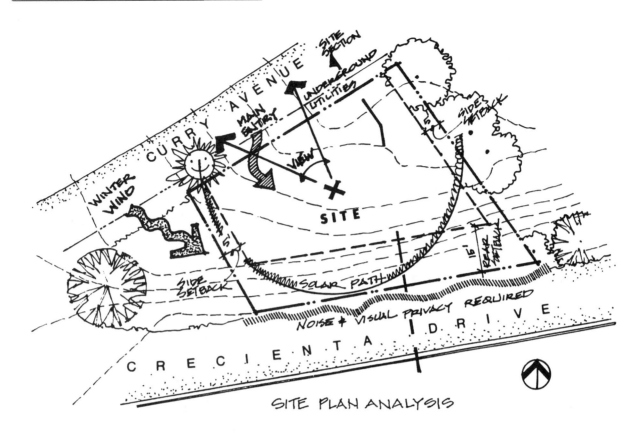

SITE PLAN ANALYSIS

Schematic analytical diagrams for site plans and site sections are frequently sketched in the design process. Influential factors on the site such as contours, traffic circulation, view, solar and wind conditions, noise, zoning regulations, and adjacent landscaping can quickly be analyzed.

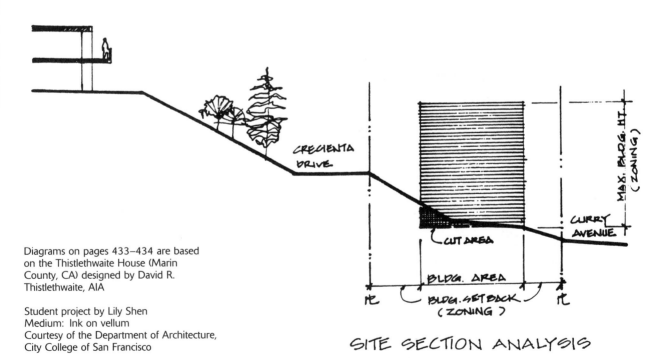

Diagrams on pages 433–434 are based on the Thistlethwaite House (Marin County, CA) designed by David R. Thistlethwaite, AIA

Student project by Lily Shen
Medium: Ink on vellum
Courtesy of the Department of Architecture,
City College of San Francisco

SITE SECTION ANALYSIS

Concept sketch

Drawings: House in
               Northern California
Medium: Pencil on trace
Courtesy of Legorreta Arquitectos,
Ricardo Legorreta, Victor Legorreta,
Noe Castro

During the design process, design drawings (diagrams, design sketches, etc.) are crucial in testing alternative schemes and themes. Design drawings document the design process. The initial stages are frequently black and white only with the goal of describing just the architectural form and its relation to the surrounding conditions. Later stages incorporate the use of color.

Every drawing type, whether two dimensional or three dimensional, can be used as a conceptual analytical diagram. Diagrams simplify information so that one can clearly examine specific aspects. As one simplifies, one abstracts reality. These graphic diagrams of a location plan, a site plan, a site section, and an elevation are precursors for the more three-dimensional diagrams of paraline and perspective sketches.

It is important that designers acquire the ability to relate the size and proportion of various architectural elements to buildings and their site conditions. Note the use of various scales in this study.

2D SITE DIAGRAMS

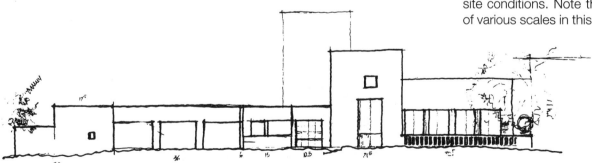

Elevation study, Scale: ⅛"=1'0"

DIAGRAMMING IDEAS

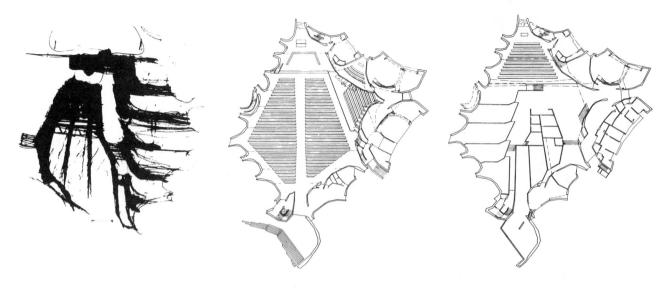

Images in the mind are first visualized (a mental act) and then sketched (a physical act). Sketching ideas on paper helps to evolve other ideas; these concepts are constantly evaluated and reevaluated. The examples show a progression from creative abstract sketches to more refined drawings.

Sketches and drawings: Kaleva Church, Tampere, Finland
Scales: upper left and bottom 1:50, upper right 1:100
Medium: Charcoal
Courtesy of Raili and Reima Pietilä, Architects

The ability to formulate mental images comes with practice. Visualizing everyday objects will form the basis for sharpening the conceptual imagination. As ideas occur, they are put on paper. This is an **ideational** drawing. An idea on paper is a visual representation of what something may conceptually look like. Some ideas will be discarded; some ideas will be changed, modified, refined, and expanded.

Reima Peitilä (1923–1993), a world-renowned Finnish architect, in the period after Alvar Aalto stated the following:

Creating architecture is a multimedia process. It involves verbal programming and directing; visualization by sketching floor plans, sections, elevations; spatialization with the help of a scale model; materialization by building . Both words and pictures are used to explain architectural form. Neither one nor the other alone is enough to make architecture as a phenomenon sufficiently comprehensible.

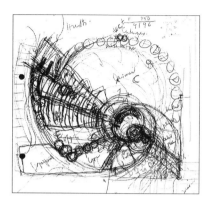 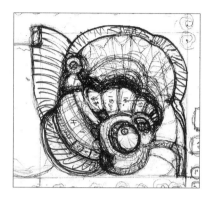 

Conceptual sketches and model photo: Tampere Main Library ("Metso"), Tampere City, Finland
Sketches 4" × 4" (10.2 × 10.2 cm), Model scale: 1:200
Courtesy of Raili and Reima Pietilä, Architects

This transparent "silk" (tracing paper) is my miraculous design medium. Almost a nonmaterial, it is cheap and of little value in the artist's permanent works. As my own design tool, this transparent, or more exactly, semitranslucent membrane functions as a catalyst, enabling visions to be fixed. The sketch has no further value after it has delivered its graphic message to the copy machine. Upon construction of the building, perhaps the production drawings go to the archives; but these sketches, though having helped mediate the path towards the form, usually get thrown in the waste paper basket before too long.

I have thought, however, that these process sketches could be of use in allowing us an insight into how architecture emerges from "scrap" or how architecture emerges almost from that indefinite 'anything' that can be behind or beneath the architectural concepts. The pictorial material of this processing design often has very little final form or character: Instead it possesses more an artistic multiple message load. Though the sketch is beyond the limited categories of logic and such consequent thinking, the sketch itself is not irrelevant or irrational. The good sketch is a multi-interpretive idea; it can give suitable impulses for feasible alternatives. We must then train ourselves to learn to read them, patiently, allowing much time.

Usually I lay sketch upon sketch, perhaps up to ten times, carefully holding the previous one as a basis for the following sketch until I feel "it is there." Usually then it is. My professional visualization opens up its possible routes through such sketch paper procedure. Architectural characteristics, features, traits, etc., are transported, transformed and transfigured via the sketches. At the end of the process, there are, of course, the final plans, sections, elevations, and details. Architectural graphics is an art where the expressive form follows the implicit function. Its latent message value is much higher than we usually assume and it is the sketch graphics that generate the spatial vision which will in turn become actual architecture.

These sketches here are merely a sample of hundreds; but it is still possible to note how, through these sketches, the building grows on the drafting table. It should be emphasized that these sketches are "conceptual tools" on the way to becoming objects and not in themselves detached objects like an artist's graphics. I would advise everyone not to break this vital growth link between these sketches and the actual building they become.
[REIMA PIETILÄ]

Notes on sketches and the architectural process
Courtesy of Raili and Reima Pietilä, Architects
Reprinted from: "PIETILÄ Intermediate Zones in Modern Architecture" with permission of Raili Pietilä
and the Museum of Finnish Architecture and the Alvar Aalto Museum

DIAGRAMMING IDEAS: THE MEDIUM

DIAGRAMMING IDEAS

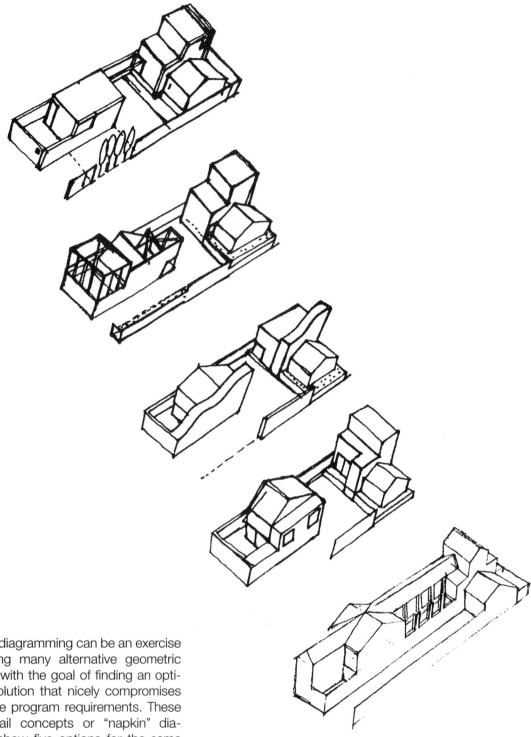

Sketch diagramming can be an exercise in testing many alternative geometric layouts with the goal of finding an optimum solution that nicely compromises all of the program requirements. These thumbnail concepts or "napkin" diagrams show five options for the same site area.

Conceptual sketches: Click Agency, West Hollywood, California
Medium: Ink on sketch paper
Courtesy of Hodgetts + Fung, Design Associates

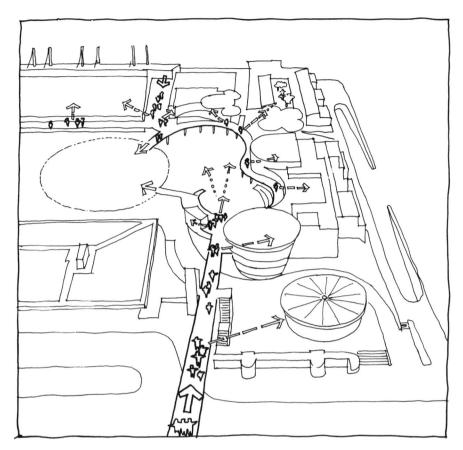

These diagrams are part of a series which were used to engage the users of the site and facilities in a public design process. Specifically, they describe routes through the site and a sequence of visual experiences. The diagrams were keyed to vignettes depicting views of the buildings and the activities observed within.
[ARCHITECT'S STATEMENT]

Movement diagrams: Yerba Buena
          Gardens Children Center
          San Francisco, California
Medium: Technical pen on vellum
6" × 6" (15.2 × 15.2 cm)
Courtesy of Adèle Naudé Santos
and Associates, Architects

These diagrams extensively use a point and a line symbol to depict pedestrian movement. The aerial bird's-eye view is much more descriptive than a site plan view in showing user circulation. Three-dimensional diagrams such as perspectives and plan obliques are generally more highly descriptive than two-dimensional diagrams. Sometimes the same diagram can be used to explain different information factors. These diagrams can be presented individually or as one set in which transparent overlays are used. A composite set should have a clear hierarchy of the informational aspects being considered.

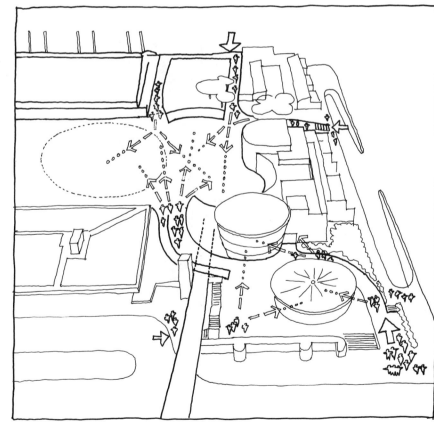

SECTION AS DIAGRAM

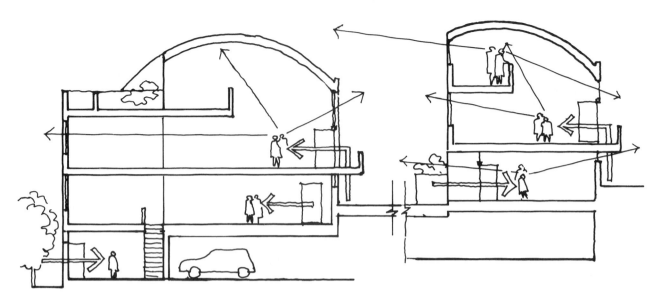

Diagram sketch: Franklin/La Brea Family Housing, Los Angeles, California
6" × 6" (15.2 × 15.2 cm), Scale: ¹⁄₁₆"=1'0"
Medium: Technical pen on Mylar
Courtesy of Adèle Naudé Santos and Associates, Architects

This section diagram clearly shows user view (thin arrowed line) and user movement (thick arrowed line).
The arrowed line is a very useful symbol in graphic diagrams.

Diagram sketch: Mixed-use Center, Turin, Italy
Medium: Black marker pen on smooth paper
Courtesy of Gunnar Birkerts and Associates, Inc., Architects

Graphic diagrams should be done with fluid and loose line strokes. This will help to give a wonderful feeling to
your conceptual ideas. Sectional diagrams should include human figures to give scale to the sketches.

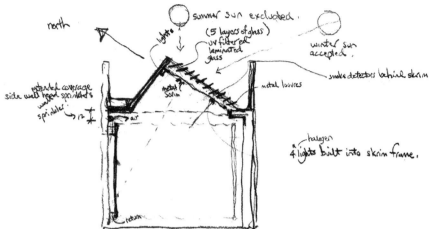

The use of light, both natural and artificial, is central to the conception of the Getty Museum and is therefore the focus of these sketches. These drawings explore the uses of light and its ability to mediate between the building's exterior and interior.
[ARCHITECT'S STATEMENT]

SECTION AS DIAGRAM

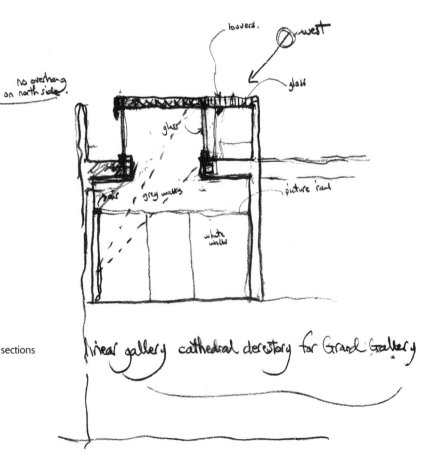

Diagrams frequently show relationships and symbolism. This diagram has a sun symbol showing the effect of winter and summer solar angles. Light direction is represented by an arrowed line (symbol) which enhances one's understanding of how light enters the museum's space. Also, note the integration of architectural design with structural and mechanical concepts.

Drawings: Conceptual sketch studies of museum sections
        The Getty Center Museum
        Los Angeles, California
Both 18" × 18" (45.7 × 45.7 cm)
Medium: graphite pencil on yellow trace
Courtesy of Richard Meier & Partners, Architects
Reprinted from The Getty Center Design Process
with permission of The J. Paul Getty Trust

PLAN AS DIAGRAM

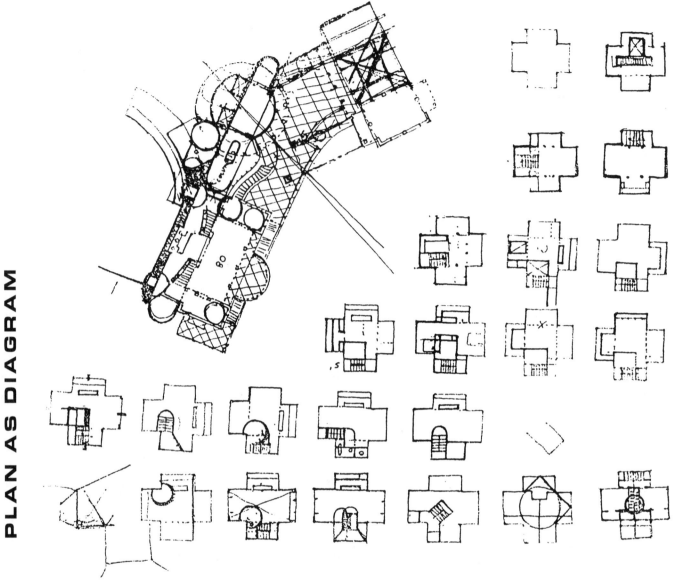

Conceptual diagrams: Villa Linda Flora (unbuilt), Bel Air, California
Medium: Ink on sketch paper, 8½" × 11" (21.6 × 27.9 cm)
Courtesy of Hodgetts + Fung, Design Associates

In any design project, there are numerous alternative solutions to be analyzed. This project shows the wide range of possible stairway types and stairway locations within the same geometric plan configuration. Frequently, diagrams are drawn with a consistent graphic format as shown above. This allows one to analyze a particular problem or focus on one specific issue (in this case, stairway location) by comparing one alternative to another.

The footprints of courthouse squares in America are remarkably similar in size. The variations of the court-house square form primarily center on the arrangement of roads around the square. Most squares are simply a block in the town grid sys-tem located at the center of the grid (Figure A). Other squares are the anomaly in the grid system so that the square is the geometric focus on the grid (Figure B). There are also some square forms that are a combina-tion of the two (Figure C). [ARCHITECT'S STATEMENT]

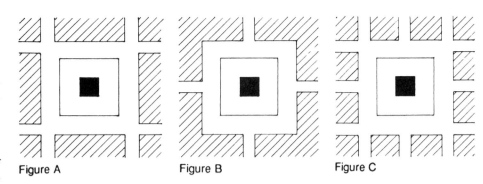

Figure A Figure B Figure C

Diagrams: The Courthouse Square
Medium: Ink
Courtesy of James F. Barker FAIA

Diagrams: Student project by Mary Vecera
Architectural Studies, Sagunto, Spain
1990, First-Open submissions
An addition to St. Patrick's Church, Cambridge
Association of Collegiate Schools of Architecture/
Precast Concrete Institute
Medium: Ink
Courtesy of the University of Texas at Arlington
School of Architecture

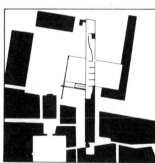

PUBLIC

BEFORE

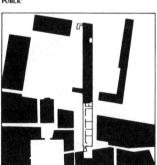

PRIVATE

OPPOSITIONS

PLAN AS DIAGRAM

These plan diagrams have been made abstractly simplistic so that one can focus on comparing specific con-cepts such as public and private spaces and before and after situations. The use of positive and negative (fig-ure and ground) spaces helps to remove other plan elements (ground textures, etc.) that would otherwise con-fuse the issues on which one wants to concentrate.

PLAN AS DIAGRAM

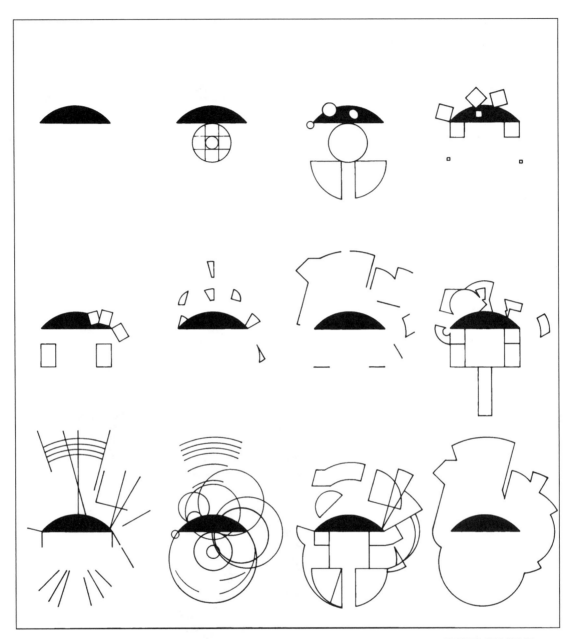

ELEMENTS   DEVELOPMENT

Diagrams: Private residence, Illinois (1988–90)
Medium: Ink
Courtesy of Stanley Tigerman, Architect

Storyboard showing the evolution of elements. The house begins with a wedge, generating other forms that tumble off of it.
[ARCHITECT'S STATEMENT]

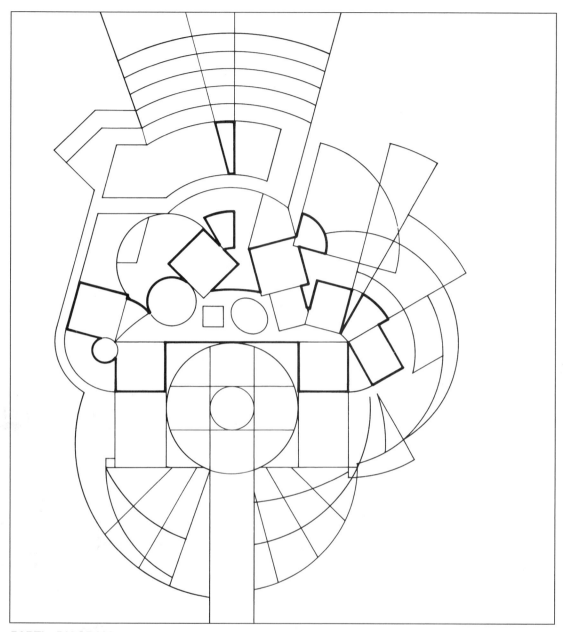

PLAN AS DIAGRAM

PARTI DIAGRAM

Diagrams: Private residence, llinois (1988–90)
Medium: Ink
Courtesy of Stanley Tigerman, Architect

In the parti diagram, the house expands into the site, and geometric repetitions radiating from the home into the landscape are indicated.
[ARCHITECT'S STATEMENT]

A **parti diagram** shows the basic schematic assumption of a plan. It is the fundamental idea (scheme) of a plan.

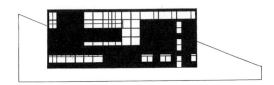

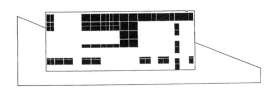

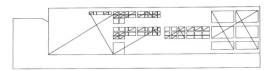

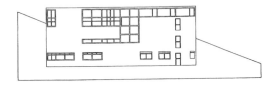

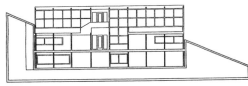

ELEVATION AS DIAGRAM

Diagrams: Student projects by Darlene Lawrence (above)
           and Karla Armas (right)
           Facade studies
Medium: Ink on Mylar
Courtesy of the University of Texas at Arlington
School of Architecture

The process of diagramming elevations is similar to that of diagramming plans. These facade studies of elevation diagrams show the strong use of figure and ground as well as solid (wall) and void (window). In a reductive manner, these diagrams allow one to concentrate on the geometric treatment of the fenestration. This simplification of the facade prevents one from being distracted by other aspects that may appear in an elevation, such as material texture on the facade.

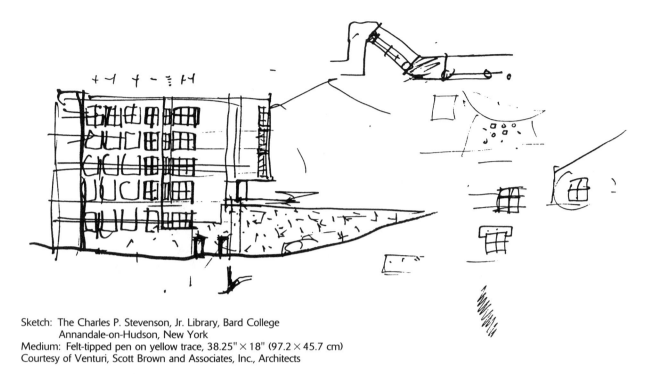

Sketch: The Charles P. Stevenson, Jr. Library, Bard College
              Annandale-on-Hudson, New York
Medium: Felt-tipped pen on yellow trace, 38.25" × 18" (97.2 × 45.7 cm)
Courtesy of Venturi, Scott Brown and Associates, Inc., Architects

A study for Stevenson Library at Bard College — a facade involving subtle rhythm as composition and turning a corner to a different kind of facade.
[ARCHITECT'S STATEMENT]

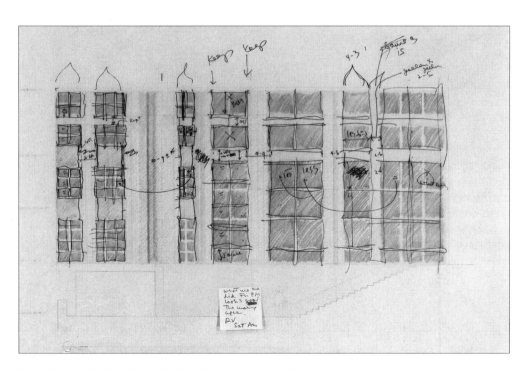

Medium: Robert Venturi annotations in red and black felt-tipped pen on Post-it note.
              Yellow trace overlaid on and attached to diazo print. 42" × 30" (106.7 × 76.2 cm)

A facade study of the same building at a late stage of development dealing in inches and referring to a previous sketch.
[ARCHITECT'S STATEMENT]

ELEVATION AS DIAGRAM

Diagram sketch: National Library, Riga, Latvia
Medium: Black marker pen on smooth paper
Courtesy of Gunnar Birkerts and Associates, Inc. Architects

THUMBNAIL SKETCH DIAGRAMS

The elevation sketches in this series are small and compact and can thus be classified as "thumbnail." They are freehand sketched elevation diagrams. The goal, as with a series of hardline elevation diagrams (p. 446), is to present conceptual ideas in a simplified format.

An ink wash produces a similar effect to that of wet marking pens. An ink wash uses a brush with an ink pen. Diluted or undiluted ink is added to water with a brush and applied in wash form over existing lines. This is an excellent technique for producing tonal variations and covering large solid areas.

This elevation sketch uses heavy wet marking pens. One should smear/smudge the ink while it's still wet. The key is to use a lot of black and contrast with lots of intensely bright colors.
[ARCHITECTURAL DESIGNER'S STATEMENT]

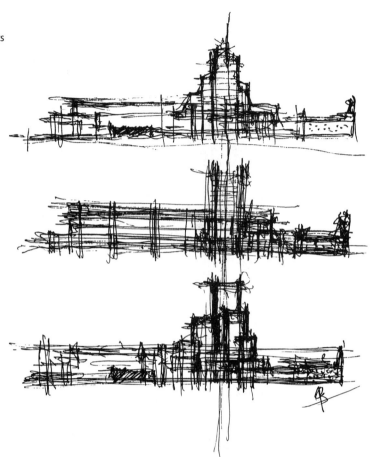

Sketch: Rajdamri, Bangkok, Thailand
Medium: Cold felt marker
Courtesy of Stan Laegreid, Senior Designer, The Callison Partnership

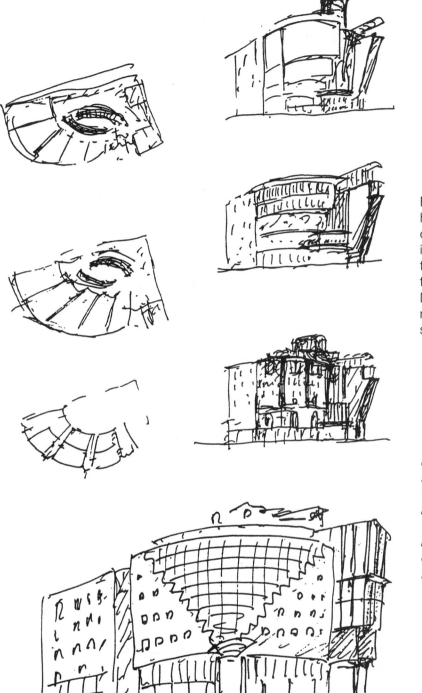

Every design professional develops his or her own language in expressing concepts graphically as a way of seeing. Concepts can be approached by thinking in plan, in elevation, in section, or in overall perspective images. Developmental sketches and the medium used for them are very personal.

These sketches show two different approaches investigated. The upper three sketches show stone facades as a veneer and a cantilevering part of the building to separate two urban spaces. The lower sketch investigates a symmetrical approach with a central entrance which was not followed up.
[ARCHITECT'S STATEMENT]

Early conceptual sketches
Haas–Haus Stephansplatz
Vienna, Austria
Medium: Ink
Courtesy of Hans Hollein, Architekt

NAPKIN SKETCH DIAGRAMS

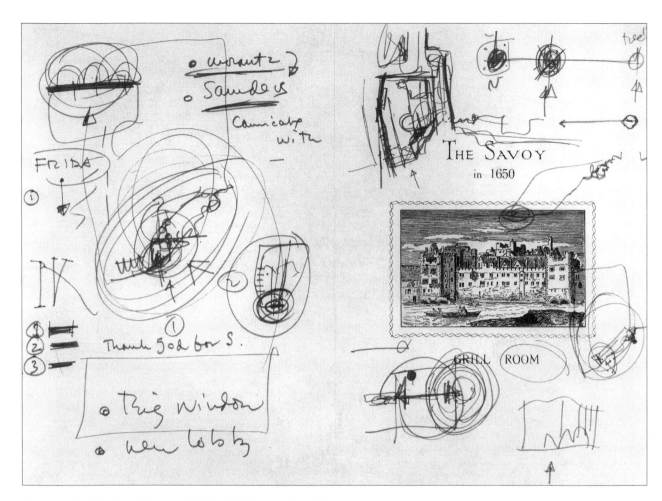

Diagrammatical sketches (both pages): National Gallery, Sainsbury Wing
London, England
Medium: Red felt-tipped pen
Courtesy of Venturi, Scott Brown and Associates, Inc., Architects

The ideal sketches are those that evolve from intuition indirectly guiding the hand more than from the mind directly guiding the hand. Also combinations of images and words enrich the process.
[ARCHITECT'S STATEMENT]

These two-dimensional napkin (in this case dinner menu) sketches were done by architect Robert Venturi. Activities such as working, playing, eating, or answering nature's call can all be times when the mind can generate creative thoughts. In other words, creative thinking is not altogether controllable and it is important for the designer to be "on guard" for the creative insight.

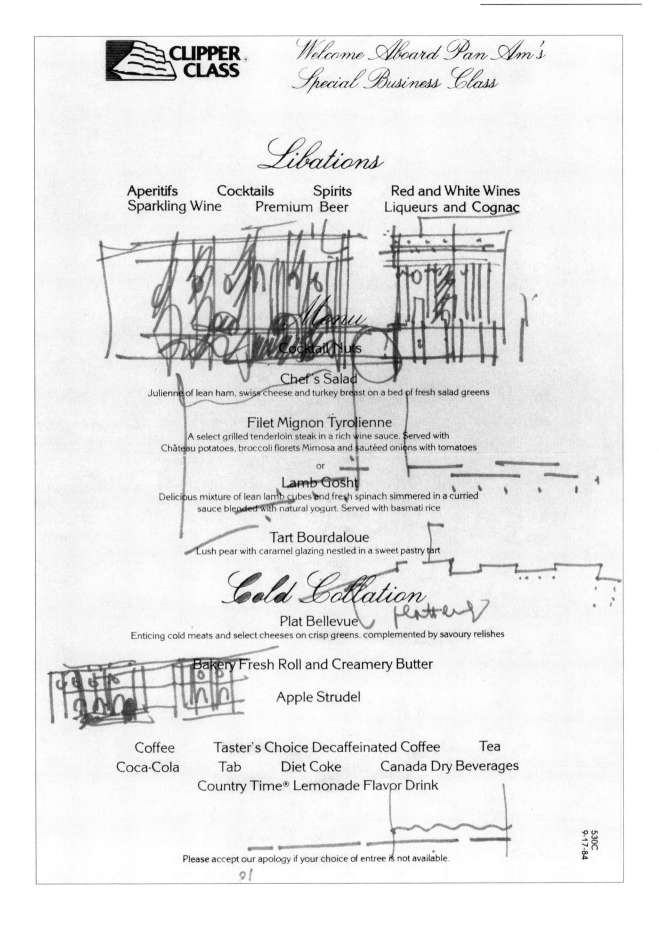

CLIPPER CLASS

Welcome Aboard Pan Am's Special Business Class

Libations

Aperitifs   Cocktails   Spirits   Red and White Wines
Sparkling Wine   Premium Beer   Liqueurs and Cognac

Menu

Cocktail Nuts

Chef's Salad
Julienne of lean ham, swiss cheese and turkey breast on a bed of fresh salad greens

Filet Mignon Tyrolienne
A select grilled tenderloin steak in a rich wine sauce. Served with
Château potatoes, broccoli florets Mimosa and sautéed onions with tomatoes

or

Lamb Gosht
Delicious mixture of lean lamb cubes and fresh spinach simmered in a curried
sauce blended with natural yogurt. Served with basmati rice

Tart Bourdaloue
Lush pear with caramel glazing nestled in a sweet pastry tart

Cold Collation

Plat Bellevue
Enticing cold meats and select cheeses on crisp greens, complemented by savoury relishes

Bakery Fresh Roll and Creamery Butter

Apple Strudel

Coffee   Taster's Choice Decaffeinated Coffee   Tea
Coca-Cola   Tab   Diet Coke   Canada Dry Beverages
Country Time® Lemonade Flavor Drink

Please accept our apology if your choice of entree is not available.

530C
9-17-84

NAPKIN SKETCH DIAGRAMS

THUMBNAIL SKETCH DIAGRAMS

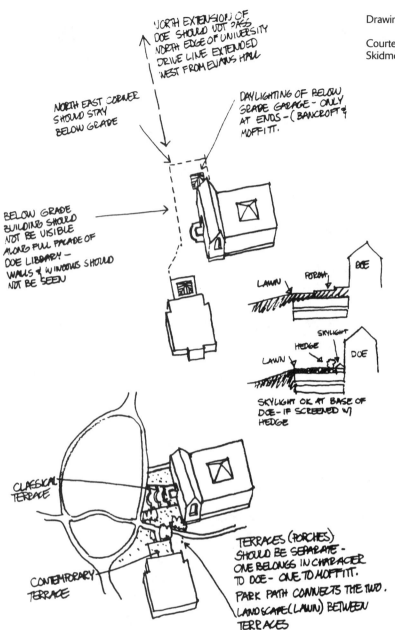

NORTH EXTENSION OF DOE SHOULD NOT PASS NORTH EDGE OF UNIVERSITY DRIVE LINE EXTENDED WEST FROM EVANS HALL

NORTH EAST CORNER SHOULD STAY BELOW GRADE

DAYLIGHTING OF BELOW GRADE GARAGE - ONLY AT ENDS - (BANCROFT & MOFFITT.

BELOW GRADE BUILDING SHOULD NOT BE VISIBLE ALONG FULL FACADE OF DOE LIBRARY - WALLS & WINDOWS SHOULD NOT BE SEEN

LAWN   PORCH.   DOE

SKYLIGHT
LAWN   HEDGE   DOE

SKYLIGHT OK AT BASE OF DOE - IF SCREENED W/ HEDGE

CLASSICAL TERRACE

CONTEMPORARY TERRACE

TERRACES (PORCHES) SHOULD BE SEPARATE - ONE BELONGS IN CHARACTER TO DOE - ONE TO MOFFITT. PARK PATH CONNECTS THE TWO. LANDSCAPE (LAWN) BETWEEN TERRACES

Drawing: A study of the Central Glade
University of California at Berkeley
Courtesy of Philip Enquist, Architect, while with
Skidmore, Owings & Merrill LLP

The drawings on these two facing pages show that two-dimensional and three-dimensional diagrams are frequently used together in analytical studies. Analytical note taking can help us to recall salient features and important objectives.

NORTH GATE   BELVEDERE   VIEW ONLY NO PATH   DOE

NORTH GATE WALK COMES TO GLADE ON AXIS W/ DOE LIBRARY. THE PATH SHOULD CONNECT TO SATHER ROAD - NO PATH SHOULD CROSS GLADE ON FORMAL AXIS WITH DOE'S FRONT DOOR.

Building Guidelines - Doe Library

Drawing: A study of the Central Glade
University of California at Berkeley
Courtesy of Philip Enquist, Architect, while with
Skidmore, Owings & Merrill LLP

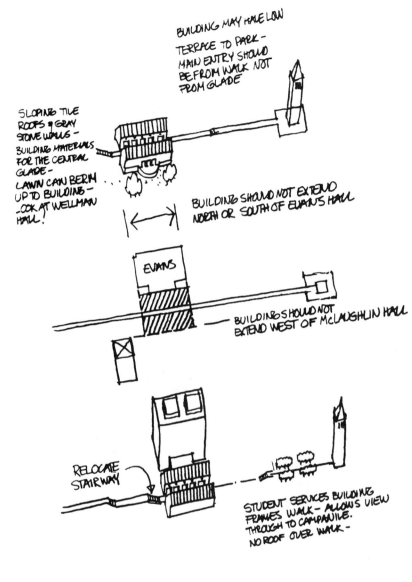

Along with the traditional wall presentation (see section on presentation formats), the report with reduced illustrations is a common mode of communicating to clients. These diagrams are part of a report. Care must always be taken to be sure that any reduced diagram or sketch "reads" well.

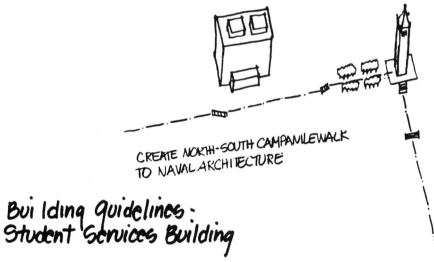

Building guidelines:
Student Services Building

DIAGRAMMING IN THE DESIGN PROCESS

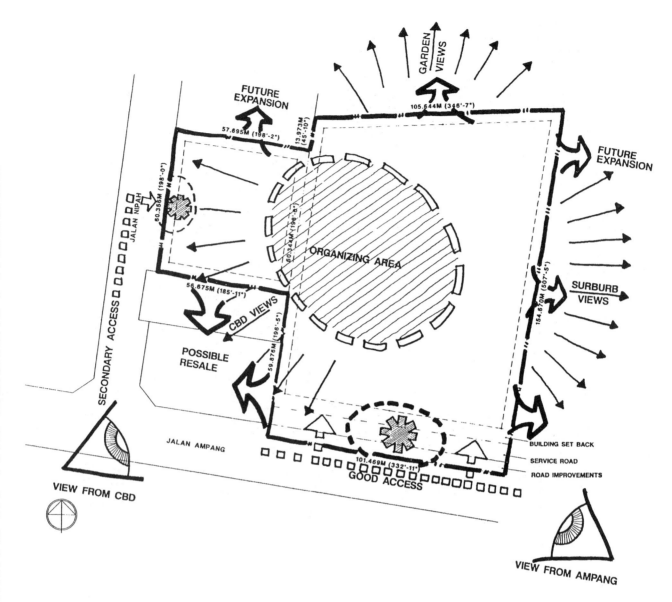

Diagram: Site analysis, Gleneagles Hospital and M.O.B., Jalan Ampang–Kuala Lumpur, Malaysia
Medium: Ink on vellum with Kroy type, 36" × 24" (91.4 × 61 cm)
Courtesy of KMD/PD Architects
Joint venture with the Architectural Network

Diagrams are generated in the earliest stages of the design process. Diagrammatic models are some of the most important types of drawing for the designer, yet paradoxically they are rarely if ever seen by the client. Diagrams are a visual means for collecting and sorting information, for testing ideas and exploring alternative solutions, for looking into the very heart of a design problem. They represent that intimate crucial conversation with oneself, a conversation conducted in a very specific language that has its own current vocabulary, grammar, and syntax.

The following sequence of six drawings shows a case study of design drawings, which include a site analysis, site massing and circulation diagrams, a selected scheme analysis, a site development plan, elevation design studies, and a conceptual elevation study.

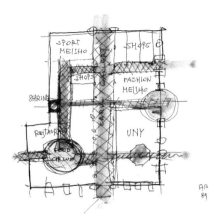

The drawing at left is a diagrammatical schematic plan sketch showing pedestrian pathways. It is a design sketch. The four different schemes sketched below were evaluated with respect to vehicular and pedestrian movement (circulation). Flow diagrams such as these can be symbolically coded (see next page). Graphic symbols for flow and bubbles are scaleless and are thus ideal for both small- and large-scale projects.

Plan sketch diagram: Shimizu Corporation
Nagoya, Aichi, Japan
Courtesy of Aldo Rossi, SDA, Architect

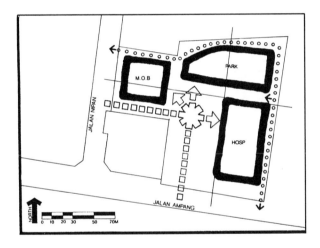

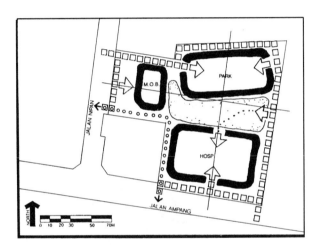

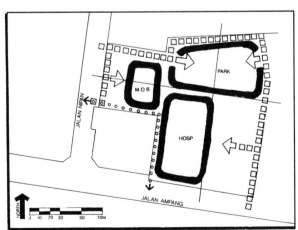

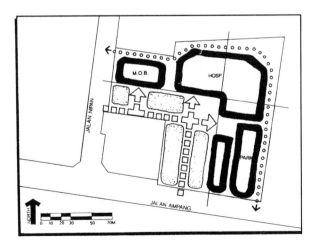

Diagrams: Four alternative schemes
Gleneagles Hospital and M.O.B.
Jalan Ampang–Kuala Lumpur, Malaysia
Each drawing 17" × 11" (43.2 × 27.9 cm), reduced and composed on 36" × 24" (91.4 × 61 cm)
Medium: Ink on bond paper
Courtesy of KMD/PD Architects
Joint Venture with the Architectural Network

DIAGRAMMING IN THE DESIGN PROCESS

DIAGRAMMING IN THE DESIGN PROCESS

KEY

☐ ☐ ☐ ☐ PUBLIC ACCESS

▨ ▨ ▨ ▨ EMERGENCY ONLY

○ ○ ○ ○ ○ SERVICE/FIRE/STAFF

• • • • • PEDESTRIAN

This is a good example of user movement or circulation (see p. 432) analysis in an early schematic stage of the design process. Note that each type of movement has a different symbol. A clear symbolic language is critical in communicating graphically important collected data to others as well as to yourself.

Diagram: Scheme C
Gleneagles Hospital and M.O.B.
Jalan Ampang–Kuala Lumpur, Malaysia
Medium: Ink on bond paper, 17" × 11" (43.2 × 27.9 cm)
Courtesy of KMD/PD Architects
Joint venture with the Architectural Network

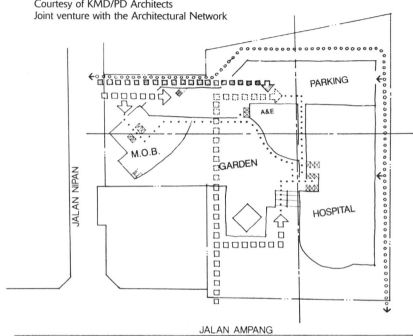

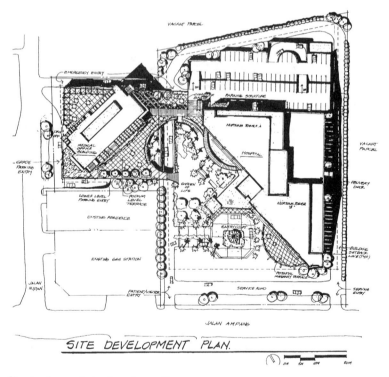

SITE DEVELOPMENT PLAN.

Site development plan for scheme C
24" × 36" (61 × 91.4 cm), Scale: 1:300
Medium: Ink on vellum

When doing conceptual diagrams, as above, or exploratory sketches (see p. 465), it is important to recognize the importance that shadows play in accentuating forms even in the early stages of the design process.

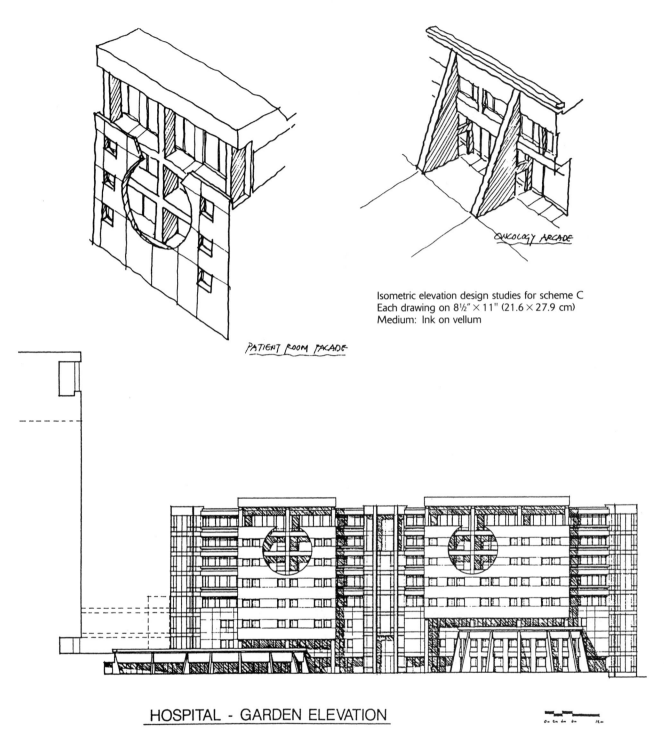

PATIENT ROOM FACADE

ONCOLOGY ARCADE

Isometric elevation design studies for scheme C
Each drawing on 8½" × 11" (21.6 × 27.9 cm)
Medium: Ink on vellum

HOSPITAL - GARDEN ELEVATION

Conceptual elevation study for scheme C
18" × 24" (45.7 × 61 cm), Scale: 1:200
Medium: Ink on vellum

DESIGN STUDIES

Exploratory sketches for design studies should always be as accurate as possible in terms of proportion and scale.

DIAGRAMMING IN THE DESIGN PROCESS

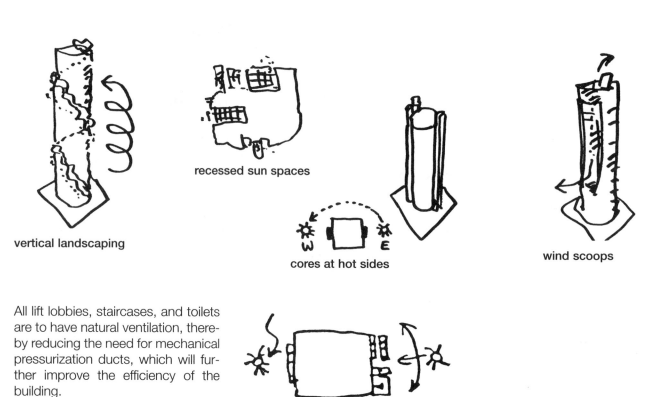

vertical landscaping

recessed sun spaces

cores at hot sides

wind scoops

All lift lobbies, staircases, and toilets are to have natural ventilation, thereby reducing the need for mechanical pressurization ducts, which will further improve the efficiency of the building.

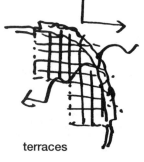

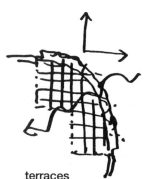

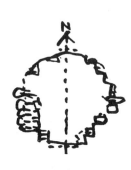

curtain wall at north and south faces

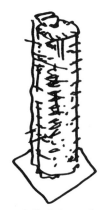

terraces

environmentally interactive wall

Diagrams: Design principles and agenda
Courtesy of T. R. Hamzah & Yeang Sdn. Bhd. Arkitek
Tengku Robert Hamzah and Dr. Kenneth Yeang, Partners

In Malaysia, the architectural firm of T. R. Hamzah & Yeang does design work that responds to regional bioclimatic design principles based on the use of low energy consumption. Being very research and development oriented, they produce quick analytical diagrams that help their designers to quickly grasp and understand their design approach. These two- and three-dimensional diagrams relate to an agenda for high-rise buildings where there is no dependency on artificial mechanical systems (air conditioning, etc.) as in highly industrialized societies. These diagrams are no more than ideograms and guidelines and are not meant to be formulae for design or hard-and-fast rules not to be broken.

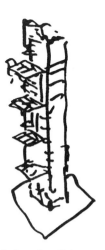

balconies & terraces

solar-collector wall

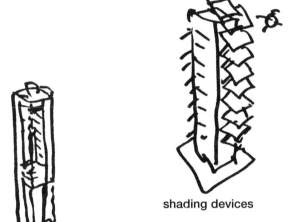

shading devices

sky courts

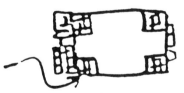

Photo: Menara Mesiniaga (IBM Tower)
Selangor, Malaysia
Courtesy of T. R. Hamzah & Yeang, Architect

Addition of "skycourts" and terraces as "sun-shading" may improve on the permissible plot ratio and give additional marketing features to the building to improve net areas of the building, in addition to controlling excessive solar gains.

Diagrams: Design principles and agenda
Courtesy of T. R. Hamzah & Yeang Sdn. Bhd. Arkitek
Tengku Robert Hamzah and Dr. Kenneth Yeang, Partners

The extensive experience acquired over time by an architect is best communicated to others by converting that experience into "expertise." Expertise simply means "transferable experience." To transfer expertise, it must be represented in a form that is easily communicable and understandable without reference back to the source.
[ARCHITECT'S STATEMENT]

DIAGRAMMING IN THE DESIGN PROCESS

DIAGRAMMING IN THE DESIGN PROCESS

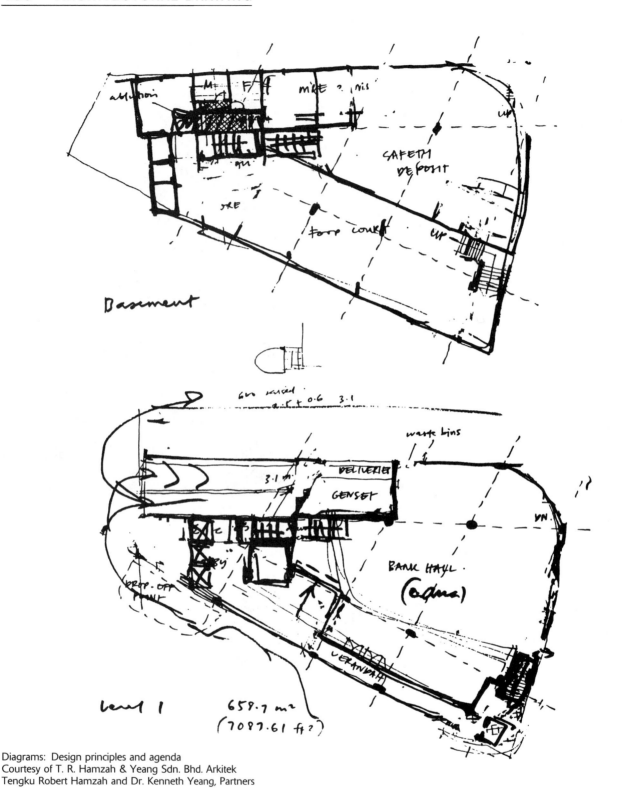

Diagrams: Design principles and agenda
Courtesy of T. R. Hamzah & Yeang Sdn. Bhd. Arkitek
Tengku Robert Hamzah and Dr. Kenneth Yeang, Partners

In a fast-track rapid-build situation, we often have to work on the design of several projects at the same time. Much like a surgeon who lets junior assistants do the preliminary preparation before he or she does the difficult incisions and operations, we have to let our assistants do the preliminary analysis and first sketches so that we can then edit and develop the design. These sketches show the editing process.
[ARCHITECT'S STATEMENT]

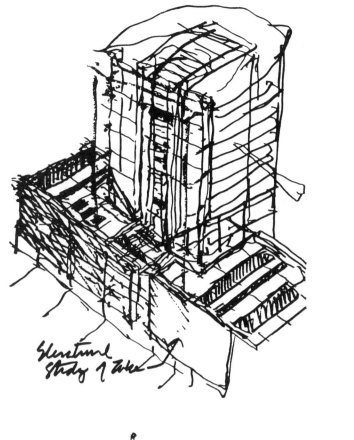

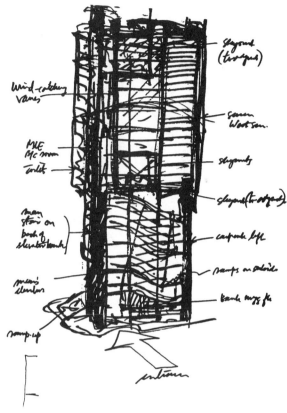

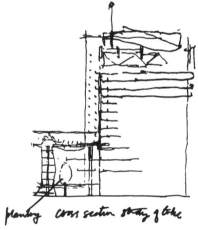

Diagrams: Design principles and agenda
Courtesy of T. R. Hamzah & Yeang Sdn. Bhd. Arkitek
Tengku Robert Hamzah and Dr. Kenneth Yeang, Partners

To properly communicate a developed sketched image to designers, who have to hard-line the drawings, it is essential to add notes to the sketches.
[ARCHITECT'S STATEMENT]

Sometimes in the midst of the design process, the client has queries on aspects of the design unclear to him or her. These sketches were prepared to explain configuration of the spaces to the client before the design has been fully completed.
[ARCHITECT'S STATEMENT]

DIAGRAMMING IN THE DESIGN PROCESS

11

Conceptual Sketching

Conceptual (or design) sketching is part of the design-drawing process. These synthetic sketches must be done quickly since they represent alternative design ideas for an imagined conception. These visualizations can be crude initial images or refined, developed drawings. Although speculative and abstract in nature, conceptual sketches are attempts to depict the reality of the design in its idealized and essential state. They are loose and flexible and quite different from hardline constructed drawings.

The intent of this chapter is to illustrate graphic methods for analytically communicating and representing conceptual ideas and design concepts, as well as to show a variety of diverse design sketch images by various architects.

Conceptual Sketching

Topic

Visualization

References

Architectural Graphics (Ching 1996, 158-163).

Drawing: A Creative Process (Ching 1990, 137–200).

Graphics for Architecture (Forseth 1980, 77–97).

Rapid Viz (Hanks and Belliston 1980, 34–45).

Topic

Design Sketching

References

Porter and Goodman. 1988. Designer Primer. Charles Scribner's Sons. 94.

Hanks and Belliston. 1977. Draw. William Kaufmann, Inc. 137–162.

Laseau, Paul. 1980. Graphic Thinking for Architects and Designers. Van Nostrand Reinhold.

Lacy, Bill. 1991. 100 Contermporary Architects: Drawings and Sketches. Abrams.

Linton, Harold. 1993. Sketching the Concept. McGraw-Hill.

Cross References

For p. 465	See pp. 84, 131
For p. 474	See pp. 339, 496
For p. 480	See pp. 433
For p. 482	See p. 434, 435,446
For p. 491	See p. 496-497

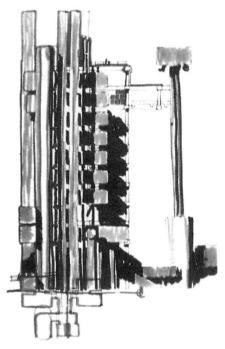

Sketch: University of Toledo's Center for the Visual Arts
Toledo, Ohio
12" × 9" (30.5 × 22.9 cm)
Medium: Ink on paper
Courtesy of Frank O. Gehry, Architect

Sketch: Lloyds of London, London, England
33" × 45.5" (83.8 × 115.6 cm)
Medium: Pen and ink on tracing paper
Courtesy of the Richard Rogers Partnership, Architects

A very early study showing plan and elevation of a satellite tower for Lloyd's of London. At this stage of the project the provision of services was considerably underestimated. In particular, the plant room was eventually more than twice the size of that shown. This free-standing tower was one of six servant satellite towers which surrounded the main atrium of the building.
[ARCHITECT'S STATEMENT]

Sketch: Pocono Pines House
Mount Pocono, Pennsylvania
17" × 11" (43.2 × 27.9 cm)
Medium: Pen and ink
Courtesy of Aldo Rossi, Studio di Architettura
New York, Architect

INTRODUCTION

The design-drawing process always begins with **rough freehand sketches.** The greatest ideas generated by architects and designers start with small thumbnail sketches. The thumbnail sketch is small and suggestive. Much is implied in the sketch which is usually used for conceptualizing and visualizing. The sketches on this page resulted in outstanding completed works by noted architects. Develop the good habit of carrying a **sketchpad** with you as you travel within the urban landscape; observe and record what you see with quick sketches and accompanying scribbled notes. Fostering this habit will eventually strengthen your ability to do problem analysis diagrams. Conceptual thinking is the crucial initial step in the design-drawing process to help you communicate ideas.

SPATIAL STRUCTURING FOR CONCEPTUAL SKETCHING

Drawng: Concept sketch for the Oxley Residence
            La Jolla, California
Courtesy of Rob Wellington Quigley FAIA

Sketch: Entry lobby and bookstore, Monterey Bay Aquarium
            Monterey, California
Medium: Ink
Courtesy of Esherick Homsey Dodge and Davis, Architects
and G. G. Chang, Architectural Illustrator

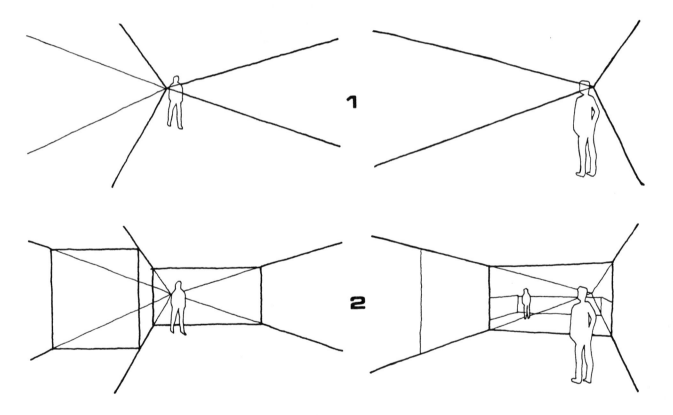

Conceptual spatial studies for accurately conveying the feeling of a possible design are best generated using the drawing type that most precisely represents what one sees, namely perspective. The most common geometric figure perceived in perspective space is cubic in nature. In an interior perspective, it is quite common to find box-like (cubic or rectilinear) structures. Likewise, many exterior building forms are box-like. Three-dimensional space can usually be structured by expanding units from a basic cube unit.

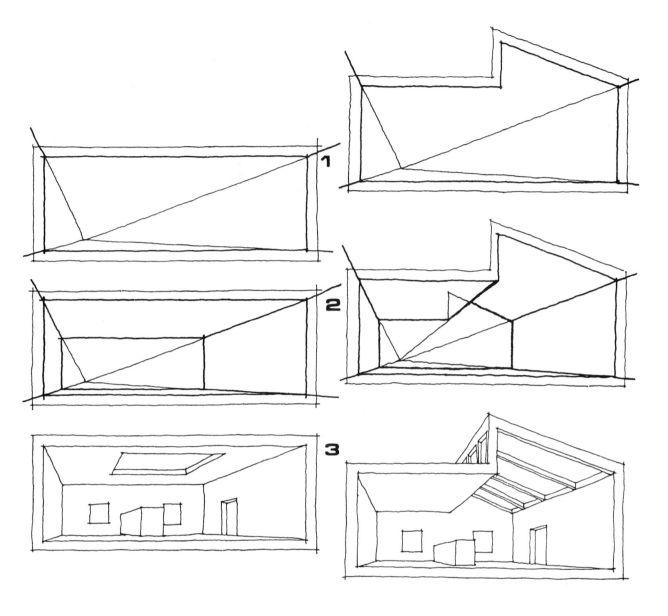

Conceptual design sketches must be done quickly. There is no time to generate accurate hardline perspectives. Perspective speculative sketches must be done freehand so that numerous alternatives can be examined. When doing freehand perspective sketches, use a box method to generate quick spatial studies. Three simple steps are needed. Lines are projected from the four corners on the true-height picture plane back into the perspective until they intersect at a vanishing point on the horizon line (1). Another plane is added for the back wall of the interior space (2) and the space is subsequently (3) structured. This method applies for both one-point and two-point (facing page) perspectives.

Often one wants to communicate the feeling of space from rudimentary, two-dimensional, schematic plan view diagrams. A series of perspective sketches is always more informative than one sketch and will enhance visualization of the concept (see pp. 166,167, and 174).

SPATIAL STRUCTURING FOR CONCEPTUAL SKETCHING

SPATIAL STRUCTURING FOR CONCEPTUAL SKETCHING

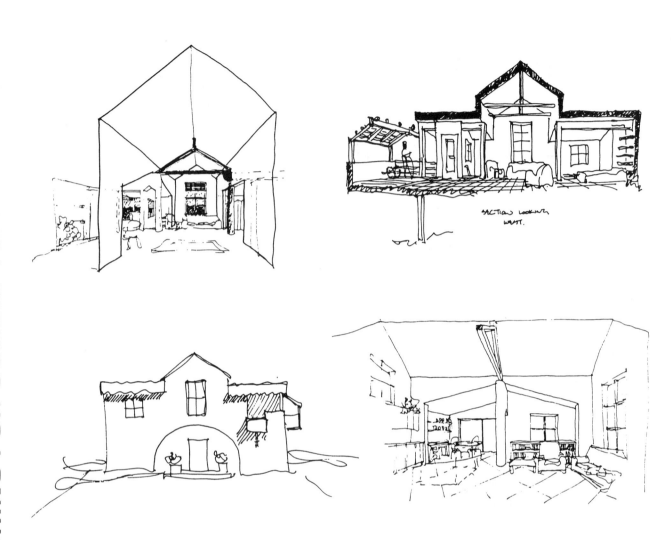

Drawing: Study Sketches, Oxley residence, La Jolla, California
Medium: Y & C stylist on trace, 17" × 11" (43.2 × 27.9 cm)
Courtesy of Rob Wellington Quigley, FAIA

As you examine the design sketches in this chapter, be aware that different types of media directly affect the feeling of space that is perceived (compare William Bruder's ink sketches [p. 481] with Robert Venturi's felt-tipped pen Sainsbury axis study [p. 487]). Architects and design professionals have adopted many traditional artistic media (graphite, ink wash, watercolor, pastel, gouache, etc.) to express their ideas; now they are beginning to exploit the medium of digital technology (see chapter on 3D modeling).

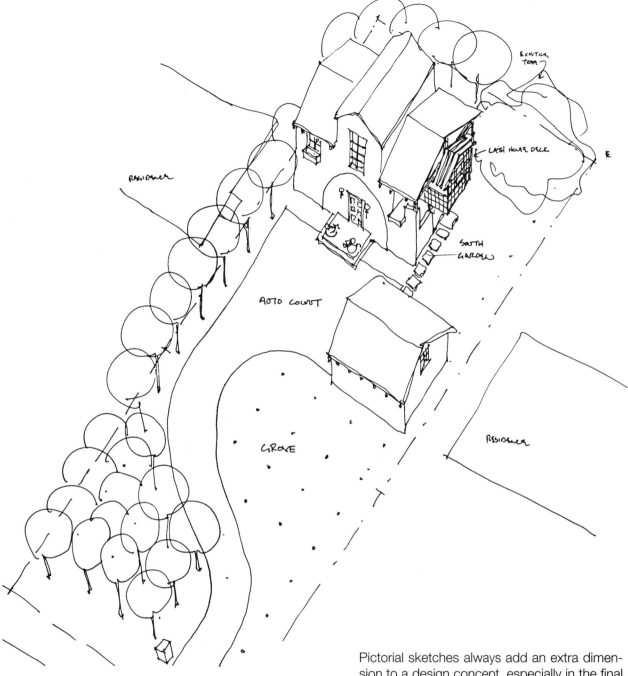

Labels in drawing:
EXISTING TREE
LATH HOUSE DECK
E
RESIDENCE
SOUTH GARDEN
AUTO COURT
GROVE
RESIDENCE

Drawing: Concept sketch for the Oxley residence, La Jolla, California
11" × 17" (27.9 × 43.2 cm)
Medium: Y & C stylist (black fine-tipped pen) on trace
Courtesy of Rob Wellington Quigley, FAIA

Pictorial sketches always add an extra dimension to a design concept, especially in the final schematic phases of any project. Spatial concepts (not seen in orthographic sketches) are more clearly revealed. These sketches aid in the development of conceiving and confirming ideas prior to the building process.

SPATIAL STRUCTURING FOR CONCEPTUAL SKETCHING

CONCEPTUAL SKETCHING

Sketches: Catholic Order of Foresters, Naperville, Illinois
Medium: Micropoint pen, various sizes montaged and
        photographically reproduced
Courtesy of Thomas R. Welch, while at Holabird and Root

These sketches explore the nature of the various components of the design and their interrelationship. By placing a number of sketches on a single page, the architect permits the viewer to understand spatial sequence, design contrasts (e.g., circle and square, glass vs. solid), and hopefully see the integration into a design totality of what at first may appear to be disparate elements.
[ARCHITECT'S STATEMENT]

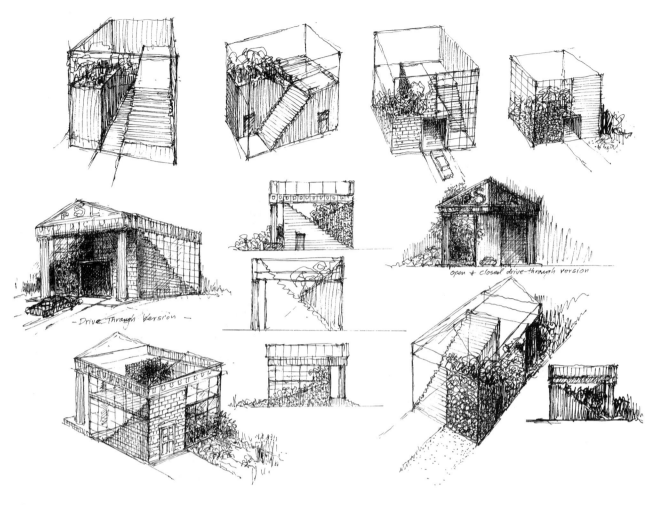

Sketches: Esquisse de details
          Perpetual Savings and Loan Bank, South Dakota
Medium: Pen and ink on paper, 14" × 11" (35.6 × 27.9 cm)
Courtesy of James Wines/SITE

CONCEPTUAL SKETCHING

This objective of trying to describe much more on paper than form and structure has always been characteristic of most of my drawings, but particularly those for the South Dakota Bank. In this case the edifice is being invaded by its natural environment and the studies try to capture this fusion of landscape and building.

As one of those who loves to draw (by hand), I frequently have to confront the question of whether we may soon become an extinct species. My office, while primitively computerized, has no sophisticated CAD capabilities; so, to avail myself of this technology, I usually collaborate with a fully equipped associate. When I find myself working for a period of time in one of these heavily committed MegaCADD environments, a day rarely passes that some zealous young computer whiz doesn't snatch a sketch off my drafting table and, with thinly veiled disdain, offer to "speed things up" by feeding it into a programmer. Under such circumstances I feel anachronisitic, as the surrounding electronic cacophony makes the gentle rustle of tracing paper under my pen stroke seem medieval. The only redeeming footnote to this kind of incident arrives later, after one of my uncooperative drawings has failed to translate well via the software and is returned to my desk with the sheepish suggestion that I should "just sketch up the idea because it might be faster." In such moments, I feel a renewed wave of relevance. This scenario can be typical of conflicts in the graphic representation of buildings and landscape architecture today.
[ARCHITECT'S STATEMENT]

CONCEPTUAL SKETCHING

Himmelsgärten

Eckstructur wird betont, um ein "feste" wand zur strasse zu schaffen

Stadtbäume

Kirchnerstrasse

Ein Wasserwand

Läden

Bänke

öffentlicher Innenraum.

kaiserplatz

Conceptual sketch: Commerzbank, Frankfurt, Germany
Medium: Pencil on paper, 297 × 209 mm (11.7" × 8.23")
Courtesy of Sir Norman Foster, Architect
Sketch by Sir Norman Foster

The sketch explores the three-dimensional geometrics that meet at this critical junction—the entrance to the public spaces. It is also mindful of the role that it can play to communicate ideas to others.
[ARCHITECT'S STATEMENT]

Freehand sketching is the most potent means of generating ideas for any type of design. It is unlikely that any medium will fully supplant the immediacy and directness of freehand drawing. In the architectural design discipline, to be able to record and evolve ideas as they occur is of utmost importance; and this oldest and most primal method of recording ideas is still essential to the designer. The designer should always record exploratory ideas with any accompanying notes (these notes are in German) in a sketchbook (log book) with bond paper that takes any kind of media. Many architects keep sketchbooks on hand at all times for the express purpose of recording their design ideas. A "sketch journal" can be an invaluable tool in the design process. You will find yourself constantly referring to this visual diary.

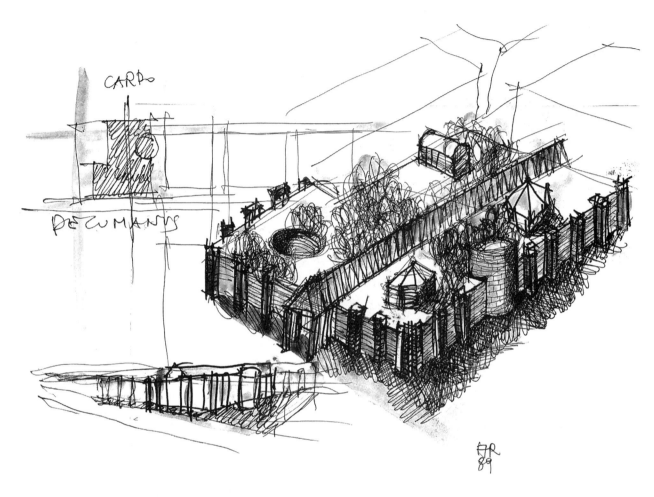

CARPO

DECUMANUS

Conceptual sketches: Shimizu Corporation, Nagoya, Aichi, Japan
Medium: Ink and watercolor
Courtesy of Aldo Rossi, SDA, New York, Architect

© Ned Matura

This early sketch for the shopping center in Nagoya, Japan, illustrates the analogy to Roman town planning which is used as a model for the project. The design is considered simultaneously in plan, axonometric, and perspective.
[ARCHITECT'S STATEMENT]

Architect Aldo Rossi's conceptual sketch is an excellent example of how architectural features on architectural subjects done in watercolor can be reinforced and enlivened by the use of ink pen lines. The watercolor wash remains fresh, while the pen delineates the details. If one wants a wash on an ink drawing, then waterproof ink is most often desirable (unless an intentional running effect is the goal, in which case use a water-soluble ink).

CONCEPTUAL SKETCHING

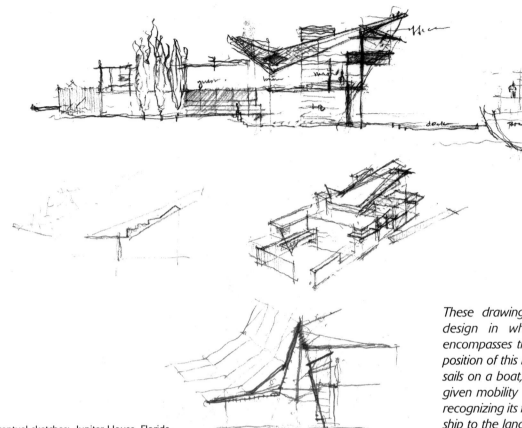

Conceptual sketches: Jupiter House, Florida
Medium: Pencil on tracing paper
Courtesy of Franklin D. Israel Design Associates Inc., Architects

These drawings delineate a design in which the roof encompasses the entire composition of this house. Like the sails on a boat, the building is given mobility and energy by recognizing its formal relationship to the land and the sea.
[ARCHITECT'S STATEMENT]

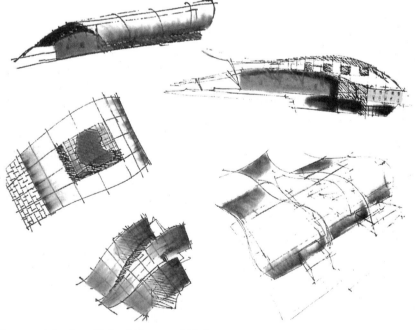

Conceptual sketches: National Museum of Marine Biology/Aquarium, Koohsiang, Taiwan, R.O.C.
Medium: Ink and watercolor
Courtesy of Esherick Homsey Dodge and Davis, Architects

In classic examples of design sketching, such as Mendelsohn's drawings for the Einstein Tower (circa 1920) or Ludwig Mies Van der Rohe's sketches for the Barcelona Pavilion (circa 1930), we again see how initial impressions often hold the essence of the subsequent, more developed design.

This community center, set in the desert near Palm Springs, is intended to evoke a retro-futuristic architecture. It is a 1990s interpretation of the dynamic modernism of the 1950s and 1960s in Southern California.
[ARCHITECTS' STATEMENT]

Conceptual sketch: Cathedral City Civic Center,
                    Cathedral City, California
8" × 5" (20.3 × 12.7 cm)
Medium: Prismacolor
Courtesy of Kanner Architects
Drawing by Stephen Kanner

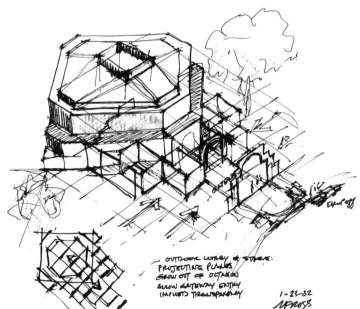

Conceptual sketch: Solvang Theatrefest, Solvang, California
10" × 13" (25.4 × 33 cm)
Medium: Pentel sign pen and Prismacolor pencils
Courtesy of Michael Franklin Ross, AIA, Design Principal,
Ross Associates and Flood, Meyer, Sutton & Associates

This is one of a series of early studies to help break down the massive scale of the theater and develop a gateway that was appropriate to the vernacular architecture of Solvang, a California city that was developed by its immigrant population to reflect their native Danish community. From the central gateway arch, layers of space are created by the projecting planes pulled away from the main theater forming outdoor lobby, performance, and gathering places. The extension of the theater to the outdoors allows a cost-effective lobby and interpenetration of the landscape with the building.
[ARCHITECT'S STATEMENT]

CONCEPTUAL SKETCHING

CONCEPTUAL SKETCHING

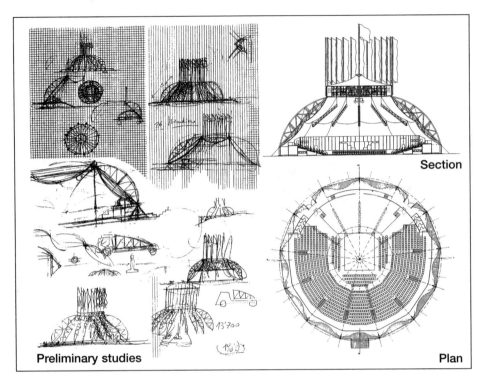

Section

Plan

Preliminary studies

Envisioning and exploring a design concept in the conceptual design stages is a time-consuming, gradual process. Quick freehand doodles and thumbnail speculative sketches are the vital images that make this process work. The preliminary sketch studies in this example typify an analysis stage, whereas the hard-line drawings typify and represent a synthesis stage.

Design sketches: Tent for the 700th Anniversary of Switzerland
Medium: Pencil
Courtesy of Mario Botta, Architect, Lugano, Switzerland

Conceptual sketches: Whitehall Ferry Terminal, New York City
Medium: Felt-tipped pen on yellow trace
Courtesy of Venturi, Scott Brown and Associates, Inc.
Sketches by Robert Venturi

...early studies for the Whitehall Ferry Terminal, featuring the big clock whose scale relates to and accommodates to its setting—including Manhattan's skyline, harbor, and the Statue of Liberty—and establishes its civic presence, and whose form symbolizes its transportation function and generates its barrel vault which monumentally shelters its interior activities.
[ARCHITECT'S STATEMENT]

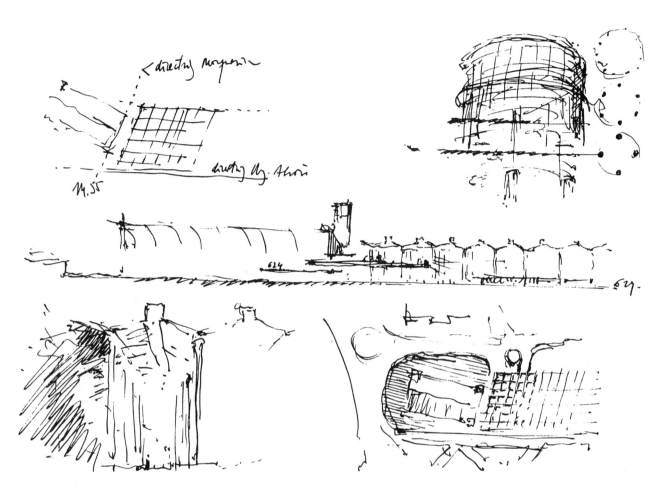

Conceptual sketches: Atocha Station
Madrid, Spain
Medium: Ink, 31.5 × 21.5 cm (12.4" × 8.5")
Courtesy of Jose Rafael Moneo, Architect

Several sketches of the Atocha Railway Station. Two of them speak about the plan and show the importance of the existing axes in defining the project. Another two are more related to the description of what a space atmosphere should be: One is related to the lantern, the other to the big hall. The sketch in the middle shows a section.
Sketches help to fix the floating ideas in the architect's mind. They often keep this early moment when architects foresee the space to come.
[ARCHITECT'S STATEMENT]

CONCEPTUAL SKETCHING

*The general program requirements were evolved in plan and section initially and continually developed during the course of massing/**parti** study. The sketches below are just a small part of a series done for daily brainstorming sessions to develop the appropriate **parti** to accommodate the technology theme and reconcile the site geometry, in this case, twin curves engaging each other in a high-tech "yin–yang" composition.*

A quick 3D AutoCAD model was developed for the variations and was used as a base for the spontaneous black Prismacolor pencil sketches. Both scaled elevational views and aerial perspectives were used as tools in conjunction with myriad quick foam study models as a basis for discussion and review. The design team was certainly not shy about generating as many options as possible for study and evaluation. Note the series of vignette sketches of how we might engage the sky plane with an appropriate communications/technology gesture.

[DESIGN ILLUSTRATOR'S STATEMENT]

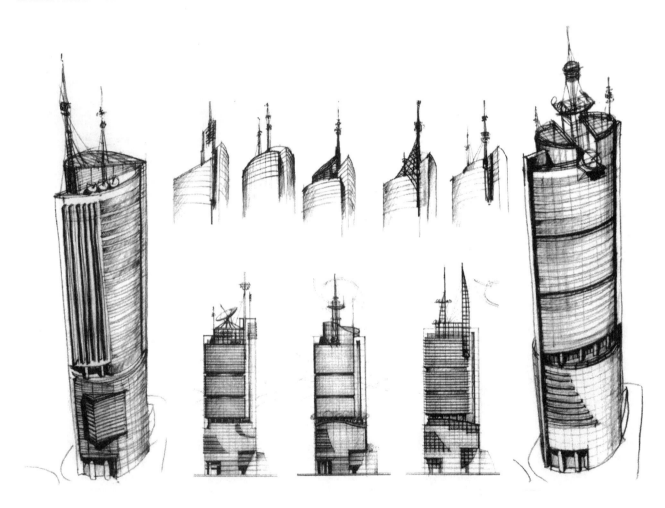

Images: Communications Center Office Tower Competition,
   Shanghai, China
Courtesy of KMD, San Francisco: Design Office
Herbert McLaughlin, Design Principal
Lawrence K. Leong, Design Illustrator
Architectural Concept Imaging, San Francisco

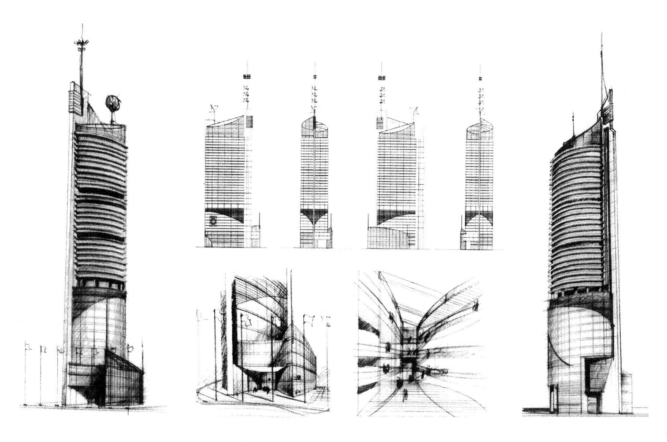

Images: Communications Center Office Tower Competition,
              Shanghai, China
Courtesy of KMD, San Francisco: Design Office
Herbert McLaughlin, Design Principal
Lawrence K. Leong, Design Illustrator
Architectural Concept Imaging, San Francisco

Once a parti *direction was decided upon, we refined the black Prismacolor 3D sketch study vignettes with a concentration on the eye-level experience and viewpoints of key locations. I used AutoCAD elevations to formalize the design conclusions and passed them on to the design team as a base for further refinement and final presentation.*
[DESIGN ILLUSTRATOR'S STATEMENT]

CONCEPTUAL SKETCHING

The axonometric, although an unrealistic view, is utilized to help my client understand the massing, proportions, and relationships of the building components, whereas the perspective portrays a humanistic view and expresses the impact of the receding facade. Soft pencil allows a varied expression of line and tone weight within a single stroke, giving an informal quality to the sketches.

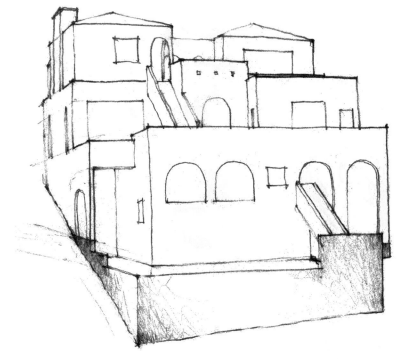

This is a conceptual massing study of a hillside residence in the area of Oakland, California. Blended within a hillside setting, it utilizes the advantage of light and view while borrowing the massing style of Tuscany.
[ARCHITECT'S STATEMENT]

These sketches, as well as those on pp. 483, 484, and 485, reflect a more advanced stage in the design sketching process.

Sketches: Woo residence, Oakland, Caifornia
Perspective: 12" × 12" (30.5 × 30.5 cm)
Axonometric: 18" × 18" (45.7 × 45.7 cm),
Scale: ⅛"=1'0"
Medium: HB pencil
Courtesy of Kenzo Handa, Architect

Sketches: Green Peace, Alameda, California
Medium: Pencil and technical pens, 12" × 18" (30.5 × 45.7 cm)
Courtesy of William P. Bruder, Architect

…pen and ink sketches developed over photo prints of existing buildings and context to show reuse potentials. This technique is a quick way to three-dimensionally present concept ideas.
[ARCHITECT'S STATEMENT]

CONCEPTUAL SKETCHING

Study the strengths and limitations of the materials you can handle, whether it be pencil, pen, brush, or crayon. In this way, you can select the appropriate medium to express the feeling and mood you want to create.

Sketch: Study for structure at the lower level of housing
tower proposal for vacant lots competition
Medium: Oil crayon on vellum, 15" × 18" (38.1 × 45.7 cm)
Courtesy of Billie Tsien, Architect
Tod Williams Billie Tsien and Associates Architects

Often drawings are done to capture feelings. This tower has a looming quality but at the same time seems ready to blast off. We were looking for a combination of weight and flight.
[ARCHITECT'S STATEMENT]

Sketch: Stairs at entry to New College
University of Virginia, Charlottesville
Medium: Felt-tipped pen on trace, 10" × 8" (25.4 × 20.3 cm)
Courtesy of Tod Williams, Architect
Tod Williams Billie Tsien and Associates, Architects

We draw thumbnail perspectives constantly to envision space. Even as it may be, it helps us to bring reality closer to concept.
[ARCHITECT'S STATEMENT]

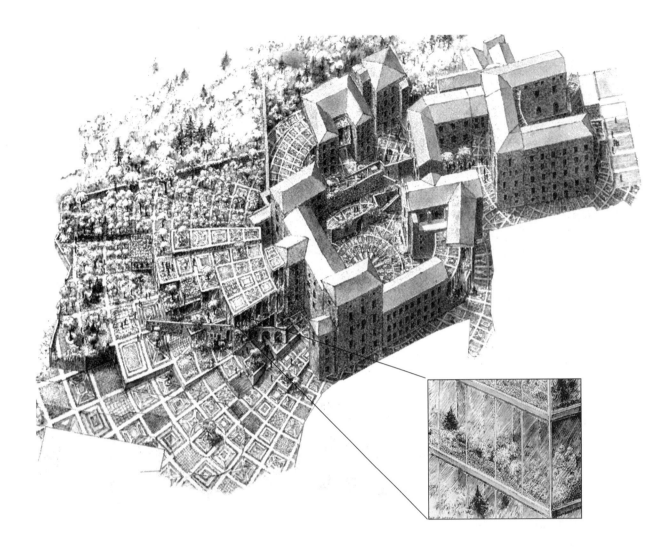

Drawing: Le Puy-en-Velay Urban Reuse Plan and New Hotel Du Department
Le Puy-en-Velay, France, 1992
Medium: Pen and ink and sepia wash
Large drawing 19" × 22" (48.3 × 55.9 cm), Detail 11" × 13.75" (27.9 × 34.9 cm)
Courtesy of James Wines/SITE

CONCEPTUAL SKETCHING

The range of drawing techniques—from Beaux-Arts watercolors to digital simulation—has become the basis of lively debate and, sometimes, a philosophical battleground. There is still a classically based group that regards all computerization as anathema and clings to the sanctity of eye and hand as the only means of describing the spirit of flux and change in nature. At the opposite pole, there are the CAD cadets who have never touched paper with pencil and look on manual rendering as hopelessly out of touch with a cybernetic future. I find myself in the middle zone and look at the ultimate value of any drawing in terms of the quality of the idea it is describing. Thus the computer printout is no different than the pencil sketch, since both can function as evidence of either processed garbage or harvested creativity.
[ARCHITECT'S STATEMENT]

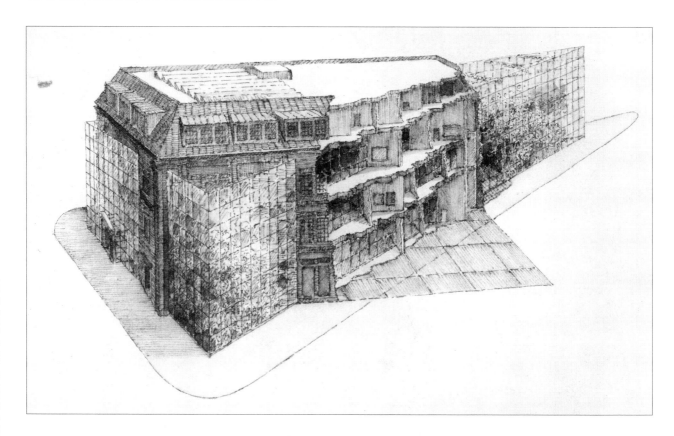

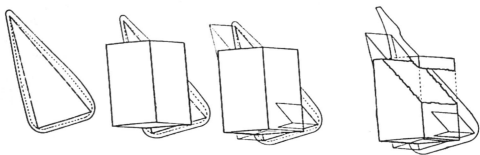

Sketch: The Frankfurt Museum of Modern Art, Frankfurt, West Germany
Medium: Pen and ink wash on paper, 14" × 17" (35.6 × 43.2 cm)
Courtesy of James Wines/SITE

Since it is necessary for the spectator to be aware of the triangular site configuration in order to understand the invasion of the rectangle, the site area is defined by an abstraction of it in glass (18 m high, supported by a space frame) which penetrates the masonry structure of the museum. This glass enclosure also defines the cafe and sculpture garden. When this ensemble of interpenetrating structures is placed on the actual site, it becomes necessary to sever one corner of the rectangular museum to allow the street to pass freely. The convention of the rough architectural cutaway is used to create a more intense dialogue between exterior and interior.
[ARCHITECT'S STATEMENT]

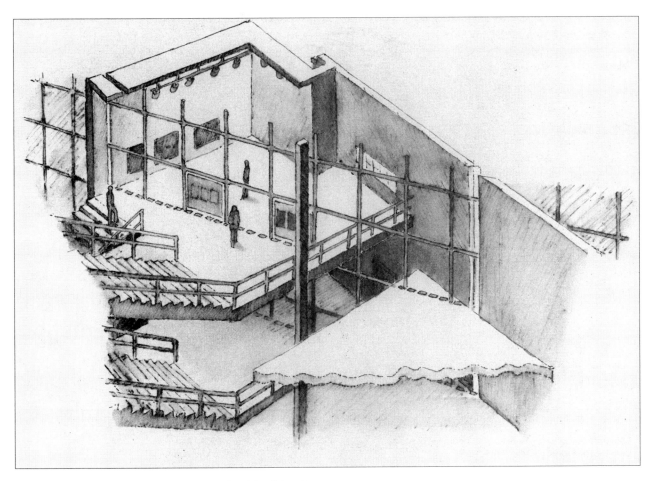

Sketch: The Frankfurt Museum of Modern Art, Frankfurt, West Germany
Medium: Pen and ink wash on paper, 13¾" × 11" (34.9 × 27.9 cm)
Courtesy of James Wines/SITE

CONCEPTUAL SKETCHING

Through this cutaway, the information on the interior of the museum has been "opened to the public." The exhibition has been extended, or expanded, literally "taken to the streets" in informational form.

To increase the free flow of watercolor and wash, I use Arches or Fabriano papers and saturate the surface with a clear matte medium. This cuts down absorbency and allows the washes to be built up gradually, with each under layer flowing easily into the next. It also increases the luminosity of the color and results in an abbreviated notational style to suggest the conditions of inversion, allusion, metaphor, dialectic, and humor.
[ARCHITECT'S STATEMENT]

CONCEPTUAL SKETCHING

When the human mind has an image, it's very hard to change; so in thinking of the form for a building, it's important to prevent having the image as long as possible, and only after all the information has been gathered.
[ARCHITECT'S STATEMENT]

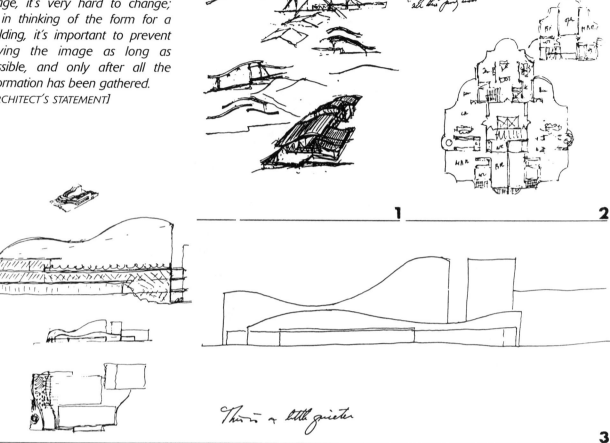

Medium: Black fine-point felt-tipped pen on white trace
Courtesy of Arthur Erickson, FAIA, FRAIC

Sketches: 1. Piney Valley Ranch
Magnus Lindholm
Eagle, Colorado
11" × 14" (27.9 × 35.6 cm)

2. "Nick & Diane, John might like all these fancy curves."
1300 West Pender
Noel Developments
Vancouver, B.C., Canada
11" × 14" (27.9 × 35.6 cm)

3. "This is a little quieter."
Performing Arts Centre
California Polytechnic State University
San Luis Obispo, California
48" × 16" (121.9 × 40.6 cm)

Conceptual sketch: Commerzbank, Frankfurt, Germany
Medium: Pencil on paper, 209 × 297 mm (8.23 × 11.7 cm)
Courtesy of Sir Norman Foster, Architect
Sketch by Sir Norman Foster

The Commerzbank, like other major German businesses, embraces "green" policies wholeheartedly. On any one floor, two of the three floor zones are offices; the third is a garden. Thus, all offices on the inner face look across the atrium to a garden and the view beyond.
[ARCHITECT'S STATEMENT]

This sketch with lines of sight done by architect Sir Norman Foster examines the view from a specific office location in the building complex.

CONCEPTUAL SKETCHING

…an early study for an axis of the interior of the Sainsbury Wing at the National Gallery in London emphasizing abstracted representations of Classical elements, false perspective in the Renaissance way, and a scenographic effect in a Baroque manner exposing lots of paintings as fragments.
[ARCHITECT'S STATEMENT]

Conceptual sketch: National Gallery, Sainsbury Wing
                      London, England
Medium: Felt-tipped pen
Courtesy of Venturi, Scott Brown and Associates, Inc., Architects
Sketch by Robert Venturi

CONCEPTUAL SKETCHING

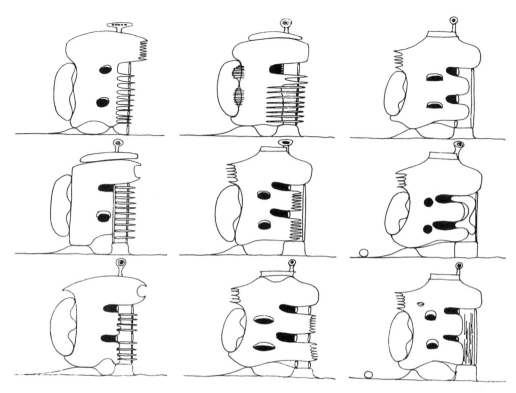

Elevation studies

Study sketches: The Smiling Lion, Mozambique, Africa
Medium: Ink
Courtesy of Amancio Guedes, Architect

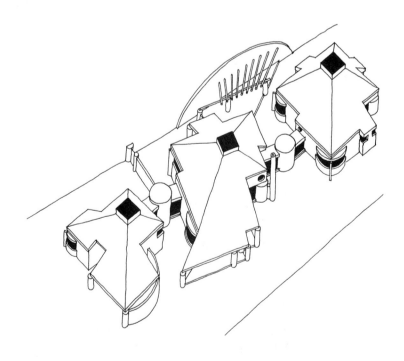

Drawing: Three Little Dancing Houses Shuffling Down a Garden in Greenside (unbuilt)
          Mozambique, Africa
Medium: Ink
Courtesy of Amancio Guedes, Architect

*Many of the ideas of my architecture orig-
inate in drawings which are common to my
paintings and sculpture. Others are para-
phrases or distorted quotations from other
artists' works and ideas. Some originate in
other kinds of sights and visions which fas-
cinate and worry me over a span of time
or remain always within me. I believe that
buildings grow out of each other, that each
artist invents his own precursors, that there
is an incessant dialogue with many pasts.
Sometimes I have ridden a track of ideas
for a time with others interspersed. Often
the ideas have crashed and turned into
others. I have instead classified my architectural inventions into a number of fami-
lies and filed them into a more or less
definitive catalogue of twenty-five architectures. Those twenty-five architectures
are my Vitruvius Mozambicanus.*
[ARCHITECT'S STATEMENT]

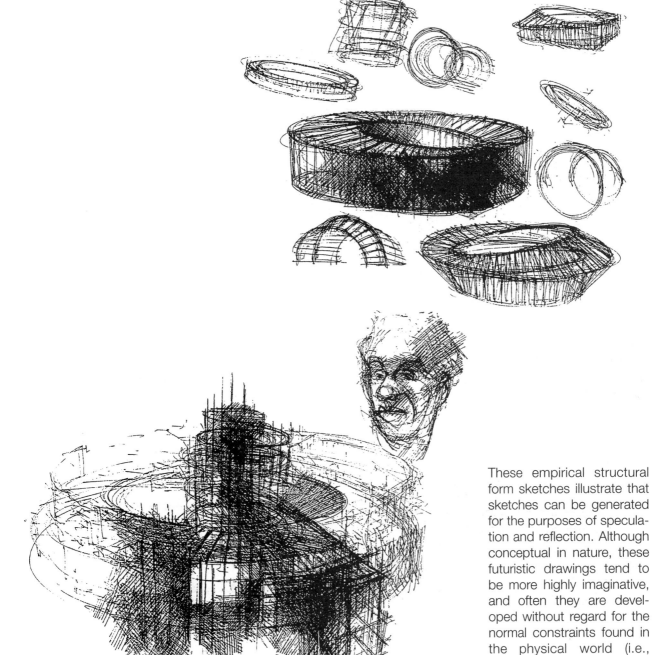

These empirical structural form sketches illustrate that sketches can be generated for the purposes of speculation and reflection. Although conceptual in nature, these futuristic drawings tend to be more highly imaginative, and often they are developed without regard for the normal constraints found in the physical world (i.e., gravtiy, climate, etc.).

Conceptual sketches: Visionary structural forms
Medium: Ink
Courtesy of Alan L. Stacell, Professor
Department of Architecture
Texas A & M University

CONCEPTUAL SKETCHING

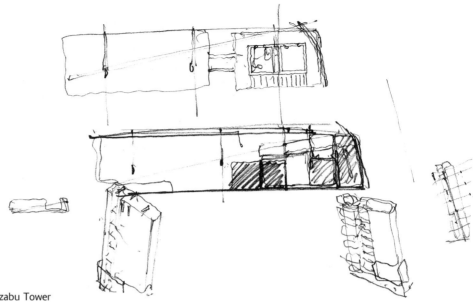

Conceptual sketches: Higashi Azabu Tower
                     Tokyo, Japan
Courtesy of Morphosis
Thom Mayne

This is a sketch from when we were first attempting to understand the nature of the problem: where the project was to be located formally. The final scheme was both an expression of and a response to the extreme limits of the site (4.5 m in width). Conceptually, it derives from the appropriation of the urban conditions within a new language.
[ARCHITECT'S STATEMENT]

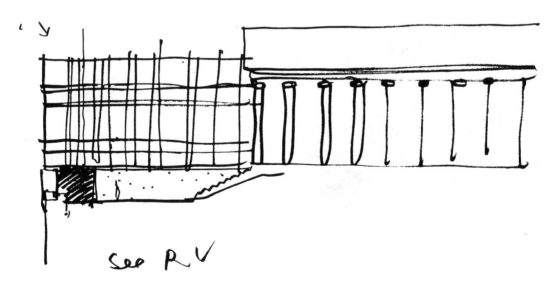

Sketch: The Charles P. Stevenson, Jr. Library, Bard College
         Annandale-on-Hudson, New York
Medium: Felt-tipped pen on yellow trace, 38" × 18" (96.5 × 45.7cm)
Courtesy of Venturi, Scott Brown and Associates, Inc., Architects

Sketch studies like this one usually focus on one element of the whole design. This sketch represents the contrasting but evolving rhythms combined within the whole composition of the front facade—of the new wing inflecting toward the old via a crescendo within its metal frame configuration—of the original Classical building whose rhythm is consistent.
[ARCHITECT'S STATEMENT]

Photo: Elevation studies and study models
The Charles P. Stevenson, Jr. Library, Bard College
Annandale-on-Hudson, New York
Courtesy of Venturi, Scott Brown and Associates, Inc.

Models are important as they expose bad things that can be hidden if you only look at drawings as you design. But they can be dangerous when you resist looking at them at eye level rather than from above. Also, if their form is sexy, you can easily forget the real building will be seen from close up as well as from far away and it needs small-scale detail as well as sculptural pizzazz.
[ARCHITECT'S STATEMENT]

Design professionals utilize not only diagrams and conceptual sketches in the design-development process, but also three-dimensional study models. The aspect of 3D modeling will be examined in the subsequent chapter.

12

3D Modeling

Buildings may be modeled in a realistic fashion by using computers with software that has the capability to describe objects with physical properties such as color, texture, etc. Computer systems may be used to design and assemble a three-dimensional digital model, assign realistic properties to the components that comprise the model, and then display various views of the model under varying lighting conditions. Using this approach, it is also possible to extract orthographic projections from the digital model and prepare plans, elevations, and sections. Additionally, any changes made to the model will automatically be reflected in the drawings extracted from the model.

The intent of this chapter is to provide an introduction to a three-dimensional, object-oriented approach to building design and communication by three-dimensional modeling with computer systems.

3D Modeling

Topic

3D Modeling

References

Sanders. 1995. The Digital Architect. John Wiley & Sons, Inc.

Bertol. 1996. Designing Digital Space. John Wiley & Sons, Inc.

Wagstaff. 1993. Macintosh 3-D Primer. MacMillan.

Guerrera 1997. Hyperrealism. McGraw-Hill.

Kvern. 1994. Real World Freehand 4. Peachpit Press, Inc.

Zampi and Morgan. 1995. Virtual Architecture. McGraw-Hill.

Porter. 1990. Architectural Drawing. Van Nostrand Reinhold. 150–155.

Knoll and Hechinger. 1993. Architectural Models: Construction Techniques. McGraw-Hill.

Moore. 1990. Model Builder's Notebook. McGraw-Hill.

Hohauser. 1984. Architectural and Interior Models: Design and Construction. Van Nostrand Reinhold.

Porter and Goodman. 1983. Manual of Graphic Techniques 3. Charles Scribner's Sons. 97–127.

Cross References

For pp. 496–497   See pp. 17–18
For p. 498   See p. 250
For p. 510   See pp. 556–557
For p. 511   See p. 196
For p. 513   See pp. 212–213
For pp. 514-515   See pp. 478–479

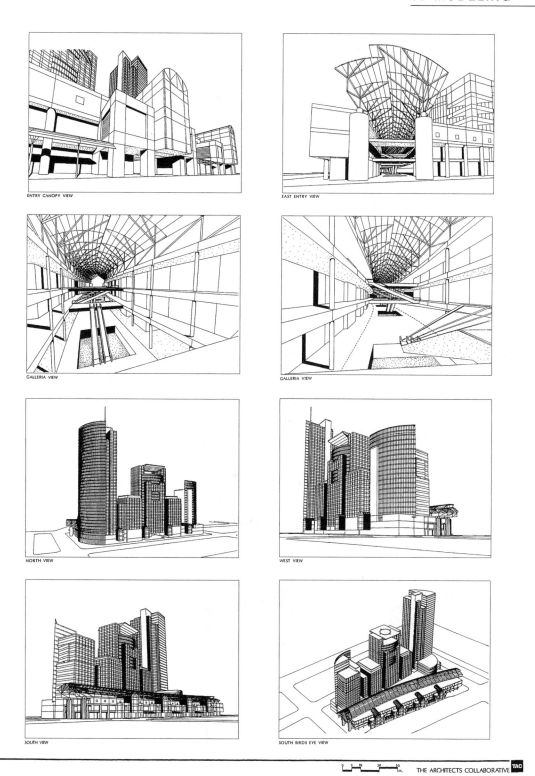

ENTRY CANOPY VIEW

EAST ENTRY VIEW

GALLERIA VIEW

GALLERIA VIEW

NORTH VIEW

WEST VIEW

SOUTH VIEW

SOUTH BIRDS EYE VIEW

THE ARCHITECTS COLLABORATIVE

Drawings: New Panchiao Station, Taipei, Taiwan
            3D Modeling of interior and exterior perspective views
Courtesy of TAC, The Architects Collaborative and
Sinotech Consulting Engineers

Traditionally, models have been built in real space to enhance the understanding of a building design. Computer 3D modeling allows for one to navigate through space and see an infinite variety of images.

3D MODELING – INTRODUCTION

MANUALLY CONSTRUCTED 3D STUDY MODELS

Before the advent of computers, 3D sketch modeling for spatial and volumetric studies was done by using scissors, X-acto knives, paper, and cardboard. Aspects such as scale, form, light, texture, color, and materials can be readily experimented with. Spatial studies are immediately tangible and can be seen from a variety of vantage points. This quick modeling technique usually involves xeroxing plans, pasting the plan on chipboard, mounting, and cutting on standard wall heights, etc. This procedure can be used for both sketch modeling (study models) and final modeling (presentation models).

With computers, presentation models can be built quickly with the utmost precision. A laser-cutting process converts hand sketches or computer drawings into parts. The laser system can do special cuts, special scoring, and special scribing in minute fine detail that is not possible with traditional model-making tools.

This model was accurately fabricated using laser techniques.

Model photos: San Francisco Bay Area buildings
Materials used: Cardboard, pantone film, colored crescent paper
Courtesy of Paul Nowicki and the Graphic Blade Studio, San Francisco

Model photos: Beth Israel, Houston, Texas
Upper left: View down Antoine Drive
Upper right: View from inside chapel
Lower left: View from west
Lower right: View from southwest
Courtesy of Solomon, Inc., Daniel Solomon FAIA

Preliminary study models lack detail and are most often massing models. These models are usually made of foamboard, chipboard, mat board, clay, or Styrofoam. Final presentation models, such as the example on this page, are commonly made of museum board, balsa wood, bass wood, and acrylics.

MANUALLY CONSTRUCTED 3D STUDY MODELS

COMPUTER-GENERATED DRAWINGS

Image: Master Bedroom/Waterpark Towers, Honolulu, Hawaii
Warner Boone AIA, Architect
Courtesy of Robert L. Montry of Media IV Design & Marketing
Services, Inc. Largo, FL

The image was created using a Macintosh IIX with 128 MB of RAM. The original 3D image was rendered in Strata Studio Pro, and finishing touches were added using Adobe Photoshop. The Strata software features extremely high resolution, affording the opportunity to achieve a detailed, photo-realistic image. The final result is a dramatic, multi-use illustration suitable for reproduction in a variety of formats including print, slide, video, and interactive computer presentation.
[ARCHITECTURAL ILLUSTRATOR'S STATEMENT]

An advantage of computer-generated drawings is that there is higher precision than manual drawings. All drawings are inputted by their exact size and, therefore, they are drawn to exact size. Consequently, scaled dimensions are not needed since actual dimensions are used. The printout is a reduction to the size desired.

Night image: Prototype for Sun Green
Homes in Japan
Courtesy of the Callison Partnership, Ltd.

3D computer modeling techniques allow designers to
bring in the element of time.
The night image above and
the day image below illustrate
a computer-rendered duplica-
tion where only the dimension
of time has changed.

Day image: Prototype for Sun Green Homes in Japan
Courtesy of the Callison Partnership, Ltd.

*Hardware: Intergraph Proprietary UNIX workstations. Rendered in Integraphmicrostation and Model View.
Outputted with Integraph RGB (proprietary format).*
[ARCHITECT'S STATEMENT]

COMPUTER-GENERATED DRAWINGS

COMPUTER-GENERATED DRAWINGS

The images are part of a larger sequence of frames put together as an animation.

These preliminary images were conceived totally by using computer modeling capabilities to generate and study the composition of the various forms. Shadow patterns were studied by selecting solar angles of Singapore and elements were added or detracted to generate a more harmonized tropical final design.
[ARCHITECT'S STATEMENT]

3D modeling through electronic imaging is not some part of a grandiose digital revolution. The process and its development evolved from refining traditional methods and means. The evolution is now in an advanced state. 3D modeling permits us to preview how conceptually designed buildings will appear and function when built. Traditional methods can always produce models to study; but new computer means are extremely efficient, and they permit the user to have more time to develop comprehensive and responsive design solutions.

Images: Pasir Ris Community Club, Singapore
Medium: Software: AutoCAD Rel 12, 3D Studio
Courtesy of The Alfred Wong Partnership Pte. Ltd.

Images: Pasir Ris Community Club, Singapore
Medium: Software: AutoCAD Rel 12, 3D Studio
Courtesy of The Alfred Wong Partnership Pte. Ltd.

Many preliminary computer-generated studies were made (opposite page) to best determine the optimum design based on our design concept for the Community Club. A study of the program requirements revealed a clear distinction of spaces; one major space of the Multi-purpose Hall and a number of smaller spaces which could be massed together in an orderly functional manner. This led to splitting one rectangular form of the building into two with an open courtyard carved in the middle. The entire complex is sheltered and capped by a series of pergolas at various levels. The natural axis and flow of traffic from the west is directed by a low curvilinear wall, housing the club name and logo with a raised garden behind it, focusing toward the entrance. This, combined with the flight of steps and layered forms of the southern edge of the building, provides the necessary impact to magnetically pull people into the Community Club. The final design image is shown above.
[ARCHITECT'S STATEMENT]

COMPUTER-GENERATED DRAWINGS

COMPUTER-GENERATED DRAWINGS

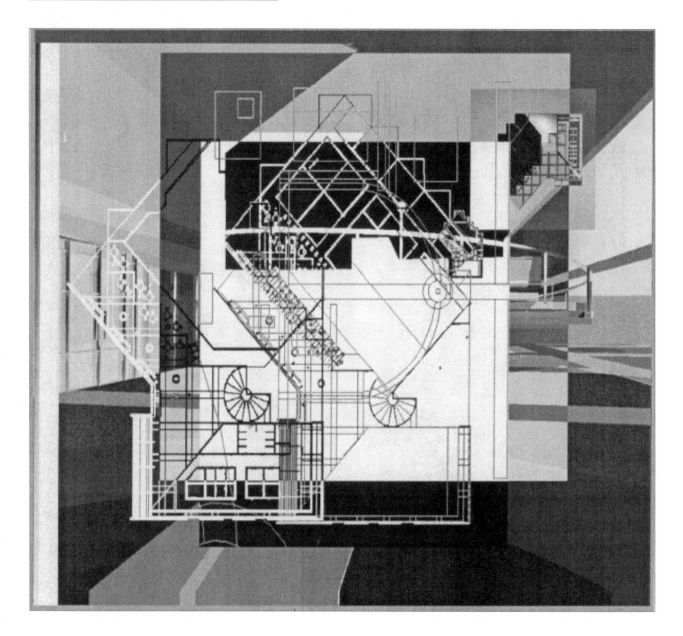

Image: Student project by Craig Hammack, Multi-Cultural Student Center
Studio Professor: Valerian Miranda, Ph.D.
Medium: Electronic Design Studio, Silicon Graphics Indigo computers with Sonata software
Courtesy of Texas A & M University, Department of Architecture

Especially for producing working drawings, computer-generated drawings have been a time and money saver for architectural offices. Also, less storage space is needed since drawing information can be stored electronically. Computers are now commonly used to generate presentation drawings and conceptual designs. Combining computer graphics with traditional drawing board methods used by both architects and artists is becoming commonplace. For example, photography can creatively be integrated with computer-generated drawings to produce spectacular realism in renderings.

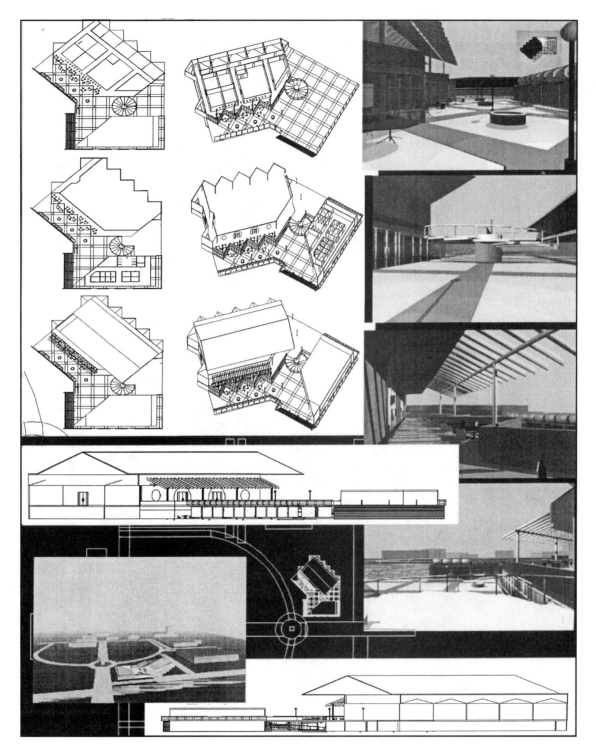

Image: Student project by Craig Hammack, Multi-Cultural Student Center
Studio Professor: Valerian Miranda, Ph.D.
Medium:Electronic Design Studio, Silicon Graphics Indigo computers with Sonata software
Courtesy of Texas A & M University, Department of Architecture

In composing a presentation, 3D computer modeling allows you to quickly choose and depict selected viewpoints from an infinite number of view choices for any architectural project. The above composite drawing shows a nice integration of drawings with photo-realistic images.

COMPUTER-GENERATED DRAWINGS

Addition to the Bauhaus School of Architecture

A steel truss skeletal structure surrounds the internal system allowing for an open floor plan.

Overall view of the design solution and existing buildings.

Interior view of the atrium space from the sixth floor looking down to the gallery and commons.

Images (this page and p. 505): Student project by Stewart Milne
Addition to the Bauhaus School of Architecture
Medium: Hardware/Software: Silicon Graphics Iris Indigo computers/Sonata software
Studio Professor: Valerian Miranda
Courtesy of the Department of Architecture, Texas A & M University

Super minicomputers using highly specialized software programs have become commonplace. Any kind of architectural drawing can be instantaneously and precisely edited with the many excellent software packages available. The time savings is enormous since continual small changes no longer require an endless flow of revised drawings.

Elements of Skin

The structure and skin of the building are inseparable and act as one.
The exoskeleton supports the
glazing making the structure visible to all inside and out.

View showing the relationship between the exterior skin and
the interior bay structure.

View of the atruim from outside showing all the steel framing

*Three-dimensional objects representing elements of the building skin, structure, staircases, elevators, roof and floor
panels, etc., were created and refined as the design progressed. The process of design involved making the elements,
placing them in the digital model, imaging and viewing the assemblies, analyzing the rendered images, and then
modifying either the individual elements or the assemblies. Presentation drawings consisted of plans, elevations,
sections, and "hidden-line" perspectives extracted from the three-dimensional, digital model composed with color,
rendered perspective views, and explanatory text and printed in color on 8½" × 11" paper.
[STUDIO PROFESSOR'S STATEMENT]*

COMPUTER-GENERATED DRAWINGS

COMPUTER-GENERATED DRAWINGS

Drawing: Storyboard, Architect: Le Corbusier
Medium: Computer, 40" × 20" (101.6 × 50.8 cm), 1993
Courtesy of Advanced Media Design, Richard Dubrow/Jon Kletzien

The building was modeled in AutoCAD Rel.12; that geometry was imported into and then rendered in 3D Studio Rel.2. Those renderings, in addition to a sky generated in Animator Pro, clouds and trees from 3D Studio, and scans done in Photoshop 2.5, were composited in Hi-Res QFX Rel.3, where the moon was added as well. All work was done on a 486-66DX2 with 64 MB of RAM.

This piece was conceived as a still representation of both the Villa Savoye and an animation that had been produced prior to this work's completion. The canvas allowed the juxtaposition of two kinds of entry sequences, the overt (the images on top) and the implied (the glowing elevation at the furthest corner).
[ARCHITECTURAL ILLUSTRATOR'S STATEMENT]

The use of color in traditional architectural renderings is generally time-consuming and expensive. However, the computer has unlimited potential in handling and manipulating the nuances of color. For this reason, color has become commonplace in computer-generated renderings.

The wire frame is the first visual representation of the 3D geometry. This simple technique allows one to correctly place the building within its environment. It requires less computer memory to place it in position. This technique also allows one to see if any changes have to be taken into account before proceeding with the final photorealistic rendering. It is much easier to move the camera within the scene in this mode.
[RENDERER'S STATEMENT]

COMPUTER-GENERATED DRAWNIGS

Macintosh Quadra 950 was used for the project with 64 MB of RAM and a 1 Gig hard drive.

Computer rendering of a 3D solid model
Project: UCSF/Mount Zion Cancer Center, San Francisco, California
Architects: HGA and ESS Architects
Rendering: Courtesy of VIEW BY VIEW Inc., San Francisco, CA

Once the design gets the green light from the client, a color photo-realistic image is generated, as seen above. Surfaces are given the appropriate attributes, such as materials, lighting, color, transparency, reflectivity, and textures, in order to achieve a photo-realistic look. Lighting is very critical in obtaining the required effect. Shadow casting is applied to simulate the sun. This image won a first prize in the 1993, AIA San Francisco Chapter computer rendering competition.
[RENDERER'S STATEMENT]

COMPUTER-GENERATED DRAWINGS

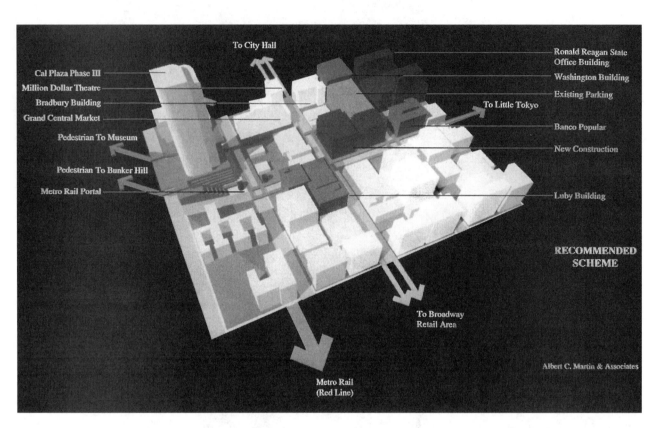

Image: Recommended Scheme — CA State Needs Assessment & M.P./L.A. Basin
Courtesy of Albert C. Martin and Associates, Planning/Architecture/Engineering

Image was created on a Macintosh Quadra 800 with 56 MB of RAM.
The image was modeled and rendered in Form-Z and saved in PICT format. The file was then opened in Photoshop 2.5 and saved in EPS. The EPS file was then placed into Pagemaker 2.5, where the lines and labels were added. The image was output as a 4K 35-mm color transparency.
[ARCHITECT'S STATEMENT]

Another area where color is strongly and boldly used in computer-generated drawings is the conceptual diagram. This schematic massing diagram effectively uses color to show orientation and direction.

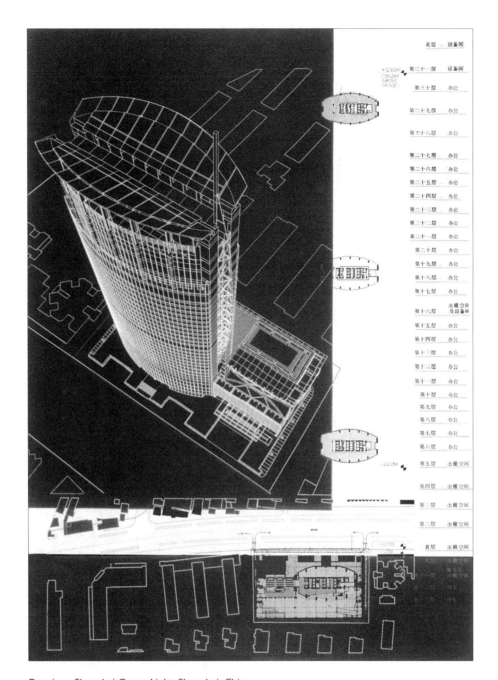

Drawing: Shanghai Ocean Light, Shanghai, China
30" × 40" (76.2 × 101.6 cm)
Medium: AutoCAD rendering (software developed by SOM and IBM)
Courtesy of Skidmore, Owings & Merrill LLP

COMPUTER-GENERATED DRAWINGS

…3D Computer model and CAD line drawings using IBM Architectural and Engineering series modeling and sheet software.

The intention is to generate a single drawing that can be used to simultaneously convey the spirit of the project as well as factual information. Dominating the composition is a perspective view of the computer model that highlights the building's soaring spire, which acknowledges and addresses the city center. Around the perspective are plans that communicate the disposition of structure and functional elements in the building. A site plan shows the project's place in the city and a sectional dimensional string indicates the height of the building and its floor-to-floor heights. The use of CAD allows this image to be automatically updated as the design process moves from schematic design to construction documents.
[ARCHITECT'S STATEMENT]

COMPUTER-GENERATED DRAWINGS

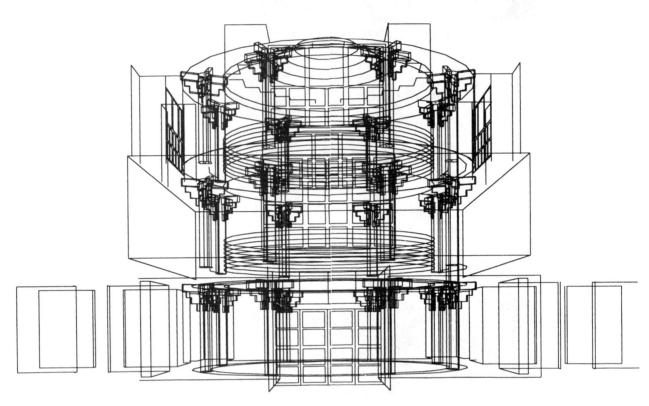

Drawing: Center for Qomolangma Nature Preserve
          Shegar, Tibet
Courtesy of William W. P. Chan, Architect, Nicholas Linehan RLA,
Don Duncan, David Segmiller, AIA

This wire frame drawing was prepared to give us a basis to look at the proportion of the space as we approach the rotunda. Since the basic formal elements are there, we can move around to study the detailed relationships between floors, columns, railings and ceilings through overlays with tracing paper. This, we think, is the objective of a wire frame drawing.
[ARCHITECT'S STATEMENT]

In perspective drawing, the main advantage of computer-generated drawings is the computer's quick ability to locate the best viewpoint (station point and angle of view). Another advantage is the efficient production of skeletal layouts which form the basis for overlays that are later modified and refined by hand.

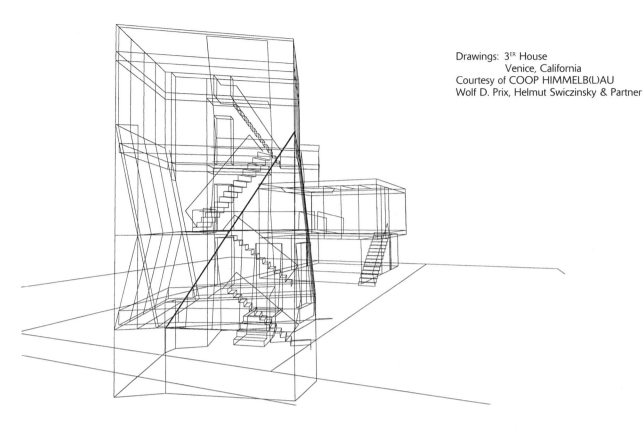

Drawings: 3ER House
Venice, California
Courtesy of COOP HIMMELB(L)AU
Wolf D. Prix, Helmut Swiczinsky & Partner

The drawings are the transformation of the three-dimensional model into a two-dimensional media [sic]. They are the intersection of imagination and planning.
[ARCHITECT'S STATEMENT]

This private residence consists of a tower (the main house) and a box (guest house on top of a garage). The tower is shaped by the environmental conditions of sun and wind as well as its orientation response to inside and outside viewpoints.

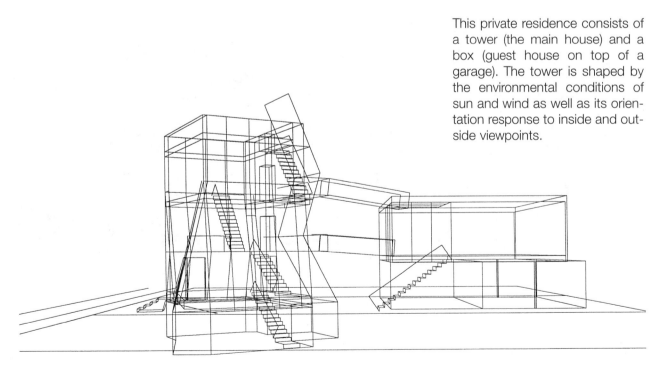

COMPUTER-GENERATED DRAWINGS

COMPUTER-GENERATED DRAWINGS

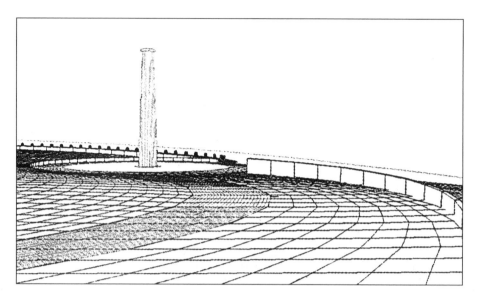

Utilizing AutoCAD R13 for Windows NT, a 3D model was constructed of both the existing site and the conceptual site plan. Perspectives were set up and studied in AutoCAD, then plotted on bond. Larry then hand-rendered the image directly on the plot media. The rendered plot was then scanned into Photoshop from which a variety of effects and manipulations could be performed. The rendered image could then be plotted out at a number of scales or presented from a variety of digital devices. [LANDSCAPE ARCHITECT'S STATEMENT]

Drawings: Landscape Charette using digital technology
        Lower Woolen Mill Park, Cleveland, Ohio
        View from Ackley
Courtesy of ATELIER ps, Landscape Architects
Design team: Chris Overdorf, David Ringstrom, and Larry Smart

This computer-generated drawing was essential to study the pyramid of the Louvre, its proportions and position, in relation to the existing building wings, the circular Place Carousel and the Arc du Carousel.
[ARCHITECT'S STATEMENT]

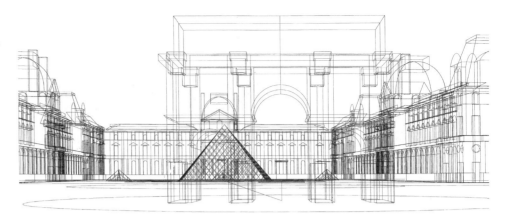

Wire frame drawing: La Pyramide du Louvre, Paris, France
Courtesy of Pei Cobb Freed & Partners, Architects

Night rendering: La Pyramide du Louvre, Paris, France
Courtesy of Pei Cobb Freed & Partners, Architects
and Paul Stevenson Oles, FAIA, Architectural Illustrator

COMPUTER-GENERATED DRAWINGS

COMPUTER-GENERATED DRAWINGS

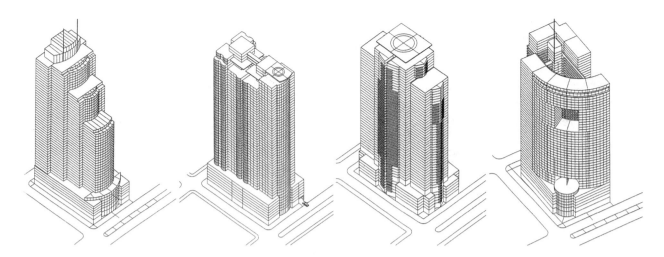

In conjunction with the design office's establishing the general space requirements within the initial building envelope, I created approximately ten massing alternatives. Above are four of the many quick wire-frame studies that were modeled in AutoCAD R12. Although AutoCAD is not necessarily the easiest software to use to create 3D geometry, I have found it to be predominantly used by architectural design and engineering offices, both locally and in Asia. Because the associate office in Manila is using AutoCAD, it makes sense to insure compatibility when transferring file information by mail, fax, or modem. The wire-frames worked well as an easily "faxable" medium as we consistently communicated overseas with the design efforts in Manila. Thus, these simple wire-frame models served the dual purposes of study and in-progress presentation of ideas for discussion.
[DESIGN ILLUSTRATOR'S STATEMENT]

Once several possible directions were selected, more developed shaded models were created by first refining the AutoCAD model and importing it to 3DSTUDIO, V3 for light source and rendering with shading. These software versions required the translation of the AutoCAD model in DXF format to input into the rendering program. Current versions of AutoCAD now allow direct saving in 3DSTUDIO's "3DS" format. At this time I chose to keep things in black and white to concentrate on the form design and not distract with color. The pictures below show just one of several shaded volumes that were created and faxed to the local office while design efforts were concurrently going on across the Pacific.
[DESIGN ILLUSTRATOR'S STATEMENT]

Lawrence Ko Leong, an architectural concept imager, serves as a design/illustrator consultant for various architectural design offices in San Francisco and in Asia. Typically working in a team-oriented setting, he uses the combination of hand-drawing and CAD skills to help visualize in-progress design ideas and to expedite the design/problem-solving process.

Images: Moldex Condominium Tower, Manila Bay, Philippines
Courtesy of Architecture International: Design Office
John Sheehy FAIA, Design Principal
Lawrence K. Leong, Design Illustrator
Architectural Concept Imaging, San Francisco

With client and design team feedback, a single direction was established. I created a more finished AutoCAD model while inputting design refinement. In AutoCAD, I used the 256-palette of colors to approximate what I thought the colors should be initially, and after importing it into the 3D STUDIO, I used the materials editor to refine the color, reflective, etc., properties with the design principal's input.

At this preliminary design phase, I did not texture map the entities as the viewpoints were such a long distance away, but by experimenting with several different color, light source, ray-trace shadow combinations, the set of CAD vignettes to the left proved effective to exhibit the design intent. (The CAD illustration became "abstract" images similar to actual physical 3D scaled architectural models.)

Note that both elevations and 3D perspectives work well together in describing the design, and that the simple black background can give drama to the design composition. Note the difference in "feel" with the eye-level perspective using a background option of a bit-mapped sky.
[DESIGN ILLUSTRATOR'S STATEMENT]

Images: Moldex Condominium Tower, Manila Bay, Philippines
Courtesy of Architecture International: Design Office
John Sheehy FAIA, Design Principal
Lawrence K. Leong, Design Illustrator
Architectural Concept Imaging, San Francisco

The final schematic design package included standard CAD plans, sections, and elevations. The highly detailed AutoCAD 3D model to the right was initially created by the local associate office of Concept International. I then worked with the design lead to fine-tune the building model in 3D STUDIO for color, light, and reflective characteristics and then in PHOTO-SHOP to further enhance contrast, color balance, surrounding buildings, palm trees, background sky, and final adjustments of different layers.

As well as any software can render, there are always going to be little areas that can be refined. It would be very time-consuming to re-render the 3D geometry over and over to get everything "perfect," versus using a photo-imaging software to make final adjustments.
[DESIGN ILLUSTRATOR'S STATEMENT]

COMPUTER-GENERATED DRAWINGS

COMPUTER-GENERATED DRAWINGS

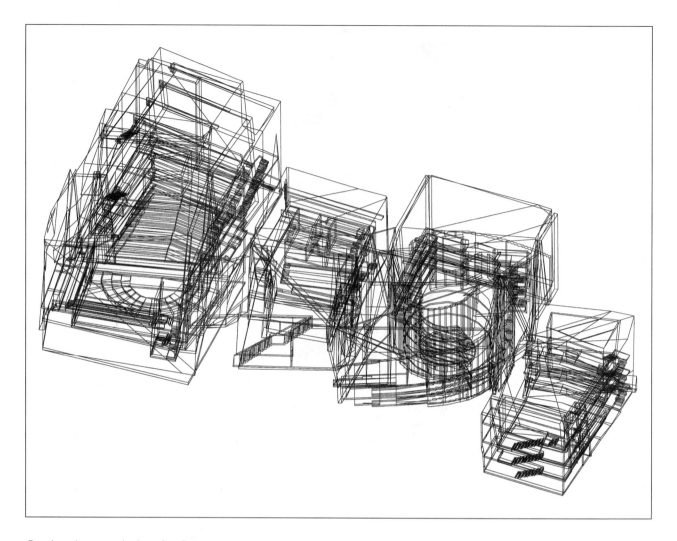

Drawing: Axonometric view of performance spaces
Center for the Arts, Emory University, Atlanta, Georgia
Medium: Computer Laser Print, 11" × 8½" (27.9 × 21.6 cm), 1993
Courtesy of Architect: Eisenman Architects PC

The building's undulating folds derive from an exploration of musical harmonics and the topographical profile of the ravines that cross the Emory campus; the folds that occur on the outside surface of the building are transformed to the inside through a mathematical and geometrical process involving computer analysis.
[ARCHITECT'S STATEMENT]

Computers are now doing not only the drawing aspects for a design but also the creative aspects. Traditionally, the creative part was always envisioned in the architect's brain. The solution to Emory's arts center complex is a spectacular example of the computer's potential to generate an architectural design. The architect fed the computer basic data and asked it to produce the ultimate design.

Drawing: Music Hall, Interior perspective looking west
Center for the Arts, Emory University, Atlanta, Georgia
Medium: Computer Laser Print, 11" × 8½" (27.9 × 21.6 cm), 1993
Courtesy of Architect: Eisenman Architects PC

The complexity of the structure required a computerized analysis of the folds and volumes to generate the precise geometric calculations needed for construction documents. In a section of the fold separated by transverse planes, for example, the four points thought to constitute a plane in fact do not lie in the same plane. This results in a surface similar to a hyperbolic paraboloid, which would pose difficulties in construction. As a solution, a trangulation system was devised using the computer to create multiple planar surfaces, each with three points; these pyramidal surfaces connect to form the cubic volumes of the building.

The building was modeled on AutoCAD R-12 with AME. The solid models were unionized on a IBM R6000RISC workstation with 256MB of RAM.
[ARCHITECT'S STATEMENT]

COMPUTER-GENERATED DRAWINGS

13

Presentation Formats

A fine set of presentation drawings is invaluable in architect/client or designer/client relationships for the purpose of graphic communication. An architectural drawing presentation usually includes a site plan, floor plans, exterior elevations, site sections, building sections, axonometrics, obliques, and perspectives. The initial stage of the design-drawing process is involved with conceptual diagrams and conceptual drawings. As the design concept evolves, more formal methods of presentation are needed. These presentation formats must effectively communicate to the targeted audience whether they be conventional or avant-garde in approach.

The intent of this chapter is to illustrate various presentation formats with respect to traditional wall presentations. The excellent books listed in the bibliography should be explored for their coverage of other presentation modes (slides, reports, models, etc.).

Presentation Formats

Topic

Architectural Presentations

Reference

Architectural Graphics (Ching 1996): 164-175.

Cross References

For p. 572   See p. 449
For p. 547   See p. 56
For pp. 553–557   See pp. 25,26,27
For pp. 566-569   See Chapter 12

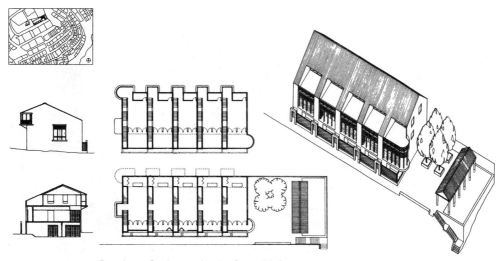

Drawings: Student project by Susan M. Stern
Row Housing, Barcelona, Spain
Courtesy of Washington University School of Architecture, St. Louis, MO

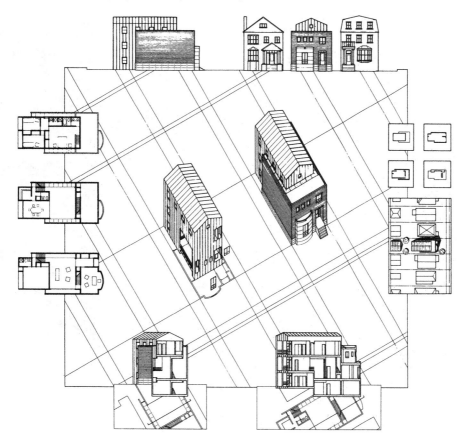

Drawing: Student project by Doug Dolezal
Central West End Townhouse
Courtesy of Washington University School of Architecure, St. Louis, MO

The primary goal of an architectural presentation is to effectively present design concepts. Implemented design concepts should be drawn and organized in an orderly structured **format.** Over the years, architects and designers have used many different formats, with the ultimate goal always being the same. This page shows both traditional and new "cutting edge" presentation methods for graphic communications.

PRESENTATION FORMATS

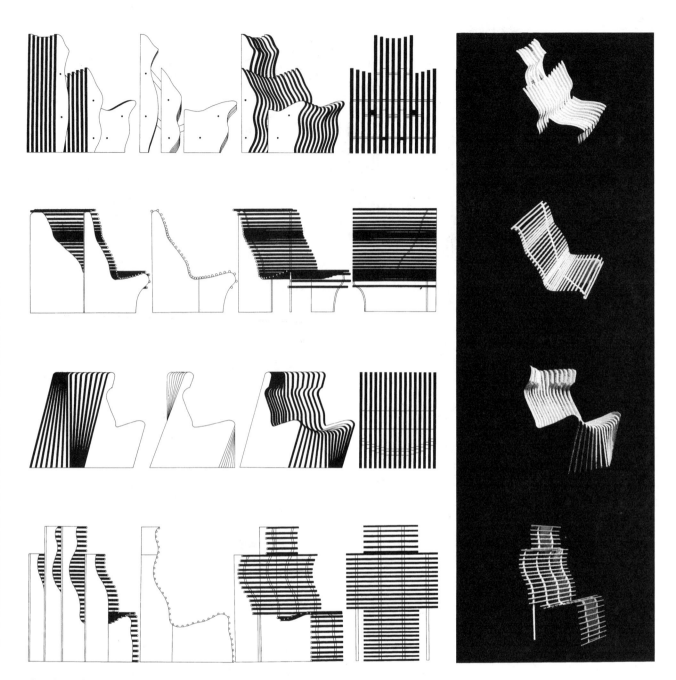

Drawings: Student project by Scott Benner, Mark Honderick, Jeff Hoeft, and Juan Lopez
Rhythms to Sit On
Medium: Ink on Mylar and photography
Courtesy of the University of Texas at Arlington, School of Architecture

Presentation formats for smaller size projects other than buildings normally do not require all of the primary architectual drawings (plan, elevation, section, etc.). This example utilizes only elevation drawings and model photographs to completely illustrate the design. Note that the projects could involve full-size mock-up models large enough for the designer to interact with his/her design. The example format on the facing page uses only drawn perspective images and accompanying text.

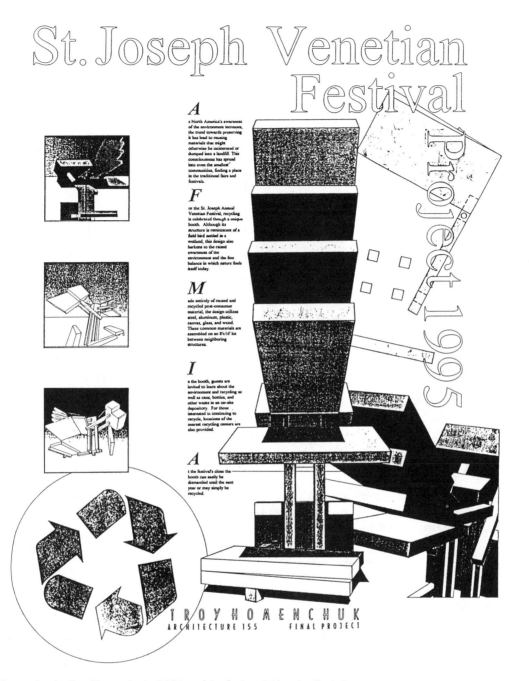

St. Joseph Venetian Festival

Project 1995

A s North America's awareness of the environment increases, the trend towards preserving materials that might otherwise be incinerated or dumped into a landfill. This consciousness has spread into even the smallest communities, finding a place in the traditional fairs and festivals.

F or the St. Joseph Annual Venetian Festival, recycling is celebrated though a unique booth. Although its structure is reminiscent of a field bird settled in a wetland, this design also harkens to the raised awareness of the environment and the fine balance in which nature finds itself today.

M ade entirely of reused and recycled post-consumer material, the design utilizes steel, aluminum, plastic, canvas, glass, and wood. These common materials are assembled on an 8'x16' lot between neighboring structures.

I n the booth, guests are invited to learn about the environment and recycling as well as cans, bottles, and other waste in an on-site depository. For those interested in continuing to recycle, locations of the nearest recycling centers are also provided.

A t the festival's close the booth can easily be dismantled until the next year or may simply be recycled.

TROY HOMENCHUK
ARCHITECTURE 155   FINAL PROJECT

Drawing: Student project by Troy Homenchuck: A Vision of the St. Joseph Venetian Festival
Media: Ink on Mylar with pastel application and 3D computer modeling images, 18" × 24" (45.7 × 61 cm)
Studio Professor: Arpad Danaiel Ronaszegi, Assistant; Tom Lowing
Courtesy of Andrews University, Division of Architecture, 1st year Graphics Studio

The project is an abstract vision on the Venetian festival. Students designed individual segments of a street and assembled it using blocks with set dimensions in interactive participation. The project duration was two weeks.
[STUDIO PROFESSOR'S STATEMENT]

PRESENTATION FORMATS

PRESENTATION FORMATS

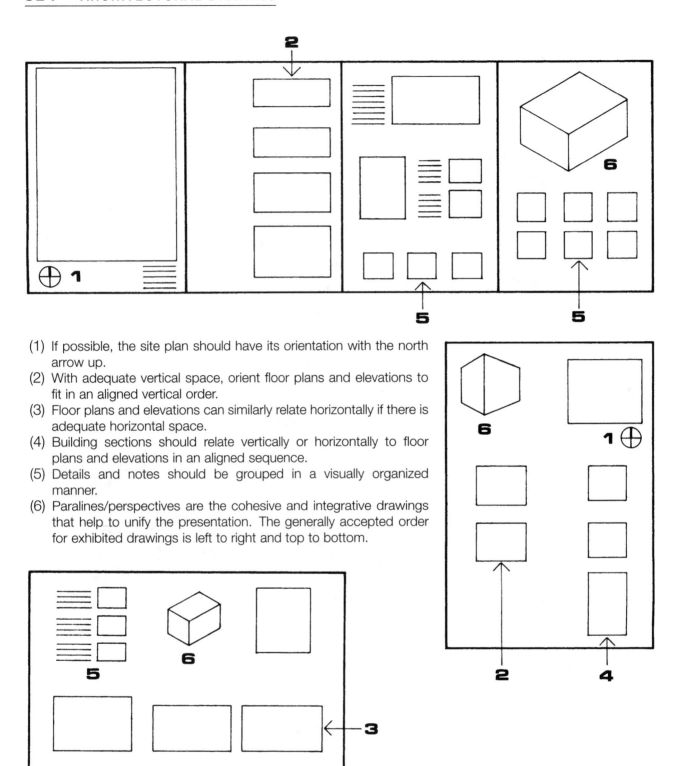

(1) If possible, the site plan should have its orientation with the north arrow up.

(2) With adequate vertical space, orient floor plans and elevations to fit in an aligned vertical order.

(3) Floor plans and elevations can similarly relate horizontally if there is adequate horizontal space.

(4) Building sections should relate vertically or horizontally to floor plans and elevations in an aligned sequence.

(5) Details and notes should be grouped in a visually organized manner.

(6) Paralines/perspectives are the cohesive and integrative drawings that help to unify the presentation. The generally accepted order for exhibited drawings is left to right and top to bottom.

In the section on conventional orthogonal terminology, the primary architectural drawings were introduced. By themselves as an isolated entity, these drawings have little importance. However, when combined as a totality in a **presentation format,** these drawings become a strong **communicative** tool. Architectural presentations are commonly done on sequential sheets or boards. The organization and composition of drawing elements is flexible as long as there is a thread of continuity and unity as well as a conceptual focus.

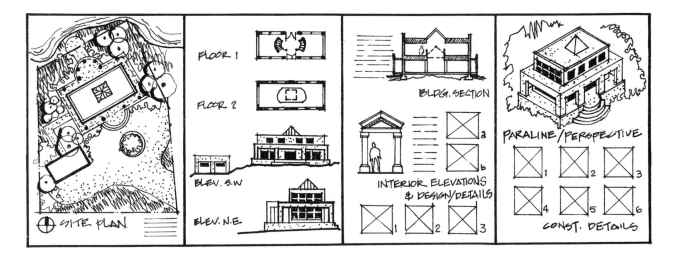

Wall presentations have the advantage of allowing a large audience to view all the drawings in context with each other. The primary components in an architectural presentation are the site plan, floor plans, elevations, sections, and paralines/perspectives. An effective presentation unifying these elements will generally require consistency in scale, orientation, and presentation technique/medium. The size of the audience and the viewing distance normally are the determinants for the choice of scale and the type of medium used.

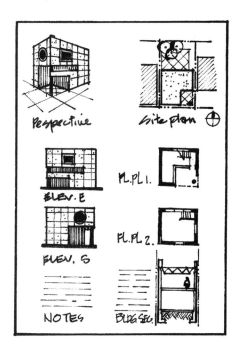

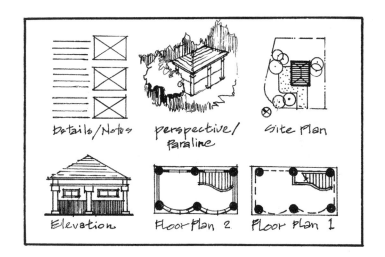

Architectural wall presentation formats are most effective when organized vertically or horizontally. The examples shown are (1) vertically oriented boards or sheets that flow and read horizontally (top row); (2) a horizontally oriented one-board or one-sheet presentation which reads as a total composition (left); and (3) a vertically oriented one-board or one-sheet presentation which reads as a total composition (right). It is often helpful to orient the site plan and floor plans in the same direction. The wall presentation is commonly supplemented with scale models, slides, reports, and the Internet (with other schools, private offices, and the lay public).

PRESENTATION FORMATS

PRESENTATION FORMATS

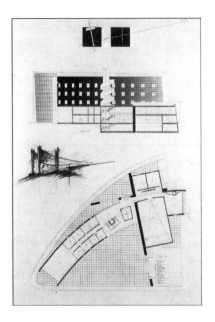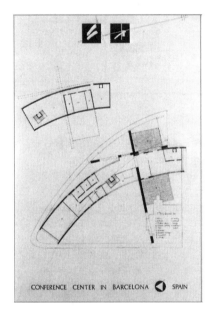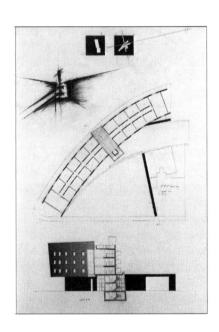

CONFERENCE CENTER IN BARCELONA ◀ SPAIN

Competition drawings: Student project by Mohd Fadzir Mohd Suhaimi
Barcelona Tile Competition, Barcelona, Spain
Courtesy of Washington University School of Architecture, St. Louis, MO

Before the 1980s, a typical set of presentation drawings usually would have each drawing (plan, elevation, section, etc.) on a separate sheet or board. The 1980s showed a movement toward having several drawing types combined into one presentation. Some examples of this type of format (termed composite drawing) follow the Hight residence. Letter size for titles and any text for architectural presentations depends on how the drawings will be viewed and used. A jury (a group of teachers, students, or peers that passes judgment on the material being presented) or client responds to the text at different viewing distances, depending on the purpose of the information. Ideally, drawings should "speak for themselves"; the inclusion of text should be minimized as much as possible. In general, use the smallest lettering size and the simplest style that is legible from the desired distance.

The following set of drawings for the Hight residence illustrates how a series of drawings can be presented in a logical sequential order. This is an example of a traditional format. Design competitions tend to be restrictive in their size requirements, which has led many contemporary competitors to design new innovative formats.

Set of drawings on pp. 527–532: Hight residence, Mendocino County,
California
24" × 36" (61 × 91.4 cm)
Medium: Pencil on Mylar
Courtesy of Bart Prince, Architect

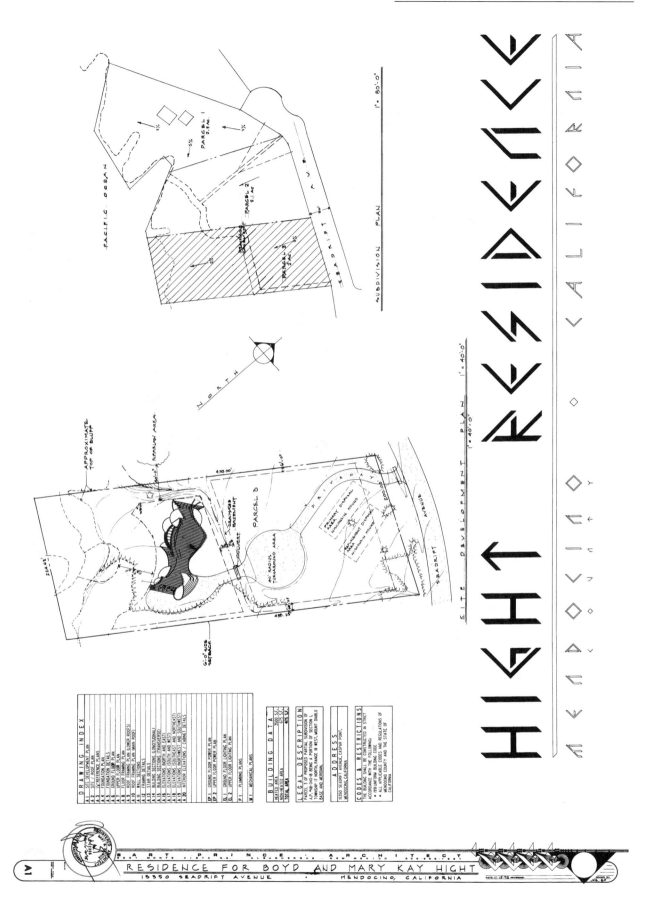

PRESENTATION FORMATS

PRESENTATION FORMATS

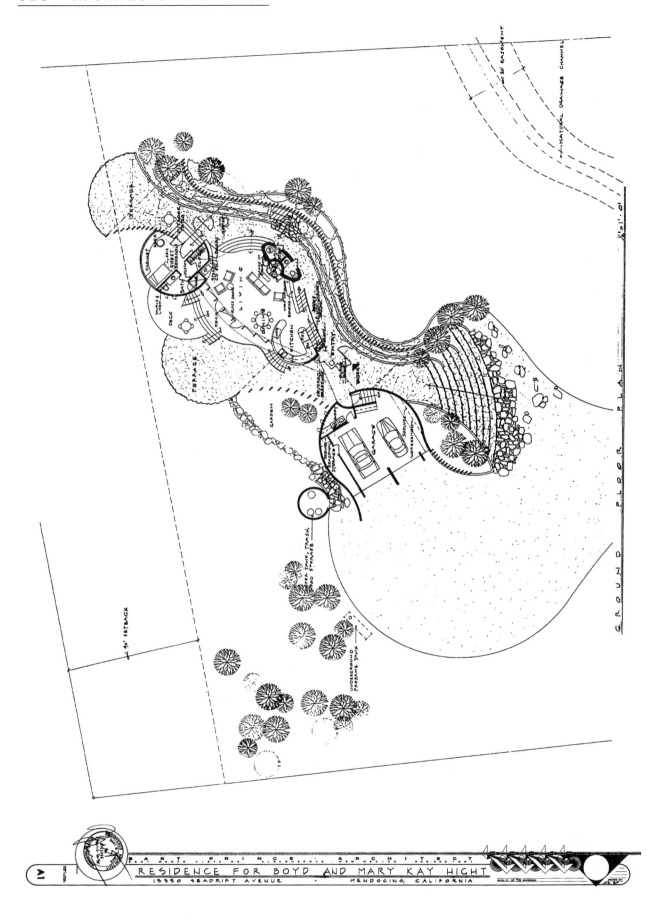

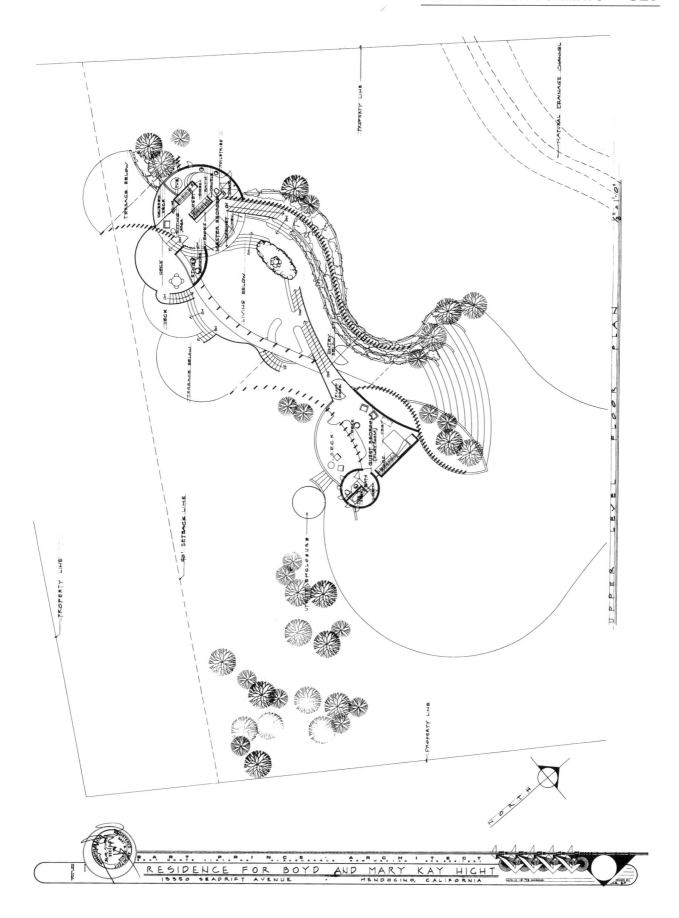

PRESENTATION FORMATS

PRESENTATION FORMATS

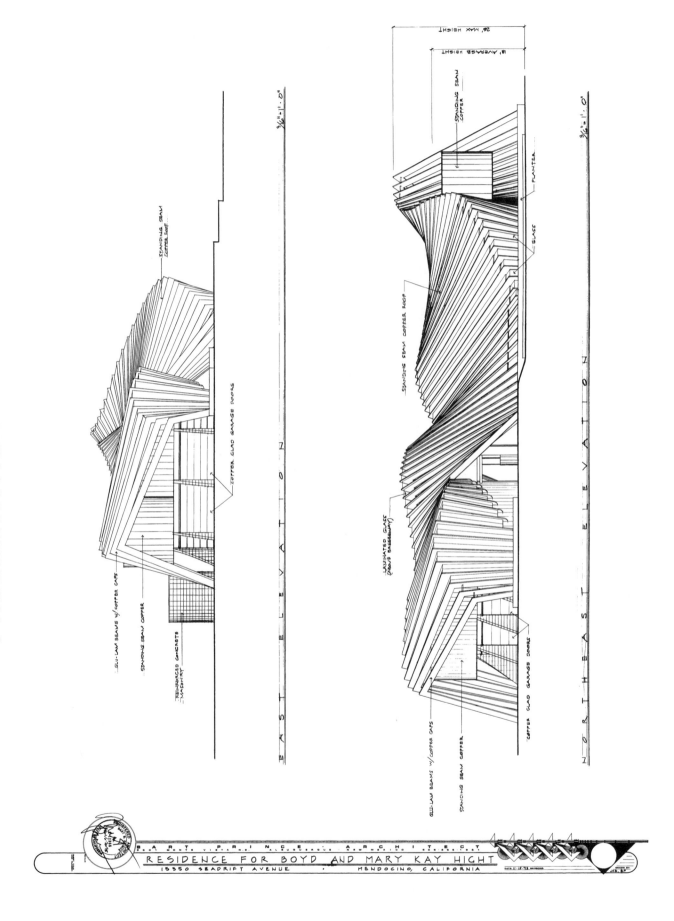

PRESENTATION FORMATS

PRESENTATION FORMATS

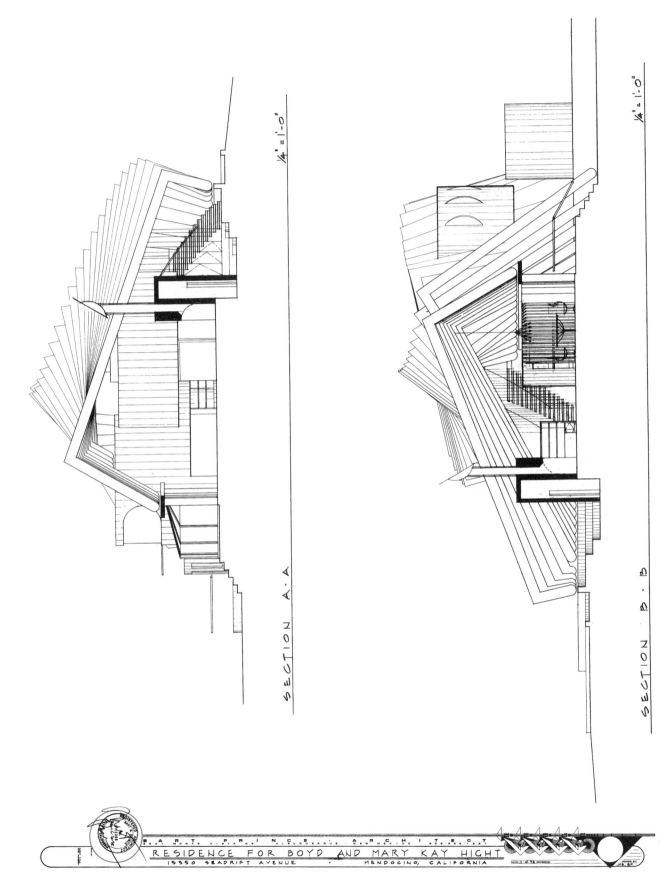

SECTION A·A   1/4"=1'-0"

SECTION B·B   1/4"=1'-0"

BART V PRINCE ARCHITECT

RESIDENCE FOR BOYD AND MARY KAY HIGHT

15350 SEADRIFT AVENUE   ·   MENDOCINO, CALIFORNIA

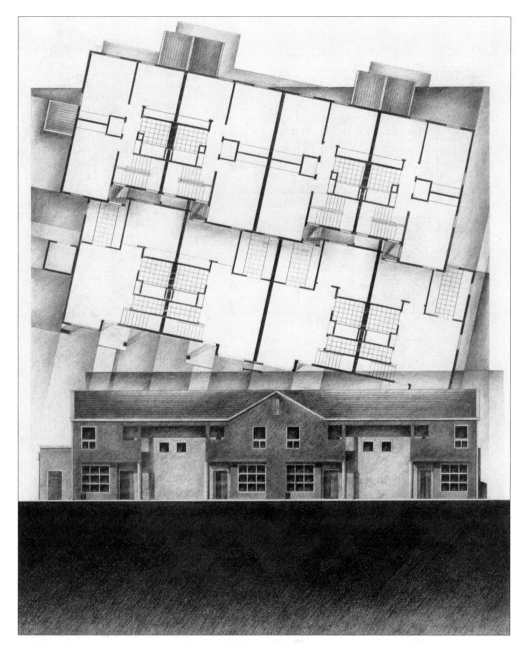

Drawings: Rancho Sespe II, Piru, California
Medium: Pencil
Courtesy of John V. Mutlow, FAIA, Architects

The previous six pages show a traditional presentation format. This page shows a more compact format. This drawing can be classified as a **composite drawing** in the sense that the plan and the elevation are composed as one presentation. Care must be taken so that each drawing can be read without losing its clarity.

The 6B pencil rendition of a two-dimensional elevation with the combination of the dwelling unit floor plans assists in an understanding of the three-dimensional quality of the facade. The design intention is to generate eight different building designs by assembling three unit types to create building identity from unit repetition (the set urban piece). The shade and shadow on the elevation quickly distinguish individual building identity.
[ARCHITECT'S STATEMENT]

PRESENTATION FORMATS

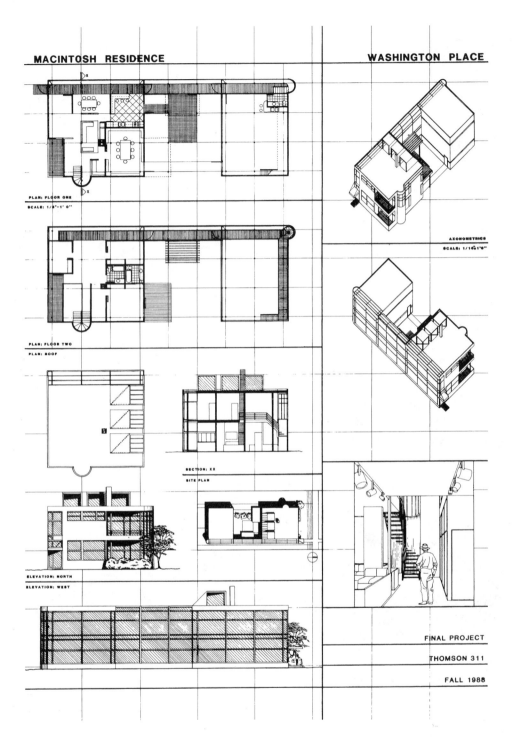

Drawing: Student project by Vaughn Dierks
Macintosh House, St. Louis, Missouri
Courtesy of Washington University School of Architecture, St. Louis, MO

This presentation was nicely laid out using a **grid** format. The grid is extremely effective in helping to organize all the drawings and bits of information that go into a comprehensive presentation. The grid should be lightly drawn. The amount of negative space between the drawings is extremely important. Too much results in drawings that "float" and too little results in a congested layout. As with any artistic composition, the proper figure–background balancing is crucial for all drawings to exist in harmony.

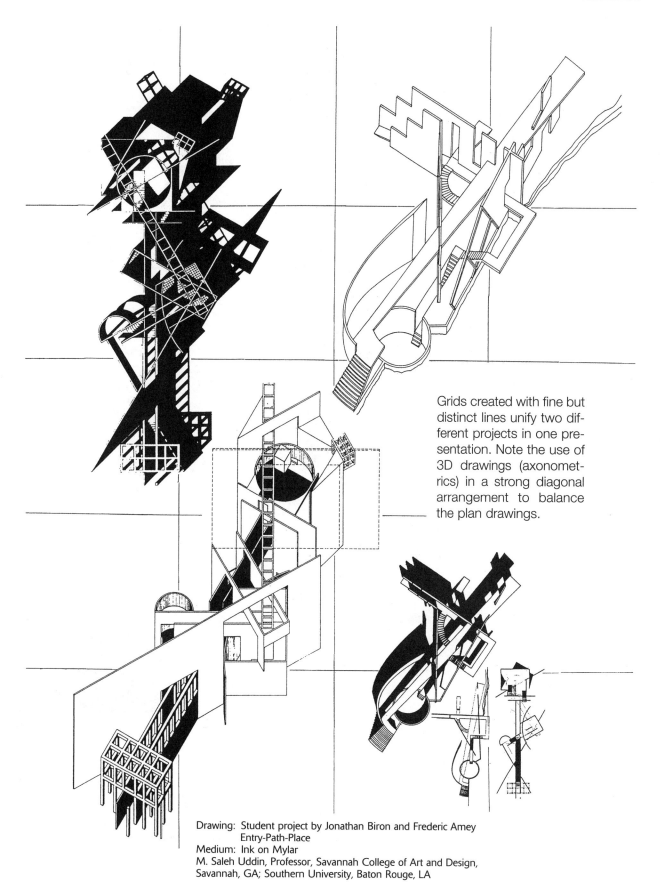

Grids created with fine but distinct lines unify two different projects in one presentation. Note the use of 3D drawings (axonometrics) in a strong diagonal arrangement to balance the plan drawings.

Drawing: Student project by Jonathan Biron and Frederic Amey
               Entry-Path-Place
Medium: Ink on Mylar
M. Saleh Uddin, Professor, Savannah College of Art and Design, Savannah, GA; Southern University, Baton Rouge, LA

PRESENTATION FORMATS

Competition drawing: Perdana Rail City, Kuala Lumpur, Malaysia
Steve Kelley, designer
Courtesy of Kaplan McLaughlin Diaz, Architects

...section elevations that started as a hardlined felt-tipped pen on trace. The drawings were scanned and then colored using Adobe Photoshop. The background foliage was also scanned, resized, and inserted using Photoshop, as were the photographic images and other sketches. All files were sent to a print service bureau via Syquest cartridge and were printed out on a large-format color printer.
[ARCHITECT'S STATEMENT]

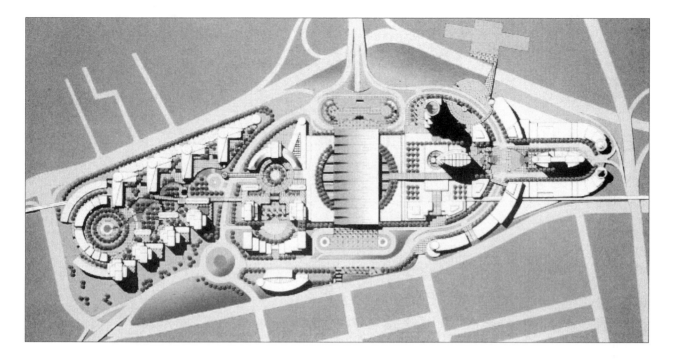

Competition drawing: Perdana Rail City, Kuala Lumpur, Malaysia
Steve Kelley, designer
36" × 24" (91.4 × 61 cm), Scale: 1:600
Medium: Ink on vellum
Courtesy of Kaplan McLaughlin Diaz, Architects

…a proposed mixed-use master plan for a rail yard site near downtown Kuala Lumpur. This site plan is an ink on vellum drawing (including shadows) that was scanned on an HP flat bed scanner. The drawing was imported into Adobe Photoshop and rendered there.
[ARCHITECT'S STATEMENT]

Drawings: Speculative Developer House (subsequent three pages)
Competition Team Architects: Edward P. Palushock, Jr. and Keith Huot
Baltimore, Maryland
Original size of all the drawings: 24" × 36" (61 × 91.4 cm)
Plan conceptual diagrams: 1/16"=1'0"
Plans, sections, elevations, and the axonometric: 1/8"=1'0"
Mediums: 2D drawings: generated and rendered utilizing AutoCAD Rel. 12
3D drawings: hand-inked on Mylar or inked freehand sketches

The design was centered around an abstraction of a single idea, and we wanted the presentation to reflect our intention clearly and rationally. Submitted for a design competition without formal requirements, we assembled a series of boards that would unfold a "story," with each board explaining a part of the concept. Individual board layouts become composed, but not intentionally overbearing. The use of the computer became an invaluable tool that allowed us to easily change, manipulate, and arrange our drawings during the design and production process.
Order of boards:

(1) Plans and Organizational Diagrams
(2) Elevation and Sections
(3) Axonometric, Perspectives, and Early Conceptual Sketches
[ARCHITECT'S STATEMENT]

PRESENTATION FORMATS

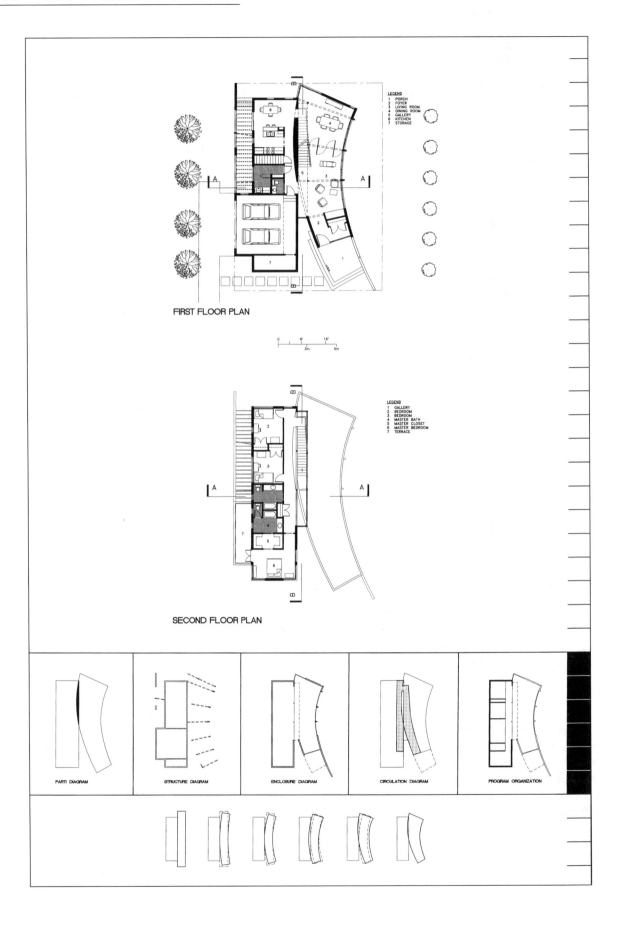

FIRST FLOOR PLAN

LEGEND
1 PORCH
2 FOYER
3 LIVING ROOM
4 DINING ROOM
5 GALLERY
6 KITCHEN
7 STORAGE

SECOND FLOOR PLAN

LEGEND
1 GALLERY
2 BEDROOM
3 BEDROOM
4 MASTER BATH
5 MASTER CLOSET
6 MASTER BEDROOM
7 TERRACE

PARTI DIAGRAM

STRUCTURE DIAGRAM

ENCLOSURE DIAGRAM

CIRCULATION DIAGRAM

PROGRAM ORGANIZATION

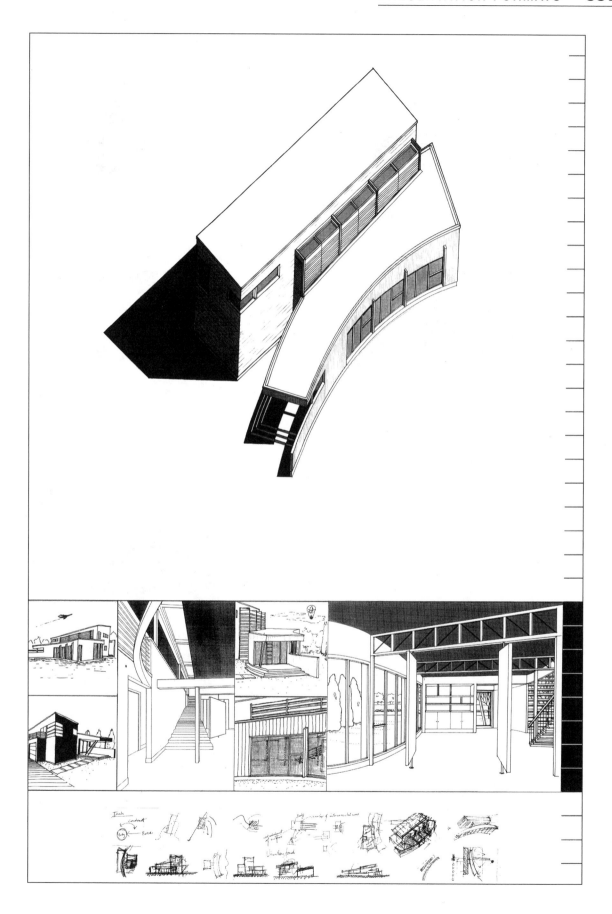

PRESENTATION FORMATS

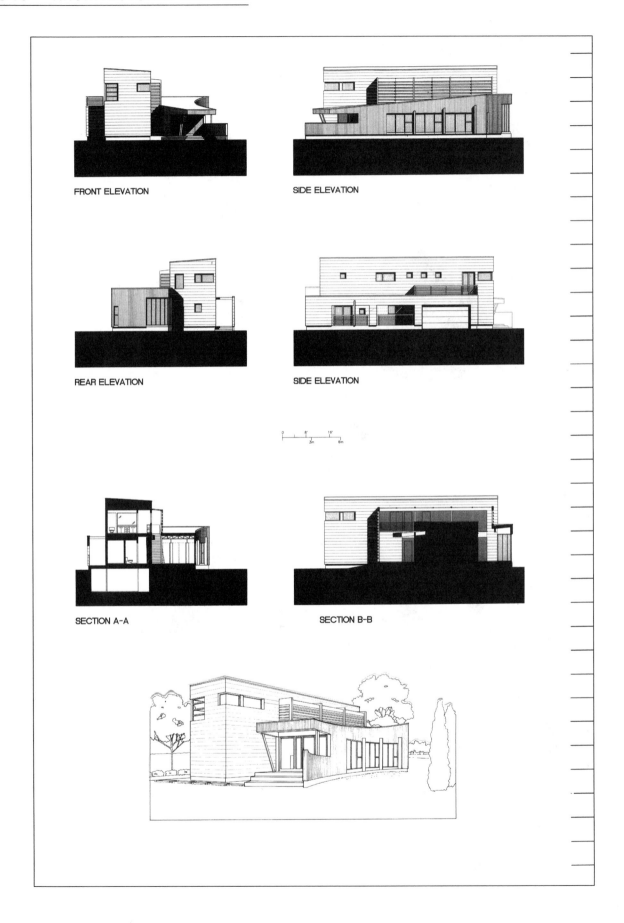

FRONT ELEVATION

SIDE ELEVATION

REAR ELEVATION

SIDE ELEVATION

SECTION A-A

SECTION B-B

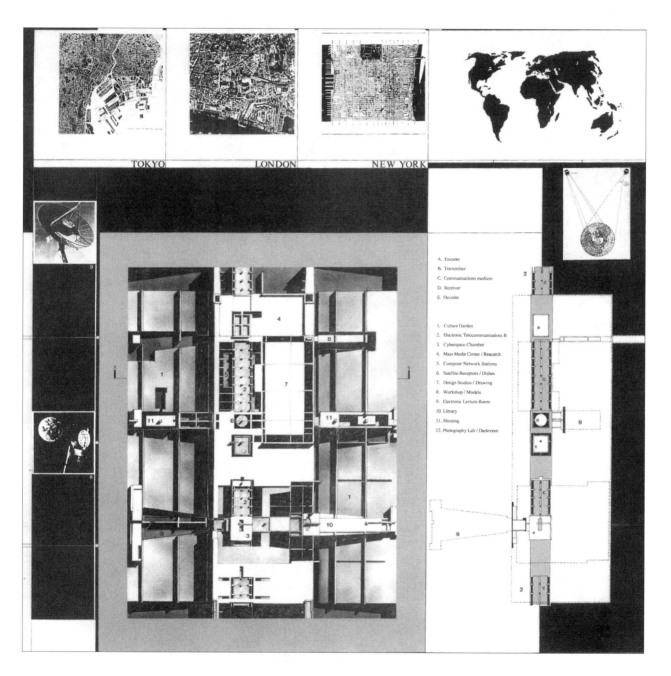

Drawing: Student project by Tim Shippey and Brian Weber
Prototype for a School of Architecture
Third Place, Central Glass Company of Japan
Courtesy of The University of Texas at Arlington
School of Architecture

This presentation nicely integrates text and photographs with drawings. See similar examples on pp. 558-559.

PRESENTATION FORMATS

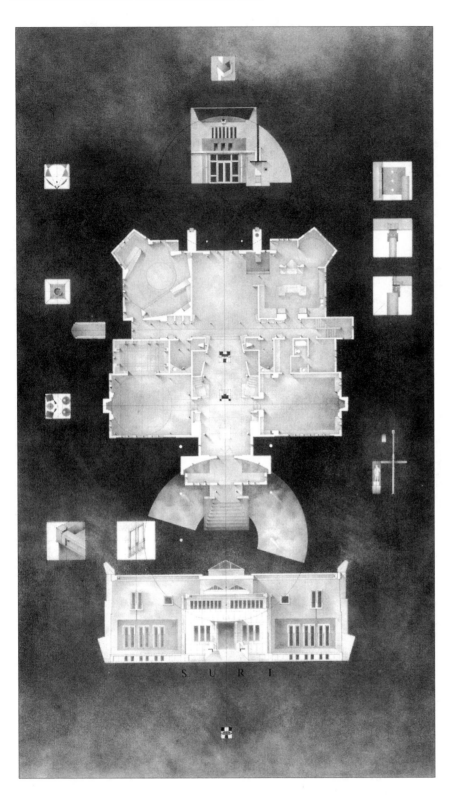

The rendering showcases the character of the building through the representation of several of its defining elements. The plan and front elevation dominate the drawing to express the overall formality of the design. Interior elevations and smaller details ring the edge of the drawing to provide a texture of scale and show off the attention to detail within the actual house. The technique of pencil on vellum, both hardline and graphite shadowing, is meant to lend a classical and stately air to the overall composition.
[ARCHITECT'S STATEMENT]

Drawing: Suri residence, Los Angeles, California
　　　　Plans, Elevations, and Details Composite.
Medium: Pencil and graphite on vellum, 32" × 54" (81.3 × 137 cm)
Scale: ³/₁₆"=1'0"
Courtesy of House + House Architects, San Francisco
Michael Banshke, Architectural Illustrator

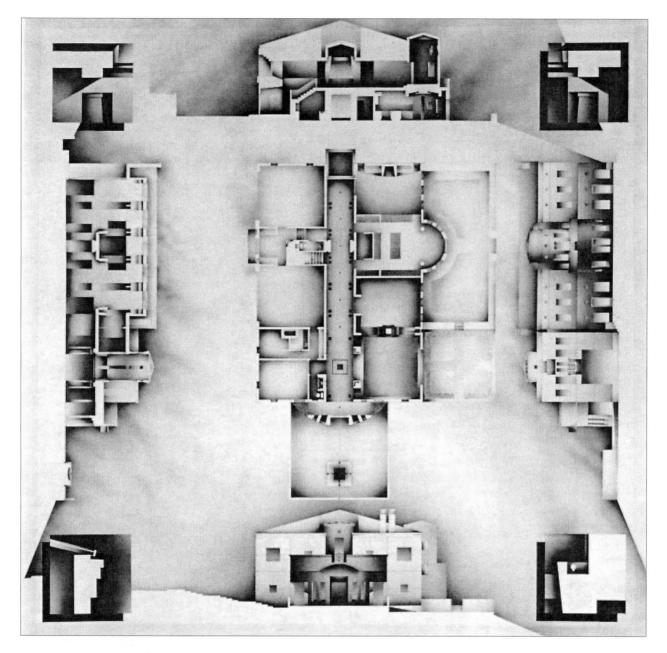

Drawing: Liu residence, Hillsborough, California
Fold-out plan, section and elevation composite
Medium: Airbrush using acrylic inks on cold-press illustration board,
40" 3 40" (101.6 3 101.6 cm)
Scale: 3/16"=1'0"
Courtesy of House + House, Architects, San Francisco
Mark David English, Inglese Architecture, Architectural Illustrator

The overall composition of the drawing emphasizes the importance of each of the four cardinal directions in the design concept and is statically balanced to reflect harmony. The plan, with white walls and lack of shadowing, illustrates its hieroglyphic nature which is literally intended to be "read." Elevations, sections, and details are carefully rendered to express the massive quality of the actual building. The four floating detail squares again emphasize the cardinal directions and pictorially bring the details closest to the viewer.
[ARCHITECT'S STATEMENT]

PRESENTATION FORMATS

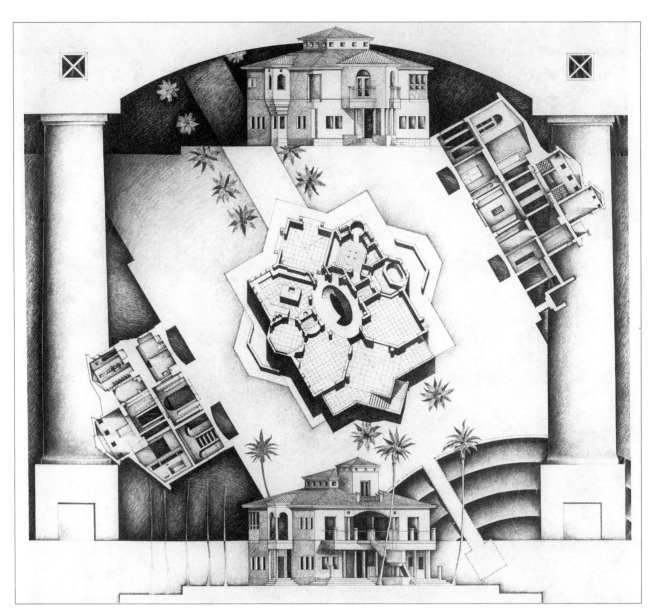

Drawing: Edwards residence, Beliz, Central America
            Fold-out sections, oblique elevations and enlarged detail frame composition
Medium: Ebony pencil on 1000H vellum, 40" × 40" (101.6 × 101.6 cm)
Scale: ³⁄₁₆"=1'0"
Courtesy of House + House Architects, San Francisco
Mark David English, Inglese Architecture, Architectural Illustrator

The overriding theme of the drawing emphasizes the importance of "stage-set design" inherent in the building itself.
Framing the main image of the drawing with an overscaled arch and column detail enhances the theatrical nature of
the drawing while solidly anchoring the dynamic elements within. The drawing is oriented to the cardinal directions
where north is the top of the page. The plan reflects its difference from north. As a result two oblique elevations can
show all facades and create a dynamic presentation.
[ARCHITECTURAL ILLUSTRATOR'S STATEMENT]

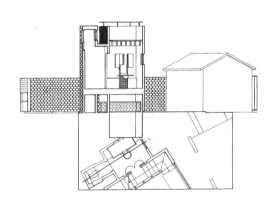

Drawings: Venice III/Bergren residence
Venice, California
21" × 31" (53.3 × 78.7 cm)
Medium: Graphite on Mylar
Courtesy of Morphosis
Thom Mayne and Kathleen Rea

This is a descriptive drawing, parallel to a model, to be used as a mechanism for evaluating a proposed solution. More abstractly, each one as a construction in itself, is the manifestation of the process by which we design.
[ARCHITECT'S STATEMENT]

PRESENTATION FORMATS

PRESENTATION FORMATS

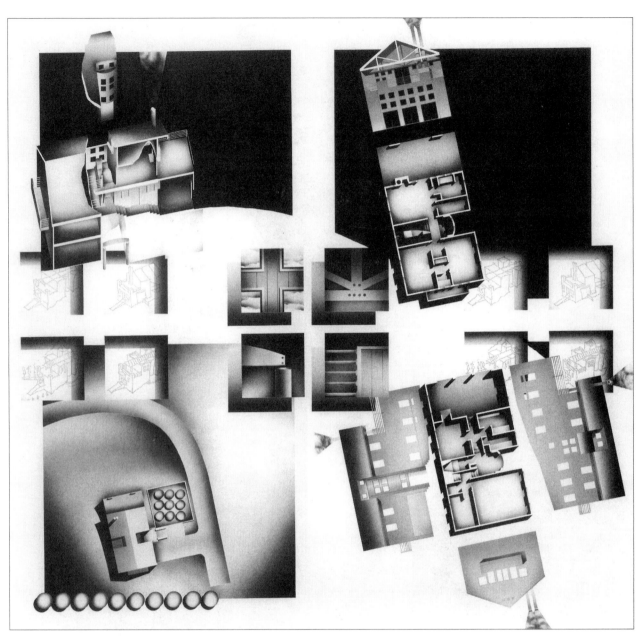

Drawing: Kerby residence, San Anselmo, California
        Exploded axonometric with details.
Medium: Airbrush using acrylic inks on cold-press illustration board. Line sketch copier image transfer using
mineral spirits, 30" × 30" (76.2 × 76.2 cm)
Scale: ⅛"=1'0"
Courtesy of House + House, Architects
Mark David English, Inglese Architecture, Architectural Illustrator

The drawing is conceived of as a collage of geometries, scales, and media arranged to represent the interaction between the very graphic building form and the natural setting. The partially exploded axonometric is small in scale to emphasize the overall prototypic "house" form, while the deviation in orientation to the drawing boundary emphasizes the natural setting. The four detail blocks contain the most important architectural "words" and lift off of the picture plane with dropped shadows in an arrangement mirroring a window pattern found as a theme in the house. The concept drawing sketches exhibit their primacy by seemingly receding into the picture plane.
[ARCHITECT'S STATEMENT]

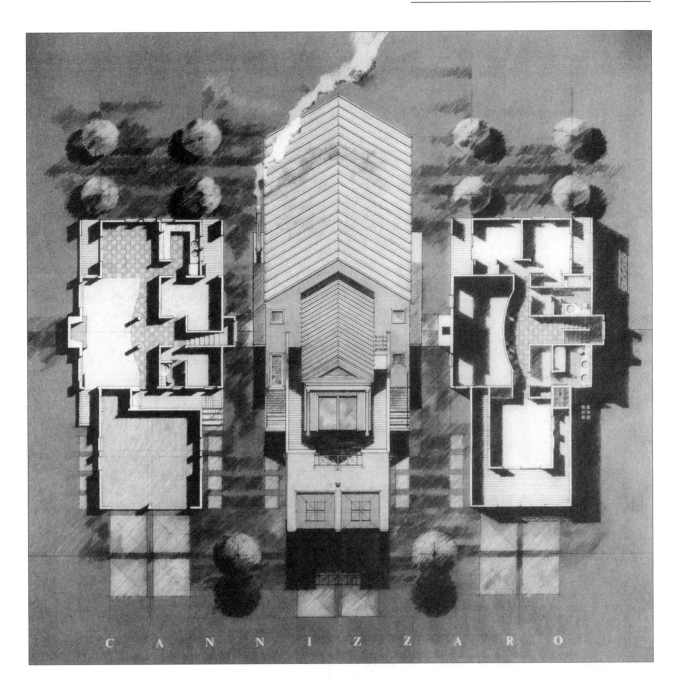

Drawing: Cannizzaro residence, Montara, California
            Plan and elevation-oblique composite.
Medium: Pencil, Prismacolor, and spray paint on vellum, 36" × 36" (91.4 × 91.4 cm)
Scale: ¼"=1'0"
Courtesy of House + House Architects
James Cathcart, Architectural Illustrator

This rendering technique was selected to emphasize the formal layout of the plan and the symmetrical nature of the front elevation. After the basic pencil work was completed, the back of the vellum was spray painted black to provide a gray background. Prismacolor was used on the back and front to create a desired soft pastel effect on the house and on the front to highlight the landscape elements.
[ARCHITECT'S STATEMENT]

PRESENTATION FORMATS

PRESENTATION FORMATS

Drawing: Hammonds residence, Berkeley, California
Medium: India ink and airbrush on Mylar
30" × 64" (76.2 × 162.6 cm)
Courtesy of House + House, Architects, San Francisco

This house was designed to replace one that was destroyed in Oakland's tragic firestorm. As in all of our projects, we began the design process by carefully analyzing the site—which in this case was a steep, narrow, downhill lot. We produced a series of relationship diagrams that studied circulation and spaces in relation to the site. We also built simple three-dimensional study models to investigate the impact of various massing alternatives. This series of axonometric sketch studies was done concurrently during the early schematic design process to analyze the building's roof shapes, open spaces, massing, fenestration, and scale. These studies were presented to our client along with our plans and models to convey our design process. We found this method of axonometric sketches a most valuable design tool.

At the conclusion of the project we decided to produce a formal rendering of the project. The final drawing consisted of three parts: an axonometric view of the house, a cross section through the house, and a series of details. Various angles were studied for the axonometric in order to best convey the building's form. When the overall layout was finalized, the final rendering was drawn with ink on Mylar. Airbursh was later applied to provide background tones and building shadows. We feel that this rendering successfully conveys the building's relationship to the land and its use of form and materials.
[ARCHITECT'S STATEMENT]

The rendering is a composite of drawings graphically laid out around the geometrics of the plan and interrelated through a system of regulating lines. By using multiple images it is possible to understand the building plan and spatial characteristics within the framework of a single drawing. The precision of pen and ink was needed to allow for the finer features to read clearly.

Design: A massive curving wall anchored in lava cliffs encircles and protects a tropical retreat on the island of Maui. By turning its back on the intense south and west sun, the house caters to clients who desired a site-specific home that utilizes the tropical island's unique character and lifestyle. Indoor and outdoor spaces are inseparably linked with disappearing walls that open each room onto outdoor lanais. Intricate screens cast glittering patterns of light and shadow as they trace the sun's path, while tropical vegetation cascades down the lava cliffs and spills inside, tying the feeling in this house to the lush, garden nature of the site. A linking tower offers distant views to the volcano of Haleakala and the Pacific Ocean beyond.
[ARCHITECT'S STATEMENT]

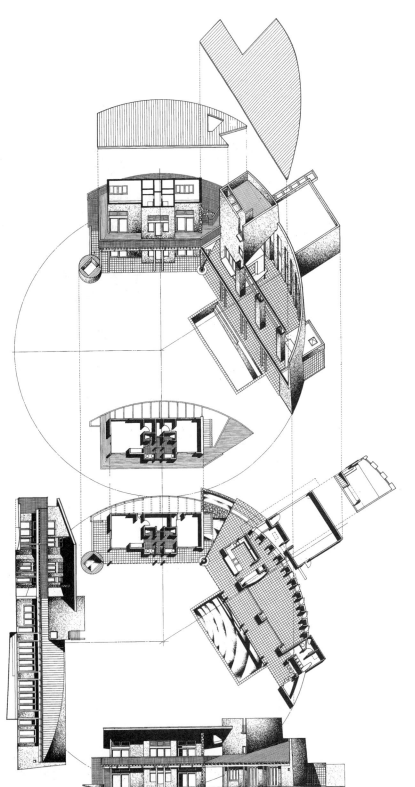

PRESENTATION FORMATS

Drawing: Ka Hale Kakuna residence, Maui, Hawaii
    Axonometric, Plan, and Elevation Composite
Medium: India ink and airbrush on mylar, 26" × 48" (66 × 121.9 cm)
Courtesy of House + House, Architects, San Francisco
David Haun, Architectural Illustrator

PRESENTATION FORMATS

This presentation uses a diagonal format, which is achieved by rotating a rectilinear grid format so that it makes an angle with the horizontal and vertical axes. This presentation format refers to the relationship between the new site and the present site of the existing facilities in the historic downtown district of Savannah, Georgia (grid pattern). The presentation is composed of the schematic diagrams on its form-evolution, the site plan, floor plans, elevations, sections, plan obliques, and descriptive text.

This presentation utilizes reversed printing in which white lines are drawn on a black background. White on black usually appears more intense than black on white.

Drawing: Student project
by Todd Heiser
Savannah Blue Print and Reprographics
Medium: Ink on Mylar
M. Saleh Uddin, Professor, Savannah College
of Art and Design, Savannah, GA;
Southern University, Baton Rouge, LA

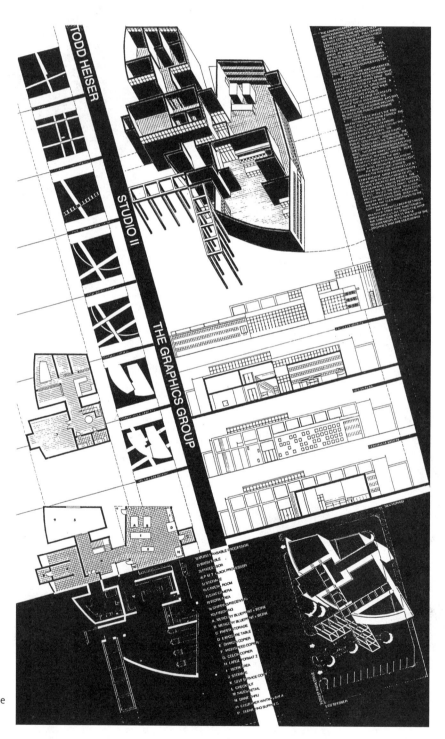

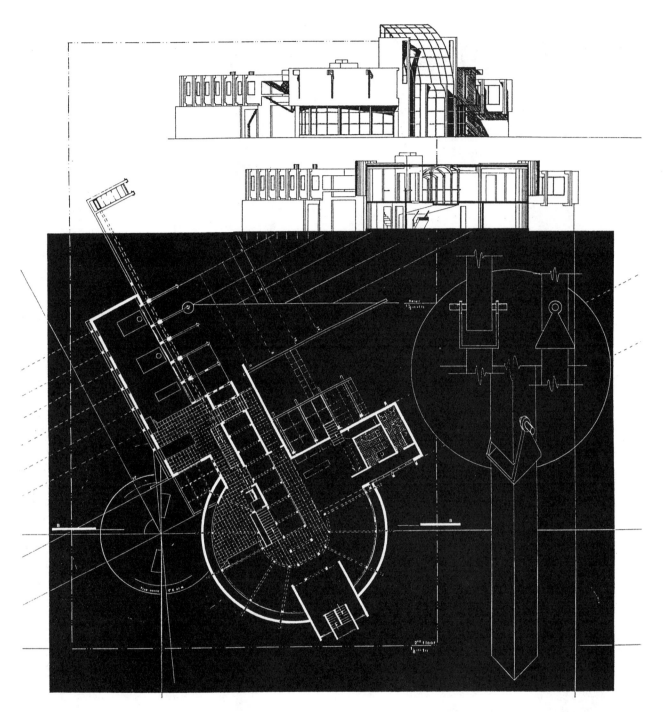

Drawing: Student project by Kevin Schellenbach
            Savannah Blue Print and Reprographics
Medium: Ink on vellum
M. Saleh Uddin, Professor, Savannah College of Art and Design,
Savannah, GA; Southern University, Baton Rouge, LA

*This presentation is one sheet of a three-sheet presen-
tation. The composition engages positive and negative
images of orthographic drawings. The reverse images of
the floor plan and the detail create a base line for the
section drawing. This particular technique effectively
separates and highlights section-elevation drawings
from floor plans and detail drawings.*
[PROFESSOR'S STATEMENT]

PRESENTATION FORMATS

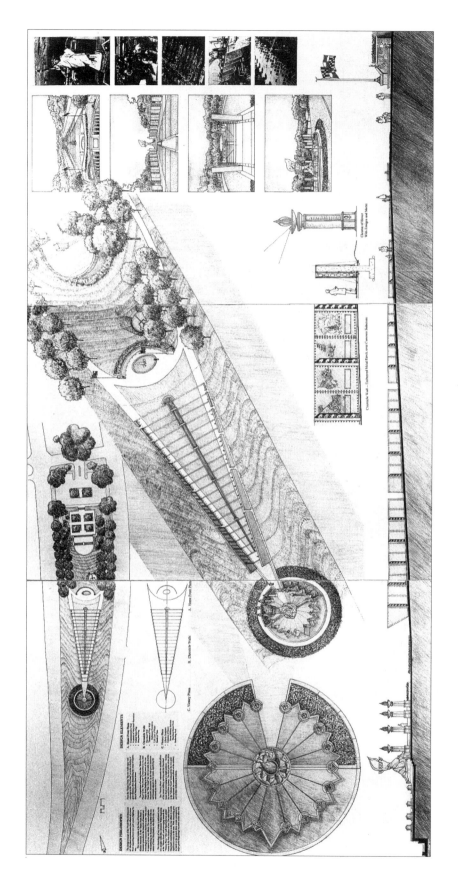

Drawings: World War II Memorial of Maryland Competition
3 Boards, 20" × 30" (50.8 × 76.2 cm) each, various scales
Medium: Felt pen and colored pencil on wheat colored yellow tracing
drymounted on Styrofoam board
Courtesy of William W. P. Chan, Don Duncan, Nicholas Linehan, and
Chris Rice, Competition team architects and designers

While there is no specific requirement for the presentation, other than the size of the boards, the designers felt strongly that an axonometric drawing should be the primary focus of the presentation. The remaining elements of the composition, such as site plan diagram, sections, details, and 3D sketches, should be positioned to visually explain the philosophy of the design. Therefore, adjacency of shapes is the key to the graphic composition.
[Competition Team Member's statement]

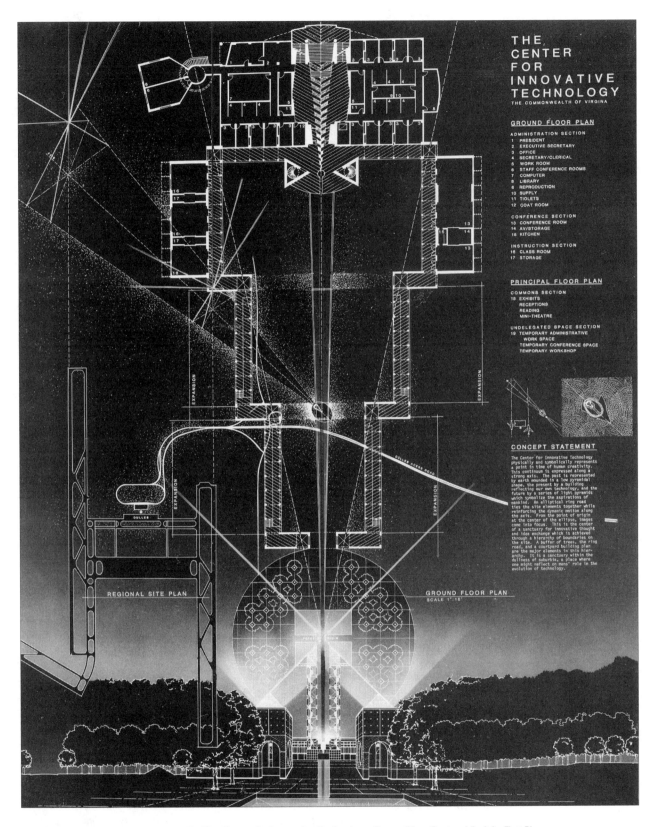

Drawings (this page and pp. 554–555): The Center for Innovative Technology Competition, Reston, Virginia, First Place
All three competition drawings: 24" × 30" (61 × 76.2 cm)
Competition Team Architects: William W. P. Chan, Peter Fillat, Rod Henderer, Tim Pellowski, and Mark Tuttle
Courtesy of William W. P. Chan, Architect

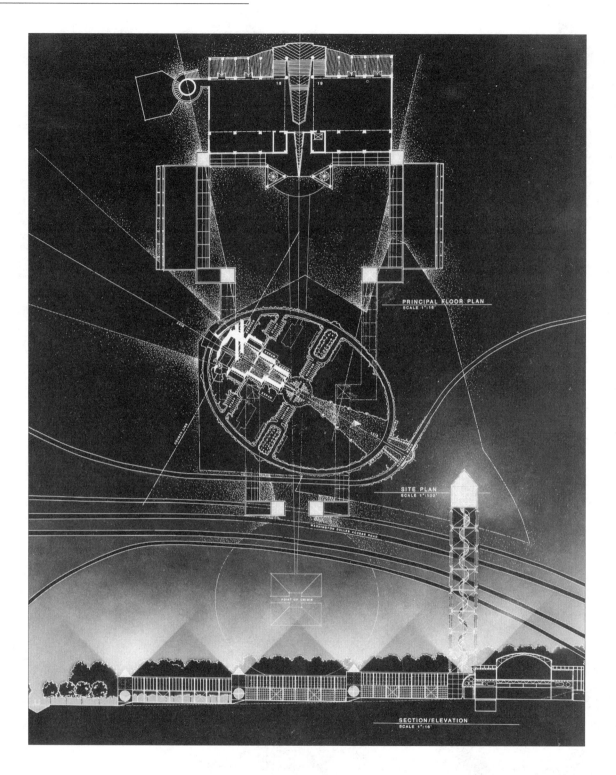

An objective of competition drawings is to achieve clarity of presentation while maintaining strong visual interest and complexity. Since the site plan, elevations, sections, plan obliques (axonometrics), and perspectives depict a specific aspect of the designed environment, we wanted to fuse them together into a graphic whole. Hence, we decided on a black background to unify these disparate elements. White lines on a pure black background appears too cold and lacking of a three-dimensional quality. A warm glow of airbrush yellow and orange was selectively sprayed onto the print to enhance the effect.
[ARCHITECT'S STATEMENT]

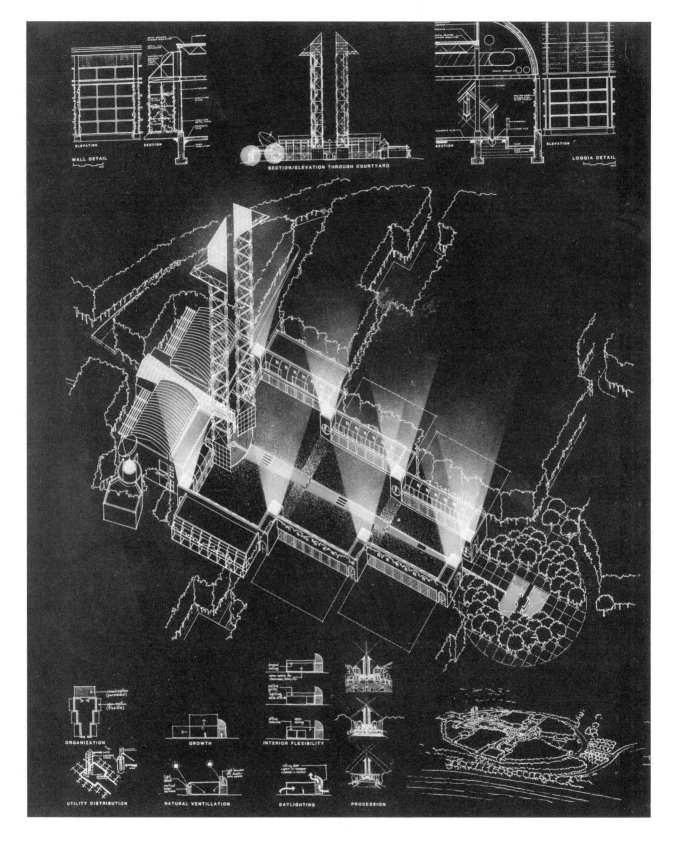

PRESENTATION FORMATS

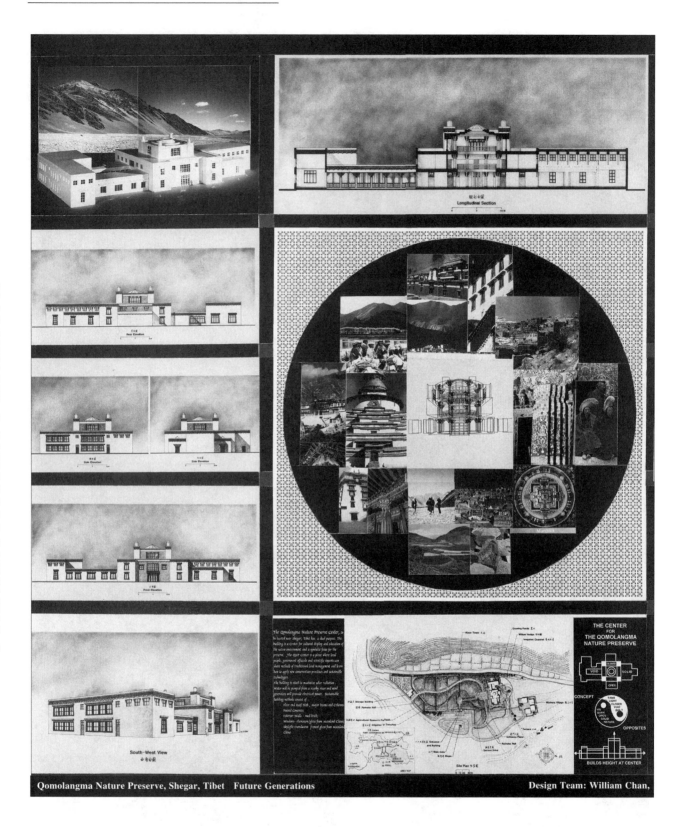

Qomolangma Nature Preserve, Shegar, Tibet   Future Generations   **Design Team: William Chan,**

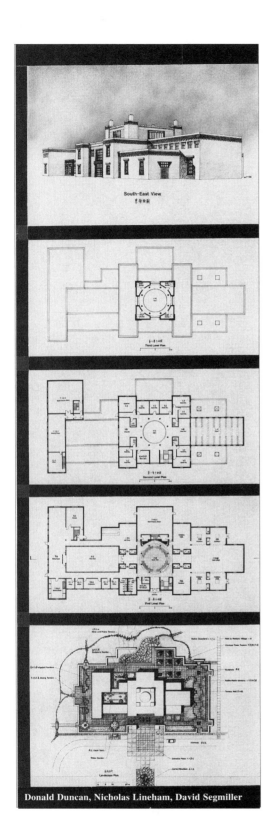

Donald Duncan, Nicholas Lineham, David Segmiller

Drawing: Center for Qomolangma Nature Preserve
          Shegar, Tibet
35" × 32" (88.9 × 81.3 cm). Scale: ⅛"=1'0"
Medium: Felt-tipped pen and Prismacolor on yellow trace
          The sky: magic marker and airbrush
Courtesy of the QNP Center Design Team
William W. P. Chan, Architect
Nicholas Linehan RLA, Don Duncan, David Segmiller, AIA

The presentation of the board is organized around the image of the "Mandala." By placing the mandala at the center of the composition, we allude to the geometry as the source of the design concept for the building. By using a photo montage of the Tibetan images, the building makes reference to its cultural heritage.
[ARCHITECT'S STATEMENT]

This presentation is based on a rectilinear grid system. In this case, the shape of the building fits nicely into rectangular units. These units can be expanded to accommodate the longitudinal section at a larger scale, the mandala image, and the site plan. Also note the clear hierarchy in the presentation typography. The largest lettering functions as the title. Progressively smaller lettering functions within the drawing format.

PRESENTATION FORMATS

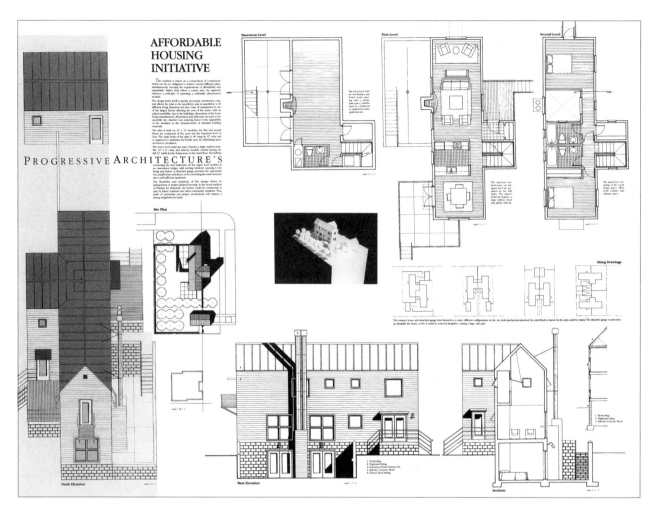

Drawing: Progressive Architecture's Affordable Housing Initiative
42" × 30" (106.7 × 76.2 cm), Scale: ¼"=1'0"
Medium: Ink and color on graphic film
Courtesy of Thomas K. Turkington, Architect,
Sandy & Babcock, Inc., Architecture & Planning

The design solution for this affordable housing study is based on a composition of components which can be re-con-figured to achieve different plans, simultaneously meeting the requirements of affordability and adaptability. Rather than follow a certain style, the approach observes a principle of repeating a uniformly dimensioned module. For this reason, the components of this drawing were laid out on a grid to achieve a regimented, orderly organization.
[ARCHITECT'S STATEMENT]

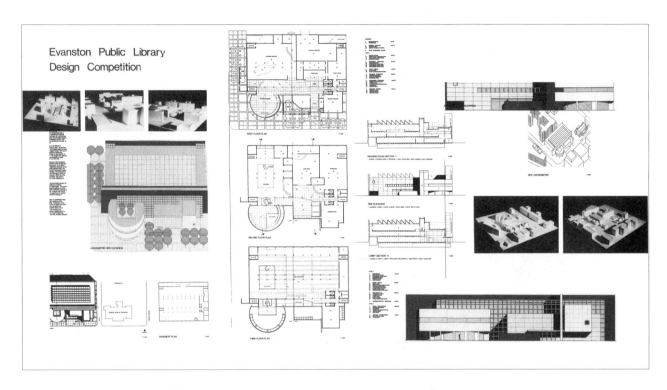

Evanston Public Library Design Competition, 72" × 36" (182.9 × 91.4 cm)
Scale of floor plans, elevations, axonometric: 1"=20'
Medium: Ink and color on graphic film
Courtesy of Michael Blakemore,
Sandy & Babcock, Inc., Architecture & Planning

*This concept for a new downtown library for the city of Evanston, Illinois, was conceived as "Library as Warehouse."
The design utilizes an orderly layout of space and separation of function, and incorporates exposed industrial materials
such as steel, glass, and brick. To further convey the design concept on this series of presentation boards, a straightforward layout has been used in which elements line up both horizontally and vertically, and an unpretentious sans serif
typestyle has been used for the titles and descriptive text.*
[ARCHITECT'S STATEMENT]

The presentation formats here and on p. 558 nicely incorporate the use of model photographs and planometric drawings.

PRESENTATION FORMATS

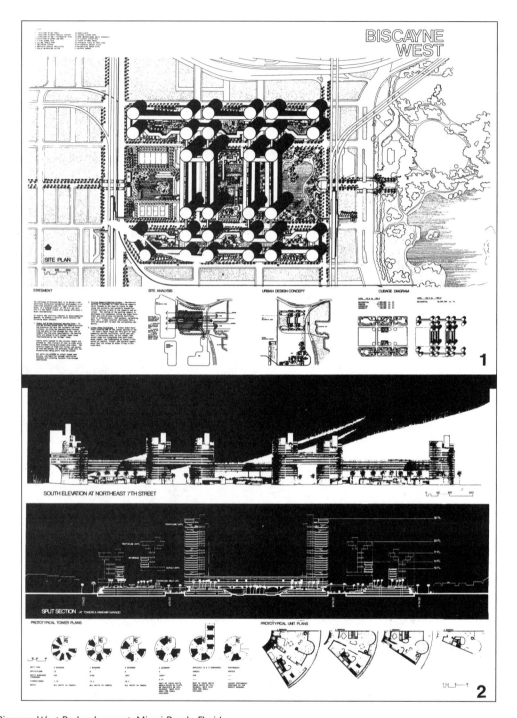

Drawings: Biscayne West Redevelopment, Miami Beach, Florida
Courtesy of Eugene Lew & Associates,
Architects, Planners, and Interior Designers

This is the design presentation for a national competition. The rules restricted the presentation to three 32" × 40" (81.3 × 101.6 cm) boards with no color allowed. To make the presentation stand out, we created a dramatic composition by using a photostat negative section, and by inking the sky black in the elevation. Small diagrams of the site plan and building plans with typed notes enabled numerous important design ideas to be conveyed in a limited board space. The design won an honorable mention.
[ARCHITECT'S STATEMENT]

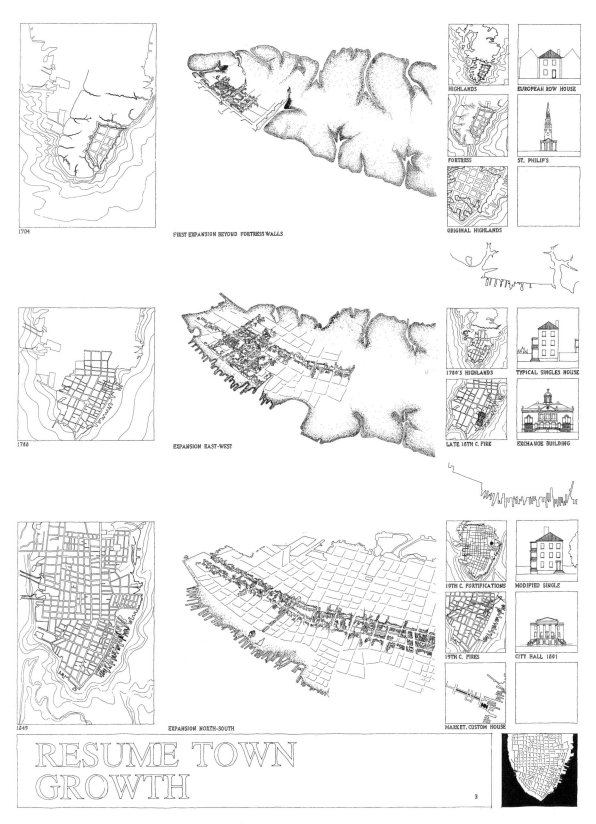

Drawings: Student projects, Charleston, South Carolina
Studio Instructor: George J. Martin and Stanley I. Hallet
Courtesy of The Catholic University of America
School of Architecture and Planning, Washington, D.C.

This is a long, linear, analytic documentation of many student projects which uses a simple grid layout format (see pp. 561–565). The pages connect sequentially.

LONG LINEAR DOCUMENT

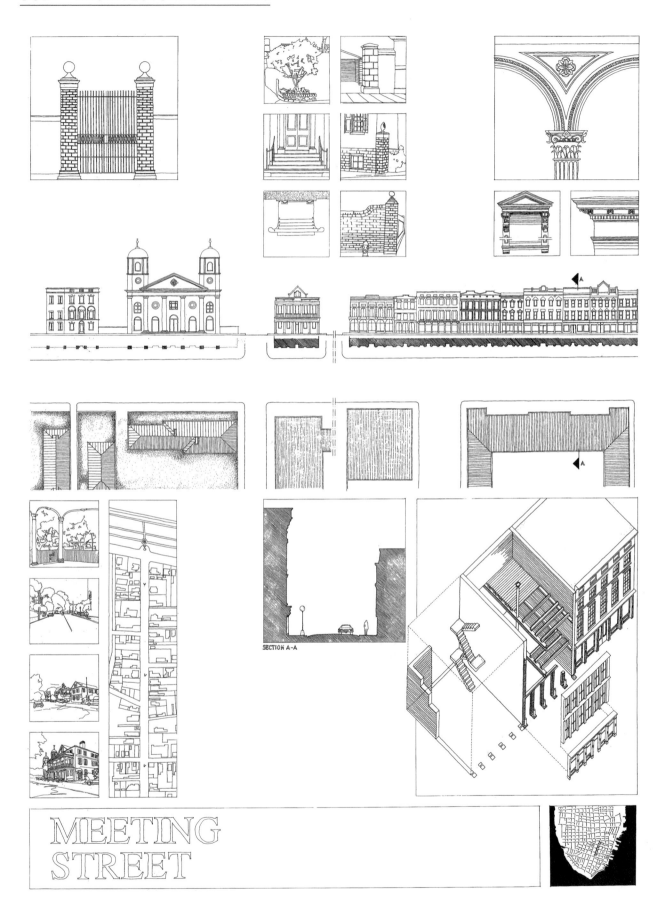

SECTION A-A

MEETING STREET

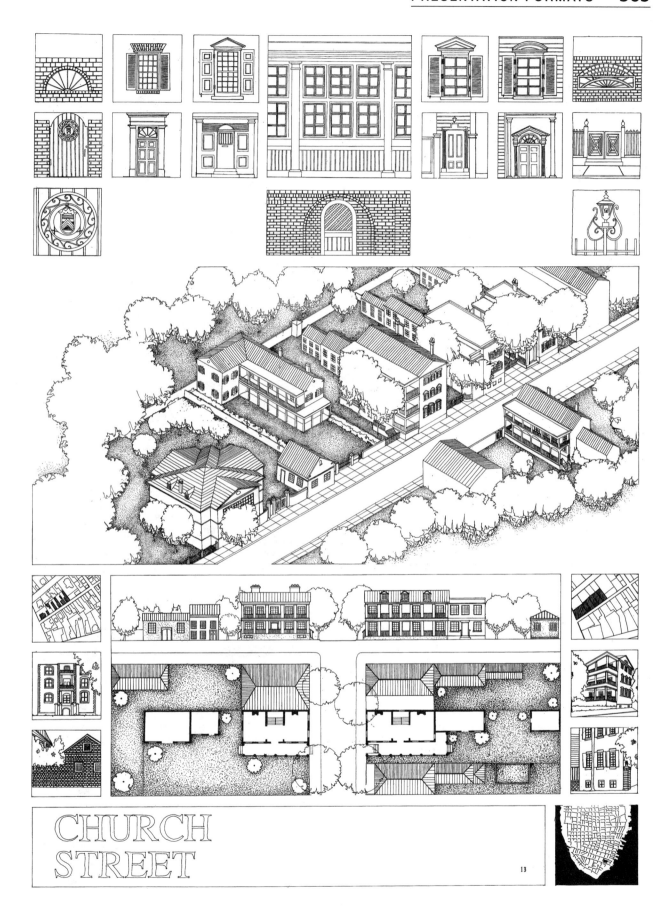

CHURCH
STREET

13

LONG LINEAR DOCUMENT

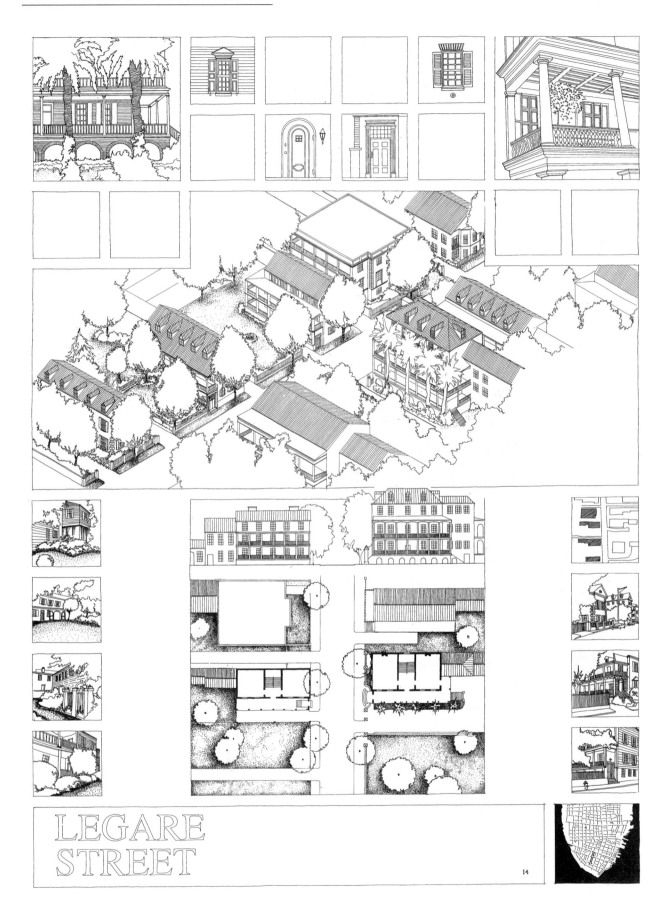

LEGARE
STREET

14

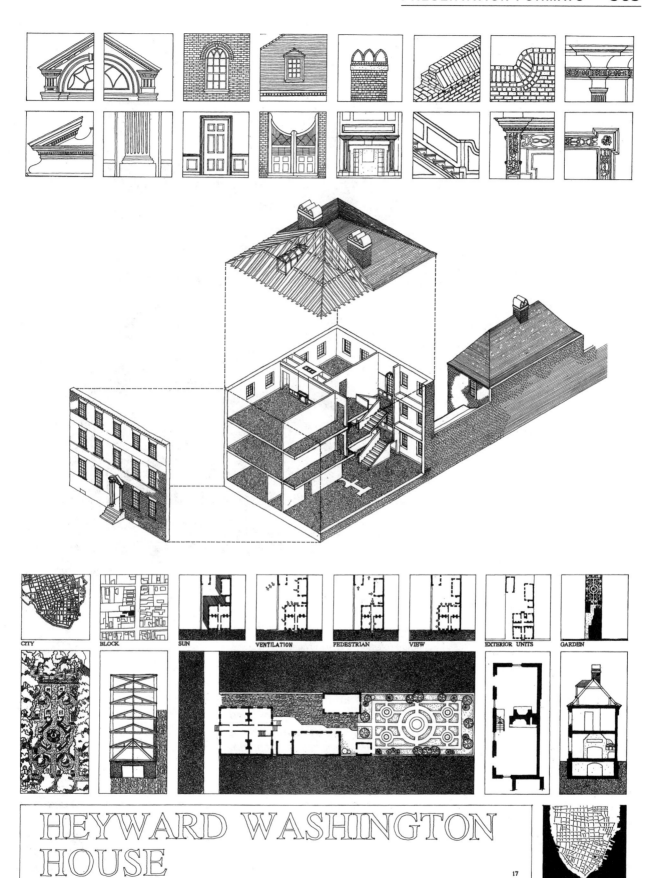

CITY   BLOCK   SUN   VENTILATION   PEDESTRIAN   VIEW   EXTERIOR UNITS   GARDEN

HEYWARD WASHINGTON HOUSE

17

LONG LINEAR DOCUMENT

ON-LINE PRESENTATION OF ARCHITECTURAL PROJECTS

Studio Professor: Valerian Miranda, Ph.D.
Courtesy of the Department of Architecture
Texas A & M University

The popularization of the information super-highway has ushered in a new medium for the presentation of architectural design. The medium has the ability to present projects consisting of hand sketches, computer-generated drawings and images, and dynamic animation of projects in an interactive manner that is not restricted by geographic boundaries. Interactivity allows geographically separated team members to contribute to the same project and also enables reviewers to offer comments about the project and presentation.

Access to the internet and the World Wide Web, a desktop computer, and a web browser are all that is necessary to participate in this medium of presentation. Essentially, digital files of drawings, images, and text are organized and linked together by HTML (HyperText Markup Language) documents accessible from a "home page." Motion can be added to three-dimensional models using VRML (Virtual Reality Modeling Language) and linked to the presentation. Additionally, sound can be added to either the static images or the animated models. Tools to assist in the preparation of on-line presentations in this new exciting medium are constantly being developed and refined, and are often available free of cost on the World Wide Web.

[STUDIO PROFESSOR'S STATEMENT]

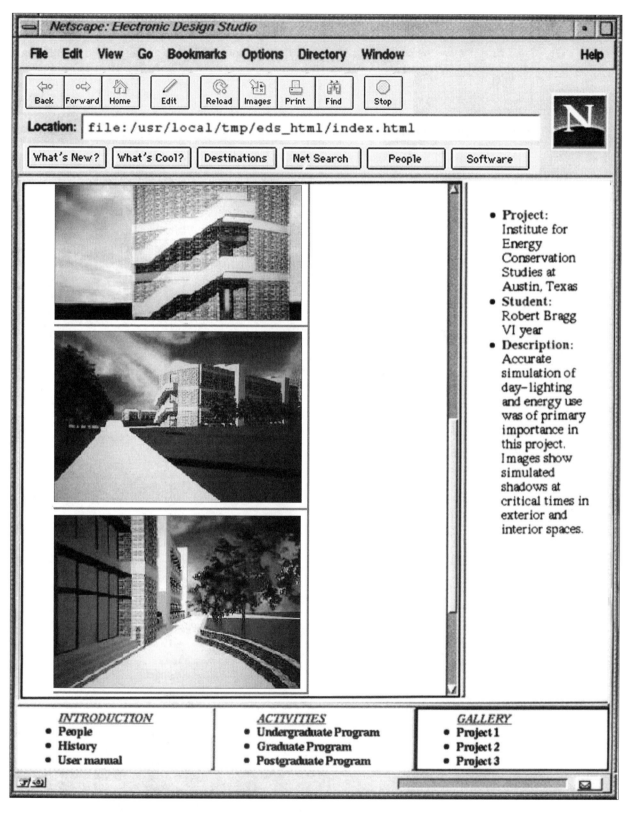

Internet images: Student project by Robert Bragg
Institute for Energy Conservation Studies, Austin, Texas
Studio Professor: Valerian Miranda, Ph.D.
Courtesy of the Department of Architecture
Texas A & M University

ON-LINE PRESENTATION OF ARCHITECTURAL PROJECTS

ON-LINE PRESENTATION OF ARCHITECTURAL PROJECTS

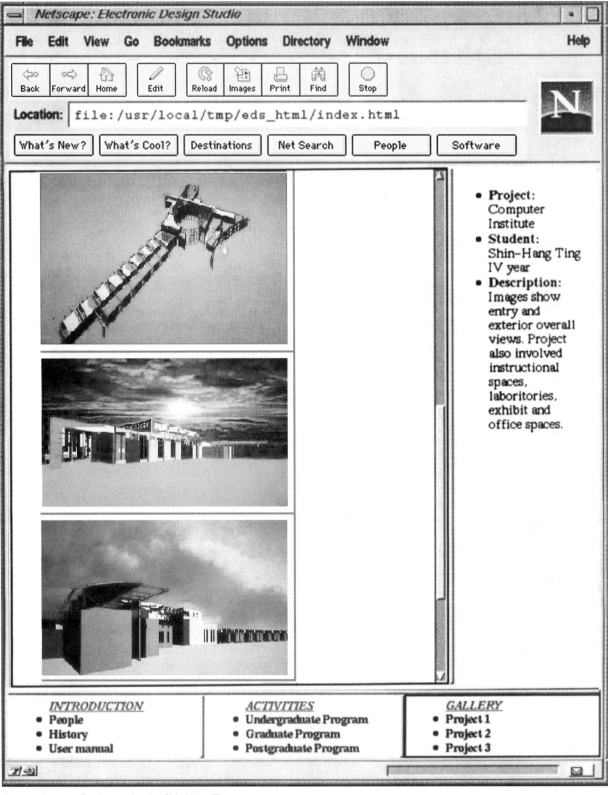

Internet images: Student project by Shin-Hang Ting
                 Computer Institute
Studio professor: Valerian Miranda, Ph.D.
Courtesy of the Department of Architecture
Texas A & M University

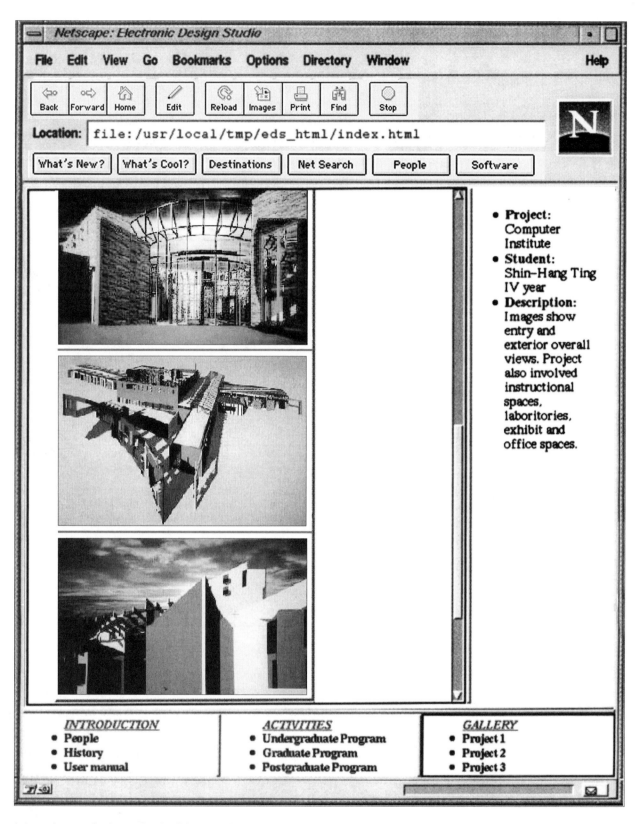

Internet images: Student project by Shin-Hang Ting
                  Computer Institute
Studio professor: Valerian Miranda, Ph.D.
Courtesy of the Department of Architecture
Texas A & M University

14

Exotics

Exotics refers to unusual presentation drawings. Recently the trend has been toward more experimentation in architectural drawing techniques. New types of composite drawings, such as see-through drawings, superimposed drawings, and hybrid drawings, are becoming commonplace in architectural design competitions. These kinds of drawings should not be attempted until you have a thorough knowledge and understanding of all of the basic drawing systems. A handful of these examples are showcased in this chapter.

Exotics

Topic

Composite Drawings

Reference

Composite Drawing. Uddin 1996. McGraw-Hill.

Cross References

For pp. 569–571   See p. 120
For p. 582   See p. 56
For p. 583   See pp. 102–103
For pp. 586–589   See pp. 114–117
For p. 593   See pp. 118–119

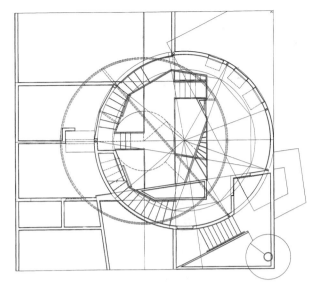

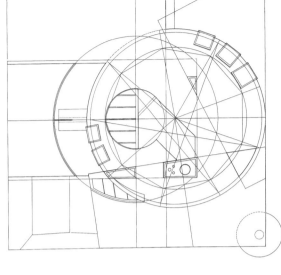

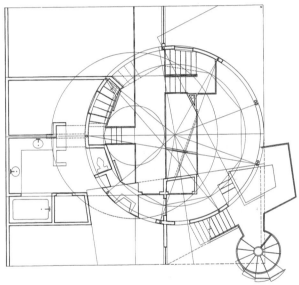

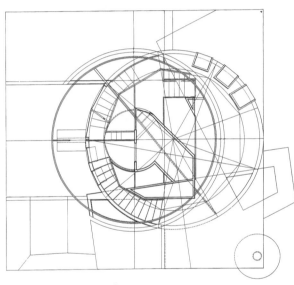

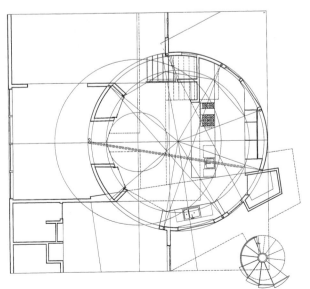

Drawings: Lawson/Westen House, Los Angeles, California
1st, 2nd, 3rd, 4th, and Roof Floor Plans
with Geometric Map Overlay
Medium: Ink on Mylar
Courtesy of Eric Owen Moss, Architects

SUPERIMPOSED PLANS

SECTION PLAN

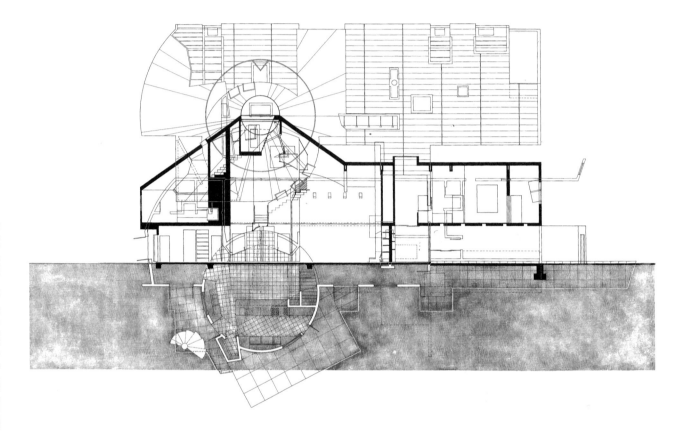

Drawing: Lawson/Westen House, Los Angeles, California
Medium: Ink on Mylar (shaded area is an ink wash)
Composite section plan
Courtesy of Eric Owen Moss, Architects

...the interrelation of the floor plan, roof plan, and section.
[ARCHITECT'S STATEMENT]

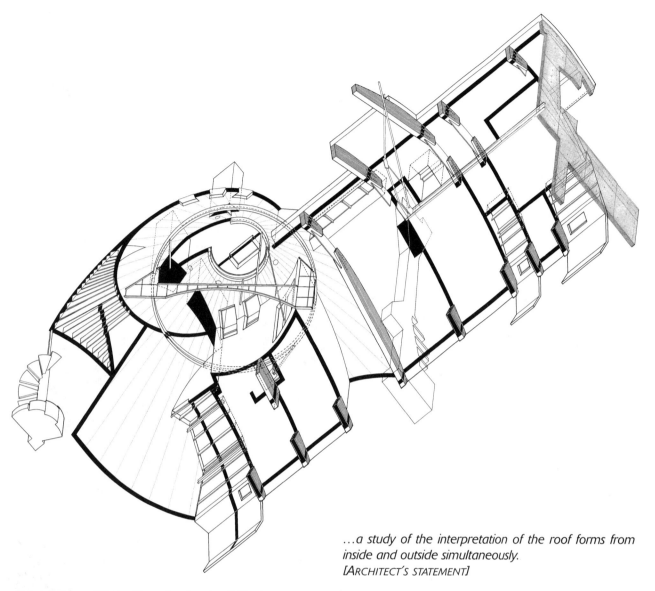

WORM'S-EYE VIEW

...a study of the interpretation of the roof forms from inside and outside simultaneously.
[*ARCHITECT'S STATEMENT*]

Drawing: Lawson/Westen House, Los Angeles, California
Medium: Ink on Mylar
Courtesy of Eric Owen Moss, Architects

Worm's-eye views are often difficult to decipher. Students and design professionals should refrain from doing this type of drawing unless they can completely understand what they have drawn. When the geometric forms of the design are complex, the interpretation of a drawn worm's-eye of that design will generally be difficult.

PERSPECTIVE CUT-AWAY VIEW

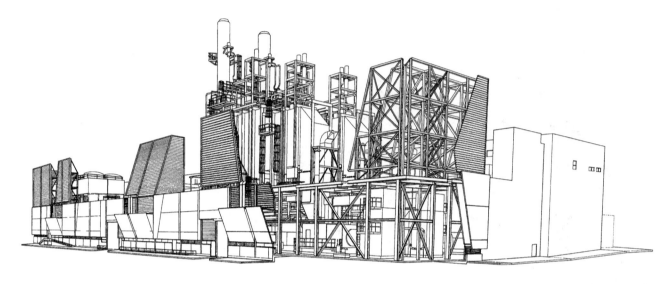

Drawing: Central Chiller Plant and Cogeneration Facility, UCLA
27" × 56" (68.6 × 142.2 cm)
Medium: Ink on Mylar
Cut-away view
Courtesy of Jones, Partners: Architecture

This project's southern facade toys with the idea of "screening" from view the equipment contained within. This drawing strips away that scrim in order to expose the building's systems and implies that the louvered screens along the cornice line are merely an extension of those systems—a manifestation of the power plant's ambivalent desires to be both prominent and anonymous. Whereas an exploded view is typically used to highlight the autonomy of individual elements, this drawings seek to confer a sense of integration to the building's varied parts.
[ARCHITECT'S STATEMENT]

The project sought to create a lobby from covered
outdoor spaces between
three buildings. Perspec-
tive sketches gave users
not accustomed to reading
plans a glimpse of what
was proposed. The plan in
perspective showed furni-
ture and wall heights for
scale and ambiance. The
vi-gnettes showed the
character of the project.
[Architect's statement]

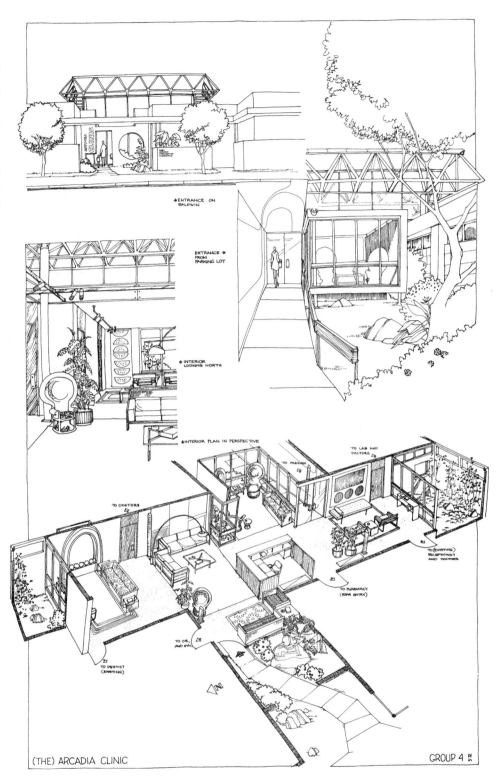

PERSPECTIVE CUT-AWAY VIEW

Drawing: Arcadia Clinic, Arcadia, California
Medium: Ink
Group Four Architecture, Research & Planning
Courtesy of Robin Chiang, Architect and Architectural Illustrator

MIRROR-IMAGE AXONOMETRIC

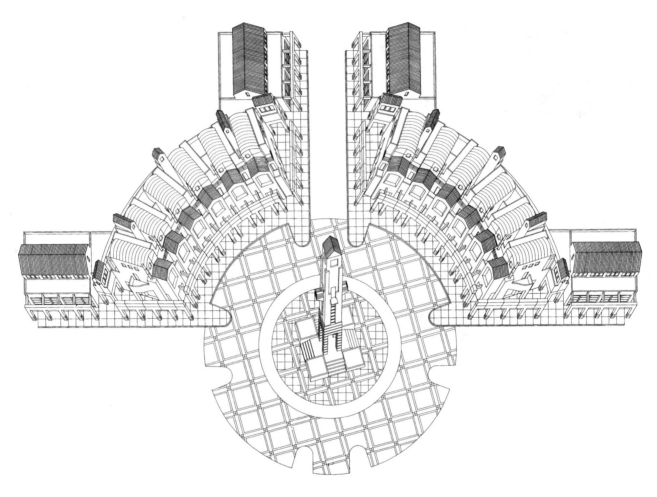

Drawing: Black Mountain Ranch, San Diego County, California
36" × 24" (91.4 × 61 cm), Scale: 1"=20'
Medium: Ink on Mylar
Courtesy of Sandy & Babcock Inc., Architecture & Planning

While this "mirror-image" axonometric drawing is unconventional, it lends itself to the symmetry of the plan and gives the impression of a more realistic birds-eye view.
[ARCHITECT'S STATEMENT]

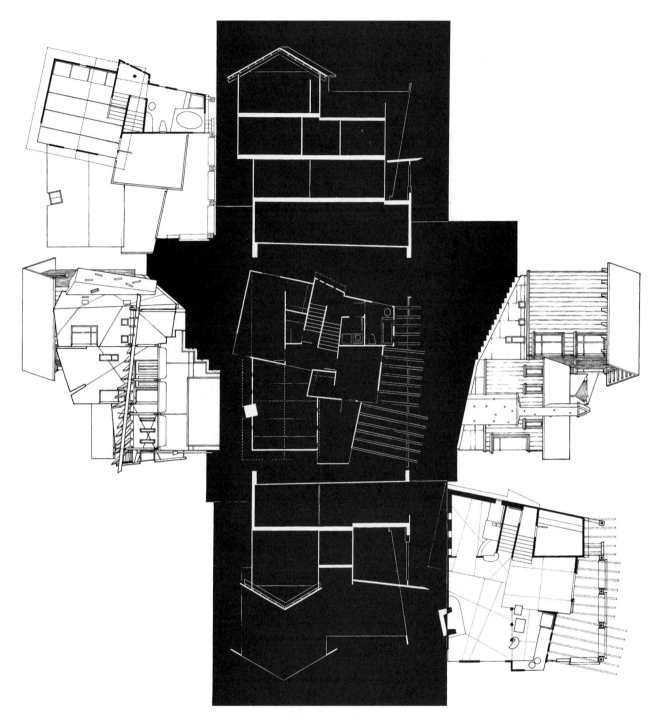

COMPOSITE DRAWING

Drawing: Revenge of the stuccoids house, Berkeley, California
24" × 36" (61 × 91.4 cm), Scale: ¼"=1'0"
Medium: Ink on canson paper
Courtesy of David Baker Associates Architects and Nancy Whitcombe

The house represented by this drawing is complex, a collage of discrete ideas and architectural strategies. The complexity of the drawing is compatible with that of the project: simple plans, elevations, and sections alone would not relate the underlying emotional content of the design. The subliminal design intent described intuitively in this composite drawing is greater than the sum of the linear information contained in the separate technical drawings that are its components.
[ARCHITECT'S STATEMENT]

COMPOSITE DRAWING

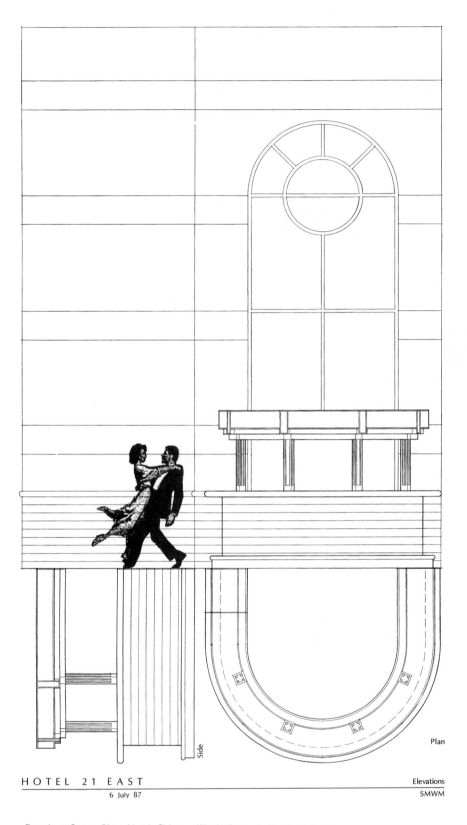

HOTEL 21 EAST

6 July 87

Side

Plan

Elevations

SMWM

This composite drawing enables the professional viewer to reach an understanding of the three-dimensional relationships of the objects. Elements of the architectural vocabulary show their clear interdependence in the total composition.
[ARCHITECT'S STATEMENT]

Drawing: Sutton Place Hotel, Chicago, Illinois (formerly Hotel 21 East)
20" × 20" (50.8 × 50.8 cm), Scale: ⅛"=1'0"
Medium: Ink on vellum (dancers—pasteup image)
Courtesy of Simon Martin–Vegue Winkelstein Moris, Interior Design
First Floor Axonometrics by Ron Aguila

Y-axis

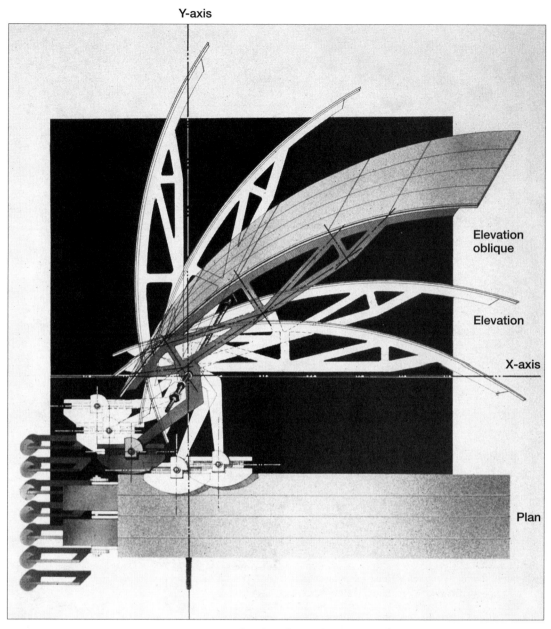

Elevation
oblique

Elevation

X-axis

Plan

Drawing: Composite plan, elevation and elevation oblique
        National Laboratories, Ltd., Dhaka, Bangladesh
Medium: Pen and ink line drawing and pattern film
Courtesy of M. Saleh Uddin, Professor,
Savannah College of Art and Design, Savannah, GA;
Southern University School of Architecture, Baton Rouge, LA

COMPOSITE DRAWING

This drawing illustrates movement of a nonstationary architectural element using a 90° sequential rotation on a horizontal axis, and incorporating a counterweight. The horizontal and vertical axes and the pivot point were established first. The middle unit showing an elevation oblique was drawn with greater detail and darker value than the other four identical units. The plan drawing was conceived as a referential drawing on a second layer. The black background below the horizontal axis was created to unify as well as to segregate the plan drawing from the rotating elevation drawings.
[PROFESSOR'S STATEMENT]

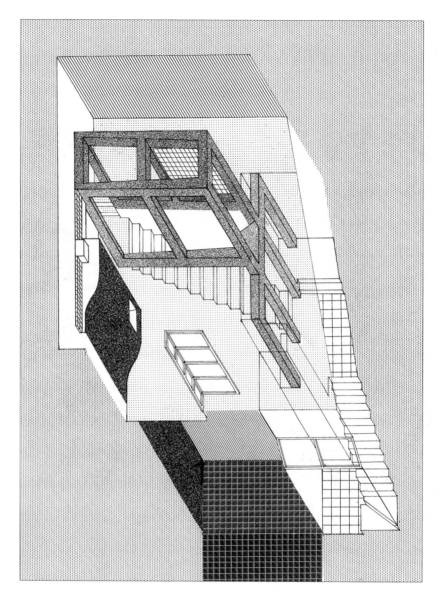

Drawing: Curtis house (1988), San Francisco, California
10⅝" × 15" (27 × 38.1 cm), Scale: ¼"=1'0"
Medium: Pen and ink (Rapidograph) and shading films
Courtesy of James Shay, AIA Architect

The primary spatial organization device in this house is the dark framework indicated in the drawing by line and shade. Secondary building elements, such as planes and shaded stairs, are indicated by line and film to establish context. [ARCHITECT'S STATEMENT]

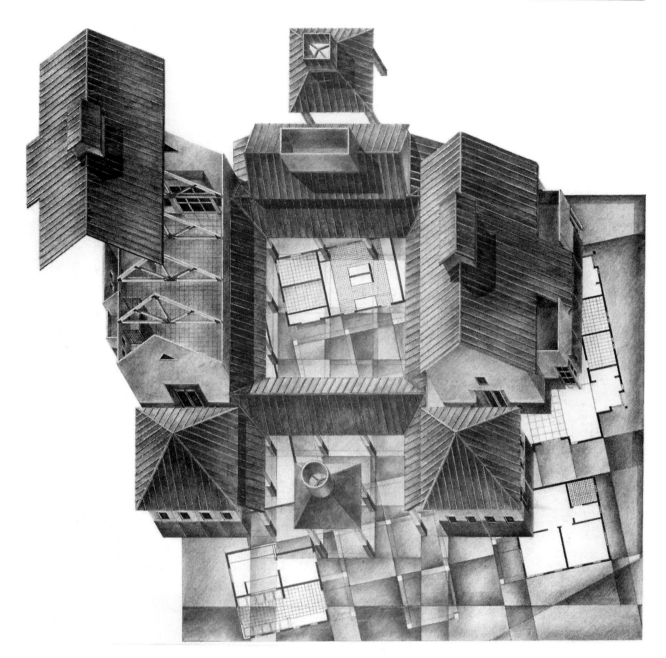

Drawing: Rancho Sespe II, Piru, California
30" × 33" (76.2 × 83.8 cm), Scale: 3/32"=1'0"
Medium: Pencil
Courtesy of John V. Mutlow, FAIA, Architects

The 6B draughtsman pencil rendering of the community building axonometric drawing with shade and shadow pro-
vides an understanding of the three-dimensional form. The axonometric drawing illustrates the roofscape and accen-
tuates the courtyard and its enclosure. The exploded roof axon and the rendered floor plan as background imply and
demonstrate the richness of the spaces and activities.
[ARCHITECT'S STATEMENT]

SUPERIMPOSED COMPOSITE DRAWING

Drawing: Blades residence, Goleta, California
Medium: Graphite on Mylar
Courtesy of Morphosis and Thom Mayne with Sarah Allan, Architects

Superimposed drawings can have the look of a beautiful artistic composition. Their drawback is that they can become confusing in the myriad array of lines and forms used to compose them. Sometimes only the originator can understand them.

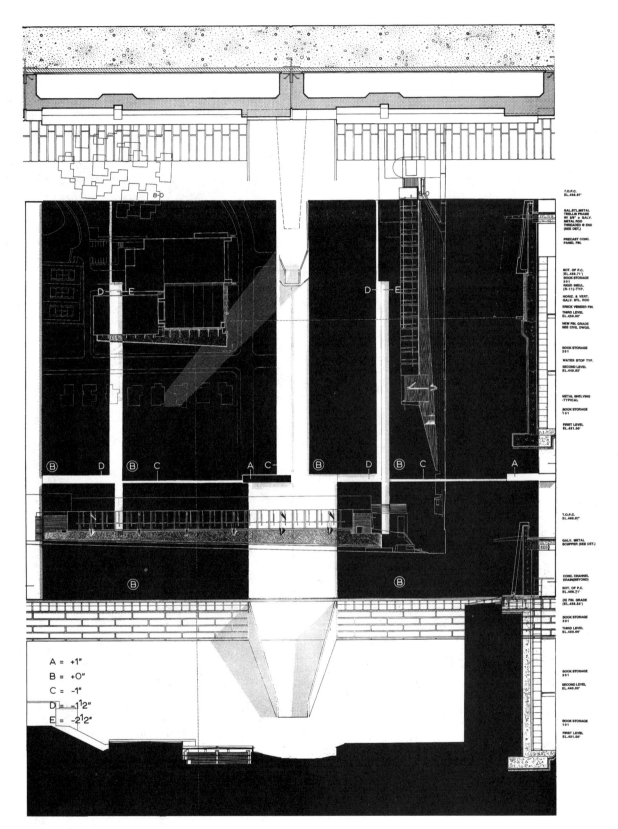

SUPERIMPOSED COMPOSITE DRAWING

A = +1"
B = +0"
C = -1"
D = -1½"
E = -2½"

Drawing: UCLA southern regional library
30" × 40" (76.2 × 101.6 cm), Scale: ⅛"=1'0"
Medium: Ink and reversed printing
Courtesy of Franklin D. Israel Design Associates, Inc., Architects

EXPLODED AXONOMETRIC AND PLAN

The colored pencil rendering of the quadruplex dwelling units axonometric drawing provides the viewer with a direct connection between the plan and the three-dimensional form of the building. The axonometric drawing illustrates how individual massing is combined to become one building. The combination of axonometric and floor plan provides an understanding of the three-dimensional form which is defined by the plan.
[ARCHITECT'S STATEMENT]

Drawing: Cabrillo Village, Saticoy, California
20" × 24" (50.8 × 61 cm), Scale: ⅛"=1'0"
Medium: Colored pencil
Courtesy of John V. Mutlow, FAIA, Architects

The drawing composite dramatically presents the main spatial ordering system of the shed-roofed volumes of the building by presenting the roof as a see-through membrane. The slope of the land is shown on the spatial section of part of the main image. The color palette is metaphorical: green for natural surfaces, pink for artificial interior surfaces, gray for artificial exterior surfaces and black as the universal background.

[ARCHITECT'S STATEMENT]

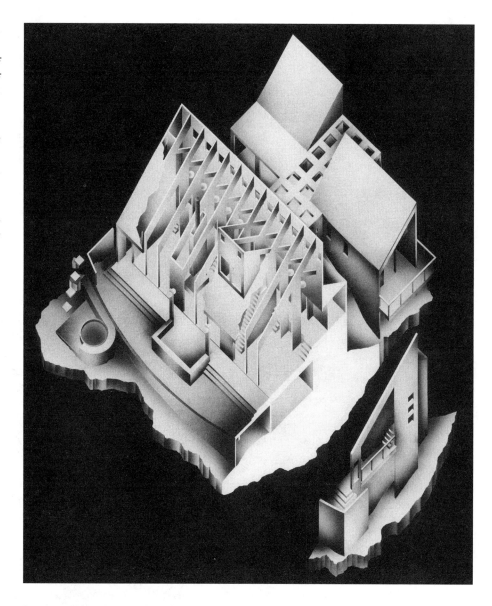

Drawing: Abbott–Elpers residence, Woodside, California
Composite: Exploded/eroded axonometric
Medium: Airbrush using india ink and acrylic inks on cold-press illustration board, 30" × 30"
(76.2 × 76.2 cm)
Scale: ¼"=1'0"
Courtesy of House + House, Architects
Mark David English, Inglese Architecture, Architectural Illustrator

EXPLODED/ERODED AXONOMETRIC

EXPLODED ISOMETRIC

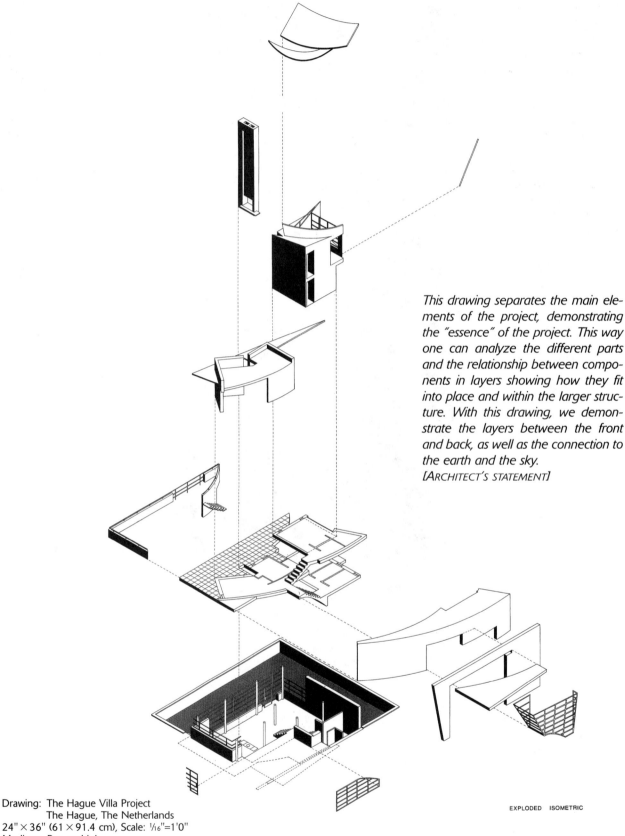

This drawing separates the main elements of the project, demonstrating the "essence" of the project. This way one can analyze the different parts and the relationship between components in layers showing how they fit into place and within the larger structure. With this drawing, we demonstrate the layers between the front and back, as well as the connection to the earth and the sky.
[ARCHITECT'S STATEMENT]

EXPLODED ISOMETRIC

Drawing: The Hague Villa Project
The Hague, The Netherlands
24" × 36" (61 × 91.4 cm), Scale: 1/16"=1'0"
Medium: Pen and ink
Courtesy of Hariri & Hariri, Architects

The element axonometric drawing is a composition of design elements: public street facade, private courtyard facade, axis, focal point, and circulation elements. The drawing visually analyzes the different design approaches to and the relationship between the public street and the private courtyard, and the sequence of circulation spaces that connect the major street to the inner courtyard, with the linkage of the street entry porch to the rotated courtyard gazebo, the axis, and the focal point. The floor plan anchors the drawing as a basic reference.

[ARCHITECT'S STATEMENT]

ELEMENT AXONOMETRIC

Drawing: Yorkshire Terrace, Los Angeles, California
34" × 42" (86.4 × 106.7 cm), Scale: ⅛"=1'0"
Medium: Ink
Courtesy of John V. Mutlow, FAIA, Architects

NONVERTICAL Z-AXIS STEPPED PLAN

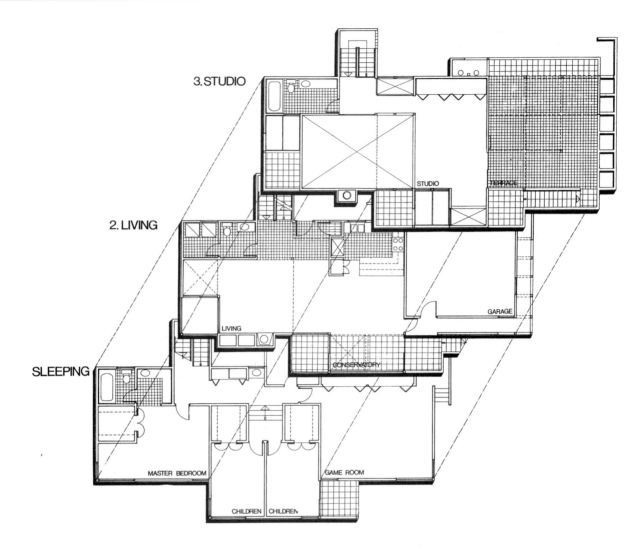

3. STUDIO

STUDIO

TERRACE

2. LIVING

GARAGE

LIVING

SLEEPING

CONSERVATORY

MASTER BEDROOM

GAME ROOM

CHILDREN CHILDREN

Drawing: Galor residence, Los Angeles, California
28" × 28" (71.1 × 71.1 cm), Scale: ¼"=1'0"
Medium: Ink
Courtesy of John V. Mutlow, FAIA, Architects

The stepped plans provide a direct interrelationship between the floors. The shaded edge of the floor identifies the service and outdoor areas and contrasts the private and public, all within the 6'8" module and 20'0" module.
[ARCHITECT'S STATEMENT]

This hybrid (see p. 604) drawing combines a one-point persective with a vertically expanded plan oblique. Note that the perspective convergence results in the plan being enlarged, allowing for a clearer view of many details.

This drawing was made in order to illustrate a relation between a plan (in this case a floor plan) and certain three-dimensional elements contained within that plan. The plan is made as a figure/ground drawing in which the central void space of the office is highlighted. It is out of that void space that the three-dimensional parts are drawn as an axonometric projection.
[ARCHITECT'S STATEMENT]

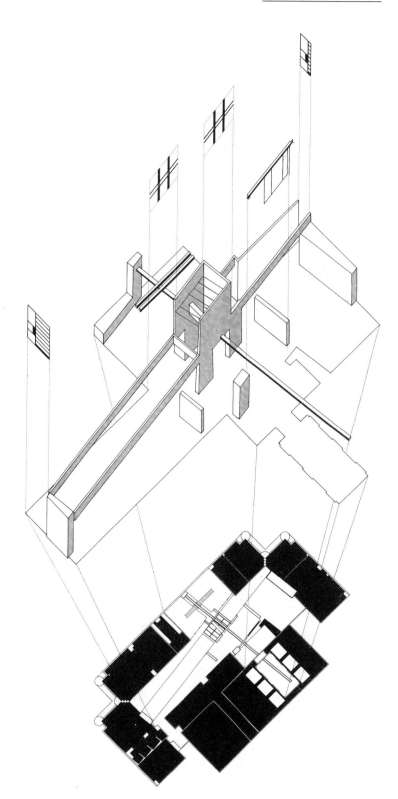

ENLARGED AND EXPANDED VIEW

Drawing: World Savings Center Executive Suite, Oakland, California
14" × 26" (35.6 × 66 cm), Scale: ⅛"=1'0"
Medium: Ink on vellum
Courtesy of Jim Jennings, Architect, of Jennings + Stout, Architects
Drawn by Jim Jennings

THE EXPLODED UP VIEW

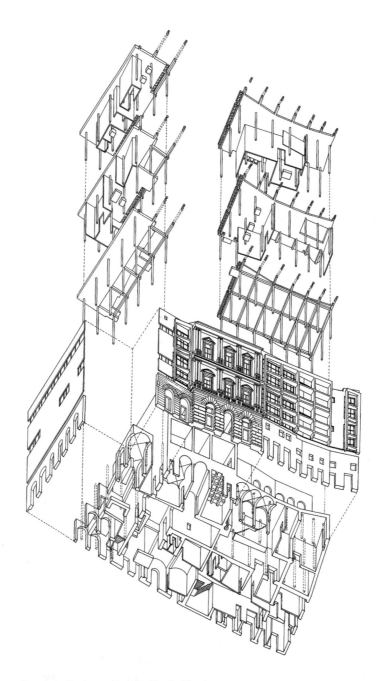

Drawing: Student project by Corvin Matei
Medium: Ink on Mylar, 12" × 20" (30.5 × 50.8 cm), Scale: ¹⁄₁₆"=1'0"
Courtesy of the University of Texas at Arlington
School of Architecture

This is an exploded worm's-eye up view with two facades exploded horizontally and three floor levels exploded vertically.

PERSPECTIVE DIAGRAM

EXPLODED AXONOMETRIC

Drawings: Click & Flick Agency, West Hollywood, California
Perspective 20" × 30" (50.8 × 76.2 cm), Scale: ⅛"=1'0"
Axonometric 24" × 30" (61 × 76.2 cm), Scale: ⅛"=1'0"
Courtesy of Hodgetts & Fung, Design Associates Architects
Lynn Batsch, project architect

This exploded axonometric up view shows that exploded or expanded elements can in turn have their own exploded or expanded parts. Compare the exploded perspective with two vanishing points on the left with the one on p. 596 which has three vanishing points.

EXPLODED PERSPECTIVE/AXONOMETRIC UP VIEWS

ASSEMBLY DRAWING

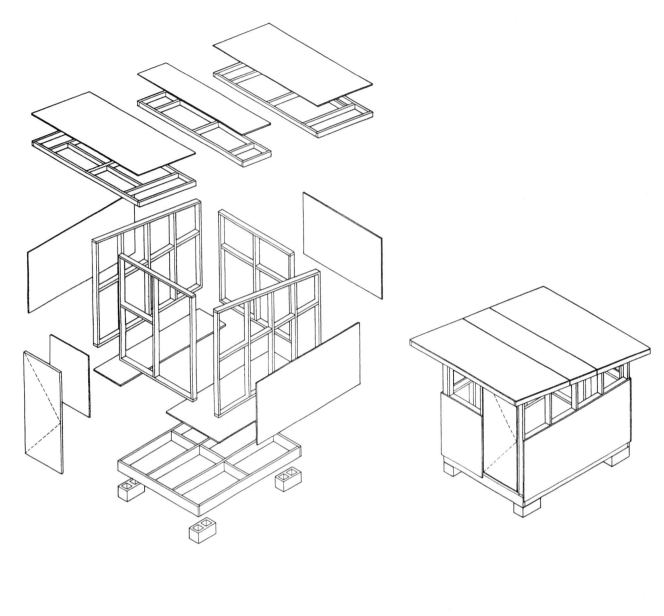

Drawing: The Mad Housers — Shelter for the homeless
            Atlanta, Georgia
24" × 36" (61 × 91.4 cm), Scale: 1½"=1'0"
Medium: Ink on Mylar
Courtesy of Tim Fish Architect

This exploded assembly drawing is drawn as an isometric, whereas the assembly drawing on the facing page is drawn as a perspective. Note the overlapping of component parts in both drawings.

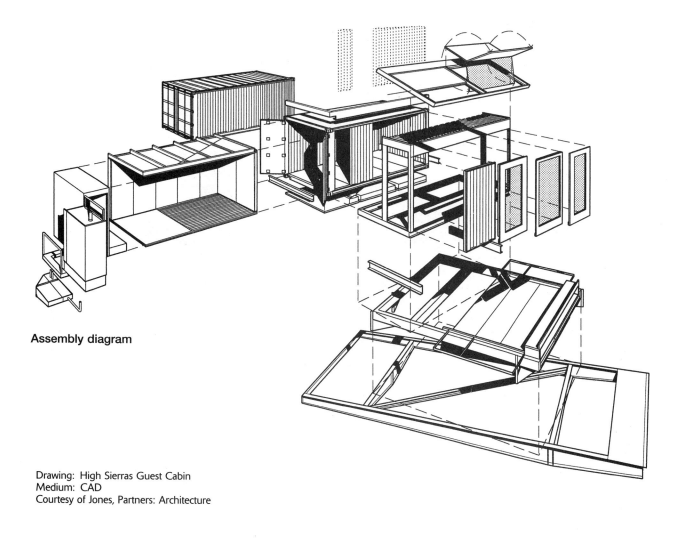

Assembly diagram

Drawing: High Sierras Guest Cabin
Medium: CAD
Courtesy of Jones, Partners: Architecture

ASSEMBLY DRAWING

The use of the exploded view highlights the nature of this structure as an assemblage of standardized parts and shows the genesis of the primary building module in the standard 20' shipping container. The primary modular assembly occupies the horizontal plane established by the existing container in the background, while accessory elements are, where possible, exploded along the vertical axis. Corrugated steel removed from the existing container is shown dotted in. [ARCHITECT'S STATEMENT]

EXPLODED PERSPECTIVE

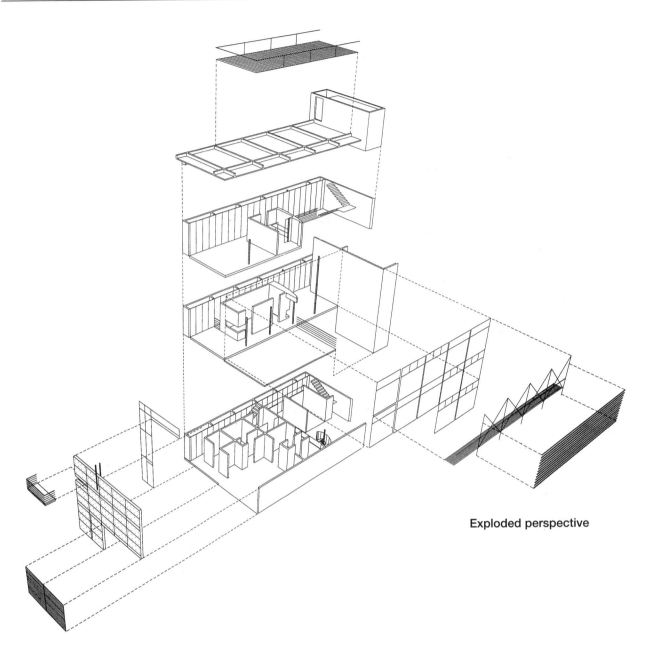

Exploded perspective

Drawing: HOUSE LE, Colonia Condesa, Mexico City, Mexico
Courtesy of TEN Arquitectos-Enrique Norten
Bernardo Gomez-Pimienta, Carlos Ordoñez, project coordinator

Each layer in this exploded perspective gives an unimpeded view of the interior and exterior details of the house. The individual layers must be far enough apart to distinguish each layer (horizontal and vertical), yet be close enough so that they "read" as a coherent whole. This same graphic strategy applies for the expanded view on the facing page.

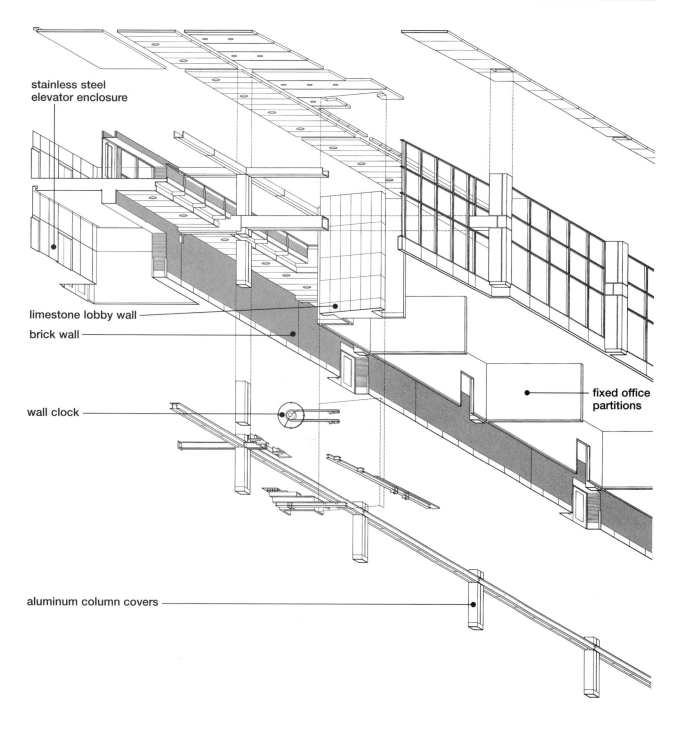

stainless steel
elevator enclosure

limestone lobby wall

brick wall

wall clock

aluminum column covers

fixed office
partitions

EXPANDED ELEVATION OBLIQUE UP VIEW

This is an expanded elevation oblique worm's-eye up view of the ground floor.

Drawing: New Office Building and Parking Garage
for the Pennsylvania Higher Education
Assistance Agency
Harrisburg, Pennsylvania
36" × 48" (91.4 × 121.9 cm)
Medium: Ink on vellum (developed as a CAD drawing)
Courtesy of Bohlin Cywinski Jackson Architects

SIMULTANEOUS UP AND DOWN VIEWS

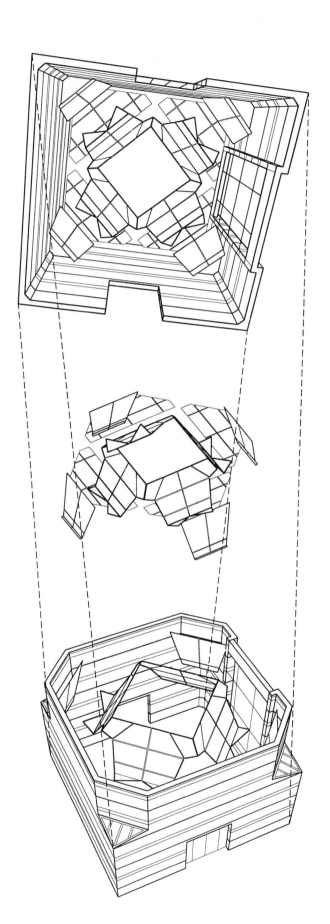

...rotated Axonometric: An "unfolding," time-lapse view of the Reading Room seen at the same time from above and from below. Drawn on AutoCAD Release 12.
[ARCHITECT'S STATEMENT]

Drawing: Ackerman Student Union, UCLA
Courtesy of Rebecca L. Binder FAIA
Drawn by Chilin Huang

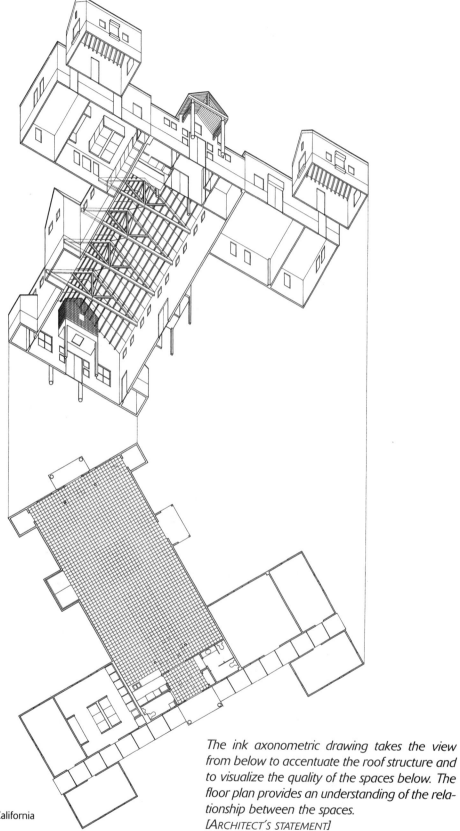

The ink axonometric drawing takes the view from below to accentuate the roof structure and to visualize the quality of the spaces below. The floor plan provides an understanding of the relationship between the spaces.
[ARCHITECT'S STATEMENT]

Drawing: Cabrillo Village, Saticoy, California
Axonometric/Floor Plan
Medium: Ink
Courtesy of John V. Mutlow, FAIA, Architects

UNFOLDED PLAN OBLIQUE

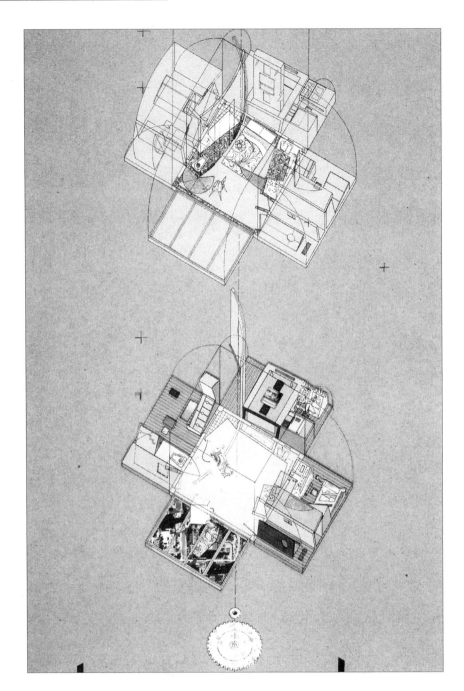

Maximized/Minimal House (Murphy Room House)
22" × 32" (55.9 × 81.3 cm), Scale: ¼"=1'0"
Courtesy of David Baker Associates Architects
Design Team: David Baker, Nancy Whitcombe, Buddy Williams

This image was drawn in ink on clear acetate. The colors and textures were achieved by the cutting out and layering of various materials: papers, Mylars, fake fur, etc., beneath the acetate drawing. This drawing was commissioned by SF Magazine *to illustrate my concept for a house of the future, the Murphy Room House. In the spirit of a Murphy bed, this drawing unfolds to illustrate figuratively the spatial concept for the room that unfolds literally. The cut paper rendering technique contributes to the abstract intention of the drawing for a project destined not to be built for a time that has not passed, realized only in the mind at the present moment.*
[ARCHITECT'S STATEMENT]

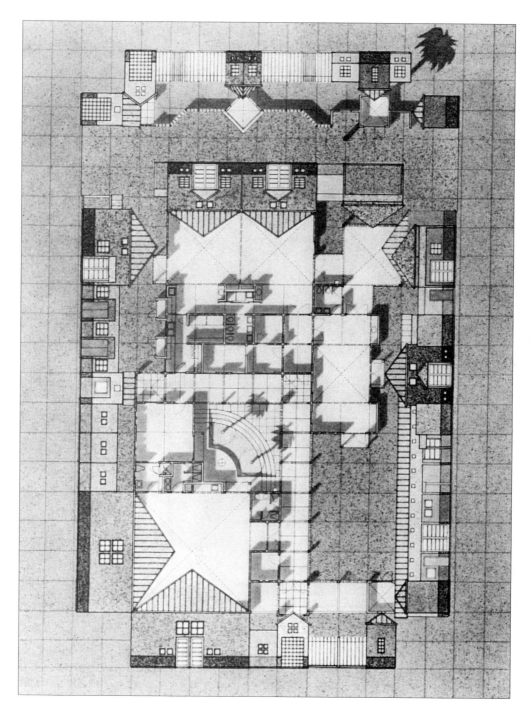

Drawing: Hoover Intergenerational Child Care Center, Los Angeles,
California
21" × 26.5" (53.3 × 67.3 cm), Scale: ⅛"=1'0"
Medium: Ink and color airbrush
Courtesy of John V. Mutlow, FAIA, Architects

The combination of floor plan and elevations in one drawing helps one to understand the direct relationship between the interior spaces and the elevation. The airbrush illustrates the color intention of the project as well as the texture of the materials.
[ARCHITECT'S STATEMENT]

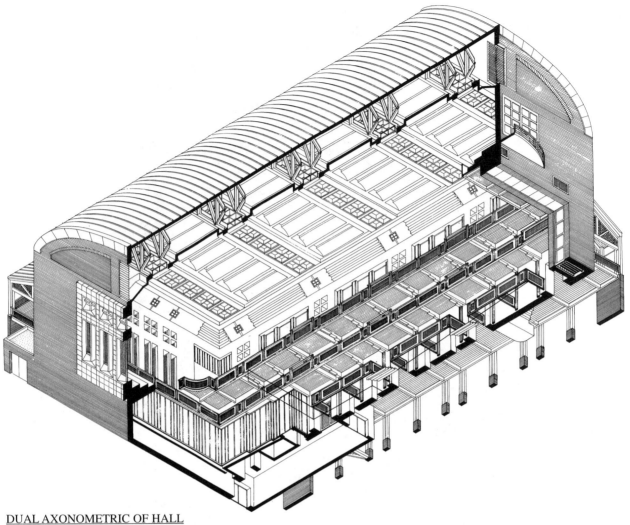

SIMULTANEOUS UP AND DOWN VIEWS

<u>DUAL AXONOMETRIC OF HALL</u>

Drawing: Seiji Ozawa Concert Hall, Tanglewood, Lenox, Massachusetts
30" × 24" (76.2 × 61 cm), Scale: ¼"=1'0"
Medium: Ink on Mylar
Courtesy of William Rawn Associates, Architects, Inc., Boston, MA

Conceptually, this drawing is a synthesis of the elemental quality of the building. Simultaneously, one is able to understand plan, section, massing, elevation, basic construction, and even detail. This technique is most useful for spaces that are bilaterally symmetrical and have enough repetition and cadence to allow one's eye to link the patterns and form.
[ARCHITECT'S STATEMENT]

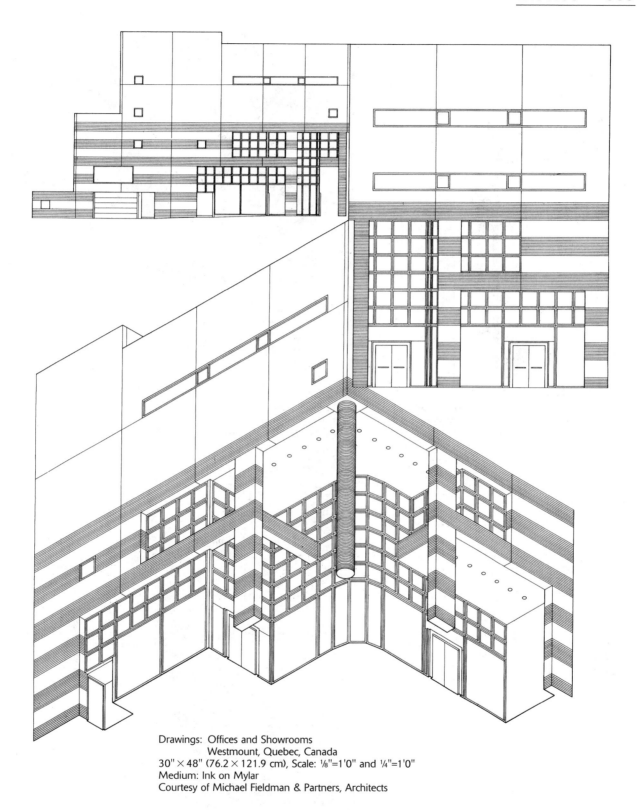

Drawings: Offices and Showrooms
Westmount, Quebec, Canada
30" × 48" (76.2 × 121.9 cm), Scale: ⅛"=1'0" and ¼"=1'0"
Medium: Ink on Mylar
Courtesy of Michael Fieldman & Partners, Architects

WORM'S-EYE VIEW: COMPOSITE ELEVATIONS

Three views at two progressive scales are composed about the pivotal corner of this design to underscore the significance of the open corner. The two drawing scales which allow for a direct measurement of the relationship between 2D and 3D views add interest.
[ARCHITECT'S STATEMENT]

HYBRID DRAWINGS

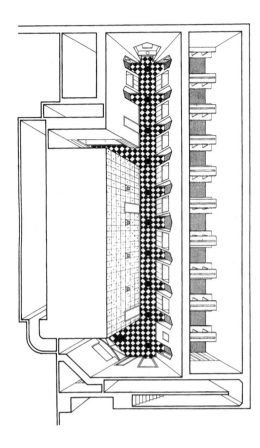

Drawing: The WEB (Work Stations in Evans Basement)
University of California, Berkeley
12" × 18" (30.5 × 45.7 cm), Scale: ⅛"=1'0"
Medium: Ink on Mylar
Courtesy of Sam Davis, FAIA, of Davis & Joyce Architects

An aerial one-point perspective shows the organization of the various rooms as would a simple plan, while also showing the volumetric relationships of the spaces. Certain liberties are necessary in the construction of such a drawing, but revealing so much conceptual information at a single glance is often valuable.
[ARCHITECT'S STATEMENT]

These hybrid drawings with unusual overhead views combine the principles of paraline and perspective drawing. At first glance, they appear to be overhead one-point perspectives. However, on closer examination, one notices many internal structural elements having infinitely parallel lines.

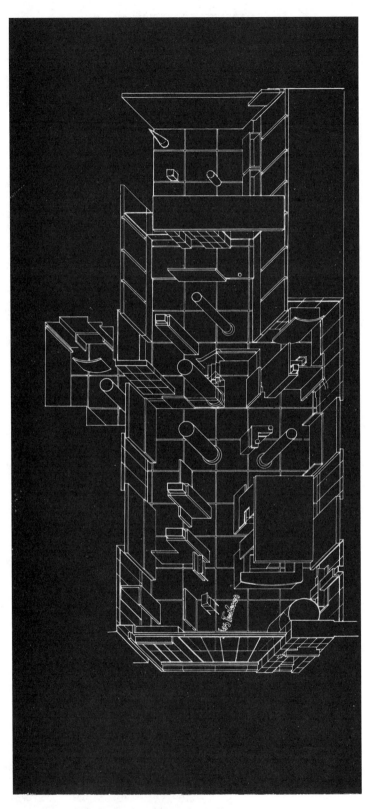

Drawing: Les Tuileries Restaurant, New York City
20" × 30" (50.8 × 76.2 cm), Scale: ¼"=1'0"
Medium: Ink and Mylar
Courtesy of Diane Lewis, Peter Mickle
and Christopher Compton, R.A., Designers

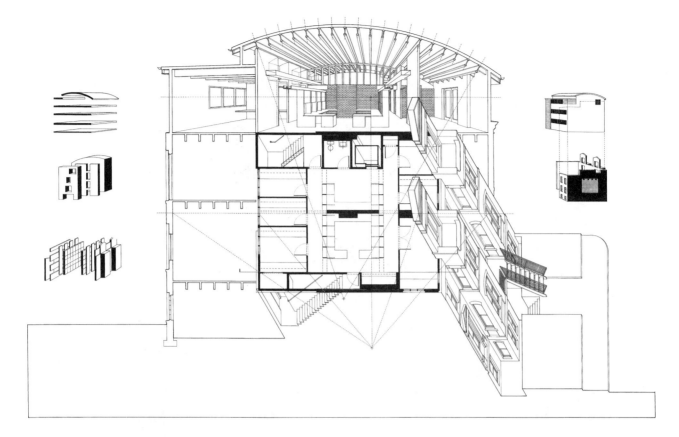

Drawing: National Minority AIDS Council, Washington, D.C.
30" × 42" (76.2 × 106.7 cm), Scale: ¼"=1'0"
Medium: Ink on Mylar
Courtesy of Vyt Gureckas/CORE

The inadequacy of representing a three-dimensional artifact in two dimensions has traditionally been overcome by generating a number of different drawings. However, the act of reconnecting the various drawings or views is left to the mind. Cubism has offered an alternative to this process by presenting simultaneous views on one surface. This drawing is an attempt to take advantage of such a strategy, but whereas Cubism relies on transparency and incidental juxtaposition, this drawing employs a more precise set of tangent lines or shared edges to graft one drawing to another. Construction lines are left in place to underscore this process of delineative reconstruction.
[ARCHITECT'S STATEMENT]

This drawing combines a perspective section with a plan and a nonvertical z-axis plan oblique (axonometric).

HYBRID COMPOSITE DRAWINGS

FISHEYE LENS BIRD'S-EYE VIEW

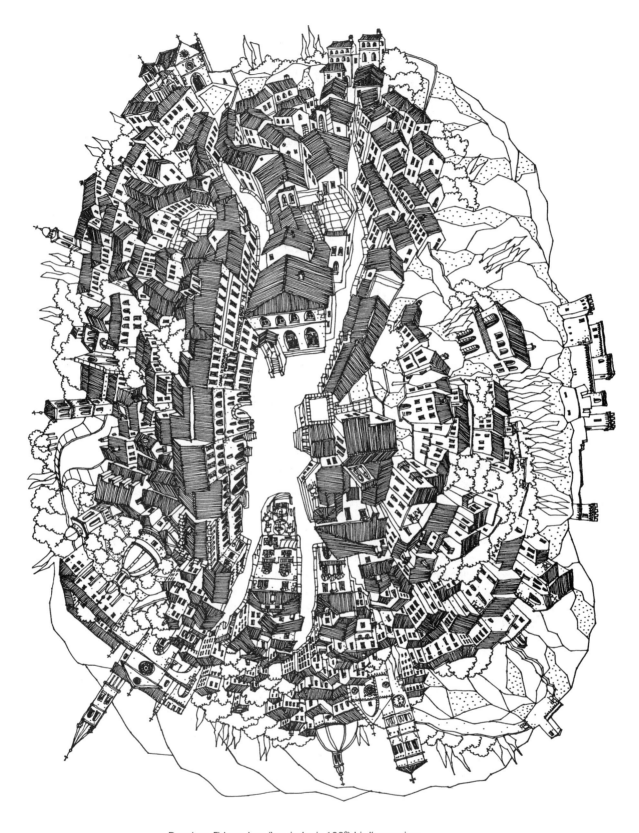

Drawing: Fisheye lens (hemispheric 180°) bird's-eye view
Assisi, Italy
Medium: Felt-tipped pen on newsprint, 16" × 24" (40.6 × 61 cm)
Courtesy of Cathi House, Architect, San Francisco

Epilogue

The primary intent of this book is to provide students and design professionals with graphic tools essential to visual communication. Architectural graphics is a powerful tool for conceptualizing, documenting, and expressing architectural communication. The variety of drawing types and methods demonstrates that a wide range of graphic tools and techniques are available for conveying architectural ideas in the design process. This primer introduces the various media currently being used, with an emphasis on black and white, with the hope that it will kindle the reader's exploratory curiosity.

With time and experience, every designer—student and professional alike—eventually settles in with the tools and techniques most suitable for him or her to express architectural ideas, whether these be freehand conceptual sketches or hardline representational drawings. Some architects/designers enjoy the feeling of a soft lead pencil on heavy white tracing paper. The softness of graphite can give a suggestive atmospheric character, especially to perspective images. Others become prolific in their expression of ideas when they use a felt-tipped pen or colored pencil on yellow tracing paper. Prismacolor pencils give a soft impressionistic feeling to architectural sketches. And still others prefer the precise feeling of ink on Mylar, especially with paraline drawings. It should be noted that every medium affects the quality of not only spatial perception but also design ideas, especially at the "design-drawing" stage. For example, charcoal causes one to almost automatically think in terms of light and shadow, whereas a fine-point pen may cause one to delineate more and to think in terms of contours, connections, and details.

As the computer and computer-generated drawings become commonplace in design education and practice, it is all the more important to maintain a strong relationship with traditional drawing media and methods, such as freehand sketching. Because of the intimate and immediate reciprocity between the human imagination and drawing, this most ancient form of expression will always remain a powerful and effective way to generate ideas.

Explore the many books (some on color drawings) listed in the bibliography which elaborate on architectural drawing as technique and/or process. Hopefully this exploration, along with a careful study of this volume, will enrich your knowledge of architectural drawing.

Bibliography

Allen, G. and R. Oliver. 1981. *Architectural Drawing: The Art and the Process.* Whitney. All chapters.

Berryman, G. 1990. *Notes on Graphic Design and Visual Communication.* Crisp Publications, Inc. Chapters 10, 11, 13.

Bertol, D. 1996. *Designing Digital Space.* Wiley. Chapter 12.

Buckles, G. M. 1995. *Building Architectural & Interior Design Models Fast!* Belpine. Chapters 1, 12.

Burden, E. 1992. *Architectural Delineation.* McGraw-Hill. Chapter 9.

————. 1981. *Entourage: A Tracing File.* McGraw-Hill. Chapter 9.

Calle, P. 1985. *The Pencil.* Ingram. Chapter 5.

Chen, J. 1994. *Architecture in Pen and Ink.* McGraw-Hill. Chapters 5, 9, 10, 11.

Chen, J. and W. T. Cooper. 1996. *Architectural Perspective Grids.* McGraw-Hill. Chapter 6.

Ching, F. 1996. *Architectural Graphics.* 3rd ed. Van Nostrand Reinhold. All chapters.

————. 1990. *Drawing: A Creative Process.* Van Nostrand Reinhold. Chapters 5, 6, 7, 8.

Clark, R. and M. Pause. 1996. *Precedents in Architecture.* Van Nostrand Reinhold. Chapters 10, 11.

Cooper, D. 1992. *Drawing and Perceiving.* Van Nostrand Reinhold. Chapters 3, 4, 6, 8.

Crowe, P. 1992. *Architectural Rendering.* McGraw-Hill. Chapter 9.

D'Amelio, J. 1964. *Perspective Drawing Handbook.* Leon Amiel. Chapters 6, 8.

Doyle, M. E. 1993. *Color Drawing.* Van Nostrand Reinhold. Chapters 5, 9.

Edwards, B. 1989. *Drawing on the Right Side of the Brain.* Tarcher. Chapter 5.

Ferriss, H. *The Metropolis of Tomorrow.* Princeton Architectural Press. Chapters 5, 10.

Forseth, K. 1980. *Graphics for Architecture.* Van Nostrand Reinhold. Chapters 3, 4, 6, 8.

Fraser, I. and R. Henmi. 1994. *Envisioning Architecture An Analysis of Drawing.* Van Nostrand Reinhold. Chapters 4, 5, 6, 10.

Friedman, J. *Creation in Space.* Kendall Hunt. Chapters 3, 8, 12.

Gill, R. W. 1990. *Rendering With Pen and Ink.* Thames and Hudson. Chapter 9.

Hanks, K. and L. Belliston. 1980. *Rapid Viz.* William Kaufman, Inc. Chapters 1, 5, 9.

Helms, M. E. 1990. *Perspective Drawing.* Prentice Hall. Chapter 6.

Herbert, D. M. 1993. *Architecture Study Drawings: Their Characteristics & Their Properties as a Graphic Medium for Thinking in Design.* Van Nostrand Reinhold. Chapters 5, 10.

Kasprisin, R. J. 1991. *Watercolor in Architectural Design.* Van Nostrand Reinhold. Chapters 5, 9.

Kautzky, T. 1960. *Pencil Broadsides.* Van Nostrand Reinhold. Chapter 5.

Kliment, S. 1984. *Architectural Sketching and Rendering.* Whitney. Chapters 5, 9, 10.

Knoll, W. and M. Hechinger. 1992. *Architectural Models: Construction Techniques.* McGraw-Hill. Chapters 1, 12.

Koplar, R. 1993. *Architectural Studies.* McGraw-Hill. Chapter 9.

Kvem, O. M. 1994. *Real World Freehand 4.* Peachpit Press, Inc. Chapters 5, 12.

Lacy, B. 1991. *100 Contemporary Architects Drawings and Sketches.* Abrams. Chapters 10, 11.

Laseau, P. 1986. *Graphic Problem Solving for Architects and Designers.* 2d ed. Van Nostrand Reinhold. Chapters 5, 10, 11.

———. 1980. *Graphic Thinking for Architects and Designers.* Van Nostrand Reinhold. Chapters 5, 10, 11.

Lin, M. W. 1993. *Drawing and Designing With Confidence: A Step By Step Guide.* Van Nostrand Reinhold. Chapters 5, 6, 9.

Linton, H. and R. Strickfaden. 1990. *Architectural Sketching in Markers.* Van Nostrand Reinhold. Chapters 5, 6, 9.

Lockhard, W. K. 1993. *Drawing as a Means to Architecture.* Van Nostrand Reinhold. Chapter 9.

———. 1993. *Design Drawing.* Pepper Publishing. Chapters 5, 10.

———. 1993. *Design Drawing Experiences.* Pepper Publishing. Chapters 5, 10.

———. 1993. *Drawing Techniques for Designers: Advocating Line and Tone Drawing.* Pepper Publishing. Chapters 8, 9.

———. 1993. *Freehand Perspective for Designers: Including Shadowcasting and Entourage.* Pepper Publishing. Chapters 5, 6, 8, 9.

Lorenz, A. and L. Lizak. 1988. *Architectural Illustration Inside and Out.* Whitney. Chapter 9.

Martin, C. L. 1968. *Design Graphics.* MacMillan. Chapters 4, 6, 8.

Mohrle, J. 1994. *Architecture in Perspective.* Whitney. Chapters 6, 9.

Moore, F. 1996. *Model Builder's Notebook.* McGraw-Hill. Chapters 1, 12.

Nichols, K., L. Burke, and P. Burke. 1995. *Michael Graves: Buildings and Projects 1990–1994.* Rizzoli. Chapters 5, 11.

Oles, P. S. 1979. *Architectural Illustration.* Van Nostrand Reinhold. Chapter 9.

———. 1987. *Drawing the Future.* Van Nostrand Reinhold. Chapter 10.

Parks, J. 1991. *Contemporary Architectural Drawings.* Pomegranate Artbooks. Chapters 5, 10, 13.

Pfeiffer, B. B. 1990. *Frank Lloyd Wright Drawings.* Abradale Press/Harry N. Abrams. Chapters 5, 11.

Porter, T. 1985. *Manual of Graphic Techniques 4.* Scribners. All chapters.

———. 1990. *Architectural Drawing.* Van Nostrand Reinhold. All chapters.

———. 1993. *Architectural Drawing Masterclass.* Scribners. Chapter 9.

Sanders, K. 1995. *The Digital Architect.* Wiley. Chapter 12.

Shen, J. and T. D. Walker. 1992. *Sketching and Rendering for Design Presentations.* Van Nostrand Reinhold. Chapters 5, 9, 10.

Sutherland, M. 1989. *Lettering for Architects and Designers.* Van Nostrand Reinhold. Chapter 2.

Szabo, M. *Drawing File.* Van Nostrand Reinhold. Chapters 5, 9.

Tanaka, E. 1990. *Architectural Presentations.* Nippan. Chapter 9.

Uddin, M. S. 1996. *Composite Drawing.* McGraw-Hill. Chapters 13, 14.

Vrooman, D. *Architecture, Perspective, Shadows, Reflections.* Van Nostrand Reinhold. Chapters 6, 7, 8.

Wagstaff, F. 1993. *Macintosh 3-D.* Hayden Books. Chapter 12.

Walker, T. D. 1989. *Perspective Sketches.* 5th ed. Van Nostrand Reinhold. Chapters 6, 7.

——— and D. Davis. 1990. *Plan Graphics.* Van Nostrand Reinhold. Chapter 9.

Wang, T. C. 1977. *Pencil Sketching.* Van Nostrand Reinhold. Chapter 5.

———. 1993. *Sketching With Markers.* Van Nostrand Reinhold. Chapters 5, 6, 9.

Watson, E. W. 1985. *The Art of Pencil Drawing.* Watson-Guptill. Chapter 5.

White, E. A. 1972. *Graphic Vocabulary for Architectural Presentation.* Architectural Media. Chapter 9.

Wright, F. L. 1983. *Drawings and Plans of Frank Lloyd Wright: The Early Period (1893–1909).* Dover. Chapters 3, 6, 9.

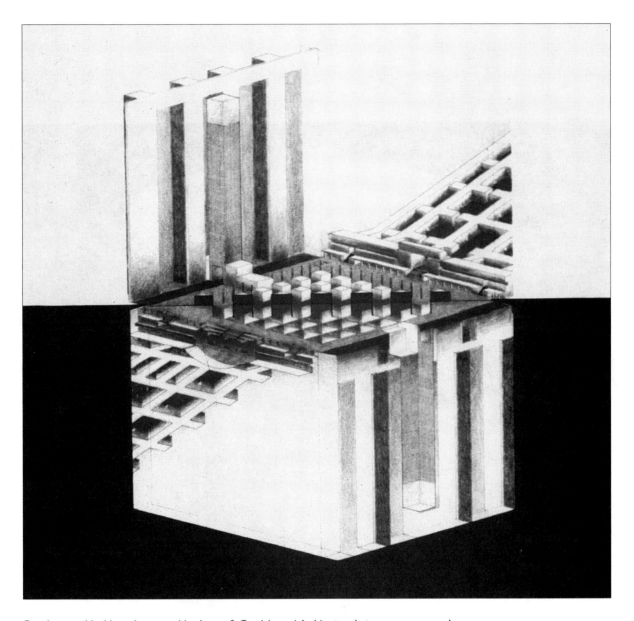

Drawings on this side and reverse side: Agrest & Gandelsonas' Architecture between memory and
amnesia, suburban center on the Mississippi, Minneapolis, Minnesota
Courtesy of Diana Agrest and Mario Gandelsonas Architects

*This project examines the relationship between the urban and suburban realms. First we consider typologies of
buildings and places that characterize the suburban landscape that are not yet part of history, the memory of
architecture. Second, we juxtapose these two opposing situations to create another kind of space. The urban
order invades the suburban disorder, but the suburban condition alters the forms and meanings of the urban
space. Moreover, the project extracts and develops new potential forms that appear when the urban and the
suburban interact and contradict each other in a close and violent way.*
[ARCHITECT'S STATEMENT]

Drawing: Urban/Suburban Intersection 2
Medium: Ink on white paper and Prismacolor 27" × 24" (68.6 × 61 cm)

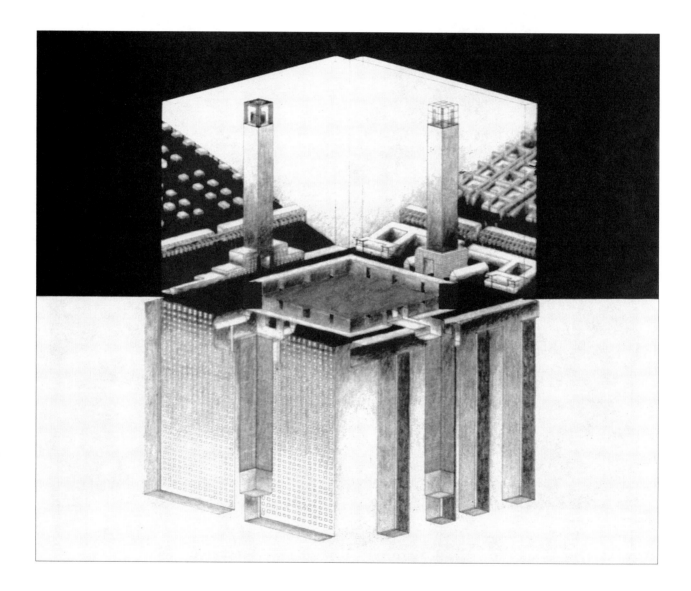

These drawings are the second and fourth of a set of four. Each of the four views shows a different consequence of the interaction of urban and suburban conditions. The decision to use the section axonometric, hinged on a mirror line and with both actual and conceptual "reflections," was made with the intention of emphasizing the coming together of, and the already inextricable link between, the existing urban and suburban typologies, as well as the creation of new forms that result from collision/interaction.
[ARCHITECT'S STATEMENT]

Drawing: Urban/Suburban Intersection 4
Medium: Ink on white paper and Prismacolor, 27" × 24" (68.6 × 61 cm)

About the Author

RENDOW YEE, Professor Emeritus, received his education at the University of California at Berkeley and Washington University in St. Louis where he received his Master of Architecture degree. He was involved with architectural education for more than 20 years at the City College of San Francisco, and there he served as Chair of the Architecture Department from 1982 to 1990. Professional organizations with which he has been affiliated include the American Society of Civil Engineers, the American Society for Engineering Education, the American Institute of Architects, and the California Council of Architectural Education.

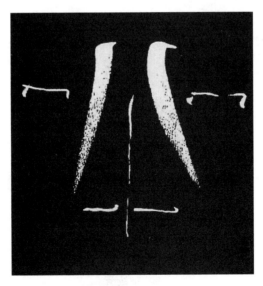

Concept sketch: Sunrise & Sunset Houses
            Sudurhlidar, Kópavogur, Iceland
7 × 7.5 cm (2.8" × 3")
Courtesy of Gudmundur Jonsson, Architect, Moval/FAI

Subject Index

Contributor Index

Photo: Cardiff Bay Opera House (1993–2000): Overhead view of opera house
London, England
Copyright: Zaha Hadid 1994/Photograph by Edward Woodman